Themis Bar Review
Multistate

Constitutional Law
Contracts & Sales
Criminal Law
Criminal Procedure
Evidence
Real Property
Torts

All other trademarks are the property of their respective companies.

The material herein is intended to be used in conjunction with the myThemis Portal™ in order to provide basic review of legal subjects and is in no way meant to be a source of or replacement for professional legal advice.

ISBN 978-1-938238-40-6
1-938238-40-0

Constitutional Law

CONSTITUTIONAL LAW

Table of Contents

PART ONE: POWERS OF THE FEDERAL GOVERNMENT 1

I.   JUDICIAL POWER 1

    A. SOURCE AND SCOPE 1

        1. SOURCE—ARTICLE III 1

        2. SCOPE 1

            a. Judicial review of congressional and executive actions 1

            b. Judicial review of state actions 1

        3. LIMITATIONS—ELEVENTH AMENDMENT 2

            a. Exceptions 2

            b. Not barred by the Eleventh Amendment 3

    B. JURISDICTION OF THE SUPREME COURT 3

        1. ORIGINAL 3

        2. APPELLATE 3

            a. Means 3

            b. Limitations 4

            c. Adequate and independent state grounds 4

    C. JUDICIAL REVIEW IN OPERATION 4

        1. STANDING 4

            a. General rule 4

            b. Taxpayer status 6

            c. Third-party standing 6

            d. Assignee standing 7

            e. Citizenship standing 7

            f. Standing to assert a Tenth Amendment violation 7

        2. TIMELINESS 8

            a. Ripeness 8

            b. Mootness 8

         3. JUSTICIABILITY—FURTHER ISSUES 9

        a. Advisory opinions 9

        b. Declaratory judgments 9

        c. Political questions 9

    4. ABSTENTION 10

        a. *Pullman* doctrine 10

        b. *Younger* abstention 10

II. THE POWERS OF CONGRESS 10

  A. COMMERCE 10

    1. INTERSTATE COMMERCE 10

        a. Power to regulate 10

        b. Construed broadly 10

    2. "SUBSTANTIAL ECONOMIC EFFECT" 11

        a. Aggregation 11

    3. NON-ECONOMIC ACTIVITY 11

  B. TAXATION AND SPENDING 11

    1. TAXING 12

        a. Power is plenary 12

        b. Uniformity 12

        c. Direct tax 12

        d. Export tax 12

    2. SPENDING 13

  C. WAR AND DEFENSE POWERS 13

    1. PROVIDING FOR THE NATIONAL DEFENSE 13

    2. COURTS AND TRIBUNALS 13

    3. NATIONAL GUARD 13

  D. INVESTIGATORY POWER 14

    1. SCOPE 14

    2. ENFORCEMENT AND WITNESS'S RIGHTS 14

  E. PROPERTY POWER 14

  F. POSTAL POWER 14

  G. POWER OVER ALIENS AND CITIZENSHIP 14

    1. ALIENS 14

       2. NATURALIZATION 14

   H. OTHER ARTICLE I POWERS 15

       1. POWER OVER THE DISTRICT OF COLUMBIA 15

       2. ELECTIONS CLAUSE 15

       3. NECESSARY AND PROPER CLAUSE 15

   I. POWER TO ENFORCE THE THIRTEENTH, FOURTEENTH, AND FIFTEENTH AMENDMENTS 15

       1. THIRTEENTH AMENDMENT—BAN ON SLAVERY 16

       2. FOURTEENTH AMENDMENT—EQUAL PROTECTION AND DUE PROCESS.........16

       3. FIFTEENTH AMENDMENT—VOTING 16

   J. QUALIFICATIONS OF MEMBERS 16

III. THE POWERS OF THE PRESIDENT 16

   A. DOMESTIC POWER..17

       1. PARDON POWER FOR FEDERAL OFFENSES..............................17

       2. VETO POWER..17

       3. APPOINTMENT AND REMOVAL OF OFFICIALS..........................17

          a. Appointment...17

          b. Removal..17

       4. AUTHORITY AS CHIEF EXECUTIVE...18

   B. FOREIGN AFFAIRS 18

       1. COMMANDER IN CHIEF...18

       2. TREATIES 18

       3. EXECUTIVE AGREEMENTS 19

IV. FEDERAL INTERBRANCH RELATIONSHIPS 19

   A. CONGRESSIONAL LIMITS ON THE EXECUTIVE.....................................19

       1. IMPEACHMENT...19

       2. APPROPRIATION...19

       3. LEGISLATIVE VETO 19

   B. DELEGATION OF LEGISLATIVE POWER 20

   C. JUDICIAL LIMITATION OF CONGRESSIONAL POWER 20

   D. IMMUNITIES AND PRIVILEGES 20

       1. JUDICIAL..20

       2. LEGISLATIVE...21

      3. EXECUTIVE 21

          a. Executive privilege 21

          b. Executive immunity 22

PART TWO: THE FEDERAL SYSTEM 23

V.   **FEDERAL AND STATE POWERS** 23

   A. EXCLUSIVE FEDERAL POWERS 23

   B. EXCLUSIVE STATE POWERS 23

   C. CONCURRENT FEDERAL AND STATE LAWS—SUPREMACY CLAUSE 23

VI.   **INTERGOVERNMENTAL IMMUNITIES** 23

   A. FEDERAL IMMUNITY 23

      1. REGULATION BY THE STATES 23

      2. TAXATION BY THE STATES 23

   B. STATE IMMUNITY 24

      1. FEDERAL REGULATION 24

          a. Congressional action 24

          b. Judicial action 24

      2. FEDERAL TAXATION 25

      3. LITIGATION INVOLVING THE UNITED STATES AND ITS OFFICERS 25

VII. **STATE REGULATION AND TAXATION OF COMMERCE** 25

   A. THE DORMANT COMMERCE CLAUSE 25

      1. GENERAL RULE 25

      2. DISCRIMINATION AGAINST OUT-OF-STATE COMMERCE 25

          a. Necessary to important state interest 26

          b. Market-participant exception 26

          c. Traditional government function exception 26

          d. Subsidy exception 26

          e. Exception—congressionally permitted discrimination 26

      3. UNDUE BURDEN ON INTERSTATE COMMERCE 27

          a. Balancing test 27

          b. "Extraterritoriality" 27

   B. STATE TAXATION OF COMMERCE 27

      1. INTERSTATE COMMERCE 27

          a. *Complete Auto* Test 27

          b. **Discrimination under other constitutional provisions**..............................28

          c. **Types of taxes** 28

      2. **FOREIGN COMMERCE**...29

   C. **ALCOHOLIC BEVERAGE REGULATION** 30

VIII. **FEDERAL PREEMPTION OF STATE LAW** 30

   A. **EXPRESS PREEMPTION** 30

      1. **NARROW CONSTRUCTION** 30

      2. **SAVINGS CLAUSE** 30

   B. **IMPLIED PREEMPTION** 31

      1. **ABSENCE OF PREEMPTION** 32

IX. **RELATIONS AMONG STATES**...32

   A. **INTERSTATE COMPACTS**...32

   B. **FULL FAITH AND CREDIT** 32

      1. **JUDGMENTS** 32

      2. **LAWS (PUBLIC ACTS)**...32

PART THREE: INDIVIDUAL RIGHTS 33

X. **STATE ACTION AND THE ROLE OF THE COURTS** 33

   A. **TRADITIONAL GOVERNMENTAL FUNCTION** 33

   B. **SIGNIFICANT STATE INVOLVEMENT** 33

   C. **INSIGNIFICANT STATE INVOLVEMENT** 33

XI. **PROCEDURAL DUE PROCESS** 34

   A. **DUE PROCESS GENERALLY** 34

   B. **PROCEDURAL DUE PROCESS APPLIED** 34

      1. **GENERAL PRINCIPLES** 34

          a. **Neutral decision maker** 34

          b. **Intentional conduct**..35

      2. **PROTECTED INTERESTS**...35

          a. **Liberty** 35

          b. **Property**..35

      3. **NOTICE AND HEARING** 36

          a. **Enemy combatants**..36

          b. Parental status 37

          c. Forfeitures 37

          d. Public employees 37

      4. COURT ACCESS 37

XII. SUBSTANTIVE DUE PROCESS 37

    A. STANDARD OF REVIEW 37

      1. STRICT SCRUTINY 38

          a. Test 38

          b. Burden of proof 38

          c. Applicability 38

      2. RATIONAL BASIS 38

          a. Test 38

          b. Burden of proof 38

          c. Applicability 39

    B. FUNDAMENTAL RIGHTS 39

      1. TRAVEL 39

          a. Interstate 39

          b. International 40

      2. VOTING AND BALLOT ACCESS 40

          a. Right to vote 40

          b. Public office and ballot access 41

      3. PRIVACY 42

          a. Marriage 42

          b. Contraception 42

          c. Intimate sexual behavior 43

          d. Abortion 43

          e. Parental rights 44

          f. Family relations 44

          g. Obscene material 44

          h. Right to refuse medical treatment 44

      4. THE SECOND AMENDMENT 44

XIII. EQUAL PROTECTION 45

A. GENERAL CONSIDERATIONS 45

    1. CONSTITUTIONAL BASIS 45

        a. State action 45

        b. Federal action 45

    2. STANDARDS OF REVIEW 45

        a. Strict scrutiny 45

        b. Intermediate scrutiny 46

        c. Rational basis 46

    3. PROVING DISCRIMINATION 47

        a. Facial discrimination 47

        b. Discriminatory application 47

        c. Discriminatory motive 47

B. SUSPECT CLASSIFICATIONS 47

    1. RACE, ETHNICITY, AND NATIONAL ORIGIN 47

        a. School integration 48

        b. Affirmative action 48

        c. Racial gerrymandering 49

    2. ALIENAGE 49

        a. Federal classification 49

        b. State classifications 49

        c. Undocumented aliens 50

C. QUASI-SUSPECT CLASSIFICATIONS 50

    1. GENDER 50

        a. Discrimination against women 50

        b. Discrimination against men 50

        c. Affirmative action (benign discrimination) 50

    2. LEGITIMACY 51

D. NONSUSPECT CLASSIFICATIONS 51

    1. AGE 51

    2. POVERTY 51

    3. SEXUAL ORIENTATION 51

E. FUNDAMENTAL RIGHTS UNIQUE TO EQUAL PROTECTION 51

        1. ONE PERSON, ONE VOTE..52
           a. Congressional districts...52
           b. State and local districts..52
           c. At-large elections...53
        2. GERRYMANDERING..53
           a. Racial discrimination...53
           b. Political discrimination...54

XIV. PRIVILEGES AND IMMUNITIES CLAUSES 54

    A. ARTICLE IV...54
        1. PROHIBITS STATE DISCRIMINATION AGAINST NONRESIDENTS 54
        2. RIGHTS PROTECTED 54
        3. EXCEPTION—SUBSTANTIAL JUSTIFICATION 55
    B. FOURTEENTH AMENDMENT—NATIONAL CITIZENSHIP 55

XV. TAKINGS CLAUSE..55

    A. PROPERTY INTEREST...56
        1. TYPES OF PROPERTY..56
        2. TYPES OF INTERESTS..56
    B. TYPES OF TAKING..56
        1. SEIZURE OF PROPERTY...56
           a. Public-use challenge 56
        2. DAMAGE TO OR DESTRUCTION OF PROPERTY 57
           a. Exception—public peril...57
        3. CHARACTERIZATION OF PROPERTY..57
        4. REGULATORY TAKING..57
           a. Public-use challenge 58
           b. Per se takings..58
           c. Post-adoption acquisition 59
        5. EXACTION AS A TAKING 59
    C. JUST COMPENSATION...59
        1. WORTHLESS PROPERTY...59
        2. ONLY PORTION TAKEN 59
        3. RETURN OF PROPERTY 60

      D. MANNER OF TAKING 60

XVI. PROHIBITED LEGISLATION 60

      A. BILLS OF ATTAINDER 60

      B. EX POST FACTO LAWS 60

      C. OBLIGATION OF CONTRACTS 61

         1. PRIVATE CONTRACTS 61

         2. PUBLIC CONTRACTS 61

XVII. FREEDOM OF RELIGION 61

      A. ESTABLISHMENT 61

         1. STANDARD OF REVIEW 61

         2. FINANCIAL AID 62

            a. Indirect aid to schoolchildren 62

            b. Direct aid to colleges and hospitals 62

            c. Tax exemptions 62

         3. SCHOOL ACTIVITIES 62

         4. RELIGIOUS DISPLAYS 63

            a. Ten Commandments 63

            b. Holiday displays 63

      B. FREE EXERCISE 63

         1. RELIGIOUS BELIEF 64

         2. RELIGIOUS CONDUCT 64

            a. Targeting religious conduct 64

            b. Generally applicable laws 64

      C. MINISTERIAL EXCEPTION TO DISCRIMINATION LAWS 64

XVIII. FREEDOM OF EXPRESSION AND ASSOCIATION 65

      A. REGULATION OF SPEECH 65

         1. EXPRESSIVE CONDUCT 65

         2. OVERBREADTH 66

         3. VAGUENESS 66

         4. PRIOR RESTRAINTS 66

         5. UNFETTERED DISCRETION 67

         6. FREEDOM NOT TO SPEAK 67

        a. **Compelled financial support**...67

   7. **GOVERNMENT SPEECH** 68

        a. **Monuments on public property** 68

        b. **Funding of private messages** 68

        c. **Speech by government employees**..68

   8. **CAMPAIGN RELATED SPEECH** 68

        a. **Political campaign contributions**...68

        b. **Political campaign expenditures** 69

        c. **Political speakers** 69

B. **REGULATION OF TIME, PLACE, AND MANNER OF EXPRESSION** 69

   1. **PUBLIC FORUM** 69

        a. **Residential areas** 70

        b. **Injunctions** 70

        c. **Public schools**...70

   2. **NONPUBLIC FORUM** 71

        a. **Viewpoint-neutral** 71

        b. **Reasonable** 71

   3. **PERSONAL PROPERTY** 71

C. **REGULATION OF CONTENT** 71

   1. **OBSCENITY AND CHILD PORNOGRAPHY**..72

        a. **Obscenity test**...72

        b. **Prohibited activities** 72

        c. **Land-use restrictions**..72

        d. **Minors**..72

        e. **Child pornography** 73

        f. **Violence**...73

   2. **INCITEMENT TO VIOLENCE**..73

   3. **FIGHTING WORDS** 73

   4. **DEFAMATION** 74

        a. **Public figure or official** 74

        b. **Public concern** 74

   5. **COMMERCIAL SPEECH** 74

    D. REGULATION OF THE MEDIA 75

        1. GENERAL CONSIDERATIONS 75

           a. Gag orders 75

           b. Attending trials 75

           c. No constitutional privilege to protect sources 75

           d. Illegally obtained and private information 75

           e. First Amendment conflict with state right of publicity 76

           f. No immunity from laws of general applicability 76

        2. BROADCAST 76

        3. CABLE TELEVISION 76

        4. INTERNET 77

  E. REGULATION OF ASSOCIATION 77

        1. PUBLIC EMPLOYMENT 77

           a. Test 77

           b. Loyalty oaths 77

        2. BAR MEMBERSHIP 78

        3. ELECTIONS AND POLITICAL PARTIES 78

           a. Voters in primary elections 78

           b. Ballot access to general election 78

           c. Fusion candidate 78

           d. Replacement candidate 79

CONSTITUTIONAL LAW

PART ONE: POWERS OF THE FEDERAL GOVERNMENT

I.   JUDICIAL POWER

A.   SOURCE AND SCOPE

1.   Source—Article III

Article III, Section 1 of the United States Constitution provides that "[t]he judicial power of the United States shall be vested in one Supreme Court and in such inferior courts as the Congress may from time to time ordain and establish."

Federal courts are generally created by the United States Congress under the constitutional power described in Article III. As noted above, Article III requires the establishment of a Supreme Court and permits the Congress to create other federal courts and place limitations on their jurisdiction. Although many specialized courts are created under the authority granted in Article I, greater power is vested in Article III courts because they are independent of Congress, the President, and the political process.

2.   Scope

Article III, Section 2 delineates the jurisdiction of federal courts as limited to **cases or controversies**:

i)   Arising under the Constitution, laws, and treaties of the United States;

ii) Affecting foreign countries' ambassadors, public ministers, and consuls;

iii) Involving admiralty and maritime jurisdiction;

iv) When the United States is a party;

v)   Between two or more states, or between a state and citizens of another state;

vi) Between citizens of different states or between citizens of the same state claiming lands under grants of different states; or

vii) Between a state, or its citizens, and foreign states, citizens, or subjects.

a.   Judicial review of congressional and executive actions

The judiciary has the power—although it is not enumerated in the text of the Constitution—to review an act of another branch of the federal government and to declare that act unconstitutional, *Marbury v. Madison*, 5 U.S. 137 (1803), as well as the constitutionality of a decision by a state's highest court, *Martin v. Hunter's Lessee*, 1 Wheat. 304 (1816). The central ideas of *Marbury v. Madison* are that (i) the Constitution is paramount law, and (ii) the Supreme Court has the final say in interpreting the Constitution.

b.   Judicial review of state actions

The federal judiciary has the power, under the Supremacy Clause (Article VI, Section 2), to review state actions (e.g., court decisions, state statutes, executive orders) to ensure conformity with the Constitution, laws, and treaties of the United States. *Fletcher v. Peck*, 10 U.S. 87 (1810).

3. Limitations—Eleventh Amendment

The Eleventh Amendment is a jurisdictional bar that prohibits the citizens of one state from suing another state in federal court. It immunizes the state from suits for money damages or equitable relief when the state is a defendant in an action brought by a citizen of another state or a foreign country. Although state officials may be enjoined from violating federal law, the Eleventh Amendment bars suits against state officials for violating ***state*** law.

The Supreme Court has expanded the amendment's reach to also preclude citizens from suing their own state in federal court. *Hans v. Louisiana*, 134 U.S. 1 (1890).

Note that the Supreme Court has also barred federal-law actions brought against a state government without the state's consent in **state** court as a violation of **sovereign immunity.** *Alden v. Maine*, 527 U.S. 706 (1999).

a. Exceptions

There are, however, a few notable exceptions to the application of the Eleventh Amendment.

1) Consent

A state may consent to suit by expressly waiving its Eleventh Amendment protection (e.g., removing the case to federal court).

2) Injunctive relief

The Eleventh Amendment bars only suits for damages, not those for injunctive or declaratory relief, unless the state itself is enjoined. When a state official is named as the defendant, the state official may be sued in federal court to prevent enforcement of an unconstitutional state statute. *Ex parte Young*, 209 U.S. 123 (1908). A state cannot invoke its sovereign immunity to prevent a lawsuit by a state agency seeking to enforce a federal right against a state official. *Virginia Office for Prot. & Advocacy v. Stewart*, 563 U.S. ___, 131 S. Ct. 1632 (2011).

3) Damages to be paid by an individual

An action for damages against a state officer is not prohibited, as long as the officer himself (rather than the state treasury) will have to pay. Such is the case when an officer acts outside the law; the action is against the officer as an individual and not in his representative capacity.

4) Prospective damages

As long as the effect of a lawsuit is not to impose retroactive damages on a state officer to be paid from the state treasury, a federal court may hear an action against a state officer, even if the action will force a state to pay money to comply with a court order.

5) Congressional authorization

Congress may abrogate state immunity from liability if it is clearly acting to enforce rights created by the Fourteenth Amendment (e.g., equal protection) and does so expressly. *Fitzpatrick v. Bitzer*, 427 U.S. 445 (1976). Congress generally may not abrogate state immunity by exercising its powers under Article I. *Seminole Tribe of Florida v. Florida*, 517 U.S. 44 (1996).

b. Not barred by the Eleventh Amendment

1) Actions against local governments

The Eleventh Amendment applies only to states and state agencies. Local governments (e.g., counties, cities) are not immune from suit.

2) Actions by the United States government or other state governments not barred

The Eleventh Amendment has no application when the plaintiff is the United States or another state.

3) Bankruptcy proceedings

The Eleventh Amendment does not bar the actions of a Bankruptcy Court that impacts state finances. *Central Cmty. Coll. v. Katz*, 546 U.S. 356 (2006).

B. JURISDICTION OF THE SUPREME COURT

1. Original

Article III, Section 2 gives the Supreme Court "original jurisdiction" (i.e., the case may be filed first in the Supreme Court) over "all cases affecting ambassadors, other public ministers and consuls and those in which a State shall be a party." Congress may not expand or limit this jurisdiction. *Marbury v. Madison*, 5 U.S. 137 (1803). It may, however, grant concurrent original jurisdiction to lower federal courts.

2. Appellate

Article III, Section 2 also provides that "in all other cases before mentioned, the Supreme Court shall have appellate jurisdiction...with such exceptions, and under such regulations as the Congress shall make."

a. Means

There are two means of establishing appellate jurisdiction in the Supreme Court: certiorari (discretionary review) and direct appeal.

1) Certiorari

Almost all cases now come to the Supreme Court by way of a petition for a writ of certiorari, i.e., discretionary review. The Court takes jurisdiction only if at least four Justices vote to accept the case (the "rule of four").

2) Direct appeal

The Supreme Court **must** hear by direct appeal only a small number of cases—those that come from a decision on injunctive relief issued by a special three-judge district court panel. 28 U.S.C. § 1253. Although these panels (and appeals) were once fairly common, they are now limited to cases brought under a few specific statutes (e.g., the Voting Rights Act).

b. Limitations

Congress has some power to limit the Supreme Court's appellate jurisdiction. *Ex parte McCardle*, 74 U.S. 506 (1868). There are constraints on this power, because to deny all Supreme Court jurisdiction over certain types of cases would undermine the constitutional system of checks and balances. *Boumediene v. Bush*, 553 U.S. 723 (2008) (Congress and President cannot remove Supreme Court's authority to say "what the law is" (quoting *Marbury v. Madison*, 5 U.S. 137 (1803))).

Note that most federal cases are filed in district court and appealed, if at all, to the courts of appeals. The jurisdiction of the federal courts is set, within the framework of Article III, by statute. For example, Congress has set the minimum amount in controversy necessary for federal jurisdiction over a case between citizens of different states at more than $75,000. 28 U.S.C. § 1332.

c. Adequate and independent state grounds

A final state-court judgment that rests on adequate and independent state grounds may not be reviewed by the U.S. Supreme Court (or it would be an advisory opinion). The state-law grounds must fully resolve the matter (i.e., be adequate) and must not incorporate a federal standard by reference (i.e., be independent). When it is not clear whether the state court's decision rests on state or federal law, the Supreme Court may hear the case, decide the federal issue, and remand to the state court for resolution of any question of state law. *Michigan v. Long*, 463 U.S. 1032 (1983).

C. JUDICIAL REVIEW IN OPERATION

Standing, timing (mootness or ripeness), and other issues of justiciability may dictate whether a case may be heard by a federal court.

1. Standing

Article III, Section 2 restricts federal judicial power to "cases" and "controversies." A federal court cannot decide a case unless the plaintiff has standing—a concrete interest in the outcome—to bring it. Congress cannot statutorily eliminate the constitutional standing requirement simply by allowing citizen suits, *Lujan v. Defenders of Wildlife*, 504 U.S. 555 (1992), but it can create new interests, the injury to which may establish standing, *Massachusetts v. EPA*, 549 U.S. 497 (2007).

a. General rule

To have standing, a plaintiff bears the burden of establishing three elements:

i) **Injury in fact**;

ii) **Causation** (the injury must be caused by the defendant's violation of a constitutional or other federal right); and

iii) **Redressability** (the relief requested must prevent or redress the injury).

See, e.g., Lujan v. Defenders of Wildlife, 504 U.S. 555 (1982); *Valley Forge Christian College v. Americans United for Separation of Church and State, Inc.*, 454 U.S. 464 (1982).

> **EXAM NOTE:** When answering questions about standing, eliminate answer choices involving only the substance of the claim and focus on whether the plaintiff is legally qualified to press a claim, regardless of merit.

1) Injury in fact

The injury must be **concrete** and **particularized.**

a) Individualized injury

When a plaintiff has been directly injured "it does not matter how many people" were also injured; when "a harm is concrete, though widely shared," there is standing. *Massachusetts v. EPA*, 549 U.S. 497 (2007). However, even though an injury may satisfy the injury-in-fact standard, the court may refuse to adjudicate a claim by the application of the principles of prudence. Under this prudential-standing principle, an injury that is shared by all or a large class of citizens (i.e., a generalized grievance) is not sufficiently individualized to give the plaintiff standing. *Warth v. Seldin*, 422 U.S. 490 (1975).

b) Type of injury

The injury need not be physical or economic. *United States v. SCRAP*, 412 U.S. 669 (1973). While a generalized harm to the environment does not confer standing, if the alleged harm affects recreational "or even mere esthetic interests," that will be sufficient. *See Summers v. Earth Island Inst.*, 555 U.S. 488 (2009).

c) Future injury

While the threat of future injury can suffice, it cannot be merely hypothetical or conjectural, but must be actual and imminent. When a future injury is alleged, damages cannot be obtained, but an injunction can be sought.

2) Causation

The plaintiff must show that the injury was fairly traceable to the challenged action—that is, that the defendant's conduct caused the injury. *Warth v. Seldin*, 422 U.S. 490 (1975).

3) Redressability

It must be likely (as opposed to speculative) that a favorable court decision will redress a discrete injury suffered by the plaintiff.

b. Taxpayer status

Usually, a taxpayer does not have standing to file a federal lawsuit simply because the taxpayer believes that the government has allocated funds in an improper way. However, a taxpayer does have standing to litigate whether, or how much, she owes on her tax bill.

> **EXAM NOTE:** The standing of taxpayers is frequently tested on the MBE. A taxpayer has standing when the taxpayer challenges governmental expenditures as violating the Establishment Clause.

1) Governmental conduct

The conduct of the federal government, or of any state government, is too far removed from individual taxpayer returns for any injury to the taxpayer to be traced to the use of tax revenues. *DaimlerChrysler Corp. v. Cuno*, 547 U.S. 332 (2006). Long-standing precedent, however, suggests that a municipal taxpayer does have standing to sue a municipal government in federal court. *Crampton v. Zabriskie*, 101 U.S. 601 (1879).

2) Exception—Establishment Clause challenge

There is an exception for a taxpayer suit challenging a **specific congressional appropriation** made under the taxing and spending powers for violation of the Establishment Clause. *Flast v. Cohen*, 392 U.S. 83 (1968). This exception does not apply to the transfer of property to a religious organization by Congress under the Property Power, *Valley Forge Christian College v. Americans United for Separation of Church and State*, 454 U.S. 464 (1982), nor to expenditures made by the President to religious organizations from monies appropriated by Congress to the President's general discretionary fund, *Hein v. Freedom From Religion Foundation*, 551 U.S. 587 (2007).

c. Third-party standing

A litigant generally has no standing to bring a lawsuit based on legal claims of a third party. There are a few notable exceptions to this rule, however:

i)   If the third parties would experience difficulty or are **unable to assert their own rights,** such as a Caucasian defendant raising equal protection and due process objections to discrimination against African-American people in the selection of grand juries, *Campbell v. Louisiana*, 523 U.S. 392 (1998);

ii) If there is a **special relationship between the plaintiff and the third parties,** such as an employer asserting the rights of its employees, a doctor asserting the rights of his patients in challenging an abortion ruling, *Singleton v. Wulff*, 428 U.S. 106 (1976), or a private school asserting its students' rights to attend despite a statute requiring attendance at public schools, *Pierce v. Society of Sisters*, 268 U.S. 510 (1925); and

iii) If a plaintiff suffers an injury, and **the injury adversely affects the plaintiff's relationship with a third party,** the plaintiff may assert the third-party's rights. *Craig v. Boren*, 429 U.S. 190 (1976).

The rule that a litigant has no standing to bring a lawsuit on behalf of a third party is based on prudential or discretionary considerations. The federal courts may refuse to hear any case on prudential-standing grounds. *Elk Grove Unified School Dist. v. Newdow*, 542 U.S. 1 (2004).

1) Organizational standing

An organization may bring an action when it has suffered an injury. In addition, an organization may bring an action on behalf of its members (even if the organization has not suffered an injury itself) if:

i) Its members would have standing to sue in their own right; and

ii) The interests at stake are germane to the organization's purpose.

Hunt v. Washington State Apple Adver. Comm'n., 432 U.S. 333 (1977). When damages are sought, generally neither the claim asserted nor the relief requested can require the participation of individual members in the lawsuit. But note that the damages limitation is not constitutionally mandated and can be waived by Congress. *United Food & Commer. Workers Union Local 751 v. Brown Group*, 517 U.S. 544 (1996).

2) Parental standing

Generally, a parent has standing to bring an action on behalf of the parent's minor child. However, after a divorce, the right to bring such an action may be limited to only one of the child's parents. Moreover, when the right to bring such an action is based on family-law rights that are in dispute, the federal courts should not entertain an action if prosecution of the lawsuit may have an adverse effect on the child. *Elk Grove Unified School District v. Newdow*, 542 U.S. 1 (2004) (noncustodial parent with joint legal custody could not challenge school policy on behalf of his daughter when the custodial parent opposed the action).

d. Assignee standing

An assignee of a claim has standing to enforce the rights of an assignor, even when the assignee is contractually obligated to return any litigation proceeds to the assignor (e.g., an assignee for collection), provided the assignment was made for ordinary business purposes and in good faith. *Sprint Commc'ns Co., L.P. v. APCC Servs., Inc.*, 554 U.S. 269 (2008).

e. Citizenship standing

Citizens do not have standing to assert a claim to enforce a constitutional provision merely because they are citizens, although a citizen may bring an action against the government to compel adherence to a specific federal statute. Even in such a case, the plaintiff must have directly suffered an injury in fact.

f. Standing to assert a Tenth Amendment violation

A party has standing to challenge the constitutionality of a federal statute on the grounds that it exceeds Congress's enumerated powers and intrudes upon the powers reserved to the states by the Tenth Amendment. *Bond v. United States*, 564 U.S. ___, 131 S. Ct. 2355 (2011) (defendant prosecuted for violation of federal statute).

2. Timeliness

An action that is brought too soon ("unripe") or too late ("moot") will not be heard.

a. Ripeness

"Ripeness" refers to the readiness of a case for litigation. A federal court will not consider a claim before it has fully developed; to do so would be premature, and any potential injury would be speculative.

For a case to be "ripe" for litigation, the plaintiff must have experienced a **real injury** (or imminent threat thereof). Hence, if an ambiguous law has a long history of non-enforcement, a case challenging that law may lack ripeness. *See Poe v. Ullman*, 367 U.S. 497 (1961).

b. Mootness

A case has become moot if further legal proceedings would have no effect; that is, if there is no longer a controversy. A **live controversy** must exist **at each stage of review,** not merely when the complaint is filed, in order for a case to be viable at that stage.

> **Example:** The classic example of mootness is the case of *DeFunis v. Odegaard*, 416 U.S. 312 (1974). The plaintiff was a student who had been denied admission to law school and had then been provisionally admitted while the case was pending. Because the student was scheduled to graduate within a few months at the time the decision was rendered, and there was no action that the law school could take to prevent it, the Court determined that a decision on its part would have no effect on the student's rights. Therefore, the case was dismissed as moot.

1) Exception—capable of repetition, yet evading review

A case will not be dismissed as moot if the controversy is a type that may often recur ("capable of repetition") but that will not last long enough to work its way through the judicial system ("yet evading review").

> **Example:** The most cited example of this exception is *Roe v. Wade*, 410 U.S. 113 (1973), when the state argued that the case was moot because the plaintiff, who was challenging a Texas statute forbidding abortion, was no longer pregnant by the time the case reached the Supreme Court. Because of the relatively short human gestation period (compared to a lawsuit), abortion litigation was readily capable of being repeated, but also likely to evade review, and the case was not dismissed as moot.

2) Exception—voluntary cessation

A court will not dismiss as moot a case in which the defendant voluntarily ceases its illegal or wrongful action once litigation has commenced. The court must be assured that "there is no reasonable expectation that the wrong will be repeated." *United States v. W.T. Grant Co.*, 345 U.S. 629 (1953).

3) Exception—class actions

If the named plaintiff's claim in a certified class action is resolved and becomes moot, that fact does not render the entire class action moot. *United States Parole Comm'n. v. Geraghty*, 445 U.S. 388 (1980).

3. Justiciability—Further Issues

Federal courts may invoke a variety of other reasons not to decide a case.

a. Advisory opinions

Federal courts may not render advisory opinions on the basis of an abstract or a hypothetical dispute. An actual case or controversy must exist.

> **EXAM NOTE:** Fact patterns involving a request for declaratory judgment are likely testing advisory opinion prohibition.

b. Declaratory judgments

The courts are not prohibited from issuing declaratory judgments, however, that determine the legal effect of proposed conduct without awarding damages or injunctive relief. The challenged action must pose a real and immediate danger to a party's interests for there to be an actual dispute (as opposed to a hypothetical one).

c. Political questions

A federal court will not rule on a matter in controversy if the matter is a political question to be resolved by one or both of the other two branches of government. *Baker v. Carr*, 369 U.S. 186 (1962).

A political question not subject to judicial review arises when:

i) The Constitution has assigned decision making on this subject to a different branch of the government; or

ii) The matter is inherently not one that the judiciary can decide.

Example: Details of Congress's impeachment procedures (constitutionally assigned to a branch other than the judiciary) and the President's conduct of foreign affairs (not within judicial competence) are examples of political questions.

Compare: The political question doctrine does not bar courts from adjudicating the constitutionality of a federal statute directing that an American child born in Jerusalem is entitled to have Israel listed as her place of birth in her U.S. passport. The Court held that the Constitution did not commit the issue to another branch of government and resolving the case would involve examining "textual, structural, and historical evidence" concerning statutory and constitutional provisions, something within judicial competence. *Zivotofsky ex rel. Zivotofsky v. Clinton*, 132 S. Ct. 1421 (2012).

4. Abstention

A federal court may abstain from deciding a claim when strong state interests are at stake:

a. *Pullman* doctrine

A court may refrain from ruling on a federal constitutional claim that depends on resolving an unsettled issue of state law best left to the state courts. *Railroad Comm'n of Texas v. Pullman*, 312 U.S. 496 (1941).

b. *Younger* abstention

A court will generally not enjoin a pending state criminal case or a state enforcement proceeding in which an especially strong state interest is involved. *Younger v. Harris*, 401 U.S. 37 (1971). The exception to this abstention is seen in cases of proven harassment or prosecutions taken in bad faith.

II. THE POWERS OF CONGRESS

Just as the federal courts are courts of limited jurisdiction, the powers of Congress are not plenary or exclusive. As the Tenth Amendment makes clear, the federal government may exercise only those powers specifically enumerated by the Constitution; it is state governments and the people, not the national government, that retain any powers not mentioned in the federal charter. Any action by the federal government must be supported by a source of power originating in the Constitution. Article I, Section 1 vests all legislative powers of the federal government in Congress.

> **EXAM NOTE:** Congress has no general police power to legislate for the health, safety, welfare, or morals of citizens. The validity of a federal statute on the bar exam may not be justified based on "federal police power."

A. COMMERCE

Article I, Section 8, Clause 3 of the Constitution, known as the Commerce Clause, empowers Congress "[t]o regulate Commerce with foreign Nations, and among the several States, and with the Indian Tribes." The term "commerce" has been defined to include essentially all activity—including transportation, traffic, or transmission of gas, electricity, radio, TV, mail, and telegraph—involving or affecting two or more states.

1. Interstate Commerce

a. Power to regulate

Congress has the power to regulate (i) the **channels** (highways, waterways, airways, etc.) and (ii) the **instrumentalities** (cars, trucks, ships, airplanes, etc.) of interstate commerce, as well as (iii) any activity that **substantially affects** interstate commerce, provided that the regulation does not infringe upon any other constitutional right. *United States v. Lopez*, 514 U.S. 549 (1995).

b. Construed broadly

The Supreme Court has upheld acts of Congress seeking to prohibit or restrict the entry of persons, products, and services into the stream of interstate commerce, as well as acts regulating the interstate movement of kidnap victims, stolen vehicles, and telephone transmissions.

2. "Substantial Economic Effect"

Congress has the power to regulate any activity, intra- or interstate, that in and of itself or in combination with other activities has a "substantial economic effect upon" or "effect on movement in" interstate commerce.

a. Aggregation

With respect to an intrastate activity that does not have a direct economic impact on interstate commerce, such as growing crops for personal consumption, as long as there is a **rational basis** for concluding that the "total incidence" of the activity in the aggregate substantially affects interstate commerce, Congress may regulate even a minute amount of that total. *Gonzales v. Raich*, 545 U.S. 1 (2005) (prohibition on personal cultivation and use of medical marijuana upheld due to effect on overall interstate trade). The practical effect of this rule is that with regard to economic activity, a substantial economic effect is presumed.

Example: The Supreme Court upheld congressional restriction of wheat production, even when applied to a farmer growing only 23 acres of wheat, primarily for personal use. The rationale behind the decision was that if every small farmer were allowed to grow an unrestricted amount of wheat, the combined effect could have an impact on supply and demand in the interstate market. *Wickard v. Filburn*, 317 U.S. 111 (1942).

3. Non-Economic Activity

Congress's power under the Commerce Clause to regulate **intrastate** activity that is not obviously economic (so-called "non-economic" activity) is limited to some degree by principles of federalism, at least when the regulation involves an area of traditional state concern. The non-economic activity must have a substantial economic effect on interstate commerce. *Nat'l Fed'n of Indep. Bus. v. Sebelius (The Patient Protection and Affordable Care Cases)*, 132 S. Ct. 2566 (2012) (requiring individuals not engaged in commercial activities to buy unwanted health insurance could not be sustained as a regulation of interstate commerce); *United States v. Morrison*, 529 U.S. 598 (2000) (federal civil remedy for victims of gender-motivated violence held invalid); *United States v. Lopez*, 514 U.S. 549 (1995) (federal statute regulating possession of a firearm within 1,000 feet of a public school struck down).

B. TAXATION AND SPENDING

Article I, Section 8 provides: "Congress shall have power to lay and collect taxes, duties, imposts and excises, to pay the debts and provide for the common defense and general welfare of the United States; but all duties, imposts and excises shall be uniform throughout the United States."

EXAM NOTE: If you see the word "appropriation" on the exam, the power to tax and spend is likely a consideration.

1. **Taxing**

A tax by Congress will generally be upheld if it has a **reasonable relationship to revenue production,** or if Congress has the **power to regulate** the activity being taxed, subject to certain limitations.

> **Example:** The Affordable Health Act's individual mandate, requiring individuals to buy health insurance or pay a penalty, merely imposed a tax on those who failed to buy insurance and therefore could be sustained under the taxing power. *Nat'l Fed'n of Indep. Bus. v. Sebelius (The Patient Protection and Affordable Care Cases)*, 132 S. Ct. 2566 (2012).

a. **Power is plenary**

Article I, Section 8 of the Constitution gives Congress the plenary (i.e., exclusive) power to raise revenue through the imposition of taxes. The government has no burden to prove that the tax is necessary to any compelling governmental interest. Instead, the General Welfare Clause has been interpreted as permitting Congress to exercise its power to tax for any public purpose. (Note: This clause has been interpreted as having the same effect on the spending power, as discussed at § II.B.2. Spending, *infra.*)

> While the General Welfare Clause gives Congress broad power in exercising its spending and taxing powers, it does not give Congress the specific power to legislate for the public welfare in general. Such "police power" is reserved for the states.

b. **Uniformity**

The requirement that all federal taxes must be uniform throughout the United States has been interpreted to mean **geographical** uniformity only; the product or activity at issue must be identically taxed in every state in which it is found. Differences in state law do not destroy this uniformity. *Fernandez v. Wiener*, 326 U.S. 340 (1945) (federal estate tax on "community property" valid despite variation in state laws regarding marital property).

c. **Direct tax**

Article I, Section 2 provides that "[r]epresentatives and direct taxes shall be apportioned among the several states," and Article I, Section 9 provides that "no...direct tax shall be laid, unless in proportion to the Census...." A direct tax (one imposed directly on property or persons, such as an ad valorem property tax) would therefore have to be apportioned evenly among the states. The difficulty of ensuring this outcome explains Congress's reluctance to enact such taxes—or perhaps the Supreme Court's reluctance to find that federal taxes are "direct." The Sixteenth Amendment gave Congress the power to lay and collect **income tax** without apportionment among the states.

d. **Export tax**

Goods exported to foreign countries may not be taxed for that reason by Congress or the states. Article I, Sections 9, 10.

2.   Spending

The spending power has been interpreted very broadly. Congress has the power to **spend for the "general welfare"**—i.e., any public purpose—not just to pursue its other enumerated powers. *U.S. v. Butler*, 297 U.S. 1 (1936). For example, Congress can provide for the public funding of presidential nominating conventions as well as election campaigns. *Buckley v. Valeo*, 424 U.S. 1 (1976). Although there are areas in which Congress cannot directly regulate, it can use its spending power to accomplish such regulation indirectly by conditioning federal funding. *See South Dakota v. Dole*, 483 U.S. 203 (1987) (statute upheld withholding federal highway funds from states unless they barred the sale of alcoholic beverages to individuals under the age of 21).

Congress cannot impose unconstitutional conditions, such as requiring distribution of the Ten Commandments to patients as a condition of Medicaid funding. *South Dakota v. Dole*, 483 U.S. 203 (1987).

C.   WAR AND DEFENSE POWERS

Article I, Section 8 gives Congress the power to declare war, raise and support armies, provide and maintain a navy, make rules for governing and regulating the land and naval forces, and provide for the organizing of a militia.

1.   Providing for the National Defense

The authority granted to Congress under the war power is very broad. Congress may take whatever action it deems necessary to provide for the national defense in both wartime and peacetime. The Court has upheld the military draft and selective service; wage, price, and rent control of the civilian economy during wartime (and even during the post-war period); and the exclusion of civilians from restricted areas.

2.   Courts and Tribunals

Congress has the power to establish military courts and tribunals under Article I, Section 8, Clause 14 and the Necessary and Proper Clause. These courts may try enemy soldiers, enemy civilians, and current members of the U.S. armed forces, but they do not have jurisdiction over U.S. civilians. U.S. citizens captured and held as "enemy combatants" are entitled, as a matter of due process, to contest the factual basis of their detention before a neutral decision maker. *Hamdi v. Rumsfeld*, 542 U.S. 507 (2004). Under the Suspension Clause of Article I, Section 9, Clause 2, all persons held in a territory over which the United States has sovereign control are entitled to habeas corpus (or similar) review of the basis for their detention, unless the privilege of seeking habeas corpus has been suspended. *Boumediene v. Bush*, 553 U.S. 723, (2008).

Because military tribunals are not Article III courts, not all constitutional protections apply (such as the right to a jury trial or grand jury indictment).

3.   National Guard

The President has the authority to order units of the National Guard into federal service without the consent of the governor of the respective state. Generally, the National Guard will be called to service to assist in times of national emergency. However, this authority extends to circumstances when no national emergency exists.

D. INVESTIGATORY POWER

Congress does not have an express power to investigate, but the Necessary and Proper Clause allows Congress broad authority to conduct investigations incident to its power to legislate. *McGrain v. Daugherty*, 273 U.S. 135 (1927).

1. Scope

The investigatory power may extend to any matter within a "legitimate legislative sphere." According to the Speech and Debate Clause of Article I, Section 6, members of Congress cannot be questioned in regard to activities such as speech or debate taking place during a session in either House of Congress in relation to the business before it. This provides an absolute immunity from judicial interference. *Eastland v. Unites States Servicemen's Fund*, 421 U.S. 491 (1975).

2. Enforcement and Witness's Rights

A subpoenaed witness who fails to appear before Congress or refuses to answer questions may be cited for contempt. The witness is entitled to certain rights, including procedural due process (e.g., presence of counsel) and the privilege against self-incrimination.

E. PROPERTY POWER

Article IV, Section 3 gives Congress the "power to dispose of and make all needful rules and regulations respecting the territory or other property belonging to the United States." There is no express limit on Congress's power to **dispose** of property owned by the United States. Under the Fifth Amendment, however, Congress may only **take** private property for public use (eminent domain) with just compensation and in order to effectuate an enumerated power.

F. POSTAL POWER

Congress has the exclusive power "to establish post offices and post roads" under Article I, Section 8, Clause 7. Congress may impose reasonable restrictions on the use of the mail (such as prohibiting obscene or fraudulent material to be mailed), but the postal power may not be used to abridge any right guaranteed by the Constitution (e.g., the First Amendment).

G. POWER OVER ALIENS AND CITIZENSHIP

1. Aliens

Congress has plenary power over aliens. *Fiallo v. Bell*, 430 U.S. 787 (1977). Aliens have no right to enter the United States and may be refused entry for reasons such as their political beliefs. *Kleindienst v. Mandel*, 408 U.S. 753 (1972). However, this power is subject to the constraints of the Fifth Amendment Due Process Clause for an alien within the United States. *Zadvydas v. Davis*, 533 U.S. 678 (2001). An alien may generally be removed from the United States, but only after notice and a removal hearing. 8 U.S.C. §§ 1229, 1229a.

2. Naturalization

Congress has exclusive authority over naturalization. Article I, Section 8, Clause 4 allows Congress to "establish a uniform rule of naturalization."

> **Example:** Children born abroad whose parents are U.S. citizens are not automatically entitled to U.S. citizenship. Congress can grant citizenship conditioned on the child's return to the U.S. within a specified timeframe or for a specified duration. *Rogers v. Bellei*, 401 U.S. 815 (1971).

However, the right of national citizenship in the Fourteenth Amendment prevents Congress from taking away the citizenship of any citizen without her consent, unless that citizenship was obtained by fraud or in bad faith. *Afroyim v. Rusk*, 387 U.S. 253 (1967) (federal statute that stripped citizenship for voting in a foreign election struck down); *Costello v. United States*, 365 U.S. 265 (1961) (citizen's willful failure to accurately state his occupation on a naturalization application resulted in loss of citizenship).

H. OTHER ARTICLE I POWERS

Congress has power over **bankruptcies, maritime matters, coining of money,** fixing of **weights and measures,** and **patents and copyrights.**

1. Power Over the District of Columbia

Article I, Section 8 provides that Congress shall have the power to: "exercise exclusive Legislation in all Cases whatsoever, over such District (not exceeding ten Miles square) as may, by Cession of particular States, and the acceptance of Congress, become the Seat of the Government of the United States." Thus, Congress has supreme authority over Washington, D.C., and may legislate freely with regard to D.C. law.

2. Elections Clause

Article I, Section 4 of the Constitution provides: "The times, places and manner of holding elections for Senators and Representatives shall be prescribed by each state legislature, but Congress may...make or alter such regulations." The Elections Clause explicitly empowers Congress to override state laws concerning federal elections.

3. Necessary and Proper Clause

Congress is given the power to enact any legislation necessary and proper to execute any authority granted to any branch of the federal government. *McCulloch v. Maryland*, 17 U.S. 316 (1819). The Necessary and Proper Clause is not an independent source of power, but it permits Congress's otherwise designated authority to be exercised fully.

> **EXAM NOTE:** Because the Necessary and Proper Clause is not an independent source of power, it is not a correct answer choice by itself unless it carries into effect other enumerated powers.

I. POWER TO ENFORCE THE THIRTEENTH, FOURTEENTH, AND FIFTEENTH AMENDMENTS

Each of the Thirteenth, Fourteenth, and Fifteenth Amendments contains a provision that authorizes Congress to pass "appropriate legislation" to enforce the civil rights guaranteed by those amendments.

1. **Thirteenth Amendment—Ban on Slavery**

   Congress has the power to adopt legislation rationally related to eliminating racial discrimination, as it is among the "badges or incidents" of slavery. *Jones v. Alfred H. Mayer Co.,* 392 U.S. 409 (1968). This power has been broadly interpreted to allow Congress to regulate both private and government action, including racial discrimination by private housing sellers, private schools, and private employers. (This is the only amendment that authorizes Congress to regulate purely private conduct.)

2. **Fourteenth Amendment—Equal Protection and Due Process**

   The Fourteenth Amendment, Section 5 Enabling Clause permits Congress to pass legislation to enforce the equal protection and due process rights guaranteed by the amendment, but not to expand those rights or create new ones. Under the separation of powers doctrine, the job of defining such rights falls to the Supreme Court. In enforcing such rights, there must be a **"congruence and proportionality"** between the injury to be prevented or remedied and the means adopted to achieve that end. *City of Boerne v. Flores,* 521 U.S. 507 (1997) (Religious Freedom Restoration Act held invalid for failure to show widespread religious discrimination and for disproportion to any purported remedial goal). Congress may override state government action that infringes upon Fourteenth Amendment rights, but it may not under this amendment regulate wholly private conduct. In the exercise of Fourteenth Amendment powers, Congress can override the Eleventh Amendment immunity of states. *Fitzpatrick v. Bitzer,* 427 U.S. 445 (1976).

3. **Fifteenth Amendment—Voting**

   The Fifteenth Amendment prohibits both the state and federal governments from denying any citizen the right to vote on the basis of race, color, or previous condition of servitude. The courts have interpreted the right to vote to include the right to have that vote meaningfully counted.

J. QUALIFICATIONS OF MEMBERS

The qualifications for members of Congress are set forth in Article I and cannot be altered by Congress or the states. *United States Term Limits, Inc. v. Thornton,* 514 U.S. 779 (1995) (state-mandated term limits for federal representatives invalid); *Powell v. McCormack,* 395 U.S. 486 (1969) (House of Representatives could not refuse to seat a scandal-plagued member who satisfied constitutional criteria for service).

III. THE POWERS OF THE PRESIDENT

Article II, Section 1 grants the "executive power" to the President. The extent of this power has been interpreted broadly by the Supreme Court, which has emphasized that the President has no power to make laws but does have the power to enforce them; this enforcement power includes the exercise of prosecutorial discretion. *Davis v. U.S.,* 512 U.S. 452 (1994). Generally speaking, the President's authority is broader in the area of foreign affairs than in domestic matters.

A. DOMESTIC POWER

1. Pardon Power for Federal Offenses

Article II, Section 2 provides the President with the power to "grant reprieves and pardons for offenses against the United States, except in cases of impeachment." This power applies only to federal cases; the President may not grant pardons for state crimes.

2. Veto Power

Article I, Section 7 gives the President the power to veto any bill presented to him (i.e., passed) by Congress. Upon presentment, the President has 10 days to act on proposed legislation. If the President signs the bill, it becomes law. The President may also veto the bill by sending it back, with objections, to the house in which it originated. Congress may override the veto and enact the bill into law by a two-thirds vote in each house.

A third option is that the President does nothing at all. If Congress is still in session at the end of the 10-day period, the bill becomes law without the President's signature. If Congress has adjourned during that time, however, the bill does not become law, because the President could not have returned it to its originating house. The President's failure to act on a bill in this situation is known as the "pocket veto" and cannot be overridden.

The President may not exercise a "line item" veto, refusing part of a bill and approving the rest, because it violates the Presentment Clause. *Clinton v. City of New York*, 524 U.S. 417 (1998).

3. Appointment and Removal of Officials

a. Appointment

Article II, Section 2 authorizes the President, **with the advice and consent of the Senate,** to appoint all "officers of the United States," including ambassadors and Justices of the Supreme Court. Congress may, however, delegate the appointment of "inferior" officials to the President alone (i.e., without Senate approval), the heads of executive departments, or the courts. "Inferior" officials are those supervised by Senate-confirmed appointees. Congress may not itself appoint members of a body with administrative or enforcement powers; such persons are "officers of the United States" and must be appointed by the President. *Buckley v. Valeo*, 424 U.S. 1 (1976) (makeup of the Federal Election Commission invalidated because a majority of its members were to be appointed by the President Pro Tem of the Senate and the Speaker of the House; the FEC's tasks were executive in nature, therefore, Congress had no right to appoint such federal officers).

b. Removal

The Constitution says nothing about the President's power to remove executive officers, but it is generally accepted that the President may remove any executive appointee without cause (and without Senate approval). Congress may not shield appointees from removal by the President by imposing a multi-tiered system in which persons at each level may be removed from office only for good cause. *Free Enterprise Fund v. Public Company Accounting Oversight Bd.,*

561 U.S. ___, 130 S. Ct. 3138 (2010) (holding 15 U.S.C.S. §§ 7211(e)(6) and 7217(d)(3) unconstitutional and invalid because the multilevel protection from removal of members of the Public Company Accounting Oversight Board was contrary to Article II's vesting of the executive power in the President and contravened the Constitution's separation of powers).

Federal judges, however, are protected under Article III, Section 1, which provides that they may "hold their offices during good behavior"; they may be removed only by impeachment.

4. Authority as Chief Executive

The scope of the President's power to issue executive orders and to govern domestic affairs is extensive but not clearly delineated. The best-known exposition holds that the President's authority varies with the degree of congressional authorization of the action. Thus, when the President acts:

i) With the express or implied authorization of Congress, presidential authority is at its highest, and the action is strongly presumed to be valid;

ii) When Congress has not spoken, presidential authority is diminished, and the action is invalid if it interferes with the operations or power of another branch of government; and

iii) When Congress has spoken to the contrary, presidential authority is "at its lowest ebb," and the action is likely invalid. *Hamdan v. Rumsfeld*, 548 U.S. 557 (2006) (military commission had no jurisdiction to proceed because the executive order authorizing the commission exceeded congressional limitations placed on the President to convene commissions).

B. FOREIGN AFFAIRS

1. Commander in Chief

Although the President is the commander in chief of the military, only Congress may formally declare war. The President may take military action without a declaration of war in the case of actual hostilities against the United States. Congress may in turn limit the President's military activities through exercise of its military appropriation (i.e., funding) power. The questions of whether and to what extent the President may deploy troops overseas without congressional approval is unsettled; presidents routinely do so, and Congress routinely asserts its authority to approve the deployment. The courts have generally left the question to the political branches.

2. Treaties

The President represents and acts for the United States in day-to-day international affairs. In addition to appointing and receiving ambassadors, the President has the exclusive power to negotiate treaties, although a treaty may only be ratified with the concurrence of two-thirds of the Senate. A ratified treaty is "the supreme law of the land," so long as it does not conflict with any provision of the Constitution, and it takes precedence over any inconsistent state law. A treaty has the same authority as an act of Congress; should the two conflict, the one most recently adopted controls. Note that a non-self-executing treaty (one that requires legislation in order to implement its provisions) does not have the same force of law as an act of Congress until legislation is passed effectuating the treaty; the treaty serves as an independent source of authority for Congress to legislate, separate from its enumerated powers. The Constitution is superior to a treaty, and any conflict is resolved in favor of the Constitution. *Medellin v. Texas*, 552 U.S. 491 (2008) (in the absence of implementing legislation by Congress, the President did not have the authority to make a non-self-executing treaty binding on the states); *Youngstown Sheet & Tube v. Sawyer*, 343 U.S. 579 (1952) (Jackson, J., conc.).

3. Executive Agreements

The President has the power to enter into executive agreements with foreign nations (e.g., reciprocal trade agreements) that do not require the approval of two-thirds of the Senate. Although not expressly provided for in the Constitution, executive agreements may be made pursuant to prior (or subsequent) congressional authorization or pursuant to the President's authority over foreign affairs.

> Conflicting federal statutes and treaties take precedence over executive agreements, but executive agreements take precedence over conflicting state laws.

IV. FEDERAL INTERBRANCH RELATIONSHIPS

The separation of powers doctrine, which is inherent in the structure of the Constitution, ensures that the executive, legislative, and judicial branches of government remain separate and distinct in order to provide a system of checks and balances.

A. CONGRESSIONAL LIMITS ON THE EXECUTIVE

1. Impeachment

Article II, Section 4 states: "The President, Vice President and all civil officers of the United States shall be removed from office on impeachment for, and conviction of, treason, bribery, or other high crimes and misdemeanors." The House of Representatives determines what constitutes "high crimes and misdemeanors" and **may impeach (i.e., bring charges) by a majority vote.** The Senate tries the impeached official, and **a two-thirds vote is necessary for conviction.**

2. Appropriation

If Congress explicitly mandates an expenditure of funds, the President has no power to impound those funds (i.e., refuse to spend them or delay the spending). The President is permitted to exercise spending discretion if the authorizing legislation so provides.

> **EXAM NOTE:** Separation of powers questions often center on the President trying to impound funds appropriated by Congress. Remember that if Congress fails to mandate that the funds are to be spent, then impoundment is not a separation of powers violation.

3. Legislative Veto

It is unconstitutional for Congress to attempt a "legislative veto" of an executive action—that is, to retain direct control over the actions of an executive agency, rather than going through the proper channels of passing a bill.

> **Example:** In *INS v. Chadha*, 462 U.S. 919 (1983), a provision of law permitted either house of Congress to overturn a decision by the Attorney General granting an alien relief from deportation. The Supreme Court held such a one-house

congressional "veto" of a matter delegated to the executive to be unconstitutional as violating the carefully wrought legislative procedures set forth in Article I, which require passage of legislation by both Houses of Congress (i.e., bicameralism) and sending to the President pursuant to the Presentment Clauses for his approval or return. Thus, the Court made clear that a two-house legislative veto would be equally unconstitutional.

B. DELEGATION OF LEGISLATIVE POWER

Because Congress is vested by Article I with "all legislative powers," it may not delegate that power to any other branch of government. This principle is known as the "nondelegation doctrine." However, delegation of some of Congress's authority to the executive branch has consistently been held constitutional, so long as Congress specifies an "intelligible principle" to guide the delegate. *Whitman v. Am. Trucking Ass'ns, Inc.*, 531 U.S. 457 (2001).

Example: The IRS has been given the power to collect taxes that are assessed under the Internal Revenue Code. Although Congress has determined the amount to be taxed, it has delegated to the IRS the power to determine how such taxes are to be collected.

Almost any legislative delegation passes the "intelligible standards" requirement, so even broadly phrased standards have been upheld.

Examples: A delegation of authority to an executive agency to regulate broadcast licenses to the extent that "public interest, convenience, and necessity require" has been upheld. *Nat'l Broad. Co. v. United States*, 319 U.S. 190 (1943). Similarly, an administrative agency could set "just and reasonable" rates for natural gas sold in interstate commerce. *FPC v. Hope Natural Gas Co.*, 320 U.S. 591 (1944).

Certain powers, however, are nondelegable, such as the power of impeachment and the power to declare war.

EXAM NOTE: Because there is almost no limitation on the ability of Congress to delegate to the executive and judiciary branches, an answer choice on the MBE indicating that Congress has "exceeded its power to delegate" is almost always incorrect.

C. JUDICIAL LIMITATION OF CONGRESSIONAL POWER

Under the doctrine of separation of powers, Congress may not reinstate the right to bring a legal action after the Supreme Court has definitely rejected that right.

Example: The Supreme Court opinion had the effect of making a pending action time-barred. Accordingly, the defendant was granted summary judgment. A statute that revived the plaintiff's right to bring the action was struck down as a violation of the separation of powers doctrine. *Plaut v. Spendthrift Farm, Inc.*, 514 U.S. 211 (1995).

D. IMMUNITIES AND PRIVILEGES

1. Judicial

A judge is absolutely immune from civil liability for damages resulting from her judicial acts, including grave procedural errors and acts done maliciously or in excess of authority unless there is a clear absence of all jurisdiction. *Butz v. Economou*, 438 U.S. 478 (1987); *Stump v. Sparkman*, 435 U.S. 349 (1978). The judge is not immune, however, to lawsuits regarding nonjudicial activities, such as hiring and firing court employees. *Forrester v. White*, 484 U.S. 219 (1988).

Prosecutors are subject to similar immunity rules. *Imbler v. Pachtman*, 424 U.S. 409 (1976). Court officers who perform ministerial duties, such as court reporters, are entitled only to qualified, not absolute, immunity. *Antoine v. Byers & Anderson*, 508 U.S. 429 (1993).

Under 42 U.S.C. § 1983, a damage claim can be brought against a state official personally for violation of constitutional rights. The Supreme Court has recognized that a similar claim can be brought against federal officials. *Bivens v. Six Unknown Named Agents of Fed. Bureau of Narcotics*, 403 U.S. 388 (1971).

2. Legislative

The Speech or Debate Clause of Article I, Section 6 protects members of Congress from civil and criminal liability for statements and conduct made **in the regular course of the legislative process,** including a speech given on the floor of Congress, committee hearings, and reports. The activities of congressional aides are also protected if a legislator performing the same acts would be immune. *Gravel v. United States*, 408 U.S. 606 (1972).

State legislators: The Speech or Debate Clause does not apply to state legislators, but under the principles of federalism, state legislators are immune from liability for actions within the sphere of legitimate legislative activity (*see* § VI.B.1.b.2, State legislators, *infra*).

This protection does not foreclose prosecution for a crime, including the taking of bribes, when the crime does not require proof of legislative acts or inquiring into the motive behind those acts. *United States v. Brewster*, 408 U.S. 501 (1972). This protection also does not apply to speeches made outside Congress, or the "re-publication" (i.e., repeating) of a defamatory statement originally made in Congress. *Hutchinson v. Proxmire*, 443 U.S. 111 (1979).

3. Executive

a. Executive privilege

Executive privilege is a privilege with respect to the disclosure of confidential information by the executive branch to the judiciary or Congress. This privilege and the more narrow presidential privilege, which applies to communications made in the performance of a president's responsibilities to shape policies and make decisions, have been recognized by the Supreme Court. The presidential privilege survives an individual president's tenure, but this privilege is not absolute. *Cheney v. United States*, 542 U.S. 367 (2004); *United States v. Nixon*, 418 U.S. 683 (1974).

1) Criminal trial

Presidential communications must be made available in a criminal case if the prosecution demonstrates a need for the information. A judge may examine the communications in camera to determine whether the communications fall within the privilege. *United States v. Nixon, supra.*

2) Civil proceedings

An executive branch decision to withhold production of information in civil proceedings will be given greater deference than in a criminal trial because the need for information is "weightier" in the latter case. In a civil case, the court may be required to consider the issue of separation of powers without first requiring the executive branch to assert executive privilege. *Cheney v. United States Dist. Court, supra.*

3) Historical preservation

Congress can require the preservation of presidential papers and tape recordings. *Nixon v. Adm'r of Gen. Servs.*, 433 U.S. 425 (1977).

4) State secrets

Claims of privilege based on national security are generally accorded enhanced deference. *United States v. Reynolds*, 345 U.S. 1 (1953) (recognizing a "state secrets" privilege). *But see In re NSA Telcoms. Records Litig.*, 564 F. Supp. 2d 1109 (2008) (the "state secrets" privilege was a common-law privilege that could be limited by congressional action).

b. Executive immunity

1) Official duties

The President may not be sued for civil damages with regard to any acts performed as part of the President's **official responsibilities.** *Nixon v. Fitzgerald*, 457 U.S. 731 (1982). The President has no immunity, however, from a civil action based on conduct alleged to have occurred **before the President took office** or completely unrelated to carrying out his job. Moreover, the President may be subject to such a suit even while in office. *Clinton v. Jones*, 520 U.S. 681 (1997).

a) Presidential advisor

A senior presidential advisor (e.g., cabinet member) is not automatically entitled to enjoy derivatively the protection of absolute executive immunity. Although the Supreme Court has stated that such an advisor may be entitled to such protection when performing special functions that are vital to national security or foreign policy, the Court has also held that an Attorney General did not qualify for absolute immunity with respect to the authorization of a warrantless wiretap for national security purposes. The burden for establishing such immunity rests with the advisor. *Harlow v. Fitzgerald*, 457 U.S. 800 (1982); *Mitchell v. Forsyth*, 472 U.S. 511 (1985).

b) Federal officials

A federal official, in performing a discretionary (as opposed to ministerial) act, is entitled to qualified immunity from liability for civil damages when the official's conduct does not violate clearly established statutory and constitutional rights of which a reasonable person would have known. This is an objective standard; a plaintiff's bare allegations of malice are insufficient to overcome this immunity. *Harlow v. Fitzgerald*, 457 U.S. 800 (1982).

> **Example:** The Attorney General, in authorizing a warrantless wiretap for national security purposes, while not entitled to absolute immunity, was entitled to qualified immunity. The unconstitutionality of this authorization was not clearly established at the time of the authorization. *Mitchell v. Forsyth*, 472 U.S. 511 (1985).

PART TWO: THE FEDERAL SYSTEM

V. FEDERAL AND STATE POWERS

The federal system, under which the federal and state governments each have exclusive authority over some areas, yet share authority over other areas, is one of the Constitution's basic checks on governmental power.

A. EXCLUSIVE FEDERAL POWERS

The Constitution explicitly provides for some powers of the federal government to be exclusive, such as the powers to coin money or enter into treaties. Other powers are by their nature exclusively federal, such as the power to declare war and the power over citizenship; a state's attempt to exercise authority in these areas would essentially subvert the power of the federal government.

B. EXCLUSIVE STATE POWERS

The Tenth Amendment provides that all powers not assigned by the Constitution to the federal government are reserved to the states, or to the people. In theory, this gives the states expansive, exclusive power. In practice, however, given the broad interpretation of the Commerce Clause and the spending power, the federal government has very broad authority, making state power rarely exclusive.

C. CONCURRENT FEDERAL AND STATE LAWS—SUPREMACY CLAUSE

It is possible (and common) for the federal and state governments to legislate in the same area. When this happens, the Supremacy Clause (Article VI, paragraph 2) provides that federal law supersedes conflicting state law (*see* § VIII. Federal Preemption of State Law, *infra*).

VI. INTERGOVERNMENTAL IMMUNITIES

A. FEDERAL IMMUNITY

1. Regulation by the States

The states have no power to regulate the federal government—for example, by imposing state wage-and-hour laws on local federal offices—unless Congress permits the state regulation or unless the state regulation is not inconsistent with existing federal policy.

2. Taxation by the States

The federal government and its instrumentalities (such as a national bank) are immune from taxation by the states. *McCulloch v. Maryland*, 17 U.S. 316 (1819).

States may, however, impose generally applicable indirect taxes so long as they do not unreasonably burden the federal government (e.g., state income taxes on federal employees).

B. STATE IMMUNITY

1. Federal Regulation

The federal government has virtually unlimited power to regulate the states.

a. Congressional action

As long as Congress is exercising one of its enumerated powers, Congress generally may regulate the states. For example, a federal minimum wage and overtime statute enacted under the commerce power can be applied to state employees. *Garcia v. San Antonio Metropolitan Transit Authority*, 469 U.S. 528 (1985). Similarly, Congress could prohibit the disclosure by state officials of personal information obtained from driver's license applications because such information constitutes an article of commerce that is being sold in interstate commerce. *Reno v. Condon*, 528 U.S. 141 (2000).

If Congress determines that a state is violating a person's civil liberties, it can place limits on that state's activities by using the power of the Fourteenth and Fifteenth Amendments. *See Oregon v. Mitchell*, 400 U.S. 112 (1970).

1) "Commandeering" limitation

Congress cannot "commandeer" state legislatures by commanding them to enact specific legislation or administer a federal regulatory program, and it may not circumvent that restriction by conscripting a state executive officer directly. *Printz v. United States*, 521 U.S. 898 (1997); *New York v. United States*, 505 U.S. 144 (1992). However, through the use of the taxing and spending powers, Congress may encourage state action that it cannot directly compel.

Example: In *South Dakota v. Dole*, 483 U.S. 203 (1987), the Court held that Congress could condition a provision of five percent of federal highway funds on the state's raising its drinking age to 21; the amount at issue did not exceed the point at which "pressure turns into compulsion."

b. Judicial action

1) Remedying constitutional violations

The federal judiciary has broad equitable powers in fashioning a remedy for a constitutional violation. For example, while a court may not directly impose a tax in order to fund a racial-discrimination remedy, it may order a local government with taxing authority to levy such a tax, and it may do so despite a state statutory limitation that would otherwise prevent such action. *Missouri v. Jenkins*, 495 U.S. 33 (1990).

2) State legislators

State legislators are absolutely immune from suit for damages and for declaratory and injunctive relief for actions within the sphere of legitimate legislative activity. *Supreme Court of Virginia v. Consumers Union of U.S., Inc.*, 446 U.S. 719 (1980); *Tenney v. Brandhove*, 341 U.S. 367 (1951).

2. Federal Taxation

States are not immune from federal taxation unless the tax would discourage essential governmental functions. *Helvering v. Gerhardt*, 304 U.S. 405 (1938). This is particularly true when the taxed state activity is a business similar to federally taxed businesses run by private individuals, such as railroads or liquor stores. *New York v. United States*, 326 U.S. 572 (1946).

3. Litigation Involving the United States and Its Officers

In suits between a state and the United States, the United States must consent before the state can file suit against it; conversely, the United States does not need to obtain consent from a state to file suit against that state. As between states, no consent is needed for one state to file suit against another state.

Suits against federal officers are limited, and generally prohibited, because such suits are considered to be brought against the United States if payment of the award will be made from the public treasury. However, if the federal officer acted outside the scope of his professional capacity, then a suit may be instituted against the officer individually.

VII. STATE REGULATION AND TAXATION OF COMMERCE

The Constitution contemplates a system of regulation of commerce and taxation that includes both the federal and state governments.

A. THE DORMANT COMMERCE CLAUSE

The Dormant Commerce Clause (sometimes referred to as the negative implication of the commerce clause) is a doctrine that limits the power of states to legislate in ways that impact interstate commerce. The Commerce Clause (Article I, Section 8, Clause 3) reserves to Congress the power "[t]o regulate commerce with foreign nations, and among the several states, and with the Indian tribes"; as a corollary, individual states are limited in their ability to legislate on such matters.

1. General Rule

If Congress has not enacted legislation in a particular area of interstate commerce, then the states are free to regulate, so long as the state or local action does not:

i) **Discriminate** against out-of-state commerce;

ii) **Unduly burden** interstate commerce; and

iii) Regulate **extraterritorial** (wholly out-of-state) activity.

2. Discrimination Against Out-of-State Commerce

A state or local regulation discriminates against out-of-state commerce if it protects local economic interests at the expense of out-of-state competitors. *See City of Philadelphia v. New Jersey*, 437 U.S. 617 (1978) (state statute prohibiting importation of out-of-state garbage discriminated in favor of local trash collectors); *Dean Milk Co. v. City of Madison*, 340 U.S. 349 (1959) (state law discriminated against out-of-state milk suppliers by requiring all milk sold in the city to be processed and bottled locally).

a. Necessary to important state interest

If a state or local regulation, on its face or in practice, is discriminatory, then the regulation may be upheld if the state or local government can establish that:

i) An important local interest is being served; and

ii) No other nondiscriminatory means are available to achieve that purpose.

Discriminatory regulation has rarely been upheld. In a few instances, a discriminatory state or local regulation that furthers an important, non-economic state interest, like health and safety, has not been struck down. *Maine v. Taylor*, 477 U.S. 131 (1986) (upheld a prohibition against importation into the state of out-of-state live baitfish that may pose contamination hazards to local waters).

b. Market-participant exception

A state may behave in a discriminatory fashion if it is acting as a market participant (buyer or seller), as opposed to a market regulator. If the state is a market participant, it may favor local commerce or discriminate against nonresident commerce as could any private business. *E.g., Reeves, Inc. v. Stake*, 447 U.S. 429 (1980) (state-owned cement plant may, in times of shortage, sell only to in-state buyers).

c. Traditional government function exception

State and local regulations may favor state and local **government** entities, though not local **private** entities, when those entities are performing a traditional governmental function, such as waste disposal. For example, an ordinance may require all trash haulers to deliver to a local **public** waste-treatment facility, but **not** to a local **private** facility. *Compare United Haulers Ass'n, Inc. v. Oneida-Herkimer Solid Waste Mgmt. Auth.*, 550 U.S. 330 (2007) (public facility), *with C & A Carbone, Inc. v. Town of Clarkstown*, 511 U.S. 383 (1994) (private facility). Similarly, a state may discriminate against out-of-state interests when raising money to fund state and local government projects. *Dep't of Revenue of Kentucky v. Davis*, 553 U.S. 328 (2008) (upholding state income tax exemption for income earned on state and local bonds, but not out-of-state bonds).

d. Subsidy exception

A state may favor its own citizens when providing for subsidy. For example, a state may offer in-state residents a lower tuition rate to attend a state college or university than out-of-state residents. *Vlandis v. Kline*, 412 U.S. 441 (1973).

e. Exception—congressionally permitted discrimination

Because Congress has exclusive authority over interstate commerce, it may explicitly permit states to act in ways that would otherwise violate the Dormant Commerce Clause. *Prudential Ins. Co. v. Benjamin*, 328 U.S. 408 (1946) (state tax only on out-of-state insurance companies upheld when Congress had enacted a law permitting states to regulate insurance in any manner consistent with federal statutes). It must be unmistakably clear that Congress intended to permit the otherwise impermissible state regulation; Congress must expressly allow or "affirmatively contemplate" such state legislation. The fact that the state policy appears to be consistent with federal policy or that the state policy furthers the goals that Congress had in mind is insufficient. *South–Central Timber Dev., Inc. v. Wunnicke*, 467 U.S. 82, 90 (1984).

3. Undue Burden on Interstate Commerce

a. Balancing test

A state regulation that is not discriminatory may still be struck down as unconstitutional if it imposes an undue burden on interstate commerce. The courts will balance, case by case, the objective and purpose of the state law against the burden on interstate commerce and evaluate whether there are less restrictive alternatives. If the benefits of the state law are grossly outweighed by the burdens on interstate commerce, then even nondiscriminatory regulation may be struck down. *Pike v. Bruce Church, Inc.*, 397 U.S. 137 (1970). This balancing test is not a cost-benefit analysis or a form of close scrutiny of state economic regulation. *United Haulers Ass'n v. Oneida-Herkimer Solid Waste Mgmt. Auth.*, 550 U.S. 330 (2007).

b. "Extraterritoriality"

States may not regulate conduct that occurs wholly beyond their borders. Thus, Connecticut could not require that beer sold in Connecticut not be priced higher than beer sold in any of the four neighboring states, because the Connecticut regime had the practical effect of regulating beer prices in those states. *Healy v. Beer Inst., Inc.*, 491 U.S. 324 (1989). There may be an exception for the regulation of the internal affairs of corporations. *CTS Corp. v. Dynamics Corp.*, 481 U.S. 69 (1987).

B. STATE TAXATION OF COMMERCE

1. Interstate Commerce

Much as with regulation, the states may tax interstate commerce only if Congress has not already acted in the particular area and if the tax does not discriminate against or unduly burden interstate commerce.

a. *Complete Auto* Test

The Supreme Court applies a four-part test to determine whether a state tax on interstate commerce comports with the Commerce Clause. *Complete Auto Transit, Inc. v. Brady*, 430 U.S. 274 (1977).

1) Substantial nexus

There must be a **substantial nexus** between the activity being taxed and the taxing state. A substantial nexus requires significant (i.e., more than minimum) contacts with, or substantial activity within, the taxing state. *E.g., Quill Corp. v. North Dakota*, 504 U.S. 298 (1992) (mailing of catalogs and shipment of goods to consumers in a state is not a sufficient nexus).

2) Fair apportionment

The tax must be fairly apportioned according to a rational formula (e.g., taxing only the state's portion of the company's business), such that interstate commerce does not pay total taxes greater than local commerce by virtue of having to pay tax in more than one state. The burden is on the taxpaying business to prove unfair apportionment.

3) Nondiscrimination

The tax may not provide a direct commercial advantage to local businesses over their interstate competitors (unless Congress specifically authorizes such a tax). A tax that is neutral on its face still may be unconstitutional if its effect is to favor local commerce. *West Lynn Creamery Inc. v. Healy*, 512 U.S. 186 (1994) (tax affecting all milk dealers, the revenue from which went to a fund used to subsidize in-state dairy farmers, violated the Commerce Clause). In addition, the denial of tax exemption to a state entity unless the entity operates primarily for the benefit of state residents may be unconstitutional. *Camps Newfound/Owatonna v. Town of Harrison*, 520 U.S. 564 (1997).

4) Fair relationship to services provided

The tax must be fairly related to the services provided by the taxing state. *Evansville-Vanderburg Airport Auth. Dist. v. Delta Airlines, Inc.*, 405 U.S. 707 (1972) (tax on airline passengers was related to benefits the passengers received from the state airport facilities).

b. Discrimination under other constitutional provisions

A discriminatory tax may violate more than just the Commerce Clause.

i) A tax that discriminates against nonresident individuals—for example, an income tax that exempts local residents—may violate the **Comity Clause** of Article IV. *Austin v. New Hampshire*, 420 U.S. 656 (1975).

ii) A discriminatory tax on out-of-state businesses, even if authorized by Congress and therefore allowed under the Commerce Clause, may still violate the **Equal Protection Clause** of the Fourteenth Amendment, if there is no rational basis to support it. *Metropolitan Life Ins. Co. v. Ward*, 470 U.S. 869 (1985).

c. Types of taxes

1) Ad valorem property tax

An ad valorem tax is based on the value of real or personal property and is often assessed at a particular time (e.g., tax day). Such taxes, which may be imposed on the full value of the property, are generally valid, but a state may **not** levy ad valorem taxes on **goods in the course of transit** (from the time the goods are delivered to an interstate carrier or begin their interstate journey until they reach their destination). *Standard Oil Co. v. Peck*, 342 U.S. 382 (1952). However, once the goods are stopped for a business purpose (i.e., obtain a "taxable situs"), they may be taxed.

A state may tax the "instrumentalities of commerce" (airplanes, railroad cars, etc.), provided that:

i)   The instrumentality has a **taxable situs** within—or **sufficient contacts** with—the taxing state (i.e., it receives benefits or protection from the state); and

ii) The tax is **fairly apportioned** to the amount of time the instrumentality is in the state.

2) Sales tax

A sales tax imposed on the seller of goods is valid as long as the sale takes place within the state. Sales tax generally does not discriminate against interstate commerce as long as there is a substantial nexus between the taxpayer and the state (e.g., his business is there), and the tax is properly apportioned.

3) Use tax

A use tax on goods purchased out of state but used within the taxing state is valid so long as the use tax rate is not higher than the sales tax rate on the same item. Even though a use tax does, on its face, seem to discriminate against out-of-state purchases, the rationale for its validity is that such a tax equalizes the tax on in-state and out-of-state goods. *Henneford v. Silas Mason Co., Inc.*, 300 U.S. 577 (1937).

4) "Doing business" taxes

Taxes levied against companies for the privilege of doing business in a state (made up of privilege, license, franchise, or occupation taxes) are valid as long as they meet the basic taxation requirements:

i)   The activity taxed must have a substantial nexus to the taxing state;

ii) The tax must be fairly apportioned;

iii) The tax may not discriminate against interstate commerce; and

iv) The tax must be fairly related to the services provided by the state.

Such a tax may be measured by a flat annual fee or by a graduated rate proportional to the amount of revenue derived from the taxing state. The burden of showing that a tax is unfairly apportioned is on the taxpayer.

2. Foreign Commerce

The Import-Export Clause of Article I, Section 10 prohibits the states, without the consent of Congress from imposing any tax on any imported or exported goods, or on any commercial activity connected with imported goods, except what is absolutely necessary for executing its inspection laws. *Brown v. Maryland*, 25 U.S. 419 (1827).

The Commerce Clause restricts state taxation of commerce with other countries because it vests in Congress the exclusive power to regulate foreign commerce. A state tax on foreign commerce must, in addition to meeting the same requirements as a tax on interstate commerce, not (i) create a substantial risk of *international* multiple taxation or (ii) prevent the federal government from "speaking with one voice" regarding international trade or foreign affairs issues. *Barclays Bank PLC v. Franchise Tax Board*, 512 U.S. 298 (1994).

C. ALCOHOLIC BEVERAGE REGULATION

The Twenty-First Amendment repealed prohibition and gave the authority to regulate the distribution of alcoholic beverages within each state to the states. However, regulations that economically favor local liquor businesses over out-of-state liquor businesses can violate the Commerce Clause. *Granholm v. Heald*, 544 U.S. 460 (2005). In addition, Congress, under the spending power, can impose conditions on the grant of federal funds that affect state regulation of alcohol. *South Dakota v. Dole, supra*.

VIII. FEDERAL PREEMPTION OF STATE LAW

The Supremacy Clause of Article VI, Section 2 provides that the "Constitution, and the laws of the United States" are the "supreme law of the land." Any state law that directly or indirectly conflicts with a federal law is void under this clause. However, the Supreme Court has frequently stated that there is a presumption against preemption, especially in areas in which states have traditionally exercised police power. *Wyeth v. Levine*, 555 U.S. 555 (2009) (health and safety).

A. EXPRESS PREEMPTION

Federal law **expressly** preempts state law in cases in which the Constitution makes the federal power exclusive (such as the powers to coin money or declare war) or when Congress has enacted legislation that explicitly prohibits state regulation in the same area (e.g., the Federal Cigarette Labeling and Advertising Act forbids state laws that regulate either cigarette labels or the "advertising or promotion" of labeled cigarettes "based on smoking and health," 15 U.S.C. § 1334).

1. Narrow Construction

An express federal preemption must be narrowly construed. *Altria Group, Inc. v. Good*, 555 U.S. 70 (2008) (Federal Cigarette Labeling and Advertising Act did not preempt a suit based on a state's general deceptive-practices statute because such a statute was not based on smoking and health).

> **Example:** The National Bank Act prohibited states to "exercise visitorial powers with respect to national banks, such as conducting examinations, inspecting or requiring the production of books or records," but it was not clear from the Act's language whether it completely prohibited the state from exercising enforcement powers when state law is violated. The Court concluded that the Act's structure and purpose differentiate between the sovereign's "visitorial powers" and its power to enforce the law. While the state could not issue administrative subpoenas to banks, it could file suit to punish violations of state banking laws. *Cuomo v. Clearing House Ass'n*, 557 U.S. 519 (2009).

2. Savings Clause

Federal law may also contain "savings clauses" that explicitly preserve or allow state laws that regulate in the same area (e.g., the Clean Water Act preserves "any right which any person (or class of persons) may have under any statute or common law," 33 U.S.C. § 1365).

B. IMPLIED PREEMPTION

Federal preemption is **implied** when any of the following circumstances exist:

i) Congress intended for federal law to **occupy the field** (*e.g., Hines v. Davidowitz*, 312 U.S. 52 (1941) (new federal law requiring registration of all aliens preempted preexisting state law requiring registration of aliens within the state));

> Intent to occupy a field can be inferred from a framework of regulation so pervasive that Congress left no room for states to supplement it or when there is a federal interest so dominant that the federal system will be assumed to preclude enforcement of state laws on the same subject. *Rice v. Santa Fe Elevator Corp.*, 331 U.S. 218, (1947). When Congress occupies an entire field, even complementary state regulation is impermissible. Field preemption reflects a congressional decision to foreclose any state regulation in the area, even if it is parallel to federal standards. *Arizona v. U.S.*, 567 U.S. ___, 132 S. Ct. 2492 (2012) (even if state may make violation of federal law a crime in some instances, it cannot do so in a field, like alien registration, that has been occupied by federal law).

ii) The state law **directly conflicts** with the federal law by, for example, requiring conduct that is forbidden by the federal law or making it impossible (or nearly so) to comply with both, *e.g., Rose v. Arkansas State Police*, 479 U.S. 1 (1986) (federal law providing that federal death benefits for state law-enforcement officers be in addition to other state benefits preempted contrary state law requiring that other benefits be reduced by the amount of death benefits); or

> **Example 1:** Under 42 U.S.C. § 1983, all persons who violate federal rights while acting under color of state law may be sued for damages. A state law shielding state corrections officers from liability under § 1983 by excluding claims brought against them from being heard in state court violated the Supremacy Clause. *Haywood v. Drown*, 556 U.S. 729 (2009).
>
> **Example 2:** Although a federal statute provides for preemption of state tort claims with regard to medical devices approved by the Federal Drug Administration, 21 U.S.C. § 360(k), there is no express preemption with regard to prescription drugs. However, a state-imposed duty on generic drug manufacturers to warn users of dangers through labeling was preempted by an FDA rule that required the label on generic drugs to match the label of the corresponding brand name drug. The court found that it was impossible for the generic drug manufacturers to comply with both federal regulations and state law. *PLIVA, Inc. v. Mensing*, ___ U.S. ___, 131 S. Ct. 2567 (2011).
>
> **Compare:** The manufacturer of a brand-name drug failed to establish preemption of a state-law duty to warn when the manufacturer was permitted under FDA regulations to change the drug label and then request FDA approval for the change. *Wyeth v. Levine, supra.*

iii) The state law **indirectly conflicts** with federal law by creating an obstacle to or frustrating the accomplishment of that law's purpose (*e.g., Perez v. Campbell*, 402 U.S. 637 (1971) (state law suspending licenses of all drivers with unpaid accident judgments frustrates the purpose of federal bankruptcy laws to provide a fresh start)).

1. Absence of Preemption

If Congress does not intend to occupy the field completely, a state is free to enact similar legislation. *Colorado Anti-Discrimination Comm'n. v. Continental Air Lines, Inc.*, 372 U.S. 714 (1963) (state statute prohibiting racial discrimination valid despite the existence of identical federal law). If there has not been federal preemption in a given area, a state is free to set more stringent standards than those imposed by the federal government. In addition, a state may recognize individual rights that exceed those granted by the federal constitution or federal statutes. *Pruneyard Shopping Ctr. v. Robbins*, 447 U.S. 74 (1980) (California's constitutional grant of greater free speech rights than the federal constitution confers upheld).

> **EXAM NOTE:** Under the Supremacy Clause, federal law sets a **floor** below which state law generally cannot go, but it does **not** set a **ceiling** beyond which state law cannot go.

IX. RELATIONS AMONG STATES

A. INTERSTATE COMPACTS

An interstate compact is an agreement, similar to a treaty or a contract, between two or more states. Article I, Section 10, Clause 3 (the "Interstate Compact Clause") allows states to enter into such agreements only with the consent of Congress. However, the only agreements that qualify as "compacts" requiring the consent of Congress are those that either affect a power delegated to the federal government or alter the political balance within the federal system.

B. FULL FAITH AND CREDIT

The Full Faith and Credit Clause of Article IV, Section 1 provides that "[f]ull faith and credit shall be given in each state to the public acts, records, and judicial proceedings of every other state."

1. Judgments

Full faith and credit requires that out-of-state **judgments** be given in-state effect. *Baker v. General Motors Corp.*, 522 U.S. 222 (1998). However, to be given full faith and credit, a decision must meet three requirements:

i) The court that rendered the judgment must have had **jurisdiction** over the parties and the subject matter;

ii) The judgment must have been **on the merits** rather than on a procedural issue; and

iii) The judgment must be **final**.

2. Laws (Public Acts)

The Full Faith and Credit Clause is "less demanding" with respect to choice of law (i.e., which state's law should apply in a situation when either might).

> **EXAM NOTE:** Approximately half of the Constitutional Law questions on the MBE will cover Individual Rights—that is, everything from here to the end of the outline.

X.   STATE ACTION AND THE ROLE OF THE COURTS

The Constitution generally protects against wrongful conduct by the government, not private parties (with the exception of the Thirteenth Amendment's prohibition against slavery, which applies to private and government action). In other words, state action is a necessary prerequisite to triggering constitutional protections. A private person's conduct must constitute state action in order for these protections to apply. For example, state action may exist in cases of private parties carrying out traditional governmental functions or significant state involvement in the activities.

A.   TRADITIONAL GOVERNMENTAL FUNCTION

State action is found when a private person carries on activities that are **traditionally performed exclusively by the state,** such as running primary elections or governing a "company town." *Terry v. Adams*, 345 U.S. 461 (1953); *Marsh v. Alabama*, 326 U.S. 501 (1946). By contrast, a shopping center that is open to the public does not thereby assume or exercise municipal functions, and therefore is not treated as a state actor. *Hudgens v. NLRB*, 424 U.S. 507 (1976) (shopping mall not required to permit picketing on its private sidewalks). Similarly, merely providing a product or service that the government **could** offer is not sufficient to make the provider a state actor. *Flagg Brothers v. Brooks*, 436 U.S. 149 (1978). However, the use of peremptory challenges, even by private litigants, constitutes state action because the selection of jurors is a traditional state function and because the judge (i.e., the government) plays a significant role in the process. *Edmonson v. Leesville Concrete*, 500 U.S. 614 (1992).

B.   SIGNIFICANT STATE INVOLVEMENT

State action may also exist if there are sufficient mutual contacts between the conduct of a private party and the government, which is a question of the degree of involvement. The Supreme Court has not laid out a test to determine what constitutes significant state involvement, but some general guidelines exist. Mere licensing or regulation of a private party does not constitute state action; the state must **act affirmatively** to facilitate, encourage, or authorize the activity. State action also exists if the actions of a private party and the government are so intertwined that a mutual benefit results, such as if the parties are involved in a joint venture. *Lugar v. Edmondson Oil Co.,* 457 U.S. 922 (1982) (state action was present when a clerk and sheriff acted together with a private citizen to obtain attachment against a property of the debtor.) Even when the state explicitly prohibits behavior that violates a person's civil rights, state action may exist if it appears the state has sanctioned the violative act.

States are constitutionally forbidden from facilitating or authorizing discrimination, but they are not required to make discrimination illegal.

C.   INSIGNIFICANT STATE INVOLVEMENT

Businesses that the government substantially regulates or to which the government grants a monopoly, such as utility companies, do not exercise state action. Further exclusions include nursing homes that accept Medicaid, schools that receive government funds but are operated by a private corporation, and congressional grants of a corporate charter.

XI. PROCEDURAL DUE PROCESS

The Due Process Clause of the **Fifth Amendment,** which applies against the **federal government,** provides that "[n]o person shall be...deprived of life, liberty, or property, without due process of law."

The Due Process Clause of the **Fourteenth Amendment,** which applies against the **states,** provides that "no state shall make or enforce any law which shall...deprive any person of life, liberty, or property, without due process of the law."

A. DUE PROCESS GENERALLY

These clauses operate at a number of levels to protect the rights of individuals and other "persons"—e.g., corporations—against the government. At the most basic level, each clause ensures that the federal and state governments must follow certain procedures before depriving any person of "life, liberty, or property." These safeguards, like notice and a hearing, are the cornerstone of **procedural due process.**

At another level, the Fourteenth Amendment, through its guarantee of rights respecting life, liberty, and property, has been interpreted to make **most provisions of the Bill of Rights** (which by its terms applies to the federal government) **applicable against the states as well.** That is, the Fourteenth Amendment Due Process Clause **incorporates** the protections of the First, Second, and Fourth Amendments, as well as most of the protections of the Fifth, Sixth, and Eighth Amendments. (However, the Fifth Amendment right to grand jury indictment and the Sixth Amendment right to a unanimous jury verdict in a criminal trial are not incorporated. While the Eighth Amendment protections against cruel and unusual punishment and excessive bail are incorporated, it has not been determined whether the Eighth Amendment protection against excessive fines is incorporated.) The Seventh Amendment right to a jury in civil trials has been held not applicable to the states.

Finally, both Due Process Clauses contain a "substantive" component that guarantees certain fundamental rights to all persons. This **substantive due process** acts as something of a catchall for rights not explicitly set forth elsewhere in the Constitution.

B. PROCEDURAL DUE PROCESS APPLIED

1. General Principles

The concept of "fundamental fairness" is at the heart of the right to procedural due process. It includes an individual's right to be **notified** of charges or proceedings against him and the opportunity to be **heard** at those proceedings. When one's liberty or property interests are adversely affected by governmental action, two questions are asked:

i)   Is the threatened interest a **protected** one?

ii)   If so, **what process** is due?

a. Neutral decision maker

Due process entitles a person to a fair decision maker. A judge must recuse herself when she has a direct, personal, substantial, pecuniary interest in a case (i.e., actual bias) or there is a serious objective risk of actual bias. In the latter instance, proof of actual bias is not required, and subjective impartiality is not sufficient to justify a refusal to recuse. *Caperton v. A. T. Massey Coal Co.*, 556 U.S. 868 (2009).

> **Example:** An attorney running for a judgeship on the state supreme court had received a $3 million contribution that had a significant and disproportionate influence on the electoral outcome. The contribution exceeded the sum total of all other contributions the attorney had received and exceeded by 50% the combined amount spent by the attorney's and his opponent's campaigns. The contribution was made by the president of a company that had received an adverse $50 million verdict in a lower court of the state prior to the election. It was foreseeable that the judgment would be appealed to the state supreme court at the time that the contribution was made. Consequently, the Due Process Clause required the judge who had received the contribution to recuse himself. *Caperton v. A. T. Massey Coal Co., supra*.

b. Intentional conduct

Due process addresses injury that results from an intentional governmental act. Mere negligent conduct by a government employee does not trigger a due process right. *Daniels v. Williams*, 474 U.S. 327 (1986) (prisoner's injury due to correction officer's negligence was not a deprivation of liberty).

2. Protected Interests

a. Liberty

An impingement on liberty is generally construed to mean **significant** governmental restraint on one's **physical freedom,** exercise of **fundamental rights** (i.e., those guaranteed by the Constitution), or **freedom of choice or action.**

Examples of loss of liberty include commitment to a mental institution, parole revocation, and loss of parental rights. Injury to reputation alone is not a deprivation of liberty, unless the injury is so great that the individual has lost **significant employment or associational rights.**

b. Property

A cognizable property interest involves more than an abstract need or desire; there must be a "legitimate claim of entitlement" by virtue of statute, employment contract, or custom. *Board of Regents v. Roth*, 408 U.S. 564, 577 (1972) (non-tenured professor with a one-year contract had no liberty or property interest in being rehired).

The rights to public education, to government-issued licenses, and to continued welfare and disability benefits are legitimate property interests. For example, although a patient may have a legitimate property interest in the continued receipt of medical benefits to pay for the patient's stay in a qualified nursing home, there is no legitimate property interest in the patient's continued residence in the nursing home of the patient's choice. As a result, a patient is not entitled to a hearing before the government disqualifies a nursing home from participating in a public benefits program. *O'Bannon v. Town Court Nursing Ctr.*, 447 U.S. 773 (1980).

There is a legitimate property interest in continued public employment only if there is an employment contract or a clear understanding that the employee may be fired only for cause. *Arnett v. Kennedy*, 416 U.S. 134 (1974). An "at will" governmental employee has no right to continued employment. *Bishop v. Wood*, 426 U.S. 341 (1976). If, however, the government gives the "at will" public employee assurances of continual employment or dismissal for only specified reasons, then there must be a fair procedure to protect the employee's interests if the government seeks to discharge the employee from his position. Such entitlement to procedural due process can also result from statutory law, formal contract terms, or the actions of a supervisory person with authority to establish terms of employment.

Note, though, that even those employees who lack any entitlement to continued employment cannot be discharged for reasons that in and of themselves violate the Constitution. Thus, an "at-will" governmental employee cannot be fired for having engaged in speech protected by the First Amendment. *Board of Regents v. Roth*, 408 U.S. 564 (1972). To be entitled to a hearing, however, the employee must make a prima facie claim that she is being discharged for reasons that violate specific constitutional guarantees. *Mt. Healthy City School Dist. Bd. of Educ. v. Doyle*, 429 U.S. 274 (1977). A dismissal will be upheld if the government can prove that the employee would have been discharged in any event for reasons unrelated to any constitutionally protected activities.

3. Notice and Hearing

If an individual's protected interest is threatened by governmental action, the next step is to determine what type of process is due. The Court considers three factors in determining the amount of process that is due:

i) The **private interest** affected by the governmental action;

ii) The risk of erroneous deprivation of that interest using current procedures and the probable **value of additional or substitute safeguards**; and

iii) The **burden (fiscal and administrative cost)** involved in providing the additional process.

Mathews v. Eldridge, 424 U.S. 319 (1976). The greater the importance of the threatened interest, the greater the likelihood that the Court will require extensive procedural safeguards prior to the termination of the interest. Generally, the person whose interest is being deprived is entitled to **notice** of the government's action by an unbiased decision maker and an **opportunity to be heard,** although the hearing need not necessarily occur before the termination of the interest.

Example: While the state must give notice and hold a hearing prior to terminating **welfare benefits,** in cases of terminating **disability benefits or public employment,** the state must give prior notice, but only a post-termination evidentiary hearing is required. *Goldberg v. Kelly*, 397 U.S. 254 (1970), *Mathews v. Eldridge, supra*.

a. Enemy combatants

United States citizens held as enemy combatants are entitled to meaningful opportunity to dispute the facts of their detention by a neutral decision maker, albeit the opportunity is adapted to reduce burdens on executive authority brought on by an ongoing military conflict. *Boumediene v. Bush*, 553 U.S. 723, (2008).

b. Parental status

Different burdens of proof are applied to termination of parental rights and paternity actions. Because termination of parental rights deprives parents of a fundamental right, the state must use clear and convincing evidence to support allegations of neglect.

When a mother or child is initiating a paternity suit, due process requires proof by only a preponderance of evidence. In a paternity action initiated by the state, the state must pay for the necessary blood work used in determining paternity.

c. Forfeitures

Forfeiture is an involuntary relinquishment of property that the government alleges is connected to criminal activity. Generally, the government is required to provide the owner with notice and a hearing prior to seizure of real property. However, the government does not need to provide notice prior to the seizure of personal property.

d. Public employees

A public employee who may be discharged only for cause has a property interest in his job and therefore is entitled to **notice** of termination and a **pre-termination opportunity to respond.** A formal hearing is not required, as long as there is pre-termination notice, an opportunity to respond to the decision maker, and a **post-termination evidentiary hearing.** *Cleveland Bd. of Educ. v. Loudermill*, 470 U.S. 532 (1985). If there is a significant reason for immediately removing a "for-cause" employee from the job, a prompt post-suspension hearing with reinstatement and back pay if the employee prevails constitutes sufficient due process. *Gilbert v. Homar*, 520 U.S. 924 (1997).

4. Court Access

The government cannot deny an indigent person access to the court system because of his inability to pay the required court fees, if such imposition of fees acts to deny a fundamental right to the indigent. Due process requires such fees to be waived. Conversely, if the matter does not involve a fundamental right, no waiver is required.

XII. SUBSTANTIVE DUE PROCESS

The guarantee of substantive due process is based upon the idea that laws should be reasonable and not arbitrary.

A. STANDARD OF REVIEW

The standard of review in substantive due process cases is generally twofold: a governmental action that infringes upon a **fundamental right** is subject to **strict scrutiny.** If the interest infringed upon is not fundamental, then there need be only a **rational basis** for the regulation.

1. **Strict Scrutiny**

   a. **Test**

   The law must be the **least restrictive** means to achieve a **compelling** governmental interest.

   1) **Least restrictive means**

   For the law to be the least restrictive means to achieve the government's interest, there cannot be a way to achieve the same interest that is less restrictive of the right at issue. A law will not fail simply because there are other methods of achieving the goal that are equally or more restrictive.

   Under strict scrutiny, the law should be neither over-inclusive (reaching more people or conduct than is necessary) nor under-inclusive (not reaching all of the people or conduct intended).

   2) **Compelling interest**

   Although there is no precise definition of what is "compelling," it is generally understood to be something that is necessary or crucial, such as national security or preserving public health or safety.

   3) **Strict in theory, fatal in fact**

   The strict scrutiny standard is very difficult to meet. The great majority of laws reviewed under strict scrutiny are struck down.

   b. **Burden of proof**

   The burden is on the government to prove that the law is necessary to achieve a compelling governmental interest.

   c. **Applicability**

   The strict scrutiny test is applied if a **fundamental right** is involved.

2. **Rational Basis**

   a. **Test**

   A law meets the rational basis standard of review if it is **rationally related** to a **legitimate** state interest. This is a test of minimal scrutiny and generally results in the law being upheld.

   b. **Burden of proof**

   Laws are presumed valid under this standard, so the burden is on the challenger to overcome this presumption by establishing that the law is **arbitrary or irrational.**

   In court, the government's stated interest in enacting the law need not be one that it offered when the law was passed. Any legitimate reason will suffice.

   This factor distinguishes rational basis review from strict scrutiny, when the government must defend the interest that it stated at the outset.

c. Applicability

The rational basis standard is used in all cases to which strict scrutiny or intermediate scrutiny does not apply. *Heller v. Doe*, 509 U.S. 312 (1993). In practice, most legislation related to lifestyle, taxation, zoning, and punitive damages is reviewed under this standard.

Although punitive damages do not violate due process, excessive damages may. The court considers whether the defendant had fair notice of the possible magnitude before it will bar a punitive-damages award.

The government cannot presume facts about an individual that will deprive that individual of certain benefits or rights. By doing so, the government creates an arbitrary classification that may violate due process as well as equal protection.

1) Retroactive legislation

The retroactive application of a statute does not in and of itself violate substantive due process. Consequently, a law that is applied retroactively must merely meet the rational basis test. *United States v. Carlton*, 512 U.S. 26 (1994) (retroactive application of estate tax law that resulted in denial of a deduction upheld). Similar treatment applies to a statutory change that is remedial in nature (i.e., affects a remedy but does not create or abolish a right). *Chase Securities Corp. v. Donaldson*, 325 U.S. 304 (1945) (lengthening of statute of limitations that permitted an otherwise time-barred lawsuit to be maintained upheld). Note, however, that the extension of a criminal statute of limitations may violate the prohibition on an ex post facto law (*see* § XVI.B. Ex Post Facto Laws, *infra*).

B. FUNDAMENTAL RIGHTS

Some rights are so deeply rooted in our nation's tradition and history that they are considered fundamental. These rights include: (i) the right to vote; (ii) the right to travel; and (iii) the right to privacy (including marriage, sexual relations, abortion, child rearing, and the right of related persons to live together). Under **strict scrutiny,** a law interfering with a fundamental right will generally be upheld only if it is **necessary** to achieve a **compelling governmental interest.**

Government infringement upon **nonfundamental rights**—those related to social or economic interests such as business, taxation, lifestyle, or zoning—requires only a **rational relationship** between the law and a **legitimate governmental interest.**

> **EXAM NOTE:** If, on a question, a fundamental right is being infringed upon for all persons, the issue is likely one of substantive due process. If the right is being denied to only a particular class of persons, then equal protection is in play.

1. Travel

a. Interstate

There is a fundamental right to travel from state to state. *Shapiro v. Thompson*, 394 U.S. 618 (1969). This includes the right to enter one state and leave another, to be treated as a welcome visitor, and, for those who wish to become permanent residents, the right to be treated equally to native-born citizens with respect to state benefits. *Saenz v. Roe*, 526 U.S. 489 (1999) (state statute denying full welfare benefits to people who had not resided in the state for one year struck down; state's interests in discouraging fraud and establishing an objective residency test were not compelling). Reasonable residency restrictions may be imposed on the receipt of government benefits (i.e., in-state tuition); however, once a person qualifies as a resident, she must be treated equally.

b. International

Although there is a right to travel internationally, it is not a fundamental right invoking strict scrutiny. Hence, the U.S. government may limit travel to Cuba, for example, as long as it has a rational basis for doing so.

2. Voting and Ballot Access

a. Right to vote

Under the Twenty-Sixth Amendment, the right to vote is fundamental to all U.S. citizens who are 18 years of age or older. This right applies to all federal, state, and local elections, including primary elections. The level of scrutiny to which a governmental restriction of this right is subject depends on the degree to which the restriction affects the exercise of this right; the more significant the impact, the greater the degree of scrutiny.

1) Residency

A governmental unit may restrict, subject to a rational basis, the right to participate in its political process to those who reside within its borders; nonresidents generally may be prohibited from voting. *Holt Civic Club v. City of Tuscaloosa*, 439 U.S. 60 (1978) (citizens who lived outside city boundaries could be denied the right to vote in city elections, even though they were subject to business licensing fees imposed by the city).

A person must be given the opportunity to prove residency before being denied the right to vote because of lack of residency. *Carrington v. Rash*, 380 U.S. 89 (1965).

a) Length of residency

A governmental unit may require, subject to strict scrutiny, that a person be a resident for a short period prior to an election in order to vote in that election. *Marston v. Lewis*, 410 U.S. 679 (1973) (50-day period upheld); *Dunn v. Blumstein*, 405 U.S. 330 (1972) (three-month and one-year periods struck down).

b) Presidential elections

Congress can supersede state residency requirements with respect to presidential elections. *Oregon v. Mitchell*, 400 U.S. 112 (1970).

2) Property ownership

Generally, property ownership is not a valid ground upon which to restrict the right to vote. *Kramer v. Union Free School District No. 15*, 395 U.S. 621 (1969) (restriction of the right to vote on school board members to property owners or parents of school-age children struck down). A limited exception exists for elections involving special-purpose entities, such as a water-storage district. *Ball v. James*, 451 U.S. 355 (1981).

3) Poll tax

Payment of a fee in order to vote (i.e., a poll tax) in an election for federal office is prohibited by the Twenty-Fourth Amendment. More broadly, the imposition of a poll tax in order to vote in any election violates the Equal Protection Clause, as a poll tax is unrelated to voter qualifications. *Harper v. Virginia Bd. of Elections*, 383 U.S. 663 (1966).

4) Voter ID

A state may require that a citizen who votes in person present a government-issued photo ID. Applying a balancing test to a facial challenge to this neutral, nondiscriminatory requirement, the state's interests, including the prevention of voter fraud and the advancement of public confidence in the integrity of the electoral process, outweighed the limited burden on the right to vote. *Crawford v. Marion County Election Bd.*, 553 U.S. 181 (2008).

5) Felon

Pursuant to Section 2 of the Fourteenth Amendment, a state may prohibit a felon from voting, even one who has unconditionally been released from prison. *Richardson v. Ramirez*, 418 U.S. 24 (1974).

6) Write-in voting

A person's right to vote does not extend to the right to vote for any possible candidate. A state may ban all write-in candidates in both primary and general elections, at least when the state provides reasonable means by which a candidate can get on the ballot. *Burdick v. Takushi*, 504 U.S. 428 (1992).

b. Public office and ballot access

There is no fundamental right to hold office through election or appointment, but all persons do have a constitutional right to be considered for office without the burden of invidious discrimination. *Turner v. Fouche*, 396 U.S. 346 (1970).

1) Property ownership

The ownership of property cannot be made a condition of holding public office. *Turner v. Fouche, supra* (appointment to local school board).

2) Filing fee

A candidate for elected public office generally may be required to pay a reasonable filing fee, but an exorbitant filing fee, such as one that imposes the entire cost of the election on the candidates, is unconstitutional. Moreover, alternative provisions must be made for a candidate who is unable to pay the fee. *Lubin v. Parish*, 415 U.S. 709 (1974); *Bullock v. Carter*, 405 U.S. 134 (1972).

3) Public support requirements

An independent candidate for elected public office can be required to obtain the signatures of voters on a petition in order to appear on the ballot, but such a requirement cannot deny independent candidates ballot access. *Jenness v. Fortson*, 403 U.S. 431 (1971) (state requirement that an independent candidate obtain five percent of the number of registered voters at the last general election for the office in question upheld); *Williams v. Rhodes*, 393 U.S. 23 (1968) (state election scheme that prohibited independent candidacies struck down). In addition, a state can deny a candidate access to the general-election ballot if the candidate failed to receive a sufficient number of votes in the primary election. *Munro v. Socialist Workers Party*, 479 U.S. 189 (1986) (minor party senatorial candidate who failed to receive one percent of the votes cast in primary election not entitled to appear on the general ballot).

4) Write-in candidates

A state may ban all write-in candidates in both primary and general elections, at least when the state provides other reasonable means by which a candidate can get on the ballot. *Burdick v. Takushi, supra*.

5) Candidate for other office

A state may prohibit a state office holder from becoming a candidate for another state office; the office holder must resign his current office in order to run for another office. *Clements v. Fashing*, 457 U.S. 957 (1982).

6) Replacement of elected official

A state may permit a political party to name a replacement for an elected public official from that party who dies or resigns while in office. *Rodriguez v. Popular Democratic Party*, 457 U.S. 1 (1982). The governor must call an election to fill a vacant congressional seat. Article I, Section 2 (House member); Seventeenth Amendment (Senator). (Note: The Seventeenth Amendment permits the state legislature to authorize the governor to appoint a temporary replacement senator.)

3. Privacy

Various privacy rights have been deemed fundamental, and any infringement upon them must be examined using strict scrutiny.

a. Marriage

The right of a man and a woman to enter into matrimony is fundamental, and substantial state interference with that right invokes strict scrutiny. *Loving v. Virginia*, 388 U.S. 1 (1967); *Zablocki v. Redhail*, 434 U.S. 374 (1978).

b. Contraception

Married persons have the right to use contraceptives, *Griswold v. Connecticut*, 381 U.S. 479 (1965), as do unmarried persons, *Eisenstadt v. Baird*, 405 U.S. 438 (1972). A state may not limit the sale of contraceptives to dispensation only by pharmacists or only to individuals older than age 16. *Carey v. Population Services International*, 431 U.S. 678 (1977).

c. Intimate sexual behavior

There is no legitimate state interest in making it a crime for fully consenting adults to engage in private sexual conduct—including homosexual conduct—that is not commercial in nature. *Lawrence v. Texas*, 539 U.S. 558 (2003).

d. Abortion

The landmark case of *Roe v. Wade*, 410 U.S. 113 (1973), established the principle that a woman has a fundamental right to an abortion. The Court acknowledged that this privacy right must be considered along with the state's compelling interests in protecting both the health of the pregnant woman and the potential life of the fetus. The resulting rule allowed for varying degrees of state restriction based on the trimester of the pregnancy. The decades since *Roe* have resulted in numerous, often conflicting, judicial opinions on the subject. The current standard is the "undue burden" test, the meaning of which depends on whether the fetus is viable (likely to survive outside the womb).

1) Pre-viability

An undue burden exists when the purpose or effect of a state law places **substantial obstacles** in the way of a woman's right to seek an abortion before the fetus attains viability. *Planned Parenthood of Southeastern Pennsylvania v. Casey*, 505 U.S. 833 (1992).

The following requirements have been held **not** to impose an undue burden:

i)   A requirement that only a licensed physician may perform an abortion;

ii) A requirement that the physician must provide the woman with truthful information about the nature of the abortion procedure, the associated health risks, and the probable gestational age of the fetus;

iii) A requirement that a woman must wait 24 hours after giving informed consent before the abortion is performed;

iv) A requirement that a minor obtain her parents' consent, or if consent is not required, provide the parents with notice of the abortion. However, this requirement has been found to be an undue burden unless, at least for mature minors, the consent requirement can be judicially bypassed. *Planned Parenthood Association of Kansas City Missouri Inc. v. Ashcroft*, 462 U.S. 476 (1983).

v)   A ban on a particular uncommon abortion technique, *Gonzales v. Carhart*, 550 U.S. 124 (2007).

An undue burden has been found when a state requires a woman to notify her husband before having an abortion.

2) Post-viability

Once the fetus reaches viability, the state may regulate, and even prohibit, abortion, as long as there is an exception to preserve the health or life of the mother. In other words, at the point of viability, the state's interest in protecting fetal life may supersede a woman's right to choose; because the state's interest in protecting fetal life cannot supersede its interest in protecting a woman's health, however, there must be an exception for the woman's health.

3) Government funding

There is no constitutional right to have the government provide indigent women with funding for an abortion or for medical care related to an abortion, even if the government does provide indigent funding for medical care at childbirth. *Maher v. Roe*, 432 U.S. 464 (1977). Furthermore, a state may prohibit all use of public facilities and public employees in performing abortions. *Webster v. Reproductive Health Services*, 492 U.S. 490 (1989).

e. Parental rights

The fundamental parental right to make decisions regarding the care, custody, and control of one's children includes the right to privately educate one's child outside the public school system, *Pierce v. Society of Sisters*, 268 U.S. 510 (1925), and to limit visitation of grandparents, *Troxel v. Granville*, 530 U.S. 57 (2000).

f. Family relations

Related persons, including extended family members, have a fundamental right to live together in a single household. *Moore v. City of East Cleveland*, 431 U.S. 494 (1977).

g. Obscene material

There is a fundamental right to possess obscene material in the privacy of one's home, *Stanley v. Georgia*, 394 U.S. 557 (1969), with the exception of child pornography, *Osborne v. Ohio*, 495 U.S. 103 (1990). The state, however, may severely restrict the sale, purchase, receipt, transport, and distribution of obscene material. *Paris Adult Theater v. Slaton*, 413 U.S. 49 (1973).

h. Right to refuse medical treatment

It is an established liberty interest that a person may not be forced to undergo unwanted medical procedures, including lifesaving measures, but the Court has not ruled on whether this right is "fundamental." *Cruzan v. Missouri Department of Health*, 497 U.S. 261 (1990).

There is no fundamental right to commit suicide; therefore, the state may ban the assistance of suicide. *Washington v. Glucksberg*, 521 U.S. 702 (1997). The Court distinguished this decision from *Cruzan* by stating that forced medication is a battery, and there is a long tradition of protecting the decision to refuse unwanted medical treatment.

4. The Second Amendment

The Second Amendment guarantees **an individual's right to possess a firearm** unconnected with service in a militia and to use that firearm for traditionally lawful purposes, such as self-defense within the home. *District of Columbia v. Heller*, 554 U.S. 570 (2008) (ban on handgun possession in the home violates Second Amendment). As mentioned previously, the Second Amendment is applicable to the states through the Fourteenth Amendment. *McDonald v. Chicago*, 561 U.S. ___, 130 S. Ct. 3020 (2010).

Like most rights, the Second Amendment right to bear arms is not unlimited. Examples of lawful regulations include imposing conditions and qualifications on the commercial sale of arms, as well as prohibitions on (i) concealed weapons, (ii) possession of firearms by felons and the mentally ill, and (iii) carrying guns in schools, government buildings, and other sensitive places are presumed to be legitimate. *District of Columbia v. Heller, supra.*

XIII. EQUAL PROTECTION

A. GENERAL CONSIDERATIONS

1. Constitutional Basis

a. State action

The Equal Protection Clause of the Fourteenth Amendment provides that "no state shall...deny to any person within its jurisdiction the equal protection of the laws." This clause applies only to states and localities.

b. Federal action

Although there is no federal equal protection clause, the Supreme Court has held that the Fifth Amendment Due Process Clause includes the rights guaranteed by the Equal Protection Clause, thereby making discrimination by the federal government subject to review under the same standards as discrimination by the states. *Bolling v. Sharpe,* 347 U.S. 497 (1954).

2. Standards of Review

When reviewing government action under equal-protection theories, the Court applies one of three levels of review, depending on the classification of persons or the type of right concerned.

a. Strict scrutiny

1) Test

The law must be the **least restrictive** means to achieve a **compelling** governmental interest.

2) Burden of proof

The burden is on the government to prove that the law is necessary. Because the strict scrutiny test is a very difficult one to pass, the government rarely meets its burden, and most laws subjected to this standard of review are struck down.

3) Applicability

The strict scrutiny test is applied if a **fundamental right** or a **suspect classification** is involved. The suspect classifications are race, ethnicity, national origin, and, if the classification is by state law, alienage. (*See* § XIII.B., *infra,* for a complete discussion of suspect classifications.)

b. Intermediate scrutiny

1) Test

To be constitutional, the law must be **substantially related** to an **important** governmental interest.

2) Burden of proof

Although the Court has not clearly stated the rule, the burden appears generally to be on the government to prove that the law in question passes intermediate scrutiny. As with strict scrutiny (and unlike rational basis review), the government must defend the interest(s) it stated when the law was enacted, not just some conceivable legitimate interest.

3) Applicability

Intermediate scrutiny is used when a classification is based on **gender** or status as a **nonmarital child** (legitimacy). Note that in gender cases there must be an "exceedingly persuasive justification" for the classification, which may bring the standard in such cases closer to strict scrutiny. *See United States v. Virginia*, 518 U.S. 515 (1996).

c. Rational basis

1) Test

A law passes the rational basis standard of review if it is **rationally related** to a **legitimate** state interest. This is a test of minimal scrutiny. It is not required that there is actually a link between the means selected and a legitimate objective. However, the legislature must *reasonably believe* there is a link.

2) Burden of proof

Laws are presumed valid under this standard, so the burden is on the challenger to overcome this presumption by establishing that the law is **arbitrary or irrational.**

3) Applicability

The rational basis standard is used in all cases in which one of the higher standards (intermediate or strict scrutiny) does not apply. Thus, rational basis review applies to laws drawing distinctions based on age, wealth, weight, or most other classifications, as well as to any distinctions drawn for business or economic reasons.

The Court generally gives extreme deference to the legislature's right to define its objectives. In order to determine the legislature's purpose, the Court will look at the statute and the preamble. If the legislative purpose is not clear from the statute, the Court may consider any conceivable purpose that may have motivated the legislature. *U.S. Railroad Retirement Bd. v. Fritz*, 449 U.S. 166 (1980).

Some classifications, although nominally subject to rational basis review, in practice receive heightened scrutiny. *See e.g., Romer v. Evans*, 517 U.S.

620 (1996) (sexual orientation); *Cleburne v. Cleburne Living Center, Inc.*, 473 U.S. 432 (1985) (developmental disability). When the government has acted out of animus toward or fear of a particular group, that action—even if not involving a suspect or a quasi-suspect classification—will be searchingly reviewed and may be struck down even under a rational basis test.

3. Proving Discrimination

To trigger strict or intermediate scrutiny, there must be **discriminatory intent** on the part of the government. The fact that legislation has a disparate effect on people of different races, genders, etc., without intent, is insufficient. Discriminatory intent can be shown facially, as applied, or when there is a discriminatory motive.

a. Facial discrimination

A law that, by its very language, creates distinctions between classes of persons is discriminatory on its face.

Example: An ordinance states that only males will be considered for a city's training academy for firefighters.

b. Discriminatory application

A law that appears neutral on its face may be applied in a discriminatory fashion. If the challenger can prove that a discriminatory purpose was used when applying the law, then the law will be invalidated.

Example: A city's ordinance concerning the police academy says nothing about gender, but in practice only men are considered for admission.

c. Discriminatory motive

A law that is neutral on its face and in its application may still result in a disparate impact. By itself, however, a disparate impact is not sufficient to trigger strict or intermediate scrutiny; proof of discriminatory motive or intent is required to show a violation of the Equal Protection Clause. *Arlington Heights v. Metropolitan Hous. Dev. Corp.*, 429 U.S. 252 (1977).

Example: A city's paramedic training school is theoretically open to both men and women, but the entrance test includes a height requirement that disproportionately excludes women.

B. SUSPECT CLASSIFICATIONS

Laws that categorize based on race, ethnicity, national origin, or (in some cases) alienage are considered suspect and therefore require closer judicial examination. Such laws are subject to strict scrutiny and are invalid unless they are **necessary** to achieve a **compelling** governmental interest.

1. Race, Ethnicity, and National Origin

Laws or regulations that intentionally disadvantage on the basis of race, ethnicity, or national origin have almost always been struck down for failing to advance a compelling state interest. One exception was *Korematsu v. United States*, 323 U.S.

214 (1944), in which the internment of Japanese-Americans during World War II was upheld in the name of national security.

a. School integration

Because discrimination must be intentional in order to violate the Constitution, only intentional (de jure) segregation in schools violates the Equal Protection Clause. *Keyes v. Sch. Dist. No. 1*, 413 U.S. 189 (1973). Moreover, a court cannot impose a remedy that involves multiple school districts unless there is evidence of intentional segregation in each district. *Milliken v. Bradley*, 418 U.S. 717 (1974); *Missouri v. Jenkins*, 515 U.S. 70 (1995) (state not compelled to create magnet schools in order to attract students from outside the district).

If a school board does not take steps to eliminate intentional racial segregation of schools, a court can order the district to implement measures, such as busing, to remedy the discrimination. Court-ordered busing is temporary, however, and must be terminated once the "vestiges of past discrimination" have been eliminated. *Bd. of Educ. v. Dowell*, 498 U.S. 237 (1991).

b. Affirmative action

Programs that favor racial or ethnic minorities are also subject to strict scrutiny. *Adarand Constructors, Inc. v. Pena*, 515 U.S. 200 (1995) (overruling application of the intermediate standard to federal discrimination).

1) Past discrimination by government

For a governmental affirmative action program to survive, the relevant governmental entity must show more than a history of societal discrimination. The government—whether federal, state, or local—must itself be guilty of specific past discrimination against the group it is seeking to favor, and the remedy must be narrowly tailored to end that discrimination and eliminate its effects. In other words, the elimination of past discrimination in a particular governmental institution is a compelling state interest; attempting to remedy general societal injustice through affirmative action is not.

2) Diversity in public universities and colleges

Race may be used as a "plus factor" (i.e., one of a range of factors to consider) in determining whether a student should be admitted to a public college or university, as there is a compelling interest in obtaining the educational benefits of a diverse student body. The use of racial quotas or of race as a determinative criterion, however, violates equal protection and is unconstitutional. *Grutter v. Bollinger*, 539 U.S. 306 (2003); *Gratz v. Bollinger*, 539 U.S. 244 (2003); *Regents of University of California v. Bakke*, 438 U.S. 265 (1978).

3) Diversity in public elementary and high schools

A school district may not assign students to schools on the basis of race unless it is necessary to accomplish a compelling interest—e.g., remedy past discrimination. However, a district may use facially race-neutral criteria that may have the same effect, such as strategic site selection for new schools or the redrawing of attendance zones. *Parents Involved in Community Schools v. Seattle School Dist. No. 1*, 551 U.S. 701 (2007).

4) Private affirmative action

Recall that the Equal Protection Clause applies only to governmental action, so private employers are not restricted by it. Discrimination by private employers is nonetheless regulated by federal statute pursuant to Congress's power under the enabling clauses of the Thirteenth and Fourteenth Amendments and the Commerce Clause.

c. Racial gerrymandering

Race may not be the predominant factor in determining the boundary lines of legislative districts (*see* § XIII.E.2.a., Racial discrimination, *infra*).

2. Alienage

Classifications based on status as a lawful resident of the United States (as opposed to a citizen) are subject to a variety of different standards, depending on the level of government and the nature of the classification.

a. Federal classification

Because Congress has plenary power over aliens under Article I, a federal alienage classification is likely valid unless it is **arbitrary** and **unreasonable.**

Example: Medicare regulations may require a five-year residency period for eligibility despite thereby excluding many lawful resident aliens. *Matthews v. Diaz*, 426 U.S. 67 (1976).

b. State classifications

1) Generally struck down

The Court will generally apply the strict scrutiny test and strike down state laws that discriminate against aliens, such as laws prohibiting aliens from owning land, obtaining commercial fishing licenses, or being eligible for welfare benefits or civil service jobs.

2) Exception—participation in government functions

A growing exception exists, however, for state laws that restrict or prohibit an alien's **participation in government functions.** Such laws need only have a **rational relationship** to a legitimate state interest. Laws prohibiting aliens from voting, serving on a jury, or being hired as police officers, probation officers, or public-school teachers have been upheld as preventing aliens from having a direct effect on the functioning of the government.

> **EXAM NOTE:** When determining whether a position or license from which aliens are excluded falls under the government function or political function exception, consider whether the position or license would allow the alien to "participate directly in the formulation, execution, or review of broad public policy" or would allow the alien to exercise "broad discretion."

c. Undocumented aliens

Undocumented aliens are not a suspect class, but the states may not deny primary or secondary public education benefits to undocumented aliens. *Plyler v. Doe*, 457 U.S. 202 (1982).

C. QUASI-SUSPECT CLASSIFICATIONS

1. Gender

Discrimination based on gender is "quasi-suspect" and subject to **intermediate scrutiny,** which is less stringent than strict scrutiny but tougher than the rational basis test. Just as with suspect classifications and fundamental rights, there must be **discriminatory intent** by the government to trigger intermediate scrutiny; disparate impact is not enough. Under intermediate scrutiny, the burden is on the state to show that a statute or regulation that treats the sexes differently is **substantially related** to an **important** governmental interest. This test applies whether the classification is invidious or benign, and it is now applied rather stringently, requiring the government to show that an "exceedingly persuasive justification" exists for the distinction, and that separate facilities (such as separate sports team facilities as state universities) are "substantially equivalent." *United States v. Virginia*, 518 U.S. 515 (1996).

a. Discrimination against women

Intentional discrimination through gender classification will generally be struck down under the intermediate scrutiny standard. For example, a state law giving preference to men over women to be administrators of decedents' estates was invalid. *Reed v. Reed*, 404 U.S. 71 (1971) (ease in determining who should serve as administrator is not an important interest). *See also United States v. Virginia*, 518 U.S. 515 (1996) (Virginia Military Institute could not exclude women from admission to public college based on overbroad generalizations about the physical capabilities and preferred educational methods of males and females).

b. Discrimination against men

Intentional discrimination against males is generally struck down for violating equal protection. However, there have been some instances of discrimination against men being upheld because of the important governmental interest:

i) Draft registration of males, but not females, *Rostker v. Goldberg*, 453 U.S. 57 (1981) (interest of preparing combat troops); and

ii) A statutory rape law that held only men criminally liable for such conduct, *Michael M. v. Sonoma County Superior Court*, 450 U.S. 464 (1981) (interest in preventing teenage pregnancy).

c. Affirmative action (benign discrimination)

The Court has upheld affirmative action regulations granting beneficial treatment to women over men (such as tax exemptions, increased social security benefits, and increased protection from mandatory armed forces discharge) because providing a remedy for past gender-based discrimination is an important governmental interest. *See Califano v. Webster*, 430 U.S. 313 (1977); *Schlesinger v. Ballard*, 419 U.S. 498 (1975).

2. Legitimacy

Classifications on the basis of status as a nonmarital child (i.e., those that distinguish between "legitimate" and "illegitimate" children) are subject to **intermediate scrutiny**—they must be **substantially related** to an **important** governmental interest. The Court will closely examine the purpose behind the distinction, and it will not uphold legislation designed to punish the offspring of a nonmarital relationship. To that end, states may not prohibit children of unmarried parents from receiving welfare benefits, *New Jersey Welfare Rights Org. v. Cahill*, 411 U.S. 619 (1973), workers' compensation benefits upon the death of a parent, *Weber v. Aetna Cas. and Sur. Co.*, 406 U.S. 164 (1972), or an inheritance from an intestate father, *Trimble v. Gordon*, 430 U.S. 762 (1977). In addition, a state cannot require a paternity action brought on behalf of an illegitimate child to be commenced within a limited time after birth in order to secure child support, while imposing a similar time limit on a legitimate child seeking child support from a parent. *Clark v. Jeter*, 486 U.S. 456 (1988).

D.   NONSUSPECT CLASSIFICATIONS

1.   Age

Age discrimination in violation of the Age Discrimination in Employment Act of 1967 does not provoke heightened scrutiny; laws and other governmental actions classifying on the basis of age are reviewed under the **rational basis** standard. *See, e.g., Massachusetts Bd. of Ret. v. Murgia*, 427 U.S. 307 (1976) (police officers may be forced to retire at age 50, even if they are as physically fit as younger officers).

2.   Poverty

Most statutes and regulations that classify on the basis of wealth (i.e., discriminate against the poor) are subject only to **rational basis** scrutiny and will be upheld. There is an exception for cases in which governmental action prohibits the poor from exercising a fundamental right because of a government-imposed fee; strict scrutiny will usually apply in those situations. For example, the availability of appeal in a criminal case cannot hinge on ability to pay for a trial transcript. *Griffin v. Illinois*, 351 U.S. 12 (1956). Also, poll taxes are unconstitutional because wealth is unrelated to a citizen's ability to vote intelligently. *Harper v. Virginia Bd. of Elections*, 383 U.S. 663 (1966).

3.   Sexual Orientation

Discrimination on the basis of sexual orientation does not provoke heightened scrutiny. The government, however, cannot impose a burden or deny a benefit on a group of persons solely based on animosity toward the class that it affects. *Romer v. Evans*, 517 U.S. 620 (1996).

E.   FUNDAMENTAL RIGHTS UNIQUE TO EQUAL PROTECTION

The fundamental rights guaranteed by substantive due process are often protected by equal protection principles as well. Thus, impingement of the right to vote, to travel, or to marry may trigger an inquiry under either the Due Process Clause or the Equal Protection Clause. However, certain rights and principles are particular to equal protection.

EXAM NOTE: The right to *travel* and the right to *vote* are the most frequently tested fundamental rights in the area of **equal protection.** (Often, both the Due Process Clause and the Equal Protection Clause will apply. Equal protection predominates if the question emphasizes denial of a right to a particular group, and it does not apply if the denial of the right is universal.)

1. One Person, One Vote

The principle of "one person, one vote" holds that one person's vote must be essentially equal to any other person's vote. To that end, when the government establishes voting districts for the election of representatives, the number of persons in each district must be approximately equal. *Reynolds v. Sims*, 377 U.S. 533 (1964). Voter approval of a redistricting plan will not justify a violation of the "one person, one vote" rule. *Lucas v. Colorado General Assembly*, 377 U.S. 713 (1964).

a. Congressional districts

When states establish districts for congressional elections, they must achieve nearly precise mathematical equality between the districts. This restriction is imposed on the states by Article I, Section 2, which requires members of the House to be chosen by "the People of the several States." An unexplained deviation of less than one percent may invalidate the statewide congressional district plan. Variations may be justified by the state on the basis of consistently applied, legitimate state objectives, such as respecting municipal political subdivision boundaries, creating geographic compact districts, and avoiding contests between incumbent representatives. In addition, variations based on anticipated population shifts may be acceptable when such shifts can be predicted with a high degree of accuracy, and population trends are thoroughly documented. *Kirkpatrick v. Preisler*, 394 U.S. 526 (1969) (variation in population of slightly less than six percent violated the "one person, one vote" rule); *Karcher v. Daggett*, 462 U.S. 725 (1983) (variation of slightly less than 0.7 percent violated the "one person, one vote" rule).

1) Congressional apportionment of House members

Congress, in apportioning members of the House among the states pursuant to Article I, Section 2, is not held to the "mathematical equality" standard. The method adopted by Congress is entitled to judicial deference and is assumed to be in good faith. *Dept. of Commerce v. Montana*, 503 U.S. 442 (1992) (Montana's loss of a congressional seat upheld, even though retention of the seat would have placed Montana closer to the ideal population size for a congressional district).

b. State and local districts

The size of electoral districts may vary much more in the case of state and local elections, as long as the variance is not unjustifiably large. A variation of less than 10% is rebuttably presumed to be a minor deviation that does not constitute a prima facie case for discrimination. *Cox v. Larios*, 300 F. Supp. 2d 1320 (N.D. Ga.), *aff'd*, 542 U.S. 947 (2004); *Brown v. Thompson*, 462 U.S. 835 (1983). When the maximum variation is 10% or greater, the state must show that the deviation from equality between the districts is reasonable and designed to promote a legitimate state interest. *Mahan v. Howell*, 410 U.S. 315 (1973) (maximum difference of 16% in size of population between state legislative districts permitted when the state respected the boundaries of political subdivisions).

1) Bodies performing governmental functions

The "one person, one vote" rule applies to local elections of entities that perform governmental functions, even when the functions are specialized rather than general in nature. *Hadley v. Junior College Dist.*, 397 U.S. 50 (1970) (election of trustees to junior college district). In addition to requiring relative equality with respect to the weight of a person's vote, the Equal Protection Clause subjects the restriction of voting of a particular class of persons to strict scrutiny, which generally results in the invalidation of the law. *Kramer v. Union Free School District No. 15*, 395 U.S. 621 (1969) (state law that restricted voting in school board election to property owners and parents with school-aged children struck down). The restriction of voting to a class of persons (e.g., landowners) and the allocation of voting weight on a basis other than personhood (e.g., the amount of land owned) has been upheld only with regard to water-district elections. *Ball v. James*, 451 U.S. 355 (1981).

c. At-large elections

While an election in which members of a governmental unit (e.g., county council members) are elected by all voters within that unit (i.e., an at-large election) does not violate the one-person, one-vote rule, it may conflict with another constitutional provision, such as the Equal Protection Clause. *Rogers v. Lodge*, 458 U.S. 613 (1982) (use of countywide system to elect county board unconstitutionally diluted the voting power of African-American citizens).

Note: Federal law bans at-large elections for congressional representatives in states that have more than one House member (i.e., the single-member district rule). 2 U.S.C.S. § 2c.

2. Gerrymandering

a. Racial discrimination

1) Vote dilution

When a state draws election districts for the purpose of scattering a racial or ethnic minority among several districts in order to prevent the minority from exercising its voting strength, the state's action is a violation of the Equal Protection Clause. *Gomillion v. Lightfoot*, 364 U.S. 339 (1960) (redrawing city boundaries to exclude African-American voters unconstitutional); *Rogers v. Lodge, supra*.

2) Majority-minority districts

Under the Equal Protection Clause, election districts for public office may not be drawn using race as the predominant factor in determining the boundary lines, unless the district plan can survive strict scrutiny. This restriction applies even when the district is drawn to favor historically disenfranchised groups. The state can use traditional factors—such as compactness, contiguity, or honoring political subdivisions—as the bases for the district, and it may only consider race if it does not predominate over other considerations. *Miller v. Johnson*, 515 U.S. 900 (1995).

A district's bizarre shape can be used as evidence that race was a predominating factor, but such a shape is not necessary for a finding of racial gerrymandering. *Shaw v. Reno*, 509 U.S. 630 (1993).

a) Voting Rights Act

The Voting Rights Act (42 U.S.C. § 1973 et seq.) requires racial gerrymandering to ensure minority success in elections by creating majority-minority districts (i.e., affirmative gerrymandering). The Act also requires federal pre-clearance for changes in voting rules, including redistricting, for specific southern states and a few other local governmental units. Receiving federal pre-clearance for a redistricting plan does not ensure that plan will avoid conflicting with the Equal Protection Clause. *Miller v. Johnson*, 515 U.S. 900 (1995).

b. Political discrimination

Partisan political gerrymandering may violate the Equal Protection Clause if the challenger can show "both intentional discrimination against an identifiable political group and an actual discriminatory effect on that group." *Davis v. Bandemer*, 478 U.S. 109, 127 (1986). However, lack of comprehensive and neutral principles for drawing electoral boundaries as well as the absence of rules to confine judicial intervention can prevent adjudication of political gerrymandering claims. *Vieth v. Jubelirer*, 541 U.S. 267 (2004).

XIV. PRIVILEGES AND IMMUNITIES CLAUSES

A. ARTICLE IV

Article IV, Section 2, known as the Comity Clause, provides that "the citizens of each state shall be entitled to all privileges and immunities of citizens in the several states."

1. Prohibits State Discrimination against Nonresidents

The Comity Clause, in essence, prohibits one state from discriminating against the citizens of another state. In this context, the term "citizen" does not include corporations or aliens.

2. Rights Protected

Nonresident citizens are protected against discrimination with respect to fundamental rights or essential activities. Examples include the pursuit of employment, transfer of property, and access to state courts.

Example: Discrimination against out-of-state residents in setting the fee for a *commercial* activity, such as a commercial shrimping license, violates the Privileges and Immunities Clause of Article IV, but similar discrimination for a *recreational* activity, such as a recreational hunting license, does not, if there is a rational basis for the fee differential. *Compare Toomer v. Witsell*, 334 U.S. 385 (1948) (fee for out-of-state commercial shrimper that was 100 times greater than the fee for an in-state shrimper unconstitutional), *with Baldwin v. Fish & Game Comm'n*, 436 U.S. 371

(1978) (fee for out-of-state resident to hunt elk that was 25 times greater than the fee for an in-state hunter constitutional).

Note that discrimination against an out-of-state resident with regard to access to a state's natural resources may violate the Dormant Commerce Clause. *New England Power Co. v. New Hampshire*, 455 U.S. 331 (1982) (prohibition on sale of hydroelectric power outside the state unconstitutional).

3. Exception—Substantial Justification

Discrimination against out-of-state citizens may be valid if the state can show a substantial reason for the difference in treatment. A substantial reason exists if:

i) The nonresidents either cause or are a part of the problem that the state is attempting to solve; and

ii) There are no less-restrictive means to solve the problem.

An example is discrimination against nonresidents with respect to the use of scarce water resources when the purpose was to preserve natural state-owned resources. *Sporhase v. Nebraska*, 458 U.S. 941 (1982).

> **EXAM NOTE:** Although the Privileges and Immunities Clause of Article IV and the Commerce Clause are not coextensive, they tend to mutually support each other; thus, consider both when analyzing a bar exam question.

B. FOURTEENTH AMENDMENT—NATIONAL CITIZENSHIP

The Fourteenth Amendment provides that "[n]o state shall make or enforce any law which shall abridge the privileges or immunities of citizens of the United States." This clause protects citizens (not corporations or aliens) from infringement by the states upon the privileges or immunities of **national** citizenship.

The privileges or immunities of national citizenship include the right to travel interstate, to petition Congress for redress of grievances, to vote for national offices, to enter public lands, to be protected while in the custody of U.S. marshals, and to peaceably assemble. *Twining v. New Jersey*, 211 U.S. 78 (1908). The guarantees of the Bill of Rights, however, are not privileges or immunities of national citizenship within the context of the Fourteenth Amendment. *Slaughterhouse Cases*, 83 U.S. 36 (1873). Therefore, those rights are protected from state action only by the Due Process Clause and the Equal Protection Clause.

This provision is seldom successfully invoked; under the limiting interpretation of the *Slaughterhouse Cases,* the rights that the clause provides are redundant to rights provided elsewhere in the Constitution. Although the Supreme Court has since relied on the clause to underscore the right to move freely among states, *Saenz v. Roe*, 526 U.S. 489 (1999) (invalidating a duration requirement for welfare benefits), there has been no subsequent expansion of use; the Fourteenth Amendment's Privileges or Immunities Clause applies, in practice, only to the right to travel.

XV. TAKINGS CLAUSE

The power of the government to take private property for public purposes is known as **"eminent domain."** The Takings Clause of the Fifth Amendment acts as a check on this power; it provides that private property may not "be taken for public use, without just compensation." The Fourteenth Amendment Due Process Clause makes the Takings Clause applicable to the states.

A.   PROPERTY INTEREST

For a person to challenge a governmental action as an unconstitutional taking, the person must have a property interest. When a person does not have an interest in the property that the government takes, the Takings Clause does not apply.

Example: An organization of homeowners challenged a beach restoration project undertaken by a state agency and local governments. The homeowners objected to the creation of land beyond the mean high water line, which represented the boundary of the homeowners' property, because this infringed upon their right as owners of property along a shore to receive accretions and because they lost the right to control public access to the shoreline. However, because, under state law, the newly created land belonged to the state, and the homeowners did not enjoy property rights with respect to this land, there was no taking of their property rights. *Stop the Beach Renourishment, Inc. v. Fla. Dep't of Envtl. Prot.*, 560 U.S. ___, 130 S. Ct. 2592 (2010). (Note: A plurality of the Supreme Court justices also found that the Takings Clause applies to a judicial taking.)

1.   Types of Property

Property that may be subject to the protection of the Takings Clause includes not only land and other real property, but also tangible personal property as well as intangible property, such as contract and patent rights and trade secrets. *Ruckelshaus v. Monsanto Co.*, 467 U.S. 986 (1984); *Lynch v. United States*, 292 U.S. 571 (1934); *James v. Campbell*, 104 U.S. 356 (1882).

2.   Types of Interests

In addition to the transfer of a fee simple interest in property, a taking may involve an easement, leasehold interest, or a lien. *Nollan v. California Coastal Commission*, 483 U.S. 825 (1987); *Armstrong v. United States*, 364 U.S. 40 (1960); *United States v. General Motors*, 323 U.S. 373 (1945). A taking may involve the rights of a property owner, such as the right to control access to the property. *Kaiser Aetna v. United States*, 444 U.S. 164 (1980) (federal government's imposition of public-access servitude on a waterway created on private property constituted a taking).

B.   TYPES OF TAKING

1.   Seizure of Property

The classic application of the Takings Clause is the seizure of private property for governmental use, such as acquiring privately held land in order to construct a courthouse or other government building. In such a case, the property owner's primary challenge to the seizure is whether he has received just compensation (*see* § XV.C., Just Compensation, *infra*).

a.   Public-use challenge

A government may seize private property not only for its own direct use but also to transfer the property to another private party. Although such a seizure is subject to challenge as not being made for a public use, the taking need merely be **"rationally related** to a **conceivable public purpose."** *Hawaii Hous. Auth. v. Midkiff*, 467 U.S. 229 (1984). This is a highly deferential standard, and the burden is on the person challenging the taking to prove a lack of legitimate interest or rational basis. In addition to traditional health, safety, and welfare justifications, economic redevelopment goals constitute a sufficient public purpose to justify the seizure. *Kelo v. City of New London*, 545 U.S. 469 (2005). Moreover, a government-mandated transfer of property from one private party directly to another (e.g., from lessor to lessee) may nevertheless be for a public use. *Hawaii Housing Authority v. Midkiff*, 467 U.S. 229 (1984).

2. Damage to or Destruction of Property

A destruction of property or property rights by the federal, state, or local government can also result in a taking. The destruction need not directly benefit the government.

Example: A federal statute that prevented the transfer by devise or descent of fractional shares of an interest in tribal land upon the death of the owner and instead provided for such interest to escheat to the tribe constituted an unconstitutional taking when there was no provision for compensation of the owner. *Hodel v. Irving*, 481 U.S. 704 (1987).

Similarly, physical damage to property or interference with a property owner's rights by governmental action can result in a taking.

Example: County ownership of an airport that resulted in an invasion of the airspace of nearby property owners by planes taking off and landing at the airport constituted a taking. *Griggs v. Allegheny County*, 369 U.S. 84 (1962).

Note: A statute that requires an owner of property rights to take action in order to preserve an unused right does not result in a taking if the owner fails to take such action. *Texaco, Inc. v. Short*, 454 U.S. 516 (1982).

a. Exception—public peril

The governmental destruction of private property in response to a public peril does not trigger the right to compensation.

Example: The owners of infected cedar trees located near apple orchards were not entitled to compensation when the cedar trees were destroyed pursuant to a state statute in order to prevent the spread of the infection to the orchards. *Miller v. Schoene*, 276 U.S. 272 (1928).

3. Characterization of Property

The Takings Clause prevents a government from recharacterizing private property as public property.

Example: Interest on the purchase price of an insolvent corporation placed by the buyer in an account with the court as part of an interpleader action involving the corporation's creditors was private property. A state court's interpretation of a statutory provision that the interest was public money constituted a taking. *Webb's Fabulous Pharmacies, Inc. v. Beckwith*, 449 U.S. 155 (1980).

4. Regulatory Taking

Generally, a governmental regulation that adversely affects a person's property interest is not a taking, but it is possible for a regulation to rise to the level of a taking.

In determining whether a regulation creates a taking, the following factors are considered:

i) The economic impact of the regulation on the property owner;

ii) The extent to which the regulation interferes with the owner's reasonable, investment-backed expectations regarding use of the property; and

iii) The character of the regulation, including the degree to which it will benefit society, how the regulation distributes the burdens and benefits among property owners, and whether the regulation violates any of the owner's essential attributes of property ownership, such as the right to exclude others from the property.

Penn Central Transportation Co. v. City of New York, 438 U.S. 104 (1978).

a. Public-use challenge

In the context of a regulation, a state or local government can act under its police power for the purposes of health, safety, and welfare. In addition, a public purpose can encompass aesthetic and environmental concerns. Moreover, it is generally inappropriate for a court to examine whether a regulation substantially advances a legitimate governmental interest. (Note, however, that an arbitrary or irrational regulation may constitute a due-process violation.) *Lingle v. Chevron U.S.A. Inc.*, 544 U.S. 528 (2005).

b. Per se takings

In two instances, a regulation clearly results in a taking.

1) Physical occupation

A taking has occurred when the governmental regulation results in a **permanent physical occupation** of the property.

Example: A law requiring a landlord to permit a cable company to install equipment on the landlord's property that would remain indefinitely constituted a taking, even though the installation had only a minimal economic impact on the landlord. *Loretto v. Teleprompter Manhattan CATV Corp.*, 458 U.S. 419 (1982).

2) No economically viable use

When a regulation results in a **permanent total loss of the property's economic value,** a taking has occurred. *Lucas v. South Carolina Coastal Council*, 505 U.S. 1003 (1992) (zoning ordinance precluding owner of coastal property from erecting any permanent structure on the land was a taking); *Tahoe-Sierra Preservation Council, Inc. v. Tahoe Regional Planning Agency*, 535 U.S. 302 (2002) (32-month building moratorium was not a taking).

Adverse economic impact: A regulation that results in a dramatic decline in the value of the regulated property does not necessarily constitute a taking.

c. Post-adoption acquisition

A person who acquires property rights after the adoption of a regulation that affects those rights may nevertheless challenge the regulation as an unconstitutional taking. *Palazzolo v. Rhode Island.*, 533 U.S. 606 (2001).

5. Exaction as a Taking

A local government may exact promises from a developer, such as setting aside a portion of the land being developed for a park in exchange for issuing the necessary construction permits. Such exactions do not violate the Takings Clause if there is:

i) An **essential nexus** between legitimate state interests and the conditions imposed on the property owner (i.e., the conditions substantially advance legitimate state interest); and

ii) A **rough proportionality** between the burden imposed by the conditions on property owner and the impact of the proposed development.

Nollan v. California Coastal Commission, 483 U.S. 825 (1987) (state-required grant of an easement across beachfront property as a condition on the issuance of a building permit was a taking due to lack of essential nexus); *Dolan v. City of Tigard*, 512 U.S. 374 (1994) (state-required dedication of land to the city for use as a greenway and pedestrian/bicycle pathway in exchange for permit to expand a store and parking lot was a taking due to lack of rough proportionality).

In determining whether there is rough proportionality between the burden and the impact, the government must make an individualized determination that the conditions are related both in nature and extent to the impact.

These requirements are limited to exactions; they do not apply to regulatory takings. *Lingle v. Chevron U.S.A. Inc., supra,* (rent cap was not an exaction taking, but instead was a valid regulation under the Takings Clause).

C. JUST COMPENSATION

The phrase "just compensation" has been interpreted to mean **fair market value,** which is the reasonable value of the property at the time of the taking. This value is measured in terms of the loss to the owner, not the benefit to the government.

1. Worthless Property

Property that is worthless to the owner but has value to the government may be taken without compensation.

> **Example:** Clients whose funds were held by lawyers and deposited in a trust account pursuant to state law to be paid to an entity in order to provide legal services for the poor were not entitled to compensation because each client's funds would not separately have earned interest. *Brown v. Legal Foundation of Washington*, 538 U.S. 216 (2003).

2. Only Portion Taken

When only a portion of an owner's property is taken, the owner may also receive compensation for any diminution in value of the remaining portion that is attributable to the taking but must reduce any compensation by the value of any special and direct benefits (e.g., a highway access) conferred on the remaining portion.

3. Return of Property

When governmental action constitutes a taking, the government cannot escape all liability by returning the property to its owner, but instead must pay the owner compensation for the period that the government possessed the property. *First English Evangelical Church v. County of Los Angeles*, 482 U.S. 304 (1987).

D. MANNER OF TAKING

Typically, when a property owner objects to the seizure of his property by the government, the government will institute condemnation proceedings, and the property owner can raise the Takings Clause as a defense to this action. When the governmental action that allegedly constitutes a taking is a statute, regulation, or ordinance, the property owner may institute a suit seeking an injunction or a declaratory judgment; this type of legal action is sometimes referred to as an inverse condemnation.

XVI. PROHIBITED LEGISLATION

A. BILLS OF ATTAINDER

A bill of attainder is a **legislative** act that declares a person or group of persons guilty of some crime and punishes them without a trial. Article I, Sections 9 and 10 forbid the federal government and the states, respectively, from enacting such "legislative trials." It applies only to criminal or penal measures.

Barring particular individuals from government employment qualifies as punishment under the prohibition against bills of attainder. *United States v. Lovett*, 328 U.S. 303 (1946).

B. EX POST FACTO LAWS

The constitutional prohibition on an "ex post facto" law is confined to a retroactive change to a **criminal or penal** law. A law that is civil in purpose is treated as a criminal law only if its punitive effect clearly overrides its civil purpose. *Smith v. Doe*, 538 U.S. 84 (2003).

Under Article I, Sections 9 and 10, a **federal or state** statute will be struck down as being ex post facto if it:

i) **Criminalizes** an act that was not a crime when it was originally committed;

ii) Authorizes, after an act was committed, the imposition of a **more severe penalty** on that act;

iii) **Deprives the defendant of a defense** available at the time the act was committed; or

iv) **Decreases the prosecution's burden of proof** required for a conviction to a level below that which was required when the alleged offense was committed.

Collins v. Youngblood, 497 U.S. 37 (1990).

Example: A change in the relevant statute of limitations that resulted in the revival of a prosecution for an act of sexual abuse for which the statute of limitations had expired violates the prohibition on ex post facto laws; the change retroactively withdrew a complete defense to the crime after it had vested. *Stogner v. California*, 539 U.S. 607 (2003).

Compare: The retroactive application of state law that required registration of convicted sex offenders and child kidnappers, and public notification of information about the convicts, including name, current address, and place of employment did not constitute an ex post facto law. The law was a nonpunitive regulatory scheme enacted for the protection of the public. *Smith v. Doe, supra*.

C. OBLIGATION OF CONTRACTS

Article I, Section 10 prohibits the states from passing any law "impairing the obligation of contracts." This prohibition applies only to **state legislation**—not state-court decisions and not federal legislation—that **retroactively** impairs contractual rights. It does not apply to contracts not yet entered into.

1. Private Contracts

State legislation that **substantially** impairs a contract between private parties is invalid, unless the government can demonstrate that the interference was **reasonable** and **necessary** to serve an **important** governmental interest. *Allied Structural Steel Co. v. Spannaus*, 438 U.S. 234 (1978); *Energy Reserves Group, Inc. v. Kansas Power and Light Co.*, 459 U.S. 400 (1983).

2. Public Contracts

Impairment by the state of a **public contract** (one to which the state or local government is a party) is subject to essentially the same "reasonable and necessary" test as private contracts, but with a somewhat stricter application. The state must show that its important interest cannot be served by a less-restrictive alternative and that the impairment it seeks is necessary because of unforeseeable circumstances. *U.S. Trust Co. v. New Jersey*, 413 U.S. 1 (1977).

Note that there is no substantial impairment if the state reserved—by statute, law, or in the contract itself—the right to revoke, alter, or amend.

XVII. FREEDOM OF RELIGION

The First Amendment provides that "Congress shall make no law respecting an establishment of religion, or prohibiting the free exercise thereof." Both the Establishment Clause and the Free Exercise Clause have been incorporated into the Due Process Clause of the Fourteenth Amendment and are therefore applicable to the states.

A. ESTABLISHMENT

When a governmental program shows preference to one religion over another, or to religion over nonreligion, strict scrutiny applies. *Bd. of Educ. v. Grumet*, 512 U.S. 687 (1994) (creation of special school district to benefit members of one religion invalid).

1. Standard of Review

Not every governmental action that impacts religion is unconstitutional. To determine whether a particular program violates the Establishment Clause, the Court may apply the three-part test developed in *Lemon v. Kurtzman*, 403 U.S. 602 (1971).

A governmental action that benefits religion is valid if:

i) It has a **secular purpose**;

ii) Its principal or primary effect **neither advances nor inhibits** religion; and

iii) It does not result in **excessive government entanglement** with religion.

Though still applied, the *Lemon* test has often been modified or set aside in the Supreme Court's more recent Establishment Clause cases.

2. Financial Aid

Programs that provide aid to religiously affiliated institutions, such as hospitals and schools, are tested under the three-part *Lemon* test and generally fall into one of the following three categories.

a. Indirect aid to schoolchildren

Financial assistance by the government that is widely available to a class of persons (not defined by religion) is likely valid, even if the aid benefits religion in some way. For example, aid to elementary- and high-school students, including students at parochial schools, in the form of textbooks, computers, standardized tests, bus transportation, and school lunches have all been upheld. Under the *Lemon* test, these forms of financial aid all have a secular primary purpose, neither advance nor inhibit religion, and have an extremely low risk of excessive entanglement.

Giving parents tuition vouchers to assist them in paying religious-school tuition does not violate the Establishment Clause if the vouchers may also be used in non-religious private schools. *Zelman v. Simmons-Harris*, 536 U.S. 639 (2002).

b. Direct aid to colleges and hospitals

Government grants to religiously affiliated colleges and hospitals are upheld only if the government requires that the aid be **used only for nonreligious purposes.** *Tilton v. Richardson*, 403 U.S. 672 (1971).

c. Tax exemptions

Property-tax exemptions for religious institutions have been held valid as being equivalent to exemptions given to other charitable organizations and therefore neither advancing nor inhibiting religion. *Walz v. Tax Comm'n*, 397 U.S. 664 (1970). Tax exemptions that are available only for religious activities or organizations, however, violate the Establishment Clause as an endorsement of religion. *Texas Monthly v. Bullock*, 489 U.S. 1 (1989).

Similarly, tax deductions given to reimburse tuition expenses only for parents of students in religious schools are invalid. If such a deduction is available to *all* parents for actual educational expenses of attending any public or private school (including parochial schools), it is valid. *Mueller v. Allen*, 463 U.S. 388 (1983).

3. School Activities

Generally, religious activities conducted in public schools violate the Establishment Clause. The following practices have been held invalid as clearly promoting religion:

i) **Prayer** and **Bible reading,** *Engel v. Vitale*, 370 U.S. 421 (1962);

ii) A designated period of silence for **"meditation or voluntary prayer,"** *Wallace v. Jaffree*, 472 U.S. 38 (1985);

iii) **Nondenominational prayer** led by a cleric at graduation ceremonies, *Lee v. Weisman*, 505 U.S. 577 (1992);

iv) Posting the **Ten Commandments** on public-school classroom walls, *Stone v. Graham*, 449 U.S. 39 (1980); and

v) **Prohibiting the teaching of Darwinism** (i.e., human biological evolution), or mandating that such teaching be accompanied by instruction regarding "creation science," *Edward v. Aguillard*, 482 U.S. 578 (1987); *Epperson v. Arkansas*, 393 U.S. 97 (1968).

If a public school allows student groups or organizations to use its facilities when classes are not in session, allowing a religious organization to use those facilities does not violate the Establishment Clause. Furthermore, to prohibit such a group from using those facilities because religious topics would be discussed would violate the First Amendment guarantee of **free speech**. *Good News Club v. Milford Central School*, 533 U.S. 98 (2001); *Widmar v. Vincent*, 454 U.S. 263 (1981). The Court has often responded to public educational institutions' Establishment Clause concerns by focusing on the free speech rights of religious students. *E.g., Rosenberger v. Univ. of Virginia*, 515 U.S. 819 (1995) (state university could not refuse to pay for printing of religious student newspaper on Establishment Clause grounds when it funded nonreligious papers).

4. Religious Displays

a. Ten Commandments

A display of the Ten Commandments on public property is an impermissible violation of the Establishment Clause if the display has a **"predominantly religious purpose."** *McCreary County v. ACLU*, 545 U.S. 844 (2005) (Ten Commandments posted in courthouse impermissible). If the display also communicates a secular moral message, or its context conveys a historical and social meaning, it may be upheld. *Van Orden v. Perry*, 545 U.S. 677 (2005) (Ten Commandments monument on the state capitol grounds displaying 17 monuments and 21 historical markers commemorating the state's "people, ideals, and events that compose its identity" was permitted because the "Ten Commandments have an undeniable historical meaning" in addition to their "religious significance." Because of the unique historical message, which is separate from any religious message, installing the Ten Commandments in a public park did not violate the Establishment Clause). This is a highly context-dependent, case-specific inquiry.

b. Holiday displays

Government holiday displays will generally be upheld unless a reasonable observer would conclude that the display is an **endorsement** of religion. The context of the display is key—a nativity scene in a courthouse under a banner reading "*Gloria in Excelsis Deo*" was struck down as endorsing religion, but a nearby outdoor display of a Christmas tree, Chanukah menorah, and other seasonal symbols was upheld as mere recognition that Christmas and Chanukah are both parts of a highly secularized winter holiday season. *County of Allegheny v. ACLU*, 492 U.S. 573 (1989).

B. FREE EXERCISE

The Free Exercise Clause of the First Amendment has been construed to include two freedoms: the freedom to believe and the freedom to act. The degree of protection that individuals are afforded from governmental interference in religion depends on whether religious belief or conduct is involved.

1.   **Religious Belief**

The freedom to believe in any religion or none at all is absolutely protected and cannot be restricted by law.   The government may not deny benefits or impose burdens based on religious belief, *Cantwell v. Connecticut*, 310 U.S. 296 (1940); it may not require affirmation of a belief, *West Virginia State Bd. of Educ. v. Barnette*, 319 U.S. 624 (1943); and it may not determine the reasonableness of a belief, although it may determine the sincerity of the person asserting that belief, *United States v. Ballard*, 322 U.S. 78 (1944).

2.   **Religious Conduct**

Religious conduct, on the other hand, is not absolutely protected.   Generally, only laws that **intentionally target** religious conduct are subject to strict scrutiny. Neutral laws of general applicability that have an impact on religious conduct are subject only to the rational basis test.

a.   **Targeting religious conduct**

Strict scrutiny applies when the government purposely targets conduct because it is religious or displays religious beliefs. *Church of the Lukumi Babalu Aye, Inc. v. City of Hialeah*, 508 U.S. 520 (1993) (city ordinance banning all ritual sacrifice of animals not for the purpose of food consumption struck down as targeting the Santeria religion).   A law that is designed to suppress activity because it is religiously motivated is valid only if it is necessary to achieve a compelling governmental interest.

Other laws that have been struck down as violating the Free Exercise Clause include compulsory school attendance for the Amish, *Wisconsin v. Yoder*, 406 U.S. 205 (1972), and denial of unemployment benefits to one whose faith prevented her from taking a job that required her to work on the Sabbath, *Sherbert v. Verner*, 374 U.S. 398 (1963).

b.   **Generally applicable laws**

Neutral laws of general applicability that have the incidental effect of interfering with one's ability to engage in religious practices are subject only to the rational basis test. *Employment Div. v. Smith*, 494 U.S. 872 (1990) (criminalization of peyote that did not contain an exception for use in Native American religious rituals upheld, as the ban was not motivated by any desire to burden religious conduct).

> **Example:** A parent's right to pray over a child who has contracted meningitis, rather than seeking medical assistance, may be limited by state child-neglect and manslaughter laws.   Parents do not have the right to endanger the lives of their children on the grounds of freedom of religion. *See Prince v. Massachusetts*, 321 U.S. 158 (1944).

C.   **MINISTERIAL EXCEPTION TO DISCRIMINATION LAWS**

Religious institutions can rely on a "ministerial exception" to federal and state employment discrimination laws in a decision to discharge a minister from employment.   The

Establishment and Free Exercise Clauses of the First Amendment bar suits brought on behalf of ministers against their churches, claiming termination in violation of employment discrimination laws. The purpose of the ministerial exception is not merely to safeguard a church's decision to discharge a minister when it is made for a religious reason but also to ensure that the authority to select and control who will serve as a minister to the church's faithful, a strictly ecclesiastical matter, is solely the church's decision. The exception operates as an affirmative defense to an otherwise cognizable claim, but not as a jurisdictional bar. *Hosanna-Tabor Evangelical Lutheran Church and School v. E.E.O.C.*, 565 U.S. ___, 132 S. Ct. 694 (2012) (employee whose responsibilities included religious instruction was "minister" within scope of ministerial exception, as such, church and school could not be held liable in E.E.O.C.'s discrimination enforcement action on her behalf).

XVIII. FREEDOM OF EXPRESSION AND ASSOCIATION

In addition to its religion clauses, the First Amendment provides that "Congress shall make no laws...abridging the freedom of speech, or of the press; or the right of the people to peaceably assemble, and to petition the Government for a redress of grievances." These aspects of the First Amendment are applicable to the states via the Fourteenth Amendment.

Freedom of expression is not absolute. While governmental regulation of the content of speech is severely constrained, governmental regulation of the time, place, and manner of speech is subject to less restriction.

A. REGULATION OF SPEECH

1. Expressive Conduct

Protected speech can include not only written, oral, and visual communication, but also activities such as picketing and leafleting. Expressive conduct (or symbolic speech) may be protected as speech, but it is subject to a lesser degree of protection. Governmental regulation of expressive conduct is upheld if:

i) The regulation is **within the government's power** to enact (e.g., through a local government's police power);

ii) The regulation furthers an **important governmental interest**;

iii) The governmental interest is **unrelated to the suppression of ideas**; and

iv) The burden on speech is **no greater than necessary.**

United States v. O'Brien, 391 U.S. 367 (1968) (prohibition against burning draft cards upheld as furthering the important governmental interest in a smoothly functioning draft system).

An example of permissible regulation of expressive conduct includes upholding a ban on public nudity, such as nude dancing in adult entertainment venues, pursuant to the important governmental interest in preventing the "harmful secondary effects" of adult entertainment on neighborhoods, which is unrelated to the suppression of expression. *City of Erie v. Pap's A.M.*, 529 U.S. 277 (2000).

Examples of impermissible regulation of expressive conduct include:

i) A ban against students wearing black armbands to protest the war in Vietnam, because the government's only interest in banning the conduct was prohibiting communication, *Tinker v. Des Moines Indep. Cmty. Sch. Dist.*, 393 U.S. 503 (1969); and

ii) A federal prohibition against burning the American flag because the law was intended to suppress messages of disapproval of governmental policy, rather than any conduct-related consequences of the burning of a flag. *United States v. Eichman*, 496 U.S. 310 (1990).

The act of signing a petition constitutes expressive conduct. Public disclosure of the petition, and, thereby, the names of the individuals who signed the petition does not violate the First Amendment because such disclosure is substantially related to the important interest of preserving the integrity of the electoral process. *Doe v. Reed*, 561 U.S. ___, 130 S. Ct. 2811 (2010).

2. Overbreadth

A law that burdens substantially more speech than is necessary to protect a compelling governmental interest is **"overbroad"** and therefore void. A statute's overbreadth must be substantial both in an absolute sense and relative to the statute's plainly legitimate reach. The mere fact that some impermissible applications of a statute can be conceived of is not sufficient to render a statute overbroad. *United States v. Williams*, 553 U.S. 285 (2008).

In order to prevent a **"chilling effect"** on protected speech (i.e., frightening people into not speaking for fear of prosecution), overbroad statutes may be challenged as **"facially invalid"** even by those who are validly regulated on behalf of those who are not. *Watchtower Bible and Tract Soc'y of New York, Inc. v. Vill. of Stratton*, 536 U.S. 150 2080 (2002) (municipal ordinance requiring a permit in order to engage in door-to-door canvassing and solicitation violated Free Speech Clause); *Bd. of Airport Comm'rs v. Jews for Jesus*, 482 U.S. 569 (1987) (administrative rule banning "all First Amendment activities" in a large airport terminal held overbroad).

3. Vagueness

A statute is **"void for vagueness"** if it fails to provide a person of ordinary intelligence with fair notice of what is prohibited. *United States v. Williams, supra*.

As with overbreadth, vagueness is impermissible for fear that constitutionally protected speech will be "chilled." In addition, the "void for vagueness" doctrine is grounded in the due process requirement of notice. Under due process principles, laws that regulate persons or entities must give fair notice of conduct that is forbidden or required. *FCC v. Fox Television Stations, Inc.*, 567 U.S. ___, 132 S. Ct. 2307 (2012), Statutes that tie criminal culpability to conduct that involves subjective judgments without providing statutory definitions, narrow context, or settled legal meanings have been struck down for vagueness. *Reno v. ACLU*, 521 U.S. 844 (1997) (indecent speech); *Coates v. Cincinnati*, 402 U.S. 611 (1971) (annoying conduct).

4. Prior Restraints

A prior restraint is a regulation of speech that occurs in advance of its expression (e.g., publication or utterance). Prior restraints are generally presumed to be unconstitutional, with limited exceptions. *Bantam Books, Inc. v. Sullivan*, 372 U.S. 58 (1963). These rare exceptions require at a minimum that:

i) There is a **particular harm** to be avoided (like publication of troop movements); and

ii) Certain **procedural safeguards** are provided to the speaker. Examples of such safeguards include:

a) The standards must be narrowly drawn, reasonable, and definite, *Butterworth v. Smith*, 494 U.S. 624 (1990);

b) The censoring body must promptly seek an injunction, *Teitel Films v. Cusack*, 390 U.S. 139 (1968); and

c) There must be a prompt and final judicial determination of the validity of the restraint, *National Socialist Party v. Village of Skokie*, 432 U.S. 43 (1977).

The **burden is on the government** to prove that the material to be censored is not protected speech. *Freedman v. Maryland*, 380 U.S. 51 (1965).

Prior restraints have been rejected even when national security was at issue, *New York Times v. United States*, 403 U.S. 713 (1971) (Pentagon Papers), and even when press coverage threatened the fairness of a trial, *Nebraska Press Ass'n v. Stewart*, 427 U.S. 539 (1976) (prior restraint must be the only way to accomplish a goal).

5. Unfettered Discretion

A law or regulation that permits a governmental official to restrict speech (e.g., requires an official to issue a permit before a rally can be held) must provide definite standards as to how to apply the law in order to prevent governmental officials from having unfettered discretion over its application. Such a law or regulation must be related to an important governmental interest and contain the procedural safeguards mentioned above. A statute that gives officials unfettered discretion is void on its face; speakers need not apply for a permit and may not be punished for violating the licensing statute. *Lovell v. City of Griffin*, 303 U.S. 444 (1938).

6. Freedom Not to Speak

The First Amendment protects not only freedom of speech, but also the freedom not to speak. One such example is a child's right not to recite the Pledge of Allegiance. *West Virginia State Board of Education v. Barnette*, 319 U.S. 624 (1943). Similarly, the private organizers of a parade cannot be compelled by the government to include in the parade a group that espouses a message with which the organizers disagree. *Hurley v. Irish-American Gay, Lesbian & Bisexual Group of Boston*, 515 U.S. 557 (1995). However, a state can compel a private entity (e.g., a shopping mall) to permit individuals to exercise their own free-speech rights when the private entity is open to the public and the message is not likely to be attributable to the private entity. *Pruneyard Shopping Center v. Robins*, 447 U.S. 74 (1980).

a. Compelled financial support

Although one can be compelled to join or financially support a group with respect to one's employment, one cannot be forced to fund political speech by that group. *Abood v. Detroit Bd. of Educ.*, 431 U.S. 209 (1977) (teacher required to pay union dues); *Keller v. State Bar of California*, 496 U.S. 1 (1990) (lawyer required to join a bar association). A student, however, can be required to pay a university activity fee even though the fee may support groups that espouse messages with which the student disagrees, at least when the fee is allocated in accord with a viewpoint-neutral scheme. *Board of Regents v. Southworth*, 529 U.S. 217 (2000).

7. Government Speech

When the government itself speaks, it is not constrained by the First Amendment. Therefore, government speech (public service announcements, agricultural marketing campaigns, etc.) need not be viewpoint-neutral. *Johanns v. Livestock Mkt'ing Ass'n*, 544 U.S. 550 (2005). This Government Speech Doctrine, however, is subject to the requirements of the Establishment Clause (*See* § XVII.A., *supra*).

a. Monuments on public property

The display of a monument on public property, even if the monument has been donated by a private person, constitutes government speech. *Pleasant Grove City v. Summum*, 555 U.S. 460 (2009) (government installed a Ten Commandments monument donated by a private person in a public park; the Court held that governmental entities may exercise "selectivity" in choosing a monument being offered by a private donor).

b. Funding of private messages

The government may fund private messages. However, it must generally do so on a viewpoint-neutral basis. *Rosenberger v. Rector and Visitors of the University of Virginia*, 515 U.S. 819 (1995). The exception to this is when the government decides to fund artists; the decision of which artist to fund is necessarily based on the content of the artist's work. *National Endowment for the Arts v. Finley*, 524 U.S. 569 (1998).

c. Speech by government employees

Attempts to fire or penalize a government employee for speech on matters of "public concern" will be strictly scrutinized. *Connick v. Myers*, 461 U.S. 138 (1983). However, speech on matters of public concern made in furtherance of the public employee's job functions receives less protection under the First Amendment than speech made by a person acting outside of his job. *Garcetti v. Ceballos*, 547 U.S. 410 (2006). Courts balance the First Amendment interest of the employee against the interest of the state, as an employer, in promoting the efficiency of the public services it provides through its employees. *Pickering v. Bd. of Educ.*, 391 U.S. 563 (1968). Speech by a government employee, including a petition for redress related to the employee's job, that does not relate to a matter of public concern, is not constitutionally protected. *Borough of Duryea v. Guarnieri*, 564 U.S. ___, 131 S. Ct. 2488 (2011).

8. Campaign Related Speech

a. Political campaign contributions

Statutes limiting campaign contributions are subject to intermediate scrutiny: they must be "closely drawn" to correspond with a sufficiently important interest. *McConnell v. Federal Election Commission*, 540 U.S. 93 (2003); *Randall v. Sorrell*, 548 U.S. 230 (2006).

1) Contributions to candidates

The government may limit contributions to individual candidates because excessive contributions to candidates create a danger of corruption and the appearance of corruption. *Buckley v. Valeo*, 424 U.S. 1 (1976). Limits on campaign contributions to candidates for state office ranging from $275 to $1,000 have been upheld. *Nixon v. Shrink Missouri Gov't PAC,* 528 U.S. 377 (2000). However, the government cannot set differential contribution limits that penalize a candidate who finances his own campaign. *Davis v. Federal Election Commission,* 554 U.S. 724 (2008)

2) Contributions to political parties

The government may limit contributions to a political party that are used to expressly advocate for the election or defeat of a particular candidate (also known as "hard money") as well as contributions that are used for other purposes, such as promoting the party itself (also known as "soft money"). *McConnell v. Federal Election Commission, supra.* In addition, the government may require a political party to disclose contributors and recipients unless the party can show that such disclosure would cause harm to the party. *Brown v. Socialist Workers '74 Campaign Committee,* 454 U.S. 112 (1982).

3) Contributions to political action committees (PACs)

The government may limit contributions to a political action committee (PAC). *California Medical Assn. v. FEC,* 453 U.S. 182 (1981).

b. Political campaign expenditures

In contrast to campaign contributions, restrictions on expenditures by individuals and entities (including corporations and unions) on communications during an election campaign regarding a candidate are subject to strict scrutiny. So long as the source of the funding is disclosed, there is no legal limit to the amount that corporations and unions may spend on "electioneering communications." *Citizens United v. Federal Election Comm'n,* 558 U.S. 310 (2010). In addition, expenditures by a candidate on her own behalf cannot be limited. *Buckley v. Valeo, supra; Davis v. Federal Election Commission, supra.*

c. Political speakers

In addition to individuals, corporations (both nonprofit and for-profit) enjoy First Amendment protection with regard to political speech. *Citizens United, supra.* Similarly, a candidate for a judgeship has a First Amendment right to express his views on disputed legal or political issues. *Republican Party of Minnesota v. White,* 536 U.S. 765 (2002).

B. REGULATION OF TIME, PLACE, AND MANNER OF EXPRESSION

The government's ability to regulate the time, place, and manner of speech varies with the forum in which the speech takes place.

1. Public Forum

A **"public forum"** may be **traditional** or **designated.** Traditional public forums are those that are historically associated with expression, such as sidewalks, streets, and parks. A designated (or limited) public forum is one that has not historically been used for speech-related activities, but which the government has opened for such use, such as civic auditoriums, publicly owned theaters, or school classrooms that the public is allowed to use afterhours. The practical difference between the two is that the government can change a designated forum to a nonpublic forum, but it cannot do the same with a traditional forum.

In either type of public forum, the government may impose reasonable restrictions on the time, place, or manner of protected speech, provided the restrictions:

i) Are **content-neutral** as to both subject matter and viewpoint (i.e., it is not necessary to hear what is said in order to apply the regulation);

ii) Are **narrowly tailored** to serve a **significant governmental interest**; and

iii) Leave open ample **alternative channels for communication** of the information.

Ward v. Rock Against Racism, 491 U.S. 781 (1989). Restrictions that are not content-neutral are subject to **strict scrutiny** (*see* § XVIII.C., Regulation of Content, *infra*).

a. Residential areas

There is no right to focus picketing on a particular single residence. However, a person may solicit charitable funds in a residential area. Door-to-door solicitation does not require a permit, as long as the solicitation is for noncommercial or nonfundraising purposes. *Cantwell v. Conn.*, 310 U.S. 296, 306 (1940).

b. Injunctions

The test for the constitutionality of injunctions in public forums depends on whether the injunction is content-neutral or content-based. If an injunction is **content-neutral**, then the test is whether it burdens **no more speech than is necessary** to achieve an **important** governmental interest. On the other hand, if the injunction is **content-based,** it must be **necessary** for the government to achieve a **compelling** governmental interest.

c. Public schools

When a public school, as a designated (limited) public forum, permits the public to use its facilities, it cannot discriminate against organizations based on its beliefs. *Lamb's Chapel v. Center Moriches Union Free School District*, 508 U.S. 384 (1993) (religious organizations); *Widmar v. Vincent*, 454 U.S. 263 (1981); *Healy v. James*, 408 U.S. 169 (1972) (political organization). Similarly, a public school may provide funding and other benefits (e.g., free use of facilities) to student groups, but it must do so on a viewpoint-neutral basis.

Example 1: A university that provided funds to various student publications could not withhold funds from a student religious publication on the grounds that the publication espoused religion. *Rosenberger v. Rector and Visitors of the University of Virginia*, 515 U.S. 819 (1995).

Example 2: A public university law school could adopt an "all comers policy" with which student organizations must comply in order to receive school funding and other benefits. Under the policy, a student organization had to admit any student as a member and permit any student to hold office in the organization. Because the policy was viewpoint-neutral, its application to a religious organization was constitutional. *Christian Legal Soc'y Chapter of Univ. of California, Hastings Coll. of Law v. Martinez*, 561 U.S. ___, 130 S. Ct. 2971 (2010).

2. Nonpublic Forum

A nonpublic forum is essentially all public property that is not a traditional or designated public forum. Examples include government offices, schools, jails, and military bases. Sidewalks on postal service property and airport terminals are also considered nonpublic forums. The government may regulate speech-related activities in nonpublic forums as long as the regulation is (i) **viewpoint-neutral** and (ii) **reasonably related to a legitimate governmental interest.**

> Note that a governmental fundraising campaign is a nonpublic forum for the expression of speech. The decision to exclude some charities (but not others) cannot be made because the government disagrees with a particular organization's political views; such a decision must be ideologically neutral. *Cornelius v. NAACP Legal Def. and Educ. Fund, Inc.*, 473 U.S. 788 (1985).

a. Viewpoint-neutral

The regulation need not be content-neutral, but it must be viewpoint-neutral. In other words, the government may prohibit speech on certain issues altogether, but it may not allow only one side of an issue to be presented. For example, while a restriction on all public speeches related to abortion on military bases would likely be upheld, a restriction only on pro-life speeches would not.

b. Reasonable

The restriction on speech-related activities in nonpublic forums must only be rationally related to a legitimate governmental interest. For example, a city may sell commercial advertising space inside city buses but refuse to sell such space for political advertising in order to avoid the appearance of favoritism and imposition on a captive audience. *Lehman v. City of Shaker Heights*, 418 U.S. 298 (1974).

3. Personal Property

Governmental regulation of speech on a person's own private property will rarely be upheld, particularly content-based regulations. While the government has some limited powers to regulate speech on private property, outright bans on certain types of speech, such as signs in a person's yard or window, are impermissible. *City of Ladue v. Gilleo*, 512 U.S. 43 (1994) (statute banning all residential signs in order to fight "visual clutter" was found unconstitutional).

C. REGULATION OF CONTENT

In general, the government may regulate the **content** of speech only if the regulation is necessary to achieve a compelling governmental interest and is narrowly tailored to meet that interest (i.e., the **strict scrutiny** test). *Brown v. Entm't Merchs. Ass'n*, 564 U.S ___, 131 S. Ct. 2729 (2011) (state law that prohibited the sale of violent video games to minors is an unconstitutional content restriction on speech); *Simon & Schuster, Inc. v. Members of the New York State Crime Victims Board*, 502 U.S. 105 (1991). The government must identify an actual problem, and the regulation of speech must be necessary to solve that problem. This standard is incredibly stringent and is not often met. *U.S. v. Playboy Entm't Group, Inc.*, 529 U.S. 803 (2000).

However, the government may restrict speech on the basis of content if the speech falls into one of the following historic and traditional categories: obscenity, subversive speech, fighting words, defamation, or commercial speech. *U.S. v. Alvarez*, 567 U.S. ___, 132 S. Ct. 2537 (2012). States are not free to create new categories of content-based restrictions without persuasive evidence that such restrictions have a long-standing history of proscription. *Brown v. Entm't Merchs. Ass'n, supra*.

1. Obscenity and Child Pornography

Neither obscene speech nor child pornography is protected by the First Amendment Free Speech Clause. *Roth v. United States*, 354 U.S. 476 (1957).

a. Obscenity test

To be considered obscene, speech must meet each part of a three-prong test developed in *Miller v. California*, 413 U.S. 15 (1973). Under the *Miller* test, the **average person,** applying **contemporary community standards,** must find that the material, **taken as a whole**:

i) Appeals to the **"prurient interest"**;

ii) Depicts sexual conduct in a **patently offensive** way; and

iii) **Lacks serious literary, artistic, political, or scientific value.**

> **EXAM NOTE:** *Standards Distinguished* – The first two prongs of this test use a contemporary **community** standard, which may be national but is generally considered to be local or statewide. A **national** standard must be applied, however, to the third prong of the test—determining the value of the work—because the work may merit constitutional protection despite local views to the contrary. *Pope v. Illinois*, 481 U.S. 497 (1987). With regard to the third prong, the judge, not the jury, determines whether this standard has been met.

Either an appellate court or a jury can assess whether the material is obscene. Evidence of similar material on newsstands is not automatically admissible, nor is expert testimony required to make such a determination.

b. Prohibited activities

The sale, distribution, and exhibition of obscene material may be prohibited. *Stanley v. Georgia*, 394 U.S. 557 (1969). However, the right to privacy precludes criminalization of possession of obscenity in one's own home. *Stanley v. Georgia, supra*.

c. Land-use restrictions

Narrowly drawn zoning ordinances may be used to restrict the location of adult theaters if the purpose of the regulation is to reduce the impact on the neighborhood of such establishments, but they may not be used to ban such establishments entirely. It does not matter that such establishments may be found in adjoining jurisdictions. *Los Angeles v. Alameda Books*, 535 U.S. 425 (2002); *City of Renton v. Playtime Theatres, Inc.*, 475 U.S. 41 (1986).

d. Minors

Material that appeals to the prurient interests of minors may be regulated as to minors, even if it would not be considered obscene to an adult audience. *Ginsberg v. New York*, 390 U.S. 629 (1968). The government may not, however, block adults' access to indecent materials in order to prevent them from reaching children. *Reno v. ACLU*, 521 U.S. 844 (1997).

e. Child pornography

The First Amendment also does not protect child pornography, which is sexually explicit visual portrayals that feature children. Because of the state's compelling interest in protecting minor children from exploitation, the sale, distribution, and even private possession of child pornography may be prohibited, even if the material would not be obscene if it involved adults. *Osborne v. Ohio*, 495 U.S. 103 (1990); *New York v. Ferber*, 458 U.S. 747 (1982).

Simulated child pornography (i.e., pornography using young-looking adults or computer-generated images) may not be banned as child pornography. *Ashcroft v. Free Speech Coalition*, 535 U.S. 234 (2002). However, offers to sell or buy simulated child pornography that contain actual depictions of children even though the sexually explicit features are simulated may be criminalized when the material is presented as actual child pornography. *United States v. Williams*, 553 U.S. 285 (2008).

f. Violence

Violence is not included in the definition of obscenity that may be constitutionally regulated. *Brown v. Entm't Merchs. Ass'n, supra*; *Winters v. New York*, 333 U.S. 507 (1948).

2. Incitement to Violence

A state may forbid speech that advocates the use of force or unlawful action if:

i)   The speech is **directed to inciting or producing imminent lawless action**; and

ii) It is **likely to incite or produce such action** (i.e., creates a clear and present danger).

Brandenburg v. Ohio, 395 U.S. 444 (1969).

Advocacy requires the use of language reasonably and ordinarily calculated to incite persons to such action. *Yates v. United States*, 354 U.S. 298 (1957). The abstract expression of ideas, including the teaching of the moral propriety or even moral necessity for a resort to force and violence, is not the same as the actual incitement of violence. There must be substantial evidence of a strong and pervasive call to violence. *Noto v. United States*, 367 U.S. 290 (1960).

3. Fighting Words

A speaker may be criminally punished for using "fighting words," which are words that **by their very nature** are likely to incite an immediate breach of the peace. *Chaplinsky v. New Hampshire*, 315 U.S. 568 (1942). Words that are simply annoying or offensive are not fighting words; there must be a genuine likelihood of imminent violence by a hostile audience. *Cohen v. California*, 403 U.S. 154 (1971).

EXAM NOTE: Attempts to forbid fighting words almost always fail as vague, overbroad, or otherwise constitutionally infirm.

Statutes designed to punish only fighting words that express certain viewpoints are unconstitutional. *R.A.V. v. City of St. Paul*, 505 U.S. 377 (1992) (the Court struck down an ordinance that applied only to fighting words that insulted or provoked on the basis of race, religion, or gender).

However, actual threats of violence are outside the protection of the First Amendment, given the need to protect individuals from (i) the fear of violence, (ii) the disruption that fear engenders, and (iii) the possibility that the threatened violence will occur. *R.A.V. v. City of St. Paul*, 505 at 388.

4. Defamation

Limits on punishment for defamatory speech may apply in cases in which the plaintiff is a public official or public figure, or when a defamatory statement involves a matter of public concern. In addition to the elements of a prima facie case of defamation, the plaintiff must in these cases prove both **fault** and the **falsity** of the statement.

a. Public figure or official

A public figure is someone who is known to the general public and includes any person who has voluntarily injected herself into the public eye. The plaintiff must prove that the defendant acted with **actual malice,** i.e., knowledge of the statement's falsity or reckless disregard for whether it was true or false. *New York Times v. Sullivan*, 376 U.S. 254 (1964). Scientists who publish in scientific journals, criminals, and spouses of wealthy persons are not considered public figures.

b. Public concern

If the plaintiff is a private figure but the defamatory statement involves a matter of public concern, then the standard is lower, but the plaintiff still must establish negligence with respect to the falsity of the statement. *Gertz v. Robert Welch, Inc.*, 418 U.S. 323 (1974).

[See the Themis Torts outline for a full discussion of defamation actions.]

5. Commercial Speech

Commercial speech—advertising and similarly economically oriented expression—is entitled to an intermediate level of First Amendment protection. Restrictions on commercial speech are reviewed under a **four-part test**:

i)   The commercial speech must **concern lawful activity** and be **neither false nor misleading** (fraudulent speech or speech which proposes an illegal transaction may be prohibited);

ii) The asserted governmental interest must be **substantial**;

iii) The regulation must **directly advance** the asserted interest; and

iv) The regulation must be **narrowly tailored** to serve that interest. In this context, narrowly tailored does not mean the least restrictive means available; rather, there must be a **"reasonable fit"** between the government's ends and the means chosen to accomplish those ends. *Board of Trustees of State University of New York v. Fox*, 492 U.S. 469 (1989).

Central Hudson Gas & Elec. v. Pub. Svc. Comm'n, 447 U.S. 557 (1980). Under this test, the Court has struck down laws prohibiting truthful advertising of legal abortions, contraceptives, drug prices, alcohol prices, and attorneys' fees and regulation of billboards on the basis of aesthetic value and safety.

> **Example:** A Massachusetts regulation that prohibited tobacco billboards within 1,000 feet of a school was struck down because the means—effectively barring most outdoor tobacco advertising in urban areas—were not narrowly tailored to the ends of protecting children. *Lorillard Tobacco Co. v. Reilly*, 533 U.S. 525 (2001).

Note that solicitation of funds, however, is recognized as a form of protected speech. *See Village of Schaumburg v. Citizens for a Better Env't*, 444 U.S. 620 (1980).

D. REGULATION OF THE MEDIA

Although the First Amendment specifically mentions freedom of the press, the media has no greater First Amendment rights than the general public.

1. General Considerations

The press has the right to publish information about matters of public concern, and the viewers have a right to receive it. This right may be restricted only by a regulation that is narrowly tailored to further a compelling governmental interest (i.e., strict scrutiny applies).

a. Gag orders

A gag order is a judicial order prohibiting the press from publishing information about court proceedings. Such orders are subject to prior-restraint analysis. Gag orders are almost always struck down because they are rarely the least restrictive means of protecting the defendant's right to a fair trial. The trial judge has other alternatives available, such as change of venue, postponement of the trial, careful voir dire, or restricting the statements of lawyers and witnesses. *Nebraska Press Ass'n v. Stuart*, 427 U.S. 539 (1972).

b. Attending trials

The public and the press both have the right to attend criminal trials, but this right is not absolute. It may be outweighed if the trial judge finds an **overriding** interest that cannot be accommodated by less restrictive means. The Supreme Court has not determined whether this right also applies to civil trials. However, the Supreme Court has held that the defendant's right to a public trial extended to voir dire, and the trial court must consider reasonable alternatives to closing the voir dire to the public in addressing the trial court's concerns. *Presley v. Georgia*, 558 U.S. ___, 130 S. Ct. 721 (2010).

c. No constitutional privilege to protect sources

A journalist has no First Amendment right to refuse to testify before a grand jury regarding the content and source of information relevant to the criminal inquiry. *Branzburg v. Hayes*, 408 U.S. 665 (1972).

d. Illegally obtained and private information

The First Amendment shields the media from liability for publishing information that was obtained illegally by a third party as long as the information involves a matter of public concern and the publisher neither obtained it unlawfully nor knows who did. *Bartnicki v. Vopper*, 532 U.S. 514 (2001).

Similarly, the First Amendment shields the media from liability for publication of a lawfully obtained private fact, e.g., the identity of a rape victim, so long as the news story involves a matter of public concern. *See Florida Star v. BJF*, 491 U.S. 524 (1989); *Cox Broadcasting v. Cohn*, 420 U.S. 469 (1975).

e. First Amendment conflict with state right of publicity

Some states recognize a right of publicity—the right of a person to control the commercial use of his or her identity. The right is an intellectual property right derived under state law, the infringement of which creates a cause of action for the tort of unfair competition. In *Zacchini v. Scripps-Howard Broad. Co.*, 433 U.S. 562 (1977), the Supreme Court considered a conflict between the First Amendment and a person's state-law right of publicity. A news program had televised a videotape of a daredevil's entire 15-second performance at a local fair when he was shot out of a cannon. The lower court held that the First Amendment protected the telecast from a tort suit regarding the right of publicity. The Supreme Court reversed, holding that the First and Fourteenth Amendments do not immunize the news media from civil liability when they broadcast a performer's entire act without his consent, and the Constitution does not prevent a state from requiring broadcasters to compensate performers. Note that a state government may pass a law shielding the press from liability for broadcasting performers' acts.

f. No immunity from laws of general applicability

As mentioned previously, the press has no greater First Amendment rights than does the general public, i.e., there is no special privilege allowing the press to invade the rights of others. As such, members of the press are not immune from the application of generally applicable laws, even if the application of such laws has a negative incidental effect on the ability to gather and report the news. *Cohen v. Cowles Media Co.*, 501 U.S. 663 (1991).

Example: A reporter who trespasses on another's property while investigating a story is not shielded from liability by the First Amendment.

2. Broadcast

Because the broadcast spectrum is a limited resource, radio and television broadcasters are said to have a greater responsibility to the public, and they therefore can be more closely regulated than print and other media. Broadcasters may be sanctioned, therefore, for airing "patently offensive sexual and excretory speech," even if such speech does not qualify as obscene under the *Miller* test, in the interest of protecting children likely to be listening. *FCC v. Pacifica Found.*, 438 U.S. 726 (1978).

3. Cable Television

The First Amendment protection provided to cable television falls somewhere between the extensive protection given to print media and the more limited protection for broadcasting. As such, a law requiring cable operators to carry local television stations is subject to intermediate scrutiny. *Turner Broad. Sys., Inc. v. FCC*, 512 U.S. 622 (1994).

Content-based regulations of cable broadcasts are subject to **strict scrutiny,** however. *United States v. Playboy Entm't. Group, Inc.*, 529 U.S. 803 (2000).

4. Internet

Because the Internet is not composed of scarce frequencies as are the broadcast media, and because of the reduced risk of an unexpected invasion of privacy over the Internet, any regulation of Internet content is subject to strict scrutiny. *Reno v. ACLU*, 521 U.S. 844 (1997).

E. REGULATION OF ASSOCIATION

Freedom of association protects the right to form or participate in any group, gathering, club, or organization virtually without restriction, although the right is not absolute. An infringement upon this right may be justified by a compelling state interest. *See, e.g., Board of Dirs. of Rotary Int'l v. Rotary Club of Duarte*, 481 U.S. 537 (1987) (discrimination against women was not in furtherance of or necessary for any of the expressive activity undertaken by the organization); *but see Boy Scouts of America v. Dale*, 530 U.S. 640 (2000) (requiring the Boy Scouts to accept leaders who acted in a manner contrary to Boy Scout principles would unduly intrude upon the Boy Scouts' expressive associational rights).

1. Public Employment

An individual generally cannot be denied public employment based simply upon membership in a political organization. *Keyishian v. Board of Regents*, 385 U.S. 589 (1967).

a. Test

A person may only be punished or deprived of public employment based on political association if that individual:

i)   Is an active member of a **subversive organization**;

ii) Has **knowledge** of the organization's illegal activity; and

iii) Has a **specific intent** to further those illegal objectives.

Scales v. United States, 367 U.S. 203 (1961) (conviction based on membership in an organization advocating the violent overthrow of the government upheld).

b. Loyalty oaths

Public employees may be required to take loyalty oaths promising that they will support the Constitution and oppose the forceful, violent, or otherwise illegal or unconstitutional overthrow of the government. *Connell v. Higgenbotham*, 403 U.S. 207 (1971). Such oaths are often found to be vague or overbroad, however. *E.g., Cramp v. Board of Public Instruction*, 368 U.S. 278 (1961) (striking down as vague a statute requiring public employees to swear that they have not and will not lend "aid, support, advice, counsel, or influence to the Communist Party"); *Shelton v. Tucker*, 364 U.S. 479 (1960) (striking down as overbroad a statute requiring teachers to file an affidavit listing every organization to which they have belonged or regularly contributed during the past five years).

2. Bar Membership

Although the state can inquire into the character of a candidate for bar admission, such admission cannot be denied on the basis of political association unless the candidate knowingly belongs to a subversive organization with specific intent to further its illegal ends. *Schware v. Board of Bar Exam'rs*, 353 U.S. 232 (1957). The state may, however, deny bar membership to a candidate who refuses to answer questions about political affiliations if that refusal obstructs the investigation of the candidate's qualifications. *Konigsberg v. State Bar of California*, 366 U.S. 36 (1961).

3. Elections and Political Parties

a. Voters in primary elections

A state cannot require a local political party to select presidential electors in an open primary (i.e., a primary in which any voter, including members of another party, may vote) when the national party prohibits nonparty members from voting. *Democratic Party v. LaFolette*, 450 U.S. 107 (1981). A state can require a semi-closed primary system, in which only registered party members and independents can vote in the party's primary, even if the party wants to permit anyone to vote. *Clingman v. Beaver*, 544 U.S. 581 (2005). On the other hand, a state may not prohibit a political party from allowing independents to vote in its primary. *Tashjian v. Republican Party of Connecticut*, 479 U.S. 208 (1986).

1) Blanket primary

A state may adopt a blanket primary system (i.e., a primary in which all voters regardless of party affiliation or lack thereof vote) that is nonpartisan. Under a nonpartisan primary system, the voters choose candidates for the general election without regard for their party affiliation. A nonpartisan blanket primary system in which a candidate identifies his own party preference or his status as an independent and that identification appears on the ballot has withstood a facial challenge, despite assertions that this self-designation violates the party's First Amendment rights as compelled speech and forced association. *Washington State Grange v. Washington State Republican Party*, 552 U.S. 442 (2008). By contrast, a partisan blanket primary system in which a party's nominees are chosen violates the party's First Amendment rights of free speech and association. *Cal. Democratic Party v. Jones*, 530 U.S. 567 (2000).

b. Ballot access to general election

A state may refuse to grant a political party's candidate access to the general-election ballot unless the party demonstrates public support through voter signatures on a petition, voter registrations, or previous electoral success. *Timmons v. Twin Cities Area New Party*, 520 U.S. 351 (1997); *Munro v. Socialist Workers Party*, 479 U.S. 189 (1986).

c. Fusion candidate

A state may prohibit a fusion candidate (i.e., a candidate who is nominated by more than one political party) from appearing on the general-election ballot as a candidate of multiple parties. This limitation on the associational rights of political parties is justified by the state's interests in ballot integrity and political stability. *Timmons v. Twin Cities Area New Party*, 520 U.S. 351 (1997).

d. Replacement candidate

When a state gives a political party the right to select an interim replacement for an elected state official who was a member of that party, the party may select the replacement through an election at which only party members may vote. *Rodriguez v. Popular Democratic Party*, 457 U.S. 1 (1982).

Contracts & Sales

CONTRACTS & SALES

Table of Contents

I.   FORMATION OF CONTRACTS 1

A.   MUTUAL ASSENT 1

   1.   OBJECTIVE THEORY OF CONTRACTS 1

   2.   OFFER AND ACCEPTANCE..1

      a.   Offer 1

      b.   Termination of offers..3

      c.   Acceptance 6

      d.   Counteroffers and mirror-image rule..9

      e.   Auction contracts 11

B.   CONSIDERATION 12

   1.   BARGAIN AND EXCHANGE 12

      a.   Legal detriment and bargained-for exchange.............................12

      b.   Gift distinguished 12

   2.   ADEQUACY OF CONSIDERATION 13

      a.   Subjective value 13

      b.   Preexisting duty rule 13

      c.   Past consideration 14

      d.   Modification...14

      e.   Accord and satisfaction 15

      f.   Illusory promises...16

      g.   Voidable and unenforceable promises 16

      h.   Requirements and output contracts 16

      i.   Settlement of a legal claim...17

C.   PROMISES BINDING WITHOUT CONSIDERATION 17

   1.   PROMISE TO PAY A DEBT BARRED BY THE STATUTE OF LIMITATIONS...........17

   2.   PROMISE TO PERFORM A VOIDABLE DUTY 17

   3.   PROMISE TO PAY BENEFITS RECEIVED—MATERIAL BENEFIT RULE.................17

   4.   PROMISSORY ESTOPPEL..18

      a. **Requirements** 18

      b. **Exception to the reliance requirement for charitable subscriptions**..........19

      c. **Construction contracts and promissory estoppel**..19

D. ENFORCEABILITY 19

  1. VOID CONTRACTS 19

  2. VOIDABLE CONTRACTS 19

  3. UNENFORCEABLE CONTRACTS 19

E. DEFENSES TO FORMATION 19

  1. MISTAKE..20

      a. **Unilateral mistake** 20

      b. **Mutual mistake**..20

      c. **Reformation for mistake** 21

  2. MISUNDERSTANDING..21

      a. **Neither party knows or should know of the misunderstanding**................21

      b. **One party knows or should know of the misunderstanding** 21

      c. **Both parties know of the misunderstanding**..21

      d. **Waiver of the misunderstanding** 22

  3. MISREPRESENTATION, NONDISCLOSURE, AND FRAUD............................22

      a. **Fraudulent misrepresentation**..22

      b. **Nondisclosure**...22

      c. **Effect** 22

      d. **Non-fraudulent misrepresentation** 23

      e. **Cure of a misrepresentation**...23

      f. **Avoidance or reformation for misrepresentation**...................................23

  4. UNDUE INFLUENCE 23

      a. **Unfair persuasion** 23

      b. **Confidential relationship—fairness and disclosure** 24

      c. **Third-party undue influence**..24

      d. **Damages**...24

  5. DURESS 24

      a. **Improper threat** 24

      b. **Deprivation of meaningful choice** 24

          c.   **Effect on the contract** 25

      6. **CAPACITY TO CONTRACT** 25

          a.   **Infancy** 25

          b.   **Mental illness** 26

          c.   **Guardianship** 26

          d.   **Intoxication** 26

          e.   **Corporate incapacity** 26

   F. **DEFENSES TO ENFORCEMENT** 26

      1. **ILLEGALITY** 26

          a.   **Effect of illegality** 27

          b.   **Exceptions** 27

      2. **UNCONSCIONABILITY** 28

      3. **PUBLIC POLICY** 28

   G. **IMPLIED-IN-FACT CONTRACTS AND QUASI-CONTRACTS** 28

      1. **IMPLIED-IN-FACT CONTRACTS** 28

      2. **IMPLIED-IN-LAW ("QUASI") CONTRACTS** 28

          a.   **In general** 28

          b.   **Requirements** 29

          c.   **Remedies** 29

          d.   **Quasi-contractual recovery by a plaintiff in breach** 29

   H. **WARRANTIES IN SALE-OF-GOODS CONTRACTS** 30

      1. **EXPRESS WARRANTY** 30

      2. **IMPLIED WARRANTY OF MERCHANTABILITY** 30

      3. **IMPLIED WARRANTY OF FITNESS FOR A PARTICULAR PURPOSE** 30

II.   **DISCHARGE** 31

   A. **IMPRACTICABILITY** 31

      1. **ELEMENTS OF IMPRACTICABILITY** 31

      2. **OTHER "EVENTS SUFFICIENT FOR DISCHARGE" OF A CONTRACT** 31

      3. **ASSUMPTION OF THE RISK** 31

      4. **PARTIAL IMPRACTICABILITY** 32

      5. **FAILURE OF A PARTICULAR SOURCE OF SUPPLY** 32

      6. **FAILURE OF AGREED-UPON METHOD OF TRANSPORTATION** 32

       B. FRUSTRATION OF PURPOSE 32

       C. RESCISSION..32

       D. RELEASE 33

       E. DESTRUCTION OR INJURY TO IDENTIFIED GOODS...................................33

III.   THIRD-PARTY BENEFICIARY CONTRACTS 33

       A. CREDITOR AND DONEE BENEFICIARIES 33

       B. INTENDED AND INCIDENTAL BENEFICIARIES...34

       C. VESTING OF BENEFICIARY'S RIGHTS 34

           1. WHEN RIGHTS VEST 34

           2. EFFECT OF VESTING ON ORIGINAL PARTIES 35

       D. DEFENSES 35

IV.   ASSIGNMENT OF RIGHTS AND DELEGATION OF DUTIES 35

       A. ASSIGNMENT OF RIGHTS 35

           1. WHEN DISALLOWED 35

           2. REQUIREMENTS 35

           3. RIGHTS OF THE ASSIGNEE...36

       B. DELEGATION OF DUTIES 36

           1. IN GENERAL 36

           2. NOVATION...36

           3. EFFECT OF DELEGATION OF PERFORMANCE 36

V.   STATUTE OF FRAUDS 37

       A. WRITING REQUIRED 37

       B. TYPES OF CONTRACTS WITHIN THE STATUTE OF FRAUDS........................37

           1. MARRIAGE PROVISION 37

           2. SURETYSHIP PROVISION 38

               a. Rule 38

               b. Exceptions 38

           3. REAL PROPERTY CONTRACTS 38

               a. Types 38

               b. Part performance 38

           4. ONE-YEAR PROVISION 39

           5. SALE OF GOODS FOR $500 OR MORE 39

		a.	Sufficiency of the writing	39
		b.	Exceptions—writing not required	40
		c.	Modifications	40
VI.	PAROL EVIDENCE RULE			40
	A.	INTEGRATION		41
		1.	TOTAL VERSUS PARTIAL INTEGRATION	41
			a. Total integration	41
			b. Partial integration	41
		2.	INTENT OF THE PARTIES	41
			a. Common-law "four corners" rule	41
			b. Second Restatement rule	41
			c. UCC rule	42
	B.	WHEN THE PAROL EVIDENCE RULE IS INAPPLICABLE	42
		1.	RAISING AN EXCUSE	42
		2.	ESTABLISHING A DEFENSE	42
		3.	SEPARATE DEAL	42
		4.	CONDITION PRECEDENT	42
		5.	AMBIGUITY AND INTERPRETATION	42
			a. Plain meaning rule	42
			b. Context rule	43
		6.	SUBSEQUENT AGREEMENTS	43
		7.	UCC RULE—TRADE USAGE AND COURSE OF DEALINGS OR PERFORMANCE	43
VII.	CONDITIONS AND PERFORMANCE			43
	A.	TYPES OF CONDITIONS		43
		1.	EXPRESS	43
		2.	IMPLIED CONDITIONS	43
	B.	TIMING OF CONDITIONS		44
	C.	SATISFACTION OF CONDITIONS		44
		1.	SATISFACTION CLAUSE	44
		2.	TIME OF PAYMENT CLAUSE	44
	D.	DISPUTES ABOUT PERFORMANCE		44
		1.	SUBSTANTIAL PERFORMANCE	45

a. Meaning 45

b. Willful failure 45

c. Damages 45

2. STRICT PERFORMANCE UNDER THE UCC 45

a. Transferring ownership 45

b. Tendering goods 46

c. Buyer's obligations 47

d. Buyer's right to inspect 48

3. DIVISIBLE OR INSTALLMENT CONTRACTS 49

a. Common law 49

b. UCC 49

E. SUSPENSION OR EXCUSE OF CONDITIONS 49

1. WAIVER 50

2. WRONGFUL INTERFERENCE 50

3. ELECTION 50

4. ESTOPPEL 50

VIII. BREACH OF CONTRACT AND REMEDIES 50

A. BREACH OF CONTRACT 50

1. COMMON LAW 50

2. UCC 51

B. ANTICIPATORY REPUDIATION 51

1. ANTICIPATORY REPUDIATION UNDER THE COMMON LAW 51

a. Repudiation of promise 51

b. Nonbreaching party's options 51

c. Retraction of repudiation 51

d. Unilateral contracts 51

2. ANTICIPATORY REPUDIATION UNDER THE UCC 51

3. PROSPECTIVE INABILITY TO PERFORM 52

a. Commercial standards for merchants 52

b. Effect of acceptance 52

C. REMEDIES: DAMAGES FOR BREACH OF CONTRACT 52

1. EXPECTATION DAMAGES 52

        a.   **In general** 52

        b.   **Partial performance**..53

        c.   **Defective performance** 54

        d.   **Waste** 54

    2. **CONSEQUENTIAL DAMAGES AND FORESEEABILITY** 55

        a.   **Consequential damages** 55

        b.   **Foreseeability** 55

        c.   **Causation**..55

        d.   **Reasonable certainty**..55

        e.   **UCC—Breach of warranty** 55

    3. **LIQUIDATED DAMAGES AND PENALTIES**...56

        a.   **Enforceability** 56

        b.   **Uncertainty of actual damages** 56

    4. **INCIDENTAL DAMAGES**...56

    5. **PUNITIVE DAMAGES** 57

    6. **NOMINAL DAMAGES**..57

    7. **MITIGATING DAMAGES** 57

D. **RESTITUTION AND RELIANCE RECOVERIES** 57

    1. **RESTITUTIONARY DAMAGES** 57

    2. **RELIANCE DAMAGES** 58

E. **SPECIFIC PERFORMANCE AND DECLARATORY JUDGMENT** 58

    1. **SPECIFIC PERFORMANCE** 58

        a.   **Factors considered** 58

        b.   **Real property**...58

        c.   **UCC** 58

        d.   **Limitations**...59

        e.   **Defenses** 59

    2. **DECLARATORY JUDGMENT** 59

F. **REMEDIES UNDER THE UCC**..59

    1. **BUYER'S REMEDIES** 59

        a.   **Failure to tender**..59

        b.   **Nonconforming tender** 60

2. SELLER'S REMEDIES 62

    a. Right to price upon acceptance..62

    b. Right to reclaim goods 62

    c. Stoppage of goods in transit 63

    d. Wrongful rejection 63

3. RISK OF LOSS..64

    a. General rules—non-identified goods, no breach 64

    b. Identified goods, no breach 65

    c. Effect of breach of contract..66

4. INSURABLE INTEREST IN GOODS...66

    a. Seller's insurable interest..66

    b. Buyer's insurable interest 66

5. TITLE AND GOOD-FAITH PURCHASERS 66

    a. Entrusting provisions 66

    b. Voidable title 67

6. STATUTE OF LIMITATIONS ON BREACH OF SALES CONTRACT 67

    a. Period of limitations 67

    b. When a cause of action accrues 67

    c. Modification of limitations period 67

CONTRACTS & SALES

EXAM NOTE: When analyzing a contracts question on the MBE, always apply common law, unless a UCC rule that differs from common law applies. In general, Article 2 of the UCC will apply whenever the transaction at issue is a sale of goods (generally, tangible personal property). When a transaction involves both the sale of goods and the rendering of services, the "predominant purpose" test applies to determine which law applies to the entire transaction. For a more extensive discussion of UCC Article 2, see the Themis *Sales* outline.

I. FORMATION OF CONTRACTS

A binding contract is created through the process of mutual assent (i.e., offer and acceptance) and consideration, and when no valid defenses to contract exist.

A. MUTUAL ASSENT

Mutual assent occurs upon acceptance of a valid offer to contract.

1. Objective Theory of Contracts

In contract law, intent is determined by the so-called "objective theory" of contracts and not by the subjective intent or belief of a party. The objective theory is key to determining whether an offer or acceptance is valid.

Whether a party intends to enter into a contract is judged by outward objective facts, as interpreted by a reasonable person. The intent of a party is what a reasonable person in the position of the other party would believe as a result of that party's objective manifestation of intent. Thus, when the other party knew or should have known that the party lacked the intent to enter into a contract, a contract is not formed, whereas the party's mere subjective lack of intent is not sufficient to prevent the formation of a contract.

Objective facts may include things that the party said when entering into the contract, the way the party acted or appeared at such time, and the circumstances surrounding the transaction. The circumstances surrounding the statement can be critical to determining what would be reasonable to believe.

2. Offer and Acceptance

a. Offer

An offer is an objective manifestation of a willingness by the offeror to enter into an agreement that creates the power of acceptance in the offeree. In other words, it is a communication that gives power to the recipient to conclude a contract by acceptance.

1) Intent

A statement is an offer only if the person to whom it is communicated could *reasonably interpret* it as an offer. It must express the **present intent** to be legally bound to a contract. As noted above, the primary test of whether a communication is an offer is based on the objective theory of contracts; i.e., whether an individual receiving the communication would believe that he could enter into an enforceable deal by satisfying the condition.

2) Knowledge by the offeree

The offeree must have knowledge of the offer in order to have the power to accept the offer.

3) Terms

For a contract to exist, the terms of the contract must be certain and definite, or the contract fails for indefiniteness. Under common law, all essential terms (i.e., the parties, subject matter, price, and quantity) must be covered in the agreement.

The UCC allows for a more liberal contract formation. Under the UCC, a contract is formed if both parties intend to contract and there is a reasonably certain basis for giving a remedy. As long as the parties intend to create a contract, the UCC "fills the gap" when a contract is silent as to a term, such as the time or place for delivery, or even the price for the goods. In addition to identifying the parties and subject matter, an agreement to sell goods generally must specify the quantity to be sold, but requirements or output contracts satisfy UCC contract formation requirements even without naming specific quantities. (Note: The UCC also implies good faith as a contract term.)

a) Duration term

In most ongoing contracts, if a duration term is not specified in the agreement, courts will imply that the contract will last for a reasonable period of time.

i) Employment contracts

If an employment contract does not state duration, there is a rebuttable presumption that the employment is "at will." In an employment-at-will relationship, either party can terminate the relationship at any time, without the termination being considered a breach of the contract (unless the termination is against public policy, such as when the employee is discharged for filing a discrimination claim).

If an employment contract provides for "permanent employment," most courts hold that, in the absence of a proven contrary intention, the employment is "at will," because the duration term in the contract is considered too vague. If the offer promises "lifetime employment," some courts hold that the agreement is for "at will" employment, while others take the term literally.

b) Missing terms

A contract may still be formed when a term, even the price term in the case of a sale of goods, is missing, if it appears that the parties intended to create a contract. The court may supply the missing term because there is a presumption that the parties intended to include a reasonable term. However, the contract must have an objective standard for the court to reference.

c) Vague terms

When the terms of the contract are vague, the same presumption cannot be made because the parties have manifested an intent that cannot be determined due to the vagueness of the terms.

4) Language

The offer must contain words of promise, undertaking, or commitment (as distinguished from words that merely indicate intention to sell or interest in buying). The offer must also be targeted to a number of people who could actually accept.

If a return promise is requested, then the contract is a bilateral contract. If an act is requested, then the contract is a unilateral contract.

5) Invitation to deal

Offers must be distinguished from invitations to deal.

Compare, for example, the question, "what is your lowest price?" with the response to that question, "we can quote you $5 per gross for immediate acceptance." The first question is merely an inquiry, whereas the second statement is an offer. (Note that for the offeree to accept the offer, the offeree must supply the quantity term in order for the contract to meet the definiteness requirement.)

Advertisements generally are considered invitations to receive offers from the public, unless associated with a stated reward. An advertisement that is sufficiently specific and limiting as to who may accept may also qualify as an offer (e.g., "Used car for sale for $5,000. First come, first served.").

> **EXAM NOTE:** Be careful not to mistake a true offer for language that sounds like an offer but is actually just an invitation to receive offers. The more definite the statement (e.g., "I will sell you X for…"), the more likely it is to be an offer.

b. Termination of offers

An offer can be accepted only when it is still outstanding (i.e., before the offer is terminated). Offers can be terminated in the following ways.

1) Lapse of time in offer

If the offer specifies a date on which the offer terminates, the offer terminates at midnight on that date. If the offer states that it will terminate after a specified number of days, the time starts to run from the time the offer is received.

If the offer does not set a time limit for acceptance, the power of acceptance terminates at the end of a reasonable period of time.

2) Death or mental incapacity

An offer terminates upon the death or mental incapacity of the offeror. An exception exists for an offer that is an option, which does not terminate upon death or mental incapacity because consideration was paid to keep the offer open during the option period, and the offer is therefore made irrevocable during that period.

Compare accepted offer: If an offer has been accepted, death of the offeror does not automatically terminate the contract. The contract may be enforceable unless there is some reason, such as impracticability, that justifies discharge of the contractual obligation.

3) Destruction or illegality

An offer involving subject matter that is destroyed is terminated. Similarly, an offer that becomes illegal is terminated.

4) Revocation

In general, an offer can be revoked by the offeror at any time prior to acceptance, even if the offer states that it will remain open for a specific amount of time. A revocation may be made in any reasonable manner and by any reasonable means, and is not effective until communicated. A revocation sent by mail is not effective until received. If the offeree acquires reliable information that the offeror has taken definite action inconsistent with the offer, the offer is automatically revoked.

Example: On day 1, A mails an offer to B. On day 2, A mails a revocation to B. If B receives the offer and accepts before receiving the revocation, a contract is formed.

The offeror's power to revoke an offer is limited by the following.

a) Option (promise not to revoke)

An option is an independent promise to keep an offer open for a specified period of time. Such promise limits the offeror's power to revoke the offer until after the period has expired, while also preserving the offeree's power to accept.

If the option is a promise not to revoke an offer to enter a new contract, the offeree must generally give separate consideration for the option to be enforceable. If the option is within an existing contract, no separate consideration is required. Note that in sale of goods contracts, however, a merchant's promise to keep an offer open need not be supported by consideration if it is in writing and signed.

b) Promissory estoppel

When the offeree detrimentally relies on the offeror's promise prior to acceptance, the doctrine of promissory estoppel may make the offer irrevocable. It must have been reasonably foreseeable that such detrimental reliance would occur in order to imply the existence of an option contract. The offeror is liable to the extent necessary to avoid injustice, which may result in holding the offeror to the offer, reimbursement of the costs incurred by the offeree, or restitution of the benefits conferred.

c) Partial performance

If the offer is for a unilateral contract, the offeror cannot revoke the offer once the offeree has begun performance. The same holds true for a bilateral contract. Once the offeree has begun performance, the contract is complete. Note, though, that the offeree must have had knowledge of the offer when she began performance.

Once performance has begun, the offeree will have a reasonable amount of time to complete performance but cannot be required to complete the performance.

d) UCC firm offer rule

Under the UCC, an offer to buy or sell goods is irrevocable if:

i) The offeror is a merchant;

ii) There are assurances that the offer is to remain open; and

iii) The assurance is contained in an authenticated writing (such as a signature, initials, or other inscription) from the offeror.

No consideration by the offeree is needed to keep the offer open under the UCC firm offer rule. UCC § 2-205.

i) Time period

If the time period during which the option is to be held open is not stated, a reasonable term is implied. However, irrevocability cannot exceed 90 days, regardless of whether a time period is stated or implied, unless the offeree gives consideration to validate it beyond the 90-day period.

ii) "Merchant" defined

For purposes of this rule, a merchant includes not only a person who regularly deals in the type of goods involved in the transaction, but also any business person when the transaction is of a commercial nature. UCC § 2-104(1), cmt. 2.

5) Revocation of general offers

A "general offer" is an offer made to a large number of people, generally through an advertisement. A general offer can be revoked only by notice that is given at least the same level of publicity as the offer. So long as the appropriate level of publicity is met, the revocation will be effective even if a potential offeree does not learn of the revocation and acts in reliance on the offer. Restatement (Second) of Contracts § 46. Note that if a person has actual knowledge of the intent to revoke but did not see the notice, then the revocation will be effective as to such person.

6) Rejection by offeree

An offer is terminated by rejection. In other words, the offeree clearly conveys to the offeror that the offeree no longer intends to accept the offer. Under the mailbox rule, a rejection is usually **effective upon receipt.** An offeree cannot accept an offer once it has been terminated.

A counteroffer acts as a rejection of the original offer and creates a new offer. An exception exists for an option holder, who has the right to make counteroffers during the option period without terminating the original offer.

> **EXAM NOTE:** Remember that a **counteroffer** is both a **rejection and a new offer.** Examine the offeree's statement closely. It may be a rejection, but it may also be only an inquiry (e.g., "Is that a 2005 model car?") or merely indecision (e.g., "Maybe not, but I should ask my wife first."), in which case the offer remains open.

7) Revival of offer

A terminated offer may be revived by the offeror. As with any open offer, the revived offer can be accepted by the offeree. For example, if A offers to paint B's house for $500, and B rejects the offer, then A can revive the offer by stating that the offer remains open. B can change her mind and accept.

c. Acceptance

Only a party to whom an offer is extended may accept (or, if the offer is extended to a class, a party who is a member of the class may accept), and the acceptance forms a contract between the parties. An acceptance is an objective manifestation by the offeree to be bound by the terms of the offer.

An offeree must know of the offer upon acceptance for it to be valid. In addition, the offeree must communicate the acceptance to the offeror.

Commencement of performance of a bilateral contract operates as a promise to render complete performance. Restatement (Second) of Contracts § 62.

1) Method of acceptance

The offeror can detail the manner of proper acceptance.

a) Bilateral versus unilateral offer

A **bilateral contract** is one in which a promise by one party is exchanged for a promise by the other. The exchange of promises is enough to render them both enforceable. An offer requiring a promise to accept can be accepted either with a return promise or by starting performance. Commencement of performance of a bilateral contract operates as a promise to render complete performance.

A **unilateral contract** is one in which one party promises to do something in return for an act of the other party (e.g., a monetary reward for finding a lost dog). Unlike in a bilateral contract, in a unilateral contract, the offeree's promise to perform is insufficient to constitute an acceptance; the offeree must perform the act to accept the offer. Note that merely starting performance is not enough to accept a unilateral contract, which requires complete performance of the act, but it will make the offer irrevocable for a reasonable period of time to allow for complete performance. Restatement (Second) of Contracts § 62.

> **EXAM NOTE:** The offeree of a unilateral contract can accept only an offer that he is aware of. In other words, if the offeree does not become aware of the offer until after acting, then his acts do not constitute acceptance.

i) Notice of acceptance

Unless notice is requested by the offeror, an offeree of a unilateral contract who accepts by rendering the requested performance is required to give notice only if the offeree has reason to know that the offeror would not learn of the requested performance with reasonable certainty and promptness. Restatement (Second) of Contracts § 54(1).

If the offeree has reason to know that the offeror would not reasonably learn of the performance, then the offeror's duty is discharged, unless:

i) The offeree exercises reasonable diligence to notify the offeror of acceptance; or

ii) The offeror learns of the performance within a reasonable time; or

iii) The offer indicates that notification of acceptance is not required.

Restatement (Second) of Contracts § 54(2).

b) An offer to buy goods for immediate shipment

If the buyer requests that the goods be shipped, then the buyer's request will be construed as inviting acceptance by the seller either by a **promise to ship** or by **prompt shipment** of conforming or nonconforming goods.

i) Shipment of nonconforming goods

If the seller ships nonconforming goods, then the shipment is both an acceptance of the offer and a breach of the contract. The seller is then liable for any damage caused to the buyer as a result of the breach.

If, however, the seller "seasonably" notifies the buyer that the nonconforming goods are tendered as an accommodation, then no acceptance has occurred, and no contract is formed. The accommodation is deemed a counteroffer, and the buyer may then either accept (thereby forming a contract) or reject (no contract formed).

c) Mailbox rule

An acceptance that is mailed within the allotted response time is effective **upon posting** (not upon receipt), unless the offer provides otherwise. The mailing must be properly addressed and include correct postage.

> **EXAM NOTE:** Keep in mind that the mailbox rule applies only to **acceptance**, and therefore it almost exclusively applies to bilateral contracts (when there is one promise in exchange for another promise), because unilateral contracts require action as acceptance.

i) Rejection following acceptance

If the offeree sends an acceptance and later sends a communication rejecting the offer, then the acceptance will generally control even if the offeror receives the rejection first. If, however, the offeror receives the rejection first and detrimentally relies on the rejection, then the offeree will be estopped from enforcing the contract.

ii) Acceptance following rejection

If a communication is sent rejecting the offer, and a later communication is sent accepting the contract, then the mailbox rule will **not** apply, and the first one to be received by the offeror will prevail. The offeror need not actually read the communication in order for it to prevail.

iii) Revocations effective upon receipt

Offers revoked by the offeror are effective upon receipt.

iv) Irrevocable offer

The mailbox rule does not apply if the offer is irrevocable, as is the case with an option contract, which requires that the acceptance be received by the offeror before the offer expires. Restatement (Second) of Contracts § 63(b), cmt. f.

v) Medium

If the acceptance is via an "instantaneous two-way communication," such as telephone or traceable fax, it is treated as if the parties were in each other's presence. Restatement (Second) of Contracts § 64. There is little case law with regard to email and other forms of modern communication. However, the Restatement focuses on whether the medium of acceptance is reasonable (e.g., whether it is reliable, used by the offeror, used customarily in the industry, or used between the parties in prior transactions). Restatement (Second) of Contracts § 65.

d) Means of acceptance

The offeror is master of the offer. As such, the offeror can dictate the manner and means by which an offer may be accepted. For example, the offeror can require the offeree to accept in writing or to accept by means of a phone call. However, unless the offeror specifically requires the offeree to accept in a particular manner or by using a particular means, the offeree can accept in any reasonable manner and by any reasonable means. UCC § 2-206. Even if the acceptance is by unauthorized means, it may be effective if the offeror receives the acceptance while the offer is still open.

2) Silence

Generally, silence does not operate as an acceptance of an offer, even if the offer states that silence qualifies as acceptance (or, more likely, implied acceptance), unless:

i) The offeree has reason to believe that the offer could be accepted by silence, was silent, and intended to accept the offer by silence; or

ii) Because of previous dealings or pattern of behavior, it is reasonable to believe that the offeree must notify the offeror if the offeree intends not to accept.

3) Notice

An offeree of a bilateral contract must give notice of acceptance. Because acceptance becomes valid when posted, a properly addressed letter sent by the offeree operates as an acceptance when mailed, even though the offeror has not yet received the notice.

Notice of acceptance of a unilateral contract is required only when the offeror is unlikely to become aware that the act is being performed or if the offeror requests such notice in the offer. Notice would be required under the same circumstances if a bilateral contract was being accepted by performance.

Unless notice is requested by the offeror, an offeree of a unilateral contract who accepts by rendering the requested performance is required to give notice only if the offeree has reason to know that the offeror would not learn of the requested performance with reasonable certainty and promptness. Restatement (Second) of Contracts § 54(1).

If the offeree has reason to know that the offeror would not reasonably learn of the performance, then the offeror's duty is discharged, unless:

i) The offeree exercises reasonable diligence to notify the offeror of acceptance;

ii) The offeror learns of the performance within a reasonable time; or

iii) The offer indicates that notification of acceptance is not required.

Restatement (Second) of Contracts § 54(2).

d. Counteroffers and mirror-image rule

1) Common-law mirror-image rule

Acceptance must mirror the terms of the offer. Any modification of the terms of the offer, or the addition of another term not found in the offer, acts as a rejection of the original offer and as a new counteroffer. Mere suggestions or inquiries, including requests for clarification or statements of intent, made in a response by the offeree do not constitute a counteroffer.

A conditional acceptance terminates the offer and acts as a new offer from the original offeree.

2) UCC rule

The UCC does not follow the mirror-image rule. Additional terms included in an acceptance of an offer do not automatically constitute a rejection of the original offer. Generally, for a sale of goods, an acceptance that contains additional terms or modifications to the terms in the offer is nevertheless treated as an acceptance rather than a rejection and a counteroffer. An exception exists when the acceptance is expressly conditioned on assent to the additional or different terms, in which case the acceptance is a counteroffer. Whether the additional or different terms are treated as part of the contract depends on whether one of the parties is a merchant. UCC § 2-207. A merchant is a person who regularly deals in the kind of goods sold or who holds himself out as having knowledge or skills particular to the practice or goods involved in the transaction. UCC § 2-104(1).

a) Both parties are not merchants

When the contract is for the sale of goods between nonmerchants or between a merchant and a nonmerchant, a definite and seasonable expression of acceptance or written confirmation that is sent within a reasonable time operates as an acceptance of the original offer. This is true even if it states terms that are additional to or different from the offer, unless the acceptance is made expressly conditional on the offeror's consent to the additional or different terms. The additional or different terms are treated as a proposal for addition to the contract that must be separately accepted by the offeror in order to become a part of the contract.

b) Both parties are merchants—battle of the forms

> **EXAM NOTE:** The MBE has consistently tested the situation in which both parties to the contract are merchants. In this situation, remember that a contract exists *under the terms of the acceptance*, unless (i) the terms materially alter the agreement, (ii) the offer expressly limits the terms, or (iii) the offeror objects to the new terms within a reasonable time after notice of the new terms is received. UCC § 2-207.

When both parties to the sale of goods are merchants, often both the offer and the acceptance are made by means of forms designed for use in the typical transactions in which the merchants engage rather than for the particular sale in question. As a consequence, the acceptance often contains different and additional terms. In this "battle of the forms" over whose terms will form the basis of the contract between the merchants, the rules may vary depending on whether the terms are additional terms or different terms.

i) **Acceptance includes additional terms**

Under the "last shot" rule, an additional term in the acceptance is **automatically included** in the contract when both parties are merchants, unless:

i) The term materially alters the original contract;

ii) The offer expressly limits acceptance to the terms of the offer; or

iii) The offeror has already objected to the additional terms, or objects within a reasonable time after notice of them was received.

If any one of these three exceptions is met, a contract is formed, but the offeror's original terms are controlling.

Examples of terms that typically are found to have materially altered the original contract include a warranty disclaimer, a clause that flies in the face of trade usage with regard to quality, a requirement that complaints be made in an unreasonably short time period, and terms that surprise or create hardship without express awareness by the other party. Terms that usually **do not** materially alter the contract include fixing reasonable times for bringing a complaint, setting reasonable interest for overdue invoices, and reasonably limiting remedies.

ii) **Acceptance includes different terms**

The courts in different jurisdictions disagree as to the result when different terms are included in the merchant offeree's acceptance. A few jurisdictions treat different terms the same as additional terms and apply the "last shot" rule, as described above. Most, however, apply the so-called **"knock-out" rule,** under which different terms in the offer and acceptance nullify each other and are "knocked out" of the contract. When there are gaps in the contract, the court uses Article 2's gap-filling provisions to patch the holes.

e. **Auction contracts**

The UCC has special rules for auction sales.

1) **Goods auctioned in lots**

If goods in an auction sale are offered in lots, each lot represents a separate sale.

2) **Completion of sale**

An auction sale is complete when the auctioneer announces its end by the fall of the hammer or in any other customary way. When a bid is made contemporaneously with the falling of the hammer, the auctioneer may, at her discretion, reopen the bidding or declare the sale completed at the fall of the hammer.

3) Reserve and no-reserve auctions

In a reserve auction, the auctioneer may withdraw the goods any time before she announces completion of the sale. An auction is with reserve unless specifically announced as a no-reserve auction.

In a no-reserve auction, the goods cannot be withdrawn by the auctioneer unless no bid is received on the item or lot.

In either type of auction, a bidder may retract her bid until the auctioneer announces the end of the bidding. A retraction, however, does not revive earlier bids.

4) When the seller bids

When an auctioneer knowingly accepts a bid by the seller or on her behalf, or procures such a bid to drive up the price of the goods, the winning bidder may avoid the sale or, at her option, take the goods at the price of the last good-faith bid prior to the end of the auction. There are two exceptions to this rule, which are that (i) a seller may bid at a forced sale and (ii) a seller may bid if she specifically gives notice that she reserves the right to bid.

B. CONSIDERATION

1. Bargain and Exchange

In addition to an offer and acceptance, some legal detriment must be bargained for in order for a contract to exist. The exchange must be a bargained-for change in the legal position between the parties. Valuable consideration must exist on both sides of the bargain to make it fully enforceable.

a. Legal detriment and bargained-for exchange

For the legal detriment to constitute sufficient consideration, it must be bargained for in exchange for the promise. The promise must induce the detriment, and the detriment must induce the promise.

Consideration can take the form of:

i) A return promise to do something;

ii) A return promise to refrain from doing something legally permitted;

iii) The actual performance of some act; or

iv) Refraining from doing some act.

b. Gift distinguished

A promise to make a gift does not involve bargained-for consideration and is therefore unenforceable.

A promise by A to give B $1,000 when B turns 21 is not enforceable because the act of attaining the age of 21 is not bargained for and is thus not sufficient consideration. There also can be no reliance on the promise (B will turn 21 regardless of A's promise), so promissory estoppel does not apply.

Alternatively, if A offers B $1,000 to quit smoking, it is assumed that A is bargaining for B's act and that B would rely on the promise of the payment when he quit smoking.

> **EXAM NOTE:** The test to distinguish a gift from valid consideration is whether the offeree could have **reasonably believed that the intent of the offeror was to induce the action.** If yes, there is consideration, and the promise is enforceable.

A party's promise to make a gift is enforceable under the doctrine of promissory estoppel if the promisor/donor knows that the promise will induce substantial reliance by the promisee, and the failure to enforce the promise will cause substantial injustice.

2. Adequacy of Consideration

The basic concept of legal detriment is that there must be something of **substance,** either an act or a promise, that is given in exchange for the promise that is to be enforced. In general, a party cannot challenge a contract on the grounds that the consideration is inadequate. A difference in economic value between the items exchanged is not grounds for finding that a contract did not exist due to inadequate consideration.

a. Subjective value

The benefit to the promisor does not need to have an economic value. Regardless of the objective value of an item, as long as the promisor wants it, the giving of it will constitute adequate consideration.

b. Preexisting duty rule

1) Common law

At common law, a promise to perform a preexisting legal duty does not qualify as consideration because the promisor is already bound to perform (i.e., there is no legal detriment). Note that if the promisor gives something in addition to what is already owed (however small) or varies the preexisting duty in some way (however slight), most courts find that consideration exists.

Partial payment of a liquidated debt is invalid for a lack of consideration, unless there is a compromise of a claim disputed in good faith. This exception applies even if it later becomes apparent that the reason for disputing the claim was invalid. Restatement (Second) of Contracts § 74.

2) Exception for a third party

There is an exception to the pre-existing legal duty rule when a third party offers a promise contingent upon performance of a contractual obligation by a party. Under the exception, the third party's promise is sufficient consideration. Restatement (Second) of Contracts § 73.

> **Example:** C contracts with P for P to install plumbing in a house being built by C for H. C subsequently becomes insolvent and walks away from the project. H contracts with P and promises to pay P the same amount P would have received from C if P installs the plumbing. P's completion of the job constitutes consideration for the promise by H, even though P was already contractually obligated to C to do the work.

c. Past consideration

Under the common law, something given in the past is typically not adequate consideration because it could not have been bargained for, nor could it have been done in reliance upon a promise.

> **Example:** A is drowning, and B dives in and saves A. Grateful to have been saved, A promises B $500. Under the common-law approach, there is no consideration, and the promise is therefore unenforceable. It is based on a mere moral obligation arising out of past conduct.

There is a modern trend, adopted by the Second Restatement, however, toward enforcing such promises when necessary to prevent injustice, unless the promisee intended his act to be a gift, or otherwise did not expect compensation. Furthermore, courts will enforce a promise only to the extent that the value of the promise is proportional to the previous benefit conferred by the promisee. *See, e.g., First National Bankshares of Beloit, Inc. v. Geisel*, 853 F.Supp. 1344 (D.Kan. 1994), Restatement (Second) of Contracts § 86.

d. Modification

1) Common law

At common law, modification of an existing contract must be supported by consideration. Agreements to modify a contract may still be enforced if:

i)   There is a rescission of the existing contract by tearing it up or by some other outward sign, and then the entering into of a new contract, whereby one of the parties must perform more than she was to perform under the original contract;

ii) There are unforeseen difficulties, and one of the parties agrees to compensate the other when the difficulties are discovered if those difficulties would make performance impracticable (*see* § II.A. Impracticability, *infra*); or

iii) There are new obligations on both sides.

2) UCC and consideration

Unlike under the common law, under Article 2, no consideration is necessary to modify a contract for the sale of goods, although there is a requirement of good faith by both parties. Thus, if one party is attempting to extort a modification, it will be ineffective under the UCC. Good faith requires honesty in fact and, in the case of a merchant, fair dealing in accordance with reasonable commercial standards.

> **EXAM NOTE:** The MBE frequently tests the different common-law and UCC rules regarding contract modification. At common law, modifications require consideration; under the UCC, they require only good faith.

> **Example:** If a party demands an increase in price because the other party has no choice but to agree, the courts will invalidate such a bad-faith modification.

a) Statute of Frauds

A contract **as modified** that falls within the Statute of Frauds must generally be in writing. However, any of the Statute of Frauds exceptions apply to take a modification out of the Statute of Frauds.

b) Parties may prohibit oral modification

A provision that modifications to a written sales contract may occur only in writing is valid and binding under the UCC. If such a provision is on a form supplied by a merchant, it must be separately signed by the other party, unless that other party is also a merchant.

i) Waiver

When an oral modification violates the Statute of Frauds or is contrary to a provision against oral modification, it may be withdrawn or retracted so long as no party has relied upon it. When one party relies on an improper modification, the other party may not avoid it by reliance on the Statute of Frauds or a no-oral-modification provision. The benefitting party is deemed to waive any challenge to the modification.

ii) Installment contracts

Generally, a party benefited by a condition under a contract may orally waive that condition without new consideration. However, in installment contracts, the beneficiary of a waiver that is not supported by consideration may retract that waiver by reasonable notification, received by the other party, that strict performance will be required, so long as the retraction would not be unjust because of a material change of position by the other party in reliance on the waiver.

e. Accord and satisfaction

Under an accord agreement, one party to a contract agrees to accept different performance from the other party than what was promised in the existing contract. Generally, consideration is required for an accord to be valid. By compromising, each party surrenders its respective claim as to how much is owed. Restatement (Second) of Contracts § 74.

When a creditor agrees to accept a lesser amount in full satisfaction of the debt, the original debt is discharged **only when there is some dispute** either as to the validity of the debt or the amount of the debt, **or when the payment is of a different type than called for under the original contract.**

A "satisfaction" is the performance of the accord agreement; it will discharge both the original contract and the accord contract. However, there is no satisfaction until performance, and the original contract is not discharged until satisfaction is complete. Therefore, if an accord is breached by the debtor, the creditor can sue either on the original contract **or** under the accord agreement.

Compare accord with a substituted contract, which is a second agreement that immediately discharges the original contract, such that the remedy for breach is limited to the terms of the second contract. Whether an agreement is an accord or a substitute contract turns on how formal the agreement is; the less formal, the more likely it is an accord.

Example 1: A contracts with B to build a barn out of cherry wood for $10,000. B instead builds the barn out of particle board. A refuses to pay, and after many discussions, finally says, "Fine. I will pay you $7,500 next week." B accepts, but when A goes to pay B the following week, B says, "I changed my mind and want the original $10,000." What is the result? The $7,500 deal was an accord, which means B can recover it or the original contract price. Once A pays the $7,500, however, the accord is satisfied and B can no longer recover under the original contract.

f. Illusory promises

An illusory promise is one that essentially pledges nothing because it is vague or because the promisor can choose whether to honor it. Such a promise is not legally binding.

Example: B promises, "I will give you $100, at my option." B's promise is an illusory promise.

A promise that is based on the occurrence of condition within the control of the promisor may be illusory, but courts often find that the promisor has also promised to use her best efforts to bring about the condition. Restatement (Second) of Contracts § 76, cmt. d. Similarly, a promise to purchase goods upon the promisor's satisfaction with the goods is not illusory because the promisor is required to act in good faith. UCC § 1-304.

g. Voidable and unenforceable promises

A promise that is voidable or unenforceable by a rule of law (e.g., infancy) can nevertheless constitute consideration. Restatement (Second) of Contracts § 78.

Example: A car dealer promises to sell a used car to a minor for $5,000. The car dealer may not escape selling the car to the minor for $5,000 on the grounds that, because the minor's promise is voidable, the car dealer did not receive consideration for its promise.

h. Requirements and output contracts

A requirements contract is a contract under which a buyer agrees to buy all that he will require of a product from the other party. An output contract is a contract under which a seller agrees to sell all that she manufactures of a product to the buyer. There is consideration in these agreements because the promisor suffers a legal detriment. The fact that the party may go out of business does not render the promise illusory.

Under the UCC, any quantities under such a contract may not be unreasonably disproportionate to any stated estimates, or if no estimate is stated, to any normal or otherwise comparable prior requirements or output.

Good faith is required under the UCC with regard to requirements and output contracts. Thus, for example, if a buyer in good faith no longer needs the goods, he may cancel the contract. Note that, except in a few states, "good faith" for a merchant includes both honesty in the transaction and "the observance of reasonable commercial standards of fair dealing in the trade." U.C.C. § 2.103(b).

i. Settlement of a legal claim

The promise not to bring a legal action or to assert a particular claim or defense in such an action generally can serve as consideration for a settlement agreement because the party making the promise is foregoing a legal right. The legal action need not be one that is certain of success. Instead, the party agreeing to forebear bringing the action must have only an honest belief as to the validity of the claim, and there must be a reasonable basis for that belief. Restatement (Second) of Contracts § 74.

C. PROMISES BINDING WITHOUT CONSIDERATION

There are a number of circumstances in which a promise will be enforceable despite the fact that it is not supported by consideration.

1. Promise to Pay a Debt Barred by the Statute of Limitations

A new promise to pay a debt after the statute of limitations has run is enforceable without any new consideration.

2. Promise to Perform a Voidable Duty

A new promise to perform a duty that is voidable will be enforceable despite the absence of consideration, provided that the new promise does not suffer from an infirmity that would make it, in turn, voidable.

Example: X, who is 15, enters into a contract with Y that is voidable because of X's infancy. Upon reaching the age of majority, X promises to perform the contract. Such promise will be enforceable without any new consideration. Note that if X reaffirmed the promise before reaching the age of majority, such promise would be voidable (because of X's continued infancy).

3. Promise to Pay Benefits Received—Material Benefit Rule

Under the material benefit rule, when a party performs an unrequested service for another party that constitutes a material benefit, the modern trend permits the performing party to enforce a promise of payment made by the other party after the service is rendered, even though, at common law, such a promise would be unenforceable due to lack of consideration.

This rule is not enforced when the performing party rendered the services without the expectation of compensation (e.g., as a gift). In addition, the promise is enforced only to the extent necessary to prevent injustice, and it is not enforceable to the extent that the value of the promise is disproportionate to the benefit received, or the promisor has not been unjustly enriched.

Example: P sees D's horse running free and knows that D is out of town. P feeds and houses the horse for two weeks at a cost of $30 while awaiting D's return. When D returns, D thanks P and promises to pay P $50 at the end of the month. At common law, this promise is unenforceable due to lack of consideration. Under the material benefit rule, the promise is not enforceable to the extent that it is disproportionate to the benefit received. Thus, P's promise can be enforced to the extent of $30.

Note: Apart from a contract remedy, the provider of services may also be able to recover under a quasi-contract theory (*see* § I.G.2., *infra*).

Requested services distinguished: If one party requests another party to perform a service but does not indicate a price, and the service is performed, this generally creates an "implied-in-fact" contract. The party who performed the requested service is generally entitled to recover the reasonable value of her services in a breach-of-contract action in which the party who enjoyed the benefit of the services refused to pay. An exception applies, however, when the services were rendered without the expectation of payment.

4. Promissory Estoppel

The doctrine of promissory estoppel (detrimental reliance) can be used under certain circumstances to enforce a promise that is not supported by consideration.

a. Requirements

A promise is binding if:

i)   The promisor should reasonably expect it to induce action or forbearance on the part of the promisee or a third person;

ii) The promise does induce such action or forbearance; and

iii) Injustice can be avoided only by enforcement of the promise.

Note that, in general, the promisee must actually rely on the promise, and such reliance must have been reasonably foreseeable to the promisor. See below, however, for an exception regarding charitable subscriptions.

The remedy may be limited or adjusted as justice requires. Generally, this results in the award of reliance damages rather than expectation damages.

Example: X, who is very wealthy, knows that her nephew Y is poor but wants to go to college. X promises to pay Y $100,000 when Y gets his diploma. Y then chooses to go to a state college and takes out $50,000 in loans to cover all tuition and expenses. In April of his senior year, Y is told by X that she won't pay anything. Y gets his degree in May and sues X. While there is no consideration for X's promise, the promise is still enforceable under the doctrine of promissory estoppel. X reasonably should have expected that Y would rely on her promise. Y did in fact rely by going to college, and it would seem unjust not to enforce the promise. Note, though, that Y's remedy can be limited "as justice requires." The proper amount would likely be $50,000 (the amount of Y's out-of-pocket expenses in reliance), not the $100,000 that X originally promised.

EXAM NOTE: Always consider whether there is a valid contract before considering promissory estoppel as the correct answer choice.

b. Exception to the reliance requirement for charitable subscriptions

Courts often apply the doctrine of promissory estoppel to enforce promises to charitable institutions. In some cases, they presume that the charity detrimentally relied on the promised contribution. A charitable subscription (i.e., a written promise) is enforceable under the doctrine of promissory estoppel without proof that the charity relied on the promise. Restatement (Second) of Contracts § 90(2).

> **Example:** A promises in writing to give a university a $10,000 donation. Under the Second Restatement, the university may enforce the promise under the doctrine of promissory estoppel, even though the university does not establish that it relied to its detriment on A's promise.

c. Construction contracts and promissory estoppel

In the construction industry, it would be unjust to permit a subcontractor to revoke a bid after inducing justifiable and detrimental reliance in the general contractor. Thus, an agreement not to revoke a sub-bid offer is enforceable under the theory of promissory estoppel.

Because the sub-bid is only an outstanding offer, the **general contractor is not bound** to accept it upon becoming the successful bidder for the general contract. A general contractor can enter into a subcontract with another subcontractor for a lower price.

D. ENFORCEABILITY

The absence of an essential element (capacity, consent, legality, form, etc.) may render the contract void, voidable, or unenforceable.

1. Void Contracts

A void contract results in the entire transaction being regarded as a nullity, as if no contract existed between the parties.

2. Voidable Contracts

A voidable contract operates as a valid contract, unless and until one of the parties takes steps to avoid it.

3. Unenforceable Contracts

An unenforceable contract is a valid contract that cannot be enforced if one of the parties refuses to carry out its terms.

> **EXAM NOTE:** Remember that a void contract cannot be enforced, but a party may opt to avoid a voidable contract.

E. DEFENSES TO FORMATION

A person who is asserted to be in breach of a contract can defend the action by showing that there has not been a valid offer and acceptance or that valid consideration was not exchanged (and no consideration substitute exists). The agreement will also not be enforced if a party can show that there was no "meeting of the minds" due to a mistake or misunderstanding, misrepresentation or fraud, undue influence or duress, or the party's own lack of capacity.

1. Mistake

A mistake is a belief that is not in accord with the facts as to a basic assumption on which the contract was made that materially affects performance. Note that the mistake must be with regard to a belief about an existing fact and not with regard to something that will happen in the future. Risks with regard to changing facts are governed by the doctrines of impracticability and frustration of purpose.

a. Unilateral mistake

When only one of the parties is mistaken as to an essential element of the contract, either party can generally enforce the contract on its terms. However, the mistaken party can void the contract if the mistaken party did not bear the risk of the mistake and either:

i) The mistake would make enforcement of the contract unconscionable; or

ii) The non-mistaken party:

a) Failed to disclose the mistake despite knowing or having a reason to know that the other party was mistaken or having a duty to disclose the fact about which the other party was mistaken; or

b) Caused the mistake.

Finally, for a unilateral mistake to form the basis for rescission, there must be an **absence of serious prejudice to the other party.** Evidence of these conditions must be clear and positive.

b. Mutual mistake

Mutual mistake occurs when both parties are mistaken as to an essential element of the contract. In such a situation, there must be a substantial difference between the deal as it was contemplated and the actual deal, with *no intent by the parties to take a risk on that element* of the transaction.

The contract will generally be **voidable** by the party that was adversely affected by the mistake if the mistake materially affects the bargain between the parties.

Example: Rescission of a contract to sell a cow was granted on grounds of mutual mistake when both parties completed the exchange of the cow on the mistaken understanding that the cow was barren. *Sherwood v. Walker*, 33 N.W. 919 (Mich. 1887).

When reformation of the contract is available to cure a mistake, neither party can avoid the contract.

1) Conscious ignorance

A party may bear the risk of a mistake, however, when she is aware, at the time of the contract, that she has only limited knowledge of the facts to which the mistake relates, and she accepts her limited knowledge as sufficient. Note that the risk created by conscious ignorance rests on the party being aware of her limited knowledge. Restatement (Second) of Contracts § 154.

2) Mistaken party's ability to void the contract

When the mistake is attributable to a party's failure to know or discover facts before entering into the contract, such failure does not bar the mistaken party from asserting the defense of mistake, unless the failure constitutes a failure to act in good faith and in accordance with the reasonable standards of fair dealing. The mistaken party's negligence with regard to the mistake is not sufficient to prevent the mistaken party from avoiding the contract. Restatement (Second) of Contracts § 157.

c. Reformation for mistake

When a writing that evidences or embodies an agreement in whole or in part fails to express the agreement because of a mistake of both parties as to the contents or effect of the writing, the court may, at the request of a party, reform the writing to express the agreement, except to the extent that rights of third parties who have relied on the document, such as good-faith purchasers for value, will be unfairly affected. Restatement (Second) of Contracts § 155.

Reformation of a writing for mistake is available if:

i) There was a prior agreement (either oral or written) between the parties;

ii) There was an agreement by the parties to put that prior agreement into writing; and

iii) As a result of a mistake, there is a difference between the prior agreement and the writing.

> Note that if one party, without the consent of the other party, intentionally omits a term from the writing that had been agreed upon by the parties, reformation would be available on the grounds of misrepresentation. (*See* § I.E.3.f. Avoidance or reformation for misrepresentation, *infra*.)

2. Misunderstanding

A misunderstanding occurs when both parties believe that they are agreeing to the same material terms, but in fact they agree to different terms.

a. Neither party knows or should know of the misunderstanding

If the misunderstanding involves a material term, and neither party knows or should know that there is a misunderstanding, then there is no contract. Restatement (Second) of Contracts § 20(1).

b. One party knows or should know of the misunderstanding

If a material term in the offer and acceptance is ambiguous, and one party knows or should know that the other party has a different understanding of the meaning of the ambiguous term, then there will be a contract formed based on the meaning of the term as understood by the unknowing party.

c. Both parties know of the misunderstanding

There is no contract if both parties at the time of contract knew that the terms were ambiguous, unless both parties intended the same meaning.

d. Waiver of the misunderstanding

Even if there is a misunderstanding, one party may waive the misunderstanding and choose to enforce the contract according to the other party's understanding.

3. Misrepresentation, Nondisclosure, and Fraud

A misrepresentation is an assertion that is contrary to the existing facts. Affirmative conduct to conceal a fact from another is equivalent to a statement that the fact does not exist. A misrepresentation may prevent the formation of the contract or make the contract voidable by the adversely affected party. The misrepresentation must be of fact and not of law or of opinion. Note that the use of an "as is" provision in a contract can shift the risk to a buyer in the absence of unconscionability.

Misrepresentation can be innocent, negligent, or fraudulent. Avoidance of a contract can be based on any of these standards, but different rules will apply. Thus, a fraudulent misrepresentation need not be material, but an unintentional misrepresentation is required to be material.

a. Fraudulent misrepresentation

Fraud exists if the misrepresentation is made:

i) Knowingly;

ii) Without confidence in the assertion; and

iii) When the person making the assertion knows that no basis exists for the assertion.

b. Nondisclosure

Nondisclosure of a known fact is tantamount to an assertion that the fact does not exist, if the party not disclosing the fact knows that:

i) Disclosure is necessary to prevent a previous assertion from being a misrepresentation or fraudulent;

ii) Disclosure would correct a mistake of the other party as to a basic assumption, and the failure to disclose would constitute lack of good faith and fair dealing;

iii) Disclosure would correct a mistake of the other party as to the contents or effect of a writing evidencing their agreement; or

iv) The other party is entitled to know the fact because of a confidential or fiduciary relationship.

c. Effect

1) Fraud in the factum

Fraud in the factum (or fraud in the execution) occurs when the fraudulent misrepresentation prevents a party from knowing the character or essential terms of the transaction. In such a case, no contract is formed, and the apparent contract is **void** (i.e., not enforceable against either party), unless reasonable diligence would have revealed the true terms of the contract.

2) Fraud in the inducement

Fraud in the inducement occurs when a fraudulent misrepresentation is used to induce another to enter into a contract. Such a contract is **voidable** by the adversely affected party if she justifiably relied on the misrepresentation in entering into the agreement.

d. Non-fraudulent misrepresentation

Even if non-fraudulent, a misrepresentation (innocent or negligent) can still render a contract **voidable** by the adversely affected party. The misrepresentation must be *material* (i.e., information that would cause a reasonable person to agree, or that the person making the misrepresentation knows would cause this particular person to agree), the adversely affected party's assent to the contract has been induced by the misrepresentation, and the adversely affected party must have justifiably relied on the misrepresentation.

e. Cure of a misrepresentation

If, following a misrepresentation but before the deceived party has avoided the contract, the facts are cured so as to be in accord with the facts that were previously misrepresented, then the contract will no longer be voidable by the deceived party.

f. Avoidance or reformation for misrepresentation

When one party misrepresents the content or legal effect of a writing to another party, the other party may elect to avoid the contract or to reform it to express what had been represented.

4. Undue Influence

A party to a contract who is a victim of undue influence can void the contract. Restatement (Second) of Contracts § 177.

a. Unfair persuasion

Undue influence is the unfair persuasion of a party to assent to a contract. It can occur by virtue of a relationship between the parties in which one party justifiably assumes that the other party will not act in a manner that is inconsistent with his welfare. It can also occur in a relationship in which one party is dominant and the other dependent, either due to lack of expertise or experience, or because the dependent person has diminished mental capacity. Such relationships include trustee-beneficiary, lawyer-client, doctor-patient, financial advisor–client, and, in some cases, parent-child.

> **Compare duress and misrepresentation:** Undue influence can provide a party with relief in circumstances in which the behavior of the other party to the contract does not rise to the level of duress or misrepresentation.

The key is whether a party has been able to exercise free and competent judgment or whether the persuasion of the other party has seriously impaired that judgment. Relevant factors can include the fairness of the bargain, the availability of independent advice, and the susceptibility of a party to being persuaded.

> **Caution:** While a person who is mentally or physically infirm may be more susceptible to persuasion, the mere existence of an infirmity is not grounds for avoiding a contract. Similarly, the existence of a confidential relationship, by itself, is not grounds for avoiding a contract.

b. Confidential relationship—fairness and disclosure

When a confidential relationship between contracting parties is established, the burden of proving that the contract is fair may be placed upon the dominant party. The dominant party to the contract may also be held to a higher standard of disclosure than she would be in a contract between arms-length parties. Restatement (Second) of Contracts § 173.

c. Third-party undue influence

When the undue influence is caused by the person who is not a party to the contract, the victim may void the contract, unless the non-victim party to the contract gave value or materially relied on the contract while acting in good faith and without reason to know of the undue influence. Restatement (Second) of Contracts § 177(3).

d. Damages

Restitution damages may be available to the party induced to enter a contract because of undue influence.

5. Duress

Duress is an **improper threat** that deprives a party of meaningful choice.

a. Improper threat

Examples of improper threats include threats of a crime, a tort, or criminal prosecution, or the threat of pursuing a civil action (when made in bad faith). In addition, it is improper to threaten to breach a contract if doing so would violate the duty of good faith and fair dealing. Restatement (Second) of Contracts § 176.

1) Threat of criminal prosecution

The threat of criminal prosecution is an improper means by which to induce a person to enter into a contract. It does not matter that the person making the threat honestly believes that the person who would be subject to criminal prosecution is guilty. Nor does it matter that the person threatened with prosecution is in fact guilty of the crime.

2) Threat of civil action

Unlike the threat of criminal prosecution, the threat of a civil action is generally not improper. The lack of success in pursuing a civil action does not make the threat improper unless the civil action is pursued in bad faith.

b. Deprivation of meaningful choice

A person is deprived of meaningful choice only when he does not have a reasonable alternative to succumbing to the threat. Thus, with regard to the threat of a civil action, a person generally has the reasonable alternative of defending against the action. However, if the threat also involves the seizure of property in conjunction with the civil action, or causes the person to be unable to fulfill other contractual obligations, then the person may be deprived of a meaningful choice. Restatement (Second) of Contracts § 175.

> **EXAM NOTE:** In assessing the effect of the threat, the test is a subjective one: Did the threat induce the person's assent?

c. Effect on the contract

When a party's agreement to enter into a contract is physically compelled by duress, such as the threat to inflict physical harm, the contract is **void.** In other instances when a party is induced to enter into a contract by duress, such as when the threat is a breach of the duty of good faith and fair dealing, the contract is **voidable.**

When the duress is caused by the person who is not a party to the contract, the victim may void the contract, unless the non-victim party to the contract gave value or materially relied on the contract while acting in good faith and without reason to know of the undue influence. Restatement (Second) of Contracts § 177(3).

Generally, restitution damages are available to the party induced to enter a contract under duress. Restatement (Second) of Contracts §§ 174, 175.

6. Capacity to Contract

Parties to a contract must be competent (i.e., have the legal capacity to be held to contractual duties). Incompetency arises because of infancy, mental illness or defect, guardianship, intoxication, and corporate incapacity.

a. Infancy

Infants (in most states, individuals who are under the age of 18) do not have the capacity to contract. When a contract is made by an infant, it is **voidable** by the infant but not by the other party. This means that the infant may either disaffirm (void) the contract and avoid any liability under it or choose to hold the adult party to the contract. The disaffirmance must be effectuated either before the infant reaches majority (or within a reasonable time thereafter). If the contract is not disaffirmed within a reasonable time after the infant reaches majority, then the infant will be held to have ratified the contract as an adult. The infant must restore any benefits received under the contract, if possible. Restatement (Second) of Contracts § 14.

1) Liability for necessities

The purpose behind the infancy doctrine is to protect minors, a class of people who are generally immature and require protection from poor judgment and advantageous adults. An exception to the infancy rule exists when the contract is based on necessities. When necessities are furnished to the infant, the infant must pay for them, but the recovery by the person furnishing the necessities is limited to the **reasonable value** of the services or goods (not the agreed upon price). Recovery is under a theory of quasi-contract.

2) Statutory exceptions

By statute, an education loan made to a minor student may not be voidable by the student but instead may be fully enforceable by the lender. Similar treatment may also be accorded an insurance contract entered into by a minor.

b. Mental illness

If an individual is adjudicated mentally incompetent, a purported contract made by the individual is **void.** On the other hand, if there has been no adjudication, a contract is **voidable** and may be disaffirmed if the individual is unable to

i)   Understand the nature and consequences of the transaction; or

ii) Act in a reasonable manner with regard to the transaction, **and** the other party has reason to know of this fact.

If a contract is made during a lucid period, the contract is fully enforceable, unless the person has been adjudicated incompetent. A mentally incompetent person may be liable for the reasonable value of necessities furnished by another party. Restatement (Second) of Contracts § 15.

c. Guardianship

If an individual's property is under guardianship by reason of an adjudication (such as for mental illness or defect, habitual intoxication, narcotics addiction), that individual has no capacity to contract, and a purported contract made by the individual is void. A person under guardianship may be liable for the reasonable value of necessities furnished by another party. Restatement (Second) of Contracts § 13.

d. Intoxication

A contract entered into while intoxicated due to alcohol or drugs is **voidable** by the intoxicated party if that person was unable to understand the nature and consequences of the transaction, and the other party had reason to know of the intoxication. The intoxicated party must act promptly to disaffirm the contract and is required to return any value received, if possible. Generally, the intoxicated party may be liable in quasi-contract for the fair value of the goods or services furnished. Restatement (Second) of Contracts § 16.

e. Corporate incapacity

When a corporation acts ultra vires (outside its powers), the contract is voidable. Most states allow recovery in quantum meruit if one party performs on the contract.

F. DEFENSES TO ENFORCEMENT

A party to a contract can assert that the nature of the agreement or the manner in which it was arrived at should prevent its enforcement.

1. Illegality

If the consideration or performance that is to occur under a contract is illegal, then the contract itself is illegal and is unenforceable. If a contract contemplates illegal conduct, it is void. If a contract becomes illegal after it is formed, the duty to perform under the contract is discharged.

> Examples of illegal contracts include contracts that are usurious, contracts for the commission of a tort or crime, or contracts in restraint of trade.

a. **Effect of illegality**

Illegal transactions are not recognized or enforceable, restitution is not awarded for consideration, and no remedy is available for partial performance.

b. **Exceptions**

1) **Ignorance**

When one party is justifiably ignorant of the facts that make the contract illegal, that party may recover if the other party to the contract acted with knowledge of the illegality.

2) **Party lacks illegal purpose**

If only one party has an illegal purpose, then the other party can recover if he did not know of the illegal purpose, or if he knew of the illegal purpose but did not facilitate that purpose, and the purpose does not involve serious moral turpitude.

> **Example:** A seller of gambling equipment can recover the price, as long as he did not become involved in illegal gambling using the equipment. *This is true even if the seller knows of the illegal purpose.*

3) **Divisible contracts**

Some contracts can be easily separated into legal and illegal parts so that recovery is available on the legal part(s) only.

4) **Licensing violation**

When a party fails to comply with a licensing, registration, or similar requirement and, as a consequence, is prohibited from performing an act, the other party's promise made in consideration for the performance of the prohibited act or a promise to perform that act is unenforceable under public-policy grounds if the requirement has a regulatory (e.g., health, safety), rather than economic (e.g., revenue-raising) purpose, **and** public policy for the requirement clearly outweighs the interest in enforcing the promise. Restatement (Second) of Contracts § 181.

5) **Restitution**

Generally, a party to an illegal contract not only cannot enforce the contract, but also is not entitled to restitution with respect to a performance rendered. Restatement (Second) of Contracts § 197.

a) **Not** *in pari delicto*

When the parties are equally at fault (*in pari delicto*), neither party is entitled to restitution for a performance rendered. But, if the parties are not *in pari delicto,* the less guilty party may be able to recover restitutionary damages. Restatement (Second) of Contracts § 198.

b) Withdrawal

A party to an illegal contract who withdraws from the transaction before the improper purpose has been achieved may be entitled to restitution for a performance that the party has rendered when the party has not engaged in serious misconduct. Restatement (Second) of Contracts § 199.

2. Unconscionability

The UCC provides that a court may modify or refuse to enforce a contract or part of a contract on the grounds that it is unconscionable. UCC § 2-302.

A contract (or part of a contract) is unconscionable when it is so unfair to one party that no reasonable person in the position of the parties would have agreed to it. The contract or part of the contract at issue must have been offensive at the time it was made. Unconscionability may also be applied to prevent unfair surprise. Boilerplate contract provisions that are inconspicuous, hidden, or difficult for a party to understand have been held unconscionable. Courts have also applied the doctrine of unconscionability when the contract is a contract of adhesion (a take-it-or-leave-it contract) and there is greatly unequal bargaining power between the parties.

The question of whether a contract is unconscionable is a question of law for the court to decide; the issue does not go to the jury.

3. Public Policy

Even if a contract is neither illegal nor unconscionable, it may be unenforceable if it violates a significant public policy (e.g., contracts in restraint of marriage).

G. IMPLIED-IN-FACT CONTRACTS AND QUASI-CONTRACTS

1. Implied-in-Fact Contracts

When words express the intent of the parties, the contract is an express contract. When conduct indicates assent or agreement, the agreement is considered implied in fact.

Example: Without paying, B joins a tour group that is walking through a downtown area learning about landmark buildings. The tour guide can charge B the fee for the tour because B's conduct of joining the group implied agreement with the contract.

2. Implied-in-Law ("Quasi") Contracts

a. In general

When one party confers a benefit on another and has a reasonable expectation of compensation, allowing the benefited party to receive the benefit without any cost would be unjust. In this case, the court can imply a contract (quasi-contract) as a method of recovery that **prevents unjust enrichment.**

b. Requirements

A court will imply a contract to prevent unjust enrichment when:

i) The plaintiff has conferred a "measurable benefit" on the defendant;

ii) The plaintiff acted without gratuitous intent; and

iii) It would be unfair to let the defendant retain the benefit because either the defendant had an opportunity to decline the benefit but knowingly accepted it, or the plaintiff had a reasonable excuse for not giving the defendant such opportunity, usually because of an emergency.

In such a case, a promise is implied that requires the defendant to make restitution to the plaintiff (such as money damages equal to the fair value of the benefit).

Implied-in-law contracts can be found in cases in which there is (i) a failed contract, (ii) no contract, or (iii) a divisible contract.

> **EXAM NOTE:** Always keep in mind the possibility of quasi-contractual relief. Even when a party is not entitled to contractual relief, if she has provided services or suffered a loss, she may be entitled to quasi-contractual relief.

c. Remedies

Generally, a successful quasi-contract action results in the award of restitution damages, although reliance damages may occasionally be awarded. Expectation damages are almost never awarded.

d. Quasi-contractual recovery by a plaintiff in breach

If a plaintiff has not substantially performed, but the defendant has still benefited from the plaintiff's performance, the plaintiff can generally recover her restitution interest less the defendant's damages for the breach. Such recovery is often referred to as "quantum meruit" ("as much as he has deserved").

To recover under quantum meruit, one must show that the recipient:

i) Acquiesced in the provision of services;

ii) Knew that the provider expected to be compensated; and

iii) Was unjustly enriched.

1) Willful breach

Most courts hold that a plaintiff in breach is permitted to recover in quasi-contract only if her breach is not willful. If the breach is willful, then she cannot recover anything in quasi-contract.

2) UCC allows for partial restitution to the breaching buyer

For contracts for the sale of goods, a defaulting buyer's right to restitution is governed by UCC § 2-718. The buyer is entitled to a refund of any payments made on the contract less damages provable by the seller and either the amount to which the seller is entitled by virtue of an enforceable liquidated damages provision or a penalty of "twenty percent of the value of the total performance for which the buyer is obligated under the contract or $500, whichever is smaller."

H. WARRANTIES IN SALE-OF-GOODS CONTRACTS

UCC Article 2 allows not only for express warranties, but also for the implied warranties of merchantability and fitness for a particular purpose.

1. Express Warranty

Any promise, affirmation, description, or sample that is part of the basis of the bargain is an express warranty, **unless it is merely the seller's opinion** or commendation of the value of the goods. The use of a sample or model will create a warranty that the goods the buyer is to receive will be like the proffered sample or model. UCC § 2-313.

An express warranty can be made subsequent to the contract for sale. Although this would modify the original agreement, under the UCC, no consideration is needed to make a modification enforceable.

Disclaimer clauses that conflict with the express warranties, such as "all warranties, express or implied, are disclaimed," are ignored. UCC § 2-316.

2. Implied Warranty of Merchantability

A warranty of merchantability is implied whenever the seller is a **merchant.** To be merchantable, goods must be **fit for their ordinary purpose** and pass without objection in the trade under the contract description. A breach of this warranty must have been present at the time of the sale. UCC § 2-314.

Unless the circumstances indicate otherwise, the warranty can be disclaimed by use of "as is," "with all faults," or similar language that makes plain that there is no implied warranty. The disclaimer may be oral, but it must use the term "merchantability" and must be conspicuous if in writing. UCC § 2-316.

If the buyer, before entering into the contract, has examined the goods or a sample or model as fully as the buyer desires, or has refused to examine the goods, then there is no implied warranty with respect to defects that an examination ought to have revealed to the buyer. UCC § 2-316(3).

3. Implied Warranty of Fitness for a Particular Purpose

A warranty that the goods are fit for a particular purpose is implied whenever the seller has reason to know (from any source, not just from the buyer) that the buyer has a particular use for the goods, and the buyer is relying upon the seller's skill to select the goods. UCC § 2-315.

Note that the seller need not be a merchant for this implied warranty to apply.

An implied warranty of fitness for a particular purpose can be disclaimed by general language (including by the use of "as is"), but the **disclaimer must be in writing and be conspicuous.** UCC § 2-316(2).

II. DISCHARGE

The promisor may not be liable for nonperformance if some supervening event or change in circumstances arises after the formation of the contract that discharges the promisor's duty to perform.

A. IMPRACTICABILITY

A party's duty to perform can be dismissed by impracticability. The defense of impracticability is available if:

i) Performance becomes **illegal** after the contract is made;

ii) The specific subject matter of the contract (e.g., the goods) is **destroyed**;

iii) In a personal services contract, the performing party to the contract **dies or becomes incapacitated**; or

iv) Performance becomes **impracticable.**

UCC § 2-615; Restatement (Second) of Contracts § 265.

If the contract is to perform services that can be delegated, it is not discharged by the death or incapacity of the party who was to perform the services.

> **Impossibility:** Traditionally, courts referred to this defense as "impossibility." Under the modern view, adopted by the Restatement, "impracticability" better expresses the extent of the increased burden that is required.

1. Elements of Impracticability

For the defense of impracticability to be available, the following conditions must also be met:

i) An **unforeseeable event** has occurred;

ii) **Non-occurrence** of the event was a basic assumption on which the contract was made; and

iii) The **party seeking discharge is not at fault.**

When performance becomes impracticable for a seller of goods, the seller must notify the buyer. Restatement (Second) of Contracts § 265.

2. Other "Events Sufficient for Discharge" of a Contract

Unforeseen natural disasters, wars, trade and military embargoes, strikes, and local crop failures have all been found sufficient to excuse performance. However, non-extraordinary increases in the cost of performance are not.

3. Assumption of the Risk

If a party assumes the risk of an event happening that makes performance impracticable, then the defense of impracticability will not apply.

> Note that impracticability is not available merely when a party has made a bad deal and will have to pay more, even a lot more, than originally contemplated. It requires some totally unexpected occurrence that completely upsets the parties' expectations. Generally, the cost increase must be extreme.

4. Partial Impracticability

When impracticability does not prevent a seller from delivering some of the goods, the goods actually produced must be apportioned among all of the buyers with whom the seller has contracted. The buyer, however, may refuse to accept and may cancel the contract. UCC §§ 2-615(b), 2-616.

5. Failure of a Particular Source of Supply

If the contract provided that a specific source of supply be used, and that source of supply fails, performance is discharged. This is so even when other sources are readily available. Courts will excuse performance when the parties have specifically identified the source in the contract.

6. Failure of Agreed-Upon Method of Transportation

If, without the fault of either party, the agreed-upon delivery facilities or method of transportation or payment become unavailable or commercially impracticable, any commercially reasonable delivery method may be tendered and must be accepted.

B. FRUSTRATION OF PURPOSE

The doctrine of frustration of purpose applies when unexpected events arise that destroy one party's purpose in entering into the contract, even if performance of the contract is not rendered impossible. The frustrated party is entitled to rescind the contract without paying damages. The event that arises must not be the fault of the frustrated party, and its nonoccurrence must have been a basic assumption of the contract. If this is the case, the party's duty to render performance is discharged, unless the language of the agreement or the circumstances otherwise indicate. Restatement (Second) of Contracts § 265.

The occurrence need not be completely unforeseeable to the parties. It must, however, be unexpected and not a realistic prospect. For the doctrine of frustration of purpose to be applicable, the frustration must be so severe that it is not within the assumed risks inherent under the contract. Restatement (Second) of Contracts §§ 261, comments b and c, 265, comment a.

Example: A contracts with B to rent B's apartment for one day in order to get a prime view of a marathon run that will occur on that day. A agrees to pay a price that is far more than the typical rental value of the apartment. The marathon run is cancelled because of a terrorist threat. A may be excused from performance under the doctrine of frustration of purpose because her essential purpose in renting the apartment has been frustrated, and the event that arose was not her fault and was completely unexpected.

C. RESCISSION

Rescission is the cancelling of a contract so as to restore the parties to their positions before the contract was made. Parties may seek to rescind a contract for a variety of reasons, including mutual mistake, fraud, misrepresentation, or even unilateral mistake, if the other party knew or should have known of the mistake. The grounds for rescission must have existed at the time the contract was made.

The non-defaulting party to a contract can cancel or rescind the contract, which requires a return of any deposits or other benefit conferred on the other party.

Rescission can also occur by the mutual agreement of the parties. The surrender of rights under the original contract by each party is consideration for the rescission by mutual agreement.

In cases of third-party beneficiaries, a contract is **not** discharged by mutual rescission if the rights of the third-party beneficiary have already vested.

D. RELEASE

A release is a writing that manifests intent to discharge another party from an existing duty. For common-law contracts, the release must generally be supported by consideration to discharge the duty.

Under the UCC, however, a claim or right can be discharged in whole or in part without consideration by a written waiver or renunciation signed and delivered by the aggrieved party. No consideration is needed to support the release.

E. DESTRUCTION OR INJURY TO IDENTIFIED GOODS

If a contract calls for the delivery of goods identified at the time the contract is made, and the goods are destroyed without the fault of either party before the risk of loss passes to the buyer, then the contract is avoided. Both parties are discharged; neither party must perform, and neither party has breached. If the goods are damaged, but not destroyed, then the contract is avoided, unless the buyer chooses to take the goods at a reduced price without any other claim against the seller. (Note: If the risk of loss has passed to the buyer, then the contract is not avoided, and the seller may demand performance by the buyer (*see* § VIII.F.3. Risk of Loss, *infra*).)

III. THIRD-PARTY BENEFICIARY CONTRACTS

A third-party beneficiary contract results when two parties enter into a contract with the understanding and intent that the performance by one of the parties is to be rendered to a third person. Jurisdictions are split as to whether the First or Second Restatement of Contracts applies.

EXAM NOTE: On the MBE, if the question is silent as to the applicable law, assume that the jurisdiction follows the Second Restatement of Contracts.

A. CREDITOR AND DONEE BENEFICIARIES

The First Restatement classifies third-party beneficiaries as creditor or donee beneficiaries. If performance of a promise would satisfy an actual, supposed, or asserted duty of the promisee to a third party, and the promisee did not intend to make a gift to the third party, then the third party is called a **creditor beneficiary.** A creditor beneficiary has the right to sue either the promisor or the promisee to enforce the contract.

Example: A agrees to paint B's house in return for B's promise to pay $500 to C because A owes C $500. C is an intended beneficiary and can recover the $500 from B.

If the promisee entered the contract for the purpose of conferring a gift on a third party, then the third-party **donee beneficiary** is given the right to sue the promisor.

Example: A pays B to build a house for C. C is a donee beneficiary of the contract between A and B.

B. INTENDED AND INCIDENTAL BENEFICIARIES

The Second Restatement abandons the donee beneficiary and creditor beneficiary categories. Instead, a third party can recover if she is an intended beneficiary. Otherwise, she is said to be an incidental beneficiary with no rights to enforce the contract.

An intended beneficiary is one to whom the promisee wishes to make a gift of the promised performance or to satisfy an obligation to pay money owed by the promisee to the beneficiary. The promisee must have an intention (explicit or implicit) to benefit the third party, or the beneficiary is incidental.

Example: If A agrees to paint B's house in return for B's promise to pay $500 to C, then C is an intended beneficiary and can recover the $500 from B.

An incidental beneficiary is one who benefits from a contract even though there is no contractual intent to benefit that person. An incidental beneficiary has no rights to enforce the contract.

Example: A promises to buy B a car manufactured by C. Here, C is an incidental beneficiary with no grounds upon which to recover if A reneged on the promise.

To bring an action for breach of a third-party beneficiary contract, the third party must establish:

i) A contract between A and B;

ii) The "clear" or "manifest" intent of A and B that the contract primarily and directly benefit the third party (or class of persons to which that party belongs);

iii) A breach of the contract by either A or B; and

iv) Damages to the third party resulting from the breach. An incidental beneficiary has no enforceable rights under a contract.

Restatement (Second) of Contracts § 302.

> **EXAM NOTE:** On the exam, if the promise indicates that the promisor will pay the third party directly to relieve the promissee from a debt, then the third party is likely an intended beneficiary. In contrast, if the promisor is to pay the promisee in order that she may pay the third party, then the third party is most likely an incidental beneficiary.

C. VESTING OF BENEFICIARY'S RIGHTS

Only an intended beneficiary has a right to bring an action on the contract. An intended beneficiary of a "gift promise" (a donee beneficiary) may sue only the promisor. If the promisee tells the donee beneficiary about the contract and should reasonably foresee reliance, and the beneficiary does so rely to his detriment, then promissory estoppel would apply. An intended beneficiary to whom the promisee owed money (a creditor beneficiary) may sue either the promisor or the promisee, or both, on the underlying obligation, but only one recovery is allowed.

1. When Rights Vest

The rights of an intended beneficiary vest when the beneficiary:

i) **Detrimentally relies** on the rights created;

ii) **Manifests assent** to the contract at one of the parties' request; or

iii) **Files a lawsuit** to enforce the contract.

2. Effect of Vesting on Original Parties

Once the beneficiary's rights have vested, the original parties to the contract are both bound to perform the contract. Any efforts by the promisor or the promisee to rescind or modify the contract after vesting are void, **unless the third party agrees** to the rescission or modification.

D. DEFENSES

The promisor can raise any defense against the third-party beneficiary that the promisor had against the original promisee. Therefore, the beneficiary also becomes liable for counterclaims on the contract that the promisor could establish against the promisee. This liability can never exceed the amount that the promisor owes under the contract.

Example: A agrees to paint B's house in return for B's promise to pay $500 to C, to whom A owes $500. If the statute of limitations (or any other contractual defense) precludes A (the promisee) from recovering against B (the promisor), then it will also preclude C (the intended creditor beneficiary) from recovering against B on the contract.

The promisor may not assert any defenses that the promisee would have had against the intended beneficiary.

Example: In the example above, if the statute of limitations precluded C from recovering against A on the debt that A owed to C, then B's obligation to C would not be affected.

IV. ASSIGNMENT OF RIGHTS AND DELEGATION OF DUTIES

A. ASSIGNMENT OF RIGHTS

"Assignment" is the **transfer of rights** under a contract, and **"delegation"** is the **transfer of duties** and obligations under a contract.

EXAM NOTE: Although the two terms are clearly distinct in concept, the term "assignment" is often used to refer to either assignment or delegation on the MBE.

Almost all contract rights can be assigned. Partial assignments are permissible, as is the assignment of future or unearned rights.

1. When Disallowed

Assignments are not allowed when they materially increase the duty or risk of the obligor or materially reduce the obligor's chance of obtaining performance. Generally, prohibitions against assignment in the contract are strictly construed, and the assignment is permissible. Even if validly prohibited by the contract, the power to assign is retained by the parties, and the only consequence is that an assignment operates as a breach of the contract.

2. Requirements

No formalities are needed for an assignment, but there must be a present intent to transfer the right immediately. No consideration is needed, but the lack of consideration would affect revocability of the assignment. If an assignment is for consideration, it is irrevocable. If no consideration supports the assignment (a gratuitous assignment), then it will generally be revocable, unless the obligor has already performed or promissory estoppel applies. If the contract right that is being assigned is evidenced by a document that symbolizes the right (e.g., a bank book, insurance policy, or stock certificates), then delivery of the document makes the assignment irrevocable. A gratuitous assignment will be automatically revoked upon the death, incapacity, or bankruptcy of the assignor. Restatement (Second) of Contracts § 332.

3. Rights of the Assignee

An assignee **takes all of the rights of the assignor as the contract stands at the time of the assignment,** but she takes **subject to any defenses that could be raised against the assignor.** The rights of the assignee are subject to set-off if the transaction giving rise to the set-off occurred prior to the time the obligor was given notice of the assignment. In addition, the rights of the assignee are subject to a set-off that arises out of the same transaction. The assignee is also subject to any modification of the contract made prior to the time the obligor obtained notice of the assignment. Thus, payment by the obligor to the assignor can be raised as a defense, provided the payment was made before the obligor had notice of the assignment.

A subsequent assignment of the same right(s) revokes any prior *revocable* assignment. If the first assignment was an *irrevocable* assignment, then the first assignee will have priority over the second assignee, unless the second assignee is a bona fide purchaser for value without notice of the first assignment, in which case the assignee who obtains payment from the obligor or judgment first will have priority. If the second assignee knows about a prior assignment, then he is estopped from asserting a claim over the first assignee even if he would have otherwise prevailed.

B. DELEGATION OF DUTIES

1. In General

Generally, obligations under a contract can be delegated. Delegation is not permitted when the other party to the contract has a substantial interest in having the delegating individual perform (for example, in a personal services contract involving taste or a special skill), or the delegation is prohibited by the contract.

When obligations are delegated, the **delegator is not released from liability,** and recovery can be had against the delegator if the delegatee does not perform.

2. Novation

A novation is the substitution of a new contract for an old one when the original obligor is released from his promises under the original agreement. A novation may be express or implied after delegation if (i) the original obligor repudiates liability to the original promisee and (ii) the obligee subsequently accepts performance of the original agreement from the delegatee without reserving rights against the obligor.

3. Effect of Delegation of Performance

Any delegation of performance under a contract for the sale of goods may be treated by the other party as creating reasonable grounds for insecurity. UCC § 2-210(5). The other party may, without prejudice to his rights against the delegator, demand assurances from the delegatee (UCC § 2-609, *see* §§ VIII.B.2–3., *infra*).

A delegation does not relieve the delegating party of her obligations under the contract unless the other party to the contract agrees to release that party and substitute a new one (a novation). Merely consenting to a delegation does not create a novation. UCC § 2-210.

A contractual assignment is typically treated as both an assignment of rights and a delegation of duties, the acceptance of which constitutes a promise to perform. Further, the promise is enforceable by either the assignor or the other party to the contract. Therefore, the UCC treats the other party as a third-party beneficiary of the assignment and delegation.

V.   STATUTE OF FRAUDS

A.   WRITING REQUIRED

Contracts that fall within the Statute of Frauds are **unenforceable** unless they are **in writing.** The memorandum must:

i)   Be in writing;

ii) Be signed by the party to be charged (i.e., the person against whom enforcement is sought); and

iii) Contain the essential elements of the deal.

The memorandum need not be formal (i.e., receipts or correspondence can serve as memoranda). The essential elements may be in more than one writing only if one of the writings references the other(s). The memorandum need not be delivered. Even if it is lost or destroyed, it still operates to satisfy the Statute of Frauds, and its prior existence can be proved by oral evidence.

> **EXAM NOTE:** Note that a memorandum sufficient to satisfy the Statute of Frauds does not need to be written at the time a promise is made and can be subsequently reduced to writing. The memorandum also does not have to be addressed to the promisee to be enforceable by the promisee.

B.   TYPES OF CONTRACTS WITHIN THE STATUTE OF FRAUDS

Most states require that these five categories of contracts be in writing:

Marriage - A contract made upon consideration of marriage;

Suretyship - A contract to answer for the debt or duty of another;

One year - A contract that cannot be performed within one year from its making;

UCC - Under the UCC, a contract for the sale of goods for a price of $500 or more; and

Real property contract - A contract for the sale of an interest in real property.

> **EXAM NOTE:** Statute of Frauds issues are often tested on the MBE. You can remember which types of contracts are governed by the Statute by using the mnemonic **Mr. SOUR** (Marriage, Suretyship, One year, UCC, Real property).

1.   Marriage Provision

Any agreement in consideration of marriage is within the Statute of Frauds, except the promises by each to marry the other (i.e., the marriage contract itself). A prenuptial agreement is the paradigm of an agreement made in consideration of marriage that is subject to the Statute of Frauds. A promise made in consideration of marriage does not become enforceable merely because the marriage has taken place in reliance on it. However, additional part performance or action in reliance may make such a promise enforceable. Restatement (Second) of Contracts § 124.

2. Suretyship Provision

a. Rule

Suretyship is a three-party contract, wherein one party (the surety) promises a second party (the obligee) that the surety will be responsible for any debt of a third party (the principal) resulting from the principal's failure to pay as agreed. A suretyship induces the second party to extend credit to the third party. A promise to answer for the debt of another must generally be in writing to be enforceable.

b. Exceptions

1) Indemnity contracts

An indemnity contract (i.e., a promise to reimburse for monetary loss) does not fall within the Statute of Frauds as a suretyship provision.

2) Main purpose exception

If the main purpose of the surety in agreeing to pay the debt of the principal is for the surety's own economic advantage, rather than for the principal's benefit, then the contract does not fall within the Statute of Frauds, and an oral promise by the surety is enforceable.

3. Real Property Contracts

a. Types

A promise to transfer or receive **any interest in real property** is within the Statute of Frauds. The Statute does not apply to the conveyance itself (which is governed by a separate statute), but it does apply to a **contract providing for** the subsequent conveyance of an interest in real property. The Statute of Frauds also applies to a promise to create an interest in real property, the assignment of a right to purchase real property, an option contract for the sale of an interest in real property, and a promise to give a mortgage or other lien as security. While leases and easements, as property interests, are generally subject to the Statute of Frauds, a lease or easement for one year or less is usually not covered by the Statute. In addition, licenses and assignments of mortgages are typically not within the Statute.

b. Part performance

Even if an oral contract for the transfer of an interest in real property is not enforceable at the time it is made, **subsequent acts** by either party that show the existence of the contract may make it enforceable, even without a memorandum. Thus, if the seller of an interest in real property conveys it to the purchaser, then the seller will be able to enforce the purchaser's oral promise to pay. Full or partial payment alone, however, would not be sufficient to take the transaction out of the Statute of Frauds. Payment must be accompanied by something more, such as possession of the property or valuable improvements, in order for the part performance doctrine to apply.

4. One-Year Provision

Contracts that **cannot** be performed within one year due to the constraints of the terms of the agreement must be in writing. The year starts **the day after** the contract is made. It is the time that the contract is made that is important, not the length of performance.

> The fact that a contract is not completed within one year does not mean that it is voidable under the Statute of Frauds. For the Statute to apply, the *actual terms* of the contract must make it impossible for performance to be completed within one year.

Full performance will generally take the contract out of the Statute of Frauds. While part performance would not take the contract out of the Statute of Frauds, restitution would be available to the party who performed.

5. Sale of Goods for $500 or More

> **EXAM NOTE:** The UCC Statute of Frauds requirements and exceptions for goods when the price is at least $500 are frequently tested on the MBE.

a. Sufficiency of the writing

When the price of goods is at least $500, the UCC requires a memorandum of the sale that must:

i) Indicate that a contract has been made;

ii) Identify the parties;

iii) Contain a quantity term; and

iv) Be signed by the party to be charged.

> The memorandum needs to be signed only by the party being sued; it does not need to be signed by both parties.

1) Type of writing required

To satisfy the Statute of Frauds, the above terms must be in writing, but that writing need not be an actual contract. It doesn't even need to be contained on one piece of paper—a series of correspondence between the parties may suffice.

2) Mistake in writing

A mistake in the memorandum or the omission of other terms does not destroy the memorandum's validity. An omitted term can be proved by parol evidence. However, enforcement is limited to the quantity term actually stated in the memorandum.

> **EXAM NOTE:** Some states have raised the threshold amount from $500 to $5,000. On the exam, assume that the amount is $500, unless stated otherwise.

b. Exceptions—writing not required

1) Specially manufactured goods

No writing is required if (i) the goods are to be specially manufactured for the buyer, (ii) the goods are not suitable for sale to others, and (iii) the seller has made "either a substantial beginning of their manufacture or commitments for their procurement." UCC § 2-201.

2) Part payment

When part of the purchase price for a single item has been paid, the contract is enforced and the partial payment falls outside the UCC Statute of Frauds only to the extent of the purchase.

3) Receipt and acceptance

The contract is outside the UCC Statute of Frauds to the extent that goods are received and accepted.

4) Judicial admission

If the party to be charged admits in pleadings, testimony, or otherwise in court that a contract was made, then the contract is enforceable only to the extent of the quantity admitted.

5) Failure to respond to a memorandum (when both parties are merchants)

If both parties are merchants and a memorandum sufficient against one party is sent to the other party who has reason to know its contents, and the receiving party does not object in writing **within 10 days,** then the contract is enforceable against the receiving party even though he has not signed it.

c. Modifications

Under UCC § 2-209(3), the requirements of the Statute of Frauds must be satisfied if the contract as modified is within its provisions. Any of the above exceptions would apply, though, to take a modification out of the Statute of Frauds.

The UCC would also enforce a provision in a contract for the sale of goods that required a modification to be in writing. Thus, even if the contract was for a sale of goods valued at less than $500 or involved one of the exceptions discussed above, if the contract specifically provided that any modification be in writing, then the UCC would enforce that requirement. *See* UCC § 2-209(2). Note that under a common-law contract, a provision requiring a modification to be in writing even though the modification would not otherwise fall within the Statute of Frauds would not be enforceable.

VI. PAROL EVIDENCE RULE

Before signing a written agreement, parties typically negotiate their contract through a series of conversations, phone calls, letters, faxes, e-mails, etc. When the written contract is finally signed, it may or may not include all of the terms of these negotiations, or it may change the terms in some way. The parol evidence rule generally prevents a party to a written contract from presenting prior extrinsic evidence that contradicts the terms of the contract as written. The rule is concerned with whether any of the earlier oral or written terms are part of the parties' contract, even though they are absent from the parties' written agreement.

A. INTEGRATION

The first step is to determine whether the parties' writing is "integrated," meaning that the parties intended it to be their final agreement. The parol evidence rule applies only to a document that is an integration.

If the document is determined not to be an integration (i.e., not to be the final expression of the parties' agreement), such as a preliminary negotiation document or tentative draft agreement, then the parol evidence rule will not apply.

1. Total versus Partial Integration

If the writing is determined to be an integration, then the second step is to decide whether it completely expresses all of the terms of the parties' agreement.

a. Total integration

If the writing completely expresses all of the terms of the parties' agreement, then it is a **total integration,** and the parties cannot introduce any extrinsic evidence (oral or written) of prior or contemporaneous understandings or negotiations.

b. Partial integration

If, on the other hand, the writing sets forth the parties' agreement about some terms, but not all terms, then it is a **partial integration.** The parties are then permitted to introduce supplementary extrinsic evidence (oral or written) of other terms as long as the evidence is **consistent** with the writing, but not if the evidence contradicts the terms of the writing.

2. Intent of the Parties

The intent of the parties determines whether there is total, partial, or no integration.

a. Common-law "four corners" rule

Under the common law, in determining whether the parties intended the written contract to be the final and complete expression of their agreement, a court was only permitted to look to the writing itself for evidence of intent. This is called the "four corners" rule because the court could not look outside the four corners of the parties' document. If the written contract appeared to be detailed, then a court would likely conclude that it was final and totally integrated. Such a conclusion was especially true if the contract had an explicit integration or "merger" clause, which usually said something like: "This contract is the final and complete expression of the parties' agreement and supersedes all prior contracts, agreements, understandings, negotiations, assurances, guarantees, or statements."

b. Second Restatement rule

The Second Restatement adopts a different approach to the parol evidence rule. If, under the circumstances, an extrinsic term of an agreement would "naturally be omitted" from a writing, then that term can be introduced, so long as it does not contradict the writing. Restatement (Second) of Contracts § 213.

c. UCC rule

In contrast to the common law and Second Restatement parol evidence rules, the UCC rule is much more lenient. The UCC essentially presumes that a written contract is only a "partial integration" of the parties' agreement, and therefore it lets in any outside terms unless a court concludes that they "certainly" would have been included in the written contract. UCC § 2-202. It is typically very difficult for courts to conclude that parties "certainly" would have included any particular term in their written contract. Thus, under the UCC, parties usually can bring in outside evidence.

B. WHEN THE PAROL EVIDENCE RULE IS INAPPLICABLE

The parol evidence rule does not apply to communications that occur after the execution of the written contract; it applies only to agreements reached before or contemporaneously with the execution of the written contract.

1. Raising an Excuse

The parol evidence rule does not apply when a party is raising an excuse, such as mistake, misunderstanding, or misrepresentation. Parties may always introduce evidence that would show that no valid contract exists or that the contract is voidable.

2. Establishing a Defense

Similarly, the parol evidence rule does not apply to evidence offered to establish a defense such as incompetence, illegality, duress, or lack of consideration. Again, if the evidence would make the contract void or voidable, then the parol evidence rule will not apply.

3. Separate Deal

Even when there is full integration, evidence may be offered if it represents a distinct and separate contract.

4. Condition Precedent

Parol evidence may also be admitted to prove a condition precedent to the existence of the contract.

5. Ambiguity and Interpretation

Evidence may be admitted for the purpose of interpreting or clarifying an ambiguity in the agreement. This can include evidence of trade usage or even local custom to show that a particular word or phrase had a particular meaning. Courts approach interpretation in two ways:

a. Plain meaning rule

This rule provides that the objective definitions of contract terms control the meaning of the contract, regardless of whether this meaning corresponds with the actual intent of the parties. Sometimes courts will go outside the document to clarify the ordinary meaning of terms that are ambiguous or overly vague.

b. Context rule

Some states permit courts to use a contextual approach to contract interpretation. Under the context rule, judges determine the contract's meaning by considering all evidence of the facts and circumstances related to the transaction. The goal is to effectuate the parties' actual contract objectives and purposes.

6. Subsequent Agreements

The parol evidence rule does not apply to evidence of agreements between the parties subsequent to execution of the writing.

7. UCC Rule—Trade Usage and Course of Dealings or Performance

Even if the terms of a written contract for the sale of goods appear to be unambiguous, a party may explain or supplement the terms by evidence of trade usage or course of dealings or performance. UCC § 2-202.

VII. CONDITIONS AND PERFORMANCE

A condition is a future and uncertain event that must take place before a party's contractual rights or obligations are created, destroyed, or enlarged. By contrast, a promise constitutes a party's obligation to act or refrain from acting.

Example: A buyer and seller enter into a contract for the sale of a house if the buyer can obtain a loan. Under the contract, the seller has promised to sell the house to the buyer, and the buyer has correspondingly promised to buy the house. However, both promises are conditioned on the buyer obtaining a loan.

Ambiguity as to whether a statement creates a promise or a condition is usually resolved in favor of a promise over a condition. Restatement (Second) of Contracts § 227.

EXAM NOTE: Remember, the failure of a **condition** relieves a party of the **obligation** to perform; the failure of a party to perform a **promise** constitutes **breach.**

A. TYPES OF CONDITIONS

A condition may be express (clearly stated in the agreement) or implied (presumed based on the nature of a transaction).

1. Express

Express conditions are expressed in the contract. Words in the contract such as "on condition that" or "provided that" are typical examples of express conditions. Express conditions must be complied with fully; substantial performance will not suffice. Arbitration clauses are enforceable, except when a consumer might be waiving an important substantive right.

2. Implied Conditions

Implied conditions are those that are deemed to be part of the contract because the nature of the agreement suggests that the parties truly intended the condition but failed to expressly include it, or because fairness requires including the condition to prevent an unjust result (also called "constructive condition"). The most common types of implied conditions are called "constructive conditions of exchange" and arise most frequently in construction and employment contracts. A court will imply that the builder or employee must perform first (at least "substantially") before the other side's performance (the payment of money) becomes due.

Substantial performance is all that is required to satisfy an implied condition.

B. TIMING OF CONDITIONS

Performance by one or both of the parties may be made expressly conditional in the contract, and the conditions may precede the obligation to perform (**condition precedent**) or may excuse the duty to perform after a particular event occurs (**condition subsequent**). A condition subsequent exists only with respect to duty that is absolute. (Note: Under the Restatement (Second) of Contracts, a condition subsequent is treated as a discharging event rather than as a condition. Restatement (Second) of Contracts §§ 224, 230.)

Example: A agrees to hire B if B passes the bar exam. B agrees to work as a clerk for C until B passes the bar exam. B's passing of the bar exam is a condition precedent to being hired by A, and a condition subsequent to B's employment with C.

If a defendant's duty is subject to a condition precedent, the plaintiff has the burden of proving that the condition occurred in order to recover. If the defendant's duty is subject to a condition subsequent, then the defendant must prove the happening of the condition to avoid liability.

C. SATISFACTION OF CONDITIONS

In most contracts, a party's duty to perform is absolute because it is easy to conclude that all conditions have been satisfied. In unusual cases, the occurrence of the condition may be more difficult to determine.

1. Satisfaction Clause

When the aesthetic taste of an individual is a condition of satisfactory performance, and that individual in good faith determines that the work is not satisfactory, then that person is not liable on the contract. Conditions requiring satisfaction of performance not involving aesthetics are examined against a reasonable person standard.

2. Time of Payment Clause

A clause in a contract making payment conditioned on the occurrence of an event is usually construed as a mere guide as to time for payment rather than as an absolute condition that must occur before payment is due.

D. DISPUTES ABOUT PERFORMANCE

A party to a contract cannot recover until performance is tendered to the other party. When parties expressly agree to a condition, they are generally held strictly to that condition, meaning that there must be full compliance. With implied conditions or constructive conditions of exchange, courts permit less than full compliance with the constructive conditions. This doctrine is known as "substantial performance."

The doctrine of substantial performance does not apply either to express conditions or to contracts for the sale of goods under the UCC.

1. Substantial Performance

a. Meaning

The doctrine of substantial performance provides that a party who substantially performs can recover on the contract even though full performance has not been tendered. If the failure of a constructive condition of exchange is minor, then it will not negate substantial performance. If the failure of a constructive condition of exchange is material, however, it will negate substantial performance.

b. Willful failure

No recovery is allowed for a willful failure, which implies some attempt to cheat the other party or to provide less than was called for by the contract.

Under the doctrine of prevention, a party must refrain from conduct that prevents or hinders the occurrence of a condition. Restatement (Second) of Contracts §§ 225, 245 cmt. a.

c. Damages

In general, the party who substantially performed the contract can recover the contract price minus any amount that it will cost the other party to obtain complete performance as had been promised. Note that even if there is no substantial performance, a party who performed to some degree and cannot recover in contract can still potentially recover through restitution.

2. Strict Performance under the UCC

Under the UCC, the basic obligations of a seller are to **transfer ownership** of the goods to the buyer and to **tender goods** conforming to the warranty obligations. In general, the UCC requires "perfect tender," and substantial performance will not suffice. Substantial performance applies to installment contracts under the UCC and when the parties agree that it applies. In addition, the UCC provides that if a buyer rejects goods as nonconforming and time still remains to perform under a contract, the seller has a right to cure and tender conforming goods.

a. Transferring ownership

The UCC implies a warranty of title in all sales contracts, providing that the seller automatically warrants that (i) it is conveying good title, (ii) the transfer is rightful, and (iii) the goods are delivered free from any security interest of which the buyer has no knowledge at the time of the contract. Actual knowledge by the buyer of a security interest on the goods nullifies the warranty of title. UCC § 2-312(1).

The UCC permits disclaimer of the warranty of title, but such disclaimer must be by specific language or circumstances that give the buyer reason to know that the seller does not claim rightful title, or that the seller is only purporting to sell such rights as the seller or a third person possesses. UCC § 2-312(2).

b. Tendering goods

The seller must tender the goods in accordance with the contract provisions or in accordance with the UCC if the contract is silent on tender. UCC § 2-503.

1) Time of tender

In the absence of a specific contract provision, the goods must be tendered within a reasonable time after the contract is made. UCC § 2-309.

2) Manner of tender

The goods are to be delivered in one delivery, unless otherwise provided in the contract, or the circumstances give either party a right to make or demand delivery in lots (as when a party would clearly have no room to store the goods if delivered all at once). UCC § 2-307.

3) Place of tender

Unless otherwise provided in the contract, the place of tender will be the seller's place of business (or residence, if the seller has no place of business), unless the goods are identified and the parties know that they are at some other location, in which case that location will be the place of tender. UCC § 2-308.

4) Method of tender

The four methods of tender are as follows.

a) Seller's place of business

If the goods are tendered at the seller's place of business, then the seller must place the goods at the disposition of the buyer and give the buyer notice, if notice is necessary to enable the seller to take delivery. UCC § 2-504.

b) Shipment contract

If the contract is a shipment contract (often identified by the words "F.O.B. (free on board) seller's place of business"), then the seller must deliver the goods to the carrier, make a proper contract for their shipment, obtain and deliver any document necessary for the buyer to obtain possession of the goods, and give the buyer notice that the goods have been shipped. UCC § 2-319(1)(a).

c) Destination contract

If the contract is a destination contract (often identified by the words "F.O.B. (free on board) buyer's place of business"), then the seller must deliver the goods to a particular place (specified in the contract) and tender them there by holding the goods at the buyer's disposition and giving the buyer notice. UCC § 2-319(1)(b).

d) Goods in the hands of a bailee

The seller must bargain for a negotiable document of title or obtain acknowledgment from the bailee of the buyer's rights in the goods. UCC § 2-509(2).

> A contract that requires the seller to ship goods to the buyer by a third-party carrier is either a shipment contract or a destination contract. When the contract is otherwise silent, a shipment contract is presumed when the contract requires shipment by a third-party carrier. UCC § 2-503 cmt. 5.

5) C.I.F. (cost, insurance, and freight) and C & F (cost and freight)

In a C.I.F. contract, the price includes the cost of the goods, the cost of transporting the goods, and the cost of insuring the goods during shipment. In a C & F contract, the price includes the cost of the goods plus the cost of shipment.

6) F.A.S. contracts

When a contract specifies F.A.S. (free alongside ship), the seller is obligated to deliver the goods **alongside** a designated vessel in a manner that comports with the ordinary course of business of the port of delivery, or at a specified dock.

c. Buyer's obligations

When a conforming tender is made, the buyer is obligated to accept and pay the price under the contract. UCC § 2-507. Rejection amounts to breach of contract.

An agreement that is otherwise sufficiently definite will not be made invalid merely because it omits details regarding the performance to be specified by one of the parties. The UCC implies an obligation of good faith within the parameter of "commercial reasonableness." UCC § 2-311(1).

When a contract fails to specify the assortment of goods, the UCC imposes a duty on the buyer to specify, whereas arrangements relating to shipment are the seller's duty to specify. UCC § 2-311(2).

If the buyer fails to specify the assortment of goods, then the seller can treat the failure as a breach by failure to accept the contracted-for goods only if the buyer's failure materially impacts the seller's performance. UCC § 2-311(3).

1) Non-carrier cases versus carrier cases

Unless otherwise specified in the contract, when goods are shipped by carrier, payment is due from the buyer at the moment the buyer receives the goods. In non-carrier cases, payment is due upon tender of delivery by the seller.

2) Shipment under reservation

A seller who ships by carrier under a contract that does not specify the method or form of payment may send the goods **under reservation,** meaning that the carrier will hold the goods until the buyer pays. This is accomplished by the seller's obtaining a negotiable or nonnegotiable bill of lading.

3) Tender of payment

a) Generally required to trigger delivery obligation

Unless otherwise agreed, tender of payment is a condition to the seller's duty to tender and complete any delivery.

b) Sufficiency of tender of payment

Tender of payment is sufficient when made by any means or in any manner consistent with the ordinary course of business, unless the seller (i) demands payment in legal tender (i.e., cash) and (ii) gives any extension of time reasonably necessary to procure such legal tender.

c) Payment by check

If payment is made by check, payment is conditional until the check is paid or dishonored.

d. Buyer's right to inspect

A buyer has a right to inspect goods that are tendered, delivered, or identified to the contract for sale, unless the contract provides otherwise.

1) Prior to payment

A buyer's right to inspect is a condition to payment. An inspection may occur at any reasonable time and place and in any reasonable manner, even when the goods are held under reservation. However, the parties can agree that inspection can occur in a particular form, time, or place. If the seller is required or authorized to send the goods to the buyer, then the inspection may be after their arrival.

2) When not entitled to inspect

Unless otherwise agreed, the buyer is **not** entitled to inspect the goods before payment of the price if the contract (i) provides for delivery "C.O.D." or (ii) is on other terms that, under the applicable course of performance, course of dealing, or usage of trade are interpreted to preclude inspection before payment. Similarly, the buyer is not entitled to inspect the goods before payment, unless otherwise agreed, if the contract provides for payment against documents of title, except when such payment is due only after the goods are to become available for inspection.

3) Expenses of inspection

Expenses of inspection must be paid by the buyer, but they may be recovered from the seller if the goods do not conform and are rejected.

3. Divisible or Installment Contracts

a. Common law

A divisible or installment contract is one in which the various units of performance are divisible into distinct parts. Recovery is limited to the amount promised for the segment of the contract performed. Damages are recoverable for breach of the other segments.

b. UCC

Special rules for installment contracts are addressed in UCC §2-612. The most important difference between installment contracts and other contracts is that the perfect tender rule does not apply; instead, the right to reject is determined by a "substantial conformity" standard.

1) Multiple shipments

Under the UCC, an installment contract is defined as one in which the goods are to be delivered in multiple shipments, and each shipment is to be separately accepted by the buyer. Parties cannot vary or contract out of this definition under the code. Payment by the buyer is due upon each delivery, unless the price cannot be apportioned. UCC § 2-612.

2) Nonconforming segment

If the seller makes a nonconforming tender or tenders nonconforming goods under one segment of an installment contract, the buyer can reject only if the nonconformity:

  i) **Substantially impairs the value** of that shipment to the buyer; and

  ii) Cannot be **cured**.

If the seller makes adequate assurances that he can cure the nonconformity, then the buyer must accept the shipment. UCC § 2-612(2).

3) Remaining segments

When there is a nonconforming tender or a tender of nonconforming goods under one segment of an installment contract, the buyer may cancel the contract only if the nonconformity **substantially impairs the value** of the entire contract to the buyer.

> **EXAM NOTE:** When presented with nonconforming goods in installment contracts, look for clues in the fact pattern as to whether a nonconformity substantially impairs the value of the entire contract.

E. SUSPENSION OR EXCUSE OF CONDITIONS

If a condition is suspended, then the condition is restored upon expiration of the suspension. If the condition is excused, then the party having the benefit of the condition can never raise it as a defense.

1. Waiver

A party whose duty is subject to the condition can waive the condition, either by words or by conduct. Courts will find waiver of a condition only if the condition is not a material part of the agreement.

The condition may be reinstated if:

i) The waiving party communicates a retraction of the waiver before the condition is due to occur; and

ii) The other party has not already suffered detrimental reliance.

2. Wrongful Interference

A duty of good faith and fair dealing is implied into **all** (both common law and UCC) contracts. Included in this duty is a duty not to hinder the other party's performance and a duty to cooperate, when necessary. Accordingly, if the party whose duty is subject to the condition wrongfully interferes with the occurrence of that condition, then the condition is excused and the party wrongfully interfering has an absolute duty to perform.

3. Election

A party who chooses to continue with a contract after a condition is broken effectively elects to waive that condition.

4. Estoppel

A party who indicates that a condition will not be enforced may be estopped from using that condition as a defense if the other party reasonably relied on the impression that the condition had been waived.

VIII. BREACH OF CONTRACT AND REMEDIES

A. BREACH OF CONTRACT

Once a duty to perform exists, nonperformance is a breach of contract unless the duty is discharged (by agreement, statute, inability to perform, waiver, etc.).

1. Common Law

Under common law, a material breach of contract (i.e., when the non-breaching party does not receive the substantial benefit of its bargain) allows the non-breaching party to withhold any promised performance and to pursue remedies for the breach, including damages. If the breach is minor (i.e., the breaching party has substantially performed), then the non-breaching party is entitled to any remedies that would apply to the nonmaterial breach. If a minor breach is accompanied by an anticipatory repudiation, then the non-breaching party may treat the breach as a material breach.

The party who commits a material breach of his contract obligations cannot sue for contract damages but would ordinarily be entitled to the fair value of any benefit conferred on the non-breaching party.

> **EXAM NOTE:** Keep in mind that under a minor breach, the non-breaching party may be able to recover damages, but also still must perform under the contract. If the breach is material, the non-breaching party does not need to perform.

2. UCC

Under the UCC, the seller generally must strictly perform all obligations under the contract or be in breach. The doctrine of material breach applies only in the context of installment contracts or when the parties so provide in their contract.

B. ANTICIPATORY REPUDIATION

1. Anticipatory Repudiation under the Common Law

a. Repudiation of promise

The doctrine of anticipatory repudiation is applicable when a promisor repudiates a promise before the time for performance arises or elapses. The repudiation must be **clear and unequivocal** (as opposed to mere insecurity) and may be by acts or words.

b. Nonbreaching party's options

Repudiation excuses the occurrence of any condition that would otherwise prevent the repudiating party's duty from being absolute. Upon repudiation, the promisee can treat the repudiation as a breach or ignore it and demand performance. If the repudiation is ignored, then continued performance by the promisee must be suspended if the performance would increase the damages of the promisor.

In a situation in which the date of performance has not passed and the only performance left is payment, the aggrieved party must wait until performance is due before filing suit (to allow the potentially breaching party to change his mind and perform). In other words, in this limited situation, anticipatory breach is inapplicable; the aggrieved party must wait for actual breach before filing suit.

c. Retraction of repudiation

Repudiation may be retracted until such time as the promisee (i) acts in reliance on the repudiation, (ii) signifies acceptance of the repudiation, or (iii) commences an action for breach of contract. Notice of the retraction must be sufficient enough to allow for the performance of the promisee's obligations.

d. Unilateral contracts

The doctrine of anticipatory repudiation *does **not** apply to unilateral contracts* and may not be used if the promisee has completed performance prior to the repudiation.

2. Anticipatory Repudiation under the UCC

According to the UCC, anticipatory repudiation occurs when there has been an **unequivocal refusal** of the buyer or seller to perform, or when a party creating reasonable grounds for insecurity fails to provide adequate assurances within 30 days of demand for assurances. UCC § 2-609. The repudiation can be retracted if the other party has not canceled the contract or materially changed position. Repudiation allows the nonrepudiating party to resort to any remedy given by the contract or code.

3. Prospective Inability to Perform

A party's expectations of performance may be diminished by an event that occurs after the contract was made.

> **EXAM NOTE:** On the exam, be reluctant to excuse a party from performing solely on the ground that the party does not expect counter-performance to be given.

Under the UCC, either party can demand assurance of performance if there are reasonable grounds for insecurity about the other party's ability or willingness to perform. Once such assurances are requested, performance may be suspended until they are provided. Failure to give adequate assurances within a reasonable time, not exceeding 30 days, can be treated as repudiation. UCC § 2-609.

a. Commercial standards for merchants

Between merchants, the reasonableness of grounds for insecurity and the adequacy of any assurance offered are determined according to commercial standards. Thus, for example, if a supplier writes to a manufacturer demanding assurances of financial solvency, and the manufacturer provides its latest audited financial statements as well as a satisfactory credit report from its banker, then that would likely constitute adequate assurances of its financial status.

b. Effect of acceptance

The acceptance of any improper delivery or payment does not preclude an aggrieved party from demanding adequate assurance of future performance.

C. REMEDIES: DAMAGES FOR BREACH OF CONTRACT

Remedies are meant to compensate the nonbreaching party for actual economic losses. Actual economic losses are calculated depending on how the contract was formed (e.g., through consideration or through promissory estoppel) and what type of contract it was (e.g., sale of goods versus services).

1. Expectation Damages

a. In general

Expectation damages are intended to put the injured party in the same position as if the contract had been performed. They are those damages that arise naturally and obviously from the breach and are normally measured by the market value of the promised performance less the consideration promised by the non-breaching party. Thus, to calculate expectation damages, subtract the contract price from the market value of performance. The market value of performance is whatever it reasonably costs to get the performance that was promised in the contract. Expectation damages must be foreseeable and the non-breaching party must be able to prove them with reasonable certainty.

Example: B breaches a contract with A to fix A's car for $500. A finds another mechanic, C, to fix A's car for $700, which is the market value of performance. A can recover $200 from B.

1) Construction contracts

In construction contracts, the general measure of damages for a contractor's failure to begin or to complete the building or other structure is the difference between the contract price and the cost of construction by another builder, plus compensation for delay in completion of the construction. The general measure of damages for the owner's failure to pay the contract price, in whole or in part, is the profits that the builder would have earned, plus any costs incurred by the builder, less the amount of any payments made by the owner to the contractor and any materials purchased by the contractor that are used by the contractor on another job.

2) Sale of goods contracts

Damages for failing to deliver goods are measured by the difference between the contract price and the market value of the goods (or the cost of cover).

3) Real estate contracts

Damages for failing to perform a real estate sales contract also are measured by the difference between the contract price and the market value.

4) Formula

The general expectation formula can be computed as follows:

Expectation Damages = loss in value + other loss − cost avoided − loss avoided

Loss in value is the difference between the performance that the non-breaching party should have received under the contract and what was actually received, if anything.

Other loss includes consequential and incidental damages, if any.

The cost avoided is the additional costs that the non-breaching party can avoid by rightfully discontinuing performance under the contract as a result of the other party's breach.

Loss avoided is the beneficial effect of the breach due to the non-breaching party's ability to salvage or reallocate resources that otherwise would have been devoted to performing under the contract. Loss avoided is subtracted only if the savings results from the injured party not having to perform rather than from some unrelated event. Restatement (Second) of Contracts § 347.

b. Partial performance

A partially performing party can generally recover for work performed, plus expectation damages for the work not yet performed.

> **Example:** B agrees to paint A's house for $500, which covers $400 in supplies and labor and $100 in profit. After B paints half of the house and incurs $200 in costs, A breaches. B can recover the $200 for costs already incurred and the $100 of profit, but not the remaining $200 for costs not yet incurred.

If at the time of a breach the only remaining duties of performance are (i) those of the party in breach and (ii) for the payment of money in installments not related to one another, then breach by nonperformance as to less than the whole, whether or not accompanied or followed by a repudiation, does not give rise to a claim for damages for total breach and is a partial breach of contract only. Restatement (Second) of Contracts § 243(3).

> **Example:** A borrows $10,000 from B. The loan is to be paid back in monthly installments with interest over a one-year period of time. A fails to make the first installment payment and tells B that he will be unable to make the other payments as well. B has a claim for partial breach of the contract but cannot sue for a total breach of the contract. (Note: Lenders circumvent this rule by including in the loan agreement an acceleration clause that causes the entire loan to become due upon the failure by the borrower to timely make an installment payment.)

c. Defective performance

1) Construction contracts

In construction contracts, damages for defective or incomplete construction are measured by the cost of repair or completion. The general measure of damages for failing to perform a construction contract is the difference between the contract price and the cost of construction by another builder.

2) Sale of goods contracts

By contrast, in contracts for the sale of goods, damages for nonconformity with the contract generally are measured by the difference between the value of the goods as warranted and the actual value of the tendered nonconforming goods.

The purpose of both measures is to place the plaintiff in as good a position as if the defendant had performed the contract according to its specifications.

d. Waste

Economic waste occurs when the amount of damages awarded is disproportional to any economic benefit or utility gained as a result of the award. If the award of expectation damages would result in economic waste, then courts may instead, at their discretion, award damages equal to diminution in value. *See Jacob & Youngs v. Kent,* 129 N.E. 889 (N.Y. 1921).

> **Example:** Landowner grants Mining Company a five-year license to remove coal from his property. In return for the license, Mining Company agreed to restore the property to its original state at the end of the five-year period. After five years, Mining Company refused to restore the land. The restoration work would cost $29,000, but, if completed, would result in only a $300 increase in the property's value. The court may elect to award only $300 in damages, instead of

the usual $29,000 expectation award. *Peevyhouse v. Garland Coal and Mining Co.,* 382 P.2d 109 (Okla. 1962).

However, if the breach is willful, and only completion of the contract will give the nonbreaching party the benefit of its bargain, then a court may award expectation damages even if that award would result in economic waste. *See Rock Island Improvement Co. v. Helmerich & Payne, Inc.,* 698 F.2d 175 (10th Cir. 1983).

2. Consequential Damages and Foreseeability

a. Consequential damages

Consequential damages are **reasonably foreseeable losses** to a nonbreaching party that go beyond expectation damages, such as loss of profits.

b. Foreseeability

Damages are recoverable if they were the natural and probable consequences of breach, or if they were "in the contemplation of the parties at the time the contract was made," or were otherwise foreseeable. *Hadley v. Baxendale,* 156 Eng. Rep. 145 (Ex. Ch. 1854).

Because it is assumed that a borrower will be able to obtain a substitute bank loan, the borrower's lost profit is considered unforeseeable at the time of contract formation.

c. Causation

A defendant can defend on the ground that the losses that the plaintiff seeks to recover would have occurred even if the defendant had not breached the contract.

d. Reasonable certainty

To recover damages, a plaintiff must prove the dollar amount of the damages with reasonable certainty. Courts are hesitant to award damages for lost profits, as they are difficult to prove. When lost profits are considered too speculative, such as with a new venture, courts often limit a party's recovery to reliance damages (i.e., reasonable expenditures made in connection with the contract).

e. UCC—Breach of warranty

While generally consequential damages for breach of warranty may be limited or excluded unless the limitation or exclusion is unconscionable, limitation of consequential damages for injury to the person in the case of consumer goods is prima facie unconscionable. Limitation of damages when the loss is commercial is not. UCC § 2-719(3).

> **EXAM NOTE:** Although courts are hesitant to award damages for lost profits and lost opportunities, such damages are still recoverable for breach of contract claims. Beware of questions on the exam that conclude in absolute terms that such damages are not recoverable. They are not likely, but they are still possible.

3. Liquidated Damages and Penalties

Liquidated damages are an amount contractually stipulated as a reasonable estimation of actual damages to be recovered by one party if the other party breaches. A term fixing unreasonably large liquidated damages is unenforceable on grounds of public policy as a penalty. A provision for liquidated damages is enforceable and not construed as a penalty if the amount of damages stipulated in the contract is reasonable in relation to either the actual damages suffered or the damages that might be anticipated at the time the contract was made. However, if the provision is construed as a penalty, then it is unenforceable.

When the contract contains a liquidated damages clause, the party seeking to repudiate that clause must show that the agreed-to damage is so exorbitant as to be in the nature of a penalty.

a. Enforceability

There is no fixed rule applicable to all liquidated damages provisions, and each is evaluated on its own facts and circumstances. To validate a liquidated damages clause, the following three-prong test must be met:

i) The **parties intended to agree** in advance to the settlement of damages that might arise from the breach;

ii) The **amount of liquidated damages was reasonable** at the time of contracting, bearing some relation to the damages that might be sustained; and

iii) **Actual damages would be uncertain** in amount and difficult to prove.

Bear Stearns Gov't Sec., Inc. v. Dow Corning Corp., 419 F.3d 543 (6th Cir. 2005).

Thus, if the liquidated damages are disproportionate to the actual damages, then the clause will not be enforced, and recovery will be limited to the actual damages proven.

b. Uncertainty of actual damages

When determining whether actual damages would be uncertain in amount and difficult to prove, courts look to the time of contracting, not to the time of breach. Additionally, the damages contained in a liquidated damages clause must be for a **specific amount for a specific breach**; the provision may not merely serve as a threat to secure performance or as a means to punish nonperformance. Although exculpatory language in the contract stating that the liquidated damages provision is not a penalty does not control, it should be given some weight.

4. Incidental Damages

Incidental damages may be awarded to the non-breaching party as compensation for commercially reasonable expenses incurred as a result of the other party's breach. In the sale of goods, such damages may include the cost of inspecting, transporting, caring for, or maintaining custody over goods.

5. Punitive Damages

Punitive damages are very rarely available in contract actions. Some statutes apply them for the purpose of punishing fraud, violation of fiduciary duty, and acts of bad faith, and for deterrence. Under the Restatement (Second) of Contracts § 355, punitive damages are not recoverable "unless the conduct constituting the breach is also a tort for which punitive damages [can be recovered]."

6. Nominal Damages

Damages do not need to be alleged in a cause of action for breach. If no damages are alleged or none are proved, the plaintiff is still entitled to a judgment for "nominal" damages (e.g., one dollar).

7. Mitigating Damages

A party to a contract must avoid or mitigate damages to the extent possible by taking such steps as to not involve undue risk, expense, or inconvenience. The non-breaching party is held to a standard of reasonable conduct in preventing loss.

Although often phrased as a "duty to mitigate damages," a non-breaching party's failure to mitigate does not give the breaching party a right to sue the non-breaching party for such failure; it only reduces the damages that may be recovered by the non-breaching party. For example, with regard to a sale of goods, a non-breaching buyer's failure to take reasonable steps to mitigate damages by buying substitute goods (i.e., cover) will prevent a claim for consequential damages but will not deprive the buyer of damages measured by the difference between the contract and market prices. In addition, the measure of damages for breach of a contract to lend money is the additional cost of obtaining a loan from another lender (e.g., the difference in cost over time between the interest rates of the original loan and the subsequent loan).

Note that reasonable expenses incurred as a result of efforts to mitigate damages can be recovered, even if the mitigation attempt was unsuccessful.

D. RESTITUTION AND RELIANCE RECOVERIES

Restitution awards the fair market value of the benefit conferred, while reliance damages are reasonable out-of-pocket losses by the non-breaching party.

1. Restitutionary Damages

Restitutionary damages restore to the plaintiff whatever benefit was conferred upon the defendant prior to the breach. Generally, the benefit may be measured by either the reasonable value of the defendant obtaining that benefit from another source or the increase in the defendant's wealth (e.g., the increase in value of property owned by the defendant) from having received that benefit. However, when justice requires, recovery may be limited to one of the two measurements. For example, if the plaintiff has breached a contract, recovery is generally limited to the increase in the defendant's wealth.

Under some circumstances, restitutionary damages may be recovered even though the plaintiff would have suffered a loss had the defendant not breached.

Thus, if A contracts with B to paint B's house for $500, and B repudiates the contract after A has done some, but not all, of the painting, and A shows that the fair value of the work that has been done is actually $1,000, most courts allow recovery of restitutionary damages ($1,000) on the theory that otherwise the defendant would be profiting from the breach.

If, however, at the time of the defendant's breach, the plaintiff has **fully performed the contract,** and the defendant owes only money and not some other kind of performance, then the plaintiff is not permitted to recover restitutionary damages and is limited to expectation damages (generally the contract price minus the cost of completion).

Restitutionary damages are also available in quasi-contract when there is no contract between the parties or when a contract is unenforceable, and a lack of any recovery would be unjust given that a benefit was conferred on the other party. Recovery is limited to the fair value of the benefit conferred.

2. Reliance Damages

Reliance damages may be recovered if a non-breaching party incurs expenses in reasonable reliance upon the promise that the other party would perform. Unlike with restitutionary damages, with reliance damages, there is no requirement that the defendant benefit from the plaintiff's expenditures. **A party cannot recover both reliance and expectation damages.**

The injured party can choose to pursue reliance damages instead of expectation damages, but those damages are then mitigated by any losses that the plaintiff would have sustained if the contract had been performed. Restatement (Second) of Contracts § 349.

E. SPECIFIC PERFORMANCE AND DECLARATORY JUDGMENT

1. Specific Performance

When damages are an inadequate remedy, the non-breaching party may pursue the equitable remedy of specific performance.

a. Factors considered

In determining whether damages are adequate, consider the:

i) Difficulty of proving damages with reasonable certainty;

ii) Difficulty of procuring a suitable substitute performance by means of money awarded as damages; and

iii) Likelihood that an award of damages will be collected.

b. Real property

Contracts involving the transfer of an interest in real property may be enforced by an order of specific performance because every parcel of **real property is considered unique.**

c. UCC

Specific performance may be granted when the goods are rare or unique, or in other circumstances—such as for breach of a requirements contract when there is not another convenient supplier. UCC § 2-716.

d. Limitations

Even if the remedy of damages is inadequate, specific performance will not be granted when the court cannot supervise enforcement. Thus, courts rarely grant specific enforcement of contracts for personal services, although they may restrain the breaching party from working for another when the contract contains a noncompete clause.

e. Defenses

Equitable defenses, such as laches (prejudicial delay in bringing the action) or unclean hands (when the non-breaching party is guilty of some wrongdoing in the transaction at issue) may be raised by the breaching party. A party may also wish to enter an injunction against the breaching party to enforce the contract.

2. Declaratory Judgment

If the rights and obligations of the parties under a contract are unclear, and an actual dispute exists between the parties concerning those rights and obligations, then either party may bring a declaratory judgment action to obtain an adjudication of those rights and duties. Declaratory judgment is not available, however, to resolve moot issues or theoretical problems that have not risen to an actual dispute.

F. REMEDIES UNDER THE UCC

The following sections more specifically address the remedies that are available to buyers and sellers under the UCC. These rules are frequently tested on the MBE.

1. Buyer's Remedies

When the seller's time for performance arises, the seller may:

i) Do **nothing** (breach by the seller);

ii) Make a **nonconforming tender** (breach by the seller); or

iii) Make a **conforming tender** (performance by the seller).

a. Failure to tender

Under the UCC, the buyer has several alternative remedies if the seller fails to tender the goods.

1) Damages

The buyer may recover the market price minus the contract price. The market price is the price that existed at the time of the breach at the place where tender was to occur under the contract. UCC § 2-713.

The UCC also permits recovery for incidental and consequential damages resulting from the seller's breach. Incidental damages are damages that are incidental to the seller's failure to perform, such as the costs of warehousing, transportation, inspection, etc. Consequential damages are any losses resulting from general or particular requirements and needs of which the seller, at the time of contracting, had reason to know and which could not be reasonably prevented by purchasing substitute goods or otherwise.

Consequential damages may be limited or excluded under the UCC unless such limitation or exclusion would be unconscionable. UCC § 2-719(3).

2) Cover

Alternatively, the buyer may purchase similar goods elsewhere and recover the replacement price minus the contract price. UCC § 2-712.

3) Specific performance

The buyer may demand specific performance for **unique** goods. In addition, specific performance may be had in other proper circumstances. An inability to cover is strong evidence of such circumstances. The court may grant specific performance on terms and conditions that the court deems just. UCC § 2-716(1).

4) Replevin

a) Payment by the buyer

When the buyer has made at least partial payment for identified goods, the buyer can obtain the undelivered goods from the seller if:

i) The seller becomes insolvent within 10 days of receiving the first payment from the buyer; or

ii) The goods were for family, personal, or household purposes, and the seller has repudiated or failed to deliver the goods as required by contract.

To obtain the goods, the buyer must tender any unpaid portion of the price to the seller. UCC § 2-502.

b) Buyer's inability to cover

The buyer can also obtain identified, undelivered goods from the seller if:

i) The buyer is unable to affect cover;

ii) The circumstances reasonably indicate that such effect will be unavailing; or

iii) The goods have been shipped under reservation, and satisfaction of the security interest in the goods has been made or tendered.

UCC § 2-716(3).

b. Nonconforming tender

Under the UCC, if either the tender or the goods are nonconforming, then the buyer has the **right to accept or reject** all or part of the goods. UCC § 2-601.

The buyer has the **right to inspect** the goods before deciding whether to accept or reject. Payment does not constitute acceptance if there is no right of inspection before payment (e.g., C.O.D., C.I.F., or C & F contracts). UCC § 2-513.

1) Rejection

a) Valid rejection

A valid rejection requires that the buyer:

   i)   Give notice to the seller;

   ii) Within a reasonable time; and

   iii) Before acceptance.

UCC § 2-602. Upon a rightful rejection, the buyer is entitled to a return of any payments made on the goods. UCC § 2-711(3).

b) Retain possession

The buyer must retain possession of rejected goods for a reasonable time to allow for the seller to reclaim them. UCC § 2-602(2).

c) Perishable and non-perishable goods

In the absence of other instructions from the seller, the buyer may store non-perishable goods at the seller's expense, reship them to the seller, or sell them for the seller's account. If the goods are perishable and the seller has no local agent to whom they can be returned, in the absence of other instructions from the seller, the buyer is required to sell the goods on the seller's behalf. UCC § 2-603.

d) Remedies

The same remedies are available to the buyer after rejection as if no tender was made by the seller, i.e., damages (including incidental and consequential damages, unless properly limited or excluded), cover, specific performance, or replevin.

Need for notice: A failure to give notice of the breach to the seller within a reasonable time after the buyer discovers or should have discovered the breach will preclude the buyer from any remedies.

i)   Conversion

The remedy for conversion is the fair market value of the goods at the time of the conversion.

2) Acceptance

Under the UCC, the buyer accepts goods by:

   i)   **Expressly stating** acceptance;

   ii) **Using** the goods; or

   iii) **Failing to reject** the goods.

UCC § 2-606.

The buyer can revoke acceptance (which amounts to rejection) if acceptance was with a reasonable expectation that the seller would cure and the seller did not cure or if the defect was hidden. The revocation must occur within a reasonable time after the nonconformity or defect was or should have been discovered, and notice must be given to the seller. UCC § 2-608.

A buyer's original refusal to accept may be withdrawn by a later acceptance if the seller indicates that he is holding the tender open. UCC § 2-601. However, if the buyer attempts to accept after his original rejection caused the seller to arrange for other disposition of the goods, then the buyer is liable for any ensuing damage. The buyer is liable even if the seller chooses to treat his action as acceptance rather than conversion. UCC § 2-601 cmt. 2.

Note that a buyer's attempts in good faith to dispose of defective goods when the seller fails to give instructions within a reasonable time are not to be regarded as an acceptance.

3) Right to cure

The seller has a right to cure a defective tender if:

i) The **time for performance** under the contract has not yet elapsed; or

ii) The seller had **reasonable grounds** to believe that the buyer would accept despite the nonconformity.

The seller must give notice of the intent to cure and make a new tender of conforming goods. If the seller had reasonable grounds to believe that the buyer would accept despite the nonconformity, the tender must be made within a reasonable time. Once cured, the tender is considered proper and valid. UCC § 2-508.

2. Seller's Remedies

a. Right to price upon acceptance

Under the UCC, the price is due after the goods are physically delivered to the buyer and the buyer has an opportunity to inspect, unless the contract provides otherwise. If the buyer refuses to pay the price, the seller may sue for the price set forth in the contract. If the contract omits a price term, then the UCC supplies a reasonable price at the time for delivery. If the contract provides that the parties will agree to a price in the future and they do not so agree, then the UCC would impose a reasonable price. UCC § 2-305.

b. Right to reclaim goods

1) Insolvent buyer

When an insolvent buyer receives goods on credit, and the seller learns that the buyer is insolvent, the seller may reclaim the goods, provided a demand is made **within 10 days** after the buyer's receipt of the goods. This 10-day limitation does not apply if the buyer has misrepresented solvency to the seller in writing within three months before delivery. Otherwise, the seller cannot base a right to reclaim goods on the buyer's fraudulent or innocent misrepresentation of solvency or of intent to pay. In addition, this right is subordinate to the rights of a buyer in the ordinary course or other good-faith purchaser, and, if exercised, precludes all other remedies with respect to the reclaimed goods. UCC § 2-702.

> **Pre-delivery insolvency:** As a condition for the seller to reclaim goods from a buyer, the buyer must have received the goods on credit while insolvent. If the buyer becomes insolvent **after** delivery, then the seller may not reclaim the goods.

2) C.O.D. sale

In a C.O.D. (cash on delivery) sale, the seller can reclaim the goods if the buyer's check bounces. UCC §§ 2-511, 512.

c. Stoppage of goods in transit

1) Buyer's breach

A seller can stop the goods in transit because of the buyer's breach; goods can be stopped in transit only if shipped in large-sized (e.g., carload, truckload) lots. The seller cannot stop goods in transit once the:

i)   Buyer has received the goods;

ii)   Carrier or warehouseman has acknowledged the buyer's rights;

iii) Goods have been reshipped by the carrier; or

iv) Title has been given or negotiated to the buyer.

UCC § 2-705(1),(2).

2) Buyer's insolvency

If the buyer becomes insolvent before the delivery of the goods, then the seller can stop goods in transit and refuse delivery except for cash. UCC § 2-705(1).

> **Compare buyer's breach:** When a buyer is insolvent, the seller can stop goods in transit, regardless of the size of the shipment.

d. Wrongful rejection

If the buyer wrongfully rejects, then the seller has three alternative remedies and would also be entitled to incidental damages and lost profits. UCC § 2-703.

1) Collect damages

The seller would ordinarily be entitled to the contract price minus the market price at the time and place for tender, together with any incidental damages, less any expenses saved as a result of the buyer's breach. UCC § 2-708(1).

If that measure does not put the seller in as good a position as performance would have done, then the measure of damages will be the profit (including reasonable overhead) that the seller would have made from full performance by the buyer, together with any incidental damages, less any payments received or the proceeds of a resale of the goods. UCC § 2-708(2).

2) Resell the goods

If the seller elects to resell and sue for the contract price minus the resale price, then the resale must be (i) only of goods identified to the contract and (ii) commercially reasonable. UCC § 2-706.

3) Recover the price

The seller can recover the price after rejection only if the goods are not sellable in the seller's ordinary course of business. UCC § 2-709.

The price is the price as defined in the contract or, if no price is defined in the contract, a reasonable price. The seller can retain deposits paid by the buyer up to the amount stated in a liquidated-damages clause, or, in the absence of such a provision, 20% of the value of performance, or $500, whichever is less.

4) Incidental damages

Note that in **addition to** any of the remedies listed above, the seller is entitled to recover incidental damages (including storage and shipping costs). UCC § 2-710.

5) Lost profits

In some circumstances, a seller cannot be made whole through resale at the contract price. This is true for volume sellers (those sellers who have an unlimited supply of the goods and who make a profit per item). Although they can resell the goods at the same price as the contract price, they have lost the opportunity to sell them in the first instance when the seller breached or repudiated. They are, therefore, entitled to those lost profits. To qualify as a "lost volume" seller, the seller needs to show only that it could have supplied both the breaching purchaser and the resale purchaser with the goods. In general, the measure of lost profit would be the list price minus the cost to the dealer or manufacturer. UCC § 2-708(2).

> **Example:** S, a high-volume maker of personal computers, contracts to sell 100 computers to B for $100,000 (their list price). B subsequently repudiates the contract, and S resells the computers to another customer. S can recover its lost profit (i.e., the list price of $100,000 minus its manufacturing cost), as well as any incidental damages from B.

3. Risk of Loss

a. General rules—non-identified goods, no breach

If the parties do not otherwise agree, if goods that have not been identified are damaged or destroyed without the fault of either party to the contract, then the risk of loss is generally on the seller until the seller satisfies the contractual delivery obligations. Upon the happening of that event, the risk of loss shifts to the buyer. UCC § 2-509.

1) Goods to be shipped by a third-party carrier

If the contract requires or authorizes the seller to ship the goods by carrier, the event necessary to shift the risk of loss is dependent upon whether the contract is a "shipment" or "destination" contract.

a) Shipment contract

If the contract does not specify the place of delivery, it is a shipment contract, and the risk of loss passes to the buyer when the seller gives possession of the goods to the carrier and makes a proper contract for their shipment. The UCC considers this the "normal" agreement involving a "normal" risk of loss. UCC § 2-509, cmt 5.

b) Destination contract

If the contract does specify delivery at a particular location, it is a destination contract, and risk of loss passes to the buyer when the seller tenders at the place specified in the contract.

> **Example:** B orders a computer from S that is identical to a display model shown on the floor of S's store. The contract specifies that the computer is to be tendered by S at B's place of residence. In transit, the computer is destroyed by the shipping company through no fault of S. S is still required to perform the contract.

> Note that "F.O.B." agreements (i.e., agreements that specify the location for delivery) additionally require the seller to give **notice** to the buyer that the goods are with the carrier before the risk of loss shifts. *See* § VII.D.2.b.4)b) Shipment contract, *supra*.

2) Goods held by a bailee

When goods that are held by a bailee are to be transferred without being moved, the risk of loss generally passes to the buyer on the buyer's receipt of a negotiable document of title covering the goods or on acknowledgment by the bailee of the buyer's right to possession of the goods.

3) All other cases

Unless the parties agree otherwise, in other cases (e.g., the buyer picks up the goods from the seller or the seller delivers the goods to the buyer), risk of loss passes to the buyer upon the taking of physical possession if the seller is a merchant; otherwise, risk passes on tender of delivery.

b. Identified goods, no breach

If the **contract deals with identified goods** (e.g., a specific painting or specifically identified items of inventory), then the seller is excused if the goods are totally destroyed without the seller's fault prior to the risk of loss being shifted to the buyer. Neither party is required to perform; neither party has breached. If the specifically identified goods are damaged, but not totally destroyed, then the contract is avoided unless the buyer chooses to take the goods at a reduced price without any other claim against the seller. UCC § 2-613.

c. Effect of breach of contract

1) Seller's Breach

If the seller delivers nonconforming goods, the risk of loss remains on the seller until the buyer accepts or there is a cure. If the buyer rightfully revokes acceptance, the risk of loss shifts back to the seller to the extent of any lack of insurance coverage by the buyer.

2) Buyer's Breach

If the **buyer repudiates or breaches** after the goods have been identified but before the risk of loss shifts, then the risk of loss is immediately shifted to the buyer to the extent of any lack of insurance coverage by the seller.

> **EXAM NOTE:** When approaching risk-of-loss problems, first ask whether the contract sets forth the risk of loss. If it does, the agreement controls. If not, ask whether there is a breach or repudiation by either party. If so, the breaching party usually bears the risk. If not, determine whether the contract is a shipment or destination contract and continue the analysis under § 2-509.

4. Insurable Interest in Goods

a. Seller's insurable interest

The seller of goods retains an insurable interest in the goods as long as the seller retains title to the goods or has a security interest in them. Unless the contract specifies otherwise, the title passes from the seller to the buyer when the seller completes his delivery obligations. At that point, the seller's insurable interest ceases unless the seller retains a security interest in the goods. When the seller alone identifies the goods, the seller may substitute other goods for those identified until default, insolvency, or notification to the buyer that the identification is final. UCC §§ 2-401; 2-501(2).

b. Buyer's insurable interest

The buyer of goods obtains an insurable interest in the goods as soon as the goods are identified to the contract. Identification can be made at any time by the parties' explicit agreement. In the absence of such an agreement, identification occurs when the contract is made if it is for the sale of goods already existing and identified; for future goods, identification occurs when the goods are shipped, marked, or otherwise designated by the seller as the goods to which the contract refers. UCC § 2-501(1).

5. Title and Good-Faith Purchasers

a. Entrusting provisions

The UCC provides that entrustment of goods by the owner to one who sells goods of that kind gives the transferee the power to convey good title to a buyer in the ordinary course. A "buyer in the ordinary course" is one who in good faith and without knowledge of a third party's ownership rights or security interest buys goods from someone selling goods of that kind. UCC § 2-403.

"Entrusting" includes any delivery and acquiescence in possession regardless of any condition expressed between the parties and regardless of whether the procurement of the entrusting or the possessor's disposition of the goods have been larcenous. UCC § 2-403(3).

b. Voidable title

When the true owner of goods sells them to another, but the sale is voidable because of fraud, because of lack of capacity, or because it was a cash sale and the buyer failed to pay or paid with a dishonored check, the buyer may transfer good title to a good-faith purchaser. UCC § 2-403.

6. Statute of Limitations on Breach of Sales Contract

a. Period of limitations

Under Article 2, an action for breach of any sales contract must be commenced within **four years** after the cause of action accrues.

b. When a cause of action accrues

In general, a cause of action accrues when the breach occurs, regardless of whether the aggrieved party knows of the breach. A breach of warranty accrues when delivery is made. If a warranty expressly extends to the future performance of the goods, the cause of action will accrue when the breach is or should have been discovered by the aggrieved party.

c. Modification of limitations period

By their original agreement, the parties may reduce the four-year limitations period of Article 2 to not less than one year, but they may not extend it.

Criminal Law

CRIMINAL LAW

Table of Contents

I.   GENERAL PRINCIPLES 1

A. *ACTUS REUS*—ACTS AND OMISSIONS 1

   1. VOLUNTARY ACT 1

   2. FAILURE TO ACT WHEN DUTY EXISTS 1

B. *MENS REA*—STATE OF MIND 2

   1. SPECIFIC INTENT CRIMES 2

   2. MALICE CRIMES 2

   3. GENERAL INTENT CRIMES 2

      a. Transferred intent 3

   4. MINORITY VIEW: MODEL PENAL CODE 3

      a. Purposely 3

      b. Knowingly or willfully 3

      c. Recklessly 3

      d. Negligently 4

      e. *Mens rea* not stated 4

   5. STRICT-LIABILITY CRIMES 4

      a. Public welfare offense 4

      b. Presumption against strict liability 4

   6. VICARIOUS LIABILITY 4

   7. CAUSATION 5

   8. MISTAKE AS A DEFENSE 5

      a. Mistake of fact 5

      b. Mistake of law 6

C. JURISDICTION 6

   1. CONSTITUTIONAL LIMITS ON AUTHORITY 6

      a. State authority 6

      b. Federal authority 6

      c. State and federal authority 6

      2. TERRITORIAL CONSIDERATIONS 7

          a. Federal 7

          b. State authority 7

  D. PARTIES TO A CRIME 7

      1. PRINCIPAL 7

      2. ACCOMPLICE LIABILITY 8

          a. Accomplice's status 8

          b. Accomplice's criminal liability 8

          c. Withdrawal 8

          d. Persons not accomplices 9

          e. Effect of the principal's status 9

      3. ACCESSORY AFTER THE FACT 9

          a. Failure to report a crime 9

          b. Misprision 9

          c. Compounding a crime 9

  E. RESPONSIBILITY 9

      1. INSANITY 9

          a. *M'Naghten* test 10

          b. Irresistible-impulse test 10

          c. *Durham* rule 10

          d. Model Penal Code test 10

          e. Burden of proof 10

      2. INTOXICATION 10

          a. Voluntary intoxication 11

          b. Involuntary intoxication 11

      3. IMMATURITY/INFANCY 11

  F. TYPES OF CRIMES 11

II. HOMICIDE 12

  A. DEFINITION 12

      1. KILLING A PERSON 12

      2. CAUSATION 12

          a. Actual cause 12

           b.   **Proximate cause** 13

           c.   **Year-and-a-day rule** 13

    B. TYPES OF HOMICIDE 13

        1. MURDER 13

           a.   **Intent to kill** 14

           b.   **Intent to inflict serious bodily harm** 14

           c.   **Depraved heart** 14

           d.   **Felony murder** 14

        2. STATUTORY CRIMES OF MURDER 16

           a.   **First-degree murder** 16

           b.   **Second-degree murder** 16

        3. VOLUNTARY MANSLAUGHTER 17

           a.   **"Heat of passion"** 17

           b.   **Causation** 17

           c.   **Imperfect defense** 17

           d.   **Transferred provocation** 18

        4. INVOLUNTARY MANSLAUGHTER 18

           a.   **Criminal negligence** 18

           b.   **Unlawful act** 18

           c.   **Causation** 18

III. OTHER CRIMES 19

    A. CRIMES AGAINST PROPERTY 19

        1. LARCENY 19

           a.   **Trespass** 19

           b.   **Taking** 19

           c.   **Carrying away (asportation)** 19

           d.   **Personal property** 19

           e.   **Another's property** 20

           f.   **Intent to permanently deprive** 22

        2. LARCENY BY TRICK 23

           a.   **False representation of material present or past fact** 23

           b.   **Reliance by the victim** 23

3. **FORGERY** 23

    a. **Fraudulent** 23

    b. **Making** 24

    c. **False writing** 24

    d. **Apparent legal significance** 24

4. **EMBEZZLEMENT** 24

    a. **Conversion** 24

    b. **Intent to defraud** 24

    c. **Type of property** 25

    d. **Another's property** 25

    e. **Lawful possession** 25

5. **FALSE PRETENSES** 25

    a. **Title must pass** 25

    b. **Type of property** 25

    c. **False factual representation** 25

    d. **Reliance by the victim** 26

    e. **Intent to defraud** 26

6. **ROBBERY** 26

    a. **Elements of larceny** 26

    b. **From the person or presence** 26

    c. **By force or intimidation** 26

    d. **Merger** 27

7. **EXTORTION** 27

    a. **Common law** 27

    b. **Modern approach** 27

8. **BURGLARY** 27

    a. **Breaking** 27

    b. **Entering** 28

    c. **Dwelling of another** 28

    d. **Nighttime** 28

    e. **Specific intent to commit a felony** 29

9. **ARSON** 29

        a. Malice 29

        b. Burning 29

        c. Another's dwelling 29

    10. POSSESSION OFFENSES..30

    11. RECEIVING STOLEN GOODS 30

    12. LEGISLATIVE CHANGES TO THEFT CRIMES 30

B. CRIMES AGAINST THE PERSON 30

    1. BATTERY..30

        a. Unlawful 30

        b. Application of force 30

        c. To the person of another 31

        d. Requisite intent 31

        e. Consent defense 31

        f. Aggravated battery 31

    2. ASSAULT 31

        a. Attempted battery 31

        b. Fear of harm 31

        c. Consent defense 32

        d. Aggravated assault 32

    3. MAYHEM 32

    4. KIDNAPPING 32

        a. Unlawful 32

        b. Confinement 32

        c. Against the victim's will 32

        d. Movement..32

        e. Hidden location 33

        f. Enhanced punishment..33

    5. FALSE IMPRISONMENT 33

        a. Unlawful 33

        b. Confinement 33

        c. Consent 33

C. RAPE AND OTHER SEX CRIMES 33

        1. RAPE 33

             a. Unlawful—exclusion of husband 34

             b. Sexual intercourse 34

             c. With a female 34

             d. Without consent 34

             e. Intent 34

        2. STATUTORY RAPE 34

        3. ADULTERY AND FORNICATION 35

        4. CRIMES AGAINST NATURE 35

        5. INCEST 35

        6. BIGAMY 35

        7. SEDUCTION 35

    D. PERJURY AND BRIBERY 35

        1. PERJURY 35

        2. SUBORNATION OF PERJURY 35

        3. BRIBERY 36

IV. **INCHOATE CRIMES** 36

    A. MERGER 36

    B. SOLICITATION 36

        1. ENCOURAGEMENT 36

        2. RELATIONSHIP TO OTHER CRIMES 36

        3. DEFENSES TO SOLICITATION 37

             a. Renunciation 37

             b. Factual impossibility 37

    C. CONSPIRACY 37

        1. AGREEMENT 37

        2. NUMBER OF CONSPIRATORS 37

             a. Feigned agreement 38

             b. Protected by statute 38

             c. Wharton Rule 38

             d. Corporation and its agents 38

             e. Prosecution of other conspirators 38

        f. **Spouses as co-conspirators** 38

    3. **UNLAWFUL PURPOSE** 38

    4. **SPECIFIC INTENT** 38

    5. **OVERT ACT REQUIREMENT** 39

    6. **SCOPE OF CONSPIRACY** 39

        a. **Crimes committed by co-conspirators** 39

        b. **Multiple crimes, single conspiracy** 39

        c. **Unknown conspirators, single conspiracy** 39

    7. **IMPOSSIBILITY** 40

    8. **WITHDRAWAL** 40

        a. **Effect on liability for conspiracy** 40

        b. **Effect on liability for substantive crimes** 40

    9. **TERMINATION** 40

    10. **PUNISHMENT** 40

D. **ATTEMPT** 41

    1. **SUBSTANTIAL STEP TEST** 41

        a. **Preparatory acts** 41

        b. **"Dangerous proximity" test** 41

    2. **SPECIFIC INTENT** 41

    3. **IMPOSSIBILITY** 42

    4. **ABANDONMENT** 42

    5. **PROSECUTION AND PUNISHMENT** 42

V. **DEFENSES** 42

A. **GENERALLY** 42

    1. **JUSTIFICATION AND EXCUSE** 42

    2. **MISTAKE OF FACT** 42

B. **SPECIFIC DEFENSES** 43

    1. **SELF-DEFENSE** 43

        a. **Deadly force** 43

        b. **Nondeadly force** 43

        c. **Retreat** 43

        d. **Imperfect right of self-defense** 43

    e. Aggressor's right to use self-defense...43

2. DEFENSE OF OTHERS 43

3. DEFENSE OF PROPERTY 44

4. ARREST..44

    a. Right to arrest 44

    b. Use of force to arrest...44

    c. Resisting unlawful arrest 44

5. PREVENTION OF CRIMES...44

6. PUBLIC AUTHORITY...44

7. PARENTAL AUTHORITY 45

8. DURESS 45

9. NECESSITY 45

10. CONSENT...45

    a. Bodily injury 45

    b. Ineffective consent 46

11. ENTRAPMENT 46

    a. Subjective approach...46

    b. Objective approach 46

12. ALIBI 46

CRIMINAL LAW

I. GENERAL PRINCIPLES

The elements of a criminal offense include the *mens rea*, or guilty mind; the *actus reus*, the bad or unlawful act; and causation. With the exception of strict liability crimes, which have no *mens rea*, every statute defining a substantive criminal offense proscribes a particular *mens rea* and *actus reus* that must be proved by the prosecution beyond a reasonable doubt for criminal liability to result.

A. *ACTUS REUS*—ACTS AND OMISSIONS

Before there can be a crime, there must be a criminal act (*actus reus*). The criminal act must be a voluntary, affirmative act that causes a criminally proscribed result. The act requirement may also be satisfied by an "omission" or failure to act under circumstances imposing a legal duty to act. A bad thought standing alone cannot result in criminal liability.

1. Voluntary Act

The criminal act must be physical and voluntary. Actions during unconsciousness, sleep, or hypnosis are not voluntary. Other acts that are not considered voluntary are reflexive or convulsive acts as well as conduct that is not the product of the actor's determination.

Example: Person A pushes Person B into a bystander, injuring the bystander. Person B cannot be held criminally liable.

If an epileptic knows of the possibility of a seizure and engages in the voluntary act of driving a car, has a seizure while driving, and causes a fatal accident, then the epileptic is criminally responsible.

Example: An epileptic may still be criminally responsible if (i) he knows of the possibility of seizure and (ii) the last act was voluntary.

The best example of when liability is not generally imposed is for acts committed while sleepwalking.

2. Failure to Act When Duty Exists

A legal duty to act and the failure to do so results in criminal liability in these five instances:

   i)   Imposed by statute (e.g., the obligation to file a tax return);

   ii) Contract (e.g., a lifeguard saving a drowning person);

   iii) Special relationship (e.g., a parent's duty to her child or the duty to one's spouse);

   iv) Detrimental undertaking (e.g., leaving a victim in worse condition after treatment); and

   v)   Causation (e.g., failing to aid after causing a victim's peril).

The defendant must have knowledge of the facts giving rise to the duty to act and yet fail to act. Additionally, it must be reasonably possible for the defendant to perform the duty.

Contrast absence of a duty: When there is not a duty to act, a defendant is not criminally liable because she fails to help others in trouble. A mere bystander has no duty to act.

B. *MENS REA*—STATE OF MIND

Mens rea is the requirement of a guilty mind or legally proscribed mental state that a defendant must possess to commit a crime. Except for strict liability crimes, a crime is committed when a criminal act (*actus reus*) is coupled with a guilty mind—both the mental and physical elements exist at the same time. Strict liability crimes have no *mens rea* requirement and require only an *actus reus*.

1. Specific Intent Crimes

Specific intent crimes require that the defendant possess **a subjective desire, specific objective, or knowledge to accomplish a prohibited result**. When dealing with specific intent crimes, it is necessary to identify specific intent for two reasons. First, the prosecution must prove the specific intent in order to prosecute the defendant; second, certain defenses (e.g., voluntary intoxication and unreasonable mistake of fact) are applicable only to specific intent crimes.

The specific intent crimes include:

i) **F**irst-degree murder;

ii) **I**nchoate offenses (attempt, solicitation, conspiracy);

iii) **A**ssault with intent to commit a battery; and

iv) **T**heft offenses (larceny, larceny by trick, false pretenses, embezzlement, forgery, burglary, robbery).

EXAM NOTE: A simple way to remember the specific intent crimes is by using the mnemonic "FIAT." Whenever a fact pattern defines the crime as requiring "the intent to...," the crime is a specific intent crime.

2. Malice Crimes

The crimes of common-law murder and arson require malice, **a reckless disregard of a high risk of harm**. Although these two crimes appear to have an "intent" requirement (e.g., intent to kill), malice requires only a criminal act without excuse, justification, or mitigation. Intent can be inferred from the accomplishment of the act.

3. General Intent Crimes

General intent crimes require only the **intent to perform an act** that is unlawful. Generally, acts done knowingly, recklessly, or negligently under the Model Penal Code are general intent crimes. Examples include battery, rape, kidnapping, and false imprisonment.

Motive is not the same as intent. The motive is the reason or explanation for the crime and is immaterial to the substantive criminal offense.

a. Transferred intent

When a defendant acts with an intent to cause harm to one person or object and that act directly results in harm to another person or object, the defendant can be liable for the harm caused under the doctrine of transferred intent.

> **Example:** D points a gun at A, intending to shoot and kill A, but accidentally shoots and kills B instead. D is guilty of two crimes: the murder of B under the doctrine of transferred intent and the attempted murder of A.

Transferred intent, also known as the unintended victim rule, is usually confined to homicide, battery, and arson. Any defenses that the defendant could assert against the intended victim (e.g., self-defense) may also transfer to the unintended victim.

> The Model Penal Code, while not specifically recognizing the doctrine of transferred intent, does recognize liability when purposely or knowingly causing a particular result is an element of an offense. This element can be established even if the actual result is not within the purpose or contemplation of the defendant, so long as the result differs from the intended or contemplated result only insofar as (i) a different person or different property is harmed or (ii) the contemplated injury or harm would have been more serious or more extensive than the harm actually caused. MPC § 203.2(2).

4. Minority View: Model Penal Code

A crime defined by statute generally states the requisite *mens rea*. The following levels of culpability are based on the Model Penal Code ("MPC"). The MPC is the minority view. The MBE tests the common-law majority position unless otherwise expressly stated in the question. The MPC has no application to federal law. The following mental states are defined by the MPC:

a. Purposely

When a defendant acts "purposely," his conscious objective is to engage in the conduct or to cause a certain result. MPC § 2.02(2)(a).

b. Knowingly or willfully

"Knowingly" or "willfully" requires that the defendant be **aware that his conduct is of the nature required by the crime** or that circumstances required by the crime exist. In other words, the defendant must be aware or know that **the result is practically certain to occur** based on his conduct. MPC § 2.02(2)(b).

c. Recklessly

"Recklessly" requires the defendant **to act with a conscious disregard of a substantial and unjustifiable risk** that a material element of a crime exists or will result from his conduct. The risk must constitute a gross deviation from the standard of conduct of a law-abiding person. MPC § 2.02(2)(c). Mere realization of the risk is not enough.

d. Negligently

A defendant acts "negligently" when that defendant should be aware of a substantial and unjustifiable risk that a material element of a crime exists or will result from his conduct. The risk must constitute a gross deviation from the standard of care of a reasonable person in the same situation. MPC § 2.02(2)(d). Furthermore, similarly to tort law, violation of a statute or ordinance may be evidence of liability.

e. *Mens rea* not stated

If the requisite *mens rea* is not stated in a criminal statute, it is established if the defendant acted purposely, knowingly, or recklessly. If the *mens rea* does not state the culpable mind applicable to all material elements of the crime, then the *mens rea* applicable to one material element is applicable to all material elements, unless noted to the contrary in the statute. MPC § 2.02(3),(4).

5. Strict-Liability Crimes

A strict-liability crime does not require a *mens rea*, rather, proof of the *actus reus* is sufficient for a conviction. Examples of strict-liability crimes include statutory rape; bigamy; regulatory offenses for public welfare; regulation of food, drugs, and firearms; and selling liquor to minors.

a. Public welfare offense

A public welfare offense is a strict-liability crime for which no *mens rea* is required. Conduct that is subject to stringent public regulation includes that which could seriously threaten the public's health or safety or is inherently dangerous.

Examples: Typical examples include adulteration of food or drugs, regulation of waste disposal, and selling liquor to minors.

b. Presumption against strict liability

Criminal offenses requiring no *mens rea* are generally disfavored. *United States v. United States Gypsum, Co.,* 438 U.S. 422, 438 (1978). Thus, courts have traditionally held that there must be some clear indication of congressional intent, express or implied, to dispense with *mens rea* as an element of the crime. In determining legislative intent, courts will often consider the severity of the associated penalty, finding crimes with relatively light penalties to be strict liability offenses, and those with more severe penalties (such as felony crimes) to have a *mens rea* element. *Staples v. United States,* 511 U.S. 600 (1994).

6. Vicarious Liability

Vicarious liability differs from strict liability in that strict-liability crimes require a personal act on the part of the defendant (*actus reus*) but not mental fault (*mens rea*). Conversely, vicarious liability crimes do not require an *actus reus*, but they do retain a *mens rea* requirement. Many times courts impose vicarious liability for strict-liability crimes. However, there generally is no indication that the legislature intended for vicarious liability to apply in strict-liability offenses. Further, imprisonment for a faultless crime may have constitutional due-process implications.

Thus, generally, vicarious-liability crimes are limited to regulatory crimes, and punishment is limited to fines.

When dealing with corporations, common law held that corporations had no criminal liability because a corporation could not form the necessary *mens rea*. Modern statutes, on the other hand, impose vicarious liability on corporations when the offensive act is performed by an agent of the corporation acting within the scope of his employment or when the act is performed by a high-ranking corporate agent who likely represents corporate policy. Under the MPC, a corporation may be held criminally liable if (i) the corporation fails to discharge a specific duty imposed by law, (ii) the board of directors or a high-ranking agent of the corporation acting within the scope of his employment authorizes or recklessly tolerates the offensive act, or (iii) the legislative purpose statutorily imposes liability on a corporation for a specific act. The individual agent of the corporation who violated the statute may also be held criminally liable, and the corporation's conviction does not preclude conviction of the individual. MPC § 2.07.

7. Causation

When intent is required, the criminal act must occur as a result of the intent. In other words, the defendant's act must cause the particular result made unlawful by statute.

8. Mistake as a Defense

a. Mistake of fact

1) Negation of intent

Mistake of fact may negate criminal intent but it must be an "honest mistake." The defense applies differently between specific- and general-intent crimes. Mistake of fact is never a defense to a strict-liability crime because strict-liability offenses do not have a *mens rea*.

2) Reasonableness of mistake

a) Specific-intent crimes

A mistake of fact is a defense to a specific-intent crime, even if the mistake is unreasonable.

> **Example:** An athlete takes an expensive gold watch from a table mistakenly thinking that it was her inexpensive black plastic sports watch. Even though the athlete's mistake of fact is unreasonable, the athlete lacks the intent to steal necessary to commit larceny, a specific-intent crime.

b) General-intent and malice crimes

A mistake of fact must be reasonable in order to be a defense to a general-intent or malice crime.

3) MPC approach

Under the Model Penal Code, a mistake of fact that negates the required state of mind for a material element of a crime is a defense. MPC § 2.04(1).

b. Mistake of law

Mistake or ignorance of the law generally is not a valid defense, except when:

i)   There is reliance on the decision of a court, administrative order, or official interpretation of the law determined to be erroneous after the conduct;

ii) A statute defining a *malum prohibitum* crime (i.e., a crime for engaging in conduct not obviously wrong, such as a failure to obtain a license) was not reasonably made available prior to the conduct; or

iii) An honestly held mistake of law negates the required intent.

> **Example:** A forcibly takes money from B to settle a debt that B owed to A. A has the mistaken belief that the law allows for self-help in such situations. A's belief negates the specific intent required for the crime of robbery (i.e., the specific intent to gain control over the property of another person).

Incorrect or bad legal advice from an attorney is not a valid mistake-of-law defense.

C.   JURISDICTION

Criminal jurisdiction addresses the authority of the federal and state governments to create criminal laws and the authority of courts to enforce those laws. (Procedural rules that affect the conduct of a trial, such as the admissibility of a defendant's confession, are discussed in the Themis Criminal Procedure outline.)

1.   Constitutional Limits on Authority

a.   State authority

State authority to create crimes is based on the states' broad, inherent police power, which is implicitly recognized by the Tenth Amendment.

b.   Federal authority

Federal authority to create crimes is limited. There is no federal common law of crimes; all crimes are statutory. Under the U.S. Constitution, Congress is granted power over only a handful of crimes, including treason and currency counterfeiting.

c.   State and federal authority

Under the Constitution, neither federal nor state governments may criminalize conduct that has already occurred (i.e., an ex post facto law) or impose punishment without a trial (i.e., a bill of attainder). The Due Process Clauses of the Fifth and Fourteenth Amendments prevent both federal and state governments from imposing criminal liability without giving clear warnings as to the conduct prohibited. *Papachristou v. City of Jacksonville*, 405 U.S. 156, 162–63 (1972) (vagrancy ordinance struck down as "void for vagueness").

Additionally, many jurisdictions are in the process of eliminating multiple convictions against a defendant with more than one offense if those multiple offenses were all part of the same criminal transaction. Some states have statutorily prohibited such convictions, while other states apply the doctrine of merger or double jeopardy to eliminate the multiple convictions.

2. Territorial Considerations

a. Federal

Congress has the power to criminalize conduct occurring over federally owned or controlled territory (national parks or the District of Columbia), conduct by United States nationals abroad, and conduct on ships or airplanes.

b. State authority

A state has the authority to prosecute a person for a crime committed within the state and for a crime that is only partly committed within the state if an element of the crime is committed within the state. In addition, the following actions may be prosecuted by the state:

i) Conduct outside the state that constitutes an attempt to commit a crime within the state;

ii) Conduct outside the state that constitutes a conspiracy to commit an offense within the state when an overt act in furtherance of the conspiracy occurs within the state;

iii) Conduct within the state to commit attempt, solicitation, or conspiracy of a crime in another jurisdiction when the state and the other jurisdiction recognize the crime; and

iv) The failure to perform outside the state a duty imposed by the state.

D. PARTIES TO A CRIME

Under the modern rule, in most jurisdictions, the parties to a crime can be a principal, an accessory before the fact, and an accessory after the fact.

At common law, the principal was called the principal in the first degree, and an accessory before the fact who was actually or constructively present at the scene of the crime was called the principal in the second degree. An accomplice who was not present at the crime scene was simply called an accessory before the fact.

1. Principal

A principal is the person whose **acts or omissions are the *actus reus*** of the crime, in other words, the perpetrator of the crime. The principal must be actually or constructively present at the scene of the crime. A principal is constructively present when some instrumentality he left or controlled resulted in the commission of the crime.

If two or more people are directly responsible for the *actus reus*, they are joint principals (i.e., co-principals).

2. Accomplice Liability

An accomplice (i.e., an accessory before the fact or a principal in the second degree) is a person who, with intent that the crime be committed, aids or abets a principal prior to or during the commission of the crime.

a. Accomplice's status

The difference between an accessory before the fact and a principal in the second degree is presence. An accomplice who is physically or constructively present during the commission of the crime is a principal in the second degree. For example, a getaway driver some distance from the scene is deemed constructively present and will be considered a principal in the second degree.

An accomplice that is neither physically nor constructively present during the commission of the crime, but who, with the requisite intent to encourage or assist in the commission of the crime, provided verbal encouragement, financial assistance, or physical assistance to the principal prior to the commission of the crime is an accessory before the fact. Mere knowledge that a crime will result is not enough to make a person an accessory before the fact or a principal in the second degree.

b. Accomplice's criminal liability

An accomplice is responsible for the crime to the same extent as the principal. If the principal commits crimes other than the crimes for which the accomplice has provided encouragement or assistance, then the accomplice is liable for the other crimes if the crimes are the natural and probable consequences of the accomplice's conduct.

Example: D encourages E to burn V's house, and E does so. The fire spreads to W's house, and it was foreseeable that it would do so. D is an accomplice to the burning of W's house.

An accomplice may be criminally liable even though she cannot be a principal.

Example: A woman who cannot commit rape as a principal can be liable for rape if she aids the male principal (e.g., restraining the victim) in his rape of the victim.

c. Withdrawal

To legally withdraw (and therefore avoid liability for the substantive crime), the accomplice must (i) repudiate prior aid, (ii) do all that is possible to countermand prior assistance, and (iii) do so before the chain of events is in motion and unstoppable.

A mere change of heart, a flight from the crime scene, an arrest by law enforcement, or an uncommunicated decision to withdraw is ineffective. Notification to the legal authorities must be timely and directed toward preventing others from committing the crime.

EXAM NOTE: Be careful not to confuse these rules with the rules regarding withdrawal for inchoate offenses such as solicitation, attempt, and conspiracy. The rules are different.

d. Persons not accomplices

A person who is a member of the class protected by a statute cannot be an accomplice. Similarly, when the crime requires another party, the other party is not, simply by engaging in the criminal act, guilty of the crime as an accomplice. For example, the buyer of drugs is not guilty of the crime of distributing drugs simply by purchasing the drugs.

e. Effect of the principal's status

At common law, the accomplice could be convicted of a crime only if the principal was also previously convicted of the crime. A small minority of jurisdictions still subscribes to this approach. By modern statute, however, in most jurisdictions, an accomplice may be convicted of a crime even if the principal is not tried, is not convicted, has been given immunity from prosecution, or is acquitted.

3. Accessory After the Fact

An accessory after the fact is a person who aids or assists a felon in avoiding apprehension or conviction after commission of the felony. An accessory after the fact must know that a felony was committed, act specifically to aid or assist the felon, and give the aid or assistance for the purpose of helping the felon avoid apprehension or conviction. An accessory after the fact is not subject to punishment for the crime committed by the felon, but instead has committed a *separate crime*, frequently labeled "obstruction of justice" or "harboring a fugitive."

a. Failure to report a crime

The mere failure to report a crime is not generally itself a crime. However, a person who gives false information to the police in order to prevent the apprehension of a felon can be an accessory after the fact.

b. Misprision

Misprision is a common-law misdemeanor that amounts to a failure to report or prosecute a known felon.

The defendant must have (i) had full knowledge that the principal committed and completed the felony alleged, (ii) failed to notify the authorities, and (iii) taken an affirmative step to conceal the crime. *U.S. v. Ciambrone*, 750 F.2d 1416, 1417 (1986).

c. Compounding a crime

A person who receives valuable consideration for agreeing not to prosecute a crime may be guilty of compounding a crime.

E. RESPONSIBILITY

1. Insanity

Insanity encompasses mental abnormalities that may affect legal responsibility. It is a legal term rather than a psychiatric term. The four tests for insanity are the *M'Naghten* test, the irresistible-impulse test, the *Durham* rule, and the Model Penal Code test. These tests expressly exclude the "sociopathic" or "psychopathic" criminals who have a tendency to commit antisocial and sometimes violent acts and are incapable of experiencing guilt. A defendant who puts his sanity at issue can be compelled to submit to psychiatric testing after being informed of his Fifth Amendment rights.

a. *M'Naghten* test

Under the *M'Naghten* test, the defendant is not guilty if, because of a defect of reason due to a mental disease, the defendant did not know either (i) the nature and quality of the act or (ii) the wrongfulness of the act.

Without knowing that the act is wrong, a defendant could not have formed the requisite criminal intent. Therefore, it is important to assess whether the defendant's actions would have been criminal if the facts, as he believed them to be, supported his delusions. However, a defendant is not exculpated simply because he believes his acts to be morally right. Loss of control because of mental illness is not a defense under this test. This is the "right from wrong" test.

b. Irresistible-impulse test

Under the irresistible-impulse test, the defendant is not guilty if he lacked the capacity for self-control and free choice because mental disease or defect prevented him from being able to conform his conduct to the law. The loss of control need not be sudden. This is an impulse that the defendant cannot resist.

c. *Durham* rule

Under the *Durham* rule, a defendant is not guilty if the unlawful act was the product of the defendant's mental disease or defect and would not have been committed but for the disease or defect. This is the "but-for" test.

d. Model Penal Code test

The Model Penal Code combines the *M'Naghten* and irresistible-impulse tests. The defendant is not guilty if, at the time of the conduct, he, as a result of a mental disease or defect, did not have substantial capacity to appreciate the wrongfulness of the act or to conform his conduct to the law. MPC § 4.01.

e. Burden of proof

The defendant is presumed sane and has the initial burden of raising the issue of mental capacity and responsibility. The burden of production then shifts to the prosecution, which also has the burden of persuasion on the issue. Depending on the jurisdiction, the level of proof required of the prosecution on the issue can be by a preponderance of the evidence, clear and convincing evidence, or beyond a reasonable doubt.

2. Intoxication

Intoxication can be caused by any substance (e.g., alcohol, drugs, or prescription medicine). There are two types of intoxication defenses: voluntary and involuntary.

a. Voluntary intoxication

Voluntary intoxication is the intentional taking of a substance known to be intoxicating; actual intoxication need not be intended.

1) Specific-intent crimes

Voluntary intoxication is a defense to specific-intent crimes if the intoxication prevents the formation of the required intent. For example, intoxication may prevent the formation of the premeditation required for first-degree murder but not second-degree murder.

2) When inapplicable

Voluntary intoxication is not a defense when the intent was formed before intoxication or when the defendant becomes intoxicated for the purpose of establishing the defense of voluntary intoxication. Voluntary intoxication is not a defense to crimes involving malice, recklessness, or negligence, or for strict-liability crimes.

Note: Although common-law murder and arson sound like specific-intent crimes because they require the "intent to kill" or the "intent to burn," they are malice crimes, and the specific-intent defenses (e.g., voluntary intoxication) do not apply.

b. Involuntary intoxication

Involuntary intoxication is a defense when the intoxication serves to negate an element of the crime, including general as well as specific-intent and malice crimes. To be considered involuntary, the intoxicating substance must have been taken:

i) Without knowledge of the intoxicating nature of the substance, including substances taken pursuant to medical advice; or

ii) Under duress.

In addition, although intoxication and insanity are two separate defenses, excessive drinking and drug use may bring on actual insanity. Thus, involuntary intoxication can give rise to an insanity defense if the requirements for that defense are met.

3. Immaturity/Infancy

At common law, a child under the age of seven could not be convicted of a crime. A child at least seven years old but less than 14 years old was rebuttably presumed to be incapable of committing a crime. A child at least 14 years old could be charged with a crime as an adult.

Modern statutes have modified this rule and provide that no child can be convicted of a crime until a certain age is reached, usually between the ages of 11 and 14.

F. TYPES OF CRIMES

There are two basic types of crimes: felonies and misdemeanors. A felony is a crime punishable by death or imprisonment for more than one year; a misdemeanor is a crime punishable by imprisonment for one year or less or by a fine or by both.

II.   HOMICIDE

A.   DEFINITION

Homicide includes the offenses of murder and manslaughter. At common law, homicide was divided into three categories: (i) homicide justified by law, (ii) criminal homicide, and (iii) excusable homicide. Criminal homicides were divided into three offenses: murder, voluntary manslaughter, and involuntary manslaughter.

Murder was defined as the unlawful killing of another living human being with malice aforethought. In most modern statutory jurisdictions "malice aforethought," which is difficult to define or approximate, has been replaced by four main categories of murder: (i) intent to kill, (ii) intent to do serious bodily injury, (iii) depraved-heart murder, and (iv) felony murder. Only the first category is an intentional killing. The remaining categories involve conduct that results in the death of another not accompanied by the intent to kill. Manslaughter includes two types: voluntary and involuntary. Voluntary manslaughter involves an intentional killing, and involuntary manslaughter is an unintentional killing.

1.   Killing a Person

For a homicide to occur, a living person must die. A body need not be found; death can be established by circumstantial evidence.

A person cannot be killed twice. Shooting a corpse is not homicide, but it can be a crime (e.g., abuse of a corpse).

At common law, a fetus is not a living person.

2.   Causation

To prove a homicide, the prosecution must show that the defendant caused the victim's death. The prosecution must prove both actual and proximate causation.

a.   Actual cause

If the victim would not have died **but for** the defendant's act, then the defendant's act is the actual cause (i.e., cause-in-fact) of the death. When the defendant sets in motion forces that led to the death of the victim, the defendant is the actual cause of the victim's death.

> **Example:** A mechanical device set up by the defendant kills an individual. The defendant is considered to have caused that individual's death.

1)   Substantial factor

Actual causation can be found when there are multiple causes, (i.e., other persons are also responsible for the victim's death) and the defendant's act was a substantial factor in causing the death.

2)   Independent cause

A defendant's act will not be deemed to be the cause of death when a victim is killed by an independent cause before the defendant's act can kill the victim. Simultaneous acts may be considered adequate causes of a single result. Additionally, a victim's preexisting condition that predisposes him to death does not break the chain of causation.

> **Example:** A plans to kill B by stabbing him. A approaches B, finding him lying on the bed in a nonresponsive state. A assumes that B is asleep and stabs him multiple times. In reality, however, B had died one hour previously due to a massive heart attack. A's actions did not cause B's death; therefore, there is no homicide (but there may be attempted murder).

3) Mercy killing

Providing a person with the **means** by which that person can commit suicide generally does not make the provider guilty of murder as an accomplice but instead guilty of a lesser crime, such as assisting a suicide. Note, however, that consent is not a defense to homicide, so a "mercy killing" (i.e., euthanasia) can be a criminal homicide even if the person was willing to die because of a painful terminal illness.

b. Proximate cause

Proximate cause (i.e., legal cause) exists only when the defendant is deemed legally responsible for a homicide. For the defendant to be legally responsible for a homicide, the death must be foreseeable. A defendant's conduct is deemed foreseeable if death is the natural and probable result of the conduct. Actions by a third party (e.g., medical malpractice by the doctor treating the victim), as well as actions by the victim (e.g., suicide to escape the pain that resulted from the injuries inflicted by the defendant), are generally foreseeable. Actions by a force of nature that are not within the defendant's control are generally not foreseeable (e.g., a lightning strike that kills a victim the defendant tied to a tree). An act that accelerates the death is a legal cause of that death.

> **EXAM NOTE:** Proximate cause is commonly tested in the context of the felony-murder rule. A frequently applied standard is that the homicide must be a natural and probable consequence of the defendant's actions.

c. Year-and-a-day rule

At common law, the defendant's act was conclusively presumed not to be the proximate cause of the killing if the victim died more than one year and one day after the act was performed. Most states either have abolished this rule or have extended the time period of responsibility.

B.   TYPES OF HOMICIDE

1.   Murder

Murder is the:

i)   Unlawful (i.e., without a legal excuse);

ii) Killing;

iii) Of a human being;

iv) Committed with **malice aforethought**.

"Malice aforethought" includes the following mental states: intent to kill, intent to inflict serious bodily injury, reckless indifference to an unjustifiably high risk to human life (depraved heart), or intent to commit certain felonies (felony murder).

a. Intent to kill

Conduct accompanied by the intent to kill that is the legal cause of the death of a living person constitutes intent-to-kill murder unless the legal circumstances surrounding the homicide are such that the crime is reduced to voluntary manslaughter. An inference of intent to kill may be made if a deadly weapon was used intentionally in the commission of the crime.

Example: A intends to kill B and, by his conduct of shooting B, kills him.

b. Intent to inflict serious bodily harm

A person who intends to do serious bodily injury or "grievous bodily harm" but actually succeeds in killing is guilty of murder despite the lack of intention to kill.

Example: A intentionally hits B over the head with a baseball bat, intending to hurt B but not kill him, and B later dies from a skull fracture.

Intent to inflict serious bodily harm is an unintentional killing that results in death.

Intent to inflict serious bodily harm can be inferred from the use of a deadly weapon to inflict the bodily injury.

c. Depraved heart

A killing that results from reckless action by a defendant that manifests an extreme indifference to human life is a depraved-heart murder.

Example: A stands on top of a highway overpass and as a joke drops a bowling ball into oncoming traffic, resulting in the death of B, a passing motorist.

Depraved-heart murder is an unintentional killing that results in death. There is a split among jurisdictions as to whether the requisite depravity exists when a defendant is unaware of the risk involved in the conduct, but even states that ordinarily follow a subjective standard allow a conviction if the reason the defendant failed to appreciate the risk was due to voluntary intoxication.

d. Felony murder

Felony murder is an unintended killing proximately caused by and during the commission or attempted commission of an inherently dangerous felony. The felonies traditionally considered inherently dangerous are: **B**urglary, **A**rson, **R**ape, **R**obbery, and **K**idnapping. [Mnemonic: **BARRK**]. (Common-law felonies also include murder, manslaughter, mayhem, and sodomy, but the BARRK crimes are most commonly tested in the context of felony murder.) To convict a defendant of felony murder, the prosecution must establish the underlying felony and that the defendant committed that felony. In addition, in most states, any aggravated felony committed with the use of a dangerous weapon is subject to the felony-murder rule.

Example: X accidentally shoots the owner of a home while committing a burglary. X could be charged with felony murder.

There is no charge of attempted felony murder if the unintended victim does not die. Generally, co-felons (including accessories) are vicariously liable for the death if the death is a foreseeable consequence of the underlying inherently dangerous felony.

If one of two co-felons kills the other during the commission or attempted commission of a dangerous felony, then this act will also constitute felony murder. If the co-felon is killed by a victim or a police officer, though, then the defendant is generally not guilty of felony murder.

Note: The underlying felony will generally merge into the crime of felony murder. For example, a defendant who kills the proprietor of a store while committing a robbery can be convicted only of felony murder; the robbery conviction would merge into the felony-murder conviction.

1) Defenses to felony murder

To defend against a felony-murder charge successfully, the defendant must establish one of the following circumstances:

i) A valid defense to the underlying felony;

ii) The felony was not distinct from or independent of the killing itself (e.g., aggravated battery);

iii) Death was not a foreseeable result or a natural and probable consequence of the felony (i.e., there was no proximate causation); or

iv) Death occurred after the commission of the felony and the ensuing flight from the scene of the crime.

2) Killing by a felony victim or the police

a) Death of a bystander

When **a third party (e.g., a bystander)** is killed by a police officer or dies as a result of resistance by the victim of the felony, the felon's liability for that death will depend on whether an agency theory or proximate-cause theory is applied. Under an agency theory, the felon will not be liable for the death of a bystander caused by a felony victim or police officer because neither person is the felon's agent. Under the proximate-cause theory, liability for the bystander's death may attach to the felon because the death is a direct consequence of the felony.

> **EXAM NOTE:** Proximate-cause theory is the majority position and should be applied on the MBE unless the question specifically indicates that the jurisdiction is an agency-theory jurisdiction.

b) Death of a co-felon

Under the *Redline* doctrine, a defendant is generally not guilty of felony murder when a victim or a police officer, acting in self-defense or trying to prevent the escape of the defendant or his co-felon, kill the co-felon.

Instead, the killing by the victim or the police officer is considered justifiable homicide. *Commonwealth v. Redline*, 137 A.2d 472 (Pa. 1958).

2. Statutory Crimes of Murder

At common law, there were no degrees of murder. Under modern statutory rules, murder is generally divided into two degrees: first-degree and second-degree murder.

> **EXAM NOTE:** Because degrees of murder do not exist at common law, the fact pattern on the MBE must supply a statute if you are to consider degrees of murder.

a. First-degree murder

First-degree murder is generally defined as a deliberate and premeditated murder. In addition, felony murder is frequently classified as first-degree murder.

1) Created by statute

Because the specific criteria for first-degree murder are established only by statute, a homicide cannot be first-degree murder without a corresponding statute.

2) Premeditation

The distinguishing element of first-degree murder is premeditation, meaning the defendant reflected on the idea of killing or planned the killing. The amount of time needed for premeditation may be brief, as long as, after forming the intent to kill, the defendant had sufficient time to become fully conscious of the intent and to consider the killing (i.e., had time for reflection). This requirement does not apply to felony murder.

3) During the commission of an inherently dangerous felony

If a murder is committed during the perpetration of an enumerated felony, then it may be first-degree murder. The most commonly enumerated felonies are **B**urglary, **A**rson, **R**ape, **R**obbery, and **K**idnapping. [Mnemonic: **BARRK**].

> **NOTE:** A homicide committed during the commission of an inherently dangerous felony may be treated as first or second-degree murder depending upon the jurisdiction.

4) Heinous murder

A murder resulting from an egregious act, such as ambush (i.e., lying in wait), torture, bombing, terrorism, or poisoning, may be classified as first-degree murder.

b. Second-degree murder

Second-degree murder is a homicide committed with the necessary malicious intent: the intent to kill, the intent to do great bodily injury, or a depraved-heart murder. In addition, a murder that occurs during the commission of a felony other than the felonies that trigger first-degree murder may statutorily be treated as second-degree murder.

> **EXAM NOTE:** Be sure to differentiate between second-degree murder and first-degree murder when answering exam questions. First-degree murder is a specific-intent crime, whereas second-degree murder, like common-law murder, is a malice crime.

3. Voluntary Manslaughter

Voluntary manslaughter is murder committed in response to adequate provocation (i.e., in the "heat of passion").

a. "Heat of passion"

The defendant acts in the heat of passion if she was provoked by a situation that would inflame the passion of a reasonable person to the extent that it would cause that person to momentarily act out of passion rather than reason. The defendant cannot have been set off by something that would not bother most people.

> **EXAM NOTE:** Remember that "heat of passion" is NOT a defense; it merely reduces murder to voluntary manslaughter.

1) Sufficient provocation

A serious battery, a threat of deadly force, or discovery of adultery by a spouse constitutes sufficient provocation. Usually words, such as taunts, do not.

2) "Cooling off"

If there was sufficient time between the provocation and the killing for a reasonable person to cool off, then murder is not mitigated to manslaughter. If there was sufficient time to cool off for a reasonable person but the defendant himself did not regain self-control, the murder is not mitigated to manslaughter.

> **Second provocation:** Even when the defendant has "cooled off," a second encounter with the victim may give rise to another situation in which the defendant acts in the "heat of passion."

b. Causation

There must be a causal connection between provocation, passion, and the fatal act. There will be no mitigation if the intent to kill was formed prior to the provocation.

c. Imperfect defense

Murder may be reduced to voluntary manslaughter even if the defendant started the altercation or the defendant unreasonably but truly believed in the necessity of using deadly force.

> While an intentional killing committed when resisting arrest is generally murder, an intentional killing can be manslaughter if the arrest is unlawful and the defendant acts in the "heat of passion."

d. Transferred provocation

When, because of a reasonable mistake of fact, the defendant is in error in identifying her provoker or accidentally kills the wrong person, she will be guilty of voluntary manslaughter if that would have been her crime if she had killed the provoker. If, however, the defendant, in her passion, intentionally kills another person known to her to be an innocent bystander, then there will be no mitigation, and murder, rather than voluntary manslaughter, will apply.

4. Involuntary Manslaughter

Involuntary manslaughter is an unintentional homicide committed with criminal negligence or during an unlawful act.

a. Criminal negligence

Criminal negligence is reckless action (or inaction when there is a duty to act) that puts another person at a significant risk of injury or death. It requires more than ordinary negligence for tort liability and something less than the extremely negligent conduct required for depraved-heart murder. For example, the failure of a parent, under a duty of care, to provide medical care to a sick minor child constitutes criminal negligence.

b. Unlawful act

The unlawful act may occur in one of two ways:

i) Under the misdemeanor-manslaughter rule, which is a killing committed in the commission of a *malum in se* (wrong in itself) misdemeanor; or

ii) A killing committed in the commission of a felony that is not statutorily treated as first-degree felony murder or second-degree murder.

The term *malum in se* means "wrong in itself," or "inherently evil," and includes crimes such as assault and battery. *Malum prohibitum* refers to wrongs that are merely prohibited (i.e., not inherently immoral or hurtful, but wrong because of a statute), such as a parking violation, smuggling, or failure to obtain a license. A homicide resulting from a wrong that is *malum prohibitum* will constitute involuntary manslaughter only if the unlawful act was willful or constituted criminal negligence.

c. Causation

There must be a causal connection between the unlawful act and the death for involuntary manslaughter to apply.

III. OTHER CRIMES

A. CRIMES AGAINST PROPERTY

1. Larceny

Larceny is the:

i) Trespassory;

ii) Taking and;

iii) Carrying away;

iv) Of the personal property;

v) Of another;

vi) With the intent to permanently deprive that person of the property (i.e., intent to steal).

a. Trespass

The property must be taken without the owner's consent. If the original taking was without consent, yet was not unlawful because there was no intent to steal at the time of the taking, then larceny may be committed at a later time if the intent to steal is later formed. Under the "continuing trespass" rule, the original trespass is deemed to be "continuing" in order for the criminal act to coincide with the criminal intent. The defendant's original taking must have been wrongful (e.g., a taking based on knowledge that the property belonged to another, such as a taking with the intent to borrow and return the property).

b. Taking

The taking (also known as "caption") requirement is satisfied by any trespassory removal of the property from the owner's possession into another's control.

1) Destruction of property in the owner's possession

The destruction of property while it is in the owner's possession (e.g., breaking an object held by the owner) is not a taking.

2) Use of an agent

A taking occurs if the defendant uses an agent, even one who is unaware of the defendant's criminal intent, to remove the property from the owner's possession.

c. Carrying away (asportation)

The carrying away requirement (also known as "asportation") is satisfied by even a slight movement of the property (e.g., inches).

d. Personal property

The property taken must be personal, not real, property. Electricity or gas supplied by a utility constitutes personal property.

1) Intangibles

Documents that represent the rights to property (e.g., stocks, bonds) are treated as personal property.

2) Services

Modern theft statutes usually criminalize obtaining services without paying for them (i.e., the theft of services).

> **EXAM NOTE:** Services taken without paying for the services (e.g., a massage) do not constitute personal property for the purposes of the MBE.

3) Real-property items

The taking of fixtures (i.e., items affixed to real property) or real-property items (e.g., trees, unharvested crops) is not larceny when the defendant's act of severance occurs immediately before the carrying away of the fixture or other real-property items. However, when the real-property items have previously been severed from the land by the owner, they become personal property (e.g., picked apples), and the carrying away of such items can be larceny.

e. Another's property

The property must be in the possession of someone other than the defendant.

Contrast with embezzlement: For embezzlement, the defendant is legally entrusted with the property by the owner, and then the defendant later fraudulently converts the property to his own use. With larceny, the initial taking must be trespassory; there cannot be lawful entrustment by the owner. This is the main difference between the two crimes.

1) Owner of property

The owner of property (i.e., a person who has title to it) can commit larceny when someone other than the owner (e.g., a lessee) is entitled to current possession of the property.

2) Thief

Larceny may even be committed against a thief. Stolen property taken from a thief can constitute larceny unless the taker has a superior possessory interest in the property (e.g., an owner or a lessee of the property).

3) Joint owners

A joint owner of property who takes possession of the property from a co-owner is not guilty of larceny because the taker has an equal right to possess the property.

4) Constructive possession

"Constructive possession" means legal possession when factual possession does not exist.

An owner has constructive possession of property when actual possession, but not title, is taken from her by fraud. The crime is called "larceny by trick." *See* § III.A.2, Larceny by Trick, *infra*.

a) Employee's control over employer's property

Low-level employees can only be guilty of larceny whereas high-level employees are typically guilty of embezzlement. An employer generally has constructive possession of property in the hands of a lower-level employee. Such an employee has custody, not possession, of the employer's property. A higher-level employee (e.g., company president) who has greater authority with respect to the employer's property may have possession of, rather than custody of, such property and may be guilty of embezzlement, rather than larceny, for taking the property.

b) Bailee possession

A bailee is guilty of larceny if, with intent to steal, the bailee opens and takes property from closed containers belonging to the bailor. Otherwise, the bailee simply has possession.

5) Abandoned versus lost property

Property that has been abandoned by its owner (i.e., the owner has surrendered all rights to the property) is not subject to larceny. Property that has been lost by its owner can be the subject of larceny if, at the time of the finding, the finder knows the owner or believes that he can locate the owner and the finder possesses the necessary intent to permanently deprive the owner of the property.

6) Mistakenly delivered property

Property that has been mistakenly delivered may be the subject of larceny if the recipient of the property realizes that a mistake has been made at the time of the receipt of the property and the recipient possesses the necessary intent to permanently deprive.

a) Special problems

When a defendant takes legitimate possession of an item, but he discovers another item enclosed in the larger item (the container), the issue arises as to whether the defendant had possession of the enclosed item at the time the defendant legitimately possessed the larger item. If so, there is no larceny because the defendant has not taken the property from another's possession. However, determining whether there is possession is a difficult task. Larceny may depend on whether the parties intended to transfer the container. If the intent is to transfer, then no larceny is committed because the defendant effectively takes immediate possession of both items. A few states hold that the defendant does not take possession of the enclosed property until he discovers it, at which point, if he forms the intent to keep the property, he is guilty of larceny.

f. Intent to permanently deprive

Larceny is a **specific-intent** crime. The intent to permanently deprive the owner of the property must be present at the time of the taking. There is no defense of restoration if the defendant later has a change of heart and restores the property to the rightful owner. The crime is complete at the time of the taking.

Examples: The intent to permanently deprive the owner of the property can occur when the defendant takes property with the intent to claim a reward, the defendant intends to throw away or abandon the property, the defendant intends to sell the property back to the owner, or the defendant intends to pledge or pawn the property without being able to redeem it.

1) Insufficient intent

The necessary specific intent does not exist when the defendant's intent is to:

    i)   Borrow property with the ability to return it;

    ii)   Pay for merchandise that she has the means to buy; or

    iii) Take money as repayment of a debt.

a) Intent to borrow

If the defendant intends only to borrow the property with the ability to do so, then larceny does not occur because there is no intent to permanently deprive the owner of the property (e.g., borrowing a car to run an errand).

If property is taken with the intent to return the property and is accidently damaged or destroyed, larceny has not occurred.

Example: D takes A's car to run an errand. On the way back to A's house, D is in a car accident, and A's car is totaled. D is not guilty of larceny.

b) Intent to pay

A defendant's intent to pay for property is not sufficient to prevent larceny when the property is not offered for sale.

c) Repayment of debt

If a defendant takes property with the honest belief that she is entitled to the property as repayment of a debt, then larceny does not occur.

d) Rewards

A defendant intending to return property in expectation of claiming a reward has not committed larceny, unless his intent is to return the property only upon receiving the reward.

2) Sufficient intent

There is sufficient intent if the defendant intends to create a substantial risk of loss of the property or if the defendant intends to sell the goods back to the owner.

3) Time for measuring intent

The intent to permanently deprive is generally measured at the time of the taking. The continuing-trespass rule may apply to stretch the time at which intent is measured. *See* § III.A.1.a, Trespass, *supra*.

2. Larceny by Trick

One who obtains possession of, but not title to, property owned by another through fraud or deceit who has the intent to unlawfully convert and who later does so convert is guilty of larceny by trick. Larceny by trick occurs when the defendant fraudulently induces the victim to deliver possession of the property to the defendant.

a. False representation of material present or past fact

The representation (whether oral, written, or by actions) must be false in fact and be of a material past or present fact. A prediction about a future event, a false promise, or an opinion, such as sales talk or puffing, is not sufficient.

b. Reliance by the victim

The victim must rely upon the false representation, and that reliance must cause the victim to give possession to the defendant. This standard is subjective, not objective.

> **Contrast with false pretenses:** Under larceny by trick, the defendant obtains possession. Under larceny by false pretenses, the defendant obtains title. *See* § III.A.5, False Pretenses, *infra.*

3. Forgery

Forgery is the:

i) Fraudulent;

ii) Making;

iii) Of a false writing;

iv) With apparent legal significance; and

v) With the intent to defraud (i.e., make wrongful use of the forged document).

a. Fraudulent

The defendant must intend to make wrongful use of the writing, (e.g., cashing a check with a forged drawer's signature). There must be intent to defraud, even if no one actually is defrauded.

b. Making

Making includes creating, altering, or fraudulently inducing another to sign a document when that person is unaware of the significance of the document. The defendant need not use the document; the crime is complete upon the "making" of the document. When property is acquired by use of the forged document, the defendant may also be guilty of another crime, such as false pretenses (*see* § III.A.5, False Pretenses, *infra*).

c. False writing

The writing itself must be false, instead of merely including false information in an otherwise genuine document. (Note: Signing another person's name on a check or other commercial paper makes the check itself false.) When there is an alteration, the alteration must be material.

d. Apparent legal significance

A document has legal significance if it has value beyond its own existence. A contract, deed, will, or check has value beyond the document itself; a painting does not.

4. Embezzlement

Embezzlement is the:

i)   Fraudulent;

ii) Conversion;

iii) Of the property;

iv) Of another;

v)   By a person who is in lawful possession of the property.

a. Conversion

Conversion is the inappropriate use of property, held pursuant to a trust agreement, which causes a serious interference with the owner's rights to the property. Interference with the owner's rights to the property can be caused by selling the property, damaging it, or unreasonably withholding possession. The defendant need not personally benefit from the conversion. No movement or carrying away of the property is required. If it is unclear whether there was a conversion of the property, then the victim must demand a return of the property, and the embezzler must refuse to return the property before a claim for embezzlement can be made.

b. Intent to defraud

The defendant must intend to defraud the owner of the property. If the defendant intends to return the exact property that is converted and has the ability to do so at the time that the intent is formed, then the defendant lacks the intent to defraud the property owner. If the defendant intends to return similar property or the cash equivalent of the value of the property, then the defendant has the intent necessary to commit embezzlement. A conversion pursuant to a claim of right also is not embezzlement.

c. Type of property

Property that is subject to larceny is also subject to embezzlement. In some states, real property, as well as personal property, may be embezzled.

d. Another's property

The property embezzled must belong to another. The inability to fulfill a contractual obligation (e.g., pay back a loan) is not embezzlement.

e. Lawful possession

The embezzler must be in lawful possession of the property at the time that the intent to defraud occurs, although some states limit embezzlement to property entrusted to the embezzler.

5. False Pretenses

The crime of false pretenses is a false representation of a past or present material fact made by the defendant with the intent to cause the victim to pass title to the defendant, and title is passed. False pretenses requires:

i) Obtaining title to the property;

ii) Of another person;

iii) Through the reliance of that person;

iv) On a known false representation of a material past or present fact; and

v) The representation is made with the intent to defraud.

a. Title must pass

Title to the property must pass from the victim to the defendant. Title can be obtained without possession of the property, but mere possession does not constitute false pretenses.

Contrast larceny by trick: Mere possession of the property without legal title by a defendant can be sufficient for larceny by trick.

b. Type of property

Generally, property that may be subject to larceny is also subject to false pretenses.

c. False factual representation

The representation must be false and must be of a material past or present fact. A prediction about a future event, a false promise, or an opinion, such as sales talk or puffing, is not sufficient. The representation may be made orally, in writing, or by actions (e.g., resetting a car's odometer). Silence does not constitute a representation, even when the defendant is aware of the owner's misunderstanding, unless the defendant caused the misunderstanding.

d. Reliance by the victim

The victim must rely upon the false representation, and that reliance must cause the victim to pass title to the defendant. This standard is subjective, not objective.

e. Intent to defraud

The defendant must know that the representation is false and specifically intend to defraud. Most courts find that a defendant acts knowingly and has knowledge of a particular fact when he is aware of a high probability of the fact's existence and deliberately avoids learning the truth. A few states require actual knowledge of a particular fact.

A defendant has the intent to defraud required to establish false pretenses when she intends that the person to whom the false representation is made will rely upon it.

6. Robbery

Robbery is:

i) Larceny;

ii) By force or intimidation;

iii) When the taking of the property is from the person or presence of the victim.

a. Elements of larceny

All of the elements of larceny are necessary for robbery. Larceny is the (i) trespassory, (ii) taking and carrying away, (iii) of the personal property of another, (iv) with the intent to steal.

b. From the person or presence

The property taken must be on the victim's person or within the victim's reach or control (i.e., in the presence of the victim). For example, if a victim is restrained by the defendant within the victim's home prior to the seizure of the property, items taken from the entire house can be treated as "from the victim's presence."

c. By force or intimidation

The taking of the property must be accomplished by force or intimidation.

1) Force

The force used by the defendant must be more than the amount necessary to effectuate taking and carrying away the property. When a pickpocket takes the victim's property without the victim's knowledge, the taking does not constitute robbery unless the victim notices the taking and resists.

> **EXAM NOTE:** The MBE often tests the degree of force necessary for robbery. Remember that slight force is sufficient, but the force must be manifested immediately before or at the same time as the taking.

2) Intimidation

The threat must be of immediate serious physical injury to the victim, a close family member, or other person present. A threat to damage or destroy property, other than the victim's home, is not sufficient.

d. Merger

Larceny, assault, and battery all merge into robbery.

> **EXAM NOTE:** Merger of these crimes is often tested on the MBE by asking, "which is the highest crime D can be convicted of?"

7. Extortion

a. Common law

At common law, extortion was the unlawful taking of money by a government officer.

b. Modern approach

Most jurisdictions have enacted statutes that more broadly define extortion as the taking of money or property from another by threat. In most jurisdictions, it is the making of threats (rather than the obtaining of the property) that is the essence of the crime. In a minority of jurisdictions, however, the accused must actually obtain the property to be guilty.

Extortion differs from robbery in two respects:

i) The threats need not be of immediate harm, nor need they be of a physical nature (e.g., threatening to expose the victim's marital infidelity in the future is sufficient); and

ii) The property intended to be taken need not be on the victim or in his presence.

8. Burglary

Common-law burglary is the:

i) Breaking and;

ii) Entering;

iii) Of the dwelling;

iv) Of another;

v) At nighttime;

vi) With the specific intent to commit a felony therein.

a. Breaking

Breaking is accomplished by using force to create an opening into a dwelling, such as by shattering a window or kicking in a door. The force used may be slight, such as opening an unlocked door or window.

Note: It is not a breaking to enter a dwelling through an open door or window, unless the opening must be enlarged to allow the entry.

1) Breaking without use of force

If entry is obtained by fraud or threat, then there is a breaking. If the defendant had consent by the owner to enter, then no breaking occurs unless the consent was obtained by fraud, or the defendant exceeded the scope of such consent.

2) Breaking within dwelling

If entry is gained with consent, a breaking can still occur if the defendant breaks into a part of the dwelling structure, such as by opening a closet door or wall safe. The mere opening of an object within the dwelling, such as a desk drawer, trunk, or box, does not constitute a breaking.

3) Use of force to exit—no breaking

The use of force to exit a dwelling does not constitute a breaking.

Most states now require only that the defendant enter the premises; a breaking is not required. The common law requires a breaking.

b. Entering

Entering occurs when any portion of the defendant's body (e.g., a hand through a broken windowpane) or an instrument used by the defendant to gain entry (e.g., a rock thrown through a window) crosses into the dwelling without permission through the opening created by the breaking.

Breaking and entering need not happen at the same time.

c. Dwelling of another

A dwelling is a structure regularly occupied for habitation. It need not be occupied at the time of the breaking, but it must not be abandoned.

All states have statutes that expand the type of structure to include non-dwellings, such as businesses, buildings, or cars, and surrounding areas, such as yards.

The dwelling must be that of another person. A person cannot burglarize his own dwelling, unless a possessory interest has been transferred to another (e.g., a tenant).

d. Nighttime

Nighttime occurs during the period of darkness between sunset and sunrise. It is not considered nighttime if there is sufficient natural daylight to see the burglar's face.

The common law required that the breaking and entering occur during nighttime. No states require that all forms of burglary be committed at night, although more severe penalties may be imposed on nighttime burglaries.

e. Specific intent to commit a felony

At the time of the breaking and entering, the defendant must have the intent to commit a felony (e.g., larceny, robbery, rape, murder) inside the dwelling.

A defendant who fails to commit the underlying felony may nevertheless be guilty of burglary as well as attempt to commit the underlying felony. If the underlying felony is completed, it does **not** merge with the burglary.

Many states have broadened the scope of the crimes intended to be committed to include misdemeanor thefts.

9. Arson

Arson is the:

i) Malicious;

ii) Burning;

iii) Of the dwelling;

iv) Of another.

a. Malice

Malice does not require ill will. The defendant is not required to intend to burn the dwelling of another; it is sufficient that the defendant performs an act with reckless disregard that creates a substantial risk of such burning.

b. Burning

The damage to the dwelling must be caused by fire. Smoke damage alone is insufficient. In addition, the damage must affect the structure of the building; mere scorching (i.e., discoloration due to heat) of the walls and burning of the contents of the dwelling are insufficient. When the dwelling is constructed of wood, there must be at least a charring of the wood (i.e., damage to the wood itself).

c. Another's dwelling

Ownership is not required. The test is whether a person has the right to possession or occupancy of the dwelling. Many states have expanded arson to include the burning of one's own dwelling. At common law, however, the burning of one's own dwelling (house burning) that was located near other houses or in a city was only a misdemeanor, and burning one's own building for insurance fraud was not considered arson.

Most states have expanded arson to include the burning of buildings other than dwellings, but burning the contents of a building alone does not constitute arson.

EXAM NOTE: The MBE has not always been consistent with regard to the definition of arson in its questions. Some questions in the past have included the burning of non-dwellings or of the defendant's own dwelling as arson, without indicating a statutory definition. If a situation looks like "arson" from a common-sense point of view, it generally will be considered arson on the MBE.

10. Possession Offenses

Possession of a prohibited object (e.g., drug paraphernalia, burglar's tools) or a substance (e.g., illegal narcotics) is unlawful if the defendant exercises control over such object or substance. The defendant is not required to be aware that possession of the object is illegal. Dominion and control must exist for a period long enough to have provided the defendant with an opportunity to cease such dominion and control.

11. Receiving Stolen Goods

Receiving stolen property is a statutory crime that requires:

i) Receiving control of stolen property;

ii) Knowledge that the property is stolen; and

iii) Intent to permanently deprive the owner of the property.

Knowledge that the property is stolen must coincide with the act of receiving the property. Only control, not possession, is necessary. The goods must have actually been stolen at the time they are received, and the defendant must believe that they have been stolen.

12. Legislative Changes to Theft Crimes

There are several changes made to the common-law property offenses under the MPC and through states' criminal codes. Larceny, false pretenses, embezzlement, and receipt of stolen goods are treated as a single statutory crime of theft. The definition of property has been expanded to cover intangibles, services, and documents. In addition, the defendant need only have unauthorized control over the property.

B. CRIMES AGAINST THE PERSON

1. Battery

Battery is the:

i) Unlawful;

ii) Application of force;

iii) To another person;

iv) That causes bodily harm to that person; or

v) Constitutes an offensive touching.

a. Unlawful

"Unlawful" means that the force is applied without legal excuse. Excessive use of force by a police officer during an arrest is unlawful.

b. Application of force

The touching, however slight, must result in bodily harm (e.g., a bruise) or an offensive touching (e.g., an unwanted kiss). The force can be applied by a third party acting under the defendant's direction or by an object controlled by the defendant (e.g., a brick thrown by the defendant).

c. To the person of another

The application of force to an object near, carried by, or attached to the victim constitutes a battery if the victim suffers bodily harm or an offensive touching.

Example: A battery occurs if a defendant kicks a cane used by a victim for support, causing the victim to fall and injure herself.

d. Requisite intent

Battery is a general-intent crime that includes not only intentional conduct but also criminal negligence (i.e., conduct that carries a high degree of risk to others).

e. Consent defense

Although consent is generally not a defense to a crime, consent may be a defense to a battery. Consent may be explicit (e.g., a signed authorization for surgery) or implicit (e.g., participation in an athletic event).

f. Aggravated battery

Battery may carry a greater penalty, by statute, when serious bodily injury is inflicted or bodily injury is caused by the use of a deadly weapon.

2. Assault

Assault is:

i) An attempt to commit a battery; or

ii) Intentionally placing another in apprehension of imminent bodily harm.

Assault requires an absence of contact with the victim. The attempted-battery assault is a specific-intent crime. The fear-of-harm assault is a general-intent crime.

Battery Distinguished: The defendant **must** actually touch the victim or something attached to his person for a battery to occur. An assault can occur even if the defendant does not touch the victim.

a. Attempted battery

The defendant must take a substantial step toward the commission of a battery. Like all attempt crimes, the defendant must have the specific intent to commit a battery.

b. Fear of harm

The "fear of harm" type of assault (also called "apprehension assault") is a general-intent crime—the defendant must intend to cause bodily harm or apprehension of such harm. The victim's apprehension must be reasonable. Unlike attempted battery, because actual apprehension is necessary, the victim's lack of awareness of the threat of harm is a defense to this type of assault.

c. Consent defense

As is the case with battery, consent may be a defense to assault.

d. Aggravated assault

Assault may carry a greater penalty, by statute, when a deadly weapon is used.

3. Mayhem

Mayhem is a common-law battery that causes the dismemberment or permanent disfigurement of a person. It is the equivalent of modern statutory aggravated battery.

4. Kidnapping

Kidnapping is the:

i) Unlawful;

ii) Confinement of a person;

iii) Against that person's will;

iv) Coupled with either:

    a) The movement; or

    b) The hiding of that person.

Note: There is no requirement for a ransom demand in order to establish kidnapping.

a. Unlawful

The unlawful requirement excludes legally sanctioned actions, such as the imprisonment of a felon by the state after his conviction.

b. Confinement

The victim's freedom of movement must be significantly restricted. It is not enough that the victim is prevented from taking a path or entering an area; the victim must be prevented from leaving an area or compelled to go to a place the victim does not want to go.

c. Against the victim's will

The confinement must be accomplished by force, threats, or fraud.

Consent of the victim to the confinement is a defense if given by a person with the capacity to consent. A child cannot consent to being taken out of the control of a parent or guardian.

d. Movement

The victim need only be moved a short distance (e.g., forced from the driver's seat into the trunk of a car). If the kidnapping occurs incident to another crime (e.g., robbery), then the movement must be more than is necessary for the commission of that crime in order for a defendant to be liable for both kidnapping and the separate offense.

e. Hidden location

Instead of movement, the victim may be concealed for a substantial period of time at a hidden location.

f. Enhanced punishment

A kidnapping that results in bodily injury, interferes with a governmental function, or is done for the purpose of collecting a ransom may be subject to enhanced punishment, by statute.

5. False Imprisonment

False imprisonment is the:

i)   Unlawful;

ii) Confinement of a person;

iii) Without consent.

a. Unlawful

The confinement is unlawful unless it is consented to or specifically authorized by law.

b. Confinement

Confinement may be effected by forcing a person to go where he does not want to or by preventing him from going where he does want so long as no alternative routes are available to him. This may be done by actual force, threat of force, or a show of force.

c. Consent

To be effective, consent must be given freely, and the one consenting must have the capacity to do so.

C. RAPE AND OTHER SEX CRIMES

1. Rape

Rape is:

i)   Unlawful;

ii) Sexual intercourse;

iii) With a female;

iv) Against her will by force or threat of immediate force.

Most modern statutes have removed the force requirement.

a. Unlawful—exclusion of husband

At common law, a husband could not rape his wife. Most states have either abolished this restriction or removed the immunity if the husband and wife have separated or filed for divorce.

b. Sexual intercourse

Actual penetration, however slight, is required; emission is not.

c. With a female

Traditionally, the victim of rape could only be a woman. Most states recognize homosexual rape as a crime labeled "sexual assault" rather than rape. Some states have defined rape in a gender-neutral manner; under such statutes, a woman could be the perpetrator of a rape.

d. Without consent

When a woman consents to sexual intercourse, rape has not occurred. Consent does not exist if intercourse is procured by force or threat of harm, or when the female is unable to consent due to a drug-induced stupor or unconsciousness.

1) Threat of harm

Consent is ineffective if a woman consents to sexual intercourse because of a threat of harm, although the harm threatened must be imminent and must involve bodily harm. Economic duress is not sufficient.

2) Fraud

Fraud rarely negates consent. Consent obtained by fraud regarding the nature of the act itself—fraud in factum (e.g., the defendant convinces the victim that the act is not intercourse but part of a medical exam)—is not a valid defense. Consent obtained by fraud in the inducement (e.g., a promise of marriage in exchange for sex) is a valid defense.

3) Resistance of the victim

Resistance of the victim is not required, but it can be evidence of the victim's lack of consent.

e. Intent

Rape is a general-intent crime requiring only the intent to commit intercourse without the consent of the female. Intent is negated if a defendant reasonably believes that the victim's lack of resistance indicates consent.

2. Statutory Rape

Statutory rape is sexual intercourse with a female under the age of consent. It is a strict-liability crime. Consent by the underage female is not a defense. A defendant's reasonable mistake of fact concerning the victim's age is not a defense.

3. Adultery and Fornication

Adultery and fornication are considered misdemeanor offenses in some states. Adultery involves sexual intercourse or cohabitation with a person who is not a spouse. Fornication is open and notorious cohabitation or sexual intercourse between unmarried persons.

4. Crimes Against Nature

There are two crimes under this category: sodomy and bestiality. Both are considered common-law felonies. However, in light of *Lawrence v. Texas*, 539 U.S. 558 (2003), it is most improbable that a defendant could be successfully prosecuted for the crime of sodomy. Because the majority in *Lawrence* held that intimate consensual sexual conduct was part of the liberty protected by the Fourteenth Amendment, *Lawrence* effectually invalidated similar laws that purport to criminalize sodomy. Bestiality (sexual intercourse with an animal by a human) continues to survive.

5. Incest

In most jurisdictions, incest is marriage or sexual acts between persons that are too closely related. However, there is no uniformity in classifying the degree of relationship. While some states restrict incest to blood relatives, many other states extend the felony to non blood relatives as well.

6. Bigamy

A strict-liability offense, bigamy is the act of marrying someone while still legally married to someone else. Common law considered a defendant guilty even when the defendant incorrectly believed that an alleged divorce was valid or that his spouse was dead.

7. Seduction

Seduction occurs when a man induces a woman to have sexual intercourse with him on the false promise of marriage. Subsequent marriage may be a defense in some jurisdictions.

D. PERJURY AND BRIBERY

1. Perjury

Perjury involves the willful act of falsely promising to tell the truth, either verbally or in writing, about material matters that affect the outcome of a case. A witness cannot be prosecuted for making two contradictory statements if they are made during the same proceeding and the witness admits, prior to the end of the proceeding, that one of the statements is false. All witnesses are absolutely immune from civil liability based on their alleged perjured testimony in litigation brought under the Civil Rights Act, 42 U.S.C. § 1983.

2. Subornation of Perjury

At common law, subornation of perjury was a separate offense committed when one persuaded or induced another to commit perjury. Some states have eliminated subornation of perjury from the perjury statute.

3. Bribery

Under common law, bribery was a misdemeanor involving the corrupt payment of something of value for the purpose of influencing the action of an official in the discharge of his public or legal duties. Under modern law, bribery can be a felony and may extend to persons who are not public officials. Mutuality is not required. Further, the offering or taking of a bribe may constitute a felony as well. In some jurisdictions, failure to report a bribe constitutes a misdemeanor.

IV. INCHOATE CRIMES

The term "inchoate" literally means "unripened." With an inchoate offense, the intended crime need not be committed for a defendant to be guilty. The inchoate offenses are solicitation, conspiracy, and attempt. Inchoate offenses are specific-intent crimes.

A. MERGER

Traditionally, under the doctrine of merger, if a person's conduct constitutes both a felony and a misdemeanor, then the misdemeanor merges into the felony, and the person can be convicted of the felony but not the misdemeanor. However, if the crimes are of the same degree, i.e., all felonies or all misdemeanors, then there is no merger of the crimes.

Modern law does not subscribe to the doctrine of merger except in cases of solicitation and attempt. A defendant may be tried, but not punished, for solicitation and the completed crime or for attempt and the completed crime. Solicitation and attempt are said to "merge" into the completed crime.

Contrast conspiracy: Unlike a solicitation and attempt conviction, a conviction for conspiracy does *not* merge into a conviction for the completed crime.

Note: The Double Jeopardy Clause generally prohibits a defendant from being convicted of both a crime and a lesser-included offense (i.e., an offense all the elements of which are also elements of the more-significant crime), such as robbery and larceny. Many jurisdictions characterize this prohibition as a "merger" of the lesser-included offense into the greater. For further discussion of double jeopardy, please refer to the Themis Criminal Procedure outline.

B. SOLICITATION

Solicitation is the:

i) Enticing, encouraging, or advising of another person;

ii) To commit a crime;

iii) With the intent that the other person commits the crime.

1. Encouragement

The encouragement may take the form of enticement, incitement, request, or command. The crime is completed upon the encouragement. The other person need not agree to commit the crime.

2. Relationship to Other Crimes

If the other person does agree, then the solicitor and the person solicited may also become co-conspirators unless the person solicited is merely feigning agreement.

3. **Defenses to Solicitation**

   a. **Renunciation**

   At common law, renunciation was no defense to solicitation. Under the Model Penal Code, voluntary renunciation may be a defense, provided the defendant thwarts the commission of the solicited crime. MPC § 5.02(3).

   b. **Factual impossibility**

   Factual impossibility is not a defense to solicitation. If a solicitor is part of a group that was meant to be exempted by the statute, then the solicitor cannot be guilty of solicitation (e.g., a minor female soliciting sex cannot be guilty of statutory rape).

C. CONSPIRACY

Conspiracy is:

   i) An agreement;

   ii) Between two or more persons;

   iii) To accomplish an unlawful purpose;

   iv) With the intent to accomplish that purpose.

The majority rule and federal law, as well as the MPC, now require the commission of an overt act, which can be legal or illegal, in furtherance of the conspiracy to complete the formation of the conspiracy. At common law, no overt act was required for the conspiracy to be complete.

> **EXAM NOTE:** Remember, unless the question specifically indicates that the majority rule is being tested, apply the rule of common-law conspiracy on the MBE. The common-law rule does not require the commission of an overt act in furtherance of the conspiracy for the crime to be complete.

1. **Agreement**

   The agreement need not be a formal document, or even in writing; an oral agreement is sufficient. An agreement need not be specifically articulated but can be inferred from a concerted action by the defendants.

2. **Number of Conspirators**

   At common law and under the majority rule, there is no such thing as a unilateral conspiracy. Two or more persons are required to form a conspiracy. The MPC, however, does permit unilateral conspiracies whereby the focus of liability is on the individual defendant and his agreement to the object of the conspiracy, but that is the minority rule. A unilateral conspiracy may be formed when only one party *actually agrees*, such as when another party merely feigns agreement, or if the alleged co-conspirators are ultimately acquitted.

a. Feigned agreement

When only one conspirator has the intent to agree, such as when the other conspirator is a governmental agent or pretends to go along with the crime to warn police, there is no conspiracy, unless another participant is involved.

b. Protected by statute

When the purpose of a criminal statute is to protect a type of person (e.g., a statutory rape statute protects underage females), there is no conspiracy between the protected party and the targeted defendant.

c. Wharton Rule

Under the Wharton Rule, if a crime requires two or more participants (e.g., adultery) there is no conspiracy unless more parties than are necessary to complete the crime agree to commit the crime. Although there is no conspiracy, the participants may be found guilty of the underlying crime itself.

d. Corporation and its agents

A corporation can conspire with its own agents with some limitations. In some jurisdictions, there can be no conspiracy between a corporation and a single agent of that corporation. A conspiracy between the corporation and multiple agents of the same corporation may, in most jurisdictions, satisfy the plurality requirement. A corporation or its agents can enter into a conspiracy with another corporation or agents of that corporation. In the federal system, there are no such limitations on a conspiracy between the corporation and its own agents.

e. Prosecution of other conspirators

A conspirator cannot be convicted of conspiracy if all other conspirators are acquitted at the same trial. In other circumstances, such as when co-conspirators are never tried or apprehended, a conspirator may be convicted of conspiracy if the prosecution proves the existence of a conspiracy.

f. Spouses as co-conspirators

Common law did not consider husband and wife as co-conspirators because the law viewed them as a single entity. However, they could, as an entity, conspire with a third person. Nearly every jurisdiction has abolished this common-law concept.

3. Unlawful Purpose

Under federal law and the modern trend, "unlawful purpose" is limited to criminal conduct. In some states, even the achievement of a lawful purpose through illegal means can be the subject of a conspiracy.

4. Specific Intent

Conspiracy is a specific-intent crime. A conspirator must have the intent to agree and the intent to commit the criminal objective. The intent to agree may be inferred from the conduct of the parties.

Example: Conspiracy to commit arson requires specific intent; the substantive offense of arson, however, is a general-intent crime. Similarly, a conspiracy to commit a strict-liability crime requires intent.

Because intent to agree and to commit the crime are elements of conspiracy, criminal liability for a conspiracy cannot be based solely on knowledge of the existence of the conspiracy. For example, a merchant who supplies goods to a conspirator knowing that the conspirator intends to use the goods in furtherance of the objective of the conspiracy is not a member of the conspiracy simply because the merchant possessed such knowledge. Instead, the merchant must take an additional step to show such intent, such as selling the goods at an exorbitant price, basing the price of the goods on a percentage of the conspiracy's "take," or ordering specially manufactured goods that the merchant does not normally sell.

5. Overt Act Requirement

An overt act was not required at common law, but it is now a required element of a conspiracy under federal law, the MPC, and in a majority of states. When an overt act is required, the conspiracy crime is not complete until the overt act is performed in furtherance of the conspiracy. The overt act can be performed by any co-conspirator, with or without the knowledge of all co-conspirators. The overt act can be lawful or unlawful.

Contrast attempt: To constitute attempt, the defendant must have taken a substantial step toward commission of the crime. A mere preparatory act is insufficient for attempt.

6. Scope of Conspiracy

a. Crimes committed by co-conspirators

Under the *Pinkerton* Rule, a conspirator can be convicted of both the offense of conspiracy and all substantive crimes committed by any other co-conspirators acting in furtherance of the conspiracy. Under the MPC, the minority view, a member of the conspiracy is not criminally liable for such crimes unless that member aids and abets in the commission of the crimes.

b. Multiple crimes, single conspiracy

A single conspiracy may have numerous criminal objectives. Not all of the co-conspirators even need to know the identities of all of the other co-conspirators or all of the details of the criminal organization. It is only necessary that all co-conspirators agree to further the common scheme or plan. Multiple conspiracies arise when the objectives and/or crimes are not committed in furtherance of the same agreement, common scheme, and plan.

c. Unknown conspirators, single conspiracy

1) Chain relationship

Persons who do not know each other can be members of the same conspiracy if there is a **community of interest** in the achievement of the object of the conspiracy. A community of interest is usually found when the activities of each person resemble links of a chain, such as a scheme to acquire and distribute drugs. In such a conspiracy, all of the members of the community of interest are liable for the acts of the others in furtherance of the conspiracy.

2) Hub-spoke relationship

A scheme that resembles a hub with spokes, such as the processing of fraudulent loans by one person that were submitted by numerous other individuals, is less likely to have a community of interest. In such a case, the "hub" and each "spoke" are usually treated as having formed a separate conspiracy with the other hubs. Thus, the common hubs will be liable for all of the other conspiracies, but the spoke members are not liable for the acts of the other conspirators.

7. Impossibility

Factual impossibility (that it was factually impossible to complete the intended crime) is not a defense to conspiracy. Legal impossibility (that the intended act is not criminal in nature) may be a defense if the object of the agreement is not a crime.

8. Withdrawal

a. Effect on liability for conspiracy

At common law, withdrawal was not a defense to conspiracy because the conspiracy is complete as soon as the parties enter into the agreement. Under the federal rule, which is also the majority rule, a conspiracy does not come into existence until an overt act has been committed. Consequently, after there has been an agreement but before an overt act has been committed, a person may avoid criminal liability for conspiracy by communicating notice of his intent not to participate to the other potential co-conspirators or by informing the police about the agreement. Upon completion of the overt act, the conspiracy is formed, and withdrawal is no longer possible. Under the MPC and the minority view, subsequent withdrawal or renunciation is possible only if there is timely notification that is sufficient to "thwart the success" of the conspiracy.

b. Effect on liability for substantive crimes

A co-conspirator may limit his liability for the substantive crimes that are the subject of the conspiracy by withdrawing from the conspiracy at any time after it is formed. For this purpose, he may withdraw by giving notice to his co-conspirators or timely advising legal authorities of the existence of the conspiracy even though such an action does not thwart the conspiracy.

9. Termination

It is important to determine when a conspiracy ends for the purposes of determining the statute of limitations and the admissibility of acts or declarations made by the conspirators in furtherance of the crime. Generally, the act of concealing the conspiracy is not treated as a part of the conspiracy.

10. Punishment

Jurisdictions vary widely with respect to penalty provisions for conspiracies. Some jurisdictions make conspiracy a misdemeanor regardless of the objective, while other jurisdictions provide maximum sentencing depending on the objective. Still others allow for a permissible maximum sentence, regardless of the objective. Nevertheless, sometimes the sentencing for conspiracy is more severe than the punishment for the crime itself.

D. ATTEMPT

An attempt requires:

i)   A **substantial step** toward the commission of a crime; coupled with

ii) The **specific intent** to commit the crime.

If the crime is successfully completed, the attempt is merged into the completed crime.

1. Substantial Step Test

A subjective test, called the "substantial step" test, is applied to determine whether an attempt has occurred. Under this test, conduct does not constitute a substantial step if it is in mere preparation; the act must be conduct that tends to effect the commission of a crime.

a. Preparatory acts

Any of the following preparatory acts may constitute a substantial step if they corroborate the defendant's criminal purpose:

i)   Lying in wait, searching for, or following the intended victim;

ii)   Unlawful entry into the place contemplated for the commission of the crime;

iii) Enticing the intended victim to go to such place;

iv) Possession of materials specially designed for committing the crime;

v)   Possession of materials to be used in the commission of the crime at or near the place of commission; and

vi) Soliciting an innocent agent to engage in criminal conduct.

b. "Dangerous proximity" test

Some states continue to apply the traditional "dangerous proximity" test. Under this test, an attempt does not occur until the defendant's acts result in a dangerous proximity to completion of the crime.

2. Specific Intent

The defendant must possess the specific intent to perform an act or attain a result, which, if completed, would constitute the target crime, even if the target crime is not a specific-intent crime.

Example: Arson is not a specific-intent crime, but attempted arson is. An attempt to commit a strict-liability crime is also a specific-intent crime.

There is no attempt to commit negligent crimes like involuntary manslaughter because a defendant's act cannot be both intentional and negligent.

3. Impossibility

Impossibility is not a defense to attempt if the crime attempted is factually impossible to commit due to circumstances unknown to the defendant. If, however, the act intended is not a crime (i.e., a legal impossibility), then the defendant is not guilty of attempt. In such a case, even when statutes purport to have done away with the impossibility defense, there is always a provision that allows for legal impossibility.

Example: D shoots V, believing that V is sleeping. V actually was already dead. D is guilty of attempted murder, but not murder.

4. Abandonment

At common law, once the defendant has taken a substantial step toward the commission of the offense, the defendant may not legally abandon the attempt to commit the crime because of a change of heart. Upon the completion of a substantial step, the crime of attempt is completed; there can be no abandonment or withdrawal.

Some states do recognize voluntary abandonment as a defense to attempt. Even then, abandonment is not voluntary if it is motivated by a desire to avoid detection, a decision to delay commission of the crime until a more favorable time, or the selection of another similar objective or victim. Abandonment by the defendant does not constitute a defense for an accomplice who did not join in the abandonment or withdrawal.

5. Prosecution and Punishment

A defendant who does not complete a crime may be charged only with attempt of the completed crime. However, if a defendant completes a crime, he may be charged either with attempt of the completed crime or with the completed crime itself. Punishment for attempt is usually less severe than the sentence for the completed offense.

V. DEFENSES

A. GENERALLY

1. Justification and Excuse

Defenses may be divided into the categories of justification and excuse. When the defendant's actions, despite being criminal, are socially acceptable, the defendant has acted justifiably. Self-defense and defense of others are examples of justification defenses. When the defendant has a disability that makes her not responsible for her actions, the defendant's criminal behavior is excused. Insanity, intoxication, and duress are examples of excuse defenses. This distinction does not affect the applicability or operation of these defenses.

2. Mistake of Fact

When a defendant is factually mistaken (e.g., the defendant thinks that the victim is holding a pistol that instead is a toy gun), the defendant may generally rely on a defense if the mistake is a reasonable one. In determining the reasonableness of the mistake, the defendant's physical characteristics, experiences, and knowledge are taken into account. An unreasonable factual mistake is a defense only to a specific-intent crime.

B. SPECIFIC DEFENSES

1. Self-Defense

One who is not the aggressor is justified in using reasonable force against another person to prevent immediate unlawful harm to himself. The harm to the defendant must be imminent, not a threat of future harm. The defendant can use only as much force as is required to repel the attack.

a. Deadly force

Deadly force is force that is intended or likely to cause death or serious bodily injury. Deadly force may be justified in self-defense only when it is reasonably necessary to prevent death or serious injury; to prevent the commission of a serious felony; or, in some cases, to apprehend a fleeing felon who may endanger the safety of the community.

b. Nondeadly force

Nondeadly force is force that is not intended or likely to cause death or serious bodily injury and may be used to repel nondeadly force.

c. Retreat

There is never an obligation to retreat before employing nondeadly force. Under the majority view, retreat is not required even when deadly force is used in self-defense. Under the minority view (states that follow the so-called "retreat doctrine"), retreat is required if it can be safely accomplished. Even under the minority view, however, retreat is never required when the person employing deadly force is in his own home.

d. Imperfect right of self-defense

Imperfect self-defense occurs when the person claiming self-defense unjustifiably kills the attacker. The purpose of the rule is to reduce the charge from murder to voluntary manslaughter. The rule is applied when, for some reason, the defendant cannot claim perfect self-defense. For example, a defendant honestly, but unreasonably, believes that deadly force is required to prevent death or serious bodily injury.

e. Aggressor's right to use self-defense

It is possible for an initial aggressor to gain the right to act in self-defense in two circumstances: (i) an aggressor using nondeadly force is met with deadly force, or (ii) the aggressor has, in good faith, completely withdrawn from the altercation and has communicated that fact to the victim.

2. Defense of Others

A person has the right to defend others under the same circumstances in which self-defense would be acceptable. Defense of others is not limited to defending family members but extends to anyone the defendant reasonably believes has the right of self-defense.

3. Defense of Property

A person in lawful possession of property that is threatened by the conduct of another, and who has no time to seek assistance from law enforcement, may take reasonable steps, including the use of nondeadly force, to protect the property. To use force, the defender must reasonably believe that the real property is in immediate danger of unlawful trespass or that personal property is in immediate danger of being carried away, and that the use of force is necessary to prevent either. The force cannot be unreasonably disproportionate to the perceived harm.

There is no right to use deadly force in defending property, with one exception. Generally, a person may use deadly force to prevent or terminate a forcible felony in the dwelling, arson, burglary, or robbery. The use of deadly force against an intruder exiting the dwelling is generally not permitted. Mechanical devices cannot be used to protect property.

4. Arrest

A police officer or a person acting under police direction is justified in using reasonable force to make a lawful arrest or to prevent the escape of one already in lawful custody.

a. Right to arrest

The right of a police officer to arrest a suspect is often specified by statute. A police officer can lawfully arrest a suspect, with or without a warrant, if the suspect has committed a crime in the officer's presence or if the officer has probable cause to believe that the defendant committed a felony offense outside of his presence. A civilian acting without police direction in making an arrest (e.g., a "citizen's arrest") who makes a mistake, even a reasonable mistake, as to the commission of the crime is not entitled to rely on this defense.

b. Use of force to arrest

A police officer can use nondeadly force to arrest a suspect. A police officer can use deadly force to arrest a suspect if the suspect represents a threat to either the officer or third parties.

c. Resisting unlawful arrest

A defendant may use nondeadly force to resist an unlawful arrest, but never deadly force. Some jurisdictions do not permit the use of force at all and require defendants to seek legal redress for an unlawful arrest.

5. Prevention of Crimes

Anyone can use deadly force to prevent the commission of a serious felony involving a risk to human life, and may use nondeadly force to prevent the commission of a felony or a breach-of-the-peace misdemeanor. A private citizen who makes a mistake, even a reasonable mistake, as to the commission of a serious felony by the victim is not entitled to rely on this defense.

6. Public Authority

Actions taken by public officials pursuant to legal authority (e.g., court-ordered seizure of property, state-sanctioned executions) are justified.

7. Parental Authority

The use of reasonable force in the exercise of parental authority (i.e., discipline) by a parent or by a person in charge of a child (e.g., a teacher) is justified if exercised for the benefit of the minor child.

8. Duress

A third party's unlawful threat that causes a defendant to reasonably believe that the only way to avoid death or serious bodily injury to himself or another is to violate the law, and that causes the defendant to do so, allows the defendant to claim the duress defense.

Duress is not a defense to intentional murder. A defendant charged with felony murder may claim duress as a defense to the underlying felony and avoid conviction for felony murder.

9. Necessity

If natural forces of nature (e.g., storm, fire) cause the defendant to commit what would otherwise be a crime, the defendant may be justified in doing so based upon necessity. The law prefers that the defendant, when faced with two evils, avoids the greater evil by choosing the lesser evil, e.g., the destruction of property to prevent the spread of a fire.

The defendant is not entitled to assert necessity if he set the natural forces in motion (e.g., set the fire) or if there is a noncriminal alternative. In addition, economic necessity does not justify theft. For example, an unemployed worker may not steal food from the grocery store.

Necessity is a result of natural forces; duress results from human actions.

EXAM NOTE: While the defendant may escape criminal liability, the defendant may be compelled by tort law to reimburse the victim for any losses.

10. Consent

Consent of the victim is not a defense to a crime unless the consent negates a required element of the crime or precludes the harm sought to be avoided by the crime. Such consent must be voluntarily and freely given, involve no fraud, and be given by one competent to consent.

Consent is a defense to rape (unless the woman is a minor), since rape is defined as sexual intercourse without consent. Consent is also a defense to kidnapping if an adult (but not a minor) consents to traveling with the defendant.

a. Bodily injury

Consent to bodily injury or to conduct that may cause bodily injury may constitute a defense when the injury is not serious or, with regard to a sporting event or similar activity, the conduct and injury are reasonably foreseeable (e.g., boxing).

b. Ineffective consent

Consent may be ineffective when given by a legally incompetent person; by a victim who is unable to make a reasonable judgment due to age, mental disease or defect, or intoxication; or by a victim whom the law seeks to protect. Consent obtained by fraud, duress, or deception may also be ineffective.

11. Entrapment

Entrapment is the conception and planning of an offense by a law-enforcement officer, and his procurement of its commission by a defendant who would not have committed that offense except for the trickery, persuasion, or fraud of the officer. If an officer merely offers an already-predisposed person the opportunity to commit a crime, it is not entrapment. In other words, the defendant must lack any predisposition to commit the crime. Entrapment can occur through the use of an undercover agent but not by a private citizen. The modern trend allows a defendant to deny participation in an event, yet still raise the defense of entrapment. Traditionally, the defendant was precluded from using the entrapment defense if he denied his participation in the event.

a. Subjective approach

The majority of states and the U.S. Supreme Court have adopted the subjective test for entrapment. Under this approach, the **focus is on the defendant**. Entrapment occurs when (i) the crime is induced by a government official or agent, and (ii) the **defendant was not predisposed** (i.e., ready and willing) to commit the crime. If a defendant is predisposed to committing the crime, then the entrapment defense is not available, even if the government agent has engaged in misconduct, such as by supplying contraband. *Hampton v. United States*, 425 U.S. 484 (1976).

b. Objective approach

Under the objective approach, which has been advanced by the MPC and adopted by a few states, the **focus is on the government's action** and the effect those actions would have on a hypothetical innocent person. This approach requires the government official or agent to have induced or encouraged the defendant to commit a crime by employing methods of persuasion or inducement that **create a substantial risk** that the crime will be committed by an otherwise law-abiding citizen.

12. Alibi

An alibi is a defense whereby a defendant denies his participation in a crime because he asserts that he was somewhere else at the time of the commission of the alleged crime.

Criminal Procedure

CRIMINAL PROCEDURE

Table of Contents

I. FOURTH AMENDMENT: APPLICATION TO ARREST, SEARCH AND SEIZURE 1

A. GENERAL FOURTH AMENDMENT PRINCIPLES 1

    1. STANDING...1

    2. THE EXCLUSIONARY RULE 1

    3. ABUSE OF DISCRETION STANDARD...1

    4. THRESHOLD OF GOVERNMENTAL ACTION 1

    5. GRAND JURY SUBPOENA 2

    6. BROADER RIGHTS POSSIBLE UNDER STATE CONSTITUTION.............................2

B. ARREST: UNREASONABLE SEIZURE OF PERSONS...2

    1. SEIZURE: OBJECTIVE TEST—NOT FREE TO LEAVE..2

        a. Intentional detention 2

    2. CONTRAST STOP AND FRISK 3

    3. ARREST WARRANTS...3

        a. Entry into home 3

    4. WARRANTLESS ARRESTS 3

        a. Crime committed in the presence of the arresting party.............................3

        b. Crime committed outside the presence of the arresting party 3

        c. Misdemeanor arrest 3

        d. Effect of invalid arrest..4

C. SEARCH AND SEIZURE...4

    1. GOVERNMENTAL ACTION..4

    2. DEFINING "SEARCH": THE VIOLATION OF A REASONABLE EXPECTATION OF PRIVACY..4

        a. Locations searched..4

        b. Objects sought 6

        c. Persons and their attributes...8

        d. Methods used to search 8

    3. SEARCH WARRANT REQUIREMENTS 9

        a. Probable cause 9

      b.   **Particularity** 10

      c.   **Anticipatory warrant** 10

      d.   **Third-party premises** 10

      e.   **Execution of warrant** 11

   4. **EXCEPTIONS TO THE WARRANT REQUIREMENT** 11

      a.   **Search incident to a lawful arrest** 12

      b.   **Exigent circumstances** 13

      c.   **Stop and frisk** 13

      d.   **Automobile exception** 15

      e.   **"Plain-view" doctrine** 16

      f.   **Consent searches** 16

      g.   **Administrative searches** 18

      h.   **Wiretapping** 20

   5. **RAISING THE ISSUE OF STANDING** 20

   6. **EXCLUSIONARY RULE** 21

      a.   **Fruit of the poisonous tree** 21

      b.   **Exceptions** 21

      c.   **Harmless error** 22

      d.   **Enforcement** 22

      e.   **Obtaining evidence by questionable methods** 23

II. **FIFTH AMENDMENT RIGHTS AND PRIVILEGES** 23

 A. **THE PRIVILEGE AGAINST COMPULSORY SELF-INCRIMINATION** 23

   1. **PERSONS** 23

   2. **TESTIMONIAL EVIDENCE** 23

   3. **COMPULSORY DISCLOSURE** 23

      a.   **Subpoena** 23

      b.   **Warrant for seizure of documents** 23

   4. **NATURE OF PROCEEDINGS** 24

   5. **INVOKING THE PRIVILEGE** 24

      a.   **Defendant's privilege** 24

      b.   **Witness's privilege** 24

   6. **COUNSELING CLIENTS TO INVOKE THE PRIVILEGE** 24

7. INVOCATION OF PRIVILEGE SHOULD NOT IMPOSE A BURDEN 24

8. WAIVING THE PRIVILEGE 25

B. THE FIFTH AMENDMENT IN A POLICE INTERROGATION CONTEXT 25

1. CUSTODIAL INTERROGATION 25

   a. "Custodial" 25

   b. "Interrogation" 26

2. COMPLIANCE 27

   a. Content 27

   b. Timing 27

   c. Right to counsel invoked 27

   d. Right to silence invoked 28

   e. Grand jury 28

3. EXCEPTIONS TO THE *MIRANDA* REQUIREMENT 28

   a. Public safety 28

   b. Routine booking 28

   c. Undercover police 28

4. WAIVER 28

5. USE OF STATEMENTS TAKEN IN VIOLATION OF *MIRANDA* 29

   a. Impeachment purposes 29

   b. Involuntary confessions 29

C. FRUITS OF A TAINTED CONFESSION 29

1. PHYSICAL EVIDENCE 29

2. SECOND CONFESSION 29

D. FIFTH AMENDMENT IN THE TRIAL CONTEXT 30

1. SCOPE OF PRIVILEGE 30

2. VOLUNTARINESS 30

3. IMMUNITY 30

   a. Transactional immunity 30

   b. Use and derivative-use immunity 30

   c. Federal and state immunity 30

4. PROSECUTORIAL COMMENT 30

III. SIXTH AMENDMENT 31

    A. APPLICABILITY: RIGHT TO COUNSEL 31

        1. TYPES OF PROCEEDINGS 31

        2. WHEN APPLICABLE 31

            a. Critical stages 31

            b. Noncritical stages 31

        3. INDIGENCE 32

        4. WAIVER 32

    B. OFFENSE-SPECIFIC 32

        1. *BLOCKBURGER* TEST 32

        2. COMPARE TO *MIRANDA* 33

    C. REMEDIES FOR DENIAL OF COUNSEL 33

        1. EFFECT ON CONVICTION 33

        2. EFFECT ON GUILTY PLEA 33

        3. EFFECT ON DENIAL OF COUNSEL AT NONTRIAL PROCEEDINGS..................33

        4. ADMISSIBILITY OF A DEFENDANT'S STATEMENTS TO INFORMANTS..............33

        5. EXCLUSIONARY RULE UNDER THE SIXTH AMENDMENT 33

            a. Fruits doctrine 33

            b. Impeachment 34

    D. INEFFECTIVE ASSISTANCE OF COUNSEL..34

        1. STANDARD OF COMPETENCE 34

        2. CONFLICT OF INTEREST 34

            a. Actual conflict..34

            b. Adverse impact...34

            c. Knowledge of the court 35

            d. Rule 44(c) 35

            e. Disqualification despite waiver 35

        3. COMMUNICATION OF FORMAL PLEA OFFER..35

        4. RIGHT TO CONFIDENTIAL COMMUNICATIONS 35

IV.   PRETRIAL PROCEDURES...36

    A. EYEWITNESS IDENTIFICATION PROCEDURES..36

        1. TYPES 36

        2. SIXTH AMENDMENT RIGHT TO COUNSEL AT LINEUPS 36

        a. **Waiver** 36

        b. **Remedy** 36

    3. **ADMISSIBILITY OF PRE- AND POST-INDICTMENT IDENTIFICATION** 36

        a. **Two-prong test** 36

        b. **Remedy** 37

    4. **NON-CORPOREAL IDENTIFICATIONS** 37

  B. **PRELIMINARY PROCEEDINGS** 37

    1. **PROBABLE CAUSE TO DETAIN (*GERSTEIN* HEARING)** 37

    2. **INITIAL APPEARANCE** 38

    3. **ARRAIGNMENT** 38

    4. **DETENTION HEARING** 38

    5. **PRELIMINARY HEARING TO DETERMINE PROBABLE CAUSE TO PROSECUTE** .38

  C. **RIGHT TO BAIL** 38

    1. **STATUTORY BAIL PROVISIONS** 38

    2. **PRESUMPTIONS PRE- AND POST-CONVICTION** 39

    3. **PRE-TRIAL DETENTION** 39

  D. **COMPETENCY** 39

  E. **GRAND JURIES** 39

    1. **INDICTMENT** 39

    2. **GRAND JURY PROCEEDINGS** 40

        a. **Defendant's rights** 40

        b. **Role of the prosecutor** 40

        c. **Witness's rights** 40

        d. **Grand jury's role** 40

  F. **STATE'S DUTY TO DISCLOSE** 41

V. **TRIAL** 41

  A. **JURY TRIAL** 41

    1. **MAXIMUM SENTENCE TO EXCEED SIX MONTHS** 41

        a. **Contempt** 41

    2. **WAIVER** 42

    3. **COMPLIANCE** 42

        a. **Jury size and unanimity** 42

      b.   **Composition of the jury**...**42**

      c.   **Impartial jury**...**44**

      d.   **Sentencing**...**44**

      e.   **Inconsistent verdicts**...**45**

B. GUILTY PLEAS..**45**

    1. KNOWING AND VOLUNTARY...**45**

      a.   **Factual basis for plea** **45**

      b.   **Effect of violation** **46**

    2. RIGHT TO COUNSEL **46**

    3. PLEA BARGAIN...**46**

      a.   **No right to bargain**...**46**

      b.   **Pressure to bargain** **46**

      c.   **No duty to disclose impeachment information** **46**

      d.   **Enforcement of the bargain** **46**

    4. EFFECT OF THE PLEA ON THE DEFENDANT'S RIGHTS.......................**47**

C. SPEEDY TRIAL..**47**

    1. COMMENCEMENT OF THE RIGHT **47**

    2. BALANCING TEST **47**

    3. REMEDY...**48**

D. PUBLIC TRIAL **48**

    1. DEFENDANT'S RIGHT **48**

    2. PUBLIC'S RIGHT...**48**

E. FAIR TRIAL **48**

    1. IMPARTIAL JUDGE **48**

    2. FAIR CONDUCT BY THE PROSECUTOR...**48**

      a.   **Examples of misconduct**..**48**

      b.   **No use of false testimony** **49**

      c.   **No suppression of favorable evidence** **49**

F. RIGHT TO CONFRONTATION **49**

    1. TRIAL **49**

    2. COMPLIANCE..**49**

      a.   **Face-to-face confrontation**..**49**

        b. Cross-examination of witnesses 50

  G. DUE PROCESS 52

     1. RIGHT TO TESTIFY 52

     2. BURDEN OF PROOF 52

        a. Presumptions 52

        b. Elements of the prosecution's case 53

        c. Affirmative defenses 53

        d. Directed verdict 53

  H. SENTENCING 53

     1. APPLICABLE RIGHTS 53

     2. ENHANCEMENT OVER THE STATUTORY MAXIMUM 53

  I. CRUEL AND UNUSUAL PUNISHMENT 54

     1. APPLICABILITY 54

     2. COMPLIANCE 54

        a. Non-death penalty 54

        b. Capital punishment 55

        c. Adequate medical care 57

VI. POST-TRIAL CONSIDERATIONS 57

  A. DOUBLE JEOPARDY 57

     1. PROTECTION AGAINST PROSECUTION AND PUNISHMENT 57

        a. Definition of "same offense" 57

        b. Acquittal 59

     2. ATTACHMENT OF JEOPARDY 59

     3. DIFFERENT JURISDICTIONS 59

     4. CIVIL ACTIONS 59

     5. GUILTY PLEA 60

     6. MISTRIAL 60

     7. APPEAL 60

        a. By the prosecution 60

        b. By the defendant 60

     8. RETRIAL OFFENSES 61

     9. RETRIAL PUNISHMENT 61

      a. Capital sentencing procedures 61

   10. COLLATERAL ESTOPPEL 61

B. APPEAL 62

C. CONVICTIONS 62

   1. WRIT OF HABEAS CORPUS 62

   2. PAROLE AND PROBATION 62

   3. ACCESS TO COURTS 63

   4. DISENFRANCHISEMENT 63

CRIMINAL PROCEDURE

I. FOURTH AMENDMENT: APPLICATION TO ARREST, SEARCH AND SEIZURE

The Fourth Amendment reads: "The right of the people to be secure in their persons, houses, papers, and effects against unreasonable searches and seizures shall not be violated, and no Warrants shall issue, but on probable cause, supported by Oath or affirmation, and particularly describing the place to be searched, and the persons or things to be seized." This amendment protects persons against unreasonable arrests or other seizures as well as unreasonable searches. In addition, when a warrant is required, it must comply with these constitutional requirements.

A. GENERAL FOURTH AMENDMENT PRINCIPLES

1. Standing

Fourth Amendment rights are personal and may not be asserted vicariously. A defendant cannot successfully challenge governmental conduct as a violation of the Fourth Amendment protection against unreasonable searches and seizures unless the defendant himself has been seized or he has a reasonable expectation of privacy with regard to the place searched or the item seized. It is not enough that the introduction as evidence of an item seized may incriminate the defendant.

Example: Defendants Al and Bob are accused of burglarizing an electronics store. Police found stolen DVD players in Al's apartment after an illegal warrantless search. Only Al has standing to raise the issue of a Fourth Amendment violation; Bob may not raise it in his own defense, as his rights were not violated.

2. The Exclusionary Rule

The right to be free from unreasonable searches and seizures must be distinguished from the remedy. The primary remedy is the "exclusionary rule," which prevents the introduction at a subsequent criminal trial of evidence unlawfully seized. This remedy is judicially created, not constitutionally mandated. The remedy provided by the exclusionary rule generally applies to criminal trials; it **does not apply** in other court proceedings, including federal habeas corpus review of state convictions, grand jury proceedings, preliminary hearings, bail hearings, sentencing hearings, and proceedings to revoke parole. Evidence will also not be excluded at trial when introduced as impeachment evidence against the defendant. Finally, the exclusionary rule is not applicable to civil proceedings. *See* § I.C.6., Exclusionary Rule, *infra,* for an expanded discussion.

3. Abuse of Discretion Standard

The judge, not the jury, resolves suppression issues raised by a pretrial motion to suppress. These issues are reviewed on appeal under the "abuse of discretion" standard.

4. Threshold of Governmental Action

The Fourth Amendment limits governmental action; it does not restrict the acts of private parties unless the private person is acting as an "instrument or agent of the government." Even if governmental action exists, there still is no constitutional violation unless the individual had a reasonable expectation of privacy and either the police did not have a valid warrant or they executed an invalid warrantless search.

> **EXAM NOTE:** Remember, the Fourth Amendment applies only to searches and seizures conducted by police or someone acting under police direction.

5. Grand Jury Subpoena

Unless a grand jury subpoena is being used for harassment or is extremely broad, requiring a person to appear before the grand jury under such subpoena does not fall under the protection of the Fourth Amendment.

6. Broader Rights Possible Under State Constitution

A state may grant broader rights under its own constitution than are granted by the federal Constitution. *See Michigan v. Long*, 463 U.S. 1032 (1983). Thus, even though the Fourth (or Fifth or Sixth) Amendment may not restrict the state government, state constitutional law may.

B. ARREST: UNREASONABLE SEIZURE OF PERSONS

1. Seizure: Objective Test—Not Free to Leave

A person is seized by the police when the officer, by means of physical force or show of authority, terminates or restrains freedom of movement; there is no seizure without actual submission. *Terry v. Ohio*, 392 U.S. 1 (1968). When the actions of the police do not show an unambiguous intent to restrain or when the individual's submission to a show of governmental authority takes the form of passive acquiescence, a seizure occurs only if, in view of the totality of the circumstances, a **reasonable person would believe he was not free to leave.** The test is whether a reasonable person would feel free to decline the officers' requests or otherwise terminate the encounter.

a. Intentional detention

The police officer must intentionally employ physical force or a show of authority in order for the officer's actions to result in a seizure.

> **Example:** During a high-speed chase, an officer forced the driver of the pursued automobile off the road. The officer's intentional use of deadly force against the driver constituted a seizure. *Scott v. Harris*, 550 U.S. 372 (2007).
>
> **Compare:** During a high-speed chase, an officer accidentally struck and killed the passenger of the pursued motorcycle when the motorcycle tipped over. The officer's accidental use of deadly force against the passenger did not constitute a seizure. *County of Sacramento v. Lewis*, 523 U.S. 833 (1998).

However, as long as the officer intentionally employs force or makes a show of authority, the officer's purpose need not be to detain the defendant in order for the defendant to be seized. Consequently, when a police officer makes a traffic stop, not only the driver but also any passengers are deemed to be seized. Therefore, the passenger as well as the driver may challenge the constitutionality of the stop. *Brendlin v. California*, 551 U.S. 249, 251 (2007).

2. Contrast Stop and Frisk

A temporary detention for the purpose of a stop-and-frisk search is not an arrest, but it may still constitute a seizure for Fourth Amendment purposes. The test is whether the officer, by means of physical force or show of authority, has in some way restrained the liberty of the citizen. Seizure includes physical restraint or an order to stop so that the officer can frisk and ask questions on the street.

3. Arrest Warrants

An arrest warrant is issued by a detached and neutral magistrate upon a finding of probable cause that a crime has been committed and that it was the particular defendant who committed the particular crime. However, an arrest made pursuant to a warrant that failed to satisfy the probable cause requirement is not illegal when the officer making the arrest independently had probable cause for making the arrest.

a. Entry into home

A warrant to arrest an individual implicitly authorizes entry into the arrestee's home to serve the warrant if the police have probable cause to believe that the arrestee is present. A police officer may not arrest a person in another person's home without a search warrant, absent exigent circumstances or valid consent. *Steagald v. United States*, 451 U.S. 204 (1981).

4. Warrantless Arrests

Unlike searches, police generally do not need a warrant to make a valid arrest **in a public place,** even if they have time to get one. *U.S. v. Watson*, 423 U.S. 411 (1976). The police, however, must have a warrant to arrest an individual in his own home, absent exigent circumstances or valid consent. *Payton v. New York*, 445 U.S. 573 (1980).

a. Crime committed in the presence of the arresting party

Either a police officer or a private individual has a right to arrest without an arrest warrant if either a felony or a misdemeanor amounting to a breach of the peace is committed in the arresting party's presence.

b. Crime committed outside the presence of the arresting party

In situations in which a **felony** has been committed outside the presence of the one making the arrest, a police officer may arrest anyone whom he reasonably believes has committed a felony, but a private individual may make an arrest only if (i) a felony has actually been committed and (ii) the private individual reasonably believes that the person being arrested is guilty.

c. Misdemeanor arrest

A warrantless arrest of a person for a misdemeanor punishable only by a fine is not an unreasonable seizure under the Fourth Amendment. *Atwater v. Lago Vista*, 532 U.S. 318 (2001). Note that the misdemeanor must have been committed in the presence of the arresting party; probable cause to believe that a misdemeanor was committed, without actually witnessing the crime, is not sufficient for a valid warrantless arrest.

d. Effect of invalid arrest

An unlawful arrest alone has **no bearing** on a subsequent criminal prosecution, and it is not a defense to the crime charged. If the police have probable cause to detain a suspect, they may do so even if they illegally arrested him (e.g., in his home without a warrant).

An unlawful arrest has legal significance, however, when there is a seizure of evidence. Evidence seized pursuant to an unlawful arrest may be suppressed at trial.

C. SEARCH AND SEIZURE

1. Governmental Action

Searches conducted by private citizens are not protected by the Fourth Amendment—there must be governmental action. However, the police may not circumvent the Fourth Amendment by intentionally enlisting private individuals to conduct a search of a suspect or areas in which the suspect has a reasonable expectation of privacy.

2. Defining "Search": The Violation of a Reasonable Expectation of Privacy

Only **unreasonable** searches and seizures are subject to the Fourth Amendment. A **search** occurs when governmental conduct violates a **reasonable expectation of privacy**. *Katz v. United States*, 389 U.S. 347 (1967). A search also may occur when the government physically intrudes upon private property for the purpose of obtaining information. *United States v. Jones*, 565 U.S. ___, 132 S. Ct. 945 (2012) (placement of GPS device on defendant's vehicle for the purpose of monitoring the vehicle's movements constituted a search).

> **EXAM NOTE:** Be aware of fact patterns that involve an individual with no expectation of privacy, such as when incriminating evidence is seized at another individual's home. Remember that the search is valid unless there is a legitimate expectation of privacy or the government trespassed upon the defendant's private property.

a. Locations searched

1) Home

Although the Supreme Court has stated that "the Fourth Amendment protects people, not places," (see *id.* at 351), the Fourth Amendment, by its terms, protects against an unreasonable governmental search of a "house." This protection extends to persons who have the right to immediate possession of a dwelling, such the renter of an apartment. *Chapman v. United States*, 365 U.S. 610 (1961).

a) Curtilage

In addition to the home itself, an area immediately surrounding the home known as the "curtilage" may be covered by the "umbrella" of the home's Fourth Amendment protection. In determining whether the area is protected, the following four-factor test applies:

i) The proximity of the area to the home;

ii) Whether the area is included within an enclosure surrounding the home;

iii) The nature of the uses to which the area is put; and

iv) The steps taken by the resident to protect the area from observation by passersby.

United States v. Dunn, 480 U.S. 294 (1987).

> **Example:** A barn was 60 yards away from the main house and 50 yards away from the innermost fence surrounding the house. The barn was not being used for domestic purposes and, despite being surrounded by a fence, was fenced in a manner that did not prevent persons from observing what lay inside the fence. Consequently, the barn and the area immediately surrounding it lay outside the curtilage. Information of illegal drug activity being conducted within the barn gained by drug enforcement agents while within that area did not constitute an unreasonable search. *Id.*

b) Open fields

Private property that lies outside the curtilage of a home, such as a farmer's field, is not protected by the home's umbrella of Fourth Amendment protection. Under the "open fields" doctrine, governmental intrusion on such property is not a search. The owner does **not** have a reasonable (i.e., objective) expectation of privacy, even though the owner may have a subjective expectation of privacy based on the fact that the land is fenced, protected from public view, and "no trespassing" signs are posted. *United States v. Oliver*, 466 U.S. 170 (1984).

c) Overnight guest in a home

While an overnight guest in a home does not have an ownership interest in the home, such a guest does have a reasonable expectation of privacy, at least as to the areas of the home to which the guest has permission to enter. *Minnesota v. Olson*, 495 U.S. 91 (1990). (As to the ability of the owner or guest to consent to a search of the home, *see* § I.C.4.f, Consent searches, *infra.*)

> **Contrast short-term use of home for illegal business purpose:** Short-term use of a home (e.g., several hours) with the permission of the owner does not give rise to a reasonable expectation of privacy, at least when the home is being used for an illegal business purpose (e.g., bagging cocaine for sale on the streets). *Minnesota v. Carter*, 525 U.S. 83 (1998).

2) Motel room

As with the search of a home, the search of a motel room by a government agent may be an unreasonable search. A motel clerk's consent to a governmental search of a room during the time it is rented is insufficient to justify the search. *Stoner v. California*, 376 U.S. 483 (1964).

3) Business premises

In general, business premises are protected by the Fourth Amendment. *G.M. Leasing Corp. v. United States*, 429 U.S. 338 (1977). However, such premises may be subjected to administrative searches, *see* § I.C.4.g., Administrative searches, *infra.*

4) Prison

A prison inmate has no reasonable expectation of privacy in his cell. The limitations on Fourth Amendment rights are justified by the need to maintain institutional security and preserve internal order and discipline. *Hudson v. Palmer*, 468 U.S. 517 (1984). Unlike a convict, a pretrial detainee may have a limited expectation of privacy in his cell. However, a detainee's cell may be subject to a routine search, and the detainee's person may be subject to a strip search or a full-body search after a contact visit with someone from the outside. *Bell v. Wolfish*, 441 U.S. 520 (1979). Jail administrators may also require all arrestees committed to the general population of a jail to undergo no-touch visual strip searches, even if the arrest was for a minor offense and even in the absence of reasonable suspicion that the arrestee possesses a concealed weapon or other contraband. *Florence v. Board of Chosen Freeholders of County of Burlington*, 566 U.S. ____, 132 S. Ct. 1510 (2012).

5) Trespass

While the fact that a governmental agent is on property without permission may make a warrantless search unreasonable (e.g., a search of a home), the fact that a governmental agent is illegally on property does not automatically make the search illegal (*United States v. Oliver*, *supra*), nor does the fact that a governmental agent is legally in a public place make the search legal (*Katz v. United States*, *supra*).

b. Objects sought

1) Papers and effects

The Fourth Amendment, by its terms, protects "papers and effects." For example, a person retains a reasonable expectation that items placed within his luggage will be free from a purposeful, exploratory physical manipulation of the luggage. *Bond v. United States*, 529 U.S. 334 (2000).

Compare smell emanating from object. A person does *not* have a reasonable expectation of privacy with regard to a smell emanating from his luggage, at least when the smell arises from an illegal substance. *United States v. Place*, 462 U.S. 696 (1983).

When papers and effects are transferred to a third party, such as checks and deposit slips given by a customer to a bank, a person no longer has a reasonable expectation of privacy in these items. Similarly, financial statements maintained by a bank are bank records in which the customer has no reasonable expectation of privacy. *United States v. Miller*, 425 U.S. 435 (1976).

2) Automobiles

Although, under the Fourth Amendment, stopping a car constitutes a seizure of the driver and any passengers, *Brendlin v. California*, 551 U.S. 249 (2007) (passenger), *Delaware v. Prouse*, 440 U.S. 648 (1979) (driver), there is a lesser expectation of privacy with regard to the automobile and its contents than with a home. *Wyoming v. Houghton*, 526 U.S. 295 (1999). Even so, officers must have an articulable, reasonable suspicion of a violation of the law in order to stop an automobile.

a) Checkpoints

Police may stop an automobile at a checkpoint without reasonable, individualized suspicion of a violation of the law if the stop is based on neutral, articulable standards and its purpose is closely related to an issue affecting automobiles. A roadblock to perform sobriety checks has been upheld, while a similar roadblock to perform drug checks has not. *Compare Michigan Dept. of State Police v. Sitz*, 496 U.S. 444 (1990) (sobriety check) *with Indianapolis v. Edmond*, 531 U.S. 32 (2000) (check for illegal drugs).

Compare random stops: Police may generally *not* stop an automobile, even for a driving-related matter, without a reasonable, individualized suspicion of a violation of the law, unless the stop is effected on the basis of neutral, articulable standards. *Delaware v. Prouse*, 440 U.S. 648 (1979) (no random stop of a driver to verify driver's license and car registration).

i) Immigration law enforcement

When the purpose of the stop relates to the enforcement of immigration laws, any car may be stopped on a random basis at the border of the United States without a reasonable suspicion of wrongdoing. *Almeida-Sanchez v. United States*, 413 U.S. 266 (1973). When a search does not occur at the border or its functional equivalent, all cars may be stopped at a fixed checkpoint without a reasonable suspicion of violation of an immigration law, but a car may not be singled out and randomly stopped without a particularized and objective basis. *United States v. Cortez*, 449 U.S. 411 (1981) (holding the stop of one car proper when officers could reasonably surmise that the car was involved in criminal immigration activity); *United States v. Martinez-Fuerte*, 428 U.S. 543 (1976) (affirming convictions based on stops at checkpoints at which all cars were stopped).

ii) Search for witnesses

A checkpoint maintained by police for the purpose of finding witnesses, rather than suspects, to a hit-and-run accident is not per se unreasonable. *Illinois v. Lidster*, 540 U.S. 419 (2004).

b) Car's VIN

The driver of a car does not have a reasonable expectation of privacy in the vehicle identification number (VIN) affixed to an automobile. *New York v. Class*, 475 U.S. 106 (1986). Consequently, a police officer's moving of papers that obstructed his view of this number did not constitute a search under the Fourth Amendment, and a gun found while doing so was admissible into evidence.

3) Abandoned property

Abandoned property is not protected by the Fourth Amendment.

Example: There is no reasonable expectation of privacy in garbage set curbside for pickup. *California v. Greenwood*, 486 U.S. 35 (1988).

c. Persons and their attributes

1) Physical characteristics

There is no expectation of privacy in one's physical characteristics; therefore, a demand for a handwriting or voice sample is not a search. *United States v. Mara*, 410 U.S. 19 (1973) (handwriting exemplar); *United States v. Dionisio*, 410 U.S. 1 (1973) (voice exemplar).

2) Government informants

Some surveillance and investigation techniques have been held not to implicate any reasonable expectation of privacy because the targets of the surveillance were regarded as having assumed the risk that the people with whom they were interacting would be government agents. There is no reasonable expectation of privacy in conversations carried on with government informants or undercover officers. Similarly, if one party to a telephone call consents to wiretapping or agrees to record the call at the government's request, such monitoring will not trigger the Fourth Amendment rights of any other party to the call. *United States v. White*, 401 U.S. 745 (1971). A person also runs the risk that a third party to whom she turns over information may disclose such information to the government. *United States v. Miller*, 425 U.S. 435 (1976).

d. Methods used to search

1) Fly-over

An inspection conducted from the air, whether by an airplane or a helicopter, does not violate a reasonable expectation of privacy and therefore is not a search for the purposes of the Fourth Amendment. *Florida v. Riley*, 488 U.S. 445 (1989) (helicopter); *California v. Ciraolo*, 476 U.S. 207 (1986) (airplane).

2) Technological device

With regard to automobiles, the Fourth Amendment does not prohibit the police from using technological devices to enhance their ability to search (e.g., radar detectors, computers to search license plates, surveillance equipment). *United States v. Knotts*, 460 U.S. 276 (1983) (placement of a tracking device on a car). However, physically intruding upon a suspect's property to install a technological device (e.g., a GPS tracker on a car) may constitute a search. *United States v. Jones, supra*.

> It is important to note the distinction between *Knotts* and *Jones*—in *Knotts*, the device was installed with the permission of the former owner (a person other than the suspect) before the car came into the defendant's possession; defendant Jones, on the other hand, owned the vehicle in question at the time the government installed the GPS device.

The use of a device or sense-enhancing technology (e.g., a thermal sensing device) that is not in use by the general public to explore the details of a dwelling that would previously have been unknowable without physical intrusion constitutes a search. *Kyllo v. United States*, 533 U.S. 27 (2001). Moreover, use of an electronic listening device to eavesdrop on a conversation made from a public phone booth can violate the speaker's reasonable expectation of privacy. *Katz v. United States, supra*.

> **Flashlight.** Because flashlights are ubiquitous, the use of a flashlight at night to illuminate the inside of a car does not constitute a search for Fourth Amendment purposes. *Texas v. Brown*, 460 U.S. 730 (1983).

3) Canine sniff

Use of a trained dog to sniff for the presence of drugs does not violate a reasonable expectation of privacy. *Illinois v. Caballes*, 543 U.S. 405 (2005) (car); *United States v. Place*, 462 U.S. 696 (1983) (luggage).

> **Officer's sense of smell:** A police officer may also rely on his own sense of smell in ascertaining the presence of illegal drugs or alcohol. *United States v. Sharpe*, 470 U.S. 675 (1985) (marijuana); *United States v. Ventresca*, 380 U.S. 102, 104, 111 (1965) (alcohol).

4) Field test of substance

A field test performed on a substance to determine if the substance is contraband is not a search for Fourth Amendment purposes. *United States v. Jacobsen*, 466 U.S. 109 (1984).

3. Search Warrant Requirements

When a search occurs, a warrant serves to protect a person's privacy interests against unreasonable governmental intrusion. A valid search warrant must be issued by a neutral and detached magistrate based on probable cause, must be supported by oath or affidavit, and must describe the places to be searched and the items to be seized.

> Warrantless searches are per se unreasonable unless the search satisfies one of seven exceptions to the warrant requirement.

a. Probable cause

Facts supporting probable cause may come from any of the following sources:

i) A police officer's personal observations;

ii) Information from a reliable, known informant or from an unknown informant that can be independently verified; or

iii) Evidence seized during stops based on reasonable suspicion, evidence discovered in plain view, or evidence obtained during consensual searches.

1) Right to attack truthfulness of affidavit

Generally, a search warrant that is valid on its face may not be attacked by a defendant as lacking in probable cause. A defendant can challenge a facially valid warrant only when the defendant can establish, by a preponderance of the evidence, that:

i) The affidavit contained **false statements** that were **made** by the affiant **knowingly, intentionally, or with a reckless disregard** for their truth; and

ii) The false statements were **necessary to** the finding of **probable cause.**

Franks v. Delaware, 438 U.S. 154 (1978).

2) Informants

Courts use the **totality of the circumstances** test to determine whether information provided by a police informant is sufficient to create probable cause. The affidavit generally does not need to include any particular information about the informant, including the informant's identity, so long as a neutral magistrate can find that, based on the informant's information and all other available facts, there is probable cause to issue the warrant. *Illinois v. Gates*, 462 U.S. 213 (1983); *McCray v. Illinois*, 386 U.S. 300 (1967).

b. Particularity

A search warrant must describe with particularity the place to be searched and the objects to be seized. *United States v. Grubbs*, 547 U.S. 90 (2006). Warrants that, in addition to describing specific documents to be seized, also refer to "other fruits, instrumentalities and evidence of the crime at this [time] unknown" are not converted into illegal general warrants by the inclusion of such language. The reference to a "crime" has been interpreted as being limited to a particular crime (e.g., false pretenses), rather than any crime. *Andresen v. Maryland*, 427 U.S. 463 (1976). A warrant need not specify the manner of its execution.

c. Anticipatory warrant

Police do not have to believe that contraband is on the premises to be searched at the time the warrant is issued. The probable cause requirement is satisfied when, at the time that the warrant is issued, there is probable cause to believe that the triggering condition will occur and, if that condition does occur, there is a fair probability that contraband or evidence of a crime will be found in a particular place. *United States v. Grubbs, supra.*

d. Third-party premises

A search warrant may be issued to search the premises of a person who is not suspected of a crime. *Zurcher v. Stanford Daily*, 436 U.S. 547 (1978).

e. Execution of warrant

1) By whom

A warrant cannot be executed by a private citizen. Generally, only a police officer may execute a warrant, but administrative warrants may be executed by the appropriate governmental official (e.g., fire inspector).

2) Timing

A warrant that is not timely executed (i.e., an unreasonable delay occurs) may be subject to challenge on the grounds that probable cause ceased to exist.

3) Manner of execution

a) Knock and announce

Most states and the federal government mandate that a police officer, when executing a warrant, must generally announce his purpose before entering. The failure to "knock and announce" will invalidate the arrest. A state may permit an exception to the rule if the entry is made under exigent circumstances, such as when there is a reasonable belief of danger to the officer or destruction of evidence. *Ker v. California*, 374 U.S. 23, 34 (1963).

Note, though, that violation of the "knock and announce" rule does not trigger the exclusionary rule (*see* § I.C.6., *infra*) with respect to evidence discovered as a result of a search conducted in violation of the "knock and announce" rule. *Hudson v. Michigan*, 547 U.S. 586 (2006).

4) Seizure of evidence not specified

A search warrant confers authority to search only the places and persons named in it. Regardless, any evidence of a crime, instrumentalities or fruits of a crime, or contraband found in plain view while properly executing the warrant, whether or not specified in the warrant, may be seized (*see* § I.C.4.e., "Plain view" doctrine, *infra*).

5) Treatment of persons not specified in the warrant

Independent justification is needed to search persons not named in a search warrant; mere proximity to a named person does not supply such justification. *Ybarra v. Illinois*, 444 U.S. 84 (1979). However, in conducting a search for contraband pursuant to a warrant, any occupant of the premises to be searched may be detained in a reasonable manner, which may include the use of handcuffs, for a reasonable time while the search is conducted. *Muehler v. Mena*, 544 U.S. 93 (2005); *Michigan v. Summers*, 452 U.S. 692 (1981).

4. Exceptions to the Warrant Requirement

EXAM NOTE: Warrantless searches are frequently tested on the MBE. Be aware of answer choices that include concepts that apply to one type of warrantless search when another is being tested.

a. Search incident to a lawful arrest

A warrantless search is valid if it is reasonable in scope and if it is made incident to a lawful arrest. If the arrest is invalid, any search made incident to it is likewise invalid. Therefore, if a suspect is stopped for a traffic offense and given a citation but not arrested, then there can be no search incident to lawful arrest. *Knowles v. Iowa*, 525 U.S. 113 (1999).

1) The *Chimel* standard

A lawful arrest creates a situation that justifies a warrantless contemporaneous search of the person arrested and the immediate surrounding area (his "wingspan") from which a weapon may be concealed or evidence destroyed. *Chimel v. California*, 395 U.S. 752 (1969). If the arrest occurs in a home, it is permissible to search "closets and other spaces immediately adjoining the place of arrest from which an attack could be launched." *Maryland v. Buie*, 494 U.S. 325, 334 (1990).

2) Time limitations (temporal unity)

A search incident to a valid arrest must take place promptly after the arrest in order to be valid.

3) Scope of search

The right to search incident to a lawful arrest includes the right to search pockets of clothing and to open containers found inside the pockets. The right also extends to containers "immediately associated" with the person (such as a shoulder bag or purse), **so long as the containers are large enough to conceal a weapon or evidence of a crime.**

4) Vehicle search incident to arrest

For many years, if the police had probable cause to arrest the driver or passenger of a vehicle, an officer could conduct a full search, incident to that arrest, of the passenger compartment and all containers therein, whether open or closed. This was known as the *Belton* rule. *New York v. Belton*, 453 U.S. 454, 460 (1981).

In 2009, the Supreme Court restricted the parameters for a warrantless vehicle search incident to arrest. *Arizona v. Gant*, 556 U.S. 332 (2009). The *Gant* Court held that, in order to justify a warrantless search of an automobile incident to arrest, the Fourth Amendment requires that law enforcement demonstrate either (i) that the arrestee is within reaching distance of the passenger compartment at the time of the search and, as a result, may pose an actual and continuing threat to the officer's safety or a need to preserve evidence from being tampered with by the arrestee or (ii) that it is reasonable that evidence of the offense of arrest might be found in the vehicle.

5) Impounded vehicle

A legally impounded vehicle may be searched, including closed containers, such as glove box or a backpack, as part of a routine inventory search. *South Dakota v. Opperman*, 428 U.S. 364, 369–71 (1976). The warrantless search need not take place at the time that the vehicle is seized.

b. Exigent circumstances

Warrantless entry into a home or business is presumed unlawful unless the government demonstrates both probable cause and exigent circumstances. In determining the existence of exigent circumstances, courts use the "totality of circumstances" test. As a corollary to this doctrine, police may also secure the premises for a reasonable time to enable officers to obtain a warrant when the police have reason to believe that the failure to do so could result in the destruction of evidence. *Illinois v. McArthur*, 531 U.S. 326 (2001).

The exigent-circumstances rule does not apply when the police create the exigency by engaging or threatening to engage in conduct that violates the Fourth Amendment. *Kentucky v. King*, 563 U.S. ___, 131 S. Ct. 1849 (2011).

1) Hot pursuit

If the police have probable cause to believe that an individual has committed a *felony* and they are pursuing him to arrest him, then they have the right to enter a private building during the pursuit, to search that building while they are present on the premises, and to seize evidence found there, even though the material found is "mere" evidence and neither fruits nor instrumentalities of a crime.

No such exigency exists in pursuing someone suspected of a nonjailable traffic offense; the hot-pursuit exception is inapplicable in that instance. *Welsh v. Wisconsin*, 466 U.S. 740 (1984).

2) Emergency situations

A search without a warrant is authorized whenever there is a reasonable apprehension that the delay required in obtaining the warrant would result in the immediate danger of evidence destruction or the threatened safety of the officer or the public, or when a suspect is likely to flee before a warrant can be obtained.

The Supreme Court has ruled that the involuntary, warrantless blood test of a drunken-driving suspect was appropriate when police could reasonably have believed that the delay necessary to obtain a search warrant would likely result in disappearance of the blood-alcohol content evidence, and the test was administered according to accepted medical practices. *Schmerber v. California*, 384 U.S. 757 (1966).

c. Stop and frisk

1) Stop—limited seizure/detention

A "stop" (also known as a "*Terry* stop") is a limited and temporary intrusion on an individual's freedom of movement short of a full custodial arrest. Merely approaching a person, but not restricting the person's movement in any way, does not constitute a detention. A stop is justified on the **reasonable suspicion,** based upon **articulable facts,** that the detainees are or were involved in criminal activity. *Terry v. Ohio*, 392 U.S. 1 (1968). Whether reasonable suspicion exists is based on the **totality of the circumstances.** It requires more than a vague suspicion, but less than probable cause, and it need not be based on a police officer's personal knowledge.

> **Example:** Police were justified in stopping a suspect who (i) was standing on a street corner in a high-crime area and (ii) fled upon noticing the police, even though neither factor alone would constitute reasonable suspicion to justify a stop. *Illinois v. Wardlow*, 528 U.S. 119 (2000).

Reasonable suspicion can be based on a flyer, a police bulletin, or an informant's tip, but only if the tip is accompanied by sufficient indicia of reliability. *United States v. Hensley*, 469 U.S. 221, 233–34 (1985).

2) Frisk—limited search

An officer who does not have probable cause to arrest may make a limited search of the person, such as a pat-down of the outer clothing, if he has **reasonable suspicion** that the suspect was or is involved in criminal activity and that the frisk is necessary for the preservation of his safety or the safety of others.

Under the **"plain feel"** exception, if an officer conducting a valid frisk feels an object that has physical characteristics that make its identity immediately obvious (i.e., he has probable cause to believe that the item is contraband), then the officer may seize the evidence. Police may also *briefly* seize items if the officers have a reasonable suspicion that the item is or contains contraband.

3) *Terry* stop of a car

Pursuant to a lawful stop of a vehicle, police may conduct a search of the passenger compartment for weapons, if:

i) The police possess a reasonable belief that the suspect is dangerous and may gain immediate control of weapons; and

ii) The search of the passenger compartment is "limited to those areas in which a weapon may be placed or hidden."

Maryland v. Buie, 494 U.S. 325, 332 (1990); *Michigan v. Long*, 463 U.S. 1032, 1048–50 (1983).

Police may order occupants out of a vehicle that they have lawfully stopped. *Maryland v. Wilson*, 519 U.S. 408 (1997).

When police lawfully detain a driver or a passenger after a traffic stop, they may frisk the person if there is reasonable suspicion that the individual has a weapon. *Arizona v. Johnson*, 555 U.S. 323 (2009).

4) Limits on time, place, and investigative method

A *Terry* stop must be temporary and last no longer than is necessary to effectuate the purpose of the stop. The investigative methods employed should be the least intrusive means reasonably available to verify or dispel the officer's suspicion in a short time.

Police may stop the person, question him for a limited period of time, and frisk him for weapons only, not evidence. Police also can require that the detained person identify himself. Failure to comply with this request can result in the arrest of the detained person.

When police hold a suspect beyond the amount of time necessary to effectuate the purpose of the stop, the seizure becomes an arrest and must be supported by probable cause.

5) Development of probable cause

If the officer conducting the stop develops probable cause, the officer may then make an arrest and conduct a full search incident to that arrest. If the stop involves a vehicle, the officer may search the passenger compartment and all containers therein, whether open or closed, if the arrestee is within reaching distance of the passenger compartment of the vehicle or if it is reasonable to believe that the vehicle contains evidence of the offense of arrest. *See* § I.C.4.a.4), Vehicle search incident to arrest, *supra,* discussing the *Gant* rule.

d. Automobile exception

The Fourth Amendment does not require police to obtain a warrant to search a vehicle if they have probable cause to believe that it contains contraband or evidence of a criminal activity. The police may search anywhere in a car that they believe there to be contraband, including the trunk and locked containers, so long as they have **probable cause** to do so. *United States v. Ross*, 456 U.S. 798, 825 (1982). The search may also extend to passengers' belongings, *Wyoming v. Houghten*, 526 U.S. 295, 302 (1999), as well as to mobile homes, *California v. Carney*, 471 U.S. 386, 393–394 (1985). Any other evidence observed in plain view may also be seized.

1) Pretextual stop

Police may use a pretextual stop to investigate whether a law has been violated, even if they have no reasonable suspicion, provided that they have probable cause to believe that the law for which the vehicle was stopped has been violated. *Whren v. United States*, 517 U.S. 806 (1996) (seizure of illegal drugs constitutional even though police stopped a car for a traffic violation as a pretext to investigate a hunch that the occupants possessed drugs).

2) Containers within a car

Probable cause to search a vehicle extends only to containers and compartments that reasonably could hold the evidence. However, if the police have probable cause to search only containers, they may search only that container, but not the entire car. *California v. Acevedo*, 500 U.S. 565, 570 (1991).

Example: A driver left a residence holding a closed paper bag, which officers had probable cause to believe contained narcotics, based on an informant's tip. The bag was placed in the trunk, and the driver drove away. Police were authorized to stop the vehicle, open the trunk, and inspect the bag. However, the search was limited to the bag only. If they did not find the bag, they could only open and search containers big enough to store the bag. *Id.* at 579–80.

3) Trunk

If police have probable cause to search the trunk, not just a container placed in the trunk, then they can search the entire trunk and every container in the trunk, even if locked.

e. "Plain-view" doctrine

1) In public view

Items in public view may be seized without a warrant because one cannot have a reasonable expectation of privacy in things that are exposed to the public (e.g., physical characteristics, vehicle identification numbers, or items in open fields).

2) In private view

In situations in which there is a reasonable expectation of privacy (e.g., in a suspect's house), a police officer may seize an item in plain view of the officer, even if it was not named in the search warrant or the discovery was not inadvertent, as long as (i) the officer is on the premises for a **lawful purpose,** and (ii) the incriminating character of the item is **immediately apparent.** If the officer is not legitimately on the premises, the plain view doctrine does not apply. *Horton v. California*, 496 U.S. 128 (1990); *Arizona v. Hicks*, 480 U.S. 231 (1987).

> **Example:** Officer Olivia was executing a valid warrant to search Defendant Doug's home for a gun suspected to have been used in a murder. On entering the premises, Olivia saw what appeared to be bags of cocaine piled on Doug's coffee table. Under the "plain view" doctrine, Olivia could properly seize the bags, even though the warrant applied only to a gun.

f. Consent searches

Consent can serve to eliminate the need for police to have probable cause as well as to first obtain a warrant in order to conduct a search.

1) Voluntary

For permission to constitute consent, the permission must be given voluntarily. Permission given under threats of harm or compulsion does not constitute consent. In determining whether a person's response constitutes consent, courts evaluate the **totality of the circumstances** in which the response is made.

a) False assertion of authority

Permission given in acquiescence to lawful authority (e.g., a warrant) is not voluntary. Consequently, if the officer conducting the search erroneously states that he has a warrant, then permission given in reliance on that statement does not constitute consent. *Bumper v. North Carolina*, 391 U.S. 543, 549 (1968).

b) Knowledge of the right to withhold consent

The failure by police to inform the person from whom consent is sought that she has the right to withhold consent does not invalidate the consent. *Schneckloth v. Bustamonte*, 412 U.S. 218, 233 (1973).

2) Third-party consent

When the person from whom consent is sought is not the defendant, in addition to the voluntariness of the permission, the authority of that person to consent can be an issue.

a) Property of a third party

Generally, a third party has the authority to consent to a search of property that she owns or occupies. As such, the defendant cannot suppress evidence seized during such a search on the grounds that he (the defendant) did not consent to the search.

b) Property of the defendant

Generally, a third party does not have the authority to consent to a search of property owned or occupied by the defendant. The defendant can suppress evidence seized during such a search unless (i) an agency relationship exists between the third party and the defendant that gives to the third party the right to consent on behalf of the defendant, or (ii) the defendant otherwise gives the third party such rights with respect to the property that the defendant assumes the risk that the third party would allow the property to be searched (e.g., a shared duffle bag). *Frazier v. Cupp*, 394 U.S. 731, 740 (1969).

c) Jointly controlled property

When the property to be searched is under the joint control of the defendant and a third party (e.g., co-tenants of an apartment, a house jointly owned by a husband and wife), the authority of the third party to consent turns on whether the defendant is present at the time of the search.

i) Defendant not present

If the property to be searched is under the joint control of the defendant and a third party, and the defendant is not present at the time of the search, then the third party has authority to consent. The third party has actual authority when she has joint access or control for most purposes. *U.S. v. Matlock*, 415 U.S. 164, 170–171 (1974). In addition, the third party's consent may be valid even though she lacks actual authority if the police reasonably believe that she has such authority. *Illinois v. Rodriguez*, 497 U.S. 177, 184 (1990).

ii) Defendant present

When the property to be searched is under the joint control of the defendant and a third party, and the defendant is present at the time of the search, then the police may not rely on third-party consent if the defendant objects to the search. *Georgia v. Randolph*, 547 U.S. 103, 114–116 (2006).

iii) Ownership versus current control

In some instances, ownership of the premises is not sufficient to confer authority to consent to a search. For example, a landlord may not consent to a search of the tenant's premises. *Chapman v. United States*, 365 U.S. 610, 617 (1961). Similarly, a hotel clerk cannot consent to the search of a guest's room. *Stoner v. California*, 376 U.S. 483, 489 (1964).

iv) Parental consent

When a child lives with a parent, the parent has the authority to consent to a search of a child's room even if the child is an adult. However, a parent may lack authority to consent to the search of a locked container inside the child's room, depending on the age of the child. *U.S. v. Block*, 590 F.2d 535, 540 (4th Cir. 1979).

3) Scope of consent

Although a search is limited to the area to which the consent applies, the search may extend to areas that a reasonable person would believe it extends. For example, consent by a driver to search his car for drugs extends to a closed container within the car that could contain drugs. *Florida v. Jimento*, 500 U.S. 248, 252 (1991).

4) Burden of proof

The prosecution must prove that the permission was freely given; the defendant is not required to show that the permission was coerced.

g. Administrative searches

Administrative search warrants are generally required for nonconsensual fire, health, or safety inspections of residential or private commercial property.

1) Probable cause

The probable cause requirement for administrative searches is less stringent than that for a criminal investigation. Evidence of an existing statutory or regulatory violation or a reasonable plan supported by a valid public interest will justify the issuance of a warrant. *Camara v. Mun. Court of San Francisco*, 387 U.S. 523, 533 (1967).

2) Use of administrative searches

The government may not use administrative searches to investigate criminal activity. However, discovery of evidence during the search does not invalidate the search. The following administrative-type searches may be validly made without a warrant:

  i) Searches of people entering an **airplane boarding area,** as long as the passenger can prevent the search by not boarding the plane;

ii) Searches of businesses in **highly regulated industries** such as liquor stores, gun shops, strip-mining operations, and automobile junkyards, because of urgent public interest and under the theory that the business impliedly consented to warrantless searches by entering into a highly regulated industry;

iii) Oral statements seized by **wiretaps,** when matters of national security are at issue;

iv) Searches of students by **public school officials,** so long as they are based on reasonable grounds (this standard is lower than probable cause and calls for only a "moderate chance" of finding the expected evidence, rather than a "fair probability" or "substantial chance"), and the measures adopted for the search are reasonably related to the objectives of the search and not excessively intrusive in light of the age and sex of the student and the nature of the infraction. *New Jersey v. T.L.O.*, 469 U.S. 325, 340–341 (1985);

> Note that searches of students by public school officials must have been initiated by the school officials and not at the request of the police in order to be valid.

v) **Special needs searches,** such as drug testing for railroad employees involved in an accident or student athletes during the athletic season. To be a special need, the state interest must be a real, current, and vital problem that can be effectively addressed through the proposed search. Even if the need exists, it must be balanced against the privacy interest at stake and the character of the intrusion. *Bd. of Educ. v. Earls*, 536 U.S. 822, 829 (2002);

vi) **Inventory searches** of items in official custody, such as impounded vehicles. After lawfully taking custody of property, police may conduct a warrantless search of other property to protect the owner's property while in custody, to protect police from claims of theft, and to protect officers from danger. Inventory searches must be performed according to standardized criteria and procedures. Subjective intent of the officer is irrelevant;

vii) **Routine international border** searches of border crossers and their belongings within the United States, including (i) stops, but not searches, by roving patrols who reasonably suspect that undocumented immigrants may be in an automobile, (ii) opening of international mail if authorities have reasonable cause to suspect contraband in the mail, and (iii) subsequent reopening of mail after the item had been resealed and delivered to the recipient;

viii) **Vehicle checkpoints and roadblocks** set up to stop cars on the basis of a neutral articulable standard and designed to serve a limited purpose closely related to the problem of an automobile's inherent mobility (e.g., to get drunk drivers off the road);

ix) **Factory searches** of the entire work force to determine citizenship of workers;

x) Searches of **government employees' file cabinets and desks** if they are justified by a reasonable suspicion of work-related misconduct or a non-investigatory, work-related need;

xi) **Detention of a traveler** whom authorities have reasonable suspicion is smuggling contraband in his stomach;

xii) Searches of **parolees and their homes,** even with no reasonable suspicion, when a parolee agrees to submit to searches by a parole officer or police officer at any time as a condition of his parole. The rationale being that because there is a greater need to search parolees since they are less likely to be law-abiding citizens, a parolee has a lower expectation of privacy;

xiii) Seizure of **contaminated or spoiled food**; and

xiv) Searches for the **cause of a fire** that occurs within a reasonable time after the fire is extinguished, but excluding searches for other evidence unrelated to the cause that would establish that the fire was attributable to arson. *Michigan v. Clifford*, 464 U.S. 287 (1984) (search of home); *Michigan v. Tyler*, 436 U.S. 499 (1978) (search of business (furniture store)).

h. Wiretapping

To obtain a warrant authorizing a wiretap, officers must satisfy the below requirements. The warrant must:

i) Be limited to a short period of time;

ii) Demonstrate probable cause that a specific crime has been or is about to be committed;

iii) Name the person or persons to be wiretapped;

iv) Describe with particularity the conversations that can be overheard; and

v) Include provisions for the termination of the wiretap.

Upon termination of the wiretap, the conversations that have been intercepted must be shown to the court. Note that a person assumes the unreliability of those to whom she speaks and has no Fourth Amendment claim if she finds out later that the listener was wired or recording the conversation. *United States v. White*, 401 U.S. 745 (1971). Furthermore, a speaker who makes no attempt to keep his conversation private has no Fourth Amendment claim. *Katz v. United States*, 389 U.S. 347 (1967).

In addition, a wiretap related to domestic security surveillance requires that a neutral and detached magistrate—not the president—make the determination that a wiretapping warrant should issue, and the wiretap must comply with the Omnibus Crime Control and Safe Streets Act. However, there is no requirement for prior authorization when a covert entry is planned to install the electronic equipment, or when a pen register is used.

5. Raising the Issue of Standing

To establish that a search violated his Fourth Amendment rights, a defendant must show a legitimate expectation of privacy with regard to the search (*see* § I.C.2., *supra*). To make such a showing, which is sometimes referred to as "standing," the defendant may have to admit facts that would incriminate him. Consequently, testimony given by the defendant to establish standing cannot be admitted as evidence against the defendant at trial.

6. Exclusionary Rule

Under the exclusionary rule, evidence obtained in violation of the Fourth, Fifth, or Sixth Amendments may not be introduced at trial to prove guilt. Under the Fourth Amendment, evidence seized during an unlawful search cannot constitute proof against the victim of the search. *Weeks v. United States*, 232 U.S. 383 (1914).

a. Fruit of the poisonous tree

Subject to some exceptions, the exclusionary rule applies not only to evidence initially seized as a result of the primary government illegality, but also to secondary "derivative evidence" discovered as a result of the primary taint, also known as the "fruit of the poisonous tree."

Example: A police officer conducts an unconstitutional search of a home, finds an address book, and uses that address book to locate a witness. The witness will not be allowed to testify, because her testimony would be a "fruit" of the unconstitutional search.

b. Exceptions

Evidence, whether primary or derivative, may still be admissible if one of the following exceptions to the exclusionary rule applies.

1) Inevitable discovery rule

The evidence would have been inevitably discovered through lawful means.

2) Independent source doctrine

The evidence was discovered in part by an independent source unrelated to the tainted evidence.

3) Attenuation principle

The chain of causation between the primary taint and the evidence has been so attenuated as to "purge" the taint. Both the passage of time and/or intervening events may attenuate the taint.

4) Good-faith exception

The good-faith exception applies to police officers who act in good faith on either a facially valid warrant later determined to be invalid or an existing law later declared unconstitutional. Good faith is limited to the objective good faith of a reasonable police officer.

This exception does **not** apply if:

i) No reasonable officer would rely on the affidavit underlying the warrant;

ii) The warrant is defective on its face;

iii) The warrant was obtained by fraud;

iv) The magistrate has "wholly abandoned his judicial role"; or

v) The warrant was improperly executed.

5) Isolated police negligence

Isolated negligence by law-enforcement personnel will not trigger the exclusionary rule. To trigger the rule, police conduct must be sufficiently deliberate such that exclusion can meaningfully deter it. The exclusionary rule serves to deter deliberate, reckless, or grossly negligent conduct or, in some circumstances, recurring or systemic negligence. *Herring v. United States*, 555 U.S. 135, 144 (2009).

Example: Defendant Don goes to the police station to pick up an impounded vehicle. Policeman Paul believes that there might be a warrant out from another county for Don's arrest and calls the other county's sheriff to check. The sheriff tells Paul that there is a warrant out for Don's arrest. Paul immediately arrests Don and in a search incident to the arrest finds illegal drugs and an illegal weapon on Don. Minutes later, the sheriff calls back to say that the warrant had actually been recalled and she had made a mistake. The exclusionary rule will not apply to the drugs and the weapon because Paul was relying in good faith on the erroneous information from the sheriff in conducting the arrest. The exclusionary rule should be applied only if there is substantial additional deterrence of police misconduct to be gained. *Herring v. United States*, 555 U.S. 135 (2009).

6) Knock and announce

The exclusionary rule does not apply to evidence discovered as a result of a search conducted in violation of the "knock and announce" rule, if the search was otherwise authorized by a valid warrant. *Hudson v. Michigan*, 547 U.S. 586 (2006).

7) In-court identification

A witness's in-court identification of the defendant is not fruit of an unlawful detention. Thus, the identification cannot be excluded. On the other hand, live testimony may be excluded as fruit of illegal police conduct if there is a sufficient link between the illegal police conduct and the testimony.

c. Harmless error

Even if the trial court wrongfully admitted illegally seized evidence, the appellate court can refuse to order a new trial if it finds that the error was harmless beyond a reasonable doubt, meaning that the erroneously admitted evidence did not contribute to the result.

Note: The denial of the right to counsel is never a harmless error.

d. Enforcement

When the defendant challenges a confession or the admissibility of evidence, by right, a hearing is held to determine whether the confession or evidence is fruit of the poisonous tree. This hearing is held outside the presence of the jury. The defendant has a right to testify at this hearing, and the state bears the burden of establishing admissibility by a preponderance of the evidence.

e. Obtaining evidence by questionable methods

Evidence obtained in a manner that shocks the conscience is inadmissible. Examples of such methods of gathering evidence include inducements by official actions that offend the sense of justice and serious intrusions into the body, such as with surgery to remove a bullet. Contrast that, however, with drawing blood, which is a reasonable intrusion because it does not generally involve trauma or pain and is a common medical procedure.

II. FIFTH AMENDMENT RIGHTS AND PRIVILEGES

A. THE PRIVILEGE AGAINST COMPULSORY SELF-INCRIMINATION

The Fifth Amendment provides that no person shall be compelled in any criminal case to be a witness against himself. It is applicable to the states through the Fourteenth Amendment.

1. Persons

A person means an individual. Artificial entities such as corporations, partnerships, and labor unions may not assert the privilege, but a sole proprietorship may. The privilege does not extend to the custodian of corporate records, even if production would incriminate the custodian individually.

2. Testimonial Evidence

The privilege protects only testimonial evidence. Nontestimonial physical evidence (such as blood or urine samples, Breathalyzer test results, handwriting exemplars, or other evidence of physical characteristics) is not protected.

3. Compulsory Disclosure

The privilege generally does not apply to an individual's voluntarily prepared business papers or to records required by law to be kept, such as tax returns. *Fisher v. United States*, 425 U.S. 391 (1976). However, a person can refuse to comply with a requirement to register or pay a tax where the requirement is directed at a select group "inherently suspect of criminal activities." *Marchetti v. United States*, 390 U.S. 39, 52 (1968) (occupational tax on bookies); *Leary v. United States*, 395 U.S. 6 (1969) (registration and tax based on transfer of marijuana).

a. Subpoena

A person who is served with a subpoena requiring the production of possibly incriminating documents may invoke the privilege if the act of turning over the documents constitutes self-incriminating testimony. *United States v. Hubbell*, 530 U.S. 27 (2000).

b. Warrant for seizure of documents

The Fifth Amendment does not prevent law-enforcement officials, pursuant to a valid warrant, from searching for and seizing documents that would incriminate a person. *Andresen v. Maryland*, 427 U.S. 463 (1976).

1) Diaries

Generally, the government may not compel **production** of a diary. The contents of a diary are similar to oral testimony, and as such are considered testimonial in nature. Because one cannot be compelled to testify against himself, the government may not compel production of documents that are similarly testimonial in nature. *See, e.g., Schmerber v. California*, 384 U.S. 757 (1966).

Note, however, that if the diary's production is not compelled, e.g., it is found incident to a lawful arrest, its contents likely are admissible (assuming the entries were made voluntarily).

4. Nature of Proceedings

The privilege extends to a defendant in any proceeding, whether civil or criminal, formal or informal, if the answers provide some reasonable possibility of incriminating the defendant in future criminal proceedings. However, the privilege cannot be invoked when the government requires civil records to be maintained and reported on for administrative purposes, because they are public records, unless those records fulfill a registration requirement of a select group of inherently suspect criminal activities and compliance would require self-incrimination. The privilege does not extend to identification requests at *Terry* stops. A violation occurs the moment the compelled statements are used against a person.

5. Invoking the Privilege

a. Defendant's privilege

A defendant who wishes to invoke the privilege simply invokes it by not taking the stand. Included in this right is the state's inability to compel the defendant to testify. The prosecution cannot bring the defendant's failure to take the stand to the jury's attention.

b. Witness's privilege

A witness, on the other hand, may be compelled to take the stand and can invoke the privilege only in response to a specific question.

6. Counseling Clients to Invoke the Privilege

Attorneys may counsel their clients to invoke the privilege and will not be held in contempt of court. Otherwise, the person invoking the privilege would be denied his Fifth Amendment protection.

7. Invocation of Privilege Should Not Impose a Burden

The state cannot penalize a defendant for invoking his right against self-incrimination by not testifying or cooperating with authorities. The prosecution cannot comment to the jury on the defendant's refusal to speak in accordance with his *Miranda* rights. A violation in this regard by the state triggers the harmless-error test. However, if during trial the defendant claims that he was not allowed to explain his story, then the prosecution may comment on the defendant's failure to take the stand.

8. Waiving the Privilege

A **defendant** waives the privilege by taking the witness stand; a **witness** waives the privilege by disclosing self-incriminating information in response to a specific question. Having taken the stand, the defendant cannot assert the privilege in response to the prosecution's proper cross-examination of his testimony, including impeachment questions.

B. THE FIFTH AMENDMENT IN A POLICE INTERROGATION CONTEXT

In the seminal case of *Miranda v. Arizona,* the U.S. Supreme Court held that a suspect has a constitutional right not to be compelled to make incriminating statements in the police interrogation process. *Miranda v. Arizona*, 384 U.S. 436 (1966). *Miranda* once was considered to be necessary in nearly every encounter with police. However, the Supreme Court has been gradually narrowing the scope and limiting the use of *Miranda.*

Any incriminating statement obtained as the result of **custodial interrogation** may not be used against the suspect at a subsequent trial **unless** the police provided procedural safeguards effective to secure the privilege against self-incrimination (i.e., informed the suspect of his *Miranda* rights). An incriminating statement includes not only a confession, but other inculpatory statements, and is subject to suppression even though the defendant intended the statement to be exculpatory.

1. Custodial Interrogation

Custodial interrogation is questioning initiated by law-enforcement officers after a person has been taken into custody.

a. "Custodial"

Custody is a substantial seizure and is defined as either a formal arrest or a restraint on freedom of movement to the degree associated with a formal arrest. *New York v. Quarles*, 467 U.S. 649, 655 (1984). A person is in custody when he is not free to leave or is otherwise deprived of his freedom in any significant way. The test is whether a **reasonable person** would **believe** that he is not free to leave. *Yarborough v. Alvarado*, 541 U.S. 652, 662 (2004). A child's age is a relevant factor to consider when determining whether the child is in custody for the purposes of *Miranda. J.D.B. v. North Carolina*, 564 U.S. ___, 131 S. Ct. 502 (2011).

> **Example:** Sarah voluntarily goes to the police station to talk about a crime. As soon as she arrives, she is informed by the officer on the case that she is free to leave at any time and is not under arrest. Even though she is speaking with the police at the police station, the totality of the circumstances establishes that she is not in "custody," and therefore *Miranda* will not apply. *See California v. Beheler*, 463 U.S. 1121 (1983); *Oregon v. Mathiason*, 429 U.S. 492 (1977).

Traffic stops generally are not considered custodial because they generally are brief and temporary. *Berkemer v. McCarty*, 468 U.S. 420 (1984).

1) Location irrelevant

There is no requirement that the interrogation take place in a police station to be deemed custodial, only that a governmental agent (e.g., police officer), not a civilian, does the interrogating.

2) Crime scene

The questioning of a person at the scene of a crime or pursuant to a field investigation does not constitute custody for *Miranda* purposes as long as the person questioned has the **right to leave** the presence of the questioning officer.

3) Effect of imprisonment

Imprisonment alone does not necessarily create a custodial situation within the meaning of *Miranda*. The questioning of a prisoner, who is removed from the general prison population, about events that took place outside the prison is not categorically "custodial" for *Miranda* purposes. A standard, objective "totality of circumstances" analysis applies when an inmate is interviewed, including consideration of the language that is used in summoning the prisoner to the interview and the manner in which the interrogation is conducted. *Howes v. Fields*, 565 U.S. ____, 132 S. Ct. 1181 (2012) (holding that defendant was not in custody for purposes of *Miranda* during seven-hour interrogation that lasted well into the night, because he was told at the outset of interrogation, and was reminded again thereafter, that he could leave and go back to his cell whenever he wanted).

b. "Interrogation"

Interrogation refers not only to express questioning, but also to any words or actions that the police know or should know are **likely to elicit an incriminating response.** *Rhode Island v. Innis*, 446 U.S. 291 (1980).

1) Voluntariness of statement

Volunteered statements are not protected by *Miranda*, as they are, by definition, not the product of interrogation.

A confession is involuntary only if the police coerced the defendant into making the confession. Whether a statement is voluntary or coerced is determined based on the totality of the circumstances (including facts such as the conduct of the police, the characteristics of the defendant, and the time of the statement). A claim that a confession should be excluded because it is involuntary must be decided by the trial judge as a preliminary question of fact, and not by the jury.

a) Trickery

Trickery by the police or false promises made to the accused by the police may render a confession involuntary. However, deceit or fraud by the interrogators (i.e., lying about a co-conspirator's confession) does not itself make the confession involuntary.

b) Character of the defendant

The defendant's age, state of health, education, or intoxication are all factors in determining the coercive nature of the confession. Although a potentially significant factor, the defendant's mental condition alone cannot violate the voluntariness standard. There must be coercive police activity for the confession to be found involuntary. *Colorado v. Connelly*, 479 U.S. 157 (1986).

2) Break in questioning

Miranda protections carry over when there is a break in the interrogation process attributed to a second police agency continuing an interrogation after the first police agency has stopped questioning the suspect.

> **EXAM NOTE:** Remember to apply the *Miranda* warnings only when an individual is subject to a custodial interrogation. If the police have no intention of questioning the individual, or if the individual is not in police custody, then the *Miranda* warnings are not applicable.

2. Compliance

Once a custodial interrogation begins, anything the defendant says is inadmissible until the defendant is informed of the *Miranda* rights **and** the defendant waives those rights.

The failure to give a suspect the *Miranda* warnings does not require suppression of physical fruits of the suspect's "unwarned but voluntary statements." *United States v. Patane*, 542 U.S. 630, 640 (2004).

a. Content

The warnings, which must be given before interrogation begins, need not be a verbatim repetition of the language used in the *Miranda* decision. Law-enforcement officials must inform defendants:

i) Of their right to remain **silent**;

ii) That any statement uttered may be **used in court**;

iii) Of their right to **consult an attorney** and to have the attorney present during an interrogation; and

iv) That an **attorney will be appointed** to represent indigent defendants.

b. Timing

The *Miranda* warning must be given before interrogation begins. If interrogation is stopped for a long duration, the warning must be given again.

c. Right to counsel invoked

The right to counsel under the Fifth Amendment is not the same as the constitutional requirement of the right to counsel under the Sixth Amendment. The right to counsel under the Fifth Amendment is not automatic. To invoke the right to counsel under the Fifth Amendment, the defendant must make a specific, unambiguous statement asserting his desire to have counsel present. If a suspect makes an ambiguous statement regarding the right to counsel, the police are not required to end the interrogation or to ask questions or clarify whether the suspect wants to invoke the right. *Davis v. United States*, 512 U.S. 452 (1994). However, once that right to counsel is invoked, **all** interrogation must stop until counsel is present. If the defendant voluntarily initiates communication with the police, a statement made by the defendant, such as a statement that the defendant spontaneously blurts out, can be admissible since it is not made in response to interrogation.

d. Right to silence invoked

As with the Fifth Amendment right to counsel, the defendant must make a specific, unambiguous statement asserting his desire to remain silent. *Berghuis v. Thompkins*, 560 U.S. ___, 130 S. Ct. 2250 (2010). If a defendant invokes his *Miranda* right to remain silent, the interrogator(s) must "scrupulously honor" that request. However, if after the defendant is released from custody, the defendant indicates a desire to speak to police, then a subsequent interrogation would be lawful, as long as the defendant was not coerced. The defendant must again receive fresh *Miranda* warnings.

e. Grand jury

There is no requirement to give *Miranda* warnings to a witness testifying for the grand jury. The witness may, however, consult with an attorney outside the grand jury room.

3. Exceptions to the *Miranda* requirement

a. Public safety

When the public's safety is at risk, the police are not required to give *Miranda* warnings before questioning a suspect.

b. Routine booking

The "routine booking question" exception allows police to ask a suspected drunken driver routine biographical questions and to videotape the driver's responses without first giving the driver *Miranda* warnings.

c. Undercover police

Miranda warnings are not required if the suspect being questioned is not aware that the interrogator is a police officer. *Illinois v. Perkins*, 496 U.S. 292, 294 (1990).

> **Example:** The police placed an undercover officer, posing as a criminal, in the defendant's jail cell, and the undercover officer engaged the defendant in a conversation designed to elicit details of the crime for which the defendant was suspected. Such statements were admissible in the absence of *Miranda* warnings. *Illinois v. Perkins, supra.*

4. Waiver

A defendant may knowingly and voluntarily waive his *Miranda* rights. The burden is on the government to demonstrate by a preponderance of the evidence that the waiver was made knowingly and voluntarily. (Keep in mind that a defendant's mental illness does not necessarily negate the voluntariness requirement; there must be coercive police activity for a confession to be involuntary. *Colorado v. Connelly, supra.*)

There can be no effective waiver, however, until the *Miranda* warnings are properly given. Silence on the part of the suspect is not sufficient to waive his *Miranda* rights. However, a suspect who has received and understood the *Miranda* warnings, and has not invoked his *Miranda* rights, waives the right to remain silent by making an uncoerced statement to the police. *Berghuis v. Thompkins*, 560 U.S. ___, 130 S. Ct.

2250 (2010). Once effectively waived, the police are not required to inform the suspect of the defense counsel's efforts to reach the defendant by telephone and need not inform counsel that the defendant is being questioned.

5. Use of Statements Taken in Violation of *Miranda*

The failure to give *Miranda* warnings is not a violation until a statement obtained without the use of warnings is used at trial. *Chavez v. Martinez*, 538 U.S. 760 (2003).

a. Impeachment purposes

Statements taken in violation of *Miranda* may be used to impeach the credibility of the criminal defendant if he takes the witness stand and gives testimony at variance with his previous admissions. *Harris v. New York*, 401 U.S. 222, 224 (1971). To be admissible for impeachment, the statement must be voluntary and trustworthy. The impeaching admissions may not be used directly in deciding ultimate issues of guilt or innocence; they may only be used in determining the defendant's veracity. The defendant's silence after being given his *Miranda* warnings cannot be used by the prosecution to oppose an insanity defense.

b. Involuntary confessions

Involuntary confessions (e.g., those produced by coercion) cannot be used either substantively or for impeachment purposes. If a coerced confession is admitted into evidence, however, reversal is not automatic; the harmless-error test is applied, and the conviction will stand if the prosecution can show other overwhelming evidence of guilt.

C. FRUITS OF A TAINTED CONFESSION

1. Physical Evidence

Derivative **physical evidence** (e.g., a gun) that has been obtained as a result of a confession that itself is inadmissible due to the failure by police to give *Miranda* warnings is admissible. *United States v. Patane*, 542 U.S. 630 (2004).

2. Second Confession

A *Miranda* violation does not automatically require the suppression of incriminating statements made by the defendant after receiving *Miranda* warnings. The giving of *Miranda* warnings generally removes the "taint" of the prior *Miranda* violation. *Oregon v. Elstad*, 470 U.S. 298, 305–306 (1985). However, a second confession may be suppressed when the circumstances indicate that the substance of *Miranda* has been drained away. For a plurality of the court, the test is an objective one—a reasonable person in the suspect's position would not have understood the *Miranda* warnings to convey a message that the suspect retained a choice about whether to remain silent. For the justice who cast the deciding vote (Justice Kennedy), the test is a subjective one—did the police act with an intent to circumvent the purpose of the *Miranda* warnings. *Miranda*; *Missouri v. Siebert*, 542 U.S. 600, 611 (2004).

D. FIFTH AMENDMENT IN THE TRIAL CONTEXT

1. Scope of Privilege

A defendant may refuse to testify at a criminal trial. He may also refuse to answer questions in other proceedings (i.e., civil depositions) when the answers might incriminate him in future criminal proceedings.

The privilege does not prevent the prosecutor from using prior conflicting statements to impeach the defendant once the defendant takes the stand. This is called "opening the door" by the defendant.

2. Voluntariness

Admissions of incriminating statements made during a court-ordered psychiatric examination are generally deemed involuntary and not admissible at trial unless the defendant is given *Miranda* warnings before the interview and waives his rights.

Business papers voluntarily prepared by an individual, or required records, such as tax returns, are not protected.

3. Immunity

The prosecution may compel incriminating testimony if it grants immunity to the individual and the individual must testify. The testimony cannot be used against the individual, directly or indirectly, in a subsequent prosecution.

a. Transactional immunity

Often called "blanket" or "total" immunity, "transactional immunity" fully protects a witness from future prosecution for crimes related to her testimony.

b. Use and derivative-use immunity

"Use and derivative-use" immunity only precludes the prosecution from using the witness's own testimony, or any evidence derived from the testimony, against the witness. The Supreme Court has held that the grant of "use and derivative-use" immunity is all that is constitutionally required to compel the testimony of a witness. *Kastigar v. United States*, 406 U.S. 441, 452–453 (1972). Testimony encouraged by a promise of immunity, however, is considered coerced and involuntary.

c. Federal and state immunity

Testimony under a grant of immunity may not be used by another U.S. jurisdiction to prosecute the defendant. *See United States v. Balsys*, 524 U.S. 666 (U.S. 1998); *Murphy v. Waterfront Comm'n*, 378 U.S. 52 (1964). Thus, a state grant of immunity will preclude admission of the testimony in a federal proceeding.

4. Prosecutorial Comment

The prosecutor may not comment on the defendant's exercise of the privilege against self-incrimination at trial. It is per se reversible error.

III. SIXTH AMENDMENT

The Sixth Amendment provides that the accused shall have the right to a public trial, the right to confront witnesses against him, the right to cross-examine witnesses, the right to be present at his own trial, and the right to "the assistance of counsel for his defense." The right to assistance of counsel encompasses not only the right to hire private counsel, but also the right to be provided with counsel without charge if the accused is unable to afford counsel.

A. APPLICABILITY: RIGHT TO COUNSEL

1. Types of Proceedings

The Sixth Amendment provides a constitutional right to counsel in any case in which actual or suspended incarceration is imposed. *Scott v. Illinois*, 440 U.S. 367 (1979).

2. When Applicable

The Sixth Amendment right to counsel applies at all **critical stages** of a prosecution, after formal proceedings have begun. The right automatically **attaches** when the State initiates prosecution with an **indictment or formal charge** and **ends at the sentencing stage** of the trial.

> **EXAM NOTE:** Unlike the Fifth Amendment right to counsel, the defendant does not need to invoke the Sixth Amendment right to counsel. The failure to provide counsel results in automatic reversal of a conviction.

a. Critical stages

The Supreme Court recently summarized its definition of "critical stage" as those proceedings between an individual and an agent of the state that amount to trial-like confrontations, at which counsel would help the accused in coping with legal problems or meeting his adversary. *Rothgery v. Gillespie County*, 554 U.S. 191, 212 (2008).

Generally, the Sixth Amendment right to counsel attaches at the following critical stages:

i) Post-indictment lineups and identifications;

ii) Post-indictment interrogations, whether custodial or otherwise;

iii) Arraignment and preliminary hearing to determine probable cause to prosecute;

iv) Plea bargaining, guilty pleas, and sentencing; and

v) Appeals as a matter of right.

b. Noncritical stages

The right to counsel generally does not apply to the following events:

i) A witness viewing photos of the alleged defendant;

ii) Precharge (investigative) lineups;

iii) Taking of fingerprints, handwriting exemplars, voice exemplars, or blood samples;

iv) Hearings to determine probable cause to detain the defendant (*Gerstein* hearing);

v) Discretionary appeals; and

vi) Post-conviction proceedings, such as parole or probation hearings (including habeas corpus).

3. Indigence

When the right to counsel exists, an indigent defendant has the right to the appointment of counsel. However, this right does not entitle an indigent defendant to the appointment of counsel of his own choosing. *See United States v. Gonzalez-Lopez*, 548 U.S. 140, 147–148 (2006) (defendant who retains his own counsel has the right to be represented by that attorney); *Wheat v. United States*, 486 U.S. 153 (1988).

4. Waiver

A defendant has the constitutional right to refuse counsel and proceed pro se at trial unless the request is untimely or the defendant is unable or unwilling to abide by the rules of procedure or protocol. *Faretta v. California*, 422 U.S. 806 (1975). A defendant who is competent to stand trial may nevertheless be found incompetent to represent himself. *Indiana v. Edwards*, 554 U.S. 164 (2009). In addition, a defendant does not have a right to proceed without an attorney on an appeal. *Martinez v. Court of Appeal*, 528 U.S. 152 (2000).

In the Fifth Amendment context, once an individual in custody asserts the Fifth Amendment right to counsel, no subsequent waiver of that right is valid in a police-initiated interrogation. *Edwards v. Arizona*, 451 U.S. 477, 484 (1981). However, police may re-open interrogation of a suspect who has asserted his Fifth Amendment right to counsel if there has been a 14-day or more break in custody (such as a the suspect's release back into the general prison population). *Maryland v. Shatzer*, 559 U.S. ___, 130 S. Ct. 1213 (2010). The Sixth Amendment right to counsel can be waived "so long as relinquishment of the right is voluntary, knowing and intelligent." *Montejo v. Louisiana*, 556 U.S. 778 (2009). Thus, as long as the defendant is given *Miranda* warnings and a valid waiver occurs, evidence obtained voluntarily from the interrogation without the presence of counsel is admissible.

> **EXAM NOTE:** Remember, even if the defendant has made a valid waiver of his right to counsel, statements made during interrogation must be **voluntary** to be admissible at trial, i.e., the police still cannot use compelled statements.

B. OFFENSE-SPECIFIC

Once the Sixth Amendment right to counsel is properly invoked, it applies **only** to the specific offense at issue in those proceedings. *McNeil v. Wisconsin*, 501 U.S. 171, 175–176 (1991).

1. *Blockburger* Test

Two crimes committed in one criminal transaction are deemed to be the same offense for Sixth Amendment purposes unless each offense requires proof of an element that the other does not. *Texas v. Cobb*, 532 U.S. 162 (2001); *Blockburger v. United States*, 284 U.S. 299, 304 (1932).

2. Compare to *Miranda*

Unlike under the *Miranda* standard, under the Sixth Amendment standard, the requirement for counsel to be present applies only to interrogations about the offense charged. However, like with *Miranda,* the defendant may make a knowing and voluntary waiver of the right to counsel being present.

> **Example:** Defendant Dave has been charged with burglary and is out on bail awaiting trial. The police also suspect Dave in an unrelated arson case, and they bring him to the police station to question him about the arson. Dave is given the *Miranda* warnings and waives his right to remain silent, but he asks to see his attorney. The police do not call Dave's attorney but continue to interrogate Dave until he confesses to the arson. While the police did violate Dave's Fifth Amendment right to have an attorney present during questioning, they did not violate his Sixth Amendment right to counsel, as the arson was unrelated to the burglary.

C. REMEDIES FOR DENIAL OF COUNSEL

1. Effect on Conviction

If a right to counsel at a trial proceeding under the Sixth Amendment is denied, the defendant's conviction should be automatically reversed, even without a specific showing of unfairness. *Gideon v. Wainwright*, 372 U.S. 335, 339 (1963). Automatic reversal also applies to a conviction obtained after a court has erroneously refused to permit an attorney chosen by the defendant to represent him, when that attorney is not supplied by the state. *United States v. Gonzalez-Lopez*, 548 U.S. 140 (2006).

2. Effect on Guilty Plea

If the defendant has pleaded guilty at a preliminary hearing, without being given the opportunity to have counsel, then the defendant has the right to withdraw the plea, and it may not be used against the defendant as an evidentiary admission. *White v. Maryland*, 373 U.S. 59, 60 (1963).

3. Effect on Denial of Counsel at Nontrial Proceedings

A denial of counsel at a nontrial proceeding, such as a lineup, is subject to harmless-error analysis. *United States v. Wade*, 388 U.S. 218, 223 (1967).

4. Admissibility of a Defendant's Statements to Informants

Post-indictment statements that a defendant makes to a police informant are inadmissible when the police intentionally create a situation likely to induce the defendant into making incriminating statements without the assistance of counsel. *United States v. Henry*, 447 U.S. 264, 274–275 (1980). There is no Sixth Amendment violation, however, if the police place an informant in the defendant's cell simply to listen and report the defendant's statements, without questioning the defendant. *Kuhlmann v. Wilson*, 477 U.S. 436, 456 (1986).

5. Exclusionary Rule Under the Sixth Amendment

a. Fruits doctrine

The fruit of the poisonous tree doctrine is applicable to violations of the Sixth Amendment right to counsel. *Nix v. Williams*, 467 U.S. 431 (1984). Both statements and physical evidence obtained as a result of a Sixth Amendment violation are inadmissible.

b. Impeachment

If the police initiate a conversation with an accused individual who has requested counsel, any incriminating statements made by the defendant may still be used for impeachment purposes, despite the fact that the improper police conduct precludes admission of the statements as part of the prosecution's case in chief. *Michigan v. Harvey*, 494 U.S. 344, 350–351 (1990).

D. INEFFECTIVE ASSISTANCE OF COUNSEL

1. Standard of Competence

The right to counsel encompasses the right to be assisted by a reasonably competent attorney and is presumed. The right to effective counsel extends to the defendant's first appeal. To reverse a conviction on the ground of ineffective counsel, the claimant has the burden to show that:

i) Counsel's representation fell below an objective standard of reasonableness; and

ii) Counsel's deficient performance prejudiced the defendant, resulting in an unreliable or fundamentally unfair outcome in the proceeding.

Strickland v. Washington, 466 U.S. 668, 687 (1984). Counsel's mere inexperience, strategy, choice of appellate issues, or even failure to produce mitigating evidence have all been found insufficient to rise to the level of ineffective counsel. *Bell v. Cone*, 535 U.S. 685 (2002); *Jones v. Barnes*, 463 U.S. 745 (1988); *United States v. Cronic*, 466 U.S. 648 (1984). The failure of defense counsel to raise a federal constitutional issue that was law at the time of the trial, but was later overruled, does not constitute ineffective assistance of counsel. *Lockhart v. Fretwell*, 506 U.S. 364 (1993).

2. Conflict of Interest

The representation of defendants with conflicting interests may amount to ineffective assistance of counsel. In general, to overturn a conviction on the basis of a conflict of interest, a defendant must show that there was an actual conflict of interest and that such conflict adversely affected the attorney's performance.

a. Actual conflict

To find an actual conflict, a court must determine that the defense attorney is subject to an obligation or unique personal interest that, if followed, would lead her to adopt a strategy other than that most favorable to the defendant.

b. Adverse impact

Adverse impact can be established by demonstrating that some plausible alternative defense strategy or tactic might have been pursued and such strategy or tactic was inherently in conflict with, or not undertaken, due to the attorney's other loyalties or interests. The conflicting character of the strategy is not sufficient if the strategy actually was rejected because another strategy was viewed as even more favorable to the accused.

c. Knowledge of the court

If an attorney representing codefendants makes a timely motion for appointment of separate counsel based on a potential conflict of interest, then the trial judge must either grant the motion or at least conduct a hearing to determine whether appointment of separate counsel is warranted under the circumstances. Failure of the judge to do so requires automatic reversal of a subsequent conviction. *Holloway v. Arkansas*, 435 U.S. 475, 484 (1978). Actual conflict and prejudice are presumed under such circumstances.

Unless the trial court knows or reasonably should know that a conflict exists, however, the court is not required to inquire about multiple representations. *Cuyler v. Sullivan*, 446 U.S. 335, 347–348 (1980). Actual conflict (rather than potential conflict) is required to be shown on appeal if the issue of separate trials was not brought up during the trial, and the defendant must show that the conflict adversely affected counsel's performance. *Mickens v. Taylor*, 535 U.S. 162, 173 (2002).

d. Rule 44(c)

When co-defendants are represented by the same attorney, Rule 44(c) of the Federal Rules of Criminal Procedure requires the court to conduct a prompt inquiry into potential conflicts of interest and advise the defendants of the right to separate representation. Failure to comply with the Rule, though, will not constitute a per se reversible error, and an appellate court will likely ask whether the end result was representation by counsel under an actual conflict.

e. Disqualification despite waiver

A trial court has the authority to disqualify a defense attorney, even over the objection of the defendant, if the court concludes that there is serious potential of a conflict of interest. *Wheat v. United States*, 486 U.S. 153, 158–159 (1988).

3. Communication of Formal Plea Offer

The right to effective assistance of counsel extends to the plea bargaining stage. Defense counsel must accurately communicate to the defendant any formal offer from the prosecution to accept a plea on terms and conditions that may be favorable to the defendant. To show prejudice once a plea offer has lapsed or has been rejected because defense counsel failed to accurately communicate the offer, a defendant must demonstrate a reasonable probability that she would have accepted the plea offer had it been accurately communicated by defense counsel. A defendant must also demonstrate a reasonable probability that the prosecutor and trial court would have accepted the plea if they had the discretion to reject it under state law. *Missouri v. Frye*, 566 U.S. ____, 132 S. Ct. 1399 (2012). Ineffective assistance of counsel at the plea bargaining stage may constitute reversible error even if the subsequent trial and conviction are fair. *Lafler v. Cooper*, 566 U.S. ____, 132 S. Ct. 1376 (2012).

4. Right to Confidential Communications

No type of discovery device may be used by the prosecution to obtain information about the defense of the case.

IV. PRETRIAL PROCEDURES

A. EYEWITNESS IDENTIFICATION PROCEDURES

1. Types

There are two types of identification procedures: corporeal and non-corporeal. Corporeal identifications are "in-person," as in lineups. Non-corporeal identifications are not in-person and involve police officers using photo arrays for a witness to identify the suspect.

2. Sixth Amendment Right to Counsel at Lineups

A defendant is entitled to have counsel present at any post-indictment lineup in which the defendant is required to participate. Testimony about a post-indictment, pre-trial identification in the absence of counsel is inadmissible at trial, but the witness may still identify the defendant at trial if the prosecution can show that the identification has independent reliability. *Kirby v. Illinois*, 406 U.S. 682, 690–691 (1972). The right to counsel does not apply to any pre-indictment eyewitness identification. *Id.*

a. Waiver

The defendant can waive the right to have counsel present, provided that waiver is made knowingly and intelligently.

b. Remedy

A violation of the defendant's right to have counsel present at a lineup results in the exclusion of the identification.

3. Admissibility of Pre- and Post-Indictment Identification

a. Two-prong test

Courts use a two-prong test to determine the admissibility of a pre- or post-indictment lineup identification: (i) the defendant must prove that the identification procedure was **impermissibly suggestive**, and (ii) the court must determine whether the testimony was **nonetheless reliable,** using five factors:

i) The witness's **opportunity to view** the defendant at the time of the crime;

ii) The witness's **degree of attention** at the time of the crime;

iii) The **accuracy of the witness's description** of the defendant prior to the identification;

iv) The **level of certainty** at the time of the identification; and

v) The **length of time** between the crime and the identification.

To prevail, the defendant must demonstrate that the procedure was impermissibly suggestive **and** that there was a substantial likelihood of misidentification. *Neil v. Biggers*, 409 U.S. 188, 199–200 (1972).

b. Remedy

1) Hearing

A suppression hearing will be held to determine the admissibility of the evidence. It usually is held outside the presence of the jury, although exclusion of the jury is not constitutionally required. The government has the burden of proving that the defendant waived counsel or that counsel was present, and the defendant has the burden of demonstrating a violation of due process.

2) Suggestiveness finding

A finding of "impermissibly suggestive procedures" will result in suppression of the out-of-court identification. However, an in-court identification of the defendant by the witness is admissible if the prosecution can establish by clear and convincing evidence that the identification at trial was reliable.

3) Standard of review

A conviction as the result of a trial in which an illegal identification was admitted will be overturned **unless,** under the doctrine of harmless error, the appellate court is convinced beyond a reasonable doubt that the improperly admitted identification did not contribute to the verdict.

4. Non-Corporeal Identifications

There is no right to counsel during a pre- or post-indictment photo spread.

A photo spread is not a critical stage of the prosecution, but the prosecution is required to turn over the photographic display in discovery, and the defendant may file a motion to suppress based upon suggestiveness of the photo array. The two-prong test for determining the validity of an in-court identification in which the witness has previously identified the defendant at a lineup (*see* § 3.a., *supra*) also applies when the witness has previously identified the defendant through a photo array.

B. PRELIMINARY PROCEEDINGS

Subsequent to the defendant's arrest, various court proceedings may be held. These pretrial proceedings, which take various forms depending on the jurisdiction, can include a hearing to determine probable cause to detain (a *Gerstein* hearing), an initial appearance, an arraignment, a detention or bail hearing, and a preliminary hearing to determine probable cause to prosecute the defendant. Some of these proceedings may be combined, and some may not be required. In addition, the defendant may make various motions, including motions to suppress evidence obtained in violation of the defendant's constitutional rights.

1. Probable Cause to Detain (*Gerstein* Hearing)

Under the Fourth Amendment, a preliminary hearing must be held after the defendant's arrest to determine whether probable cause exists to hold the defendant, unless such determination has already been made before the defendant's arrest through a grand jury indictment or the judicial issuance of an arrest warrant. *Gerstein v. Pugh*, 420 U.S. 103 (1975). This hearing, known as a *Gerstein* hearing, need not be adversarial. There is no right to counsel at this hearing, and hearsay evidence may be introduced, but a hearing not held within 48 hours after arrest is presumptively unreasonable. *County of Riverside v. McLaughlin*, 500 U.S. 44 (1991). However, the failure to hold this hearing does not affect the prosecution of the defendant for the charged offense, other than the exclusion of any evidence discovered as a consequence of the unlawful detainment. Under the Fifth Amendment, all felony charges must be by indictment of a federal grand jury, unless waived by the defendant.

2. Initial Appearance

Soon after the defendant is arrested, the defendant must be brought before a judge who advises the defendant of the charges against him and of his rights and who appoints counsel if the defendant is indigent. During this initial appearance, which may be held in conjunction with a *Gerstein* hearing, the judge may also determine whether the defendant should be released prior to trial and the conditions of the release (e.g., bail), accept a plea from the defendant, and set a date for a preliminary hearing.

3. Arraignment

At an arraignment, the court informs the defendant of the crime with which the defendant has been charged and elicits the defendant's response (i.e., plea) to those charges. At this time, the court may appoint counsel for an indigent defendant. These events may also take place at the initial appearance.

4. Detention Hearing

In conjunction with the defendant's initial appearance or at a separate hearing, the court may determine whether to release the defendant and any conditions upon such release. At such time, the court may set bail (*see* § C. Right to Bail, *infra*).

5. Preliminary Hearing to Determine Probable Cause to Prosecute

Subsequent to the defendant's initial appearance, a preliminary hearing may be held to determine whether there is probable cause to believe that the defendant has committed a specific crime. At this hearing, which is an adversarial proceeding, the defendant has the right to counsel. *Coleman v. Alabama*, 399 U.S. 1 (1970). A defendant who has been indicted by a grand jury is not entitled to this hearing.

C. RIGHT TO BAIL

There is no explicit constitutional right to bail. However, any denial of bail must comply with the Due Process Clause. Therefore, the setting of excessive bail or the refusal to set bail is immediately appealable. Furthermore, bail set higher than an amount reasonably calculated to ensure the defendant's presence at trial is "excessive" under the Eighth Amendment.

1. Statutory Bail Provisions

The Bail Reform Act of 1984 governs release or detention determinations in federal courts in criminal proceedings. Many states have modeled similar statutory bail provisions on the Act.

2. Presumptions Pre- and Post-Conviction

There is a presumption in favor of pre-trial release. A detention hearing must be held at the initial appearance for there to be a release. However, there is a presumption against bail post-conviction, pending appeal. The Federal Rules of Evidence do not apply at detention hearings.

3. Pre-Trial Detention

Certain pretrial detention practices that are reasonably related to maintaining jail security are permissible and do not violate due process or the Fourth Amendment. These include routine inspections of inmates' cells, prohibiting receipt of outside food or personal belongings, body-cavity searches, and double bunking.

D. COMPETENCY

Incompetency is a bar to trial. The judge has a constitutional duty to investigate and determine the competence of the defendant to stand trial if such evidence is apparent to the judge. A separate hearing is held to assess the defendant's competency. The test for whether a defendant is competent to stand trial is the same test for determining whether the defendant is competent to plead guilty: whether the defendant comprehends the nature of the proceedings against him and has the ability to consult with a lawyer with a reasonable degree of rational understanding.

If the defendant is declared mentally incompetent to stand trial, and the charge is a serious criminal offense, then the government may administer antipsychotic drugs. Three conditions must be met before the defendant can receive these drugs:

i)   The treatment should not cause serious side effects that would affect the fairness of the trial;

ii) The treatment is necessary and there is no less intrusive method to further the government's important interest; and

iii) The treatment is medically appropriate.

Insanity Defense Distinguished: The insanity defense considers the defendant's mental condition at the time of the crime, whereas incompetence concerns the defendant's mental condition at the time of the trial. Detention also varies depending on whether it is based on incompetency or insanity. In a successful insanity defense, the defendant may be detained in a mental hospital for a longer term than incarceration requires. If a defendant is found to be incompetent, confinement in a mental hospital must be limited to a brief period of time for evaluation.

The conviction of a legally incompetent defendant or the failure of the trial court to provide an adequate competency determination violates due-process principles by depriving the defendant of the constitutional right to a fair trial. State courts may place the burden of proving incompetence on the defendant, but they may not require the defendant to prove it by clear and convincing evidence.

E. GRAND JURIES

1. Indictment

After hearing the prosecution's evidence, the grand jury decides whether there is probable cause to charge a particular defendant with a particular crime and, if so, returns a "true bill" of indictment. (This formal charging process is mandated by the

Fifth Amendment under the federal system for felonies and is used in most eastern states, but a state is not constitutionally required to use this process, as the Fifth Amendment Grand Jury Clause has not been incorporated by the Fourteenth Amendment. In most western states, the charging process is initiated by filing an information by a prosecutor.)

2. Grand Jury Proceedings

a. Defendant's rights

The grand jury is a non-adversarial proceeding. The proceedings are conducted in secret, and the defendant has no right to present or confront witnesses or to introduce evidence. The defendant is not entitled to a dismissal due to a procedural defect in grand jury proceedings, unless the defect substantially impacted the grand jury's decision to indict. However, the defendant (or any other witness) may make a motion to seal the grand jury report if he believes that he has been defamed.

1) Double jeopardy

Because jeopardy does not attach until a trial begins, the Double Jeopardy Clause does not apply to grand jury proceedings. The refusal of a grand jury to indict a defendant with respect to a specific crime does not prevent the indictment of the defendant for the same crime by another grand jury. *United States v. Williams*, 504 U.S. 36, 49 (1992). (*See* § VI.A., Double Jeopardy, *infra*.)

b. Role of the prosecutor

The prosecutor is the advisor to the grand jury. As such, the prosecutor's role is to advise the grand jury with respect to the law and assist the grand jury in its job of issuing subpoenas for witnesses and evidence. The prosecutor has no legal obligation to present evidence exculpating the defendant to the grand jury. Thus, a grand jury indictment cannot be dismissed for the prosecutor's failure to present exculpatory evidence, unless the prosecutor violated a preexisting constitutional or legislative rule. The prosecutor is subject to the grand jury secrecy rules.

c. Witness's rights

A grand jury witness has no right to counsel in the grand jury room. The witness may request permission to consult with counsel outside of the jury room before answering a grand jury question. A prosecutor's failure to give a *Miranda* warning to a witness who then lies to a grand jury does not prevent the prosecution of the witness for perjury. *United States v. Wong*, 431 U.S. 174 (1977). Further, a witness who is a target of an investigation and may become a defendant is not entitled to a warning of his putative defendant status; the failure to receive such a warning does not protect a lying witness from a perjury conviction. *United States v. Washington*, 431 U.S. 181 (1977).

d. Grand jury's role

The grand jury has subpoena power to investigate matters before it or to initiate criminal proceedings. The subpoena can be quashed by the opposing party if he can demonstrate that the evidence sought is not relevant to the investigation.

However, the witness or defendant cannot attack the subpoena based on the grand jury's lack of probable cause. The grand jury is not restricted to hearing evidence that would be admissible at trial; an indictment may generally be based on hearsay or illegally obtained evidence. *United States v. Calandra*, 414 U.S. 338, 348 (1974) (illegally seized evidence admissible in grand jury proceeding); *Costello v. United States*, 350 U.S. 359 (1956) (hearsay evidence admissible in grand jury proceeding). (Note: By federal statute, information obtained from an illegal wiretap cannot be presented to a grand jury. 18 U.S.C. 2515.) The grand jury may not exclude members of minority races, regardless of whether they are the same race as the defendant. Such exclusion will lead to a reversal of the indictment without regard to the harmlessness of the error. *Campbell v. Louisiana*, 523 U.S. 392 (1998); *Vasquez v. Hillery*, 474 U.S. 254 (1986).

F. STATE'S DUTY TO DISCLOSE

The prosecution has an affirmative duty to disclose any material evidence favorable to the defendant and relevant to the prosecution's case in chief that would negate guilt or diminish culpability or punishment. *Brady v. Maryland*, 373 U.S. 83 (1963). Failure to make such a disclosure violates the Due Process Clause and is grounds for reversal, regardless of whether the failure to disclose was intentional, if the defendant can show that (i) the evidence is favorable to the defendant (i.e., is exculpatory or impeaches) and (ii) the failure to disclose caused prejudice against the defendant. *Strickler v. Green*, 527 U.S. 263, 281-282 (1999); *United States v. Bagley*, 473 U.S. 667, 675 (1985). This duty does not extend to disclosure of impeachment evidence prior to a plea bargain agreement, *United States v. Ruiz*, 536 U.S. 622 (2002), or to post-conviction proceedings.

V. TRIAL

A. JURY TRIAL

In the federal system, the Sixth Amendment provides the right to jury trials. States are obligated under the Fourteenth Amendment to provide jury trials in criminal cases involving only serious offenses. *Duncan v. Louisiana*, 391 U.S. 145 (1968). States have wide latitude, though, to determine the conduct and details of jury use.

1. Maximum Sentence to Exceed Six Months

There is a constitutional right to a jury trial for **serious offenses**—those that carry an authorized sentence of **more than six months of imprisonment,** regardless of the actual penalty imposed. *Baldwin v. New York*, 399 U.S. 66 (1970). The right to a jury trial attaches for crimes punishable by six months of imprisonment or less only if additional statutory or regulatory penalties make the offense a "serious offense." *United States v. Nachtigal*, 507 U.S. 1 (1993) (a misdemeanor for which the maximum punishment was six months in prison and a $5,000 fine or probation not to exceed five years was not a serious offense). There is no right to trial by jury for multiple petty offenses (those that carry a combined total maximum term exceeding six months); the prison terms imposed for such convictions are not aggregated.

a. Contempt

In a civil contempt case, there is no jury trial requirement if the witness can avoid the punishment by complying with the court order. In a criminal contempt case that has no statutorily authorized punishment, the right to a jury trial is determined by the actual penalty imposed. Thus, a sentence of over six months would trigger the right to a jury trial. However, an alleged contemnor is not entitled to a jury trial simply because a strong possibility exists that upon conviction he will face a substantial term of imprisonment regardless of the punishment actually imposed. Moreover, if a sentence is imposed for contempt and it is more than six months, an appellate court may reduce the sentence to six months or less to protect the conviction against constitutional attack for lack of a jury. There is no right to a jury trial when the sentence imposed is probation, regardless of the length of the probation, at least when imprisonment following revocation of probation does not exceed six months.

2. Waiver

A defendant may waive the right to a jury trial and opt for a trial by judge, known as a "bench trial," if the waiver is freely and intelligently made. *Adams v. United States ex rel McCann*, 317 U.S. 269 (1942). However, the defendant does not have an absolute right to a bench trial. The court or prosecutor may compel the defendant to submit to a jury trial, unless the defendant would be denied a fair trial. *Singer v. United States*, 380 U.S. 24 (1965).

3. Compliance

a. Jury size and unanimity

A jury of less than six members is a denial of due process, and a unanimous verdict is constitutionally required if a jury is made up of only six members. For juries of seven or more, the vote need not be unanimous, but there is no strict rule as to how many votes are required for conviction.

Federal Rule of Criminal Procedure 23(b) requires a 12-member jury unless waived in writing and approved by the court. A verdict by 11 jurors is permitted if the 12th juror is excused for good cause after deliberations begin.

b. Composition of the jury

1) Representative cross-section of the community

The Equal Protection Clause bars racial discrimination in the selection of juries, including grand juries. The requirement that a jury be selected from a representative cross-section of the community also extends to sexual discrimination. However, the actual jury selected need not represent a fair cross-section of the community. *Holland v. Illinois*, 493 U.S. 474, 480 (1990).

2) All defendants may challenge jury selection discrimination

The defendant has standing to challenge the jury-selection process, regardless of any showing of actual bias. *Powers v. Ohio*, 499 U.S. 400, 410–411 (1991).

3) Prima facie case

The prima facie case for absence of a representative cross-section can be established by showing that:

i) The group allegedly excluded is a **"distinctive" group** in the community;

ii) The group was not **fairly represented** in the venire from which the jury was chosen; and

iii) The underrepresentation resulted from a **systematic exclusion** of the group in the jury-selection process.

To rebut, the prosecution must show that the disproportionate exclusion manifestly and primarily advances a significant governmental interest.

4) State's right to use neutral principles

In response to a claim of intentional racial discrimination in jury selection, the state has the right to apply neutral, nonracial principles to jury selection, even though it results in a smaller percentage of minorities on juries. The state must prove "absence of discriminatory intent."

5) Peremptory challenges

Peremptory challenges are requests by both parties during the voir dire jury-selection process to disqualify potential jurors without the need to show cause.

a) Discriminatory use

The Fourteenth Amendment Equal Protection Clause prohibits both the criminal defendant and the prosecutor from exercising peremptory challenges solely based on race or gender. *J.E.B. v. Alabama*, 511 U.S. 127 (1994); *Batson v. Kentucky*, 476 U.S. 79, 84 (1986). The defendant need not be a member of the excluded group in order to have standing to contest the prosecution's use of its peremptory challenges.

If the explanation for striking a juror is deemed pretextual, then it gives rise to an inference of discriminatory intent that makes it difficult for the challenge to survive. *Snyder v. Louisiana*, 552 U.S. 472, 485 (2008).

The United States Supreme Court has set forth a three-prong test (the "*Batson*" test) to determine whether a **peremptory challenge** has been exercised on the basis of race, in violation of the Equal Protection Clause of the Fourteenth Amendment. The test requires that:

i) The moving party establishes a **prima facie case of discrimination**;

ii) The party who exercised the challenge provides a **race-neutral explanation** for the strike;

iii) The moving party carries her burden of **proving that the other party's proffered reason was pretextual** and that the strike was indeed motivated by purposeful discrimination.

Once the party who exercised the challenge offers a race-neutral explanation and the trial court has ruled on the ultimate question of intentional discrimination, the preliminary issue becomes moot. **The ultimate burden of persuasion regarding racial motivation rests with the opponent of the strike.**

b) Not constitutionally required

The loss of a peremptory challenge does not violate the right to an impartial jury. *Ross v. Oklahoma*, 487 U.S. 81, 88 (1988). A defendant's exercise of peremptory challenges is not denied or impaired when the defendant chooses to use such a challenge to remove a juror who should have been excused for cause. *United States v. Martinez-Salazar*, 528 U.S. 304, 307 (2000).

c) Harmless-error doctrine

The Constitution allows states to choose between harmless-error review and automatic reversal when a judge, acting in good faith, erroneously denies a defendant's peremptory challenge. *Rivera v. Illinois*, 556 U.S. 148 (2009). Thus, if state law permits harmless-error review of the erroneous seating of the juror, there is no constitutional requirement for automatic reversal of the defendant's conviction.

c. Impartial jury

The Sixth Amendment provides that an accused person is entitled to a trial by an impartial jury. Claims of juror bias and misconduct are subject to the harmless-error rule.

1) Views on race

A defendant is entitled to inquire on voir dire into ethnic or racial prejudice of possible jury members only when the issues to be tried involve allegations of racial or ethnic prejudice, or whenever race is "inextricably bound up in the case." *Ristiano v. Ross*, 424 U.S. 589, 597 (1976).

2) Views on capital punishment

Prospective jurors who are opposed to the death penalty may be removed for cause if their opposition to the death penalty is so strong as to prevent or substantially impair the performance of their duties at the sentencing phase of the trial. *Wainwright v. Wirr*, 469 U.S. 412, 424–425 (1985); *Adams v. Texas*, 448 U.S. 38, 44 (1980).

An improper exclusion of a juror from a jury that imposed a death sentence is subject to automatic reversal. *Gray v. Mississippi*, 481 U.S. 648, 668 (1987).

d. Sentencing

1) Enhancements

When a sentence may be increased if additional facts are established, a jury must determine the existence of such facts. Enhancement of a defendant's sentence by a judge without such a determination violates the defendant's right to a jury trial. *Apprendi v. New Jersey*, 530 U.S. 466, 476 (2000). This limitation on a judge's ability to impose an enhanced sentence also applies when the defendant has entered a guilty plea. *Blakely v. Washington*, 542 U.S. 296 (2004). However, the harmless-error test applies to determine whether a sentence enhanced in violation of a defendant's right to a jury trial must be reversed. *Washington v. Recuenco*, 548 U.S. 212 (2006).

2) Concurrent versus consecutive sentences

Judges can decide whether sentences for multiple crimes run concurrently or consecutively without violating this right. *Oregon v. Ice*, 555 U.S. 160 (2009).

e. Inconsistent verdicts

If a jury renders a verdict that a defendant is guilty of certain offenses but not guilty of other related offenses, then the verdict is not reviewable on the grounds of inconsistency, even when the jury acquits the defendant of an offense that is a predicate offense to an offense for which the same jury finds the defendant guilty. *United States v. Powell*, 469 U.S. 57 (1984). This rule, which permits inconsistent verdicts, is also applicable when a defendant is convicted of an offense for which a co-defendant, who is tried at the same time, is acquitted, even though the facts would logically dictate the same verdict for each defendant. *United States v. Dotterweich*, 320 U.S. 277 (1943). This rule extends to bench as well as jury trials. *Harris v. Rivera*, 454 U.S. 339 (1981). (Note: The defendant may challenge a jury verdict on the grounds that there was insufficient evidence to establish the defendant's commission of a crime.)

B. GUILTY PLEAS

A guilty plea is an admission of facts contained in the charging document (e.g., indictment, information).

1. Knowing and Voluntary

Because a guilty plea constitutes both a confession and a waiver of various constitutional rights, the plea must be both intelligent and voluntary. *Boykin v. Alabama*, 395 U.S. 238 (1969); *McCarthy v. United States*, 394 U.S. 459 (1969). The record must reflect that the judge has determined that the defendant knows and understands the following:

i) The nature of the charges and their essential elements;

ii) The consequences of the plea (i.e., the maximum and minimum possible sentences); and

iii) The rights that the defendant is waiving (e.g., right to a trial).

(Note: The judge does not personally need to explain each element of the crime. It is sufficient for the defendant's counsel to explain the nature and elements of the crime to him. *Bradshaw v. Stumpf*, 545 U.S. 175 (2005).) The judge must also determine that the plea did not result from force or improper threats or from promises other than those contained in the plea agreement.

a. Factual basis for plea

Although the federal rules of criminal procedure require a judge to ascertain that there is factual basis for the defendant's plea, a judge is generally not constitutionally required to ascertain that there is a factual basis for the plea, nor does the defendant need to admit guilt. However, when the defendant, despite entering a plea, also asserts his innocence, the judge must determine that there is a factual basis for the plea. *North Carolina v. Alford*, 400 U.S. 25, 37 (1970).

b. Effect of violation

When the court fails to ensure that the plea was knowing and voluntary, the defendant is entitled to withdraw his plea.

2. Right to Counsel

In entering a plea, a defendant has the right to counsel. *White v. Maryland*, 373 U.S. 59 (1963).

3. Plea Bargain

A plea bargain between the prosecutor and the defendant is treated as a contract. The bargain may involve the crimes with which the defendant has been charged, such as a promise by the prosecutor to drop specific charges in exchange for the defendant's promise to plead guilty to other charges, or the defendant's sentence, such as a promise by the prosecutor to recommend a particular sentence in exchange for the defendant's guilty plea.

a. No right to bargain

A defendant cannot compel the prosecutor to bargain; the defendant does not have a constitutional right to plea bargain. *Weatherford v. Bursey*, 429 U.S. 545 (1977).

b. Pressure to bargain

A defendant's plea made in response to the prosecution's threat to bring more serious charges does not violate the protection of the Due Process Clause against prosecutorial vindictiveness, at least when the prosecution has probable cause to believe that the defendant has committed the crimes. *Bordenkircher v. Hayes*, 434 U.S. 357 (1978). Similarly, the bringing of felony charges against a defendant after the defendant asserted his right to a jury trial for misdemeanor offenses related to the same incident does not in itself constitute prosecutorial vindictiveness. *United States v. Goodwin*, 457 U.S. 368 (1982).

c. No duty to disclose impeachment information

The prosecution is not required to disclose impeachment information or information related to an affirmative defense to a defendant when the defendant enters into a plea bargain agreement prior to trial. The failure to disclose such information does not render the defendant's plea bargain involuntary. *United States v. Ruiz*, 536 U.S. 622 (2002).

d. Enforcement of the bargain

1) Court

When entering into a plea bargain, the agreement is enforceable against the defendant and the prosecutor, but not against the judge. If the judge is not satisfied with the bargain, he can reject the plea. A defendant does not have a constitutional right to have his plea accepted by the court.

2) Prosecution

Should the prosecution violate the provisions of the plea bargain, the judge decides whether specific performance of the plea is required or whether the defendant can withdraw his plea. *Santobello v. New York*, 404 U.S. 257 (1971).

3) Defense

If a defendant fails to abide by the plea agreement (e.g., fails to testify in another trial), then the prosecution can have the sentence vacated and reinstate the original charge. *Ricketts v. Adamson*, 483 U.S. 1 (1987).

4. Effect of the Plea on the Defendant's Rights

Generally, a defendant, by entering a guilty plea, waives his constitutional rights, such as the right to a trial, the privilege against self-incrimination, and the right to confront his accusers. However, a defendant may challenge a guilty plea on the due-process grounds that it was not a knowing and voluntary waiver of such rights. *Boykin v. Alabama*, 395 U.S. 238 (1969). In addition, a guilty plea does not constitute a waiver of a double jeopardy challenge unless the waiver is agreed to in the plea agreement. *Menna v. New York*, 423 U.S. 61 (1975). A defendant may also attack a guilty plea that is due to ineffective assistance of counsel. *Hill v. Lockhart*, 474 U.S. 52 (1985). (Note: A defendant may also challenge a guilty plea on the grounds that the court lacked jurisdiction. *Menna v. New York, supra.*)

C. SPEEDY TRIAL

The Due Process Clause and federal statutes protect defendants from intentional and prejudicial **pre-accusation** delay. The Sixth Amendment speedy trial guarantee, the Fourteenth Amendment, the Speedy Trial Act of 1974, and other federal and state statutes protect defendants from undue **post-accusation** delay.

1. Commencement of the Right

Statutes of limitations are the primary safeguards against pre-accusation delay. However, the Due Process Clause may be violated if the delay was used to obtain a tactical advantage for the prosecution or to harass the defendant. *United States v. Marion*, 404 U.S. 307 (1971). Delay resulting from an investigation conducted in good faith does not violate the Due Process Clause. *United States v. Lovasco*, 431 U.S. 783 (1977).

Under the Sixth and Fourteenth Amendments, the time period commences at the time of arrest or formal charge, whichever comes first. The defendant need not know about the charges against him for the right to attach.

2. Balancing Test

The factors to be considered in determining whether the defendant has been deprived of a speedy trial post-accusation are the:

i) Length of the delay;

ii) Reason for the delay;

iii) Defendant's assertion of a right to a speedy trial; and

iv) Prejudice to the defendant.

Courts weigh these factors and determine whether the state made a "diligent, good-faith effort" to bring the defendant to trial. *Barker v. Wingo*, 407 U.S. 514, 530 (1972). A delay caused by the inaction of an attorney assigned by the state to represent the defendant may be attributable to the defendant, but a delay caused by the court's failure to promptly appoint replacement counsel when an assigned attorney withdraws or by a breakdown in the public-defender system is attributable to the state. *Vermont v. Brillon*, 556 U.S. 81 (2009).

3. Remedy

If the defendant's right to a speedy trial is violated, the charges are dismissed with prejudice.

D. PUBLIC TRIAL

1. Defendant's Right

The Sixth Amendment guarantees a criminal defendant the right to a public trial. The defendant may waive the right and request a closed proceeding. However, because the request also implicates the First Amendment right of access of the press and the public, the court must consider several factors, and the likelihood of a closed proceeding is slight. The court may even allow the proceedings to be televised over the defendant's objection.

The right to a public trial extends to preliminary hearings and suppression hearings. A suppression hearing may be closed if (i) there is an overriding interest likely to be prejudiced by an open trial, (ii) the closure is not in excess of the interest, (iii) other alternatives have been considered, and (iv) the court enters adequate findings to support closure.

2. Public's Right

Regardless of the wishes of the defendant or prosecutor, a trial must be public unless there is either a *substantial likelihood* of prejudice to the defendant or a need to limit access to ensure an orderly proceeding. *Press-Enterprise Co. v. Superior Court of CA (Press-Enterprise I)*, 464 U.S. 501, 509–10 (1984).

E. FAIR TRIAL

1. Impartial Judge

Due process requires that a judge possess neither actual nor apparent bias. If actual or apparent bias exists, the judge must follow a recusal process in the federal or state jurisdiction. The impermissible bias or prejudice usually must stem from an extrajudicial source.

2. Fair Conduct by the Prosecutor

a. Examples of misconduct

A prosecutor may not:

i) Make material misstatements of law or fact;

ii) Elicit information from the defendant outside the presence of his counsel;

iii) Express opinions about the defendant's guilt or innocence;

iv) Make unfair or improper remarks about the defendant, his counsel, or witnesses;

v) Comment on the defendant's failure to testify at trial; or

vi) Make improper remarks to the jury to inflame their passions to convict for an improper reason.

b. No use of false testimony

A prosecutor may not knowingly use perjured or false testimony for the case in chief, for sentencing, or to impeach the credibility of a witness.

c. No suppression of favorable evidence

As discussed in IV.F., *supra,* due process requires the prosecution to disclose evidence favorable to the accused when such evidence is material to guilt or punishment. Evidence is material if there is a "reasonable probability" that disclosure would have changed the outcome of the proceeding; a reasonable probability is "a probability sufficient to undermine confidence in the outcome." *United States v. Bagley*, 473 U.S. 667, 682 (1985). The prosecution's failure to disclose evidence in its possession both favorable and material to the defense entitles the defendant to a new trial. *Brady v. Maryland,* 373 U.S. 83 (1963). Under *Bagley*, the prosecution's failure to turn over specifically requested evidence will seldom, if ever, be excused.

Similarly, police violate due process when, in bad faith, they destroy evidence that would have been useful to the defendant at trial. The defendant does not, however, have the right to require police to preserve all evidence if it is not certain that the evidence would have been exculpatory.

F. RIGHT TO CONFRONTATION

1. Trial

The accused has the right to directly encounter adverse witnesses, to cross-examine adverse witnesses, and to be present at any stage of the trial that would enable the defendant to effectively cross-examine adverse witnesses as guaranteed by the Sixth and Fourteenth Amendments. Not only does this right allow the defendant to cross-examine the adverse witness, but it also allows the defendant to observe the demeanor of the adverse witness. A witness may invoke the right against self-incrimination; however, such an invocation after testimony has already been made may violate the defendant's right to confrontation, guaranteed by the Sixth and Fourteenth Amendments, because the witness's invocation will prevent adequate cross-examination by the defendant. If the defendant was instrumental in preventing a witness from testifying, then he forfeits his right to confrontation.

2. Compliance

a. Face-to-face confrontation

Face-to-face confrontation is not an absolute right. A criminal defendant has the right to confront witnesses against him under the Sixth Amendment, unless preventing such confrontation is necessary to further an important public policy and the reliability of the testimony is otherwise assured. A defendant who voluntarily leaves the courtroom or a disruptive defendant whom the judge removes from the courtroom has not had his right to confrontation violated. This is to be determined on a case-by-case basis.

> The state's interest in protecting child witnesses from more than *de minimis* trauma as a result of testifying in the defendant's presence is considered an important public purpose under this rule. *Maryland v. Craig*, 497 U.S. 836, 855–856 (1990).

b. Cross-examination of witnesses

The right to confrontation means more than being allowed to confront the witness physically. The principal purpose of confrontation is to secure for the defendant the opportunity of cross-examination of the prosecution's witnesses.

1) Impeachment for bias

A denial of the opportunity to cross-examine a prosecution witness with regard to bias violates the Confrontation Clause. *Delaware v. Van Arsdall*, 475 U.S. 673, 679 (1986). However, such denial is subject to harmless-error analysis. Moreover, trial judges retain wide latitude to impose reasonable limits on such cross-examination based on concerns about, among other things, harassment, prejudice, confusion of the issues, the safety of the witness, or interrogation that is repetitive or only marginally relevant. *Id.*

2) Memory loss by the witness

The fact that a witness has a memory loss does not by itself violate the Confrontation Clause. *Delaware v. Fensterer*, 474 U.S. 15, 19–20 (1985). The Supreme Court has held that the Confrontation Clause does not bar testimony concerning a prior out-of-court identification when the identifying witness is unable, because of memory loss, to explain the basis for the identification. A defendant may conduct an effective cross-examination if given the opportunity to address the very fact of the poor memory of the witness. *United States v. Owens*, 484 U.S. 554, 564 (1988).

3) Confrontation Clause and the hearsay rule

The Confrontation Clause limits the use of hearsay evidence in a criminal trial. Out-of-court statements by witnesses that are "testimonial" are barred under the Confrontation Clause, unless the witnesses are unavailable and the defendant had a prior opportunity to cross-examine those witnesses, regardless of whether such statements are deemed reliable by the court. If, however, the declarant appears for cross-examination at trial, then the Confrontation Clause places no constraints at all on the use of the declarant's prior out-of-court testimonial statements. *Crawford v. Washington*, 541 U.S. 36, 59 (2004).

Out-of-court testimonial statements are not barred by the Confrontation Clause when they are used for a purpose other than establishing the truth of the matter asserted (i.e., when they are not used for a hearsay purpose). *Id. See also Tennessee v. Street*, 471 U.S. 409, 417 (1985).

The Confrontation Clause has no application to "non-testimonial" out-of-court statements. *Whorton v. Bockting*, 549 U.S. 406, 420 (2007).

a) Testimonial statements

A statement is considered "testimonial" if the declarant would reasonably expect it to be used in a prosecution. Such statements include affidavits, custodial examinations, prior testimony, and statements given in response to police interrogation. *Crawford v. Washington*, 541 U.S. 36, 40 (2004). The Supreme Court has also held that certificates of analysis, which state the results of state laboratory tests, are testimonial evidence that may not be admitted without accompanying live testimony by the analyst who conducted the tests. *Melendez-Diaz v. Massachusetts*, 557 U.S. 305, 340 (2009). It is not sufficient to substitute the testimony of another analyst who is familiar with the testing protocol but did not perform or observe the tests or sign the report. *Bullcoming v. New Mexico*, 564 U.S. ___, 131 S. Ct. 2705 (2011).

b) Non-testimonial statements

The Confrontation Clause permits the admission of non-testimonial statements, even if they lack indicia of reliability. *Whorton v. Bockting,* 549 U.S. 406, 411 (2007). Statements made for the primary purpose of assisting the police in the investigation of an ongoing emergency are not testimonial. Examples of non-testimonial statements include statements made to a 911 operator during a domestic dispute, *Davis v. Washington*, 547 U.S. 813, 822 (2006), and statements made to police officers by the victim of a mortal gunshot wound as he lay in a gas-station parking lot. *Michigan v. Bryant*, 562 U.S. ___, 131 S. Ct. 1143 (2011).

4) Witness unavailable

The right of confrontation is satisfied if the defense counsel had a right to cross-examine the witness at an earlier hearing, provided that the prosecution failed in a good-faith effort to produce the witness at the trial and the declarant is now unavailable. However, if the witness is unavailable because of the defendant's conduct, then testimonial hearsay is admissible. *Giles v. California*, 554 U.S. 353, 373 (2008).

5) Confession of a non-testifying co-defendant at a joint trial

a) *Bruton* rule

The admission of a confession by a non-testifying co-defendant at a joint trial against the defendant violates the Sixth Amendment, even when it merely corroborates the defendant's own confession. *Bruton v. United States*, 391 U.S. 123, 132 (1968). A limiting instruction will not cure the defect. If the co-defendant testifies, then the rule does not apply. The rule does not apply at a bench trial. *Lee v. Illinois*, 476 U.S. 530, 539 (1986). It also does not apply to the statements of an accomplice who is not tried as a co-defendant or to a co-defendant who takes the stand and denies making such a statement. *Nelson v. O'Neil*, 402 U.S. 622, 629–630 (1971); *Dutton v. Evans*, 400 U.S. 74, 88–89 (1970).

b) Harmless error

Admission of a co-defendant's statement in violation of *Bruton*, however, is subject to harmless-error analysis. *Schneble v. Florida*, 405 U.S. 427, 430 (1972).

c) Severance

The accused may assert a demand for a severance of the trial of his case from a co-defendant's case whenever the prosecution intends to introduce a confession that is hostile to one co-defendant, and the confession:

i) Implicates the confessing defendant but is not admissible against the non-confessing defendant; and

ii) Cannot be edited to exclude inculpation of the non-confessing defendant.

Bruton v. United States, 391 U.S. 123, 132 (1968). The prosecutor may avoid severance if the court denies the use of the statement or the prosecutor chooses not to use it at trial.

G. DUE PROCESS

1. Right to Testify

A defendant has a right to testify and to present evidence on his own behalf.

2. Burden of Proof

a. Presumptions

1) Presumption of innocence

While a defendant is not automatically entitled to a jury instruction apprising the jury of the presumption of innocence doctrine, the presumption is a basic tenet of a fair trial, and it may be required when necessary for a fair trial. *Kentucky v. Whorton*, 441 U.S. 786, 789 (1979).

2) Presumptions of facts

a) Permissive presumption

A permissive presumption (i.e., a presumption that the trier of fact is not compelled to accept and that does not shift the burden of proof) regarding an element of an offense does not violate the due-process requirement that the prosecution must prove each element of an offense unless the presumption is irrational. A presumption is not irrational if it is more likely than not to flow from the proven fact on which it depends. *County Court v. Allen*, 442 U.S. 140, 163–164 (1979) (upholding the statutory presumption that the occupants of a car in which firearms are found are in possession of the firearms).

b) Mandatory presumption

A mandatory presumption (i.e., a presumption that the trier of fact is compelled to accept or that shifts the burden of proof) regarding an element of an offense violates the due-process requirement. *Sandstrom v. Montana*, 442 U.S. 510, 522 (1979) (jury instruction that a person intends the ordinary consequences of his voluntary acts constituted a mandatory presumption when the crime—deliberate homicide—required proof of intent).

b. Elements of the prosecution's case

The Due Process Clause requires that the prosecution prove all of the elements of the case beyond a reasonable doubt. Due process does not require the court to use any particular words to advise the jury of the government's burden of proof. In some jurisdictions, the failure to instruct on reasonable doubt may result in reversible error, whereas in other jurisdictions, the lack of such an instruction is per se reversible error.

> Sentencing factors need not be proved beyond a reasonable doubt unless the fact is being used to increase the penalty beyond the proscribed statutory maximum, in which case proof beyond a reasonable doubt is required. *Apprendi v. New Jersey*, 530 U.S. 466, 492 (2000).

c. Affirmative defenses

The state is not forbidden by the Due Process Clause from placing the burden of proving an affirmative defense—such as insanity, self-defense, entrapment, or duress—on the defendant. *Dixon v. United States*, 548 U.S. 1, 13 (2006).

d. Directed verdict

In a criminal case, a judge may order a directed verdict only for acquittal; the power to convict is reserved to the jury.

H. SENTENCING

1. Applicable Rights

Sentencing is considered a critical stage triggering the Sixth Amendment right to counsel. A defendant may have the right to confrontation and cross-examination at sentencing, particularly in death-penalty cases, or when a sentence is based upon a finding of new facts beyond those necessary to prove the offense charged. *Gardner v. Florida*, 430 U.S. 349, 358 (1977); *Specht v. Patterson*, 386 U.S. 605, 610 (1967).

2. Enhancement Over the Statutory Maximum

Any fact, other than a prior conviction, that can be used to increase a sentence beyond the statutorily prescribed maximum must be charged in an indictment, submitted to a jury, and established beyond a reasonable doubt. A fact is considered an element of a crime, as opposed to a sentencing enhancement, when it can increase the maximum sentence imposed. The failure to abide by the above procedure is a violation of the defendant's due-process rights under the Fifth Amendment and Sixth Amendment rights to notice and a jury trial, both of which are incorporated against the states through the Fourteenth Amendment. *Apprendi v. New Jersey*, 530 U.S. 466, 476 (2000).

It is not a Sixth Amendment violation for a judge to impose consecutive sentences based on facts that were not found by the jury, but rather by the judge. *Oregon v. Ice*, 555 U.S. 160 (2009). The rule of *Apprendi v. New Jersey, supra,* is thus limited to sentencing for single crimes, not to the arrangement for punishing multiple offenses.

Harmless-error analysis applies in deciding whether or not to overturn a sentence for a judge's failure to submit a sentencing factor to the jury. *Washington v. Recuenco*, 548 U.S. 212, 222 (2006).

I. CRUEL AND UNUSUAL PUNISHMENT

1. Applicability

The Eighth Amendment to the U.S. Constitution prohibits the federal government from imposing cruel and unusual punishment for federal crimes, or "such punishment as would amount to torture or barbarity, any cruel and degrading punishment not known to the common law, or any fine, penalty, confinement, or treatment so disproportionate to the offense as to shock the moral sense of the community." U.S. Const. amend. VIII.

2. Compliance

a. Non-death penalty

1) Physical conditions of incarceration

The physical conditions of incarceration amount to cruel and unusual punishment only if the prisoner can show that prison officials had actual knowledge of a substantial risk to the prisoners.

2) Physical force

A prisoner need not show serious injury to recover for a violation of the Eighth Amendment prohibition against cruel and unusual punishment. The inquiry is whether the physical force was applied in a good-faith effort to maintain or restore discipline, rather than applied maliciously and sadistically to cause harm.

3) Sentence proportionality

A sentence that is grossly disproportionate to the crime constitutes cruel and unusual punishment. However, a lengthy sentence does not necessarily violate the Eighth Amendment. *Compare Weems v. United States*, 217 U.S. 349 (1910) (reversing punishment of 20 years' imprisonment for falsifying a public record) *with Harmelin v. Michigan*, 501 U.S. 957 (1991) (upholding punishment of life imprisonment without the possibility of parole for drug dealing based on possession of more than 650 grams of cocaine) *and Ewing v. California*, 538 U.S. 11 (2003) (upholding punishment of an indeterminate sentence of 25 years to life for theft of merchandise valued at about $1,200 after conviction of at least two other felonies, at least one of which was serious or violent).

4) Equal protection limitations on punishment

A jail sentence is impermissible if it is imposed only because the defendant was unable to pay a fine. If a defendant has made reasonable bona fide efforts to pay the fine, then revocation of probation without consideration of alternative punishments is fundamentally unfair under the Fourteenth Amendment.

5) Repeat offenders

Some jurisdictions have statutes imposing mandatory indeterminate life sentences (e.g., 25 years to life) on defendants who commit three felonies, even if the felonies are non-violent property-related offenses. These recidivist statutes are not unconstitutional under either the Double Jeopardy Clause of the Fifth Amendment or the Cruel and Unusual Punishment Clause of the Eighth Amendment. *Ewing v. California*, 538 U.S. 11 (2003).

6) Defendant's perjured testimony

If a trial judge believes that the defendant perjured himself during the trial, then the judge may take this belief into consideration when determining the sentence.

b. Capital punishment

The death penalty may be imposed only under a statutory scheme that provides:

i) Clear and objective standards;

ii) Specific and detailed guidance; and

iii) An opportunity for rational review of the process.

1) Homicide crimes

a) Aggravating circumstances

A defendant in a homicide case cannot be sentenced to death unless the trier of fact convicts the defendant of murder and finds at least one "aggravating circumstance" at either the guilt phase or penalty phase. *Brown v. Sanders*, 546 U.S. 212, 218–19 (2006). The aggravating circumstance must meet two requirements:

i) It must not apply to every defendant convicted of murder; and

ii) It must not be unconstitutionally vague. (For example, "especially heinous, atrocious, or cruel" conduct definition is unconstitutionally vague.)

The trier of fact can consider both statutory and non-statutory aggravating circumstances, but the death penalty cannot be imposed without one statutorily defined aggravating factor being found.

b) Mitigating circumstances

A death sentence violates the Eighth and Fourteenth Amendments if the sentencing judge refuses to review or admit mitigating evidence.

Mitigating evidence must be presented if it meets a low threshold test for relevance. *Woodson v. North Carolina*, 428 U.S. 280, 316 (1976).

> **Note:** When the death penalty is not imposed (e.g., when the defendant receives a sentence of life in prison without parole), a mandatory sentence may be imposed without the presentation of mitigating evidence. *Harmelin v. Michigan*, 501 U.S. 957, 965 (1991).

2) **Non-homicide crimes**

Punishment that is disproportionately excessive in relation to the crime committed is prohibited by the Eighth Amendment. The death penalty is considered excessive in a rape case when the victim was an adult woman or a child, *Coker v. Georgia*, 433 U.S. 584 (1977); *Kennedy v. Louisiana*, 554 U.S. 407 (2008), and in felony-murder cases when the defendant did not intend to kill or intend that lethal force be used.

3) **Defendant insane**

The Eighth Amendment prohibits states from inflicting the death penalty on a prisoner who is insane or can "demonstrate a severe mental disorder." *Panetti v. Quarterman*, 551 U.S. 930, 960 (2007).

4) **Mental retardation of the defendant**

The Eighth Amendment prohibits execution of mentally retarded persons. *Atkins v. Virginia*, 526 U.S. 504 (2002).

5) **Age of the defendant**

The Eighth Amendment prohibition against "cruel and unusual punishment" prohibits the execution of a defendant who was younger than 18 years of age at the time of the commission of a crime. *Roper v. Simmons*, 543 U.S. 551, 569 (2005). In addition, the Eighth Amendment prohibits the imposition of a sentence of life without the possibility of parole on a defendant who was younger than 18 years of age at the time of the commission of the crime if the crime was not a homicide. *Graham v. Florida*, 560 U.S. ___, 130 S. Ct. 2011 (2010). If the crime was a homicide, the juvenile cannot be subject to a **mandatory** sentence of life imprisonment without the possibility of parole. Under such circumstances, the sentencing judge must be permitted to take the defendant's youth and other relevant circumstances into consideration when imposing punishment. *Miller v. Alabama*, 567 U.S. ___, 132 S. Ct. 2455 (2012).

6) **Fairness of sentencing proceedings**

To minimize the risk of arbitrary action, a capital sentencing process must satisfy, at a minimum, two general requirements:

i) The process must channel or limit the sentencer's discretion in order to genuinely narrow the class of persons eligible for the death penalty and reasonably justify the imposition of a more severe sentence on the defendant compared to others found guilty of murder; and

ii) The court must allow the jury to consider any relevant mitigating evidence that might lead the sentencer to decline to impose the death penalty. The sentencer is also allowed to take into consideration victim impact statements.

7) Racial discrimination claims

Under *McCleskey v. Kemp*, 481 U.S. 279 (1987), the Supreme Court held that despite serious statistical evidence of racial disparity in the imposition of the death penalty (e.g., African-American defendants who kill white victims are more likely to receive the death penalty), it was not imposed as a result of unconstitutional discrimination.

8) Lethal injection

Lethal injection is not considered cruel and unusual punishment because there is only a mere possibility that the condemned may receive an improperly administered shot that would cause him unnecessary pain.

c. Adequate medical care

Although prison inmates have a right to adequate medical care, such care constitutes "cruel and unusual punishment" under the Eighth Amendment only when there is a deliberate indifference to the serious medical needs of an inmate. Mere negligence in assessing an inmate's medical condition or in providing treatment is not sufficient to trigger a constitutional violation. *Estelle v. Gamble*, 429 U.S. 97, 104–105 (1976).

VI. POST-TRIAL CONSIDERATIONS

A. DOUBLE JEOPARDY

The Fifth Amendment protection against double jeopardy applies to the federal government. It has been incorporated by the Due Process Clause of the Fourteenth Amendment, and consequently it also applies to the states. *Benton v. Maryland*, 395 U.S. 784 (1969).

1. Protection Against Prosecution and Punishment

The Fifth Amendment Double Jeopardy Clause provides three protections:

i) Protection against a second prosecution for the same offense after acquittal;

ii) Protection against a second prosecution for the same offense after conviction; and

iii) Protection against multiple punishments for the same offense.

a. Definition of "same offense"

1) Shared elements

If a defendant's conduct may be prosecuted as two or more crimes, then the *Blockburger* test is applied to determine whether the crimes constitute the same offense for double jeopardy purposes. Under this test, each crime must require the proof of an element that the other does not in order for each to be considered as a separate offense. *Blockburger v. United States*, 284 U.S. 299, 304 (1932).

Example 1—No Jeopardy: A defendant robs a store and shoots and kills the store clerk. The state prosecutes the defendant for premeditated murder. The defendant is acquitted. The state then brings charges against the defendant for robbery. The protection against double jeopardy does not apply because robbery and murder each require the proof of an element that the other does not. Robbery requires, among other elements, the proof that the defendant took the victim's personal property; murder requires, among other elements, the death of the victim.

Example 2—Jeopardy: A defendant robs a store and shoots and kills the store clerk. The state prosecutes the defendant for felony murder based on the robbery. The defendant is acquitted. The state then brings charges against the defendant for robbery. The protection against double jeopardy applies because the state, in order to prove felony murder in the first trial, had to prove that the defendant committed a robbery. *Harris v. Oklahoma*, 433 U.S. 682, 683 (1977).

As a consequence of *Blockburger,* the Double Jeopardy Clause generally bars successive prosecutions for greater and lesser included offenses. A lesser included offense is one that does not require proof of an element beyond those required by the greater offense.

2) Occurrence of a necessary subsequent event

When jeopardy has attached with respect to a lesser included offense prior to the occurrence of an event necessary to establish the greater offense, the defendant may be subsequently tried for the greater offense.

Example: If a defendant who physically harms a victim is tried for a crime such as battery, and the victim subsequently dies as a consequence of the defendant's conduct, then the defendant may be tried for murder without running afoul of the Double Jeopardy Clause. *Diaz v. United States*, 223 U.S. 442, 449 (1912).

3) Statutory offenses

At a single trial, a defendant may be convicted of two offenses, one of which is a lesser included offense of the other, if both offenses are statutory and the legislature has specifically authorized cumulative punishment. *Missouri v. Hunter*, 459 U.S. 359, 368–369 (1983) (first-degree robbery and armed criminal action).

4) Conspiracy

An offense and the conspiracy to commit that offense are not the same offense for double-jeopardy purposes because each requires proof of different elements. *United States v. Felix*, 503 U.S. 378, 389 (1992).

5) Sentence enhancement use

The use of a defendant's prior conviction to enhance the sentence imposed on a defendant for a current conviction does not violate the Double Jeopardy Clause. *Witte v. United States*, 515 U.S. 389, 400 (1995).

b. Acquittal

A defendant who has been acquitted of a crime generally may not be retried for the same crime. A grant of a demurrer or motion to dismiss in favor of the accused at the close of the state's case is the equivalent of an acquittal. There must be a final verdict of acquittal, however, for the Double Jeopardy Clause to apply. *See Blueford v. Arkansas*, 566 U.S. ____, 132 S. Ct. 2044 (2012) (holding that defendant could be retried for murder even though jury in first trial had announced in open court that they had unanimously voted against murder charges, because declaration in open court was not equivalent to verdict of acquittal since jury was sent back to deliberate on lesser-included charges of manslaughter and negligent homicide and might have revisited decision on murder charges).

2. Attachment of Jeopardy

The protection against double jeopardy is not triggered until jeopardy attaches. In a jury trial, jeopardy attaches when the jury is empaneled and sworn in. In a bench trial, jeopardy attaches when the first witness is sworn in.

3. Different Jurisdictions

Under the dual-sovereignty doctrine, the protection against double jeopardy does not preclude prosecution of a crime by both federal and state governments. Consequently, a defendant may be charged and convicted for the same type of crime in a federal court and a state court. Similarly, a defendant may be prosecuted by two different states for the same conduct. However, a state and state-created entity, such as a municipality, cannot both prosecute a defendant for the same conduct. *Waller v. Florida*, 397 U.S. 387, 394 (1970) (municipality's conviction of defendant for violation of city ordinance for destruction of city property precluded state prosecution for grand larceny).

4. Civil Actions

The Double Jeopardy Clause does not preclude a criminal punishment and civil penalty for the same conduct. Therefore, even if a defendant has been found guilty in a criminal action, the state may still bring a civil action against the defendant that arises out of the same conduct. The protection does not apply to administrative proceedings such as a disciplinary hearing stemming from criminal conduct, nor does it apply to a parole, probation, or bond-revocation hearing related to a criminal charge or punishment.

A civil penalty may be treated as a criminal punishment when the penalty amount is grossly disproportionate to governmental loss and it serves only a deterrent or retributive purpose. *Dep't of Revenue of Montana v. Kurth Ranch*, 511 U.S. 767, 783 (1994) (tax imposed on possession of illegal drugs after satisfaction of state and federal fines and forfeitures). However, a civil forfeiture proceeding is typically not punitive in nature. *United States v. Ursery*, 518 U.S. 267, 275 (1996) (forfeiture of property used in the commission of drug crimes).

Note: Juvenile adjudicatory proceedings are criminal, not civil, actions for purposes of the Double Jeopardy Clause. A minor who is subject to an adjudicatory hearing regarding conduct that would constitute a crime if committed by an adult cannot subsequently be tried as an adult for a crime based on such conduct. *Breed v. Jones*, 421 U.S. 519, 541 (1975).

5. **Guilty Plea**

A defendant does not automatically waive her double-jeopardy rights by entering a guilty plea, but the plea agreement may include a provision that the charges against the defendant may be reinstated if the defendant breaches the agreement. *Ricketts v. Adamson*, 483 U.S. 1, 11 (1987). A guilty plea to a lesser included offense does not preclude prosecution for a greater offense if the greater offense has been charged before the plea is entered. *Ohio v. Johnson*, 467 U.S. 493, 501 (1984).

6. **Mistrial**

The Double Jeopardy Clause does not prohibit a retrial following a mistrial if "taking all the circumstances into consideration, there is a manifest necessity for [declaring a mistrial]." *United States v. Perez*, 22 U.S. 579, 580 (1824). For example, if a mistrial is declared because the judge or a juror is ill or dies, or because of a hung jury, then the defendant generally may be retried. On the other hand, if the judge grants an acquittal instead of declaring a mistrial after there has been a hung jury, then a retrial is not permitted. Moreover, if the prosecution asks for a mistrial because of its inability to locate a witness, then double jeopardy prevents a retrial.

If the defendant asks for or consents to a mistrial, then she generally can be retried, unless the request is based on bad-faith conduct by the prosecutor or judge directed toward goading the defendant into seeking a mistrial. The manifest necessity standard does not apply when the defendant requests a mistrial. *United States v. Dinitz*, 424 U.S. 600, 606–607 (1976).

7. **Appeal**

   a. **By the prosecution**

   The government may appeal an adverse ruling in a criminal case only when authorized by statute. If the trial judge grants an acquittal on an issue that does not relate to the defendant's guilt or innocence, such as the failure to give the defendant a speedy trial, then the prosecution may appeal and, if the appeal is successful, the defendant may be retried. In addition, a prosecutor may appeal an order dismissing an indictment or suppressing evidence, a bail determination, the sentence imposed on a defendant, and a post-verdict new-trial order.

   b. **By the defendant**

   The Double Jeopardy Clause generally does not prevent the retrial of a defendant after an appeal on the basis of an error made at trial, such as the admission of improper hearsay evidence or improper jury instructions. *Lockhart v. Nelson*, 488 U.S. 33, 38 (1988). This is true even when a conviction is overturned due to the weight of the evidence. *Tibbs v. Florida*, 457 U.S. 31, 42 (1982). However, a retrial after reversal of a conviction due to **insufficiency** of the evidence is barred by the Double Jeopardy Clause. A conviction is based upon insufficient evidence if the evidence presented, when viewed in the light most favorable to the prosecution, is such that **no rational fact-finder** could have found the defendant guilty beyond a reasonable doubt. *Burks v. United States*, 437 U.S. 1, 18 (1978).

8. **Retrial Offenses**

A defendant who was tried for a crime but convicted only of a lesser included offense may not be retried on the originally charged crime even if the conviction is reversed. *Price v. Georgia*, 398 U.S. 323, 329 (1970).

Example: A defendant on trial for murder is found guilty of voluntary manslaughter. The conviction is overturned on appeal due to trial error. The defendant's retrial for murder violates the Double Jeopardy Clause, even if on retrial the defendant again is convicted only of voluntary manslaughter.

9. **Retrial Punishment**

The Double Jeopardy Clause generally does not preclude a greater sentence from being imposed on a defendant upon reconviction after a successful appeal. However, the Due Process Clause does prevent the imposition of a greater sentence upon reconviction if the greater sentence is imposed as a penalty for the exercise of a statutory right to appeal or to seek a collateral remedy. Consequently, when imposing a greater sentence upon reconviction, the judge must articulate reasons for the greater sentence that are based on objective information concerning identifiable conduct by the defendant that occurred after the original sentencing proceeding. *Alabama v. Smith*, 490 U.S. 794 (1989). In a jurisdiction where a jury rather than the judge determines the sentence, the jury in the retrial may impose a greater sentence unless it has been told of the defendant's original sentence. *Chaffin v. Stynchcombe*, 412 U.S. 17, 24 (1973).

a. **Capital sentencing procedures**

The Double Jeopardy Clause is applicable to capital sentencing proceedings when there is a determination that the government failed to establish an aggravating factor that would justify the death penalty. Consequently, if a jury imposes a life sentence rather than the death penalty, then the defendant, upon retrial, may not be sentenced to death. *Bullington v. Missouri*, 451 U.S. 430, 445 (1981).

A capital-sentencing procedure under which the sentencing judge may override the jury's recommendation and impose the death penalty does not violate the Double Jeopardy Clause.

10. **Collateral Estoppel**

The Double Jeopardy Clause recognizes the doctrine of collateral estoppel. For collateral estoppel to apply, the earlier decision must have necessarily determined the issue on which collateral estoppel is sought by the defendant.

Example 1: Several victims were robbed at the same time. The defendant is initially tried for the crime with respect to only one of the victims. The sole contested issue at the trial is whether the defendant was a perpetrator of the crime. The defendant is acquitted of the crime. The acquittal prevents the defendant's prosecution for the robbery with respect to any other victim. The fact that the jury determined that the defendant was not a perpetrator of a robbery estops the government from trying the defendant for robbery of any of the other victims. *Ashe v. Swenson*, 397 U.S. 436 (1970).

If a jury renders a verdict against a defendant on one crime but deadlocks on another crime that contains the same element, then the jury's verdict may serve to prevent retrial on the crime over which the jury was deadlocked. In such a case, issue preclusion applies to the issue(s) that the jury did determine.

> **Example 2:** A defendant was charged with both insider trading and fraud. An element of both crimes is the possession of insider information. The jury acquitted the defendant of fraud but deadlocked over insider trading. By acquitting the defendant, the jury determined that the defendant did not possess insider information. Consequently, under the doctrine of collateral estoppel, the government could not retry the defendant for fraud. *Yeager v. United States*, 557 U.S. 110, (2009).

The burden is on the defendant to prove that the jury's verdict **necessarily** determined the issue that the defendant seeks to foreclose. Because a jury usually renders a general verdict in a criminal trial, it is rare that a defendant will be able to meet this burden.

B. APPEAL

The Constitution neither provides for nor guarantees an individual the right to appeal. Nevertheless, appeals are commonplace in the U.S. justice system. Individuals are guaranteed certain rights during their appeal, among them equal protection and the right to counsel. However, despite this latter right, if an attorney believes that the appeal is frivolous, she may withdraw so long as the appellant's right to counsel continues to be protected. There is also no right of self-representation during an appeal.

C. CONVICTIONS

1. Writ of Habeas Corpus

Defendants may attack their convictions, even if their appeal was unsuccessful or not available, by challenging the lawfulness of the detention under a writ of habeas corpus. The defendant does not have to be in custody; she may be out on bail, probation, or parole. However, if the defendant's sentence has expired and her prior conviction is being used to enhance a later one, then the defendant does not satisfy the in-custody requirement to petition for the habeas writ.

A writ of habeas corpus proceeding is civil in nature. Therefore, the "beyond a reasonable doubt" standard is not applicable. The petitioner must demonstrate only the unlawfulness of the detention by a preponderance of the evidence. If the petitioner is granted the writ, then the state may appeal, and double jeopardy does not apply to either the appeal or the retrial after the granting of the writ. An indigent person does not have a right to have counsel appointed to assist in perfecting her habeas petition.

2. Parole and Probation

If a new sentence will be imposed upon the revocation of parole, then the right to counsel is activated, and the parolee is entitled to representation to the same extent as a trial. On the other hand, if an already-imposed sentence is triggered by parole revocation, then the right to counsel is limited. The right to counsel applies only if it is necessary for a fair hearing.

3. **Access to Courts**

Reasonable access to courts, with no unreasonable limitations on presenting arguments, is a right of prison inmates. In addition, inmates cannot be prohibited from consulting with other inmates if there is no reasonable alternative in the prison, such as a law library.

4. **Disenfranchisement**

Some states disenfranchise a convicted felon. This prohibition on voting does not violate the Fourteenth Amendment, even when it applies to felons who have been released from incarceration. *Richardson v. Ramirez*, 418 U.S. 24, 54 (1974).

Evidence

EVIDENCE

Table of Contents

I.   PRESENTATION OF EVIDENCE..1

    A.   INTRODUCTION OF EVIDENCE 1

       1.   ROLE OF JUDGE AND JURY 1

          a.   Judge 1

          b.   Jury 2

       2.   CHALLENGE TO EVIDENCE RULING 2

          a.   Objection to admission of evidence 2

          b.   Offer of proof for exclusion of evidence..2

          c.   Consequence of a definitive ruling 2

          d.   Plain error rule 2

       3.   LIMITED ADMISSIBILITY 3

       4.   COMPLETENESS RULE 3

       5.   JUDICIAL NOTICE 3

          a.   Facts subject to judicial notice..3

          b.   Procedure 4

    B.   MODE AND ORDER OF PRESENTATION OF EVIDENCE 5

       1.   TRIAL PROCESS 5

          a.   Judicial control of process...5

          b.   Judicial presentation of evidence...5

       2.   EXAMINATION OF WITNESS...5

          a.   Scope of cross-examination 5

          b.   Additional examination 5

          c.   Examination of a defendant 5

       3.   FORM OF QUESTIONS 6

          a.   Leading questions 6

          b.   Improper questions...6

       4.   EXCLUSION OF WITNESSES 7

    C.   BURDENS AND PRESUMPTIONS 7

       1. BURDEN OF PROOF 7

          a. Burden of production 7

          b. Burden of persuasion 8

       2. PRESUMPTIONS 8

          a. Rebuttable 8

          b. Conclusive 9

          c. Diversity cases 9

       3. DESTRUCTION OF EVIDENCE 9

II.   RELEVANCE 9

   A. GENERAL CONSIDERATIONS 9

       1. DIRECT AND CIRCUMSTANTIAL EVIDENCE 10

          a. Direct evidence...10

          b. Circumstantial evidence 10

       2. EXCLUSION OF RELEVANT EVIDENCE 10

       3. RELEVANCE DEPENDENT ON EXISTENCE OF FACT 10

       4. ADMISSION OF IRRELEVANT EVIDENCE—CURATIVE ADMISSION 10

       5. LAYING A FOUNDATION 11

   B. CHARACTER EVIDENCE..11

       1. CIVIL CASES 11

          a. Inadmissible to prove conforming conduct 11

          b. Character at issue 11

       2. CRIMINAL CASES 11

          a. Defendant's character 11

          b. Victim's character 12

       3. METHODS OF PROVING CHARACTER 13

       4. IMPEACHMENT 13

   C. BAD ACTS...13

       1. ADVANCE NOTICE 14

       2. INTRODUCTION OF SPECIFIC ACTS AS CHARACTER EVIDENCE 14

          a. Civil cases...14

          b. Criminal cases 14

          c. Cross-examination of character witness.......................14

    D. HABIT EVIDENCE 15

III.   WITNESSES 15

    A. COMPETENCE 15

        1. PERSONAL KNOWLEDGE 15

        2. OATH OR AFFIRMATION 15

        3. JUDGE AS WITNESS 15

        4. JUROR AS WITNESS..15

            a. At trial...15

            b. After trial 16

        5. CHILD AS WITNESS...16

        6. DEAD MAN'S STATUTES..16

            a. Protected parties..16

            b. Disqualified witnesses 17

            c. Interested person 17

            d. Waiver 17

    B. IMPEACHMENT 17

        1. WHO MAY IMPEACH A WITNESS 17

        2. WITNESS'S CHARACTER FOR TRUTHFULNESS 17

            a. Reputation and opinion testimony..17

            b. Truthful character evidence 17

            c. Specific instances of conduct 18

        3. CRIMINAL CONVICTION 19

            a. Crimes involving dishonesty or false statement 19

            b. Crimes not involving dishonesty or false statement..........................19

            c. Convictions more than 10 years old..19

            d. Effect of pardon..20

            e. Juvenile adjudications...20

            f. Manner of proof..20

            g. Pendency of appeal 20

        4. PRIOR INCONSISTENT STATEMENTS 20

            a. Disclosing the statement to the witness...20

            b. Extrinsic evidence 20

5. BIAS OR INTEREST 21

6. SENSORY COMPETENCE 21

7. IMPEACHMENT OF A HEARSAY DECLARANT...21

8. REHABILITATION OF A WITNESS 22

9. RELIGIOUS OPINIONS AND BELIEFS 22

10. IMPEACHMENT BY CONTRADICTORY EVIDENCE 22

11. COLLATERAL ISSUES 22

C. RECOLLECTION REFRESHED...22

1. PRESENT RECOLLECTION REFRESHED 22

    a. Adverse party's options...23

    b. Failure to produce or deliver the writing 23

2. PAST RECOLLECTION RECORDED 23

D. OPINION TESTIMONY...23

1. LAY WITNESS 23

2. EXPERT WITNESS..24

    a. Subject matter of testimony 24

    b. Qualified expert..24

    c. Ultimate issue...24

    d. Basis of opinion 24

    e. Court-appointed expert..25

    f. Interpreter 25

IV. TANGIBLE EVIDENCE..25

A. AUTHENTICATION 25

1. PHYSICAL OBJECTS...25

    a. Personal knowledge 25

    b. Distinctive characteristics 25

    c. Chain of custody..26

    d. Reproductions and explanatory evidence 26

    e. X-ray images and electrocardiograms 26

2. DOCUMENTARY EVIDENCE 26

    a. Ancient documents and data compilations..26

    b. Public records...26

      c. **Reply letter doctrine** 26

      d. **Handwriting verification** 27

      e. **Self-authenticating documents** 27

      f. **Attesting witness** 28

   3. **ORAL STATEMENTS** 28

      a. **Voice identification** 28

      b. **Telephone conversations** 28

B. **BEST EVIDENCE RULE** 28

   1. **CONTENTS AT ISSUE** 29

   2. **"ORIGINAL"** 29

   3. **EXCEPTIONS** 29

      a. **Duplicates** 29

      b. **Original unavailable** 29

      c. **Public records** 30

      d. **Summaries** 30

      e. **Admission by party** 30

   4. **ROLE OF COURT AND JURY** 30

C. **PAROL EVIDENCE RULE** 30

   1. **GENERAL RULE** 30

      a. **Complete integration** 31

      b. **Partial integration** 31

   2. **EXCEPTIONS** 31

   3. **APPLICABLE EVIDENCE** 31

D. **DEMONSTRATIVE AND EXPERIMENTAL EVIDENCE** 31

V. **PRIVILEGES AND OTHER POLICY EXCLUSIONS** 31

A. **PRIVILEGES** 31

   1. **CONFIDENTIAL COMMUNICATION** 31

      a. **Presence of third party** 32

      b. **Waiver** 32

   2. **SPOUSAL PRIVILEGE** 32

      a. **Spousal immunity** 32

      b. **Confidential marital communications** 33

        c.   Exceptions 33

   3. ATTORNEY-CLIENT PRIVILEGE..33

        a.   Elements...33

        b.   Exceptions 34

        c.   Effect of disclosure on waiver 35

   4. PHYSICIAN-PATIENT PRIVILEGE 36

   5. PSYCHOTHERAPIST-PATIENT PRIVILEGE 36

   6. SELF-INCRIMINATION...37

        a.   In general 37

        b.   Comment and inference 37

        c.   Immunity...37

   7. OTHER PRIVILEGES..37

        a.   Clergy-penitent 37

        b.   Accountant-client 37

        c.   Professional journalist 37

        d.   Governmental privileges 38

  B. PUBLIC POLICY EXCLUSIONS..38

   1. SUBSEQUENT REMEDIAL MEASURES.....................................38

   2. COMPROMISE OFFERS AND NEGOTIATIONS............................38

        a.   Exceptions 38

        b.   No immunization of evidence...39

        c.   Prohibition on all parties 39

   3. OFFERS TO PAY MEDICAL EXPENSES 39

   4. PLEA NEGOTIATION 39

        a.   Exceptions 39

        b.   Waiver 39

   5. LIABILITY INSURANCE 40

   6. SEXUAL CONDUCT...40

        a.   Victim's conduct 40

        b.   Defendant's conduct 41

VI.   HEARSAY...42

  A. WHAT IS HEARSAY 42

    1. DECLARANT—PERSON 42

    2. STATEMENT—ASSERTION 42

    3. OFFERED TO PROVE THE TRUTH OF THE MATTER ASSERTED 42

        a. Legally operative facts 43

        b. Effect on recipient 43

        c. State of mind 43

        d. Impeachment 43

    4. MULTIPLE HEARSAY 43

  B. WHAT IS NOT HEARSAY 43

    1. PRIOR STATEMENTS 44

        a. Prior inconsistent statements 44

        b. Prior consistent statements 44

        c. Prior statement of identification 44

    2. OPPOSING PARTY'S STATEMENT 44

        a. Judicial admission 45

        b. Adoptive admission 45

        c. Vicarious statements 45

VII. HEARSAY EXCEPTIONS 46

  A. DECLARANT UNAVAILABLE AS A WITNESS 46

    1. UNAVAILABLE DECLARANT 46

    2. FORMER TESTIMONY 46

    3. DYING DECLARATION 46

    4. STATEMENT AGAINST INTEREST 47

    5. STATEMENT OF PERSONAL OR FAMILY HISTORY 47

    6. STATEMENT AGAINST PARTY THAT CAUSED DECLARANT'S UNAVAILABILITY47

  B. DECLARANT'S AVAILABILITY AS A WITNESS IMMATERIAL 47

    1. PRESENT SENSE IMPRESSION 48

        a. Res gestae 48

    2. EXCITED UTTERANCE 48

    3. STATEMENT OF MENTAL, EMOTIONAL, OR PHYSICAL CONDITION 48

        a. State of mind 48

        b. Physical condition 49

    4. STATEMENT MADE FOR MEDICAL DIAGNOSIS OR TREATMENT........................49

        a. Statement made to a person other than a physician 49

        b. Statement made by a person other than the patient...............................49

    5. RECORDED RECOLLECTION 49

    6. RECORDS OF REGULARLY CONDUCTED ACTIVITY (BUSINESS RECORDS) 50

        a. Authentication..50

        b. Lack of trustworthiness...50

        c. Medical records 50

        d. Police reports 51

        e. Absence of a record 51

    7. PUBLIC RECORDS...51

        a. Lack of trustworthiness...51

        b. Absence of a record 51

        c. Public record or vital statistics..51

    8. LEARNED TREATISES 52

    9. JUDGMENT OF PREVIOUS CONVICTION...52

    10. OTHER EXCEPTIONS 52

  C. RESIDUAL EXCEPTION..53

VIII. CONSTITUTIONAL LIMITATIONS 53

  A. HEARSAY EVIDENCE RESTRICTIONS 53

    1. SIXTH AMENDMENT—CONFRONTATION CLAUSE AND HEARSAY EVIDENCE ...53

        a. Testimonial statements...53

        b. Unavailability of the declarant 54

    2. FOURTEENTH AMENDMENT—DUE PROCESS CLAUSE 54

  B. FACE-TO-FACE CONFRONTATION 54

EVIDENCE

EXAM NOTE: Watch out for MBE questions with answer choices that would be correct under common law but are inconsistent with the Federal Rules. Remember, aside from the rules related to evidentiary privileges and constitutional limitations, the Federal Rules govern the MBE.

I. PRESENTATION OF EVIDENCE

With some exceptions, the Federal Rules apply to all civil and criminal proceedings before United States district courts, courts of appeal, Bankruptcy Court, and Claims Court, and in proceedings before United States magistrates. Fed. R. Evid. 1101(a).

The Federal Rules do not apply to:

  i) The court's determination of a preliminary question of fact governing admissibility (*see* § I.B.1.a. Judicial control of process, *infra*);

  ii) Grand jury proceedings; and

  iii) Criminal proceedings for the following purposes:

   a) The issuance of a search or arrest warrant or a criminal summons;

   b) A preliminary examination in a criminal case;

   c) Extradition or rendition;

   d) Consideration of bail or other release;

   e) Sentencing; and

   f) Granting or revoking probation or supervised release.

Fed. R. Evid. 1101(c), (d).

A. INTRODUCTION OF EVIDENCE

1. Role of Judge and Jury

In a jury trial, the jury is traditionally the trier of fact and the judge the trier of law.

a. Judge

The trial judge generally decides **preliminary questions** regarding the competency of evidence, including the admissibility of evidence, whether privilege exists, and whether a person is qualified to be a witness. The court is not bound by the Federal Rules in deciding these questions, except with respect to privileges, and it may consider otherwise inadmissible evidence. Fed. R. Evid. 104(a). With respect to preliminary questions, the party offering the evidence ordinarily bears the burden to persuade the trial judge by a preponderance of the evidence. *Bourjaily v. United States*, 483 U.S. 171 (1987) (confession of co-conspirator as admission of party opponent); *Daubert v. Merrell Dow Pharm.*,

509 U.S. 579 (1993) (expert opinion); Rule 702, Notes of Advisory Committee (2000).

Hearings on preliminary matters must be conducted outside the presence of the jury when the hearing involves the admissibility of confessions, when a defendant in a criminal case is a witness and so requests, or when justice requires it. Fed. R. Evid. 104(c).

b. Jury

A party has the right to present evidence (e.g., bias) that is relevant to the weight and credibility of other evidence (e.g., the testimony of a witness). Once evidence has been admitted, it is the role of the jury to determine the **weight and credibility** of the evidence. Fed. R. Evid. 104(e).

2. Challenge to Evidence Ruling

A party may challenge an evidentiary ruling as erroneous only if the ruling affects a substantial right of a party, and the party notifies the judge of the error. There are two ways to call the court's attention to the error—objection and offer of proof. Fed. R. Evid. 103(a). (Note: While the judge in a jury trial must permit a party to challenge the court's ruling, the judge must also conduct the trial to the extent practicable so that inadmissible evidence is not suggested to the jury. Fed. R. Evid. 103(d).)

a. Objection to admission of evidence

If the ruling **admits** evidence, a party must make a timely **objection** or motion to strike and must usually state the specific ground for the objection or motion in order to preserve the admissibility issue for appeal. A party is not required to state the ground if it is apparent from the context. Fed. R. Evid. 103(a)(1).

b. Offer of proof for exclusion of evidence

If the ruling **excludes** evidence, a party must make an **offer of proof** in order to preserve the evidence for appellate review of the ruling. An offer of proof is an oral or written explanation of the relevance and admissibility of the evidence made on the record. The court may direct that an offer of proof be made in question-and-answer form. An offer of proof is not necessary if the substance of the evidence is apparent from the context. Fed. R. Evid. 103(a)(2),(c).

c. Consequence of a definitive ruling

Once a judge has made a definitive ruling on the admissibility of evidence, a party need not renew an objection or offer of proof, even if the ruling was made before the trial began. Fed. R. Evid. 103(b).

d. Plain error rule

A plain error—an error that affects a substantial right—is grounds for reversal, even if no objection or offer of proof was made. Fed. R. Evid. 103(e). A court may take notice of a plain error to prevent a miscarriage of justice or to preserve the integrity and the reputation of the judicial process.

3. Limited Admissibility

Evidence may be admissible for one purpose but not for another (e.g., for impeachment but not substantive purposes), or against one party but not against another. In these cases, if a party makes a timely request, the court must restrict the evidence to its proper scope and instruct the jury accordingly. Fed. R. Evid. 105.

4. Completeness Rule

Under the rule of completeness, when a party introduces part of a writing or recorded statement, an adverse party may compel the introduction of an omitted portion of the writing or statement if, in fairness, it should be considered at the same time, such as when the omitted portion explains or clarifies the admitted portion. This rule also applies to a separate writing or recorded statement that relates to the introduced writing or recorded statement, such as the original letter when the reply letter has been introduced. Fed. R. Evid. 106. The rule of completeness does not require the admission of irrelevant portions of a statement. *United States v. Kopp*, 562 F.3d 141 (2d Cir. 2009).

Timing of introduction of omitted evidence: While the rule of completeness permits an adverse party to compel the immediate introduction of evidence during the presentation of related evidence, the rule does not *require* the adverse party to do so. The adverse party may instead choose to present the omitted evidence subsequently, such as during cross-examination.

5. Judicial Notice

Judicial notice is the court's acceptance of a fact as true without requiring formal proof. The Federal Rules only address judicial notice of adjudicative facts, which are the facts of the case at hand—those that relate to the parties and their activities, and that typically are decided by the jury. The Federal Rules do not apply to judicial notice of legislative facts, which are policy facts related to legal reasoning and the lawmaking process. Fed. R. Evid. 201.

Example (adjudicative fact): A witness testifies that an accident happened on a Saturday. The accident report indicates that the accident happened on July 21, 2007. Whether July 21, 2007, was indeed a Saturday is an adjudicative fact.

Example (legislative fact): A judge must decide whether to recognize an exception to the common-law marital privilege. The fact that allowing the exception would undermine the sanctity of marriage is a legislative fact.

a. Facts subject to judicial notice

Not all adjudicative facts are subject to judicial notice. Judicial notice may be taken of an adjudicative fact only if it is **not subject to reasonable dispute** because (i) it is **generally known** within the territorial jurisdiction of the trial court, or (ii) it can be **accurately and readily determined** from sources whose accuracy cannot reasonably be questioned. Fed. R. Evid. 201(b).

1) Generally known facts within jurisdiction

A fact does not need to be known by everyone to be "generally known"; it must only be well known within the community. Fed. R. Evid. 201(b).

> **Example:** A judge could take judicial notice that a bank provides a checking account customer with a monthly account statement. *Kaggen v. IRS*, 71 F.3d 1018 (2d Cir. 1995).

Despite being termed "judicial notice," a judge may not take notice of a fact based solely on his own personal knowledge.

> **Example:** A judge could not take judicial notice of informal judicial procedures for the issuance of court orders within a jurisdiction. *Switzer v. Coan*, 261 F.3d 985 (10th Cir. 2001).

2) Accurately and readily determined facts

A fact that can be accurately and readily determined need not be generally known as long as it can be determined from a source whose accuracy cannot be reasonably questioned, such as a geographic and historical fact obtained from a respected reference source.

> **Example:** A judge could take judicial notice of the state's statutory rate for post-judgment interest in determining the appropriate interest rate for pre-judgment interest. *Fox v. Kane-Miller Corp.*, 398 F. Supp. 609 (D. Md. 1975).

> **Contrast:** A judge could not take judicial notice of information about a company found on the company's website, because such information is often self-serving and subject to puffery. *Victaulic Co. v. Tieman*, 499 F.3d 227 (3d Cir. 2007).

b. Procedure

A court may take judicial notice at any time during a proceeding, including on appeal, whether upon request of a party or by the court's own initiative. Note, however, that a court may not take judicial notice against a criminal defendant for the first time on appeal. *U.S. v. Jones*, 580 F.2d 219 (6th Cir. 1978). If a party makes a request and the court is supplied with the necessary information, then the court must take notice of the fact. Fed. R. Evid. 201(c), (d).

1) Party's opportunity to be heard

When a party makes a timely request, the judge must give the party an opportunity to be heard on the propriety of taking judicial notice and the nature of the fact to be noticed. This right to be heard exists even if the court has taken judicial notice of a fact before notifying the party. Fed. R. Evid. 201(e).

2) Instructing the jury

a) Civil case

In a civil case, the jury must be instructed to accept the noticed fact as **conclusive**. Fed. R. Evid. 201(f).

b) Criminal case

In a criminal case, the jury must be instructed that it **may or may not accept** any judicially noticed fact as conclusive. Fed. R. Evid. 201(f).

B. MODE AND ORDER OF PRESENTATION OF EVIDENCE

1. Trial Process

A trial traditionally begins with the plaintiff's case-in-chief, followed by the defendant's case, followed by the plaintiff's rebuttal.

a. Judicial control of process

Subject to the evidentiary rules, a party is generally free to present evidence in the manner and order that the party feels is most effective. The order of the witnesses and presentation of the case, however, are within the discretion of the court, in order to effectively determine the truth, avoid wasting time, and protect witnesses from harassment. Fed. R. Evid. 611(a).

b. Judicial presentation of evidence

A judge may question, or even call, a witness. If the judge calls a witness, all parties may cross-examine that witness. A party objecting to the judge's calling or interrogation of a witness may wait to object until the next opportunity when the jury is not present. Fed. R. Evid. 614.

2. Examination of Witness

A party who calls a witness may examine the witness subject to the evidentiary rules. Another party may then cross-examine that witness.

a. Scope of cross-examination

The scope of cross-examination generally is limited to the subject matter of the direct examination and the credibility of the witness; however, the court may allow inquiry into additional matters. Fed. R. Evid. 611(b).

b. Additional examination

After cross-examination, the party who called the witness may engage in redirect examination, ordinarily to reply to any significant new matter raised on cross-examination. Recross-examination is also generally permissible with respect to significant new matters brought up during redirect examination. For both redirect and recross, the court has discretion to permit inquiry into other matters.

c. Examination of a defendant

The Fifth Amendment privilege against self-incrimination protects a defendant in a criminal case from being compelled to testify. A defendant in a criminal case who testifies as to a preliminary question, such as the voluntariness of the defendant's confession, has not opened himself up to cross-examination on other issues in the case. Fed. R. Evid. 104(d).

3. Form of Questions

a. Leading questions

1) Direct examination

On direct examination of a witness, a leading question—that is, a question that suggests the answer within the question—generally is not permitted. Fed. R. Evid. 611(c).

> **Example:** The question "Didn't you start the fire at 10:00?" suggests when the person being questioned started the fire. In contrast, the question "When did you start the fire?" does not suggest the answer.

a) Exceptions

A leading question is permitted on direct examination when it is necessary to develop the witness's testimony. For example, a leading question is usually permitted to elicit preliminary background information that is not in dispute. In addition, a leading question is typically permitted on direct examination of a witness who has difficulty communicating due to age or a physical or mental condition. Finally, when a party calls a witness who is likely to be antagonistic, such as an adverse party or a person associated with an adverse party, or a witness who presents adverse testimony (i.e., a hostile witness), even if such testimony is unanticipated, then the party ordinarily is permitted to use leading questions.

2) Cross-examination

There is no restriction on the use of leading questions during cross-examination. Fed. R. Evid. 611(c).

b. Improper questions

1) Compound question

A question that requires answers to multiple questions is compound and is not permitted.

> **Example:** "Didn't you leave the house at 7:00, lock the door behind you, get in your car, and drive away?" (A "no" answer could mean that the witness did not leave at all, left at a time other than 7:00, did not lock the door, etc.)

2) Assumes facts not in evidence

A question that assumes as true facts that have not been established is not permitted.

> **Example:** "When did you stop beating your wife?" (The question assumes that the witness is married and used to beat his wife. If neither fact has been established, this question is objectionable.)

3) Argumentative

A question that is intended to provoke an argument, rather than elicit a factual response, is not permitted.

Example: "You don't really expect the jury to believe you, do you?"

4) Calls for a conclusion or opinion

A question that requires the witness to draw a conclusion or state an opinion that he is not qualified to make is not permitted.

Example: "How did your mother feel after you told her the news?" (The witness cannot know how her mother felt and would have to give an opinion to answer the question.)

5) Repetitive

A question that has been asked and answered is not permitted, although judges may allow some repetition, particularly on cross-examination.

4. Exclusion of Witnesses

At a party's request or upon the court's own initiative, the court must exclude witnesses from the courtroom so that they do not hear the testimony of other witnesses. Some witnesses, however, may not be excluded under this rule, including:

i) A party who is a natural person;

ii) An officer or employee of a party that is not a natural person, after the individual has been designated as the party's representative by its attorney;

iii) A person whose presence is essential to a party's presentation of its case, such as a police officer in charge of the investigation in a criminal case; or

iv) A person, such as a victim, whose presence is permitted by statute.

Fed. R. Evid. 615. Note that a victim may be excluded if the court determines, by clear and convincing evidence, that the victim's testimony would be materially altered by the victim hearing other testimony. 18 U.S.C. § 3771.

C. BURDENS AND PRESUMPTIONS

1. Burden of Proof

The burden of proof comprises two distinct burdens: the burden of production and the burden of persuasion.

a. Burden of production

The party with the burden of production (or burden of going forward) must produce legally sufficient evidence as to each element of a claim or defense, so that a reasonable trier of fact could infer that the alleged fact has been proved. In meeting this burden, a plaintiff or prosecutor has made a **prima facie** case. Failure to meet this burden can result in a directed verdict against the party bearing the burden. The determination of whether it has been met rests with the court. The burden of production may shift during trial.

> **Example:** In a negligence action in which the plaintiff produces uncontroverted evidence of the defendant's negligence, the defendant who does not have an affirmative defense bears the burden of producing evidence that challenges the case made by the plaintiff.

b. Burden of persuasion

The burden of persuasion (or standard of proof) is the degree to which legally sufficient evidence must be presented to the trier of fact. For example, in a civil case, this burden usually lies with the plaintiff to prove the allegations in the complaint and with the defendant to prove any affirmative defenses. This burden does not shift. Typically, determination of whether it has been met rests with the trier of fact.

1) Civil standards

The standard in most civil cases is a **preponderance of the evidence.** A fact is proven by a preponderance of the evidence if it is more likely to exist than not.

A higher standard used in some civil cases (such as fraud) is **clear and convincing evidence.** Under this standard, the existence of a fact must be highly probable or reasonably certain.

2) Criminal standard

In criminal cases, the prosecution must prove each element of a crime **beyond a reasonable doubt** to overcome the defendant's presumption of innocence. *In re Winship*, 397 U.S. 358 (1970).

2. Presumptions

A presumption is a conclusion that the trier of fact is required to draw upon a party's proof of an underlying fact or set of facts (i.e., basic facts). For example, a presumption arises that a person is dead when a party establishes that the person has been missing and not heard from for more than seven years. A rebuttable presumption may be overcome by evidence to the contrary; a conclusive presumption may not.

a. Rebuttable

A rebuttable presumption shifts the burden of production, but not the burden of persuasion, to the opposing party. Under the "bursting bubble" approach followed by the Federal Rules in a civil case, a presumption "bursts" (i.e., no longer has a preclusive effect) after the introduction of sufficient evidence by the opposing party to sustain a contrary finding. If no contrary evidence is introduced, the judge must instruct the jury to accept the presumption. If contrary evidence is introduced, the burden of persuasion remains on the party who had it originally. While the presumption no longer has preclusive effect after the introduction of contrary evidence, a judge may instruct the jury that it may, but is not required to, draw the conclusion (e.g., a person is dead) from the basic facts (e.g., the person has been missing for seven years). Fed. R. Evid. 301.

> **Limitation:** The "bursting bubble" approach does not apply when a federal statute or another Federal Rule of Evidence, such as Federal Rule 302 (*see* § c. Diversity cases, *below*), provides otherwise.

b. Conclusive

Conclusive (or irrebuttable) presumptions are treated as rules of substantive law and may not be challenged by contrary evidence, no matter how strong the proof. One example is the presumption in some states that a child under the age of four lacks the ability to form the intent necessary to commit an intentional tort; no evidence to the contrary is permitted to disprove this assumption.

c. Diversity cases

In a federal diversity action, the federal court generally applies the Federal Rules to determine the resolution of evidentiary issues. However, when state substantive law is determinative of the existence of claim or defense under the *Erie* doctrine, then state law, rather than the Federal Rules, also governs the effect of a presumption related to the claim or defense. Fed. R. Evid. 302.

3. Destruction of Evidence

In general, the intentional destruction of evidence relevant to a case raises a presumption or inference that such evidence would have been unfavorable to the party that destroyed the evidence. To be entitled to such an inference, the alleged victim of the destruction of the evidence must establish that (i) the destruction was intentional, (ii) the destroyed evidence was relevant to the issue about which the party seeks such inference, and (iii) the alleged victim acted with due diligence as to the destroyed evidence. The presumption that arises from the destruction of evidence is rebuttable.

II. RELEVANCE

A. GENERAL CONSIDERATIONS

As a rule, evidence must be relevant to be admissible, and all relevant evidence is admissible unless excluded by a specific rule, law, or constitutional provision. Fed. R. Evid. 402. Evidence is relevant if:

i) It has any tendency to make a fact more or less probable than it would be without the evidence (i.e., **probative**); and

ii) The fact is of consequence in determining the action (i.e., **material**).

Fed. R. Evid. 401.

> **Sufficiency Distinguished:** To be relevant, evidence need not, by itself, establish an element that a party must prove (e.g., the death of an individual in a homicide prosecution) or serve to refute such an element (e.g., a defendant's lack of a duty in a negligence action). The test of sufficiency of a party's evidence focuses on all evidence submitted by a party and admitted by the court. By contrast, under the test of relevancy, evidence is admissible even if it is only a single brick that is part of a wall of evidence establishing a party's position. Fed. R. Evid. 401, Notes of Advisory Committee, referring to Professor McCormick's famous statement, "A brick is not a wall."

1. **Direct and Circumstantial Evidence**

   a. **Direct evidence**

   Direct evidence is identical to the factual proposition that it is offered to prove. An eyewitness who testifies that she saw the defendant shoot the victim dead is an example of direct evidence that the defendant committed a homicide.

   > **Conviction without direct evidence:** There is no rule that requires the presentation of direct evidence in order to convict a defendant. In other words, a defendant can be convicted solely upon circumstantial evidence.

   b. **Circumstantial evidence**

   Evidence that tends to indirectly prove a factual proposition through inference from collateral facts is circumstantial. An eyewitness who testifies that, moments before entering a room, she heard a shot, and upon entering the room saw the defendant standing over the body of the victim holding a smoking gun is circumstantial evidence that the defendant committed a homicide.

   > **Compare direct evidence:** While it is sometimes said that direct evidence is better than circumstantial evidence, circumstantial evidence may have greater probative value. For example, testimony as to the identity of a thief based on a fleeting glimpse by an eyewitness with poor vision may not be as persuasive as testimony that the stolen item was found in the defendant's home.

2. **Exclusion of Relevant Evidence**

   Relevant evidence may be excluded if its probative value is **substantially outweighed** by the danger of unfair prejudice, confusing the issues, misleading the jury, undue delay, wasting time, or needlessly presenting cumulative evidence. This exclusion is often denominated by the applicable rule; that is, it is referred to as a "Rule 403" exclusion. Fed. R. Evid. 403.

   > **Matter of degree:** Evidence may be admissible even if the danger of prejudice or other factors outweigh the probative value, so long as the danger does not do so **substantially.**

3. **Relevance Dependent on Existence of Fact**

   When the relevance of evidence depends upon whether a fact exists, proof must be introduced sufficient to support a finding that the fact does exist. The court may admit the proposed evidence on the condition that the proof is introduced later. Fed. R. Evid. 104(b). In making its determination that sufficient evidence has been introduced, the court must examine all of the evidence and decide whether the jury could reasonably find the conditional fact by a preponderance of the evidence; the court itself is not required to find that the conditional fact exists by a preponderance of the evidence. *Huddleston v. United States*, 485 U.S. 681 (1988).

4. **Admission of Irrelevant Evidence—Curative Admission**

   Generally, irrelevant evidence is inadmissible. However, when a court admits evidence that is not relevant, the court may permit the introduction of additional irrelevant evidence to rebut the previously admitted evidence. Known as a curative admission, such evidence is admitted when necessary to remove unfair prejudice.

The failure of a party to object to the admission of the initial irrelevant evidence is a factor to be considered in determining whether the party was unfairly prejudiced by it. *United States v. Hall*, 653 F.2d 1002 (5th Cir. 1981); *Crawford v. United States*, 198 F.2d 976 (D.C. Cir. 1952).

5. Laying a Foundation

Various types of evidence are admissible subject to the existence of a necessary predicate (i.e., a foundation), such as the authentication of tangible evidence. The failure of the proponent of the evidence to establish that foundation may be challenged by an objection for lack of proper foundation.

B. CHARACTER EVIDENCE

Character evidence, which is generalized information about a person's behavior—such as information that the defendant is a criminal, a bad parent, or an inattentive driver—is generally inadmissible.

1. Civil Cases

a. Inadmissible to prove conforming conduct

In a civil case, evidence of a person's character (or character trait) generally is inadmissible to prove that the person acted in accordance with that character (or character trait) on a particular occasion. Fed. R. Evid. 404(a)(1).

> **Example:** A plaintiff cannot introduce evidence that the defendant is a reckless driver to prove that the defendant drove recklessly on the day in question.

Evidence concerning past sexual assault or child molestation by a *defendant* in a case in which the claim for relief is based on the defendant's sexual misconduct is admissible. Evidence concerning the past sexual behavior of a victim of sexual misconduct (e.g., rape) is admissible in limited circumstances (*see* § V.B.6. Sexual Conduct, *infra*).

b. Character at issue

Character evidence is admissible, however, when character is an **essential element** of a claim or defense, rather than a means of proving a person's conduct. Character is most commonly an essential element in defamation (character of the plaintiff), negligent hiring or negligent entrustment (character of the person hired or entrusted), and child-custody cases (character of the parent or guardian). Fed. R. Evid. 404(b); 405.

2. Criminal Cases

a. Defendant's character

1) By prosecution—defendant's bad character

In general, the same rule that applies in a civil action applies to the prosecution in a criminal case. The prosecution is not permitted to introduce evidence of a defendant's **bad character** to prove that the defendant has a **propensity** to commit crimes and therefore is likely to have committed the crime in question. Fed. R. Evid. 404(a)(1).

> **Example:** A defendant is charged with brutally murdering his wife. The prosecution may not present evidence of the defendant's violent nature.

2) By defendant—defendant's good character

A defendant is **permitted** to introduce evidence of his **good character** as being inconsistent with the type of crime charged.

> **Example 1:** A defendant is charged with brutally murdering his wife. The defendant may present evidence of his peaceable nature.

The defendant's character evidence must be pertinent to the crime charged.

> **Example 2:** A defendant is charged with embezzling money from her employer. The defendant may not present evidence of her peaceable nature.

Proof of good character offered by the defendant must be in the form of **reputation** testimony or **opinion** testimony. Reputation evidence is defined as a defendant's reputation in the community. "Community" includes people with whom the defendant engages on a regular basis.

3) Defendant "opens the door"

Although the prosecution cannot introduce evidence of the defendant's bad character, the defendant makes his character an issue in the case if he offers evidence of his good character. When the defendant **"opens the door,"** the prosecution is free to rebut the defendant's claims by attacking the defendant's character. Fed. R. Evid. 404(a)(2)(A).

> **Defendant as witness:** The defendant does not "open the door" to character evidence merely by taking the stand, but as a witness, the defendant is subject to impeachment.

In addition, the defendant "opens the door" for the prosecution to introduce evidence of his bad character by introducing evidence of the victim's bad character. The prosecution's evidence regarding the defendant must relate to the same character trait (e.g., violence) that the defendant's evidence about the victim did. Fed. R. Evid. 404(a)(2)(A).

b. Victim's character

1) By defendant—victim's bad character

A criminal defendant may introduce reputation or opinion evidence of the alleged victim's character when it is relevant to the defense asserted. Fed. R. Evid. 404(a)(2)(B). (Note: The introduction of evidence of the character of an alleged victim of sexual misconduct in a criminal case, however, is subject to significant limitations (*see* § V.B.6. Sexual Conduct, *infra*).)

> **Example:** A defendant is charged with assault. The defendant may offer evidence of the alleged victim's character trait of violence to support a claim of self-defense by showing that the alleged victim was the aggressor.

2) By prosecution—victim's good character

Generally, the prosecution may offer rebuttal evidence of the alleged victim's good character only after the defendant has introduced evidence of the alleged victim's bad character. Fed. R. Evid. 404(a)(2)(B).

> **Example:** A defendant is charged with assault. The defendant presents evidence of the alleged victim's character trait of violence to support a claim of self-defense. The prosecution may then rebut the defendant's evidence with evidence of the alleged victim's character trait of peacefulness. Note: The prosecution may also offer evidence of the defendant's character trait of violence.

In a homicide case, the prosecution may also offer evidence of the alleged victim's trait for peacefulness to rebut evidence that the alleged victim was the first aggressor. Fed. R. Evid. 404(a)(2)(C).

3. Methods of Proving Character

When character evidence is admissible, it may always be proved by testimony about the person's reputation or in the form of the witness's opinion. Fed. R. Evid. 405(a). For use of specific instances of conduct, *see* § II.C.2. Introduction of Specific Acts as Character Evidence, *infra*.

4. Impeachment

Character evidence is admissible for impeachment purposes. Character evidence about the witness may be introduced to show that the witness is not a person whose testimony should be believed. In such instances, the witness's character for untruthfulness is relevant. When permitted, the witness's testimony may be supported by testimony as to the witness's character for truthfulness. Fed. R. Evid. 404(a)(3). *See* § III.B. Impeachment, *infra*.

C. BAD ACTS

In addition to general evidence of a person's character (or character trait), evidence of a prior bad act is not admissible to prove a person's character in order to show that the person acted in accordance with that character on a particular occasion. Fed. R. Evid. 404(b)(1).

> **Example 1:** A driver is sued to recover for injuries inflicted on the plaintiff allegedly due to the driver's negligent failure to stop at a stop sign. The plaintiff cannot introduce testimony by a witness that the driver failed to stop at the same stop sign the day before the accident in question for the purpose of proving that the plaintiff failed to stop at the stop sign on the day of the accident.

Although a defendant's crimes or other wrongful acts are not admissible to show his criminal propensity in order to prove that he committed the crime for which he is charged, such bad acts are admissible for another purpose, such as proving motive, opportunity, intent, preparation, plan, knowledge, identity, absence of mistake, or lack of accident. Fed. R. Evid. 404(b)(2).

Example 2: A defendant is charged with murder. Evidence that the defendant was previously convicted of robbery is likely admissible if the murder victim was the prosecutor on the robbery case against the defendant. Such evidence establishes the defendant's motive for killing the victim.

MIMIC evidence: This type of evidence is sometimes referred to as "MIMIC" evidence (**M**otive, **I**ntent, absence of **M**istake, **I**dentity, or **C**ommon plan), but it is important not to treat this list as all-inclusive. Subject to the other restrictions on the admissibility of evidence (e.g., relevancy, Rule 403 exclusion), a defendant's bad act may be introduced for any purpose so long as that purpose is not to prove that, because the defendant had a propensity to commit crimes, the defendant committed the charged crime.

1. Advance Notice

When a criminal defendant requests, the prosecution must provide reasonable notice of the general nature of such evidence that the prosecution intends to offer at trial. Such notice must generally be given before trial, but it can be given during trial when the court, for good cause, excuses the lack of pretrial notice. Fed. R. Evid. 404(b)(2).

2. Introduction of Specific Acts as Character Evidence

a. Civil cases

When character evidence is admissible as evidence in a civil case (i.e., evidence that is an essential element of a claim or defense), it may be proved by specific instances of a person's conduct as well as either by testimony about the person's reputation or by testimony in the form of an opinion. Fed. R. Evid. 405(b).

b. Criminal cases

Generally, when character evidence is admissible as evidence in a criminal case (e.g., evidence of good character introduced by the defendant), specific instances of a person's conduct are not admissible. Character must be proved by either reputation or opinion testimony. Fed. R. Evid. 405(a).

Non-propensity use: When a defendant's bad act is not used to show the defendant's criminal propensity but for another purpose (e.g., motive, identity), such instance of conduct may be admissible for that purpose.

c. Cross-examination of character witness

When a character witness is cross-examined, the court may allow a party to inquire into specific acts committed by the person about whom the witness is testifying. Fed. R. Evid. 405(a).

Rule 403: Keep in mind that evidence of a prior bad act that is otherwise admissible is especially subject to challenge under Federal Rule 403, which permits the court to exclude evidence when its probative value is substantially outweighed by the danger of unfair prejudice (*see* § II.A.2. Exclusion of Relevant Evidence, *supra*).

D. HABIT EVIDENCE

Evidence of a **person's habit** or an **organization's routine** is admissible to prove that the person or organization acted in accordance with the habit or routine on a particular occasion. A habit is a person's particular routine reaction to a specific set of circumstances.

> **Example:** A person drives the same route to work and parks in the same spot every day.

Habit evidence may be admitted without corroboration and without an eyewitness. Fed. R. Evid. 406.

> **EXAM NOTE:** Habit is more specific than character evidence. On the MBE, words like "always" or "every time" generally refer to habit, whereas "often" or "frequently" are more likely to imply character evidence.

III. WITNESSES

A. COMPETENCE

Generally, every person is presumed to be competent to be a witness. Common-law prohibitions on a witness's ability to testify because of a lack of religious belief or conviction of a crime are inapplicable in proceedings governed by the Federal Rules. Questions of mental competence go to the weight rather than the admissibility of the testimony. However, in cases that turn on state law, such as diversity cases, a witness's competency is determined by state law. Fed. R. Evid. 601.

1. Personal Knowledge

A non-expert witness must have personal knowledge of a matter in order to testify about that matter. Personal knowledge may be established by the witness's own testimony as well as through other means. Fed. R. Evid. 602.

2. Oath or Affirmation

A witness must give an oath or affirmation to testify truthfully. The oath or affirmation must be in a form designed to impress that duty on the witness's conscience. Fed. R. Evid. 603. An interpreter must give an oath or affirmation to make a true translation. Fed. R. Evid. 604.

3. Judge as Witness

The presiding judge is absolutely barred from testifying as a witness in the trial. A party is not required to object in order to preserve the issue. Fed. R. Evid. 605.

4. Juror as Witness

a. At trial

A juror may not testify as a witness at trial in front of the members of the jury. If a juror is called to testify, the opposing party must be given the opportunity to object outside the presence of the jury. A juror may be called to testify outside the presence of the other jurors as to matters that occur during the trial, such as the bribery of a juror or a juror's failure to follow the court's instruction (e.g., discussing the case with family members). Fed. R. Evid. 606(a).

b. After trial

During an inquiry into the validity of a verdict, a juror generally may not testify about:

i) Any statement made or incident that occurred during the course of the jury's deliberations (e.g., refusal to apply the court's instructions);

ii) The effect of anything upon that juror's, or any other juror's, vote; or

iii) Any juror's mental processes concerning the verdict.

Fed. R. Evid. 606(b).

1) Exceptions

A juror may testify about whether:

i) Extraneous prejudicial information was brought to the jury's attention (e.g., the circulation of a newspaper article not introduced into evidence about the trial and the defendant's guilt);

ii) An outside influence was improperly brought to bear on a juror (e.g., a threat on the life of a juror's spouse); or

iii) A mistake was made in entering the verdict onto the verdict form.

The mistake exception, item iii above, does not extend to mistakes about the consequences of the agreed-upon verdict. Fed. R. Evid. 606(b).

Grand jury: The same rule applies with regard to a challenge to the validity of an indictment by a grand jury.

5. Child as Witness

The competence of a child depends on his intelligence, his ability to differentiate between truth and falsehood, and his understanding of the importance of telling the truth. *Wheeler v. United States*, 159 U.S. 523, 524, 526 (1895) (finding a five-year-old child competent to testify at a capital murder trial). A witness who is so young that he is unable to understand the requirement to tell the truth would be disqualified. There is, however, no specific age at which a person becomes competent. The decision with regard to competency is one for the court.

6. Dead Man's Statutes

At common law, a party with a financial interest in the outcome could not testify in a civil case about a communication or transaction with a person whose estate was party to the case and the testimony was adverse to the estate, unless there was a waiver. Dead Man's Statutes do not apply in criminal cases.

The Federal Rules do not include such a restriction, but most jurisdictions have adopted such "Dead Man's Statutes," which may be applicable in federal cases when state law applies (i.e., diversity cases).

a. Protected parties

The rationale of a Dead Man's Statute is to protect a decedent's estate from parties with a financial interest in the estate. Therefore, protected parties generally include an heir, a legatee, a devisee, an executor, or an administrator of an estate.

b. Disqualified witnesses

Any person directly affected financially by the outcome of the case may be disqualified as a witness under a Dead Man's Statute. A predecessor in interest to the party may be disqualified in order to prevent circumvention of the statute by transference of property to a relative or friend.

c. Interested person

A personal representative of the decedent or a successor in interest may also be protected under a Dead Man's Statute as an interested person.

d. Waiver

An interested person or protected party may waive the protection afforded by a Dead Man's Statute in several ways, including (i) failing to object to the introduction of testimony by a disqualified witness or (ii) introducing evidence of a conversation or transaction to which the statute applies.

B. IMPEACHMENT

A witness may be impeached by calling into question her credibility. Typically, a witness's testimony is challenged based on her character for truthfulness, bias, ability to perceive or testify accurately, or prior statement that contradicts the witness's testimony at trial. In addition, a witness may be impeached by another witness or by evidence that contradicts the witness's testimony.

1. Who May Impeach a Witness

Any party, including the party that called the witness to testify, may attack the credibility of a witness. Fed. R. Evid. 607.

2. Witness's Character for Truthfulness

a. Reputation and opinion testimony

A witness's credibility may be attacked by testimony regarding the witness's character for untruthfulness. Generally, this testimony must be about the witness's **reputation** for having a character for untruthfulness or in the form of an **opinion** of the witness's character for untruthfulness. Fed. R. Evid. 608(a).

b. Truthful character evidence

The credibility of a witness may not be bolstered. Evidence of the truthful character of the witness is admissible only after the witness's character for truthfulness has been attacked. Evidence that impeaches the witness but does not specifically attack the witness's character for truthfulness, such as testimony that the witness is biased, does not constitute an attack. As with evidence regarding a witness's character for untruthfulness, evidence as to a witness's character for truthfulness is generally admissible only in the form of reputation or opinion testimony. Fed. R. Evid. 608(a).

c. Specific instances of conduct

Generally, a specific instance of conduct (e.g., lying on a job application) is not admissible to attack or support the witness's character for truthfulness. However, on cross-examination, a witness may be asked about specific instances of conduct if it is probative of the truthfulness of (i) the witness or (ii) another witness about whose character the witness being cross-examined has testified. Fed. R. Evid. 608(b).

1) Limitations

The judge may refuse to allow such questioning of a witness under either Federal Rule 403 (the probative value is substantially outweighed by the danger of unfair prejudice) or Federal Rule 611 (protection of the witness from harassment or undue embarrassment). In addition, the lawyer who examines the witness must have a good-faith basis for believing that the misconduct occurred before asking the witness about it. *United States v. Davenport*, 753 F.2d 1460 (9th Cir. 1985).

2) Arrest

Because an arrest for misconduct is not itself misconduct, a witness may not be cross-examined about having been arrested solely for the purpose of impeaching the witness's character for truthfulness; however, the witness may be cross-examined about the underlying conduct that lead to the arrest. *See Michelson v. United States*, 335 U.S. 469 (1948).

3) Use of extrinsic evidence

When, on cross-examination, the witness denies a specific instance of conduct, extrinsic evidence is not admissible to prove that instance in order to attack or support the witness's character for truthfulness. This prohibition also bars references to any consequences that a witness may have suffered because of the conduct (e.g., suspension from a governmental job for improper personal use of governmental property). (An exception exists for criminal convictions, *see* § 3. Criminal Conviction, *below*.)

Note, however, that extrinsic evidence of specific conduct can be admissible to impeach the witness on other grounds, such as bias. Fed. R. Evid. 608(b), Notes of Advisory Committee (2003).

While a document is generally considered to be extrinsic evidence, *United States v. Elliott*, 89 F.3d 1360, 1368 (8th Cir. 1996), when the foundation for the document is established through the witness being impeached, it is possible that the document might be admissible to impeach the witness's character for truthfulness. Kevin C. McMunigal & Calvin W. Sharpe, *Reforming Extrinsic Impeachment*, 33 Conn. L. Rev. 363, 372–73 (2001).

4) Privilege against self-incrimination

By testifying on another matter, a witness does not waive the privilege against self-incrimination for testimony that relates only to the witness's character for truthfulness. Fed. R. Evid. 608(b).

3. Criminal Conviction

A witness's character for truthfulness may be impeached with evidence that the witness has been convicted of a crime, subject to the limitations discussed below. It does not matter whether the conviction is for a state or federal crime. Fed. R. Evid. 609.

a. Crimes involving dishonesty or false statement

Subject to the 10-year restriction (*see below*), **any witness** may be impeached with evidence that he has been convicted of **any crime**—felony or misdemeanor—**involving dishonesty or false statement,** regardless of the punishment imposed or the prejudicial effect of the evidence. A crime involves dishonesty or false statement if establishing the elements of the crime requires proof (or admission) of an act of dishonesty or false statement, such as perjury, fraud, embezzlement, or false pretense. Crimes of violence, such as murder, assault, and rape, are not crimes involving dishonesty or false statement, even though the perpetrator acted deceitfully in committing the crime of violence. Fed. R . Evid. 609(a)(2).

b. Crimes not involving dishonesty or false statement

Subject to the 10-year restriction (*see below*), a conviction for a crime not involving fraud or dishonesty is admissible to impeach a witness only if the crime is **punishable by death or imprisonment for more than one year** (typically, a felony). Fed. R. Evid. 609(a)(1).

1) Criminal defendant

When the witness is a criminal defendant, evidence of a felony conviction for a crime not involving dishonesty or false statement is admissible **only if** its probative value outweighs the prejudicial effect to that defendant. This stricter-than-usual balancing test gives extra protection to a criminal defendant who takes the stand in his own defense.

2) Other witnesses

For witnesses other than a criminal defendant, such evidence generally must be admitted. The court does have the discretion, however, to exclude the evidence when the party objecting to the impeachment shows that its probative value is **substantially outweighed** by its prejudicial effect (i.e., the Rule 403 standard).

c. Convictions more than 10 years old

If more than 10 years have elapsed since the conviction (or release from confinement, whichever is later), then evidence of the conviction is admissible only if:

i) The probative value of the conviction, supported by specific facts and circumstances, **substantially outweighs** its prejudicial effect; and

ii) The proponent gives an adverse party reasonable written notice of the intent to use such evidence so that the adverse party has a fair opportunity to contest the use of such evidence.

Fed. R. Evid. 609(b).

d. Effect of pardon

Evidence of a witness's conviction is not admissible if the conviction has been the subject of a pardon, annulment, or other action based on a finding of innocence. This rule also applies to an action based on a finding that the witness has been rehabilitated, provided that the witness has not been convicted of a later crime punishable by death or imprisonment in excess of one year (typically, a felony). Fed. R. Evid. 609(c).

e. Juvenile adjudications

Evidence of a juvenile adjudication is not admissible to impeach a defendant. When the witness is not the defendant, evidence of a juvenile adjudication can be used to impeach the witness's character for truthfulness only if:

i) It is offered in a criminal case;

ii) An adult's conviction for that offense would be admissible to attack the adult's credibility; and

iii) Admitting the evidence is necessary to fairly determine guilt or innocence.

Fed. R. Evid. 609(d).

> **Used to show bias:** Under the Sixth Amendment Confrontation Clause, evidence of a witness's juvenile adjudication can also be used by a criminal defendant to impeach a witness's credibility by showing bias, such as when the witness's juvenile adjudication could provide a motive for the witness to lie. *Davis v. Alaska*, 415 U.S. 308 (1974).

f. Manner of proof

Evidence of a prior conviction may be produced by way of an admission by the witness, whether during direct testimony or on cross-examination, as well as by extrinsic evidence (e.g., a record of the conviction). Fed. R. Evid. 609, Notes of Advisory Committee (1990).

g. Pendency of appeal

A witness's conviction may be used for impeachment purposes even if an appeal is pending. Evidence of the pendency is also admissible. Fed. R. Evid. 609(e).

4. Prior Inconsistent Statements

A witness's prior statement that is inconsistent with a material part of the witness's testimony may be used to impeach the witness.

a. Disclosing the statement to the witness

A party who is examining a witness about the witness's prior statement is not required to show it or disclose its contents to the witness, but the statement must be shown, or its contents disclosed, to an adverse party's attorney upon request. Fed. R. Evid. 613(a).

b. Extrinsic evidence

Extrinsic evidence of a witness's prior inconsistent statement may be introduced only if the witness is given the opportunity to **explain or deny** the statement, and the opposing party is given the opportunity to **examine the witness** about it. The witness's opportunity to explain or deny the statement need not take place before the statement is admitted into evidence.

1) Exceptions to the opportunity to explain

The opportunity to explain or deny a prior inconsistent statement does not apply when the statement (i) impeaches a hearsay declarant (*see* § 7. Impeachment of a Hearsay Declarant, *below*) or (ii) qualifies as an opposing party's statement under Rule 801(d)(2) (*see* § VI.B.2., "Opposing Party's Statement," *infra*). Fed. R. Evid. 806, 613(b).

2) Collateral matter

Extrinsic evidence of a prior inconsistent statement cannot be used to impeach a witness regarding a collateral (i.e., irrelevant) matter; the questioning party is bound by the witness's answer.

5. Bias or Interest

Because a witness may be influenced by his relationship to a party (e.g., employment), his interest in testifying (e.g., avoidance of prosecution), or his interest in the outcome of the case (e.g., receipt of an inheritance), a witness's bias or interest is always relevant to the credibility of his testimony, and consequently, a witness may be impeached on that ground.

Although the Federal Rules do not expressly require that a party ask the witness about an alleged bias before introducing extrinsic evidence of that bias, many courts require that such a foundation be laid before extrinsic evidence of bias can be introduced.

> **EXAM NOTE:** MBE questions typically test bias in the form of witnesses who are employed by one of the parties, or witnesses for the prosecution who testify in exchange for reduced or dropped charges.

6. Sensory Competence

A witness may be impeached by showing a deficiency in her testimonial capacities to perceive, recall, or relate information. This can be achieved by demonstrating that the witness is physically or mentally impaired, or through evidence of outside interference with the witness's abilities, such as thunder impeding the ability to hear or darkness impeding the ability to see.

7. Impeachment of a Hearsay Declarant

When a hearsay statement is admitted into evidence, the credibility of the declarant may be attacked (and, if attacked, supported) by any evidence that would be admissible if the declarant had testified as a witness. The declarant need not be given the opportunity to explain or deny any inconsistent statement or conduct, whether such statement or conduct occurred before or after the hearsay statement. If the party against whom a hearsay statement has been admitted calls the declarant as a witness, then the party is entitled to examine the declarant on the statement as if under cross-examination. Fed. R. Evid. 806.

Similar impeachment treatment is accorded a nonhearsay statement made by a co-conspirator, agent, or authorized spokesperson for an opposing party that has been admitted into evidence.

8. Rehabilitation of a Witness

A witness who has been impeached may be "rehabilitated" by the introduction of rebuttal evidence by either party to support the witness's credibility. Rehabilitation may be accomplished by:

i) **Explanation** or clarification on redirect examination;

ii) Reputation or opinion evidence of his **character for truthfulness,** if the witness's character was attacked on that ground under Fed. R. Evid. 608(a); or

iii) A **prior consistent statement** offered to rebut an express or implied charge that the witness lied due to improper motive or influence.

Fed. R. Evid. 801(d)(1)(B).

9. Religious Opinions and Beliefs

Evidence of a witness's religious opinions or beliefs is not admissible to attack or support a witness's credibility. Fed. R. Evid. 610. However, such evidence may be admissible to show bias or interest, such as when the witness is affiliated with a church that is a party to a lawsuit.

10. Impeachment by Contradictory Evidence

A witness may be impeached by evidence that contradicts the witness's testimony. Impeachment may be by extrinsic evidence as well as by cross-examination.

Example: The plaintiff in a negligence action based on a car accident testifies that, due to the defendant's reckless driving, the plaintiff's car was damaged. The defense may introduce a record of an insurance claim filed by the plaintiff prior to the accident for such damage due to another incident. Alternatively, the defense attorney may cross-examine the plaintiff about that claim.

11. Collateral Issues

While the Federal Rules do not explicitly prohibit impeachment on collateral issues, a court may refuse to admit evidence related to a collateral issue under the Rule 403 balancing test. Generally, a party may not impeach the credibility of a witness by introducing extrinsic evidence of a collateral matter. Instead, the party must accept the witness's testimony.

Example: A defendant is charged with assault. A prosecution witness testifies that the defendant assaulted the victim, who was wearing a plaid shirt. The defense may not call another witness to testify that the victim was wearing a striped shirt in order to establish the type of shirt that the victim was wearing.

C. RECOLLECTION REFRESHED

1. Present Recollection Refreshed

A witness may examine any item (e.g., writing, photograph) to "refresh" the witness's present recollection. The witness's testimony must be based on the witness's refreshed recollection, not on the item itself (e.g., the witness cannot read from the refreshing document).

a. Adverse party's options

When the item used to refresh a witness's recollection is a writing, the adverse party is entitled to have the document produced, to inspect the document, to cross-examine the witness about it, and to introduce any relevant portion into evidence. If the producing party claims that the document contains unrelated matter, the court may examine the document in camera and delete any unrelated portion before ordering that the rest be delivered to the adverse party. The adverse party may object to the deletion, in which case the deleted portion must be preserved in the record. Fed. R. Evid. 612(b).

Evidentiary purpose: When an adverse party seeks to introduce a writing used to refresh a witness's memory, the writing typically will be admissible for only the purpose of impeaching the witness's credibility. It will be admissible for substantive purposes only if it satisfies the other restrictions on admissibility, such as the hearsay rule.

When the refreshing of a witness's memory with a writing takes place before the witness testifies, the court may permit an adverse party to utilize these options, if justice so requires. Fed. R. Evid. 612(a).

b. Failure to produce or deliver the writing

In a criminal case, if the prosecution refuses to comply with a court order to produce or deliver a writing, the court must strike the witness's testimony, or may, when justice requires, declare a mistrial. In other circumstances, the court is free to issue any appropriate order. Fed. R. Evid. 612(c).

2. Past Recollection Recorded

A memorandum or record about a matter that a witness once had knowledge of but now has insufficient recollection of to testify to it may be admissible under a hearsay exception (*see* § VII.B.5. Recorded Recollection, *infra*). Although the record may be read into evidence, it is received as an exhibit only if offered by an adverse party.

Refreshed and recorded recollections distinguished: The item used to refresh a witness's present recollection is generally not admitted into evidence, but a document introduced under the recorded recollection hearsay exception may be.

D. OPINION TESTIMONY

1. Lay Witness

A lay (non-expert) witness is generally not permitted to testify as to his opinion. However, lay opinions are admissible with respect to common-sense impressions such as appearance, intoxication, speed of a vehicle, or another's emotions. To be admissible, the opinion must be:

i) Rationally **based on the perception** of the witness; and

ii) Helpful to a **clear understanding** of the witness's testimony or the determination of a fact in issue.

Additionally, the opinion must **not** be based on scientific, technical, or specialized knowledge. Fed. R. Evid. 701.

2. Expert Witness

a. Subject matter of testimony

Before an expert witness may testify, the court must first determine that the subject matter of the witness's testimony:

i) **Is scientific, technical, or other specialized knowledge,** which focuses on the *reliability* of the testimony; and

ii) Will **help the trier of fact** understand the evidence or determine a fact in issue, which focuses on the *relevance* of the testimony.

b. Qualified expert

Once the testimony is determined to be reliable and relevant, an expert witness may testify as to her opinion, provided:

i) The witness is **qualified as an expert** by knowledge, skill, experience, training, or education;

ii) The testimony is based on **sufficient facts or data**;

iii) The testimony is the product of **reliable principles and methods** (i.e., the factual data, principles, and methods used as a basis for the testimony are of the type reasonably relied on by experts in the field, although the data need not be admissible itself); and

iv) The witness **applied the principles and methods reliably to the facts** of the case.

Fed. R. Evid. 702. The expert must also possess a reasonable degree of certainty in her opinion, which may be expressed using language such as "probably." *United States v. Mornan*, 413 F.3d 372 (3d Cir. 2005); *see also, Kumho Tire Co. v. Carmichael*, 526 U.S. 137 (1999); *Daubert v. Merrell Dow Pharm.*, 509 U.S. 579 (1993).

c. Ultimate issue

Generally, an expert's opinion may be admissible even though the opinion embraces an ultimate issue in the case (including the defendant's state of mind). However, an expert **may not** state an opinion about whether a criminal defendant had the **requisite mental state** of any element of the crime charged or of a defense. That determination lies in the province of the trier of fact. Fed. R. Evid. 704.

d. Basis of opinion

The expert's opinion may be based on facts and data that the expert has personally observed or about which the expert has been made aware. When such facts and data are not admissible, the opinion itself may nevertheless be admissible if experts in the particular field would reasonably rely on those kinds of facts and data in forming an opinion on the subject. If such facts are inadmissible, the proponent nevertheless may disclose them to the jury if their probative value in helping the jury evaluate the opinion substantially outweighs their prejudicial effect. Fed. R. Evid. 703.

1) Disclosure of underlying facts and data

An expert may state an opinion and give the reasons for it without first testifying as to the underlying facts or data, unless the court orders otherwise. Another party, when cross-examining the expert, may, of course, require the expert to disclose those facts or data. Fed. R. Evid. 705.

2) Use of hypothetical

In making facts known to the expert at trial, use of a hypothetical question is not required.

e. Court-appointed expert

The court may appoint an expert witness and must inform the expert, either orally or in writing, of the expert's duties. Such a witness must advise each party of any findings. Each party may depose the witness, call the witness to testify, and cross-examine the witness. The court may authorize disclosure to the jury that the court appointed the expert. In a criminal case, the expert is paid by funds provided by law; in most civil cases, the expert's compensation is paid by the parties. Fed. R. Evid. 706.

f. Interpreter

An interpreter is subject to the rules for expert witnesses. Fed. R. Evid. 604.

IV. TANGIBLE EVIDENCE

Tangible evidence is evidence that is not presented in the form of testimony by a witness; it includes both documentary evidence (e.g., a written contract, a letter) and physical objects (e.g., a gun, torn clothing, an injured foot, a sound recording).

A. AUTHENTICATION

All tangible evidence must be authenticated. To authenticate an item, the proponent must produce sufficient evidence to support a finding that the thing is what its proponent claims it is. This is a lesser standard than a preponderance of the evidence. Fed. R. Evid. 901(a).

1. Physical Objects

a. Personal knowledge

A physical object may be authenticated by testimony of **personal knowledge** of the object. Fed. R. Evid. 901(b)(1).

Example: The owner of a stolen pocket watch may authenticate the watch by simply identifying it, "Yes, that is my pocket watch that was stolen."

b. Distinctive characteristics

A physical object may be authenticated by testimony of its **distinctive** characteristics. Fed. R. Evid. 901(b)(4).

c. Chain of custody

Authentication by chain of custody must be used with respect to a physical object that could easily be tampered with or confused with a similar item, such as a blood sample. The witness testifying must account for the whereabouts of the item from the time it was obtained up until its introduction at the trial.

d. Reproductions and explanatory evidence

When reproductions (e.g., photographs, diagrams, maps, movies) are introduced into evidence, they may be authenticated by the testimony of a witness with personal knowledge that the object accurately depicts what its proponent claims it does. It is generally not necessary to call the person who created the reproduction to authenticate it. However, the creator may be called to authenticate the reproduction and may do so by testifying that the reproduction method produces an accurate result. Fed. R. Evid. 901(b)(9).

e. X-ray images and electrocardiograms

X-ray images, electrocardiograms, and similar items are physical representations of things that cannot otherwise be seen (i.e., the inner workings and functionality of a human body), and, as such, unlike other reproductions, they cannot be authenticated merely by the testimony of a witness that they are accurate reproductions of the facts. To authenticate such an item, it must be shown that an accurate process was used, that the machine used was working properly, and that the operator of the machine was qualified to operate it. The chain of custody must also be established.

2. Documentary Evidence

Documentary evidence is commonly authenticated by stipulation, testimony of an eyewitness, or handwriting verification.

a. Ancient documents and data compilations

A document or data compilation, including data stored electronically, is considered authentic if it is (i) at least **20 years old,** (ii) in a **condition unlikely to create suspicion** as to its authenticity, and (iii) **found in a place where it would likely be** if it were authentic. Fed. R. Evid. 901(b)(8).

b. Public records

A public record may be authenticated by evidence that the document was recorded or filed in a public office as authorized by law or that the document is from the office where items of that kind are kept. Fed. R. Evid. 901(b)(7).

c. Reply letter doctrine

A document may be authenticated by evidence that it was written in response to a communication, so long as it is unlikely, based on the contents, that it was written by someone other than the recipient of the first communication.

d. Handwriting verification

There are two methods by which handwriting verification may be used to authenticate a writing.

1) Comparison

An expert witness or the trier of fact may compare the writing in question with another writing that has been proven to be genuine in order to determine the authenticity of the writing in question. Fed. R. Evid. 901(b)(3). This method may also be used for authenticating other items, such as fingerprints, cloth fibers, and hair.

2) Non-expert opinion

A lay witness with personal knowledge of the claimed author's handwriting may testify as to whether the document is in that person's handwriting. The lay witness must not have become familiar with the handwriting for the purposes of litigation. Fed. R. Evid. 901(b)(2).

e. Self-authenticating documents

The following items of evidence are self-authenticating—they do not require extrinsic evidence of authenticity in order to be admitted:

i) Public documents bearing a governmental seal and a signature of an authorized governmental official or that are not sealed but are signed by an authorized governmental official and certified by another authorized governmental official;

ii) Certified copies of public records;

iii) Official publications issued by a public authority;

iv) Newspapers and periodicals;

v) Trade inscriptions (e.g., labels affixed in the course of business that indicate ownership);

vi) Notarized (acknowledged) documents;

vii) Commercial paper (including the signature thereon, and related documents);

viii) Any document, signature, or other item declared by federal statute to be authentic; and

ix) Records of a regularly conducted activity (e.g., a business) certified by a custodian of the records.

Although a proponent of a self-authenticating document generally is not required to give an adverse party advance notice of the intent to introduce the document, the proponent of business records (item ix, *above*) must give an adverse party reasonable written notice prior to the trial or hearing of the intent to offer the record and must make the record available for inspection so that the party has a fair opportunity to challenge them. Fed. R. Evid. 902.

f. Attesting witness

The testimony of a witness who attests or subscribes to a document generally is not required to authenticate a document. However, such testimony may be required by state law, such as to authenticate a will. Fed. R. Evid. 903.

3. Oral Statements

Oral statements may need to be authenticated as to the identity of the speaker in cases in which that identity is important (e.g., an opposing party's statement).

a. Voice identification

A voice can be identified by **any person** who has heard the voice **at any time** (including one made familiar solely for the purposes of litigation, in contrast to the rule for handwriting verification). It makes no difference whether the voice was heard firsthand or through mechanical or electronic transmission or recording. Fed. R. Evid. 901(b)(5).

b. Telephone conversations

A party to a telephone conversation may authenticate statements made during that conversation by testifying that:

i) The caller recognized the speaker's voice;

ii) The speaker knew facts that only a particular person would know;

iii) The caller dialed a number believed to be the speaker's, and the speaker identified himself upon answering; or

iv) The caller dialed a business and spoke to the person who answered about business regularly conducted over the phone.

Fed. R. Evid. 901(b)(4)–(6).

B. BEST EVIDENCE RULE

The best evidence rule (also known as the original document rule) requires that the original document (or a reliable duplicate) be produced in order to prove the contents of a writing, recording, or photograph, including electronic documents, x-rays, and videos. A "writing" is defined as "letters, words, numbers or their equivalent set down in any form." A "recording" and "photograph" are similarly broadly defined. Fed. R. Evid. 1001(a)–(c).

This rule applies only when the **contents of the document are at issue** or a witness is **relying on the contents of the document** when testifying. Fed. R. Evid. 1001–08.

Caution: Despite its name, the best evidence rule does not require a party to present the most persuasive evidence, nor does it require the presentation of documentary evidence instead of a witness's testimony simply because a document is available.

Example: A witness writes down her observations of an accident immediately after it happens. The best evidence rule does not prevent the witness from testifying about the event simply because a writing of her observations exists.

EXAM NOTE: The best evidence rule is frequently an incorrect answer choice on the MBE.

1. Contents at Issue

The contents of a document are at issue when:

i) The document is used as proof of the happening of an event, such as with a photograph of a bank robbery;

ii) The document has a legal effect, such as with a contract or a will; or

iii) The witness is testifying based on facts learned from the writing (as opposed to personal knowledge), such as with an x-ray image.

Fed. R. Evid. 1002, Notes of Advisory Committee.

2. "Original"

An original of a writing or recording includes any counterpart intended to have the same effect as the original by the person who executed or issued it. If the information is stored electronically, any legible printout (or other output readable by sight) that reflects the information accurately is an original. An original of a photograph includes the negative and any print made from it. Fed. R. Evid. 1001(d).

3. Exceptions

a. Duplicates

A duplicate is a counterpart produced by any process or technique that accurately reproduces the original. Fed. R. Evid. 1001(e). A duplicate is admissible to the same extent as an original unless:

i) There is a genuine question as to the authenticity of the original; or

ii) The circumstances make it unfair to admit the duplicate, such as may be the case when only part of the original is duplicated.

Fed. R. Evid. 1003.

Handwritten copies: Handwritten copies of an original are not duplicates and are admissible only when the original or duplicate is lost, destroyed, or in the possession of an adversary who fails to produce it.

b. Original unavailable

The original is not required, and other evidence of its contents is admissible if:

i) All of the originals are lost or destroyed, and not by the proponent acting in bad faith;

ii) The original cannot be obtained by any available judicial process;

iii) The party against whom the original would be offered (a) had control of the original, (b) was at that time put on notice that the original would be the subject of proof at the trial or hearing, and (c) failed to produce it at the trial or hearing; or

iv) The writing, recording, or photograph is not closely related to a controlling issue (i.e., it is a collateral matter).

In such cases, once the party has accounted for the absence of an original, the party may prove the contents of the writing, recording, or photograph by other means. Fed. R. Evid. 1004.

c. Public records

The contents of a public record (i.e., an official record or a document recorded or filed in a public office as authorized by law) may be, and generally are, proved by a certified copy rather than by the original record. Alternatively, a public record may be proved by a copy of the record plus the testimony of a person who has compared the copy with the original. If a certified or compared copy cannot be obtained by reasonable diligence, the contents may be proved by other evidence. Fed. R. Evid. 1005.

d. Summaries

The contents of voluminous writings, recordings, or photographs may be presented in the form of a chart, summary, or calculation, if such contents cannot be conveniently examined in court. The proponent must make the originals or duplicates available for examination and copying by other parties at a reasonable time and place. The court may order the proponent to produce the originals or duplicates in court. Fed. R. Evid. 1006.

e. Admission by party

The proponent may prove the contents of a writing, recording, or photograph by the testimony, deposition, or written statement of the party against whom the evidence is offered. In such a case, the proponent does not need to account for the original. Fed. R. Evid. 1007.

Oral out-of-court statement: If a party against whom a document is offered admits to the contents of the document in an oral statement made out of court (other than during a deposition), the best evidence rule applies. The proponent must account for the original before using the adverse party's oral statement to prove the contents of the document.

4. Role of Court and Jury

Ordinarily, the court determines whether the proponent has fulfilled the conditions for admitting other evidence of the content of a document. In a jury trial, however, the jury determines any issue as to whether:

   i) An asserted writing, recording, or photograph ever existed;

   ii) Another writing, recording, or photograph produced at trial is the original; or

   iii) Other evidence of content correctly reflects the content.

Fed. R. Evid. 1008.

C. PAROL EVIDENCE RULE

1. General Rule

The parol evidence rule operates to exclude evidence that, if introduced, would change the terms of a written agreement. The rule is based on the assumption that a written contract represents the complete agreement between the parties.

a. Complete integration

If a written agreement is a complete integration (i.e., contains all of the terms to which the parties agreed), then the parol evidence rule is in effect, and no extrinsic evidence may be introduced.

b. Partial integration

A contract that contains some, but not all, of the terms to which the parties agreed is a partial integration. In this case, extrinsic evidence that **adds to** the writing may be admitted. Evidence that **contradicts** the writing may not be admitted.

2. Exceptions

Extrinsic evidence can always be admitted for the following purposes:

i) To clarify an ambiguity in the terms of the writing;

ii) To prove trade custom or course of dealings;

iii) To show fraud, duress, mistake, or illegal purpose on the part of one or both parties; or

iv) To show that consideration has (or has not) been paid.

3. Applicable Evidence

Only evidence of **prior or contemporaneous negotiations** is subject to the parol evidence rule. In other words, evidence of negotiations conducted **after** the execution of the written contract is not prohibited by the parol evidence rule and may be offered to prove subsequent modifications of the agreement.

D. DEMONSTRATIVE AND EXPERIMENTAL EVIDENCE

A court may allow demonstrations and experiments to be performed in the courtroom. This may include exhibition of injuries in a personal injury or criminal case. A court has discretion to exclude evidence of personal injuries if the demonstration of such severe injuries would result in unfair prejudice. A court may also exclude a demonstration that cannot be effectively cross-examined. Science experiments are permitted but may be excluded if they will result in undue waste of time or confusion of the issues.

V. PRIVILEGES AND OTHER POLICY EXCLUSIONS

A. PRIVILEGES

The Federal Rules have no specific privilege provisions but instead defer to common-law privileges, except in diversity cases, when state rules generally apply. Fed. R. Evid. 501. A claim of privilege applies at all stages of a case or proceedings. Fed. R. Evid. 1101(c).

1. Confidential Communication

For a privilege to apply, there must be a confidential communication.

a. Presence of third party

Generally, if the communication is overheard by a third party, the privilege is destroyed. However, the presence of the third party does not destroy the privilege if:

i) The first two parties do not know that the third party is present (e.g., an unknown eavesdropper); or

ii) The third party is necessary to assist in the communication (e.g., a translator).

b. Waiver

A privilege may be waived if the person who holds the privilege:

i) Fails to assert the privilege in a timely manner (i.e., when the testimony is offered);

ii) Voluntarily discloses, or allows another to disclose, a substantial portion of the communication to a third party, unless the disclosure is privileged; or

iii) Contractually waives the privilege in advance.

A wrongful disclosure without the privilege holder's consent does not constitute a waiver. For limitations on waiver of the attorney-client privilege due to inadvertent disclosure, *see* § 3.c. Effect of disclosure on waiver, *below*.

2. Spousal Privilege

"Spousal privilege" comprises two distinct privileges: spousal immunity and confidential marital communications.

a. Spousal immunity

The general rule is that the spouse of a **criminal defendant** may not be called as a witness by the prosecution. Nor may a married person be **compelled** to testify against his spouse in any criminal proceeding, including a grand jury proceeding, regardless of who is the defendant.

1) Holder of the privilege

a) Federal courts

In federal courts (and a minority of states), the **witness spouse** holds the privilege and may choose to testify but cannot be compelled to do so.

b) State courts

In many jurisdictions, the **party spouse** (as opposed to the witness spouse) holds the privilege and may prevent the witness spouse from testifying, even if the witness spouse wants to testify.

2) Period to which the privilege applies

The spousal immunity privilege applies to testimony about events that occurred **before and during the marriage.**

3) Time limit on assertion of the privilege

The spousal immunity privilege can be asserted **only during a valid marriage.** The right to assert the privilege expires upon divorce or annulment.

b. Confidential marital communications

Communication made between spouses **while they were married** is privileged if the communication was made **in reliance on the sanctity of marriage.**

1) Holder of the privilege

The majority view is that the privilege is held by **both spouses.** Some courts, however, have taken the position that only the communicating spouse can assert the privilege. *See* 1 Kenneth S. Broun et al., McCormick on Evidence § 83 (6th ed. 2006).

2) Scope of the privilege

This privilege applies only to communications made **during marriage.** This privilege applies to both **civil and criminal cases.**

3) Lack of time limit on assertion of the privilege

The time for asserting this privilege extends **beyond the termination of the marriage.** Thus, either party may assert the privilege—by refusing to testify or by preventing the other party from doing so—at any time, even after divorce or the death of one spouse.

> **Comparison of timing:** Spousal immunity applies to events occurring before marriage but ends when the marriage does, whereas the confidential communication privilege begins with marriage but continues beyond the length of the marriage.

c. Exceptions

Neither of the spousal privileges applies in cases in which one spouse is suing the other, or when one spouse is charged with a crime against the other spouse or the children of either.

3. Attorney-Client Privilege

A confidential communication between a client and an attorney for the purpose of seeking legal advice or representation is privileged.

a. Elements

1) Confidential

The communication must be intended to be confidential in order to be privileged. A communication made in the presence of a third party generally is not privileged, but the presence of, or communication by or through, a representative of the client or the attorney does not destroy the attorney-client privilege.

2) Communication

The communication must be **for the purpose of seeking legal advice or representation,** but the attorney does not need to give advice or agree to the representation for the privilege to exist.

a) Non-privileged statements

A statement made to an attorney that is not about legal advice or services sought by the client is not privileged. This includes statements regarding the fact of employment, the identity of the client, and the fee arrangements for the representation. If providing such information would divulge a confidential communication or incriminate the client, then it may be protected.

Furthermore, the attorney-client privilege does not protect disclosure of the underlying facts. A client cannot be compelled to answer the question "What did you say to your attorney?" but cannot refuse to reveal a fact within her knowledge merely because she told that fact to her attorney. *Upjohn Co. v. United States*, 449 U.S. 383 (1981) (quoting *Philadelphia v. Westinghouse Electric Corp.*, 205 F.Supp. 830, 831 (E.D. Pa. 1962)).

Finally, communications are not privileged when they are made to an attorney who is acting in a capacity other than as an attorney, such as a tax preparer, business partner, or witness to a will.

b) Corporate client

When an attorney represents a corporation, some states limit the privilege to communications received by the attorney from a member of the "control group" of the corporation (employees in a position to control or take a substantial part in a decision). *See, e.g., Consolidation Coal Co. v. Bucyrus-Erie Co.*, 432 N.E.2d 250 (Ill. 1982). However, in cases in which federal law controls, the privilege extends to communications by a non-control-group employee about matters within the employee's corporate duties made for the purpose of securing legal advice for the corporation. *Upjohn Co. v. United States*, 449 U.S. 383 (1981) (protecting communications by lower-level employees who were directed by their superiors to communicate with the corporation's attorney).

3) Client holds the privilege

The client holds the privilege and is the only one who may waive it. The attorney, however, must assert the privilege on the client's behalf to protect the client's interests. The privilege exists until it is waived, and it can survive the client's death.

b. Exceptions

The attorney-client privilege does not protect these confidential communications:

i) Communications made to enable or aid the commission of what the client **knew or should have known** was a crime or fraud;

ii) Communications relevant to a dispute between attorney and client (e.g., a malpractice allegation);

iii) Communications relevant to a dispute between parties who claim through the same deceased client; and

iv) Communications between former co-clients who are now adverse to each other.

> **Work product documents:** Documents prepared by an attorney for his own use in connection with the client's case are not covered by the attorney-client privilege because **they are not communications.** However, such documents are protected under the "work product" doctrine and are not subject to discovery unless the party seeking disclosure (i) demonstrates a substantial need for the information, and (ii) cannot obtain the information by any other means without undue hardship. The mental impressions, conclusions, and trial tactics of an attorney are always protected from discovery. Fed. R. Civ. P. 26(b)(3).

c. **Effect of disclosure on waiver**

Although the Federal Rules generally do not address the existence or scope of common-law privileges, there is one exception. Federal Rule 502 addresses the effect that a litigation-related disclosure of protected information has on the waiver of the attorney-client privilege, drawing a distinction between an intentional disclosure and an unintentional disclosure. The rule applies to confidential communications as well as material protected by the work-product doctrine. Fed. R. Evid. 502.

1) **Inadvertent disclosure—no waiver**

When made during a federal proceeding, the inadvertent disclosure of privileged communication or information does not waive the privilege if the holder of the privilege:

i) Took reasonable steps to prevent disclosure; and

ii) Promptly took reasonable steps to rectify the error.

Fed. R. Evid. 502(b). In determining whether the holder took reasonable steps to prevent disclosure, factors such as the number of documents to be reviewed, the time constraints for production, or the existence of an efficient records-management system may be relevant.

2) **Intentional disclosure—limitation on the scope of waiver**

When made during a federal proceeding, the intentional disclosure of privileged material operates as a waiver of the attorney-client privilege. The waiver extends to undisclosed information only in those unusual situations in which (i) the disclosed and undisclosed material concern the same subject matter and (ii) fairness requires the disclosure of related information because a party has disclosed information in a selective, misleading, and unfair manner. Fed. R. Evid. 502(a).

3) **Effect of disclosure made in a state proceeding**

When privileged material is disclosed in a state proceeding and the state and federal laws are in conflict as to the effect of the disclosure, the disclosure does not operate as a waiver in a subsequent federal proceeding if the disclosure (i) would not be a waiver had it been made in a federal proceeding or (ii) is not a disclosure under the law of the state where it was made. In other words, the federal court must apply the law that is most protective of the privilege. This rule does not apply if the state court has issued an order concerning the effect of the disclosure; in such a case, the state-court order would be controlling. Fed. R. Evid. 502(c).

4) Controlling effect of a federal confidentiality order

A federal court may order that the privilege or protection is not waived by disclosure connected with the pending litigation (i.e., a confidentiality order). In such a case, the disclosure does not constitute a waiver in any other federal or state proceeding. Fed. R. Evid. 502(d).

5) Parties' agreement

An agreement between the parties regarding the effect of a disclosure binds only the parties unless the agreement is incorporated into a court order. Fed. R. Evid. 502(e).

4. Physician-Patient Privilege

Although there is no common-law privilege covering statements made by a patient to a doctor, many states protect such communications by statute, so long as the communications were made for the purpose of obtaining medical treatment. The patient holds the privilege; thus, only the patient may decide whether to waive it.

The privilege does not exist if:

i) The information was acquired for **reasons other than treatment**;

ii) The patient's **physical condition is at issue**;

iii) The communication was made as part of the **commission of a crime or tort**;

iv) A **dispute exists** between the physician and the patient;

v) The patient contractually **agreed to waive** the privilege; or

vi) A **case is brought in federal court** and state law does not apply (e.g., most cases that involve a federal question).

If an attorney requests that a physician consult with his client, then the physician-patient privilege applies only if treatment is contemplated during the consult.

5. Psychotherapist-Patient Privilege

The federal courts and most states recognize a privilege for confidential communications made between a psychiatrist, psychologist, or licensed social worker and a patient. The patient holds the privilege, but the psychotherapist must assert the privilege in the patient's absence.

The privilege does not exist if (i) the patient's mental condition is at issue, (ii) the communication was a result of a court-ordered exam, or (iii) the case is a commitment proceeding against the patient.

The psychotherapist-patient privilege is more widely recognized than the traditional physician-patient privilege.

6. **Self-Incrimination**

   a. **In general**

   The Fifth Amendment protection against self-incrimination allows a witness in any proceeding to refuse to give testimony that may tend to incriminate the witness. The protection covers only current (not prior) statements, and it does not apply to physical characteristics or mannerisms. The privilege belongs only to human beings. A corporation or other organization is not able to assert the privilege. *Bellis v. United States*, 417 U.S. 85 (1974).

   b. **Comment and inference**

   In a criminal case, a prosecutor may not comment on the defendant's failure to take the stand and may not argue that the jury should draw a negative inference from the assertion of the privilege. *Griffin v. California*, 380 U.S. 609 (1965).

   In a civil case, however, it is proper for the opposing party to ask the jury to draw an adverse inference from a witness's claim of privilege.

   c. **Immunity**

   A witness may be compelled to provide incriminating testimony if the government grants him immunity from prosecution. The witness is not entitled to "transactional" immunity, i.e., protection against prosecution for the entire transaction about which he was testifying; instead, the government is constitutionally required to offer mere "use" immunity, which prohibits only the use of the compelled testimony against the witness. *Kastigar v. United States*, 406 U.S. 441 (1972). If the government does prosecute the witness in such a case, the government has the burden to show that the compelled testimony did not provide an investigatory lead that was helpful to the prosecution.

   A witness may lose the right to invoke the privilege if the danger of incrimination has been removed through acquittal or conviction of the underlying charge. If the questioning about the adjudicated crime can lead to prosecution for other crimes, however, the privilege can be invoked.

7. **Other Privileges**

   a. **Clergy-penitent**

   In some jurisdictions, a confidential communication made by a penitent to a member of the clergy is privileged. The penitent holds the privilege, but the clergy member must assert the privilege on the penitent's behalf.

   b. **Accountant-client**

   Although not available at common law, many jurisdictions recognize a privilege for confidential communications made by a client to his accountant. The privilege operates similarly to the attorney-client privilege.

   c. **Professional journalist**

   There is no federal privilege protecting a journalist's source of information, but some states have enacted statutes extending some protection to journalists.

d. Governmental privileges

The government, at all levels, is privileged against disclosing:

i)   The identity of an informant in a criminal case; and

ii) The communication of **official information** (i.e., information that relates to the internal affairs of the government and is not open to the public) by or to public officials.

B.   PUBLIC POLICY EXCLUSIONS

1.   Subsequent Remedial Measures

When measures are taken that would have made an earlier injury or harm less likely to occur (e.g., repairing an area where a customer slipped), evidence of the subsequent measures is **not admissible to prove negligence, culpable conduct, a defective product or design, or the need for a warning or instruction.** However, evidence of subsequent remedial measures may be admissible for other purposes, such as impeachment or—if disputed—ownership or control of the cause of the harm (e.g., a car) or the feasibility of precautionary measures. Fed. R. Evid. 407.

Product liability: The exclusion of evidence of a subsequent remedial measure applies to product liability actions based on negligence and those based on strict liability. To be excluded, the remedial measure must be undertaken **after** the plaintiff is injured; a remedial measure made after a product was manufactured but **before** the plaintiff was injured is not subject to exclusion under this rule. Fed. R. Evid. 407, Notes of Advisory Committee (1997).

2.   Compromise Offers and Negotiations

Compromise offers made by any party, as well as any conduct or statements made during compromise negotiations, are not admissible to prove or disprove the **validity or amount of a disputed claim,** nor may they be admitted for impeachment by prior inconsistent statement or contradiction. Fed. R. Evid. 408.

Lack of dispute: If the claim is not disputed as to its validity or amount (e.g., a party admits to both), then a statement made in connection with an offer to settle for a lesser amount is admissible. Fed. R. Evid. 408, Notes of Advisory Committee.

a.   Exceptions

1)   Negotiation with a governmental agency

A person's conduct or statements made during compromise negotiations with a governmental agency (e.g., the IRS) during the exercise of its regulatory, investigative, or enforcement authority may be introduced in a subsequent criminal case against the person.

2)   Admissibility for other reasons

Evidence of settlement offers and negotiations is admissible to prove bias or prejudice of a witness, to negate a claim of undue delay, or to prove obstruction of a criminal investigation or prosecution.

b. No immunization of evidence

Evidence may be admissible through means other than as an admission made during compromise negotiations. A party does not immunize (i.e., protect from admission) evidence simply by discussing it during compromise negotiations. Fed. R. Evid. 408, Notes of Advisory Committee (2006).

c. Prohibition on all parties

Compromise evidence is not admissible on behalf of **any party** who participated in the compromise negotiations, even the party who made the settlement offer or statement. The protection of this rule cannot be waived unilaterally. Moreover, when there are more than two parties, a settlement agreement entered into by a party with an adverse party cannot be used by a remaining adverse party to prove or disprove the validity or amount of an unsettled claim. Fed. R. Evid. 408, Notes of Advisory Committee (2006); *Branch v. Fid. & Cas. Co.*, 783 F.2d 1289 (5th Cir. 1986).

3. Offers to Pay Medical Expenses

Evidence of the payment, offer to pay, or promise to pay medical or similar expenses resulting from an injury is **not admissible to prove liability for the injury.** Fed. R. Evid. 409.

Compare compromise: Unlike a compromise negotiation, any conduct or statement that accompanies the payment, offer to pay, or promise to pay medical expenses is admissible.

4. Plea Negotiation

In a civil or criminal case, evidence of the following is generally not admissible against the defendant who made the plea or participated in the plea discussions:

i) Withdrawn guilty pleas;

ii) Pleas of no contest (i.e., a *nolo contendere* plea);

iii) Statements made while negotiating a plea with a prosecutor (e.g., an offer to plead guilty); and

iv) Statements made during a plea proceeding (e.g., a Rule 11 proceeding under the Federal Rules of Criminal Procedure).

Fed. R. Evid. 410(a).

a. Exceptions

Statements made during pleas or negotiations are admissible, however, if another statement made during the same plea or negotiation has already been admitted, and fairness requires that the statement in question also be admitted. Such statements also are admissible in a subsequent perjury prosecution if they were false statements made under oath, on the record, and with counsel present. Fed. R. Evid. 410(b).

b. Waiver

A defendant may waive the protection of Rule 410 if the waiver is knowing and voluntary. *United States v. Mezzanatto*, 513 U.S. 196 (1995).

5. Liability Insurance

Evidence that a person was or was not insured against liability is not admissible to prove whether the person acted negligently or otherwise wrongfully. However, such evidence may be admissible for another purpose, such as to prove agency, ownership, or control, or to prove a witness's bias or prejudice. Fed. R. Evid. 411.

6. Sexual Conduct

a. Victim's conduct

Under the "rape shield" rule, evidence offered to prove the sexual behavior or sexual predisposition of a victim (or alleged victim) generally is not admissible in any civil or criminal proceeding involving sexual misconduct. The exclusion applies to the use of such evidence for impeachment as well as substantive purposes.

Sexual behavior includes not only sexual intercourse or contact but also activities that imply such sexual intercourse or contact, such as the use of contraceptives or the existence of a sexually transmitted disease. Sexual predisposition can include the victim's mode of dress, speech, or lifestyle. Fed. R. Evid. 412(a), Notes of Advisory Committee (1994).

1) Exceptions

a) Criminal cases

In a criminal case involving sexual misconduct, evidence of specific instances of a victim's sexual behavior is admissible to prove that someone other than the defendant was the source of semen, injury, or other physical evidence. In addition, evidence of sexual behavior with the person accused of sexual misconduct is admissible if offered by the defendant to prove consent or if offered by the prosecution. Fed. R. Evid. 412(b)(1).

> Note that, in contrast with the general preference under the Federal Rules for reputation or opinion testimony over evidence of specific acts, in criminal cases involving sexual misconduct, reputation or opinion evidence of a victim's sexual behavior or predisposition is not admissible.

Finally, any evidence whose exclusion would violate the defendant's constitutional rights is admissible under Rule 412. For example, under the Sixth Amendment Confrontation Clause, a defendant in a rape case may be able to cross-examine an alleged victim who testified that she lived with her mother about her cohabitation with another man in order to show that the alleged victim denied having consensual sex with the defendant in order to protect her relationship with the other man. *Olden v. Kentucky*, 488 U.S. 227 (1988).

b) Civil cases

In a civil case, evidence offered to prove a victim's sexual behavior or predisposition is admissible if its probative value **substantially outweighs** the danger of harm to any victim and of unfair prejudice to any party. Evidence of a victim's reputation is admissible only when it has been placed in controversy by the victim. Fed. R. Evid. 412(b)(2).

> The restriction on evidence of a victim's sexual behavior or predisposition applies only when the party against whom the evidence is offered can be characterized as a victim of sexual misconduct. For example, a plaintiff in a defamation action based on a statement about the plaintiff's sexual behavior is not a victim of sexual misconduct. By contrast, a plaintiff who brings a Title VII sexual harassment action can be characterized as a victim of sexual misconduct. Fed. R. Evid. 412, Notes of Advisory Committee (1994).

c) Procedure for admission

In a criminal or civil case, the party intending to offer evidence of the victim's sexual behavior or predisposition must file a motion describing the evidence and stating the purpose for its introduction. The motion must be filed at least 14 days before trial unless the court sets a different time. The motion must be served on all parties, and the victim (or the victim's guardian or representative) must be notified. The court must conduct an *in camera* hearing and give the victim and the parties the right to attend and to be heard. Unless the court orders otherwise, the record of the hearing is sealed. Fed. R. Evid. 412(c).

b. Defendant's conduct

In a criminal case in which a defendant is accused of sexual assault, attempted sexual assault, or conspiracy to commit sexual assault, evidence that the defendant committed any other sexual assault is admissible to prove any relevant matter. Similarly, in a criminal case in which a defendant is accused of child molestation, evidence that the defendant committed any other child molestation is admissible to prove any relevant matter. A similar rule applies in civil cases alleging sexual assault or child molestation. Fed. R. Evid. 413–15.

> **Propensity evidence:** Unlike Federal Rule 404(b), which applies to other crimes or bad acts committed by a defendant, these rules permit the use of a defendant's previous commission of a sexual assault or child molestation as evidence of the defendant's propensity to commit the charged sexual assault or child molestation. Consequently, for example, a defendant's prior conviction for rape can be used as evidence of the defendant's propensity to commit the charged rape, but a defendant's prior conviction for robbery cannot be used as evidence of the defendant's propensity to commit the charged robbery.

The court does have discretion to exclude such evidence under Rule 403 when the probative value is substantially outweighed by the danger of unfair prejudice. *United States v. Kelly*, 510 F.3d 433 (4th Cir. 2007); *Johnson v. Elk Lake Sch. Dist.*, 283 F.3d 138 (3d Cir. 2002).

1) Not limited to convictions

An arrest or even testimony of an incident that was unreported to the authorities may be admitted as evidence that a defendant has committed sexual assault or child molestation. Moreover, unlike Rule 609 regarding the use of a conviction to impeach a witness, there is no specific time restriction on the use of such evidence. *See, e.g.*, *United States v. Horn*, 523 F.3d 882 (2008).

2) Pretrial disclosure

The prosecutor or plaintiff who intends to introduce such evidence must disclose it to the defendant at least 15 days before trial unless the court, for good cause, allows a later disclosure. Fed. R. Evid. 413(b), 414(b), 415(b).

VI.   HEARSAY

A.   WHAT IS HEARSAY

Hearsay is a statement that the declarant makes at a time other than while testifying at the current trial or hearing (i.e., an out-of-court statement) that is offered to prove the truth of the matter asserted. Fed. R. Evid. 801(c). Hearsay evidence generally is inadmissible unless it falls within an exception or exclusion set out in the Federal Rules, a federal statute, or a Supreme Court rule. Fed. R. Evid. 802.

1.   Declarant—Person

The declarant (i.e., the maker of the statement) must be a person. Evidence generated by a machine or an animal is not hearsay. Fed. R. Evid. 801(b). Examples of such nonhearsay evidence include:

i)   A dog's bark;

ii)   An automatically generated time stamp on a fax;

iii)   A printout of results of computerized telephone tracing equipment; and

iv)   Raw data (such as blood-alcohol level) generated by a forensic lab's diagnostic machine.

Witness as declarant: A witness's own prior statement may be hearsay, and if hearsay, the witness may be prohibited from testifying as to her own statement unless an exception or exclusion applies.

2.   Statement—Assertion

A statement is a person's oral or written assertion, or it may be nonverbal conduct intended as an assertion. Fed. R. Evid. 801(a). An example of assertive conduct is a defendant nodding his head up and down to indicate a "yes" answer to a question.

Contrast nonassertive conduct: Nonassertive conduct is not hearsay. An example of nonassertive conduct is a pilot's act of flying an airplane, when such evidence is offered as evidence of the plane's safety.

3.   Offered to Prove the Truth of the Matter Asserted

Statements offered to prove something other than the truth of the matter asserted are not hearsay.

EXAM NOTE: A statement that is not hearsay is not automatically admissible. For exam purposes, it is important to keep in mind that the statement must be admissible under the other rules restricting admission, such as the rules on privileges.

a. Legally operative facts

A statement offered to prove that the statement was made, regardless of its truth, is not hearsay.

Example: In a slander action, the defendant's statement that the plaintiff is a murderer may be admissible to prove that the defendant made the statement but not to prove that the plaintiff is a murderer.

b. Effect on recipient

A statement offered to show the effect on the person who heard it is not hearsay.

Example: In a negligence action, the defendant's statement to the plaintiff that the sidewalk in front of the defendant's house was icy may be admissible to show that the plaintiff had notice of the danger but not to show that the sidewalk was actually icy.

c. State of mind

A statement offered as circumstantial evidence of the declarant's mental state is not hearsay.

Example: A testator's statement, "I am the queen of England," is not admissible to show its truth, but it is admissible to prove that the testator is not of sound mind.

d. Impeachment

A statement offered solely to impeach a witness is not being introduced for its truth and therefore is not hearsay.

4. Multiple Hearsay

A statement that contains hearsay within hearsay may be admissible as long as each part of the combined statement conforms to a hearsay exception. Fed. R. Evid. 805.

Example: A plaintiff sues a defendant for battery, claiming that the defendant struck the plaintiff's kneecaps with a baseball bat. At trial, the plaintiff seeks to introduce as evidence a hospital record, which consists of a note from a physician that the plaintiff told the physician that the plaintiff's injury was caused by being struck with a baseball bat. Both the plaintiff's statement to the physician and the note are hearsay; they are out-of-court statements being offered to prove the truth of the matter asserted—the cause of the plaintiff's injury. However, because each part of the statement falls within a hearsay exception (the plaintiff's statement is a statement made for the purpose of obtaining medical treatment, and the doctor's note is a business record), the hospital record may be admissible.

B. WHAT IS NOT HEARSAY

The following types of statements, which otherwise would qualify as hearsay, are expressly defined as nonhearsay. Fed. R. Evid. 801(d).

1. **Prior Statements**

   The Federal Rules identify three types of prior statements that are not hearsay. In all three cases, the witness who made the statement must testify at the present trial or hearing and be subject to cross-examination concerning the statement in order for it to be admissible. Fed. R. Evid. 801(d)(1).

   a. **Prior inconsistent statements**

      A prior inconsistent statement **made under penalty of perjury** at a trial, hearing, or other proceeding, or in a deposition may be admissible to **impeach** the declarant's credibility and as **substantive evidence.** Statements made in a prior legal action that is unrelated to the current action may be admitted under this rule. Fed. R. Evid. 801(d)(1)(A).

      Statement not made at a former proceeding: An inconsistent statement that was not made under penalty of perjury may be admissible to impeach a witness but is not admissible under this provision as substantive evidence.

   b. **Prior consistent statements**

      A prior consistent statement, whether made under oath or not, may be admissible to rebut an express or implied charge that the declarant recently fabricated it or acted from a recent improper influence or motive in testifying. Such a statement is admissible only if it was made **before the declarant had reason to fabricate or the improper influence or motive arose.** Fed. R. Evid. 801(d)(1)(B).

   c. **Prior statement of identification**

      A previous out-of-court identification of a person after perceiving that person (e.g., lineup or photo array) is not hearsay and may be admissible as substantive evidence. Fed. R. Evid. 801(d)(1)(C).

      EXAM NOTE: Beware of fact patterns involving prior out-of-court identifications by a witness who is not testifying at the current trial and therefore is not subject to cross-examination. This rule cannot apply, for instance, if the witness is dead or otherwise unavailable to testify.

2. **Opposing Party's Statement**

   A statement made by a **party to the current litigation** is not hearsay if it is offered by an opposing party. The statement may have been made by the party in his individual or representative capacity (e.g., trustee). Fed. R. Evid. 801(d)(2)(A). This type of statement traditionally was known as an admission of a party-opponent.

   Contrast statement against interest exception: Unlike with the statement against interest hearsay exception (*see* § VII.A.4. Statement Against Interest, *infra*), an opposing party's statement need not have been against the party's interest at the time that it was made.

   Unlike most testimony by a lay witness, an opposing party's statement may be admitted even if it is not based on personal knowledge. In addition, an opposing party's statement in the form of an opinion may be admitted, even if the statement is about a matter that normally would be beyond the scope of lay witness opinion testimony. Fed. R. Evid. 801(d)(2), Notes of Advisory Committee.

a. Judicial admission

An admission made during the discovery process or a stipulation otherwise made during a proceeding is conclusive evidence, as is a statement made in a pleading, unless amended. Otherwise, although a statement in a pleading or an admission or stipulation made in another proceeding is usually admissible, it may generally be rebutted.

Note: A *withdrawn* guilty plea is generally not admissible in a subsequent civil or criminal proceeding (*see* § V.B.4. Plea Negotiation, *supra.*)

b. Adoptive admission

An adoptive admission is a statement of another person that a party expressly or impliedly adopts as his own. Fed. R. Evid. 801(d)(2)(B). Silence in response to a statement is considered an adoptive admission if:

i) The person was present and heard and understood the statement;

ii) The person had the ability and opportunity to deny the statement; and

iii) A reasonable person similarly situated would have denied the statement.

Post-arrest silence by a defendant who has received *Miranda* warnings may not be used as an adoptive admission of a statement made by another person (e.g., a police officer). *Doyle v. Ohio*, 426 U.S. 610 (1976).

c. Vicarious statements

A statement made by one person may be imputed to another based on the relationship between them. In determining whether a statement constitutes an opposing party's statement, the statement is considered, but the statement itself cannot establish the necessary relationship between the parties.

1) Employee or agent

A statement made by a party's agent or employee constitutes an opposing party's statement if it was made concerning a matter **within the scope of and during the course of the relationship.** Fed. R. Evid. 801(d)(2)(D).

2) Authorized speaker

A statement about a subject that is made by a person who is **authorized** by a party to make a statement on the subject constitutes an opposing party's statement. Fed. R. Evid. 801(d)(2)(C).

3) Co-conspirators

Although a statement made by one co-party is not admissible against another co-party based solely on their status as co-parties, a statement made by a co-conspirator **during and in furtherance of** the conspiracy is admissible as an opposing party's statement against other co-conspirators. Fed. R. Evid. 801(d)(2)(E). A statement made by a co-conspirator after being arrested is not admissible, since it was not made during the conspiracy.

VII. HEARSAY EXCEPTIONS

Although hearsay generally is inadmissible, the Federal Rules identify some situations in which hearsay is allowed, either because of necessity (i.e., the declarant is unavailable) or because the statements are inherently trustworthy, in which case the declarant's availability is immaterial.

A. DECLARANT UNAVAILABLE AS A WITNESS

There are five exceptions to the hearsay rule that apply only if the declarant is unavailable as a witness: former testimony, dying declaration, statement against interest, statement of personal or family history, and statement offered against a party that wrongfully caused the declarant's unavailability.

1. Unavailable Declarant

An unavailable declarant is a person who:

i) Is exempt on the grounds of privilege;

ii) Refuses to testify despite a court order to do so;

iii) Lacks memory of the subject matter of the statement;

iv) Is unable to testify due to death, infirmity, or physical or mental disability; or

v) Is absent and cannot be subpoenaed or otherwise made to be present.

A declarant is not deemed unavailable if the unavailability is due to the procurement or wrongdoing of the proponent of the statement in order to prevent the declarant from testifying at or attending the trial. Fed. R. Evid. 804(a).

2. Former Testimony

Testimony that was given **as a witness** at a trial, hearing, or lawful deposition is not excluded as hearsay if the party against whom the testimony is being offered (or, in a civil case, a party's predecessor-in-interest) had an **opportunity and similar motive** to develop the testimony by direct examination, redirect examination, or cross-examination. This exception applies whether the testimony was given during the current proceeding or during a different one, but the witness who gave the testimony must now be unavailable. Fed. R. Evid. 804(b)(1).

Grand jury testimony generally does not fall within the former testimony exception, but it may be admissible nonhearsay evidence as a prior inconsistent statement.

3. Dying Declaration

A statement qualifies as a "dying declaration" if:

i) The declarant **believes that her death is imminent**; and

ii) The statement pertains to the **cause or circumstances** of her death.

Under this exception to the hearsay rule, although the declarant must be unavailable, the declarant need not have actually died in order for the statement to avoid exclusion as hearsay. The dying-declaration exception applies **only in homicide prosecutions and civil cases.** Fed. R. Evid. 804(b)(2).

4. **Statement Against Interest**

A statement made by a declarant who is unavailable to testify is not excluded as hearsay if the statement:

i) Was against the declarant's interest at the time it was made; and

ii) Would not have been made by a reasonable person unless he believed it to be true.

Under this exception to the hearsay rule, the statement must have been against the declarant's proprietary or pecuniary interest, have invalidated the declarant's claim against someone, or have exposed the declarant to civil or criminal liability. A statement that would subject the declarant to criminal liability is not admissible unless corroborating circumstances clearly indicate the trustworthiness of the statement. Fed. R. Evid. 804(b)(3).

Opposing party's statement distinguished: A **statement against interest** may be made by a non-party, the declarant must be unavailable, and the statement must have been against the declarant's interest at the time it was made. An **opposing party's statement,** on the other hand, must have been made by a party, and the statement need not have been against the party's interest when it was made (*see* § VI.B.2. Opposing Party's Statement, *supra*).

5. **Statement of Personal or Family History**

A statement concerning the unavailable declarant's own birth, adoption, marriage, divorce, legitimacy, familial relationship, or other similar fact of personal or family history is not excluded as hearsay. Fed. R. Evid. 804(b)(4).

6. **Statement Against Party That Caused Declarant's Unavailability**

Formerly known as the "forfeiture against wrongdoing" exception, a statement offered against a party that wrongfully caused the declarant's unavailability is not excluded as hearsay. Under this exception, the wrongful party forfeits the right to object to the admission of the declarant's statement as hearsay. The wrongdoing, which need not be criminal, may be accomplished by a deliberate act or by acquiescing to another's act, but must be done with the intent of preventing the witness from testifying. This exception applies to all parties, including the government. Fed. R. Evid. 804(b)(6).

Note: For the effect of the Confrontation Clause on this exception, *see* § VIII.A.1.b. Unavailability of the declarant, *infra*.

B. **DECLARANT'S AVAILABILITY AS A WITNESS IMMATERIAL**

The following hearsay exceptions do not require that the declarant be unavailable because the circumstances under which the statements were made suggest that the statements are inherently trustworthy. Fed. R. Evid. 803.

1. **Present Sense Impression**

   A statement describing or explaining an event or condition that is made **while or immediately after the declarant perceived it** is not excluded as hearsay. Fed. R. Evid. 803(1).

   a. **Res gestae**

      A common-law hearsay exception labeled "res gestae" (meaning "things done") existed for a statement that was precipitated by an event or was about a contemporaneous condition. The Federal Rules do not contain a general res gestae exception but instead recognize several distinct, related exceptions, including exceptions for a present sense impression; an excited utterance; a dying declaration; a statement of mental, emotional, and physical condition; and a statement made for purposes of medical treatment or diagnosis.

2. **Excited Utterance**

   A statement made about a startling event or condition **while the declarant is under the stress of excitement that it caused** is not excluded as hearsay. Under this exception to the hearsay rule, the event must shock or excite the declarant, and the statement must relate to the event, but the declarant need not be a participant in the event (i.e., the declarant can be a bystander). Fed. R. Evid. 803(2).

   Present sense impression distinguished: A present sense impression must be a **description** of the event, whereas an **excited utterance** need only **relate to** the exciting event.

   Example 1: Adele looks out the window and states, "It sure is raining hard tonight." She has made a statement of present sense impression, which is admissible to prove that it rained on the night in question.

   Example 2: Bob discovers that he has a winning lottery ticket and shouts, "I just won a million dollars!" He has made an excited utterance, which is admissible to prove that he won the money.

   Note: There is some overlap between these exceptions, and a statement, such as one describing a murder made immediately after the murder took place, could fall into both categories.

3. **Statement of Mental, Emotional, or Physical Condition**

   A statement of the declarant's **then-existing** state of mind or emotional, sensory, or physical condition is not excluded as hearsay. Fed. R. Evid. 803(3).

   a. **State of mind**

      A statement of **present intent, motive, or plan** can be used to prove **conduct in conformity** with that state of mind. A statement of a memory or past belief is inadmissible hearsay when used to prove the fact remembered or believed, unless the statement relates to the validity or terms of the declarant's will.

EXAM NOTE: Do not confuse this "state of mind" hearsay exception with circumstantial evidence of the declarant's state of mind, which is not hearsay. (*See* § VI.A.3.c. State of mind, *supra*.) To fall under the hearsay exception, the statement must be offered to prove that the declarant acted in accordance with his stated intent.

b. Physical condition

When a declarant's physical condition at a particular time is in question, a statement of the declarant's mental feeling, pain, or bodily health made **at that time** can be used to prove the **existence** of that condition but not its cause.

In most states, a statement made by a patient to a doctor relating to a **past** condition is not admissible under this exception. Under the Federal Rules, such a statement is admissible under the hearsay exception for statements for purposes of medical diagnosis or treatment (*see* 4. Statement Made for Medical Diagnosis or Treatment, *below*).

4. Statement Made for Medical Diagnosis or Treatment

A statement describing medical history or past or present symptoms is not hearsay if it is made for medical **diagnosis or treatment.** A statement of the cause or source of the condition is admissible as an exception to the rule against hearsay if it is reasonably pertinent to diagnosis or treatment. Fed. R. Evid. 803(4).

Effect of physician-patient privilege: A statement that falls within this hearsay exception still may be inadmissible if it is protected by the physician-patient privilege.

a. Statement made to a person other than a physician

The statement need not be made to a physician to fall under this exception. Statements to other medical personnel, including hospital attendants and ambulance drivers, or even to family members, may be included. Fed. R. Evid. 803(4), Notes of Advisory Committee.

b. Statement made by a person other than the patient

Under this hearsay exception, the statement need not necessarily be made by the patient, so long as it is made for the purpose of medical diagnosis or treatment. The relationship between the declarant and the patient usually determines admissibility—the closer the relationship, the stronger the motive to tell the truth, and, as such, the more presumably reliable the statement. The court must assess the probative value of the statement pursuant to Rule 403, weighing that value against the risk of prejudice, confusion, or waste of time. *See Weinstein's Evidence*, Vol. 4 (1993), p. 803-145.

5. Recorded Recollection

If a witness is unable to testify about a matter for which a record exists, that record is not excluded as hearsay if the following foundation is established:

i) The record is on a matter that the witness once knew about;

ii) The record was made or adopted by the witness when the matter was fresh in the witness's memory;

iii) The record accurately reflects the witness's knowledge; and

iv) The witness states that she cannot recall the event well enough to testify fully and accurately, even after consulting record on the stand.

Under this exception, the record, if admitted, may be read into evidence, but it may be received as an exhibit only if offered by an adverse party. Fed. R. Evid. 803(5).

Present recollection refreshed distinguished: An item—which need not be a writing—used to refresh a witness's recollection is not admitted into evidence (*see* § III.C.1. Present Recollection Refreshed, *supra*), so there is no hearsay problem.

6. **Records of Regularly Conducted Activity (Business Records)**

A record (e.g., memorandum, report, data compilation) of an act, event, condition, opinion, or diagnosis is not excluded as hearsay if:

i) The record was kept in the course of a regularly conducted activity of a business, organization, occupation, or calling;

ii) The making of the record was a regular practice of that activity; and

iii) The record was made at or near the time by (or from information transmitted by) someone with knowledge.

Although this exception is commonly referred to as the "business records" exception, it extends to any regularly conducted activity of an organization, including a nonprofit organization. Fed. R. Evid. 101(b)(4); 803(6)(A)–(C).

Recorded recollection exception distinguished: Unlike the recorded recollection exception, the business records exception does not require the inability to remember, but it does require that the record be kept in the course of a regularly conducted business activity.

a. **Authentication**

For the record to be admissible under the business records hearsay exception, the custodian of the record or other qualified witness may testify that the above requirements have been met. Alternatively, a record may be self-authenticated if properly certified (*see* § IV.A.2.f. Self-authenticating documents, *supra*). Fed. R. Evid. 803(6)(D).

b. **Lack of trustworthiness**

A business record that otherwise qualifies under this hearsay exception is nevertheless inadmissible if the source of information for the record or the method or circumstances of its preparation indicate a lack of trustworthiness. Fed. R. Evid. 803(6)(E).

Anticipation of litigation: Records prepared in anticipation of litigation, such as an employee's accident report, may not qualify under this exception due to a lack of trustworthiness. *Palmer v. Hoffman*, 318 U.S. 109 (1943).

c. **Medical records**

Medical records are considered business records to the extent that the entries relate to diagnosis or treatment. Statements related to fault associated with the cause of injury generally do not qualify under the business records exception.

d. Police reports

A police report can qualify under the business records exception, but a statement made by a witness that is contained in the report does not generally qualify because the witness is not acting on behalf of the police in making the statement. The statement may, however, qualify under another hearsay exception, such as an opposing party's statement.

e. Absence of a record

Evidence that a **matter is not included in a record** of a regularly conducted activity may be admissible to prove that the matter did not occur or exist, provided that a record was regularly kept for a matter of that kind. The circumstances, including the possible source of the information, must not indicate a lack of trustworthiness. Fed. R. Evid. 803(7).

7. Public Records

A hearsay exception applies to a record or statement of a public office or agency that sets out:

i)   The **activities** of the office or agency;

ii) An **observation** of a person under a duty to report the observation (except for an observation of a law enforcement officer offered in a criminal case); or

iii) **Factual findings of a legal investigation,** when offered in a civil case or against the government in a criminal case.

Fed. R. Evid. 803(8).

Investigative reports: In addition to factual findings, opinions, evaluations, and conclusions contained in an investigative report that are based on factual findings are included in the public records exception. *Beech Craft Corp. v. Rainey*, 488 U.S. 153 (1988).

a. Lack of trustworthiness

As with the business records exception, the court may exclude any evidence offered under this exception if the source of the information or other circumstances indicate a lack of trustworthiness. Fed. R. Evid. 803(8)(B).

b. Absence of a record

Similarly, testimony that a diligent search failed to disclose a public record or statement may be admitted to prove that the record or statement does not exist, or that a matter did not occur or exist, if a public office regularly kept a record of statements for a matter of that kind. Fed. R. Evid. 803(10).

c. Public record or vital statistics

A record of a birth, death, or marriage is not excluded as hearsay if the event is reported to a public office in accordance with a legal duty. Fed. R. Evid. 803(9).

8. Learned Treatises

A statement contained in a treatise, periodical, or pamphlet is not excluded as hearsay if:

    i) An expert witness **relied on the statement during direct examination** or it was **called to the expert's attention on cross-examination**; and

    ii) The publication is established as a **reliable authority** by admission or testimony of the expert witness, by another expert's testimony, or by judicial notice.

If admitted, the statement is read into evidence, but the publication itself may not be received as an exhibit. Fed. R. Evid. 803(18).

9. Judgment of Previous Conviction

Evidence of a final judgment of conviction is not excluded as hearsay if:

    i) The judgment was entered after a trial or guilty plea, but not a plea of no contest (i.e., *nolo contendere*);

    ii) The conviction was for a crime punishable by death or imprisonment for more than one year; and

    iii) The evidence is offered to prove any fact essential to sustain the judgment.

If the prosecutor in a criminal case offers evidence of a final judgment of conviction for a purpose other than impeachment, the judgment must have been against the defendant. Fed. R. Evid. 803(22).

> **Traffic offense:** A driver's guilty plea to a traffic offense that is punishable by a fine or imprisonment for one year or less cannot be used as evidence of the driver's negligence under this hearsay exception.

10. Other Exceptions

Other hearsay exceptions for which the declarant's availability is immaterial include:

    i) A statement concerning personal or family history, such as a birth, death, marriage, or divorce contained in a regularly kept record of a religious organization (Fed. R. Evid. 803(11));

    ii) A statement of fact in a marriage or baptismal certificate (Fed. R. Evid. 803(12));

    iii) A statement of fact about personal or family history contained in a family record, such as a Bible or an engraving on a ring (Fed. R. Evid. 803(13));

    iv) Records of, and statements in, documents affecting an interest in property (Fed. R. Evid. 803(14), (15));

    v) Statements in ancient documents (i.e., authenticated documents in existence at least 20 years) (Fed. R. Evid. 803(16));

    vi) Market reports and similar commercial publications generally relied upon by the public (Fed. R. Evid. 803(17));

    vii) Reputation concerning personal or family history, boundaries or general history, or character (Fed. R. Evid. 803(19)–(21)); and

viii) A judgment admitted to prove a matter of personal, family, or general history or a boundary, if the matter was essential to the judgment and could be proved by evidence of reputation. Fed. R. Evid. 803(23).

C. RESIDUAL EXCEPTION

There is a "catch-all" exception for a statement that is not otherwise covered by the Federal Rules. A hearsay statement may be admissible under this exception if:

i)   The statement has equivalent circumstantial guarantees of trustworthiness;

ii) It is offered as evidence of a material fact;

iii) It is more probative on the point for which it is offered than any other evidence that the proponent can reasonably obtain; and

iv) Admission will best serve the purposes of the Federal Rules and the interests of justice.

The proponent must give an adverse party reasonable notice before the trial or hearing of the intent to offer the statement as well as its particulars, including the declarant's name and address. Fed. R. Evid. 807.

VIII. CONSTITUTIONAL LIMITATIONS

A. HEARSAY EVIDENCE RESTRICTIONS

Hearsay evidence has successfully been challenged on two constitutional grounds.

1.   Sixth Amendment—Confrontation Clause and Hearsay Evidence

In a criminal trial, the Confrontation Clause of the Sixth Amendment requires that, in order to admit an out-of-court testimonial statement of a declarant (i.e., hearsay) against a defendant:

i)   The declarant must be unavailable; and

ii) The defendant must have had a prior opportunity to cross-examine the declarant.

Crawford v. Washington, 541 U.S. 36 (2004).

Note: The Supreme Court suggested in dicta in *Crawford* that the Confrontation Clause does not preclude the admission of a dying declaration as hearsay, even if the statement is testimonial, since this common-law exception predates the Confrontation Clause. *Crawford v. Washington*, 541 U.S. 36, 56, n.6 (2004).

a.   Testimonial statements

In determining whether a statement is testimonial, an objective analysis of the circumstances, rather than the subjective purpose of the participants, is key. A statement made during a police interrogation that had the primary purpose of ascertaining past criminal conduct is testimonial, as is a certificate of a governmental laboratory analyst that a substance was an illegal drug. *Melendez-Diaz v. Massachusetts*, 557 U.S. 305 (2009).

By contrast, a statement made to police during the course of questioning with the primary purpose of enabling police to provide assistance to meet an ongoing emergency (e.g., a 911 call) is not testimonial, *Davis v. Washington*, 547 U.S.

813 (2006), nor is a statement made by a fatally wounded victim as to the identity of his assailant in response to police questioning, because the statement was made to assist the police in addressing an on-going emergency, *Michigan v. Bryant*, 562 U.S. ___, 131 S. Ct. 1143 (2011).

b. Unavailability of the declarant

The Confrontation Clause mandates that the use of hearsay evidence based on the forfeiture-by-wrongdoing exception requires the defendant to have acted with the particular purpose of making the witness unavailable. The mere fact that the declarant is unavailable due to the defendant's act (e.g., murder of the witness) is not sufficient to establish such a purpose when the defendant is on trial for the act that made the witness unavailable. *Giles v. California*, 554 U.S. 353 (2008).

2. Fourteenth Amendment—Due Process Clause

The Due Process Clause of the Fourteenth Amendment may prevent application of a hearsay rule when such rule unduly restricts a defendant's ability to mount a defense.

Example: Application of a state evidentiary rule that prevents a defendant from using a witness's hearsay statements to impeach the defendant's in-court testimony operated to deny the defendant the ability to present witnesses in the defendant's own defense. *Chamber v. Mississippi*, 410 U.S. 284 (1973).

B. FACE-TO-FACE CONFRONTATION

The Confrontation Clause reflects a preference for face-to-face confrontation of a defendant and a witness in court.

Example: A defendant who is charged with committing a sex crime against a child can force the child victim to testify in open court rather than from behind a screen that blocks the witness's view of the defendant. *Coy v. Iowa*, 487 U.S. 1012 (1988).

This type of confrontation may be denied, however, if there is an important public interest at stake, such as protecting a child.

Example: A child victim of a sex crime could testify via a one-way closed circuit television when there was a specific finding that the child witness would suffer serious emotional distress if the witness was required to testify in open court. *Maryland v. Craig*, 497 U.S. 836 (1990). The Court in *Coy*, above, refused to recognize a *presumption* of trauma to witnesses who were victims of sexual abuse.

Real Property

REAL PROPERTY

Table of Contents

I.   **OWNERSHIP** **1**

   A.   **PRESENT ESTATES** **1**

       1.   **FEE SIMPLE ABSOLUTE** **1**

       2.   **DEFEASIBLE FEES**...**1**

          a.   **Fee simple determinable** **1**

          b.   **Fee simple subject to condition subsequent**............................**2**

          c.   **Fee simple subject to executory interest** **2**

       3.   **FEE TAIL** **3**

       4.   **LIFE ESTATE** **3**

          a.   **Measuring life is grantee**...**3**

          b.   **Measuring life is third party** **4**

          c.   **Rights and obligations**...**4**

          d.   **Waste** **4**

   B.   **CONCURRENT ESTATES** **5**

       1.   **TENANCY IN COMMON** **5**

       2.   **JOINT TENANCY** **5**

          a.   **Four unities** **5**

          b.   **Severance**..**5**

       3.   **TENANCY BY THE ENTIRETY** **6**

       4.   **RIGHTS AND OBLIGATIONS**...**6**

          a.   **Possession** **6**

          b.   **Third-party rents** **7**

          c.   **Operating expenses**..**7**

          d.   **Repairs and improvements** **7**

          e.   **Fiduciary obligation**...**7**

          f.   **Partition**..**8**

   C.   **FUTURE INTERESTS**..**8**

       1.   **REVERSION** **8**

2. POSSIBILITY OF REVERTER 8

3. RIGHT OF REENTRY 8

4. REMAINDER 9

    a. Class interests 9

    b. Contingent remainder 10

    c. Rule in *Shelley's Case* 10

    d. Doctrine of Worthier Title 10

5. EXECUTORY INTERESTS 11

    a. Shifting executory interest 11

    b. Springing executory interest 11

6. TRANSFERABILITY OF REMAINDERS AND EXECUTORY INTERESTS 11

7. CLASSIFICATION OF INTERESTS 11

8. RULE AGAINST PERPETUITIES 12

    a. Affected future interests 12

    b. Measuring lives 13

    c. Creation events 13

    d. "Vest or fail" requirement 13

    e. Effect of violation 13

    f. Special rule for transfer to a class 13

    g. Exceptions 14

    h. Common violations 15

    i. Statutory changes 16

II. LANDLORD AND TENANT 16

A. TYPES OF TENANCIES 17

1. TENANCY FOR YEARS 17

    a. Term 17

    b. Creation 17

    c. Termination 17

2. PERIODIC TENANCY 17

    a. Term 18

    b. Creation 18

    c. Termination 18

     3. TENANCY AT WILL 19

        a. Term 19

        b. Creation 19

        c. Termination 19

     4. TENANCY AT SUFFERANCE 19

B. DUTIES OF TENANT 19

     1. DUTY TO PAY RENT 20

        a. Destruction of premises 20

        b. Material breach of lease by landlord 20

     2. DUTY TO AVOID WASTE 20

        a. Ameliorative waste 20

        b. Permissive waste 20

     3. CONTRACTUAL DUTY TO REPAIR 21

     4. OTHER DUTIES 21

     5. LANDLORD'S REMEDIES FOR TENANT'S BREACH 21

        a. Failure to pay rent 21

        b. Abandonment 21

        c. Holdover tenant 21

C. DUTIES OF LANDLORD 22

     1. GIVE POSSESSION 22

     2. DUTY TO REPAIR 22

     3. WARRANTY OF HABITABILITY 22

     4. COVENANT OF QUIET ENJOYMENT 23

        a. Actual eviction 23

        b. Partial eviction 23

        c. Constructive eviction 23

        d. Retaliatory eviction 24

D. TORT LIABILITIES 24

     1. TENANT 24

     2. LANDLORD 24

E. ASSIGNMENT AND SUBLETTING 24

     1. ASSIGNMENT VERSUS SUBLEASE 24

      2. ASSIGNEE'S RIGHTS AND LIABILITIES 24

      3. SUBLESSEE'S RIGHTS AND LIABILITIES 24

      4. ORIGINAL TENANT'S RIGHTS AND LIABILITIES 25

      5. LANDLORD ASSIGNMENTS 25

      6. LIMITATIONS ON ASSIGNMENT AND SUBLETTING.......................25

           a. Prohibition 25

           b. Landlord's permission 25

           c. Waiver by landlord 25

   F. CONDEMNATION 25

   G. FAIR HOUSING AND DISCRIMINATION 26

      1. PROTECTED CLASSES 26

      2. PROHIBITED PRACTICES 26

      3. ENFORCEMENT AND COMPLIANCE 26

      4. COMPLAINT PROCESS 27

III. DISPUTES ABOUT OWNERSHIP IN LAND 27

   A. ADVERSE POSSESSION 27

      1. CONTINUOUS 27

           a. Tacking 27

           b. Disability of owner 27

      2. ACTUAL, OPEN AND NOTORIOUS...28

      3. HOSTILE 28

      4. EXCLUSIVE 28

      5. SCOPE OF POSSESSION 28

           a. Constructive adverse possession 28

           b. Below surface area 28

           c. Future interests 28

   B. THE LAND SALE CONTRACT 28

      1. FORMATION 28

           a. Statute of Frauds...29

           b. Exceptions to Statute of Frauds 29

           c. Rescission of contract 29

      2. PERFORMANCE..29

    a. Marketable title 29

    b. Time of the essence...30

    c. Implied warranty of fitness or suitability (new homes) 30

    d. Disclosure duty (all homes) 31

    e. Tender of performance...32

    f. Merger 32

3. REMEDIES FOR BREACH 32

    a. Damages...32

    b. Specific performance...32

4. EQUITABLE CONVERSION 33

    b. Risk of loss 33

    c. Insurance 33

    d. Effect of buyer's or seller's death.......................................33

5. SECURITY INTEREST..34

    a. Mortgage 34

    b. Mortgage alternatives 35

    c. Effect of transfer by mortgagor 35

    d. Effect of transfer by mortgagee 36

    e. Pre-foreclosure...36

    f. Foreclosure and its effect on interests.................................38

    g. Non-judicial foreclosure 39

    h. Priority in foreclosure actions 39

    i. Personal liability of mortgagor..40

    j. Defenses...40

    k. Discharge...41

6. OPTIONS AND RIGHTS OF FIRST REFUSAL 41

    a. Option contract 41

    b. Right of first refusal 41

    c. Rule Against Perpetuities..42

    d. Restraints against alienability...42

    e. Marketable title 42

7. REAL ESTATE BROKER..42

     a. **Seller's agent** 42

     b. **Buyer's agent** 43

     c. **Dual agent** 43

     d. **Transaction brokers** 43

C. **DELIVERY AND RECORDING OF DEED**.....................................43

  1. **INTENT TO TRANSFER (DELIVERY)** 43

     a. **Retention of deed by grantor** 44

     b. **Transfer of deed to grantee** 44

     c. **Transfer of deed to third party**................................44

     d. **Acceptance** 46

  2. **VALID DEED** 46

     a. **Parties** 46

     b. **Words of transfer** 46

     c. **Description of property** 46

  3. **RECORDING ACT** 47

     a. **Types of statutes** 47

     b. **Paid value** 48

     c. **Notice** 49

     d. **Priorities** 50

     e. **Rule application**..50

     f. **Chain-of-title problems** 51

  4. **TYPES OF DEEDS** 52

     a. **General warranty deed**..52

     b. **Special warranty deed**...54

     c. **Quitclaim deed** 54

D. **FIXTURES**...54

  1. **STRUCTURES AND ITEMS INCORPORATED INTO STRUCTURES** 54

  2. **ATTACHMENT OF CHATTEL** 54

  3. **REMOVAL OF CHATTEL**...54

     a. **Fee simple owner of real property** 54

     b. **Other possessors of real property** 55

     c. **Trespassers**...55

       d. Mortgagee versus secured party 55

       e. Sale of fixtures by property owner 55

  E. CONVEYANCE BY WILL AND BY OPERATION OF LAW 55

    1. IN GENERAL 56

    2. ADEMPTION 56

    3. LAPSE 56

    4. EXONERATION OF LIENS 56

    5. ABATEMENT 57

       a. Specific 57

       b. General 57

       c. Demonstrative 57

       d. Residuary 57

       e. Pro rata abatement 58

  F. CONVEYANCE BY TRUST 58

    1. PRIVATE TRUSTS 58

    2. CHARITABLE TRUSTS 58

  G. RESTRAINTS ON ALIENATION 59

    1. RESTRAINTS ON LEGAL INTERESTS 59

       a. Forms of restraint..59

       b. Permissible restraints 59

    2. RESTRAINTS ON EQUITABLE INTERESTS 60

IV. DISPUTES ABOUT THE USE OF LAND...60

  A. EASEMENTS...60

    1. CLASSIFICATION OF EASEMENTS..60

       a. Easements by grant and reservation 60

       b. Easements appurtenant and profit in gross......................60

    2. TYPES OF EASEMENTS 61

       a. Express easements..61

       b. Easements by necessity and implication...........................61

       c. Easements by prescription 62

       d. Easements by estoppel..62

       e. Negative easements 62

   3. **TRANSFER** 62

      a. **Easement appurtenant** 62

      b. **Easement in gross** 63

   4. **TERMINATION** 63

      a. **Release** 63

      b. **Merger** 63

      c. **Severance** 63

      d. **Abandonment** 63

      e. **Destruction and condemnation** 63

      f. **Prescription** 64

      g. **Estoppel** 64

      h. **Sale to bona fide purchaser** 64

   5. **SCOPE OF EASEMENT** 64

      a. **Express easements** 64

      b. **Implied easements** 64

   6. **PROFITS** 64

   7. **LICENSES** 65

   8. **DUTY TO MAINTAIN** 65

B. **COVENANTS RUNNING WITH THE LAND** 65

   1. **REQUIREMENTS TO RUN** 65

      a. **Writing** 66

      b. **Intent** 66

      c. **Touch and concern** 66

      d. **Notice—burden only** 66

      e. **Privity** 66

      f. **Specific examples** 67

   2. **EQUITABLE SERVITUDES** 67

      a. **Requirements** 67

      b. **Implied reciprocal servitudes** 67

   4. **TERMINATION OF COVENANTS** 68

   5. **CHANGED CIRCUMSTANCES** 68

C. **WATER RIGHTS** 68

       1. THEORIES 68

           a. Riparian rights 68

           b. Prior appropriation 68

       2. WATERWAYS 69

       3. GROUNDWATER 69

       4. SURFACE WATER 69

       5. SUPPORT RIGHTS 69

           a. Lateral support 69

           b. Subjacent support 70

       6. AIR RIGHTS 70

       7. REMEDIES FOR INTRUSION ONTO LAND 70

   D. GOVERNMENT REGULATION OF LAND 70

       1. ZONING 70

           a. Exemptions and variances 70

           b. Relationship to covenants 71

       2. EMINENT DOMAIN 71

   E. NUISANCE 71

       1. PRIVATE NUISANCE 71

           a. Substantial 71

           b. Unreasonable 71

       2. PUBLIC NUISANCE 72

       3. REMEDIES 72

           a. Damages 72

           b. Injunctive relief 72

   F. DEDICATION 72

V. OTHER TYPES OF OWNERSHIP 72

   A. COMMON-INTEREST COMMUNITIES 72

       1. CONDOMINIUMS 72

       2. COOPERATIVES 72

   C. EMBLEMENTS (CROPS) 73

       1. CONVEYANCE OF CROPS 73

       2. EXCEPTIONS 73

REAL PROPERTY

I. OWNERSHIP

Ownership of real property may be transferred by sale, gift, or upon death by devise or intestate succession. The seller or donor is called the grantor, and the buyer or recipient is called the "grantee." This section will discuss both present and future possessory interests in land (which are subject only to the rights of others), and other sections will discuss non-possessory interests in land (which are subject to specific restrictions as to the use of the land).

A. PRESENT ESTATES

To be categorized as a freehold, an estate must be (i) immobile (either land or some interest derived from or affixed to land) and (ii) for an indeterminate duration (as opposed to a leasehold, which is for a limited duration). The owner of a present estate has the right to currently possess the property.

1. Fee Simple Absolute

Fee simple absolute is the most common form of property ownership and the broadest ownership interest recognized by law. It is absolute ownership of potentially infinite duration, is freely alienable (i.e., easily bought or sold), and has no accompanying future interest. Although common law required words of limitation (e.g., "and heirs"), conveyances that are ambiguous are now considered fee simple by default (e.g., "to B").

Example: A conveys Blackacre "to B and his heirs." C conveys Whiteacre to "B." Both conveyances give B a fee simple absolute estate in the property.

The fee simple absolute is a present estate that does not terminate unless the owner dies intestate without heirs, in which case the property escheats to the state.

2. Defeasible Fees

As with a fee simple absolute estate, a defeasible fee is ownership of potentially infinite duration. But, unlike a fee simple absolute estate, a defeasible fee **may be terminated by the occurrence of an event**.

a. Fee simple determinable

A fee simple determinable is a present fee simple estate that is **limited by specific durational language** (e.g., "so long as," "while," "during," "until"), such that it terminates automatically upon the happening of a stated condition and full ownership of the property is returned to the grantor. The fee simple determinable is freely alienable, devisable, and descendible, but it is always subject to the stated condition.

> **EXAM NOTE**: Be certain that the language limits the duration, not merely the purpose, of the transfer before concluding that a fee simple determinable was created. If the language limits only the purpose, it is treated as creating a fee simple absolute.

1) Possibility of reverter

Upon the occurrence of the stated condition, the estate automatically reverts back to the grantor. The grantor's retained future interest is called a **"possibility of reverter."** A possibility of reverter is freely alienable by the grantor, both during his life and upon his death.

> **Example:** A conveys Blackacre "to B and his heirs, until B gets married." The estate reverts back to A if B gets married. Therefore, B has a fee simple determinable in Blackacre, with a possibility of reverter in A.

b. Fee simple subject to condition subsequent

A fee simple subject to a condition subsequent is a present fee simple that is **limited in duration by specific conditional language.**

> **EXAM NOTE:** Typical language that indicates a fee simple subject to a condition subsequent: "provided that," "on condition that," "but if."

1) Compare to fee simple determinable

As with a fee simple determinable, the fee simple subject to a condition subsequent is freely alienable by the owner during his life, and upon his death, devisable and descendible.

Unlike a fee simple determinable, termination of a fee simple subject to a condition subsequent is not automatic. Upon occurrence of the stated condition, the present fee simple **will terminate only if the grantor affirmatively demonstrates intent to terminate** (e.g., by bringing an action to recover possession).

If the language in the conveyance is ambiguous, courts typically adopt a preference for the fee simple on condition subsequent.

2) Right to terminate

In the conveyance, the grantor must explicitly retain the right to terminate the fee simple subject to a condition subsequent (known as the **"right of entry," "right of re-entry,"** or **"power of termination"**). In most states, this right is devisable and descendible, but it cannot be transferred during the owner's lifetime. The owner may waive this right, but the mere failure to assert it does not constitute a waiver.

> **Example:** A conveys Blackacre "to B and his heirs, but if B gets married, then A can reenter Blackacre." B will retain ownership until A exercises his right to reenter. B has a fee simple subject to a condition subsequent in Blackacre, and A has a right of re-entry. (Even if B gets married, B will retain his current possessory estate in Blackacre until A exercises his right to terminate B's estate.)

c. Fee simple subject to executory interest

A fee simple subject to an executory interest is a present fee simple estate that is limited in duration by either conditional language or durational language, such that it will terminate upon the occurrence of the specified condition, and **title will pass to a third party** (i.e., someone other than the grantor).

Upon occurrence of the stated condition, the present fee simple terminates automatically. The future interest held by the third party is an **executory interest**.

> **Example:** A conveys Blackacre "to B for as long as the property is used as a hospital, then to C." In Blackacre, B has a fee simple subject to an executory interest, C has an executory interest, and A does not have an interest. (Note: C's interest is subject to the Rule Against Perpetuities.)

For a more detailed discussion, *see* § I.C.5., Executory Interests, *below*.

3. Fee Tail

A fee tail is a freehold estate that limits the estate to the grantee's lineal blood descendants by specific words of limitation (e.g., "heirs of the body"). The fee tail estate has been eliminated in most states because it is treated as a fee simple absolute.

4. Life Estate

A life estate is a present possessory estate that is limited in duration by a life. The language must be clear, and must be measured in terms of a life, not a number of years (e.g., "to A for life"). Upon the end of the measuring life, title reverts to the grantor or specified remainderman. This future interest is known as a reversion.

> **Example 1:** A conveys Blackacre "to B for the life of B." B has a life estate in Blackacre, which terminates upon B's death. A has a reversion; upon B's death, ownership of Blackacre reverts to A.
>
> **Example 2:** A conveys Blackacre "to B for B's life, and then to C." B has a life estate in Blackacre, which terminates upon B's death. C has a remainder; upon B's death, ownership of Blackacre vests in C.

The life estate is not subject to the Rule Against Perpetuities.

a. Measuring life is grantee

To be a life estate, the interest granted must be measured by the life of a human being and be qualified only by non-time limitations. Unless otherwise specified, the measuring life is the grantee.

> **Example:** A conveys Blackacre to "B for life." B has a life estate that is measured by his own life.

A life estate is fully transferable during the life of the person by whom the life estate is measured. Because the interest terminates at the death of the person by whom the life estate is measured, a life estate measured by the grantee's life is generally neither devisable nor descendible. If the life estate is received by will or intestacy, the life tenant may renounce the estate if he so chooses. In the states that have done away with the common-law curtesy and dower custom, a surviving spouse has a statutory right to take a portion of the estate.

In states that continue dower and curtesy, a conveyance from the husband to a bona fide purchaser without the wife's joining in the conveyance does not defeat dower. Similarly, a wife's dower rights are not defeated by the husband's creditors.

b. Measuring life is third party

A life estate measured by the life of a third party is also called a "life estate *pur autre vie*."

> **Example:** A conveys Blackacre to "B for the life of C." A granted a life estate to B for the life of C.

c. Rights and obligations

A life tenant has the right of possession, the right to all rents and profits during possession, and the right to lease, sell, or mortgage the property (right of alienation). To the extent that the property can produce income, life tenants have the obligation to pay all ordinary taxes on the land and interest on the mortgage. If the property is not producing an income, the life tenant is responsible for taxes and mortgage interest to the extent of the reasonable rental value of the land. The life tenant also has the duty not to commit waste.

The life tenant is under no obligation to insure the land for the benefit of the remainderman and is not responsible for damage caused by third-party tortfeasors.

> **EXAM NOTE:** Remember that the life tenant is responsible only for the interest of a mortgage on the life estate, whereas the remainderman is responsible for the mortgage itself.

d. Waste

The rights of a holder of any estate except a fee simple may be limited by the doctrine of waste. The particular rules of waste depend on the type of estate held by the present tenant and the type of waste created.

Any remainderman or grantor with a reversionary interest may enter upon the land to inspect for waste and seek an injunction to prevent waste.

1) Affirmative waste

Affirmative (or voluntary) waste is the result of overt conduct that causes a decrease in the value of the property. The holder of the vested remainder interest may bring suit for damages, and either a vested or contingent remainder holder may bring suit for an injunction. Limited exceptions exist for the exploitation of minerals and timber if such use was authorized by the grantor, was in effect at the time the tenancy began, or is necessary to maintain the property.

2) Permissive waste

Permissive waste is the result of neglect, a failure to keep up the property, or a failure to reasonably protect the property. To maintain the property and avoid permissive waste, the tenant is required only to spend the amount of income generated by the property. The tenant's responsibilities include paying any property taxes and mortgage interest associated with the property.

3) Ameliorative waste

At common law, a life tenant was prohibited from engaging in acts that changed the property's value (even those that enhanced the value), unless all future interest holders were known and consented. The current majority rule allows life tenants to physically alter structures on the property when necessary to make reasonable use of the property.

B. CONCURRENT ESTATES

A concurrent estate (or co-tenancy) is ownership or possession of real property by two or more persons simultaneously. The most common concurrent estates are tenancy in common, joint tenancy, and tenancy by the entirety.

1. Tenancy in Common

Any tenancy with two or more grantees creates a tenancy in common (and is thus considered the "default" or "catch-all" co-tenancy when neither joint tenancy nor tenancy in the entirety exists). Equal right to possess or use the property (unity of possession) is required, and **no right of survivorship** exists. Each co-tenant holds an undivided interest with unrestricted rights to possess the whole property, regardless of the size of the interest. Without the right of survivorship, each tenant can devise or freely transfer his interest to anyone. A tenant in common may also transfer his interest to another by a lease. The other tenants in common are entitled to share possession with the lessee and to receive a share of the rental profits from the lessor-tenant in common. In most states, there is a presumption that a conveyance to two or more persons creates a tenancy in common rather than a joint tenancy.

2. Joint Tenancy

A joint tenancy exists when two or more individuals own property **with the right of survivorship** (i.e., upon the death of a joint tenant, the interest terminates and automatically goes to the surviving joint tenants). Modern law calls for a clear expression of intent along with survivorship language.

> **EXAM NOTE:** To determine if a joint tenancy was created, look for survivorship language.

a. Four unities

The joint tenancy must be created with each joint tenant having an equal right to possess or use the property (unity of **p**ossession), with each interest equal to the others (unity of **i**nterest), at the same time (unity of **t**ime), and in the same instrument (unity of **t**itle). [*Mnemonic–"PITT"*].

Unlike a joint tenancy, a tenancy in common requires only the unity of possession.

b. Severance

Although an interest in a joint tenancy cannot be devised, joint tenants can convey all or part of their individual interests during their lifetimes (*inter vivos*) to a third party, thereby severing the joint tenancy.

1) Effect of severance on remaining joint tenants

Once the joint tenancy interest is transferred inter vivos, the right of survivorship to that interest is destroyed and converted to a tenancy in common. A conveyance by only one of more than two joint tenants does not destroy the joint tenancy of the remaining joint tenants.

Note that any lien against one joint tenant's interest also terminates upon that tenant's death, such that the lien does not encumber the surviving tenants' interests.

2) Mortgages

A joint tenant may grant a mortgage interest in the joint tenancy property to a creditor. In **lien theory** states (the majority), the mortgage is only a lien on the property and does not sever the joint tenancy absent a default and foreclosure sale. In **title theory** states (the minority), the mortgage severs title, and the tenancy between the joint tenants and creditor is converted into a tenancy in common.

3) Leases

There is a split among jurisdictions with respect to how to handle joint tenancies when one joint tenant leases his interest. Some jurisdictions hold that the lease destroys the unity of interest and thus severs the joint tenancy, while other jurisdictions believe that the lease merely temporarily suspends the joint tenancy, which would resume upon expiration of the lease.

4) Intentional killings

When one co-tenant intentionally kills the other co-tenant, some states allow the felonious joint tenant to hold the property in constructive trust for the deceased joint tenant's estate. This means that the surviving joint tenant does not profit from the felony but can keep his interest in the property. Other jurisdictions have statutes that sever the joint tenancy upon a felonious killing of one joint tenant by another joint tenant.

3. Tenancy by the Entirety

Tenancy by the entirety is a joint tenancy between married persons with a right of survivorship. The same rules for joint tenancy apply to tenancy by the entirety, plus the joint tenants must be married when a deed is executed or the conveyance occurs (the fifth **unity of person**). Neither party can alienate or encumber the property without the consent of the other. Tenancy by the entirety is used in many states and is analogous to community property in the states that recognize that type of property ownership.

4. Rights and Obligations

a. Possession

Unless there is an agreement to the contrary, each co-tenant has the right to possess all of the property. A co-tenant is generally not required to pay rent to the other co-tenants for the value of her own use of the property, even when the other co-tenants do not make use of the property. Similarly, a co-tenant is generally not required to share profits earned from the use of the property, such as from a business conducted on the property.

As a consequence of each tenant's right to possess the entire property, a co-tenant's exclusive use of the property does not, by itself, give rise to adverse possession of the interest of another cotenant.

1) Ouster

When a co-tenant refuses to allow another co-tenant access to the property, the ousted co-tenant may bring a court action for ouster to gain access to the property and to recover the value of the use of the property for the time during which the co-tenant was denied access to the property.

2) Natural resources

A co-tenant is entitled to the land's natural resources (e.g., timber, minerals, oil, gas) in proportion to her share.

b. Third-party rents

A co-tenant must account to other co-tenants for rent received from third parties but can deduct operating expenses when calculating net proceeds. Third-party rents are divided based on the ownership interest of each tenant.

c. Operating expenses

A co-tenant can collect contribution from the other co-tenants for paying more than his portion of necessary or beneficially spent operating expenses (e.g., taxes or mortgage interest) unless he is the only one in physical possession of the property, and the value of his use of it is equal to or outweighs the overpayment. Note that a co-tenant in sole possession can collect only for the amount that exceeds the rental value of the property.

d. Repairs and improvements

A co-tenant does not have a right to be reimbursed by other co-tenants for repairs made to the property, even when those repairs are necessary. However, the majority view is that contribution for necessary repairs can be compelled in actions for accounting or partition. A co-tenant may, in some jurisdictions, maintain a separate action for contribution, as long as the other co-tenants have been notified of the need for the repair.

Similarly, except in actions for accounting or partition, a co-tenant does not have a right to reimbursement for improvements made to the property. As noted, when a third party is occupying the property, the co-tenant who collects rent from the third party can subtract expenses for necessary repairs from the rent received before sharing the rent with the other co-tenants.

e. Fiduciary obligation

In general, co-tenants do not owe fiduciary duties to each other. However, co-tenants who became co-tenants at the same time (e.g., by the same deed or will) can have a fiduciary obligation to each other, such that if one co-tenant buys back his property at a tax or mortgage foreclosure sale, the other co-tenants can reacquire their original interests by paying their due contributions.

Co-tenants share a duty of fair dealing, such that an acquisition by one co-tenant that impacts the estate owned by all co-tenants is considered an acquisition by all co-tenants.

f. Partition

1) Who may partition

A tenant in common or a joint tenant generally has the right to unilaterally partition the property, but a tenant by the entirety *does not* have this right. Property can be partitioned either voluntarily (if the co-tenants agree in writing on the division of land) or involuntarily (by court action).

The holder of a future interest who shares that interest with another (e.g., jointly held remainder interest) does not have the right to immediate possession and therefore cannot maintain an action for involuntary partition.

2) Effect of partition

In a partition action, the court divides the jointly owned property into distinct portions, or, if division of the property is not practicable or fair, the court may sell the property at a public auction and distribute the proceeds among the co-tenants in accordance with their ownership interests.

3) Restriction on partition

An agreement by co-tenants not to seek partition is enforceable. However, the agreement must be clear, and the time limitation must be reasonable.

C. FUTURE INTERESTS

A future interest is an interest in presently existing property or in a gift or trust, which may commence in use, possession, or enjoyment sometime in the future.

1. Reversion

A reversion (or "reverter") is the future interest held by the grantor who grants a life estate or estate for years but does not convey the remaining future interest to a third party. Reversions are not subject to the Rule Against Perpetuities.

2. Possibility of Reverter

A possibility of reverter is automatically retained by a grantor when a fee simple determinable is conveyed.

3. Right of Reentry

A right of reentry (also called "right of entry" or "power of termination") is a future interest held by the grantor after a fee simple on condition subsequent is granted.

4. Remainder

A remainder is a future interest created in a grantee that is capable of becoming possessory upon the expiration of a prior possessory estate of known fixed duration that is created in the same conveyance in which the remainder is created. A remainder can either be vested or contingent. If a survivorship contingency is stated in a conveyance, then the majority view is that the contingency applies at the termination of the interest that precedes distribution of the remainder. A minority approach interprets a survivorship contingency to require surviving only the testator and not the life tenant.

a. Class interests

A class interest consists of a group of unspecified persons whose number and identity and share of the interest is determined in the future (e.g., at the death of the donor). Usually, the group is of children.

Example: A conveys a gift "to my children." Here, A conveys a class gift to an unspecified group because the recipients (i.e., those who will qualify as A's children upon A's death) are not known until A dies.

1) Vested remainder

A vested remainder is an interest that is not subject to any conditions precedent and is created in an ascertainable grantee.

Example: A conveys Blackacre "to B for life, and then to C and his heirs." Here, the grantee, C, is ascertainable.

a) Vested subject to open

If a conveyance grants a remainder to a class of grantees and at least one of the grantees receives a vested remainder at the time of the conveyance, then that vested remainder is subject to open (i.e., the property interest is uncertain because other grantees may become vested, and able to share in the grant).

Example: A conveys "to B for life, and then to B's children as they turn 18." B has three children upon death, X (10 years old), Y (15 years old), and Z (20 years old). Z has a vested remainder subject to open because the property interest may be shared if Y and/or X become vested (i.e., reach age 18).

Once a class closes, any person who might otherwise have become a class member (e.g., later-born siblings) cannot claim an interest in the property as a class member.

Although those born after the class closes are generally not part of the class, *those already in gestation upon closing are* included in the class.

Absent a closing date, the rule of convenience closes the class when any member of the class becomes entitled to immediate possession of the property.

> **Example:** A conveys "to B for life, and then to C's children." If the conveyance does not specify when the class closes, then the class closes when B dies, regardless of any of C's children born after B's death.

b) Vested subject to complete

A vested remainder subject to complete indicates that the occurrence of a condition subsequent will completely divest the remainder interest.

> **Example:** A conveys "to B for life, and then to C; but if C has no children, then to D's children." C has a vested remainder interest, but if he is not survived by his children at the time of B's death, then C's interest will be divested.

b. Contingent remainder

A remainder is contingent if it is created in a grantee that is unascertainable, or if it is subject to an express condition precedent to a grantee's taking. This normally occurs in one of two circumstances: (i) when the property cannot vest because the beneficiary is unknown, or (ii) when the property cannot vest because the known beneficiary is subject to a condition precedent that has not yet occurred.

> **Example:** A conveys "to B for life, remainder to C's heirs." If C is alive at the conveyance, C's heirs are not yet ascertainable, and the remainder is contingent.

Contingent remainders were destroyed at common law if they had not vested by the time the preceding estate terminated. In such a situation in most states today, the grantor's reversion becomes possessory, and the person holding the contingent remainder takes a springing executory interest (see *below*), which becomes possessory if and when the condition precedent is met.

c. Rule in *Shelley's Case*

At common law, the rule in *Shelley's Case* prevented contingent remainders in the grantee's heirs by defeating the grantor's intent and changing the interest that the grantor purported to give to the grantee and his heirs to a vested remainder in the grantee. The rule in *Shelley's Case* changes the state of the title to two successive freehold estates in the grantee. Under the doctrine of merger, both the present and future interests are merged so that the grantee takes in fee simple absolute. Most jurisdictions have abolished the rule in *Shelley's Case*, and the parties now take the present and future interests according to the language in the deed.

> **Example:** A conveys "to B for life, remainder to B's heirs." If the rule in *Shelley's Case* applies, then after the merger, B will receive the property in fee simple absolute. If the rule in *Shelley's Case* has been abolished, then B has a life estate and B's heirs have a contingent remainder in the subject property.

d. Doctrine of Worthier Title

The Doctrine of Worthier Title is a rule of construction similar to the rule in *Shelley's Case*, except that it prevents against remainders in the grantor's heirs, and still applies in some states. The presumption is in a reversion to the grantor.

5. Executory Interests

An executory interest is a future interest in a third party that is not a remainder and that cuts the prior estate short upon the occurrence of a specified condition. **Executory interests are transferable** and are subject to the Rule Against Perpetuities.

Most courts hold that executory interests are freely transferable, although they were not transferable inter vivos at common law.

The two types of executory interests are shifting executory interest and springing executory interest.

a. Shifting executory interest

A shifting executory interest divests the interest of the grantee by cutting short a prior estate created in the same conveyance. The estate "shifts" from one grantee to another on the happening of the condition.

Example: A conveys "to B and his heirs, but if C returns from Paris, then to C." This conveyance creates a fee simple subject to an executory limitation in B and a shifting executory interest in C.

b. Springing executory interest

A springing executory interest divests the interest of the grantor or fills a gap in possession in which the estate reverts to the grantor.

Example: A conveys "to B for life, and one year after B's death to C and his heirs." This conveyance creates a life estate in B, a one-year reversion in A (in fee simple subject to an executory limitation), and a springing executory interest in C.

EXAM NOTE: Any interest held by a third party that follows a fee is always an executory interest because a remainder *never* follows a fee.

6. Transferability of Remainders and Executory Interests

Vested remainders are fully transferable inter vivos, devisable by will, and descendible by inheritance. Today, executory interests and contingent remainders are transferable inter vivos in most jurisdictions, although under common law they were not transferable; both are devisable and descendible. It is important to note that most states permit any transferable future interest to be reached by creditors, except for those interests held by unascertainable or unborn persons.

7. Classification of Interests

It is important to classify the various interests in a disposition clause in order (i.e., from left to right) because the characterization of the first interest usually determines the characterizations of the following interests. For example, a contingent remainder can follow a contingent remainder but cannot follow a fee simple.

Example 1: A conveys Blackacre "to B for life, then to C if C survives B; but if C does not survive B, on B's death to D."

B has a present life estate. C has a future interest, which is a remainder because it can become possessory upon the termination of the preceding possessory interest (i.e., B's life estate), and is a contingent remainder because C's taking is conditioned on C surviving B. D also has a future interest, which is a remainder because it can become possessory upon the termination of B's life estate; it is a contingent remainder because D's taking is contingent on C not surviving B.

Now consider the following language that results in the same outcome (i.e., C owns Blackacre if C survives B, and D owns Blackacre if C does not) but different property interests for C and D immediately after the conveyance.

Example 2: A conveys Blackacre "to B for life, and on B's death to C. But if C predeceases B, on B's death to D." B has a present life estate. C has a future interest, which is a remainder because it can become possessory upon the termination of B's life estate. C's remainder is vested because C is ascertainable **and** there is no condition precedent that C must satisfy to take Blackacre. However, C's vested remainder is subject to complete if a condition subsequent (C predeceasing B) occurs. D has a future interest, but it is not a remainder because C's interest is not an estate of a fixed duration, but is instead a fee simple estate, which has an unlimited duration. However, if the condition subsequent occurs, D would be entitled to take possession of Blackacre, thereby cutting short C's interest. Consequently, D has a shifting executory interest.

The above two examples demonstrate the importance of examining each clause independently and classifying each interest in the proper order.

8. **Rule Against Perpetuities**

Under the Rule Against Perpetuities ("Rule"), specific future interests are valid only if they must vest or fail by the end of a life in being, plus 21 years.

Example 1: A conveys Blackacre "to B for life, and then to the first male descendant of B, then to C." This provision violates the Rule because it may be many generations before there is a male descendant of B, if at all.

Example 2: A conveys Blackacre "to B for life, and then to B's first son who reaches the age of 18, then to C." This provision is valid because any son of B will attain age 18 within 21 years after B's death.

Note the difference in the examples above. In Example 1, the opportunity for B to have a male descendant does not end after he dies. Because there is a possibility that the devise will neither vest nor fail within a life in being plus 21 years, the Rule is violated.

On the other hand, in Example 2, once B dies, his opportunity to have children ends, and so the clock starts. If, when he dies, B has at least one son under the age of 18, then it is certain to be less than a life in being plus 21 years before the condition either vests (son reaches 18) or fails (son dies).

a. **Affected future interests**

The Rule applies only to the following interests: contingent remainders, vested remainders subject to open, executory interests, powers of appointment, rights of first refusal, and options. It does *not* apply to future interests that revert to the grantor (i.e., reversion, possibility of reverter, right of reentry).

1) Trust interests

Even though a beneficiary of a trust holds only an equitable interest in the trust property, such an interest may be subject to the Rule.

b. Measuring lives

The application of the Rule is determined by one or more measuring (or, validating) lives. A measuring life must be human, but there can be more than one measuring life, provided the number of such lives is reasonable. If a measuring life is not specified, then the measuring life is the life directly related to the future interest that is subject to the Rule.

> **Example 1:** A devises Blackacre "to B for life, and then to B's children who reach the age of 25." B's life is the measuring life.

If there is not a measuring life, then the applicable testing period is 21 years from the time that the future interest is created.

> **Example 2:** A devises Blackacre "to a charity for so long as the property is used as an animal shelter, and then to C." Since there is not a measuring life, C's interest must vest or fail within 21 years of the creation of C's interest in order to satisfy the Rule. Since there is not a guarantee regarding the future use to which Blackacre is put, C's interest violates the Rule.

c. Creation events

The Rule tests the future interest as of the time that it is created. For example, a future interest created by a will is tested as of the testator's death.

d. "Vest or fail" requirement

The Rule requires that the future interest either vest or fail to vest within the applicable time period. If there is *any possibility* that it will not be known whether the interest will vest or fail within that period, then the Rule has not been satisfied.

e. Effect of violation

If a future interest fails to satisfy the Rule, then **only the offending interest fails**. In the rare case when the voiding of the future interest undermines the grantor's intent, the entire transfer is voided.

> **EXAM NOTE:** The MBE often tests the Rule by presenting answer choices relating to the result of a failed interest. Be sure to analyze the estate without the offending interest and to consider the grantor's intent.

f. Special rule for transfer to a class

If the transfer of a future interest is made to a class, and the Rule voids a transfer to any member of a class, then the transfer is void as to all class members, even those whose interests are already vested (i.e., "bad as to one, bad as to all").

> **Example:** A devises Blackacre "to B for life, and then to B's children who have graduated from college." At the time of A's death, B had two children: X, who had graduated from college, and Y, who had not. X has a vested remainder subject to open; Y, as well as any after-born children of B, has a contingent remainder. At the time of B's death, Y has also graduated from college, and B has had a third child, Z, who is in elementary school. Because it may take Z more than 21 years to graduate college and thereby vest his interest, not only is Z's interest void under the Rule, but X and Y's interests are also void.

1) Rule of convenience as a savior

The rule of convenience can operate to prevent the application of the Rule to a class transfer.

> **Example 1:** A conveys Blackacre "to B for life, and then to C's children." At the time of the conveyance, C has one child, X. X has a vested remainder subject to open. Although C may have children more than 21 years after B's death, the class will close upon B's death since C has a child, X. Consequently, X and any other children born to C prior to B's death will take Blackacre. The Rule will not apply to void their interests in Blackacre.

The application of the rule of convenience to a class transfer does not automatically forestall the application of the Rule.

> **Example 2:** In the example at f, *supra*, (A devises Blackacre "to B for life, and then to B's children who have graduated from college"), although the class closes upon B's death because both X and Y have vested remainder interests, Z, as a child of B, is also a member of the class. Because Z's interest may not vest within 21 years of B's death, the remainder interests of all of B's children are void because of the Rule.

> **EXAM NOTE:** Beware of fact patterns with class gifts to grandchildren of an inter vivos grantor instead of a testator. An inter vivos transfer is more likely to violate the Rule because there is a greater chance that a donor will have later-born children than a testator.

2) Exceptions

There are two main exceptions to the "bad as to one, bad as to all" rule for class transfers. Both transfers of a specific dollar amount to each class member (e.g., "$50,000 to each grandchild who survives his parent") and transfers to a subclass that vests at a specific time (e.g., "to the children of B, and upon the death of each, to that child's issue") are tested separately. Any person who is entitled to the transferred interest is not prohibited from taking that interest simply because there are other members of the class who are prohibited from taking the interest.

g. Exceptions

1) Charity-to-charity exception

If property passes from one charity to another charity, then the interest of the receiving charity is not subject to the Rule.

> **Example:** Blackacre is conveyed "to charity B, as long as the premises are used for a school, and then to charity C." The executory interest of charity C may not vest within the time allotted by the Rule, but, because the Rule does not apply to charity-to-charity transfers, C's executory interest is valid.

> **EXAM NOTE:** The Rule applies to property that passes between a charity and a non-charity.

2) Current tenant's option exception

The Rule does not apply to an option to purchase the property that is held by a current leasehold tenant. If the current tenant can transfer such an option, then this exception does not apply to a subsequent holder of the purchase option.

h. Common violations

1) Class transfers—"survival beyond age 21" condition

If a transfer to a class is conditioned on the class members surviving to an age beyond 21 and the class is open, then the transfer to the class violates the Rule.

> **Example:** A conveys Blackacre "to B for life, and then to B's children who reach the age of 30." At the time of the conveyance, B has one child, X, who is 35 years old. X has a vested remainder subject to open; B's potential children have a contingent remainder. The contingent remainder violates the Rule because it is possible that B could have another child who would not attain the age of 30 until more than 21 years after B's death. Because the contingent remainder is invalid, X's vested remainder subject to open is also invalid as a consequence of the "bad as to one, bad as to all" rule for class transfers.

2) Fertile octogenarian

Anyone, regardless of age or physical condition, including an 80-year-old woman (i.e., the fertile octogenarian) is deemed capable of having children for the purposes of the Rule. Some states have set an age limit (e.g., 55 years old) beyond which it is rebuttably presumed that a woman cannot have a child.

> **Example:** A conveys Blackacre "to B for life, then to B's children who reach the age of 30 years old." At the time of the conveyance, B is 90 years old, with one child, X, who is 35 years old. X has a vested remainder subject to open, since B, despite her age, is assumed to be capable of having another child. Because the contingent remainder in that child would violate the Rule, X's interest is also void under the "bad as to one, bad as to all" rule.

3) Unborn spouse

If an interest following a widow's life estate cannot vest until the widow dies, then it violates the Rule.

> **Example:** A conveys Blackacre "to B for life, then to B's widow for life, then to B's children who are then living." The contingent remainder in B's children

violates the Rule because B's widow may be someone who is not yet alive at the time of the conveyance. The contingent remainder would not violate the rule if the life estate was conveyed to a particular person (e.g., B's current spouse) instead of "B's widow."

4) Defeasible fee followed by an executory interest

An executory interest that follows a defeasible fee violates the Rule, unless there is a time limit on the vesting of the executory interest that satisfies the Rule.

If the limit on the defeasible fee is durational (e.g., "so long as," "while"), then the striking of the executory interest leaves the grantor with the possibility of reverter. If the limit on the defeasible fee is a condition subsequent (e.g., "but if," "upon the condition that"), then the striking of the executory interest leaves the holder of the defeasible fee with a fee simple absolute interest in the property.

Example 1: A conveys Blackacre "to B for so long as the property is used for residential purposes; if it is not, then to C." B has a fee simple subject to an executory interest; C has an executory interest. Because C's executory interest could become possessory after the expiration of the testing period for the Rule, C's interest is stricken, and A has a possibility of reverter in Blackacre.

Example 2: A conveys Blackacre "to B; but if the property is used for residential purposes, then to C." B has a fee simple subject to an executory interest; C has an executory interest. Because C's executory interest could become possessory after the expiration of the testing period for the Rule, C's interest is stricken, and B owns Blackacre in fee simple absolute.

5) Conditional passage of interest

If there is a condition imposed on the passing of a future interest subject to the Rule that is not confined to a specified time limit that meets the Rule's testing period, such as probating the will or termination of a current military conflict, then the future interest runs afoul of the Rule.

i. Statutory changes

A majority of the states have adopted the Uniform Statutory Rule Against Perpetuities, which adopts a "wait and see" stance with respect to the applicability of the Rule. Under this stance, an otherwise invalid interest is valid if it does in fact vest within 90 years of its creation. A few states have simply repealed the Rule altogether.

II. LANDLORD AND TENANT

The relationship between a landlord and a tenant can create four different estates. This relationship is generally governed by a contract, called the "lease," and contains the covenants of the parties. The promises are generally independent of each other. In other words, each party must perform his promises regardless of whether or not the other party performs his promise.

A. TYPES OF TENANCIES

There are four types of landlord-tenant estates:

i) Tenancy for years;

ii) Periodic tenancy;

iii) Tenancy at will; and

iv) Tenancy at sufferance.

1. Tenancy for Years

A tenancy for years is an estate measured by a fixed and ascertainable amount of time.

a. Term

A tenancy for years may be any length of time (e.g., one week, six months, five years).

b. Creation

A tenancy for years is created by an agreement between the landlord and the tenant. The Statute of Frauds applies to a tenancy for years that is longer than one year; such agreements must be in writing. A lease subject to the Statute of Frauds is voidable until the tenant takes possession and the landlord accepts rent from the tenant.

c. Termination

1) At end of term

Termination occurs automatically upon the expiration of the term; no notice is required. Any right to renew the agreement must be explicitly set out in the lease.

2) Prior to end of term

Termination may also occur before the expiration of the term, such as when the tenant surrenders the leasehold (i.e., the tenant offers and the landlord accepts return of the leasehold). In addition, although at common law the doctrine of independent covenants usually prevented the breach of a covenant in the lease by a tenant or landlord from giving the other party the right to terminate the lease, most states recognize that the breach of certain specific leasehold covenants (i.e., the tenant's payment of the rent, and the landlord's covenants of quiet enjoyment and implied warranty of habitability) can give rise to a right to terminate the lease.

2. Periodic Tenancy

A periodic tenancy is a repetitive, ongoing estate measured by a set period of time (e.g., a month-to-month lease) but with no predetermined termination date.

a. Term

A periodic tenancy automatically renews at the end of each period until one party gives a valid termination notice. The Statute of Frauds does not apply to a periodic tenancy because its nature is that it is for a non-fixed term.

b. Creation

A periodic tenancy can be created by express agreement, implication (e.g., the failure of an express agreement to mention a termination date), or operation of law (e.g., a hold-over tenant, *see* § II.B.5.c., Holdover tenant, *below*).

c. Termination

Because a periodic tenancy automatically renews, notice is required to terminate.

1) At end of term

Notice of termination must be given before the beginning of the intended last period of the periodic tenancy.

Example 1: A landlord who wants to terminate a month-to-month tenancy as of March 31st must give notice of the termination to the tenant before the first day of March.

Notice that is given late is generally treated as effective for the subsequent period.

Example 2: A landlord who wanted to terminate a month-to-month tenancy that began on January 1st as of March 31st gave notice of the termination to the tenant on March 5th. The notice is effective to terminate the month-to-month tenancy as of the end of April.

A notice of termination is generally effective only as of the last day of the period (e.g., the end of the month for a month-to-month tenancy that began on the first day of the month).

Example 3: A landlord wanted to terminate a month-to-month tenancy that began on January 1st as of March 15th. The landlord gave notice of the termination to the tenant on February 14th. The notice is effective to terminate the month-to-month tenancy as of the end of March.

EXAM NOTE: The termination of year-to-year tenancy requires notice only six months rather than one year in advance.

In addition, many states have reduced the advance notice period for all periodic tenancies even further (e.g., one month).

2) Prior to end of term

The same circumstances discussed with regard to a tenancy for years may also give rise to the termination of a periodic tenancy prior to the end of a term.

3. Tenancy at Will

a. Term

A tenancy at will is a leasehold estate that does not have a specific term and continues until terminated by either the landlord or tenant.

b. Creation

A tenancy at will can be created by the express agreement of the parties or by implication if a person is allowed to occupy the premises, such as when the parties are negotiating a lease. Note that, unless this tenancy is expressly created, the payment of rent by the tenant converts a tenancy at will into a periodic tenancy.

c. Termination

At common law, a tenancy at will could be terminated by either party without advance notice, but the tenant had to be given a reasonable time in which to vacate the premises. By statute, most states now require that a party give advance notice in order to terminate a tenancy at will, and some states allow only the tenant to terminate the lease at will. A tenancy at will can also be terminated by the death of either party, waste or assignment by the tenant, and transfer or lease of the property to a third party by the landlord. Restatement Second of Property: Landlord-Tenant §1.6.

If it is not clear from the language of the lease that it is a tenancy at will, it may be construed as a determinable estate (e.g., an estate for years determinable). A tenancy that is terminable at the will of one party only may be unconscionable. Restatement Second of Property: Landlord-Tenant §1.6, cmt. g.

4. Tenancy at Sufferance

A tenancy at sufferance is the period of time after the expiration of a lease during which the tenant remains on the premises. During a tenancy at sufferance, the tenant is bound by the terms of the lease that existed before expiration, including payment of rent.

> **EXAM NOTE:** Know the difference between a tenancy at will, which is created by the agreement of the landlord and the tenant, and a tenancy at sufferance, which is created by the actions of the tenant alone.

A tenancy at sufferance can be terminated by the departure of the tenant from the premises, by the eviction of the tenant from the premises by the landlord, or by the landlord's decision to lease the premises to the tenant for another term. Thus, the landlord's remedies may include eviction, creation of a periodic tenancy, or forcible entry in some states.

B. DUTIES OF TENANT

The tenant has two basic duties: to pay rent and avoid waste. The duty to pay rent arises as a consequence of the agreement between the tenant and the landlord (i.e., a lease), which usually takes the form of a written contract. The duty to avoid waste is the same duty imposed on any holder of a current possessory property interest with respect to the holders of other interests in the same property. The duty to avoid waste may be modified by contractual or other legal obligations regarding repair of the premises.

1. Duty to Pay Rent

Although a tenant may enjoy a leasehold estate without having to pay rent (e.g., if the tenant is a relative of the landlord), most tenants are required to pay rent. Although rent was not apportionable under common law, most states today allow the tenant to pay a proportionate amount of the rent if the leasehold terminates prematurely. In addition, the landlord may require a deposit (either as security or a future rent payment) prior to commencing the leasehold.

This duty to pay rent is subject to two major exceptions: destruction of the premises and a material breach by the landlord.

a. Destruction of premises

The lease is terminated and the tenant is excused from paying rent if the premises are destroyed, such as by flood, as long as the tenant is not at fault for the destruction. At common law, the tenant's duty to pay rent was not excused simply because the leasehold premises were destroyed.

b. Material breach of lease by landlord

At common law, the doctrine of independent covenants usually prevented the tenant from avoiding the obligation to pay rent despite the landlord's material breach of the lease. However, even at common law, a landlord who breached the covenant of quiet enjoyment could give the tenant the right to terminate the lease and cease paying rent. In addition, most states give tenants various options with regard to the payment of rent if a landlord violates the implied warranty of habitability **in a residential lease** (e.g., establishment of an escrow account into which the rent is paid, deducting the cost of repairs incurred by the tenant from the rent paid).

2. Duty to Avoid Waste

At common law, a tenant was held to the same standards of waste imposed on a life tenant, including the duty not to commit affirmative waste (i.e., damage to property), ameliorative waste (i.e., alterations to property, even if the value of the property increases), or permissive waste (i.e., failure to prevent or repair damage).

a. Ameliorative waste

A tenant is entitled to make changes to the physical condition of the leased property that are reasonably necessary for the tenant to use the property in a reasonable manner, unless the landlord and tenant agree otherwise. Restatement (Second) of Property: Landlord and Tenant § 12.2(a).

b. Permissive waste

A tenant has a duty, unless relieved by the terms of the lease, state statute, or local ordinance, to repair the premises to the extent necessary to maintain the premises in their pre-rental condition. An exception exists for **normal wear and tear**, unless the tenant contracts otherwise.

3. Contractual Duty to Repair

If a **non-residential lease** specifies that the tenant must "repair and maintain" the property, then the tenant is generally liable for all damage to the property, unless the landlord caused the damage. If the damage is significant (e.g., structural damage due to a fire) and such damage was not caused by the tenant, then the modern trend is to narrowly read the tenant's duty to repair and to find that it does not cover such damage.

A **residential lease** provision that places the burden of repair on the tenant is generally void, but the tenant may be required to notify the landlord of the need for such repairs.

4. Other Duties

A tenant may have other contractual duties, such as a duty to avoid excessive noise or to use the premises only for a specified type of business. In addition, a tenant who uses the premises for illegal purposes on a regular basis (e.g., drug distribution) may violate an implied duty. Violation of such duties can give the landlord the right to terminate the lease.

5. Landlord's Remedies for Tenant's Breach

a. Failure to pay rent

If the tenant fails to pay rent, then the landlord can sue both for damages and to remove the tenant from the property. An agreement to pay rent on or by a certain date is a material term of a lease and, thus, late payment of rent is considered a material breach of the lease. Thus, a landlord may bring an action for damages.

b. Abandonment

At common law, if the tenant unjustifiably abandoned the leasehold, then the landlord could treat the abandonment as an offer of surrender and could accept by **retaking the premises**.

1) Duty to mitigate

Alternatively, the landlord may re-rent the premises on the tenant's behalf and hold the tenant liable for any deficiency. The majority rule today requires a landlord to mitigate damages by making an effort to re-rent the premises.

2) Anticipatory breach

Although the landlord can sue a tenant for rent as it becomes due, a landlord cannot sue for future rent due under the lease because the doctrine of anticipatory breach does not apply to leases.

c. Holdover tenant

When a tenant continues to occupy the premises without the landlord's agreement after the original lease expires, the tenant is considered to be a "holdover tenant." The landlord can continue the relationship by treating the holdover tenant as a periodic tenant or a tenant at sufferance. Alternatively, the landlord may file a lawsuit for unlawful detainer if the holdover tenant remains after serving a written notice to vacate (or "quit").

The tenant is not considered to be a holdover tenant if the tenant leaves a few articles of personal property behind or the tenant's occupation is only for a few hours. Circumstances out of the tenant's control (e.g., severe illness) and seasonal leases are also exempt from the holdover doctrine.

1) Periodic tenant

By accepting rent after the termination of a lease, the landlord creates a periodic tenancy, the terms of which mirror the previous terminated lease. Notwithstanding the foregoing, no periodic lease of a residence can be implied for greater than one month, and of a commercial structure no longer than one year, due to Statute of Frauds requirements.

2) Tenant at sufferance

If the landlord refuses to accept rent from a holdover tenant, then the tenant is considered wrongfully in possession and the landlord may evict the tenant without notice. *See* § II.A.4, Tenancy at Sufferance, *above.*

3) Self-help

Most states no longer allow the landlord to use self-help, but he must instead (i) properly serve the tenant with notice of a lawsuit and (ii) obtain a court judgment of possession.

4) Rent

A landlord can impose a higher rent on a holdover tenant if the landlord informed the tenant of the new rent prior to the expiration of the old lease. Otherwise, the rent of the old lease applies.

C. DUTIES OF LANDLORD

1. Give Possession

In most states, a tenant is relieved of the obligation to pay rent if the landlord fails to deliver actual possession of the leasehold premises. The minority rule requires only that the landlord deliver legal possession.

2. Duty to Repair

The contract can place the duty to repair on the tenant of a commercial lease. The landlord has the duty to repair under a residential lease, even when the lease attempts to place the burden on the tenant, except for damages caused by the tenant.

3. Warranty of Habitability

There is an implied warranty of habitability to most **residential** leases, particularly when the dwelling is multi-family. The landlord must maintain the property such that it is reasonably suited for residential use. The landlord's failure to comply with applicable housing code requirements constitutes a breach of this warranty, particularly with regard to violations that substantially threaten the tenant's health and safety. This warranty generally cannot be waived by the tenant, either by express language in the lease or by taking possession of the property with knowledge of the conditions.

If the premises are not habitable, then the tenant may choose to (i) refuse to pay rent, (ii) remedy the defect and offset the cost against the rent, or (iii) defend against eviction. Generally, before the tenant can withhold the rent or remedy the defect, she must first notify the landlord of the problem and give him a reasonable opportunity to correct the problem.

4. Covenant of Quiet Enjoyment

Every lease (both commercial and residential) contains an implied covenant of quiet enjoyment, which is breached only when the landlord, someone claiming through the landlord, or someone with superior title disrupts the possession of the tenant. Off-premises actions of third parties will not suffice.

The landlord is not liable for acts of other tenants, but he has a duty to take action against a tenant's nuisance-like behavior and to control the common areas. Any actions by the landlord that breach this covenant amount to an **actual or constructive eviction** of the tenant.

Not every interference with the use and enjoyment of the premises amounts to a constructive eviction. Temporary or *de minimis* acts not intended to amount to a permanent expulsion do not amount to constructive eviction.

a. Actual eviction

If the landlord removes the tenant from the premises, then the total eviction terminates the lease and ends the tenant's obligation to pay rent.

b. Partial eviction

If the tenant is prevented from possessing or using a portion of the leased premises, then the tenant may seek relief for a partial actual eviction. The type of relief granted depends on who prevented the possession.

1) Landlord

The tenant is completely excused from paying rent for the entire premises if the landlord is responsible for partial eviction.

2) Third parties

The tenant must pay the reasonable rental value of the premises occupied if the partial eviction is by a third party with a superior claim to the property.

The tenant is not excused from paying rent if a third-party adverse possessor/trespasser partially evicts the tenant.

c. Constructive eviction

If the landlord substantially interferes with the tenant's use and enjoyment of the leasehold (e.g., fails to provide heat or water), then the tenant's obligation to pay rent is excused due to constructive eviction **only if the tenant gives notice and vacates** the property within a reasonable amount of time.

d. Retaliatory eviction

A landlord may not evict a residential tenant for failure to pay rent as retaliation for the tenant's reporting a housing code violation to the appropriate authorities.

D. TORT LIABILITIES

1. Tenant

The tenant is the possessor of the leasehold who owes a duty of care to invitees, licensees, and foreseeable trespassers and may be liable for dangerous conditions or activities on the leased property. However, this duty is not violated by a failure to remove a natural accumulation of snow or ice, unless an act or failure to act caused the condition to worsen.

2. Landlord

Under common law, the landlord is responsible for injuries occurring only in **common and public areas**, or non-common areas under the landlord's control, or those occurring as a result of a **hidden defect** or **faulty repair** completed by the landlord.

The modern trend is to hold landlords to a general duty of reasonable care. This means that a landlord may be liable for (i) existing defects prior to the tenant's occupation of the premises, (ii) failure to make repairs required by a housing code, and (iii) at times, the criminal activity of third persons who injure tenants.

See the Themis Torts outline for a further discussion of the liability of owners and possessors of land.

E. ASSIGNMENT AND SUBLETTING

Absent any language to the contrary, a lease can be freely assigned or sublet. Because a lease is both a contract and a conveyance, these can be independent grounds for liability.

1. Assignment versus Sublease

An assignment is a complete transfer of the tenant's remaining lease term. Any transfer for less than the entire duration of the lease is a sublease.

2. Assignee's Rights and Liabilities

Assignee tenants are in privity of estate with the landlord, and are thus liable to the landlord for the rent and any other covenants in the lease that run with the lease. However, if the assignee tenant reassigns the leasehold to a subsequent tenant, then the assignee tenant's privity with the landlord ends. Thus, he is no longer liable because the subsequent tenant is now in privity with the landlord.

3. Sublessee's Rights and Liabilities

Because the sublessee is not in privity of estate or contract with the landlord, the sublessee is not liable to the landlord for the rent or any other covenants in the lease but is liable to the lessee. However, if the sublessee expressly assumes the rent covenant (or any other covenants), then he becomes personally liable to the landlord. While the sublessee can enforce all covenants made by the original lessee in the sublease, the sublessee cannot enforce any covenants made by the landlord.

4. Original Tenant's Rights and Liabilities

The privity of estate held by the original tenant terminates upon a successful assignment by the tenant to the assignee. Because the original tenant remains in privity of contract with the landlord (both are parties to the lease agreement), however, the original tenant remains liable for all the covenants in the lease—even after a successful assignment. Absent an agreement by the landlord to release the original tenant from liability (i.e., a **novation**), the original tenant remains liable to the landlord for the entire duration of the lease.

5. Landlord Assignments

A landlord may assign his ownership interest, usually through a deed, to a third party without the tenant's consent. The tenant is required to continue his rent obligation and any other covenant under his lease to the new landlord, provided that the covenants touch and concern the land. Likewise, the assignee landlord, as well as the original landlord, is bound to the tenant by the covenants of the lease.

6. Limitations on Assignment and Subletting

a. Prohibition

When a lease prohibits the tenant from assignment or subletting the leasehold, the tenant may nevertheless assign or sublet the premises. However, the landlord generally can then terminate the lease for breach of one of its covenants and recover any damages.

b. Landlord's permission

When a lease prevents assignment or subletting of the leasehold without the permission of the landlord, and the lease is silent as to a standard for exercising that permission, the majority rule is that the landlord may withhold permission only on a *commercially reasonable ground*. The minority position is that the landlord may withhold permission at his discretion. Non-assignment and non-sublease clauses are valid but narrowly construed.

> A clause that prohibits assignment does not automatically also prohibit subleasing.

c. Waiver by landlord

An assignment or sublease may be waived if the landlord knows of either the assignment or sublease and does not object. When a landlord consents to an assignment or waives her right to object, she cannot then object to a subsequent assignment. This prohibition on an objection to a subsequent assignment does not apply to subsequent subleases, and a minority of jurisdictions does not impose such a prohibition even on a subsequent assignment.

F. CONDEMNATION

Condemnation is the taking of land either for public use or because it is unfit for use, and it can be a partial taking or a complete forfeiture. If the condemnation is partial, meaning that only a portion of the leased property is condemned or the property is temporarily condemned, then the tenant must continue to make his rent payments. However, he is entitled to compensation for the portion of the property that was condemned or the time that he was dispossessed from the leased property.

If the condemnation is complete, meaning that the entire leased property is taken for the balance of the lease term, then the tenant is discharged from his rent obligation and is entitled to compensation.

G. FAIR HOUSING AND DISCRIMINATION

The Fair Housing Act ("FHA") (Title VIII of the Civil Rights Act of 1968), 42 U.S.C.S. § 3601 *et seq.*, prohibits discrimination in the sale, rental, and financing of homes and in other housing-related transactions (such as advertising, homeowner's insurance, and zoning). Owner-occupied buildings with no more than four units and single-family housing sold or rented without the use of a broker may be exempted from the FHA in certain circumstances.

1. Protected Classes

The FHA prohibits discrimination on the basis of race, color, religion, national origin, sex, disability, and familial status. Protected familial status includes having or securing custody of children under the age of 18 and being pregnant. Exemption from familial status protection exists for certain housing for older persons.

2. Prohibited Practices

The Act prohibits taking any of the following actions on the basis of a protected characteristic:

i)   Refusing to rent or sell housing;

ii) Making housing unavailable;

iii) Providing different housing services or facilities;

iv) Setting different terms for sale or rental of a dwelling;

v)   Falsely denying that housing is available;

vi) Refusing to make a mortgage loan or imposing different terms or conditions on a loan;

vii) Refusing to allow a disabled tenant to make reasonable modifications to the dwelling or common-use areas at his own expense;

viii) Refusing to make reasonable accommodations in rules, policies, practices, or services if necessary for the disabled person to use the housing (e.g., refusing to allow a visually impaired tenant to keep a guide dog in an apartment with a "no pets" policy);

ix) Threatening, coercing, intimidating, or interfering with anyone exercising a fair housing right; and

x)   Advertising or making any statement that indicates a limitation or preference based on protected characteristics.

3. Enforcement and Compliance

The U.S. Department of Housing and Urban Development ("HUD") plays the lead role in administering the FHA. A person who believes that a violation of the FHA has occurred may file a complaint with HUD and/or file suit in federal court (a court-appointed attorney may be available). Available relief includes actual damages (including humiliation, and pain and suffering), injunctive or other equitable relief (such as making the housing available), and reasonable attorney's fees and costs. If the case is resolved by an administrative hearing, then a civil penalty to vindicate the public interest may be assessed. A federal court may award punitive damages.

4. Complaint Process

Complaints filed with HUD are first investigated by the Office of Fair Housing and Equal Opportunity ("FHEO"). If it finds reasonable cause to believe that discrimination occurred, then the case is heard in an administrative hearing within 120 days, unless either party elects for the case to be heard in federal court.

Before an administrative hearing is ordered, HUD attempts to reach an agreement among the parties, and any conciliation agreement will cease action on the complaint. For a conciliation agreement to cease action on the complaint, however, it must protect both the complainant and the public interest. The breach of a conciliation agreement may result in suit by the attorney general.

III. DISPUTES ABOUT OWNERSHIP IN LAND

A. ADVERSE POSSESSION

The doctrine of adverse possession allows ownership to be granted to a person who exercises exclusive physical possession of a piece of property for a certain amount of time. Title acquired by adverse possession is as good as title traceable to a prior record owner. For possession to ripen into title, possession must be continuous, actual, open and notorious, hostile, and exclusive. Government-owned land cannot be adversely possessed.

1. Continuous

Possession must be continuous and uninterrupted for a period of time as defined by statute (or 20 years at common law). Seasonal or infrequent use may be sufficiently continuous if it is consistent with the type of property that is being possessed (e.g., land at a summer camp).

a. Tacking

An adverse possessor may tack on his predecessor's time in order to satisfy the statutory period, as long as there is privity satisfied by any non-hostile nexus (such as blood, contract, deed, or will). The periods of possession must pass directly from one possessor to the next without any gaps.

Tacking is not allowed when there is an actual, wrongful exclusion of a party entitled to possession from the property (ouster).

b. Disability of owner

The statute of limitations will not run against a true owner who is afflicted with a disability (e.g., insanity, infancy, imprisonment) at the inception of the adverse possession.

2. Actual, Open and Notorious

Possession must be open and notorious, such that a reasonable true owner would become aware of the claim. Uses that are hidden (such as underground wiring or piping) are insufficient to satisfy this requirement.

3. Hostile

The adverse possessor must possess the land without the owner's permission and with the intent to claim the land as his own against the claims of others for it to be considered "hostile." The majority of jurisdictions do not require that the possession be hostile in the sense that the possessor purposefully seeks to defeat the owner's title. The intent of the possessor is irrelevant in many jurisdictions. Most jurisdictions that consider intent will grant title to a possessor who, in good faith, thought he had the legal right to possess (i.e., believed that the property was not owned or thought that he owned the property).

4. Exclusive

Possession cannot be shared with the true owner, although two or more people can join together to create a tenancy in common by adverse possession.

5. Scope of Possession

a. Constructive adverse possession

If a person enters property under color of title (a facially valid will or deed) and actually possesses only a portion of the property, then constructive adverse possession can give title to the whole. The amount possessed must be a reasonable portion of the whole.

b. Below surface area

The adverse possessor acquires the rights to the subsurface (e.g., mineral rights), unless those rights belong to a third party.

c. Future interests

The adverse possessor acquires the estate held by the person who has legal possession at the time that the adverse possession began. In other words, the adverse possession period does not run against future interests that exist at the time that the adverse possession begins, but it does apply to future interests created from a fee simple absolute estate after the adverse possession has begun.

B. THE LAND SALE CONTRACT

1. Formation

A contract for the sale of real property is generally negotiated by a real estate broker who acts as an intermediary between sellers and buyers of real estate. Generally, the broker has the duty of a fiduciary and must follow the same requirements as for the formation of any contract (i.e., offer, acceptance, and consideration), and the contract is subject to the Statute of Frauds.

a. Statute of Frauds

The land sale contract must:

i) Be in writing;

ii) Be signed by the party to be charged; and

iii) Contain all of the essential terms (i.e., parties, property description, terms of price and payment).

b. Exceptions to Statute of Frauds

1) Part performance

Under the doctrine of part performance, either party may seek specific performance when the acts of performance constitute persuasive evidence of the existence of a contract. Among the acts that may constitute such evidence are:

i) Payment of all or part of the purchase price;

ii) Possession by the purchaser; or

iii) Substantial improvement of the property by the purchaser.

2) Detrimental reliance

Specific performance may also be permitted when the party seeking enforcement has reasonably relied on the contract and would suffer such hardship that the other party will be estopped from asserting the Statute of Frauds as a defense to the contract.

3) Admission

A party may be able to enforce an oral land sale contract when the other party admits the existence of the contract.

c. Rescission of contract

While a writing is generally required to create an enforceable land sale contract, a majority of states permit the oral rescission of a land sale contract.

2. Performance

a. Marketable title

Absent contrary language, an implied covenant of marketable title (i.e., a title free from defects) is part of a land sale contract, regardless of the type of deed created. Marketable title is a title that is free from an unreasonable risk of litigation. Unless otherwise agreed, the seller is not required to deliver marketable title until the closing. In the case of an installment land contract, marketable title is not required to be given until delivery occurs.

Once the deed is delivered, the terms of the contract merge with the deed, and the deed controls. This is known as "merger." After merger takes place, the purchaser is not able to enforce provisions of the purchase contract.

1) Defects

Defects in title rendering title unmarketable include:

    i)   Title acquired by adverse possession that has not yet been quieted (i.e., supported by a judicial decree);

    ii) Future interests wherein the holders of such interests have not agreed to the transfer;

    iii) Private encumbrance (e.g., mortgage, covenant, option, or easement);

    iv) Violation of a zoning ordinance; or

    v) Significant physical defect (an encroachment on the land that is incurable).

The above defects may be waived in the contract of sale.

> **EXAM NOTE:** Remember that once the deed takes effect, the terms of the contract merge with the deed, and the deed controls.

2) Remedies for unmarketable title

A buyer may rescind and recover payments, sue for breach, or bring an action for specific performance with an abatement of the purchase price (e.g., price adjustment to compensate the buyer for the defect), but she usually cannot do so until the date of closing.

b. Time of the essence

Generally, a court will assume that time is not of the essence in a real estate contract, unless the contract specifically states that time is of the essence, circumstances indicate that this was the intention of the parties, or one party gives the other party notice that time is of the essence. Such notice must be given at a reasonable time before the date designated for closing.

If time is not of the essence, strict adherence to the closing date set in the contract will not be required in equity. Thus, a failure to perform will generally not be grounds for rescission of the contract. A party can sue for specific performance, though, as long as the party was ready to perform within a reasonable time from the date set for performance.

Regardless of whether time is of the essence in a real estate contract, though, the party that fails to render performance on the date set for closing in the contract will be in breach and liable for damages in an action at law.

c. Implied warranty of fitness or suitability (new homes)

Replacing the doctrine of caveat emptor ("let the buyer beware"), a warranty of fitness or suitability (or implied warranty of quality, workmanlike construction, performance, habitability) is implied in a land sale contract for the purchase of a newly constructed residence. In some jurisdictions, the warranty extends to repair and remodeling of an existing residence and even to related structures (such as a detached garage or a retaining wall).

1) Construction defects

Under this warranty, the seller asserts that he used adequate materials and good workmanship in working on the residence. The implied warranty generally covers latent construction defects (i.e., defects that cannot be discovered by reasonable observation or inspection), such as a defective electrical, plumbing, or mechanical system, or a leaky roof or drainage problem that does not manifest itself until after the sale. While the buyer has a duty to conduct a reasonable inspection of the residence for patent defects, the buyer is not required to employ an expert home inspector.

2) Parties

a) Defendants

Generally, the warranties are implied against commercial builders, developers, and contractors of residences.

b) Plaintiffs

A majority of jurisdictions permit not only the initial homeowner-purchaser but also subsequent purchasers who do not contract directly with the commercial developer or builder to recover damages.

3) Timing

Generally, a suit for breach of this warranty must be brought within a reasonable time after discovery of the defect. When the warranty is statutory, a fixed time is generally specified (generally from one year to 10 years), may vary with the type of defect (e.g., structural defects, foundation problems), and may begin to run with the completion of the residence or the initial buyer's possession of it rather than with the discovery of the defect.

4) Damages

Damages are generally based on the cost of repairs to bring the residence into compliance with the warranty. However, when the defects cannot be corrected without substantial destruction of the residence, damages may be based on the difference between the value of the residence with the warranty and the value of the residence as built.

5) Disclaimer and waiver

This implied warranty may be disclaimed by the builder or waived by the homeowner if done so with language that is clear and unambiguous, but a general disclaimer (e.g., "property is sold as is") is generally not sufficient.

d. Disclosure duty (all homes)

In a majority of jurisdictions, a seller of a residence has a duty to disclose all known material physical defects to the buyer. The defect must not be readily observable or known to the buyer. To be material, the defect must substantially affect the value of the residence, impact the health or safety of a resident, or affect the desirability of the residence to the buyer. When a seller fails to make such disclosures, the buyer may rescind the sale or seek damages. Some states limit this duty to commercial sellers (e.g., builders); other states impose this duty on all sellers.

Even in a jurisdiction that does not require an affirmative disclosure by the seller, a buyer can sue the seller for misrepresentation or fraudulent concealment. General disclaimers (e.g., property sold as is) are not sufficient to preclude the seller's liability.

e. Tender of performance

The seller's and the buyer's performance are concurrent conditions. Therefore, one is not obligated to perform without the other's performance. When one party, either the buyer or the seller, repudiates the contract, the non-repudiating party is excused from performing. However, if both parties fail to perform, then the closing date is simply extended until one of the parties performs. On the other hand, the inability of the seller to produce a marketable title does not automatically create a breach; rather, the buyer must give the seller sufficient time to cure the title defect.

f. Merger

Under the doctrine of merger, obligations contained in the contract of sale, such as the seller's duty to deliver marketable title, are merged into the deed and cannot thereafter be enforced unless the deed contains the obligation. However, this doctrine generally is not applicable to obligations that are collateral to and independent of the conveyance itself, such as the obligation of the buyer to perform some act on the property after acquisition.

(Note: The term "merger" is used in other real property contexts, such as the merger of property interests (e.g., acquisition of both the land that is subject to and the land that is benefited by a restrictive covenant). Such a merger results in the extinguishment of the property right (e.g., the restrictive covenant).)

3. Remedies for Breach

a. Damages

Both the buyer and the seller can recover damages based on the difference between the contract price and the market value on the date of performance. If the seller breached but acted in good faith, then damages are limited to the buyer's out-of-pocket expenses.

A non-breaching seller may also collect liquidated money damages for costs relating to reselling the property, but courts likely will not enforce liquidated damage clauses if the seller suffered no loss (such as if the value of the property actually increased).

b. Specific performance

The buyer is entitled to specific performance for a seller's breach of a contract to sell land because the buyer's remedy at law is considered inadequate due to the unique nature of land. Under the theory of mutualities of remedies, the seller is also permitted to seek specific performance and force the buyer to purchase the land, even though the seller typically receives money rather than land. When the buyer seeks specific performance with respect to property for which there is a title defect (e.g., an encumbrance), the buyer may also obtain an abatement in purchase price to compensate the buyer for the defect.

4. **Equitable Conversion**

Under the doctrine of equitable conversion, although the seller retains legal title to real property during the pendency of the land sale contract, equitable title passes to the buyer upon entering the contract. The seller effectively holds the property in trust for the buyer, and has a duty to keep up the property. However, as the holder of legal title, the seller has the right to possess the property.

a. **Action against seller**

When an action is maintained against the seller for a claim that arose prior to the execution of the contract, a judgment obtained against the seller after the execution of the contract is not enforceable against the real property. Under the doctrine of equitable conversion, the seller's interest is converted by the contract into an interest in the proceeds from the sale; it is no longer an interest in the real property itself.

b. **Risk of loss**

Most states, following the logic of the doctrine of equitable conversion, place the risk of loss during the time between the execution of the contract and the closing **on the buyer**, regardless of whether the buyer takes possession of the property. An exception is recognized when the loss is attributable to the seller's intentional or negligent actions. The Uniform Vendor and Purchaser Risk Act (adopted by a minority of jurisdictions) keeps the risk of loss with the seller, unless and until the buyer takes possession or title is transferred. For the Act to apply, a material part of the property must be destroyed.

c. **Insurance**

Unless the contract requires otherwise, the seller does not have a duty to carry casualty insurance. Because the buyer has an equitable interest in the property, the buyer may obtain such insurance. When the risk of loss is on the buyer and the seller has casualty insurance, the seller is generally required to give the buyer credit against the purchase price in the amount of the insurance proceeds when a casualty occurs.

d. **Effect of buyer's or seller's death**

When one of the contracting parties dies prior to the performance date of the contract, the seller's interest may be treated as personal property and the buyer's interest may be treated as a real property interest for the purposes of distributing the property pursuant to either's will.

1) **Seller's death**

When the seller-decedent has devised his real property interests, the proceeds from the sale of the property under contract are treated as personal property that passes to the devisee of the seller-decedent's personal property. The devise of the real property itself is treated as having been adeemed. In jurisdictions that have adopted an anti-ademption statute, the devisee of the seller-decedent's real property is entitled to the sale proceeds.

2) Buyer's death

The person entitled to buyer-decedent's real property, such as the devisee of the buyer-decedent's real property pursuant to the buyer-decedent's will, can compel the transfer of the property to herself.

5. Security Interest

a. Mortgage

Lenders and buyers use mortgages as security devices to secure repayment of a debt. Two such devices are purchase-money mortgages and future advance mortgages. A **purchase-money mortgage** is used when a person takes out a loan for the purpose of purchasing property. A **future advance mortgage** (sometimes considered a second mortgage on property used to secure the loan) is a line of credit often used for home equity, construction, business, and commercial loans.

The promise to repay the debt is usually contained in the mortgage note, which sets out the terms of the transaction. This document reflects only the personal obligation of the debtor and need not be filed in order to enforce the mortgage. An agreement without a writing that encumbers property as security for a debt is an equitable mortgage that may be proven by parol evidence.

If the debtor fails to repay the debt, then the lender has the power to force a judicial foreclosure sale to satisfy the debt.

1) Severance

The **majority rule** (the lien theory) treats the mortgage interest as a lien that does not affect a joint tenancy.

The **minority rule** (the title theory) severs joint tenancy upon the granting of a mortgage and converts it to a tenancy in common.

2) Statutory redemption

After the foreclosure sale is complete, some states still allow the debtor/mortgagor to redeem the property for a limited time. A statutory redemption by the mortgagor essentially nullifies the foreclosure sale because it ends the purchaser's title and restores title to the debtor/mortgagor.

Statutory redemption by the mortgagor is final.

Example: A sold Blackacre to B for $300,000. B made a down payment of $100,000, and A carried a mortgage for the remaining balance. A mortgage was executed as security for a $200,000 promissory note due in 2015 with 7% interest per year. B stopped making payments on the mortgage in 2007, and A forced a foreclosure sale to settle the debt. Before the foreclosure sale, B could pay off the debt and reclaim Blackacre. After the foreclosure sale, however, B could reclaim only by statutory redemption.

b. Mortgage alternatives

1) Deed of trust

In some states, a deed of trust (or trust deed) is used in place of a mortgage. The debtor (landowner) makes a note to a third-party trustee as collateral security for the payment of the note to the beneficiary (lender), with the condition that the trustee re-conveys the title to the debtor upon payment of the note. Upon default, the beneficiary instructs the trustee to sell the land to repay the note. In a defective transfer of a deed-of-trust transaction, an equitable lien can be argued when a property is transferred without proper payment of the mortgage.

2) Installment land contract

An installment land contract is a contract for deed. The seller retains title until the buyer makes the final payment under an installment payment plan. Usually, installment land contracts allow the seller to keep all installment payments and retake possession if the buyer fails to make a payment.

States vary in their methods to assist purchasers in default. Some jurisdictions treat an installment land contract as a mortgage, requiring the seller to foreclose on the property rather than have the purchaser forfeit payments. Other jurisdictions offer equity of redemption, similar to mortgage law. Still others provide for a combination of forfeiture and restitution of payments.

3) Sale-leaseback

In a sale-leaseback, the property is simultaneously sold and leased back to the seller, usually for long-term continued use.

4) Absolute deed

An absolute deed (also known as a "Deed of Absolute Sale") is free of all liens and encumbrances and is used to transfer unrestricted title to property. Unlike a mortgage deed, an absolute deed does not transfer title back to the mortgagee when the terms of the mortgage have been fulfilled.

c. Effect of transfer by mortgagor

1) Assuming mortgage—personal liability attaches

If the buyer assumes the mortgage, then, upon default, the lender may seek payment from both the original debtor and the buyer for payment of the debt. The original debtor is relieved of all liability, however, if there is any modification of the obligation after the mortgage is assumed. (Note: Most jurisdictions do not require that an assumption agreement be in writing; if proven, an oral agreement is enforceable.)

2) "Subject to" mortgage

If the buyer takes title "subject to" an existing mortgage, then the buyer is not personally liable upon default, although absent a novation, the original debtor is personally liable. The property remains subject to the security interest held by the lender. If a deed is silent, then the grantee is considered to have taken subject to the mortgage.

3) Due-on-sale clauses

Mortgages employ due-on-sale and due-on-encumbrance clauses to prevent the transfer of mortgages. These clauses are enforceable and allow acceleration of the mortgage (i.e., when the principal and interest become due immediately).

4) Subrogation and suretyship

A surety, also known as a guarantee, is a promise by a borrower's guarantor to assume the obligation to pay the debt upon default by the borrower. Subrogation provides for the substitution of a surety in the place of a creditor so that the surety succeeds to the rights, claims, and remedies of the creditor in relation to the debt to recover the cost of making payment or performing on the borrower's behalf.

d. Effect of transfer by mortgagee

1) Transfer mortgage without note

Jurisdictions are split with regard to transferring mortgages without the note. Because the note is the principal evidence of the debt, many states hold that a transfer of the mortgage alone has no legal validity and is void. Other jurisdictions, however, consider the note and the mortgage something of a single entity. Thus, they hold that the note is automatically transferred along with the mortgage, unless expressly stated to the contrary.

2) Transfer note without mortgage

Conversely, transferring the note without the mortgage is possible because the mortgage follows the note. Although it is customary for the transferee to obtain and record a mortgage assignment, no separate written assignment is necessary.

If the promissory note given by the mortgagor is a negotiable instrument, then the mortgagor is generally obligated to pay the holder of the note. This is true even when the mortgagor does not have notice that the original mortgagee has transferred to the note to a third party. However, most promissory notes given in connection with a mortgage are not negotiable instruments. In such cases, the traditional view follows the rule for a promissory note (that it is a negotiable instrument), but the modern trend is that the mortgagor may pay the original mortgagee until the mortgagor receives notice of the transfer. Restatement (Third) of Property: Mortgages § 5.5.

e. Pre-foreclosure

1) Possession

Whether the mortgagee may take possession depends on the theory of title that the jurisdiction follows.

In a **lien theory state**, the mortgagee cannot take possession prior to foreclosure because the mortgagor is considered to be the owner of the land until foreclosure.

In a **title theory state**, legal title is in the mortgagee until the mortgage has been fully satisfied. Thus, the mortgagee is entitled to take possession at any time and can certainly take possession as soon as default occurs. As such, the mortgagee can make repairs, take rent, prevent waste, and lease out vacant space. While in practice this may seem advantageous, few mortgagees take advantage of this right because of the liability risks involved. A mortgagee in possession assumes a duty to take reasonable care of the property, and incurs liability as if she were the owner. Instead, some mortgagees opt to have the court appoint a receiver to manage the property and intercept the rents prior to foreclosure.

A minority of jurisdictions follow the **intermediate theory**, which in practice is similar to the title theory. In actuality, the intermediate theory combines both lien and title theories. It allows the mortgagor to retain legal title (lien theory) until default, and, on the mortgagor's default, it vests legal title in the mortgagee (title theory).

2) Waste

The mortgagor has a duty not to commit waste at least to the extent that the waste impairs the mortgagee's security. This duty exists even if the mortgagor is not otherwise in default.

3) Equity of redemption

After the default, but ***prior to*** a foreclosure sale, the mortgagor may regain clear title to the property under the doctrine of equity of redemption by paying the full debt plus any accrued interest.

Statutory right of redemption: Many states also permit the mortgagor to reclaim the property ***after*** a foreclosure sale. In these jurisdictions, during a fixed period of time (typically between three months and two years), the mortgagor has the right to reimburse the party who purchased the property at the foreclosure sale to reclaim the property.

a) Deed in lieu of foreclosure

In lieu of foreclosure, a mortgagor may convey all interest in the property to the mortgagee ("deed in lieu of foreclosure"). This permits the mortgagee to take immediate possession of the property without any further legal formalities, but it requires the consent of both the mortgagor and the mortgagee.

b) Clogging

A mortgagor may waive his right to redeem after the mortgage is executed in exchange for good and valuable consideration. However, courts routinely reject attempts by the mortgagee to deny the mortgagor this right (i.e., to "clog" the equity of redemption) prior to default, such as by the inclusion of a waiver clause in the mortgage.

f. Foreclosure and its effect on interests

The two most common types of foreclosure are by judicial sale and power of sale. Judicial sale provides for the sale of mortgaged property under the supervision of a court in which all proper parties are notified. Foreclosure by power of sale is held by the mortgage holder. A few jurisdictions adhere to the strict foreclosure method, in which a court orders the mortgagor to pay the mortgage within a certain time period. If the mortgagor does not pay within the time period, then the mortgagor takes title free and clear.

Purchasers at a foreclosure sale take the property free and clear of any interests created after the creation of the interest being foreclosed, and they take subject to any mortgages or liens that are senior to the lien of the foreclosing party. If the bid at the sale is less than the debt, even if it is for fair market value, then the lender may be granted a deficiency judgment for the balance of the debt against the debtor.

1) Junior interests

All interests that are junior to the mortgage that is being foreclosed are destroyed. Thus, all junior interests must be given notice of the foreclosure and made necessary parties to the foreclosure action. This provides the junior interest with an opportunity to redeem the property by paying off a senior interest. If a subordinate interest is not made party to the action, her interests will be safeguarded, regardless of the foreclosure action.

Generally, a creditor whose debt is secured by a mortgage on multiple properties can elect which property to subject to a foreclosure sale. However, when a senior mortgage is foreclosed and the mortgage covers multiple properties, the holder of a junior mortgage on some but not all of these properties can petition the court to apply the equitable doctrine of **"marshalling of assets."** Under this doctrine, the holder of the senior mortgage may be compelled to first foreclose on the properties for which only that holder possess a mortgage in order to protect the security interest of the holder of the junior mortgage, so long as it does not prejudice the interest of the holder of the senior mortgage or a third party. If there are multiple junior interests, property subject to the more recently created interests is subject to foreclosure prior to property subject to the more remotely created interests (i.e., **the "inverse order rule"**).

2) Senior interests

A purchaser at a foreclosure sale takes subject to any mortgages or liens that are senior to the lien of the foreclosing party. A senior interest is generally any interest created before the interest being foreclosed, but classification of interests is subject to the applicable recording act and any subordination agreements between the mortgagees.

3) Omitted party

If a subordinate interest is not made party to the action, his interests will be safeguarded, regardless of the foreclosure action. As a result, the purchaser does not acquire an interest in the property free of the subordinate's rights.

4) Subrogation

A person who pays off another person's mortgage obligation may become the owner of the obligation and the mortgage to the extent necessary to prevent unjust enrichment. Subrogation is appropriate when the payor is under a legal duty to do so, or when he does do so to protect an interest in the property subject to the mortgage or on account of misrepresentation, mistake, duress, fraud or undue influence.

5) Deficiency and surplus

If a foreclosure sale takes place and the proceeds are not enough to pay the outstanding mortgage balance, costs, and liens on the property, then there is a deficiency. The homeowner is then responsible for paying the deficiency even though she no longer owns the property. Even if the bid is for fair market value, the lender may still be granted a deficiency judgment for the balance of the debt against the debtor.

If the proceeds from the sale exceed the mortgage balance, outstanding liens, and foreclosure costs, then there is a surplus of proceeds from the sale against which the homeowner may make a claim.

g. Non-judicial foreclosure

If a mortgage contains a "power of sale" clause that calls for the sale of property to pay off the balance on a loan in the event of default, then a non-judicial (private) foreclosure is authorized.

h. Priority in foreclosure actions

The money from a foreclosure sale is applied first to the costs associated with the sale, second to the balance and interest of the mortgage obligation being foreclosed, and finally to the mortgage obligations owed to all junior interest holders. Any residue is paid to the debtor. If the successful bid at the sale is less than the debt, then the lender may be granted a deficiency judgment.

When multiple interests must be paid out of the proceeds, generally, the earliest mortgage placed on the property has priority over the other interests. There are, however, some exceptions as noted below.

1) Exceptions

a) Purchase-money mortgage exception

A purchase-money mortgage (i.e., a mortgage used to finance the purchase of the property) has **priority over all other** non-purchase-money mortgages, even those recorded earlier. A seller's purchase-money mortgage has priority over those of third-parties (and the priority of third-party purchase-money mortgages is determined chronologically).

b) Unrecorded senior mortgage exception

A senior mortgage (i.e., one that is first in time) is not given priority over junior mortgagees who paid value for the mortgage without actual inquiry or constructive notice of the senior mortgage.

c) Subordination agreement between mortgagees

When a senior mortgagee agrees to subordinate his interest to a junior mortgagee, such agreement will be enforced unless the mortgage is not sufficiently described or specified.

d) Mortgage modifications

A senior mortgagee who enters into an agreement with the landowner to modify the mortgage by making it more burdensome subordinates his interest only as to the modification. The senior mortgagee's original mortgage will otherwise remain superior.

Similarly, when a senior mortgagee makes an optional advance of funds after the mortgage is executed, and a junior mortgage is placed on the property with the senior mortgagee's knowledge, the advance will be subordinate to the junior interest. Otherwise, if the junior interest is placed on the property without the senior mortgagee's knowledge, then the optional advance will have the same priority as the original mortgage.

e) Future-advances mortgages

A future-advances mortgage (line of credit often used for home equity, construction, business, and commercial loans) can provide for obligatory advances or optional advances. If payments are obligatory, a junior lien is junior to amounts loaned both before and after the junior lien was recorded. If, however, the payments under a future-advances mortgage are optional, the junior lien has priority over payments made after the junior lien is recorded.

i. Personal liability of mortgagor

When the mortgagor signs a note and gives a mortgage, in most states, the mortgagee is permitted to bring an action based on the note itself before bringing an action to foreclose on the mortgage. In addition, after bringing a foreclosure action, the mortgagee is permitted by many states to bring a deficiency action against the mortgagor. Some states disallow this action when the mortgagee forecloses via a private foreclosure sale or when the mortgage is a purchase-money mortgage. In addition, some states limit the amount that may be recovered in a deficiency action to the fair market value of the property when the value of the property falls below the amount of the deficiency.

j. Defenses

Mortgages are subject to the same defenses as the underlying obligation secured by the mortgage (e.g., mistake, duress, failure of consideration, or fraud). In addition, the following valid defenses can affect the application of all or part of a mortgage.

1. Usury

Usury is the act of lending money at an interest rate in excess of the legal limit. If a bank or association is a usurious lender, only the interest, not the principal, is forfeited.

2. Competency

If the parties lack the legal capacity to contract, because of minority or mental incapacity, a mortgage may be invalidated.

k. Discharge

A mortgage may be discharged by payment of the debt secured by the mortgage, acceptance by the mortgagee of a deed in lieu of foreclosure, or by the merger of the equitable and legal interests.

6. Options and Rights of First Refusal

An option to purchase real property (or a right of first refusal with respect to the transfer of property) involves special considerations. As an interest in property, each is subject to the Statute of Frauds and the applicable recording act.

a. Option contract

In an option contract, one party acquires the right to purchase property, typically during a specific time period, in exchange for consideration.

1) Protection against revocation and termination

An option contract removes the ability of a grantor to revoke the option. Otherwise, an offeror is free to withdraw the offer, even despite a promise to the contrary, unless the offeree has detrimentally relied on the offer. In addition, as a contract, the option does not terminate upon the death or incapacity of the grantor of the option, unlike the termination of an offer upon the death of the offeror.

2) Counter-offer without rejection

The holder of an option can make an offer to the grantor of the option that otherwise would constitute a counteroffer (and thereby a rejection of the original offer) without losing the right to exercise the option.

3) Acceptance

The holder of an option must exercise the option pursuant to the terms of the contract. The mailbox rule, which treats an acceptance as valid when mailed, does not apply. The holder's decision to exercise the option must be received by the grantor of the option within any time period specified in the contract.

b. Right of first refusal

A right of first refusal is a preemptive right that gives its holder the opportunity to acquire property prior to its transfer to another, and is valid unless it is unreasonable. The right may be limited in various ways, such as the time period during which the right exists, the transactions to which it applies, and its transferability to another person.

c. Rule Against Perpetuities

The Rule Against Perpetuities does not apply to an option or right of first refusal granted to a current leasehold tenant. A significant minority of jurisdictions, following the modern trend, do not apply the rule to an option contract or a right of first refusal when the property right is created in a commercial transaction. Restatement (Third) of Property: Servitudes § 3.3, cmt. a. Under the Uniform Statutory Rule Against Perpetuities, options in commercial transactions are exempt from the rule. See § I.C.8.i. Statutory changes, *supra*.

d. Restraints against alienability

As partial restraints on the alienability of property, both an option contract and a right of first refusal are subject to the rule of reasonableness. Under this rule, the utility of the purpose served by the restraint is balanced against the likely harm that would result from its enforcement. Restatement (Third) of Property: Servitudes § 3.4, cmt. c.

e. Marketable title

A right of first refusal as well as an option contract can constitute an encumbrance that prevents the seller of property from providing marketable title.

7. Real Estate Broker

In many instances, the sale of real property involves a real estate broker or agent. The rights and duties of the broker are generally governed by contract.

a. Seller's agent

Typically, a real estate broker serves as the seller's agent. There is usually a listing agent, who deals directly with the seller and who may help to set the selling price and assume primary responsibilities for advertising the property for sale. There is also a selling agent, who serves as a sub-agent of the listing agent and finds a buyer for the property. Generally, the listing agent and the selling agent share in the commission paid by the seller.

1) Entitlement to commission

a) Procurement of buyer

In general, to be entitled to a commission, the selling agent's efforts must be the procuring cause for the buyer's purchase of the property. In other words, the resulting sale must be induced primarily by those efforts.

b) "Ready, willing, and able" buyer

Most contracts provide for payment of a commission to the real estate broker upon the procurement of a buyer who is ready, willing, and able to purchase the property on terms that are agreeable to the seller. Consequently, a broker generally has a right to a commission when the contract of sale is executed or, if the contract is subject to conditions, when the conditions are satisfied, despite the fact that the sale does not take place. Traditionally, it made no difference whether the nonoccurrence of the sale was due to the seller or the buyer. However, in a minority of states, the broker is not entitled to a commission when the buyer, after entering into a contract, defaults ("no sale, no commission" rule), but the broker may be entitled to a share of any recovery gained by the seller from the defaulting buyer (e.g., retention of a deposit).

While entering into a contract usually establishes that the buyer is both ready and willing, when the buyer's contractual duty to pay is subject to a condition precedent, the failure of that condition to be met will prevent the broker from being entitled to the commission.

b. Buyer's agent

More recently, a real estate broker may serve as the buyer's agent. Typically, such an agent also receives a commission-based fee in an amount similar to the selling agent.

c. Dual agent

A dual agent serves as agent for both the buyer and seller of real property. Many states prohibit a person from serving as a dual agent, due to the likelihood of a conflict of interest.

d. Transaction brokers

In a few states, unless the parties to a real estate transaction specify otherwise in a written contract, the broker serves as a facilitator of the transaction but does not act as an agent for either the seller or the buyer. As a transaction broker, the broker may be subject to statutory rules as well as some ethical duties, such as fair dealing, honesty, care and competence, in assisting the parties with the transaction (e.g., securing a title search).

C. DELIVERY AND RECORDING OF DEED

To transfer a real property interest, the grantor must demonstrate the intent to make a present transfer of the interest (e.g., delivery of the deed) and the grantee must accept the interest. In addition, pursuant to the Statute of Frauds, the transfer of a real property interest must be evidenced by a writing (e.g., a valid deed). Finally, the grantee may be able to protect his property interest against others' claims by recording the deed.

1. Intent to Transfer (Delivery)

The grantor must, at the time of transfer, intend to make a present transfer of a property interest to the grantee. Note that the interest itself may be a future interest, such as when a parent retains a life estate in a residence and transfers a remainder interest to an adult child.

Typically, this intent is manifested by delivery of the deed. Delivery may be completed by physically handing or mailing the deed to the grantee or the grantee's agent. However, intent can be implied from the words and conduct of the grantor, such as when the grantor drafts and records a deed.

Although it is often stated that a deed must be delivered in order for a real property interest to pass (i.e., a delivery requirement), the term "delivery" is used as shorthand for the existence of the necessary grantor intent. Physical transfer of a deed is not required and is not conclusive evidence of the grantor's intent.

a. Retention of deed by grantor

When the grantor keeps the deed, intent to transfer is not presumed. Instead, parol evidence is admissible to establish whether the grantor had the intent to make a present transfer of the property interest.

b. Transfer of deed to grantee

Transfer of a deed to the grantee creates a presumption that the grantor intended to make a present transfer of the property interest. Parol evidence is admissible to show that the grantor lacks such intent (e.g., the grantor intended only to create a mortgage not to effect an outright transfer). However, when the grantor transferred the deed to the grantee subject to an oral condition (i.e., a condition that does not appear in the deed), parol evidence is not admissible and the condition is not enforceable.

c. Transfer of deed to third party

1) Grantor's agent

When the grantor transfers the deed to her own agent (e.g., an attorney), the transfer is treated as if the grantor had retained the deed, even when the grantor has instructed the agent to deliver the deed to the grantee at some future time or upon the happening of an event. Until the grantor's agent delivers the deed to the grantee, the grantor can demand that the agent ignore the prior instruction and return the deed to the grantor.

2) Grantee's agent

When the grantor transfers the deed to the grantee's agent, the transfer is treated as if it had been made to the grantee herself.

3) Independent agent—gift

If the grantor purportedly gives property to a grantee through a third party and places a condition on the transfer of the deed by the third party to the grantee, whether delivery has taken place depends on the grantor's language. If the grantor retains an absolute right to recover the deed, then no valid delivery exists because transfer of title was not clearly intended.

Example 1: A executes a deed that transfers real property to B. The deed itself contains no conditions. A gives the deed to C to hold and says, "Give this deed to B on his 21st birthday, unless I ask for the deed back before then." Because A retained an absolute right to recover the deed, A did not have the intent to make a present transfer.

If the grantor does not retain a right to retrieve the deed, then the key is whether the grantor intends to make a present gift of a property interest. If so, the grantor cannot later void the gift. Instead, the conditional transfer is treated as creating a future property interest in the grantee.

Example 2: A executes a deed that transfers real property to B. The deed itself contains no conditions. A gives the deed to an independent third party, C, and says, "I want B to have this property when she has her first child. Please give the deed to her then." Since A gave C the deed with the intent of presently creating an executory interest in B, B currently has an executory interest in the real property.

When the third party's transfer of the deed to the grantee is conditioned on the death of the grantor, the grantor's transfer of the deed to the third party must evidence the intent to make a present gift. When the grantor's intent is that the gift itself be effective only upon the grantor's death, the transfer can be ineffective due to a failure to comply with the requirements for a testamentary transfer (i.e., the Statute of Wills).

Example 3: A executes a deed that transfers real property to B. The deed itself contains no conditions. A gives the deed to an independent third party, C, saying, "I want B to have this property upon my death. Please give the deed to her then." Because A gave C the deed with the intent of presently creating a remainder interest in B, the transfer is effective.

Example 4: A executes a deed that transfers real property to B. The deed itself contains no conditions. A gives the deed to an independent third party, C, saying, "I want B to have this property if she outlives me. Please give the deed to her then." Because A gave C the deed with the intent of making a testamentary transfer (i.e., requiring that B survive A in order to take the property), the transfer is ineffective unless the requirements for a testamentary transfer were satisfied.

4) Independent agent—contract

When a contract for the sale of real property calls for the seller to give the deed to an independent third party (i.e., an escrow agent) and conditions the release of the deed to the buyer on the happening of an event, typically payment of the purchase price, the escrow agent is obligated to transfer the deed to the buyer if and when the condition occurs.

a) Retrieval by grantor

When there is a written contract, the grantor cannot require the escrow agent to return the deed prior to the failure of the condition to occur. When the contract is oral, the grantor can reclaim the deed from the escrow agent because the Statute of Frauds requires a writing for a land sale contract to be enforceable.

b) Escrow agent

When the escrow agent delivers the deed to the buyer prior to the performance of the condition, title to the property remains with the seller. This is true even when the buyer then transfers the property to a third party, even a person who purchases the property in good faith (i.e., a bona fide purchaser). An exception exists when the seller permits the buyer to possess the property.

c) Time of transfer

In general, title to the property remains in the seller until the condition is satisfied. Once the condition is satisfied, title automatically vests in the buyer. The date of transfer can relate back to the date that the grantor deposited the deed in escrow when, before the condition is satisfied, the grantor dies, becomes incapacitated or marries, or the grantee dies.

d. Acceptance

Acceptance is required for a transfer to be complete, and the grantee is generally presumed to have accepted any beneficial conveyance. Acceptance relates back to the time the deed was transferred, unless a bona fide purchaser or creditor of the grantor would be negatively affected by doing so.

If the grantee rejects the deed, no title passes and the grantor holds the title. If the grantee accepts the deed and then changes his mind even a moment later, however, an entirely new deed must be created in order for the grantee to convey the title back to the original grantor.

2. Valid Deed

Valid deeds abide by the Statute of Frauds and include all necessary terms, such as the grantor's signature, named grantee, words of transfer, and a description of the property. Unlike a contract, **consideration is not required.**

a. Parties

The **grantor** and **grantee** must be identified. In addition, the grantor's signature is required, but in most states, it need not be witnessed nor acknowledged (notarized). The grantee need not sign the deed.

A deed that does not identify the grantee is ineffective until the grantee's name is added or determined.

Example: A executed a deed conveying Blackacre "to my neighbors." Until the intended neighbors are determined by extrinsic evidence, the deed has no effect.

b. Words of transfer

The portion of a deed that contains the words that transfer an interest from the grantor to the grantee is called a "granting clause" (e.g., "do grant and convey"). Any language evidencing a present intent to transfer will suffice.

c. Description of property

The description of the property must be reasonably definite, but extrinsic evidence is admissible to clarify. A habendum clause (e.g., "to have and to hold") in a deed defines the interest conveyed. When there is an irreconcilable difference between the granting clause and the habendum clause, the granting clause prevails.

Descriptions by metes and bounds or by street address are acceptable but not required to sufficiently describe the property. When there is a conflict between descriptions of the property in the deed, descriptions based on monuments (e.g., from oak tree east to tool shed) are given priority over area descriptions (e.g., "100 acres").

Fraudulent documents are ineffective to convey title, even if they are relied upon by bona fide purchasers. Deeds executed through duress, mistake, or undue influence, or by minors or persons who are otherwise incapacitated, are deemed voidable.

3. Recording Act

A deed need not be recorded to be valid and convey good title. The common law rule was "first in time, first in right," meaning that a grantee could not lose title to a subsequent grantee.

All states have enacted recording acts, which establish priorities among conflicting claims to land and promote certainty of title. Nearly all types of property interests may be recorded, including easements, covenants, leases, and mortgages. Some state statutes also require that the grantor acknowledge the deed before a notary public, in an attempt to prevent fraudulent transfers.

a. Types of statutes

The three types of recording statutes are notice, race, and race-notice.

> **EXAM NOTE:** Notice and race-notice statutes are the most frequently tested types of recording statutes on the MBE.

1) Notice statute

A purchaser need only purchase without notice of the prior interest to prevail under a notice statute. (See *infra* for a discussion of what constitutes notice.) Notice statutes tend to protect subsequent purchasers against interest holders who could have, but failed to record documents describing their interests.

> **EXAM NOTE:** Notice statutes are commonly tested on the MBE and usually contain words like "in good faith" or "without notice."

> **Example of a notice statute:** "No conveyance or mortgage of real property shall be good against subsequent purchasers for value and *without notice* unless the same be recorded according to law."

> **EXAM NOTE:** Remember that a bona fide purchaser need not record in order to prevail over a prior interest in a notice jurisdiction, but must record to prevail against a subsequent purchaser.

2) Race statute

A minority of states have race statutes, when the purchaser who records first prevails, regardless of his knowledge of any prior conflicting interests.

> **Example of a race statute:** "No conveyance or mortgage of real property shall be good against subsequent purchasers for value unless the same be *first recorded* according to law."

3) Race-notice statute

A race-notice statute requires a subsequent purchaser to take the interest without notice of a prior conflicting interest **and** be the first to record.

Example of a race-notice statute: "No conveyance or mortgage of real property shall be good against subsequent purchasers for value and *without notice* who shall *first record*."

b. Paid value

Only a grantee who pays value for an interest in real property is entitled to protection under the recording statutes.

1) Mortgages

Mortgagees are considered to have "paid value" and are protected by the recording acts, unless the mortgage is not given simultaneously with a loan (such as when the mortgage is given after the loan is created).

2) Judgment liens

Creditors are protected only against claims that arise after a judgment lien against the debtor is recorded, unless otherwise indicated by statute. However, the majority of jurisdictions protect purchasers of property at a judicial sale against all unrecorded interests subject to the recording act.

Example: B purchases Blackacre from A (the record owner), but B does not record the deed. C, a creditor of A, not knowing of the deed to B, then records a judgment lien against Blackacre. A judicial sale of Blackacre is scheduled. A sells Blackacre to D, who promptly records the deed.

In this example, C is protected against D's claim because D purchased after C recorded the judgment lien. In the majority of jurisdictions, C is not protected against B's unrecorded interest (which preceded the recording of C's lien) unless C purchases Blackacre at the judicial sale (in which case C takes A's original title).

3) Donees, heirs, and devisees

Grantees who acquire title of property by gift, intestacy, or devise are not protected by the recording act against prior claims, even those who fail to record their claims to the same property.

Example: A sells Blackacre to B, who forgets to record the deed. In the interim, A gives a deed to his daughter, C, who promptly records her deed. C will not defeat B's ownership because C did not pay value for the property.

4) Shelter rule

Grantors who are protected by the recording act protect (or "shelter") their grantees who would otherwise be unprotected. The **exception** to the shelter rule is that a purchaser who is not a bona fide purchaser cannot convey to a bona fide purchaser and then buy back the property to obtain the status of a bona fide purchaser.

c. Notice

As discussed *supra*, only purchasers who give value in good faith and without notice of a prior claim will prevail in notice or race-notice jurisdictions. "Notice" can be actual, by inquiry, or constructive.

1) Actual notice

A grantee possessing actual, personal knowledge of a prior interest cannot prevail under a notice or race-notice recording statute.

2) Inquiry notice

If a reasonable investigation would have disclosed the existence of prior claims, then the grantee is considered to possess inquiry notice, and cannot prevail against those prior claims. The purchaser is charged with whatever knowledge a reasonable inspection of the property would have disclosed. In most states, taking a quitclaim deed does not in itself create inquiry notice of prior claims.

> **EXAM NOTE:** Examples of situations that typically give rise to inquiry notice on the MBE are (i) when someone other than the grantor has possession of the property (e.g., a tenant) or (ii) when documents are referenced in the chain of title.

Example: A's deed to B references a restrictive covenant entered into by A and B at the time of the deed. The deed is recorded, but the covenant is not contained in the deed. Any purchaser in A's chain of title will be charged with knowledge of the covenant and its contents.

3) Constructive notice

Grantees are held to have constructive notice of all prior conveyances that were properly recorded.

a) Tract index

All properties in a tract index system are listed by location on a separate page that includes all conveyances and encumbrances.

b) Grantor—grantee indexes

Each yearly index is usually alphabetized by the last names of grantors and grantees.

When searching the chain of title, the potential purchaser must first search for the grantor's name as a grantee (to ensure good title) in the grantee index, and must then search for the name of the grantor's grantor must be searched as a grantee, and so on, until the title has been searched back to its inception (common law rule) or as far back as the recording statute provides. Some states have search cut-off dates. Then, the grantors are searched as grantors to verify the chain of title.

c) Related searches

Title searches also should include a search of tax assessment and judgment lien records, as well as the marriage, divorce, and probate records for every named grantor and grantee.

d. Priorities

Interests are placed in order of priority based on the relevant statute (notice, race, and race-notice). The protected interest that is first in time is satisfied first, followed by the junior interests in order of time.

e. Rule application

Example 1: First, O conveys Blackacre to A, but A does not record. Second, O then conveys Blackacre to B, who has no notice of the earlier conveyance to A. Next, A records. Then, B records. B sues A to quiet title in Blackacre. What is the result?

i) Under a race statute, the first in time to record prevails. In the situation above, A wins because A was the first to record.

ii) Under a notice statute, regardless of who records first, those who in good faith purchase without notice prevail. So, in the above scenario, B wins because B took without notice.

iii) In a race-notice jurisdiction, B is unable to prove that he had both no notice **and** recorded first. Because A recorded first, A wins.

Example 2: First, O conveys an easement in Blackacre to A, but A does not record. Second, O then conveys Blackacre in fee simple absolute to B, who knows of the earlier conveyance to A. Next, B records. Then, A records. B sues A for title to Blackacre. What is the result?

i) Under a race statute, B wins, and the easement is extinguished because B recorded first.

ii) Under a notice statute, A wins because B had notice of A's rights at the time of purchase.

iii) In a race-notice jurisdiction, A prevails and can enforce the easement against B because B is unable to show that he both recorded first **and** purchased without notice of A's prior claim.

Example 3: First, O promises A in writing that O will use Blackacre only for residential purposes, and the parties intend that this burden will run with the land. A does not record the promise. O then conveys Blackacre in fee simple absolute to B, who has no notice of O's earlier promise to A. Next, B records. Then, A records the promise. B then conveys a fee simple absolute estate in Blackacre to C, who has actual knowledge of O's promise to A. C uses Blackacre for non-residential purposes. A sues C to enforce O's promise to A, seeking damages and an injunction. What is the result?

i) Under a race statute, C wins, even though C records after A. In this situation, A's recording is outside C's chain of title, so it does not constitute "winning the race" for the purposes of a race statute. Also, because B's interest in Blackacre "wins" over A's, and C relies on B's title, C wins.

ii) Under a notice statute, C wins even though C had notice. The shelter doctrine shelters C by making B's title marketable, because B was a good-faith purchaser. Therefore, B passes his title to C, and C takes B's status as a good-faith purchaser.

iii) In a race-notice jurisdiction, C wins because the shelter doctrine applies.

f. Chain-of-title problems

1) Wild deed

Although an instrument is recorded and indexed in the recording office, it may not be recorded in such a way as to give notice to subsequent purchasers (i.e., the deed may not be in the "chain of title"). A deed not within the chain of title is a "wild deed."

> **Example 1:** First, O conveys Blackacre to A, but A does not record. Second, A conveys Blackacre to B, and B records. O then conveys Blackacre to C, who has no notice of the earlier conveyances to A or B. Next, C records. Then, A records the deed from O to A. B sues A for title to Blackacre. What is the result?

i) Under a race statute, C prevails even though B recorded the deed from A to B before C recorded the deed from O to C, because the deed from A to B was a "wild deed," outside C's chain of title. In performing a standard title search, C would have searched in the grantor index for deeds listing O as the grantor from the date the deed granting Blackacre to O was executed to the date C recorded the deed from O to C. No deed from O to A would have been discovered in such a search, and without finding a deed from O to A, B would not be expected to look for a deed from A to B.

ii) Under a notice statute, C prevails because he had no actual notice of the conveyances from O to A and from A to B, and the deed from A to B did not give him constructive notice because it was a wild deed.

iii) In a race-notice jurisdiction, C prevails for a combination of the two reasons above: C had no actual or constructive notice of O's deed to A, and B's prior recording of the deed from A to B does not count because it is a wild deed.

2) Deed recorded late

> **Example 2:** O conveys Blackacre to A, but A does not record. Next, O conveys Blackacre to B, who has actual notice of the conveyance from O to A, and B records. Then, A records. Next, B conveys to C, who has no actual notice of the O-to-A conveyance. C sues A for title to Blackacre. What is the result?

i) Under a race statute, C prevails even though A recorded the deed, because A's deed was recorded outside C's chain of title. Remember that under the standard title search, C would only research the grantor index under O's name until the date that B recorded the deed from O to B. Because O's deed to A was filed after that date, it is not considered "duly recorded" for the purposes of a race statute.

    ii) Under a notice statute, C wins because C had no notice and because A's deed was recorded outside C's chain of title.

    iii) In a race-notice jurisdiction, C wins because both race and notice requirements are met.

3) Deed recorded early (estoppel by deed)

Under the "estoppel by deed" doctrine, a grantor who conveys an interest to land by warranty deed before actually owning it is estopped from later denying the effectiveness of her deed. Consequently, when the grantor does acquire ownership of the land, the after-acquired title is transferred automatically to the prior grantee.

However, under the majority rule, a subsequent purchaser from the same grantor who takes without notice can obtain good title—despite the doctrine of estoppel by deed—in a notice or race-notice jurisdiction. The purchaser is generally required to search the grantee index for a grantor's name only as far back as the date on which the grantor's name appears as a grantee (i.e., the date on which the grantor acquired the property). That date is the earliest date that a grantor's name must be searched on the grantor index for a conveyance by the grantor. The recording of a transfer made by the grantor before that date is not treated as giving the purchaser constructive notice of the transfer.

4) Title insurance

Title insurance protects owners or lenders against the actual monetary loss due to such matters as title defects and lien problems. Title defects are most often created as the result of errors in the title-examining process, as well as title-recording errors. Forged instruments and undelivered deeds also create title defects because they do not transfer title and are void.

Lien problems result from the invalidity or unenforceability of mortgage liens. Additionally, tax liens and judgments create defects that do not allow for the proper transference of title.

4. Types of Deeds

a. General warranty deed

The grantor of a general warranty deed guarantees that he holds six covenants of title, which are discussed below.

1) Present covenants

Present covenants embodied in the general warranty deed are the covenant of seisin, the covenant of the right to convey, and the covenant against encumbrances.

The covenant of seisin warrants that the grantor owns the land as it is described in the deed. The covenant of the right to convey guarantees that the grantor has the right to transfer title. The covenant against encumbrances guarantees that the deed contains no undisclosed encumbrances.

2) Future covenants

Future covenants run with the land, and the statute of limitations does not begin to run until the grantee's rights are encroached. The grantor of a general warranty deed promises to protect the grantee against subsequent lawful claims of title or encroachment (the covenant of quiet enjoyment and the covenant of warranty).

In some jurisdictions, the grantor also promises to do whatever is necessary to pass title to the grantee if it is later determined that the grantor omitted something required to pass valid title (future covenant of further assurances).

3) Breach of covenant

a) Time of breach

Breach of the present covenants occurs at the time of conveyance. A breach of the covenants of seisin and right to convey arises when the grantor is not the owner. A property that is encumbered at the time of conveyance creates a breach of the covenant against encumbrances. In most states, these present covenants do not run with the land. Consequently, a subsequent grantee cannot sue to enforce them against the original grantor. However, some states allow a remote grantee to sue the original grantor for breach of the covenant against encumbrances. *See* Uniform Land Transactions Act § 2-312.

Conversely, a breach of future covenants occurs only upon interference with possession and runs to successive grantees. The party seeking liability must provide the covenantor with notice of the claim.

b) Recovery

A buyer can recover for breach of the covenant against encumbrances the lesser of the difference in value between title with and without the defect, or the cost of removing the encumbrance.

Recovery for the covenants of enjoyment or warranty is the lesser of the purchase price or the cost of defending title.

Recovery for the covenants of seisin, right to convey, or further assurances is the lesser of the purchase price or the cost of perfecting title.

c) After-acquired title

When a person who purports to transfer real property that he does not own subsequently becomes the owner of that property, the after-acquired title doctrine provides that title to the property automatically vests in the transferee. Most often, this doctrine is applied to the grantor of a warranty deed. A related doctrine, estoppel by deed, prevents the grantor from asserting ownership of the after-acquired property. For the interplay of estoppel by deed and the recording acts, *see* § III.C.3.f.3), Deed recorded early (estoppel by deed), *supra*.

b. Special warranty deed

A special warranty deed contains the same covenants of title but only warrants against defects arising during the time the grantor has title.

c. Quitclaim deed

Unlike a warranty deed, a quitclaim deed promises **no covenants of title.**

A common form of quitclaim deed is the tax deed, which is used by government authorities when selling properties seized for nonpayment of taxes.

The grantee in a quitclaim deed (or a grant deed or warranty deed) receives no better title than what the grantor possessed.

D. FIXTURES

A fixture is tangible personal property (i.e., chattel) that is attached to real property in a manner that it is treated as part of the real property when determining its ownership.

1. Structures and Items Incorporated into Structures

Structures built on real property (e.g., walls, dams) and materials incorporated into a structure (e.g., bricks used in making a wall) become part of the realty. The owner of the real property is generally also the owner of the structure on the real property (e.g., an improvement), including any materials used in constructing the structure. Once incorporated into the structure, such materials become an integral part of the real property and are not subject to a separate security interest. UCC § 9-334(a).

2. Attachment of Chattel

The fee simple owner of real property is free, subject to governmental land-use restrictions, to make improvements to the real property, including fixtures. For the holder of a life estate or a tenant, the right to make improvements to real property (ameliorative waste) is somewhat circumscribed. *See* § I.A.4.d.3, Ameliorative waste, *supra*, regarding life estate holders, and § II.B.2., Duty to Avoid Waste, *supra*, regarding tenants.

3. Removal of Chattel

a. Fee simple owner of real property

A fee simple owner of real property typically intends for the chattel to become a fixture by attaching chattel to real property. Such intent is judged by applying an objective, reasonable person standard that examines such factors as the importance of the chattel to the real property, whether the chattel was specially designed for use on the real property, and the amount of damage to the real property that removal of the chattel would cause.

When the chattel is a fixture, the buyer of the real property is generally entitled to the chattel unless the seller reserves the right to remove the fixture in the contract of sale. Similarly, the mortgagee is entitled to the chattel upon foreclosure of the mortgage unless the mortgage provides otherwise.

b. Other possessors of real property

Absent an agreement to the contrary, a non-freehold tenant, such as a tenant under a tenancy for years or a periodic tenancy, can remove a fixture that the tenant has attached to the leased property if (i) the leased property can be and is restored to its former condition after the removal, and (ii) the removal and restoration is made within a reasonable time. If the leased premises cannot be restored to its former condition, then the tenant can remove the fixture only with the consent of the landlord. This rule applies to commercial tenants and the removal of trade fixtures, as well as to residential tenants and the removal of personal items, such as bookshelves attached to the wall. Restatement (Second) of Property: Landlord and Tenant § 12.2(4), (5).

A licensee and a life tenant are generally also subject to this rule.

A reasonable time for removal generally does not extend beyond the termination of the lease, but it may do so when (i) the termination is not due to a breach by the tenant, and (ii) the date of termination is not foreseeable by the tenant sufficiently far enough in advance to permit removal before the termination of the lease or unless equitable factors (such as illness of the tenant) justify an extension. Restatement (Second) of Property: Landlord and Tenant § 12.3.

c. Trespassers

Under common law, a trespasser (such as a holdover tenant) is prohibited from removing a fixture attached to the land. Many jurisdictions now allow a trespasser to remove a fixture that was attached in good faith or at least to recover the value added to the property by the improvement.

d. Mortgagee versus secured party

When there is a conflict between the mortgagee of real property and the holder of a security interest in a fixture attached to the real property, the general rule is that the first to record has priority. An exception exists when the security interest is a purchase-money security interest (i.e., a security interest given in connection with the acquisition of the goods). In such cases, the secured party who records her security interest before or **within 20 days** after the goods become a fixture has priority over a prior recorded mortgage. UCC § 9-334.

e. Sale of fixtures by property owner

A contract for the sale of a structure or its materials is a contract for the sale of goods governed by the UCC when the structure or material is to be severed by the seller. A contract for the sale of other things that are attached to real property and are capable of severance without material harm to the real property is a contract for the sale of goods regardless of whether the seller or buyer effects the severance. UCC § 2-107(1), (2).

E. CONVEYANCE BY WILL AND BY OPERATION OF LAW

Real property can be conveyed by will and by statutes that govern intestate succession for property that does not pass by will.

1. In General

A transfer of ownership of real property at death through a will can take effect through a specific devise (e.g., "I leave my residence to my son") or residuary clause (e.g., "I leave all other property to my daughter") when the property is not specifically mentioned in the will. When a decedent does not leave a valid will or the will does not specify a taker of the real property, the property is transferred pursuant to the applicable state law of intestate succession. While the intestacy rules vary by state, preference is typically given to the decedent's immediate family (e.g., spouse, children). When a decedent has no heir, as determined under state law, the property typically escheats to the state.

2. Ademption

A devise of real property may fail (or be "adeemed") because the testator no longer owns the property upon death (i.e., because the property was sold, destroyed, or given away before death). If the testator gives the property to the intended beneficiary while the testator is still alive, then the devise is adeemed by satisfaction. Once a devise is adeemed, the beneficiary named in the will takes nothing.

> **EXAM NOTE:** Remember that ademption can occur only with a specific devise, such as real property, and not with a general devise, such as money.

> **Example:** A executes a will under which Blackacre is devised to B but then sells Blackacre to C. When A dies, the gift is adeemed and B takes nothing.

3. Lapse

Under common law, a devise of real property can also fail (lapse) if the beneficiary under a will dies before the testator and no alternate beneficiary is named. When the testator indicates a clear intent that the devise survive the death of the beneficiary, the devise will not fail. In addition, all jurisdictions have anti-lapse statutes, which prevent a gift from lapsing if the gift is made to the parties specified by the statute (usually immediate relatives of the testator). A lapsed gift becomes part of the residuary estate.

> **Example:** By will, A devises her car to B, Blackacre to C, and the remainder of her property (the residuary estate) to D. A does not name any alternate beneficiaries. If C dies before A and the devise does not qualify for protection under the anti-lapse statute, then Blackacre becomes part of the residuary estate and passes to D, along with all of A's property other than the car, which goes to B. If C is related to A such that the anti-lapse statute applies, then Blackacre passes to C's descendants.

When a devise is made to a class (e.g., "my children") and one member of the class dies before the testator, only the surviving class members take the property. However, if an anti-lapse statute applies because the class members were related to the testator, then the descendants of the predeceased class member also share in the devise. Most states apply the anti-lapse rule first before applying the class gift rule.

4. Exoneration of Liens

Under the exoneration of liens doctrine, if a testator makes a specific devise of real property that is subject to an encumbrance, such as a mortgage or a lien, the devisee is entitled to have the land "exonerated" by payment of the encumbrance from the remaining assets in the testator's estate. Although this is the majority view, many states have abolished this doctrine. In such states, the property passes subject to the encumbrance unless the will specifically requires payment of the encumbrance.

5. **Abatement**

A devise is reduced or abated when the assets of the estate are insufficient to pay all debts and satisfy all devises. If the testator does not choose to indicate her intended order of abatement, then gifts are sacrificed to satisfy funeral expenses, expenses of administration, and creditors' claims in the following order:

i) Property not disposed of by will;

ii) Residuary devises;

iii) General devises; and

iv) Specific devises.

Some states further break down abatement to favor various devisees, such as the testator's relatives or surviving spouse, or a type of property (e.g., real property, cash), within a particular class (e.g., specific devises).

a. **Specific**

A specific devise is a devise of property that can be distinguished with reasonable accuracy from other property that is part of the testator's estate (e.g., a car, a house).

Example: "I give my diamond wedding ring to A."

b. **General**

A general devise is a devise of personal property that the testator intends to be satisfied from the general assets of his estate.

Example: "I give $100,000 to A."

c. **Demonstrative**

A demonstrative devise is a general devise that is to be paid from a particular source.

Example: "I give $100,000 from my First Federal bank account to A."

A demonstrative devise is treated as a specific devise for abatement purposes to the extent that it can be satisfied from the specified source, and otherwise it is treated as a general devise.

d. **Residuary**

A residual devise is a devise of the estate remaining after all claims against the estate and all specific, general, and demonstrative devises have been satisfied.

Example: "I give all the rest and residue of my property, wheresoever situated, whensoever acquired, and whether known to me or not, to A."

e. Pro rata abatement

Within each class, the amount abated is allocated on a pro rata basis among the devisees in proportion to the amount of property each would have received if a full distribution had been made.

> **Example:** In her will, a testator made a general devise of $10,000 to her daughter and a general devise of $20,000 to her son. At the time of her death, the testator's estate consisted of $21,000 in cash. The devises exceed the estate by $9,000 ($10,000 + $20,000) – $21,000). The daughter's devise is reduced by $3,000 ($9,000 x ($10,000/$30,000)) to $7,000 ($10,000 – $3,000). The son's devise is reduced by $6,000 ($9,000 x ($20,000/$30,000) to $14,000 ($20,000 – $6,000).

F. CONVEYANCE BY TRUST

A trust is essentially a situation in which property is managed by one person or entity for the benefit of another.

1. Private Trusts

The trust must have:

i)   A **settlor**, the person who creates the trust;

ii) A **trustee**, the person or entity who holds legal title to the property;

iii) **Res**, the property that is subject to the trust; and

iv) **Beneficiaries**, those *identifiable* persons for whose benefit the trust is created and who hold equitable title to the property.

An inter vivos trust is created when the settlor conveys his property (res) to the trustee while the settlor is alive. Alternatively, the settlor may simply declare that he is holding certain property in trust for certain beneficiaries, without there being an actual conveyance of the property. Remember that any conveyance of real property must satisfy the Statute of Frauds.

Another form of conveyance occurs when the settlor creates a trust by language in his will and transfers the property by devise in his will. This type of trust is called a "testamentary trust" and comes into being only on the death of the settlor. Finally, the settlor may create an inter vivos trust but not fund the trust until his death by devise in his will. In this case, property "pours over" into the trust.

2. Charitable Trusts

A differentiating factor between a private trust and a charitable trust is the beneficiaries. As noted above, a private trust must have identifiable beneficiaries, whereas in a charitable trust, the beneficiaries must be reasonably numerous and unidentifiable. Another important distinction is that the Rule Against Perpetuities does not apply to trusts that are entirely charitable. Moreover, if a charitable trust no longer serves the purpose for which it was created, then the court may redirect the trust to a different purpose. This is called the "doctrine of cy pres." The attorney general of the state also has the power to enforce a charitable trust but not a private trust.

G. RESTRAINTS ON ALIENATION

1. Restraints on Legal Interests

Generally, a restraint on the right of alienation is void when it purports to prohibit alienation of the estate and render any conveyance by the grantee void. If the restraint is valid, then any attempt to alienate the property in violation of the restraint is null and void. If void, the restraint is rejected, and the property could be alienated in violation of the void restraint. Restatement (Second) of Property § 4.1.

Sometimes restraints restrict the power to transfer the interest only under certain specific circumstances. In such cases, the restraint may be valid if it is for a limited time and for a reasonable purpose. However, any restraint based on a person's race, ethnicity, or religion is not enforceable. Further, such discriminatory restraints are considered state action and are forbidden by the Fourteenth Amendment. In addition, the federal Fair Housing Act prohibits housing discrimination on the basis of race, color, religion, gender, disability, familial status, and national origin. Among the prohibited activities are refusing to rent or sell housing or setting different terms or conditions for the sale or rental of a dwelling on a prohibited basis. There are various exceptions, including an exemption for a residential sale by an owner and a lease of an owner-occupied dwelling with four or fewer units.

a. Forms of restraint

1) Disabling restraint

A disabling restraint is a prohibition on the transfer of the property interest by its owner. Such a restraint is always void.

2) Forfeiture restraint

A forfeiture restraint effects the loss of property (i.e., the property is forfeited) if the interest owner attempts to transfer his interest. Such a restraint on a future interest or a life estate can be valid.

3) Promissory restraint

A promissory restraint is a promise by the property interest holder not to transfer the property interest. Such a restraint is enforceable by an injunction against the transferor/promisor to prevent the transfer or by a suit seeking damages from the transferor/promisor for having violated the promise. Such a restraint on a life estate can be valid.

b. Permissible restraints

A restraint that is limited in time and purpose may be valid. In addition, a right of first refusal, which gives the holder of the right the opportunity to purchase the property interest if sold, is usually upheld, as are restrictions on the transfer of a lease (e.g., a prohibition on assignment). Other permissible restraints are those found in commercial transactions when the basis for the restraint is found in the parties' contractual obligations.

Compare restraints on use: Unlike restraints on the transfer of legal property interests, restraints on the *use* of property (e.g., covenants) are generally permissible.

2.   Restraints on Equitable Interests

A restriction on the transferability of an equitable property interest (e.g., a beneficial property interest held in trust), such as a spendthrift clause, is valid.

IV.   DISPUTES ABOUT THE USE OF LAND

The most commonly tested disputes about the use of land revolve around use of another's land (by easement, profit, or license) or restriction of use of one's own land (by covenants running with the land or equitable servitude). Other disputes concern who has the right to own or possess land; ownership is decided by a quiet-title action, while possession (often between a landlord and tenant) is decided by an action for ejectment.

A.   EASEMENTS

An easement is the right held by one person to make specific, limited use of land owned by another. The land that is subject to the easement is the servient estate, whereas the land that benefits from an easement on a servient estate is the dominant estate.

> **EXAM NOTE:** When a fact pattern involves the use of another's land, consider three questions:
>
> 1. Was an easement created?
>
> 2. If so, was the easement terminated?
>
> 3. What is the scope of the easement?

1.   Classification of Easements

a.   Easements by grant and reservation

An affirmative easement gives another the right to use the land for a specific purpose.

An easement by reservation is created when a grantor conveys land but reserves an easement right in that land for his own use and benefit (and not for a third party).

b.   Easements appurtenant and profit in gross

Easements are presumed to be appurtenant (i.e., tied to the land) unless there are clear facts to the contrary. The benefits of an easement must correspond directly to the use and enjoyment of the possessor of the dominant estate.

An easement is in gross if it was granted to benefit a particular person (as opposed to the land).

> **Example:** A owns lakefront property and grants B, who lives in a town across the lake, an easement to gain access to the lake at a certain point on A's property. A created an easement in gross because it benefits B, not any land owned by B.

2. Types of Easements

a. Express easements

An express easement arises when it is affirmatively created by the parties in a writing that is in compliance with the Statute of Frauds.

b. Easements by necessity and implication

1) Easement by necessity

An easement by necessity is generally created only when property is virtually useless (e.g., landlocked) without the benefit of an easement across neighboring property. In addition, for an easement by necessity to be created, both the dominant and servient estates must have been under common ownership in the past. Also, the necessity must have arisen at the time that the property was severed and the two estates were created. However, unlike an easement by implication, a quasi-easement need not have existed at the time that both estates were under common ownership (i.e., there need not be a showing of prior use). Restatement (Third) of Property: Servitudes § 2.15.

Example: B owns an undeveloped parcel of land, which B subdivides into two lots. B sells one of the lots to A and retains the other lot for himself. The only access to a public road from the lot purchased by A is through the lot retained by B. Even though the deed makes no mention of an easement across B's lot and there has not been a prior path from A's lot across B's lot to the public road, A has an easement by necessity across B's lot to the road.

EXAM NOTE: On the exam, if it is not absolutely clear that an easement is required for use, then it is not an easement by necessity.

2) Easement by implication

If an easement was previously used on the servient estate by an earlier owner, then the court may find that the parties intended the easement to continue if the prior use was continuous, apparent (open and obvious), and reasonably necessary to the dominant land's use and enjoyment (distinguish from an easement by necessity, which requires strict necessity).

a) Quasi-use

Because an owner cannot have an easement on his own land, this is considered a "quasi" easement. The scope of a quasi-easement is determined by the prior use that gave rise to the easement, but it can change over time if the changes are reasonably foreseeable at the time of conveyance.

b) Recorded plat

Easements may also be implied without an existing use in a conveyance of lots sold in a subdivision with reference to a recorded plat or map that details streets leading to lots. An easement may be implied from a subdivision map or plat, may be created through eminent domain, and may arise by actual or implied dedication. Individuals who buy lots have an implied easement to be able to get to their lots that does not expire even if a public easement held by the city or county is vacated in the future.

c. Easements by prescription

Easements can be obtained by prescription similarly to the way land can be acquired by adverse possession. There must be continuous, actual, open, and hostile use for the statutory period (or 20 years). Unlike adverse possession, the use need not be exclusive (such as a public easement to access a beach).

The scope of an easement by prescription is limited to the nature and extent of the adverse use.

d. Easements by estoppel

Good-faith, reasonable, detrimental reliance on permission by a servient estate holder, may create an easement by estoppel to prevent unjust enrichment.

Example: A allows B to use a road on A's land to gain access to B's land, and B builds his house with the road being its main access point, improving the road with pavement and foliage. Thereafter, A tells B that he can use the road only if B pays $500; A closes off the road when B refuses. B likely has an easement by estoppel because he relied on the ability to use the road when he built his house, and unjust enrichment may otherwise result.

Distinguish this example from easement by prescription, which requires that the use be hostile (i.e., no permission was given). To prove an easement by estoppel, there must be permission to use the property, plus detrimental reliance on that permission (as in the example above).

e. Negative easements

A negative easement (or "restrictive covenant") prevents the owner from using land in particular ways. To be valid, a negative easement must be expressly created by a writing signed by the grantor, and it is typically recognized only in relation to restricting use of light, air, support, or stream water from an artificial flow.

Example: A conveys a lot adjacent to his own to B, with an agreement that no structure will be built that would obstruct the light and air of A's land. This is a negative easement of light and air because it deprives B from enjoying the property to the fullest extent. Negative easements are really restrictive covenants (see full discussion, *infra*).

3. Transfer

a. Easement appurtenant

An easement appurtenant is transferred with the land to which it relates. Consequently, the benefit is transferred automatically with the transfer of the dominant estate, and the burden likewise is transferred automatically with the transfer of the servient estate.

b. Easement in gross

Traditionally, an easement in gross could not be transferred, but most courts now look to the intent of the parties to determine whether the parties intended only the holder of the easement in gross to enjoy the right, in which case it is not transferable, or whether the parties intended the holder to be able to transfer it.

Whether a transferable easement in gross can be apportioned turns on whether the easement in gross is exclusive or non-exclusive. A non-exclusive easement may not be divided up, but an exclusive easement may be. However, the division of an exclusive easement in gross is subject to the one stock rule. Under this rule, the use that the transferees make of the easement collectively is limited by the use that the transferor made of the easement (i.e., his "stock").

4. Termination

a. Release

An easement can terminate by a writing that expressly releases the easement right and complies with the Statute of Frauds.

b. Merger

An easement is terminated if the owner of the easement acquires fee title to the underlying estate (and the easement is said to "merge" into the title). Under such circumstances, the easement is not automatically revived unless a new grant is made.

Note that the easement does not merge if the owner acquires less than fee title, and merger is applicable only to easements appurtenant.

c. Severance

Any attempt to convey an appurtenant easement separate from the land it benefits terminates (or "severs") the easement.

d. Abandonment

An easement can be terminated if the owner of the easement acts in an affirmative way that shows a clear intent to relinquish the easement right.

Mere statements of intent without affirmative conduct are insufficient to constitute abandonment but may constitute estoppel (*infra*). Mere non-use of the easement is also not sufficient to extinguish the easement right.

Example: B is the owner of an easement across A's land for access to a beach. B does not like the beach and builds a brick wall across his land, blocking the entranceway to the easement. B's easement is terminated by abandonment.

e. Destruction and condemnation

Destruction of a structure on the servient estate by natural forces can terminate an easement if the easement is related to the structure (e.g., access to a lighthouse). Condemnation of the servient estate also terminates an easement.

Note that some courts permit the holder of the easement to receive compensation because of the condemnation.

f. Prescription

If an easement holder fails to protect his easement against a trespasser for the statutory period, his easement right may be terminated by prescription.

g. Estoppel

If the servient estate owner changes position to his detriment in reliance on statements or conduct of the easement holder that the easement is abandoned, then the easement holder may be estopped from asserting the easement.

h. Sale to bona fide purchaser

If a **written easement** is granted but not recorded against the servient estate, then the easement is not enforceable against a bona fide purchaser (i.e., a purchaser with no notice of the easement). The easement is not actually terminated, but rather becomes unenforceable.

5. Scope of Easement

a. Express easements

The scope of an express easement is defined in the first instance by its terms. If the terms are ambiguous, courts look to the intent of the original parties, which may be indicated by the easement's original purpose.

When the language of an express easement is ambiguous, changes in the use of an easement are tested under a reasonableness standard, with the understanding that the original parties most likely contemplated not only its present use but also its future use.

b. Implied easements

The scope of an easement by necessity or implication is determined by the extent of the necessity. In other words, courts examine the circumstances surrounding the easement and will consider the easement's future foreseeable use, so long as any changes in use are reasonable. The scope of an easement by prescription is limited to the nature and extent of the adverse use.

6. Profits

A profit is an easement that confers the right to enter another's land and remove specific natural resources (such as oil, gas, minerals, timber, or game).

Although a profit can be either exclusive or non-exclusive, most are construed as non-exclusive. If the profit is exclusive, then the holder of the profit has an unlimited and exclusive right to take the subject matter of the profit from the land. If it is non-exclusive, then the right to take the profit is either limited by quantity, time, or use or shared with another. Exclusive rights may be assigned and apportioned, as long as the apportionment is not wholly inconsistent with the original agreement.

Non-exclusive rights are assignable, but apportionment is not permitted when the burden on the servient estate is increased. Under the "one stock" rule, the transferees are limited to the amount of material taken by the transferor (i.e., his "stock"), and this quantity is divided up by transferees taking the profit.

Profits are created and analyzed similarly to easements, except that profits cannot be created by necessity.

7. Licenses

As with an easement, a license is a non-possessory right to enter another's land for some delineated purpose. Unlike an easement, a license is freely revocable unless coupled with an interest or detrimentally relied on (e.g., if money is spent in furtherance of the license). Examples of licenses are tickets to amusement parks, theaters, or other public venues. A license coupled with an interest occurs when, for example, a grantor creates a life estate for A with the remainder to B. During A's life tenancy, B has an irrevocable license to enter the land and inspect for waste, because of his future interest in the land.

A license may be created without consideration or a writing. Because no writing is required, a license is created when there is an oral attempt to create an easement or written attempt otherwise fails due to the Statute of Frauds.

In addition to a specific revocation by the licensor, a license is revoked when the licensor dies or the servient estate is transferred. Traditionally, a license could not be transferred by the licensee, and the attempt to do so resulted in the loss of the license.

8. Duty to Maintain

The owner of the easement has the right and the duty to maintain the easement for its purpose unless otherwise agreed between the owner of the easement and the owner of the servient land. The duty to contribute, however, is dependent upon the reasonableness of the repair. Specifically, the repairing party must give the contributing parties adequate notification and a reasonable opportunity to participate in decisions regarding the repairs. Moreover, the repairs must be performed adequately, properly, and at a reasonable price. *See* Restatement (Third) of Property § 4.13 (2000).

B. COVENANTS RUNNING WITH THE LAND

Unlike easements, profits, and licenses (which grant affirmative rights to use land), real covenants and equitable servitudes restrict the right to use land. When damages are sought to enforce the covenant, the covenant is called a "real covenant." When an injunction is sought to enforce a covenant, it is called an "equitable servitude." The requirements discussed below are necessary for both the benefit and the burden to run with the land, unless otherwise indicated.

1. Requirements to Run

Covenants run with the land (subsequent owners may enforce or be burdened by the covenant).

> **EXAM NOTE:** The requirements for a covenant to run with the land have been tested on nearly every MBE.

a. Writing

For a covenant to be enforceable, it must first comply with the Statute of Frauds. The only exception is an implied reciprocal servitude, which does not require a writing.

b. Intent

The parties must intend for the rights and duties to run with the land. Look for either explicit language, like "and his heirs and assigns," or implication from the totality of the document and circumstances.

c. Touch and concern

The covenant must "touch and concern the land," which generally means that the person seeking enforcement must establish that the benefit or burden affects both the promisee and the promisor as owners of land and not merely as individuals.

Most courts would find that an affirmative covenant to maintain insurance for improvements on the land touches and concerns the servient estate. However, generally, most courts are hesitant to find that affirmative covenants touch and concern the land for fear that the covenant will unnecessarily encumber the land.

The modern trend shifts the burden by superseding the touch-and-concern requirement. Instead, the covenant is presumed valid unless it is contrary to public policy, imposes an unreasonable restraint on alienation or trade, or is unconscionable. If not, the covenant is valid unless illegal or unconstitutional. Restatement (Third) of Property: Servitudes § 3.2.

d. Notice—burden only

Under the recording acts, a subsequent purchaser without notice of a burdening covenant is not bound by it. Such notice can be constructive (recorded in the chain of title), actual (awareness that the covenant exists), or inquiry (duty to find out).

e. Privity

1) Horizontal privity—burden only

For the burden to run, the original parties to the covenant must have privity of estate at the time the agreement creating the covenant is entered into. This means that there must be some shared property interest apart from the covenant itself. (Note: Horizontal privity is not required for the benefit to run.)

2) Vertical privity

The successor to property can be held to the covenant (i.e., the burden runs) only if title to the entire servient estate (as measured durationally (e.g., a fee simple interest), not geographically (e.g., 20 acres)) can be traced back to the promisor. The successor to the property can enforce the covenant (i.e., the benefit runs) as long as the property interest possessed by the successor is at least some portion of the property interest held by the promisee. Consequently, a covenant granted by the holder of a fee simple interest cannot be enforced against a successor interest that holds only a life estate, but the life estate holder can enforce a covenant given to the holder of the fee simple interest.

3) Modern trend: no privity required

The Restatement of Property relies less on privity to determine running of the benefit and the burden than on a distinction between affirmative and negative covenants. The benefits and burdens of an affirmative covenant run to the successor of an estate of the same duration as the estate of the original party. Negative covenants, on the other hand, are analyzed similarly to easements.

f. Specific examples

There are certain burdens that come with their own specific problems. First, **money** that is used in connection with the land, such as association fees, as a general rule will run with the land. With **covenants not to compete**, although the burden of restricting land use touches and concerns the land, some courts have refused to permit the benefit to run with the land because the covenant does not affect the land's physical use. Finally, a **racially based covenant** that disallows an owner from transferring his property to another because of the person's race is never enforceable because to enforce it would violate the Fourteenth Amendment.

2. Equitable Servitudes

Equitable servitudes are covenants about land use that are enforced at equity by injunction.

a. Requirements

For a servitude to be enforced at equity, it must be in writing and meet the following requirements.

i) There must be **intent** for the restriction to be enforceable by successors in interest for the benefit to run and enforceable against successors in interest for the burden to run;

ii) The servitude must **touch and concern** the land; and

iii) The person against whom the servitude is to be enforced must have notice (whether **actual, record, or inquiry notice**) of the servitude.

Unlike with a real covenant, with an equitable servitude, a party seeking to enforce it need not show privity, but the party is limited to equitable remedies.

> **EXAM NOTE:** When a party has established the existence of a real covenant entitling him to money damages, remember that the promise may also be enforced as an equitable servitude entitling the party to equitable relief.

b. Implied reciprocal servitudes

Most jurisdictions impose the following requirements to enforce an implied reciprocal servitude: (i) there must be **intent to create** a servitude on all plots (i.e., the promise must be reciprocal), (ii) the servitude must be **negative** (i.e., a promise to refrain from doing something), and (iii) the party against whom enforcement of the servitude is sought must have actual, record, or inquiry **notice**. To establish intent, a common scheme must be established. Note that no writing is required for an equitable servitude created by implication.

> **EXAM NOTE:** Equitable servitudes in subdivisions (also called "mutual rights of enforcement" and "reciprocal negative servitudes") are typically tested in a situation involving an owner subdividing a large tract of land into smaller lots to create a common scheme of development by:
>
> i) **Recording a map** showing the scheme;
>
> ii) **Telling purchasers** of the lots about the plan; or
>
> iii) Including a **common building restriction** in most of the lot deeds.

4. Termination of Covenants

Like easements, covenants, equitable servitudes, and implied reciprocal servitudes terminate upon written release, merger of title, abandonment, estoppel, condemnation, or sale to a bona fide purchaser.

5. Changed Circumstances

> **EXAM NOTE:** Typical equitable defenses are applicable to actions for equitable servitudes or implied reciprocal servitudes (such as laches or unclean hands), but "**changed circumstances**" is the most commonly tested.

If a restriction on a property no longer makes sense to enforce due to drastic changes in the surrounding area since the restriction was first contemplated, the restriction will not be enforced. A good indication that the neighborhood has changed is a variance in zoning ordinances.

Example: A small subdivision restricts lots to residential use. Forty years later, the subdivision is next to a major thoroughfare, and the land in the surrounding area is largely commercial and industrial. The restriction for residential use will likely be unenforceable on the theory that its value was lost with the drastic change of the neighborhood.

C. WATER RIGHTS

1. Theories

a. Riparian rights

The riparian doctrine states that water belongs to those who own the land bordering the water course (riparians). Riparians share the right of reasonable use of the water. One riparian is liable to another for unreasonable interference with the other's use. Domestic use trumps commercial use and can be unlimited.

b. Prior appropriation

Most western states have adopted the doctrine of prior appropriation, which states that the water belongs initially to the state, but the right to divert and use it can be acquired by an individual, regardless of location. Rights are determined by priority of beneficial use. The norm for allocation is first in time, first in right.

Any productive or beneficial use of the water, including use for agriculture, is sufficient to create appropriation rights.

2. Waterways

Rights in navigable waters are limited by the government's right to protect the use of the waterway for transportation. Rights to non-navigable waters vary in their treatment depending on the theory to which the jurisdiction subscribes. Most jurisdictions, including those that have adopted the doctrine of reasonable use, treat non-navigable water (including all underground water) rights in the same manner as surface water rights. Some jurisdictions that have adopted an appropriation system have also applied it to non-navigable waters, including underground ponds and lakes. At least one jurisdiction has adopted a correlative rights standard, which gives a landowner a proprietary right to the portion of water that correlates to his proportion of land over the underground waterway.

3. Groundwater

The majority view allows the surface owner to make "reasonable use" of the groundwater. Contrast this with the doctrine of absolute ownership followed by some eastern states, which allows the surface owner total and complete discretion over water extraction and use. The western states, on the other hand, tend to follow the prior appropriation doctrine.

4. Surface Water

Surface water (traditionally called "diffused surface water") is, as the name implies, water that lies on the surface of the land but that is not part of a lake or waterway. Usually, the water derives from rain or melted snow. In about half of the states, the landowner may make changes or improvements to his land to combat the flow of surface water ("common enemy doctrine"). Some jurisdictions limit this right to prohibit unnecessary harm to another's land. On the other hand, about half of the states prevent the landowner from altering the rate or natural flow of water ("natural flow theory"). However, most of those states have mitigated the rule to permit **reasonable** changes in water flow. This is a growing trend and requires balancing the harm against the utility.

5. Support Rights

A landowner has the right to have the land supported in its natural state.

a. Lateral support

A landowner is strictly liable for damages to adjoining land caused by the landowner's excavation of his land, unless the adjoining land was improved in a way that contributed to the damage.

In other words, when adjoining land is in its natural state (i.e., undeveloped), a landowner who excavates on his own land is strictly liable for any damage to the adjoining land caused by the excavation. If the adjoining land has been improved (i.e., is not in its natural state), the excavating landowner is strictly liable for any damage caused by the excavation only if the land **would have collapsed in its natural state** (regardless of the improvement). However, if the weight of an improvement on adjoining land contributes to the land's collapse, then the excavating landowner is not strictly liable. Instead, the adjoining landowner may recover only if the excavating landowner was negligent.

> **Example 1:** Owner and Neighbor have adjoining parcels of land. Owner excavates on his land, causing Neighbor's undeveloped land to collapse. Owner is strictly liable.
>
> **Example 2:** Owner and Neighbor have adjoining parcels of land. Owner's excavation of his land causes Neighbor's barn and the land under it to collapse. Owner is strictly liable unless the weight of Neighbor's barn contributed to the collapse. In that case, Neighbor may recover only if Owner was negligent in his excavation.

b. Subjacent support

The right to subjacent support (i.e., support from beneath the surface of the land) arises when the owner of land grants the right to mine on his land to a third party. The owner of the mineral rights is strictly liable for any failure to support the land and any buildings on the land at the time the rights were conveyed. The owner is liable only for negligence for damage to any improvements built after the conveyance of the rights.

6. Air Rights

A landowner has the right to have the air above his land be free from excessive noise and aircraft transit. This is not an exclusive right, but such intrusions may constitute a trespass.

7. Remedies for Intrusion onto Land

The possessor of land has a right to exclude trespassers and to be free from noise and odors that substantially limit his right to use and enjoy the land. He may seek an injunction in equity or damages at law as compensation for the intrusion.

D. GOVERNMENT REGULATION OF LAND

The following testable concepts should be read in conjunction with the detailed discussion of the Fifth and Fourteenth Amendments in the Themis Constitutional Law outline.

1. Zoning

State and local governments may regulate the use of land through zoning laws, subject to the limitations of the Fifth and Fourteenth Amendments of the Constitution.

Zoning laws may be used to segregate incompatible uses from developing in the same area. They are enacted for the protection and safety of the communities' citizens. Single-family residences are normally considered the highest and best use in zoning ordinances. Commercial and industrial uses are lower uses and generally incompatible with residential neighborhoods. Unusual uses, like funeral homes, require special-use permits, even if the district authorizes that type of use.

a. Exemptions and variances

In certain situations, an owner may be exempt from a zoning ordinance. If an owner can demonstrate that a particular zoning ordinance exacts a unique hardship on him, then he may request a variance as long as the variance is not contrary to the public welfare.

b. Relationship to covenants

A zoning restriction establishes a "ceiling" beyond which a private covenant cannot go, but it does not set a "floor" below which a private covenant cannot go.

> **Example**: A zoning ordinance requires that a residence be set back at least 50 feet from the edge of the property. A covenant that requires a setback of 100 feet is enforceable. A covenant that requires a setback of 25 feet does not override the zoning restriction and cannot justify the location of a residence that is set back only 35 feet.

> **EXAM NOTE:** Fact patterns about zoning ordinances that contain standard restrictions are typically not far enough outside the norm to be constitutional violations.

2. Eminent Domain

A taking occurs when the government takes title to land, physically invades land, or severely restricts the use of land. Courts look to whether an essential nexus exists between the legitimate state interest stated as the justification for the taking/restriction and any conditions imposed on the property owner.

Valid exercises of police power include regulations that have the purpose of protecting the public from harm, or ensuring a public benefit.

A landowner can recover damages equal to the reduction in value to his property resulting from a partial taking.

E. NUISANCE

See a more detailed discussion of Nuisance in the Themis Torts outline.

1. Private Nuisance

A private nuisance is a **substantial, unreasonable** interference with another individual's use or enjoyment of his property. The interference need not be intentional or even negligent to constitute nuisance. Anyone with possessory rights in the property may bring a nuisance claim.

a. Substantial

A substantial interference is one that would be offensive, inconvenient, or annoying to an average person in the community.

b. Unreasonable

The interference is unreasonable if the injury caused outweighs the usefulness of the defendant's actions.

2. Public Nuisance

A public nuisance is an unreasonable interference with the health, safety, or property rights of the community. To recover for a public nuisance, a plaintiff must show that he suffered a different kind of harm than that suffered by the rest of the community.

3. Remedies

a. Damages

The usual remedy for nuisance is damages. Damages include any depreciation in the value of the property, and may be apportioned among multiple defendants. All resulting harm is recoverable, including personal harm (e.g., diseases acquired from inhaling fumes), and harm to property.

b. Injunctive relief

If money damages are inadequate or unavailable, courts may impose injunctive relief. In determining whether an injunction is appropriate, the courts will balance the potential hardships of the two parties. However, the court need not consider the relative hardships if the defendant's conduct was unreasonable.

F. DEDICATION

Dedication is the giving of land by the lawful owner to the government for use by the public. The owner still retains the fee, but the public essentially holds an easement in trust such that the owner does not retain any rights that are inconsistent with the complete exercise and enjoyment of the public uses to which the property has been committed. The dedication may be express (through a deed), implied, or by adverse use by the public, but it must be accepted by the public entity (which can be implied by use).

V. OTHER TYPES OF OWNERSHIP

A. COMMON-INTEREST COMMUNITIES

Most common-interest communities are created by a declaration, which serves to both impose servitudes and provide for mandatory membership in an association of property owners. To be a common-interest community, the common property must be appurtenant to the separately-owned property. Restatement (Third) of Property: Servitudes § 6.2.

1. Condominiums

Condominium unit ownership is fee ownership. However, it differs from most other types of property ownership in that in a condominium, the owner owns the interior of his unit and an undivided interest in the common elements and exterior of the building. Each unit owner carries his own mortgage and is responsible for taxes, insurance, and expenses related to the upkeep of the unit and the building.

2. Cooperatives

Cooperatives are a type of housing in which the land and buildings are owned by corporations that lease the individual apartments to its shareholders. Residents who live in cooperatives are not fee owners of the units they live in; rather, they are tenants who own shares of the stock in the building. As a result, the residents are restricted from transferring their interest in the building. Tenants also have a legitimate concern about the other tenants' ability to pay their mortgage. Unlike condominiums, in which each owner is responsible for his own mortgage, a cooperative has a blanket mortgage. This mortgage takes priority over occupancy leases, and each tenant pays a share of the mortgage. Although a tenant is not personally liable on the mortgage, a default by any tenant could initiate foreclosure proceedings on the property, which could in turn terminate all leases. Maintenance expenses in a cooperative are treated the same as in a condominium.

C. EMBLEMENTS (CROPS)

Fructus industriales and *fructus naturales* are two types of crops that, with some exceptions, are conveyed along with the land conveyance. *Fructus industriales* are produced through cultivation and are considered personalty. *Fructus naturales* are perennial; they do not require planting because they are produced by nature alone. Title to *fructus naturales* passes automatically with the land because this crop is considered real property.

1. Conveyance of Crops

Generally, both *fructus naturales* and *fructus industriales* are conveyed along with the land conveyance because the owner of the land is presumed to be the owner of both types of crops. Because this presumption is based on the intent of the parties, a contrary intent may be shown to rebut the presumption.

2. Exceptions

Harvested crops, or crops that have been severed from the land, are not conveyed with the land. Thus, the prior owner can remove the crops and has the right to reenter the land.

Some courts also treat ripened *fructus industriales* as being constructively severed from the land because they no longer draw sustenance from the soil. Thus, in some jurisdictions, these crops are not conveyed with the land.

When crops are planted by a tenant, if the tenant's lease is for an uncertain duration and the lease is terminated through no fault of the tenant, then the tenant has a right to reenter the land and remove, harvest, and cultivate crops planted prior to the termination of his tenancy. This "doctrine of emblements" applies unless there is a provision to the contrary in the lease, or the one who planted the crops is a trespasser. However, adverse possessors who plant under a claim of right are entitled to the same rights as tenants.

Torts

TORTS

Table of Contents

I.   **INTENTIONAL TORTS INVOLVING PERSONAL INJURY** 1

   A.   **GENERALLY** 1

      1.   **ACT** 1

      2.   **INTENT** 1

          a.   Children and the mentally incompetent 1

          b.   Transferred intent 1

   B.   **BATTERY** 2

      1.   **ELEMENTS** 2

      2.   **LACK OF CONSENT** 2

      3.   **HARMFUL OR OFFENSIVE CONTACT** 2

      4.   **PLAINTIFF'S PERSON** 2

      5.   **CAUSATION** 3

      6.   **INTENT** 3

      7.   **DAMAGES** 3

   C.   **ASSAULT** 3

      1.   **BODILY CONTACT** 3

      2.   **REASONABLE APPREHENSION** 4

      3.   **IMMINENCE** 4

      4.   **MERE WORDS** 4

      5.   **INTENT** 4

      6.   **DAMAGES** 4

   D.   **INTENTIONAL INFLICTION OF EMOTIONAL DISTRESS** 4

      1.   **INTENT** 5

      2.   **EXTREME OR OUTRAGEOUS CONDUCT** 5

      3.   **ACTS DIRECTED TOWARD THIRD PARTIES** 5

      4.   **CAUSATION** 5

      5.   **DAMAGES** 6

     E. FALSE IMPRISONMENT...6

           1. CONFINED WITHIN BOUNDARIES..6

           2. METHODS OF CONFINEMENT...6

           3. TIME...7

           4. INTENT...7

           5. DAMAGES..7

II.   DEFENSES TO INTENTIONAL TORTS INVOLVING PERSONAL INJURY...........................7

     A. CONSENT...7

           1. EXPRESS CONSENT 7

                 a. Mistake 7

                 b. Fraud 7

                 c. Duress..7

            2. IMPLIED CONSENT 8

                 a. Emergency situation...8

                 b. Injuries arising from athletic contests.......................8

                 c. Mutual consent to combat...8

            3. CAPACITY..8

     B. SELF-DEFENSE 8

           1. USE OF REASONABLE FORCE 8

            2. USE OF DEADLY FORCE 8

            3. OBLIGATION TO RETREAT 9

            4. INITIAL AGGRESSOR 9

            5. THIRD-PARTY INJURIES 9

     C. DEFENSE OF OTHERS 9

     D. DEFENSE OF PROPERTY 9

           1. REASONABLE FORCE ALLOWED 9

           2. USE OF DEADLY FORCE NOT ALLOWED 9

           3. REASONABLE FORCE TO PREVENT INTRUSION UPON REAL PROPERTY............9

           4. RECAPTURE OF CHATTELS 10

           5. FORCE TO REGAIN POSSESSION OF LAND 10

     E. PARENTAL DISCIPLINE 10

     F. PRIVILEGE OF ARREST 10

		1.	FELONY	10
			a. Arrest by private citizen	10
			b. Arrest by police officer	10
		2.	MISDEMEANOR	10

III. HARMS TO PERSONAL PROPERTY AND LAND 11

A. TRESPASS TO CHATTELS 11

1. DEFINITION 11

2. INTENT 11

3. APPROPRIATE PLAINTIFFS 11

4. MISTAKE 11

5. DAMAGES 11

6. REMEDY 11

B. CONVERSION 11

1. DEFINITION 11

2. INTENT 12

3. INTERFERENCE 12

4. DISTINGUISHING CONVERSION FROM TRESPASS TO CHATTELS 12

5. DAMAGES 12

C. TRESPASS TO LAND 12

1. INTENT 13

2. PHYSICAL INVASION 13

3. APPROPRIATE PLAINTIFFS 13

4. DISTINGUISHED FROM NUISANCE 13

5. DAMAGES 13

6. NECESSITY AS A DEFENSE TO TRESPASS 13

a. Private necessity 14

b. Public necessity 14

c. Application to torts affecting damages to chattels 14

D. NUISANCE 15

1. PRIVATE NUISANCE 15

a. Definition 15

b. Nature of defendant's conduct 15

   c. **Appropriate plaintiffs** 15

   d. **Substantial interference** 15

   e. **Unreasonable interference** 15

   f. **Distinguished from trespass** 15

   g. **Access to light** 16

   h. **Defenses to private nuisance** 16

  2. **PUBLIC NUISANCE** 16

   a. **Definition** 16

   b. **Applying principles derived from the law of private nuisance** 17

  3. **REMEDIES FOR NUISANCES** 17

   a. **Damages** 17

   b. **Injunctive relief** 18

  4. **ABATEMENT** 18

   a. **Private nuisance** 18

   b. **Public nuisance** 18

IV. **NEGLIGENCE** 18

 A. **DEFINITION** 18

  1. **STANDARD OF CARE** 19

   a. **Traditional approach** 19

   b. **Restatement (Third) approach** 19

  2. **ELEMENTS OF NEGLIGENCE** 19

 B. **DUTY** 19

  1. **FAILURE TO ACT** 19

  2. **FORESEEABILITY OF HARM** 20

  3. **FORESEEABILITY OF HARM TO THE PLAINTIFF** 20

   a. **Cardozo (majority) view** 20

   b. **Andrews (minority) view** 20

  4. **SPECIFIC CLASSES OF FORESEEABLE PLAINTIFFS** 20

   a. **Rescuers** 20

   b. **Intended beneficiaries** 20

   c. **Fetuses** 21

  5. **AFFIRMATIVE DUTY TO ACT** 21

        a. **Assumption of duty** 21

        b. **Placing another in peril** 21

        c. **By contract** 21

        d. **By authority** 21

        e. **By relationship** 21

C. **THE STANDARD OF CARE** 21

    1. **REASONABLY PRUDENT PERSON** 21

        a. **Mental and emotional characteristics** 22

        b. **Physical characteristics** 22

        c. **Intoxication** 22

        d. **Children** 22

    2. **COST-BENEFIT ANALYSIS** 22

    3. **CUSTOM** 23

        a. **Within community or industry** 23

        b. **Safety codes** 23

        c. **Professionals** 23

        d. **Physicians** 23

    4. **NEGLIGENCE *PER SE*** 24

        a. **Basic rule** 24

        b. **Proof of defendant's compliance not dispositive** 24

        c. **Defenses** 24

        d. **Violation by plaintiff** 25

    5. **STANDARDS OF CARE FOR SPECIFIC CLASSES OF DEFENDANTS** 25

        a. **Common carriers and innkeepers** 25

        b. **Automobile drivers** 25

        c. **Bailors and bailees** 26

        d. **Modern trend** 26

        e. **Emergency situations** 26

    6. **POSSESSORS OF LAND** 26

        a. **Two approaches** 27

        b. **Trespassers** 27

        c. **Invitees: traditional approach** 28

     d.   **Licensees: traditional approach** 29

     e.   **Invitees and licensees: modern and Restatement approach** 29

     f.   **Liability of landlords and tenants** 30

     g.   **Off-premises victims** 30

     h.   **Sellers of real property** 30

D. BREACH OR VIOLATION OF DUTY OF CARE 30

   1. BURDEN OF PROOF 30

   2. *RES IPSA LOQUITUR* 31

     a.   **Traditional requirements** 31

     b.   **Modern trends** 31

     c.   **Third Restatement** 32

     d.   **Procedural effect of *res ipsa loquitur*** 32

E. CAUSATION 32

   1. CAUSE IN FACT 32

     a.   **"But-for" test** 32

     b.   **Multiple and/or indeterminate tortfeasors** 33

     c.   **Loss of chance of recovery** 34

   2. CAUSAL LINKAGE 34

   3. PROXIMATE CAUSE (SCOPE OF LIABILITY) 34

     a.   **Limitation on liability** 35

     b.   **Extent of damages** 36

     c.   **Intervening and superseding causes** 36

F. DAMAGES 37

   1. ACTUAL DAMAGES 37

   2. COMPENSATORY DAMAGES 37

   3. MITIGATION OF DAMAGES, AVOIDABLE CONSEQUENCES 37

   4. PERSONAL INJURY: CATEGORIES OF DAMAGES 38

   5. PROPERTY DAMAGE 38

     a.   **General rule** 38

     b.   **Cost of repairs** 38

     c.   **Household items** 38

   6. COLLATERAL-SOURCE RULE 38

       a. Traditional rule 38

       b. Modern trend 38

   7. PUNITIVE DAMAGES 39

G. SPECIAL RULES OF LIABILITY 39

   1. NEGLIGENT INFLICTION OF EMOTIONAL DISTRESS 39

       a. Threat of impact 39

       b. Zone of danger 39

       c. Witnessing harm to close relative 39

       d. Physical symptoms required 39

       e. Exceptions to physical-injury requirement 40

       f. "Parasitic" damages 40

   2. WRONGFUL DEATH AND SURVIVAL ACTIONS 40

       a. Wrongful death actions 40

       b. Survival actions 40

   3. RECOVERY FOR LOSS ARISING FROM INJURY TO FAMILY MEMBERS............41

       a. Spouses 41

       b. Parent-child 41

       c. Limitations..41

   4. "WRONGFUL LIFE" AND "WRONGFUL BIRTH" CLAIMS 41

       a. Wrongful life..41

       b. Wrongful birth 41

H. VICARIOUS LIABILITY 41

   1. LIABILITY OF EMPLOYER FOR EMPLOYEE'S TORTS 42

       a. Employer's right of control 42

       b. Scope of employment 42

       c. Negligent hiring...42

   2. TORTS COMMITTED BY INDEPENDENT CONTRACTORS 43

       a. Generally no vicarious liability 43

       b. Distinguished from employee 43

       c. Non-delegable duties 43

       d. Negligence in hiring 43

   3. BUSINESS PARTNERS 43

	4.	AUTOMOBILE OWNERS	43
		a. Negligent entrustment	43
		b. Family purpose doctrine	43
		c. Owner liability statutes	44
	5.	PARENTS AND THEIR CHILDREN	44
		a. No vicarious liability	44
		b. Negligence of parents	44
	6.	"DRAM SHOP" LIABILITY	44
	7.	BAILMENT LIABILITY	45

I. LIMITATION OF LIABILITY RESULTING FROM DEFENDANT'S IDENTITY OR RELATIONSHIPS ("IMMUNITIES") 45

	1.	LIABILITY OF THE GOVERNMENT AND ITS OFFICERS	45
		a. Federal government	45
		b. State governments	45
		c. Municipalities	46
		d. Government officials	46
	2.	INTRA-FAMILY IMMUNITY	47
		a. Interspousal immunity	47
		b. Parent-child immunity	47
	3.	CHARITABLE IMMUNITY	47

J. SHARING LIABILITY AMONG MULTIPLE DEFENDANTS 47

	1.	JOINT AND SEVERAL LIABILITY	47
		a. Definition	47
		b. Application	48
	2.	CONTRIBUTION	48
		a. Determining "fair shares"	48
		b. Intentional tortfeasor	48
	3.	SEVERAL (PROPORTIONATE) LIABILITY	48
	4.	SATISFACTION AND RELEASE	48
	5.	INDEMNIFICATION	49
		a. Vicarious liability	49
		b. Complete reimbursement	49

K. DEFENSES TO NEGLIGENCE 49

    1. CONTRIBUTORY NEGLIGENCE 49

        a. Contributory negligence: traditional rule...49

        b. Last clear chance..50

        c. Comparative fault...50

        d. Imputed contributory negligence 52

        e. Distinguishing comparative fault, contribution, and several liability 52

    2. ASSUMPTION OF THE RISK..53

        a. Exculpatory clauses in contracts..53

        b. Participants and spectators in athletic events.................................53

        c. Unreasonably proceeding in face of known, specific risk 53

V.   STRICT LIABILITY 54

  A. ABNORMALLY DANGEROUS ACTIVITIES 54

    1. BASIC RULE 54

    2. DEFINITION OF "ABNORMALLY DANGEROUS"....................................54

    3. SCOPE OF RISK 55

    4. AIRPLANES..55

  B. THE RULE OF *RYLANDS V. FLETCHER* 55

  C. ANIMALS...55

    1. WILD ANIMALS 55

        a. Dangerous propensity 56

        b. Plaintiff's fearful reaction 56

        c. Liability to trespassers 56

    2. DOMESTIC ANIMALS...56

        a. Known to be dangerous 56

        b. "Dog-bite" statutes 56

    3. OWNER'S ANIMALS ON ANOTHER'S LAND 56

    4. PLAINTIFF'S CONDUCT 56

    5. LANDLORD'S LIABILITY...57

  D. DEFENSES TO STRICT LIABILITY 57

    1. CONTRIBUTORY NEGLIGENCE...57

    2. COMPARATIVE FAULT 57

    3. ASSUMPTION OF THE RISK..57

       4. STATUTORY PRIVILEGE 57

VI.   PRODUCTS LIABILITY 57

    A. NEGLIGENCE 58

       1. DUTY 58

       2. BREACH 58

       3. CAUSATION 58

       4. DAMAGES 58

       5. DEFENSES 58

    B. STRICT PRODUCTS LIABILITY 58

       1. ELEMENTS OF CLAIM 59

       2. DEFECTIVE PRODUCT 59

          a. Manufacturing defect 59

          b. Design defect...59

          c. Failure to warn 59

          d. Inference of defect..60

       3. PLAINTIFFS 60

       4. DEFENDANTS...60

          a. Business of seller...60

          b. Chain of distribution...60

          c. Even if not responsible for the defect 61

          d. Seller of component part...61

          e. Indemnification 61

          f. Lessor 61

          g. Products and services...61

          h. Exclusions...61

       5. DAMAGES 61

       6. DEFENSES..62

          a. Comparative fault...62

          b. Contributory negligence...62

          c. Assumption of risk..62

          d. Product misuse, modification, or alteration by the user.............62

          e. Substantial change in product 62

   f. **Compliance with governmental standards**..................................63

   g. **"State of the art"**...63

   h. **Statute of limitations issues**..63

   i. **Contract disclaimers, limitations, and waivers**............63

  C. **WARRANTIES**...63

   1. **IMPLIED WARRANTIES**...64

    a. **Two types**..64

    b. **Claims**..64

   2. **EXPRESS WARRANTIES**..64

   3. **DEFENSES TO WARRANTY CLAIMS**....................................64

    a. **Disclaimers**..64

    b. **Tort defenses**...65

VII. **DEFAMATION, INVASION OF PRIVACY, AND BUSINESS TORTS**............65

  A. **DEFAMATION**...65

   1. **DEFAMATORY LANGUAGE**...65

   2. **"OF OR CONCERNING" THE PLAINTIFF**.............................66

   3. **PUBLICATION**..66

    a. **To a third party**...66

    b. **Republication**...66

    c. **Internet service providers**......................................66

   4. **CONSTITUTIONAL REQUIREMENTS**...................................66

    a. **Public official**..67

    b. **Public figure**..67

    c. **Private individual**...67

   5. **FALSITY**...67

    a. **Matters of public concern**......................................67

    b. **Private individual plaintiff/not a matter of public concern**........68

    c. **Opinion**...68

   6. **FAULT**...68

    a. **Public official or public figure**..............................68

    b. **Private individual/matter of public concern**........68

    c. **Private individual/not a matter of public concern**........68

    7. **LIBEL AND SLANDER DISTINGUISHED**..68

        a. **Libel**..68

        b. **Slander**..69

    8. **CONSTITUTIONAL LIMITATIONS ON DAMAGES**............................70

        a. **Public-official or public-figure plaintiffs**..............................70

        b. **Private individual/matter of public concern**........................70

        c. **Private individual/not a matter of public concern**..............70

    9. **DEFENSES**..71

        a. **Truth**..71

        b. **Consent**...71

        c. **Absolute privileges**..71

        d. **Qualified (conditional) privilege**...71

B. **INVASION OF PRIVACY**..72

    1. **MISAPPROPRIATION OF THE RIGHT TO PUBLICITY**.....................72

    2. **UNREASONABLE INTRUSION UPON THE PLAINTIFF'S PRIVATE AFFAIRS**.......72

    3. **PLACING THE PLAINTIFF IN A FALSE LIGHT**.................................73

    4. **PUBLIC DISCLOSURE OF PRIVATE FACTS ABOUT A PLAINTIFF**......73

        a. **Elements**...73

        b. **Publicity**..73

        c. **Disfavored tort**...73

        d. **Disclosure of dated material**...74

    5. **DAMAGES**..74

    6. **DEFENSES**..74

        a. **Defamation defenses**...74

        b. **Consent**...74

C. **INTENTIONAL MISREPRESENTATION**..74

    1. **DEFENDANT'S FALSE REPRESENTATION**.....................................74

    2. **SCIENTER**...75

    3. **INTENT**..75

    4. **CAUSATION**...75

    5. **JUSTIFIABLE RELIANCE**...75

    6. **DAMAGES**..75

D. NEGLIGENT MISREPRESENTATION 75
    1. ELEMENTS AND SCOPE 75
    2. DEFENSES 76
    3. DAMAGES 76
    4. DISTINGUISHED FROM ORDINARY NEGLIGENCE 76
E. INTENTIONAL INTERFERENCE WITH BUSINESS RELATIONS 76
    1. INTENTIONAL INTERFERENCE WITH CONTRACT 76
        a. Elements 76
        b. Nature of contractual relationship 76
        c. Interference with performance other than inducing breach 76
        d. Justification 77
    2. INTERFERENCE WITH PROSPECTIVE ECONOMIC ADVANTAGE 77
    3. THEFT OF TRADE SECRETS 77
F. INJURIOUS FALSEHOODS 77
    1. TRADE LIBEL 77
    2. SLANDER OF TITLE 78
G. WRONGFUL USE OF THE LEGAL SYSTEM 78
    1. MALICIOUS PROSECUTION 78
    2. ABUSE OF PROCESS 78

TORTS

I. **INTENTIONAL TORTS INVOLVING PERSONAL INJURY**

A. **GENERALLY**

A prima facie case for any intentional tort, including those not involving personal injury, must include proof of an **act**, **intent**, **and causation**.

1. **Act**

The act must be voluntary, meaning that the defendant must have directed the physical muscular movement.

2. **Intent**

The defendant acts **intentionally** if:

i) The defendant acts with the **purpose** of causing the consequences of his act; or

ii) The defendant acts knowing that the consequence is **substantially certain** to result.

Restatement (Third) of Torts: Liability for Physical and Emotional Harm § 1 (2010). (Hereinafter, "Rest. 3d § xx.")

a. **Children and the mentally incompetent**

A majority of courts hold that both **children** and those who are **mentally incompetent** can be held **liable for intentional torts** if they either act with a purpose or know the consequences of their acts with a substantial certainty.

b. **Transferred intent**

Transferred intent exists when a person intends to commit an intentional tort against one person, but instead commits either:

i) A **different intentional tort** against that person;

ii) The intended tort **against a different person**; or

iii) A different intentional tort against a different person.

Example 1: When the defendant throws a hardball in the direction of the plaintiff, intending only to scare her (assault), but the ball strikes the plaintiff, the defendant is liable to the plaintiff for the battery. **The intent to commit one intentional tort** (the assault) **suffices to satisfy the intent requirement for another intentional tort**, the battery. Conversely, if the defendant intends to strike the victim and cause contact but instead misses and scares the plaintiff, the intent to cause the battery suffices for the intent required for the assault.

Example 2: If the defendant throws a punch intending to strike the man standing next to him, but misses and instead strikes a third party, the intent to commit a battery on the man suffices to complete the intent requirement for the battery to the third party under the doctrine of **transferred intent.**

Example 3: If the defendant throws a punch intending to strike the man standing next to him and misses both that man and a third party who is standing nearby, but causes that third party to experience apprehension of an imminent harmful or offensive bodily contact, the intent to commit a battery on the man "transfers" and suffices to complete the tort of assault against the third party.

Transferred intent applies only when the intended tort and the resulting tort are among the following: battery, assault, false imprisonment, and trespass to chattels. Note in particular that it **does not apply** to intentional infliction of emotional distress.

B. BATTERY

1. Elements

A defendant is liable to the plaintiff for **battery** when he:

   i) Causes a **harmful or offensive contact** with the person of another; and

   ii) Acts **with** the **intent** to cause such contact or the apprehension of such contact.

2. Lack of Consent

There is no battery if the plaintiff consented to the act, either expressly or by virtue of participating in a particular event or situation (such as being bumped on a crowded subway or playing in a football game). *See* § II.A., *infra*.

3. Harmful or Offensive Contact

Contact is harmful when it causes injury, physical impairment, pain, or illness.

Contact is **offensive when a person of ordinary sensibilities** (i.e., a reasonable person) would find the contact offensive (objective test).

Note that a **defendant may be liable if he is aware that the victim is hypersensitive but proceeds to act nonetheless**. In such a case, the fact that a reasonable person would not find the conduct offensive is not a defense.

The plaintiff need not be aware of the contact when it occurs in order to recover.

Example: If an operating room attendant inappropriately touches the patient while she is under the effects of anesthesia, there may be a battery even though the patient was not aware of the touching.

4. Plaintiff's Person

Contact with anything **connected to** the plaintiff's person qualifies as contact with the plaintiff's person for the purposes of battery (e.g., a person's clothing, a pet held on a leash, a bicycle ridden by the plaintiff).

5. **Causation**

   The act must in fact result in contact of a harmful or offensive nature. A defendant who sets in motion a chain of events that causes contact with the plaintiff, whether the contact is direct or indirect, is liable (e.g., a trip wire set by the defendant that causes the plaintiff to fall).

6. **Intent**

   To act intentionally, a defendant must act with either (i) the purpose of bringing about the consequences of that act or (ii) the knowledge that the consequences are substantially certain to occur.

   In some cases, depending on the jurisdiction and the factual context, a defendant may be liable if he intends merely to bring about the contact. While the contact must be harmful or offensive, the defendant need not intend that result (single intent rule). In other cases, depending on the jurisdiction and the factual context, a defendant may be required to intend not only to bring about a contact but must also intend that the contact be harmful or offensive (double intent rule).

   The doctrine of transferred intent applies to battery.

7. **Damages**

   No proof of actual harm is required; the plaintiff may recover nominal damages even though no actual damage occurred (to vindicate his right to physical autonomy).

   Many states allow recovery of **punitive damages** if the defendant acted outrageously or with malice (i.e., a wrongful motive, or a conscious or deliberate disregard of a high probability of harm). *See* § IV.F.7., *infra*.

   Under the **thin ("eggshell") skull/shabby millionaire rule**, the defendant is not required to foresee the extent of damages in order to be held liable for all damages.

   Example: If the defendant inappropriately pinches a stranger on a bus, he will be liable for battery. If it turns out that the victim is a hemophiliac and bleeds to death, the defendant will be liable for all damages appropriately awarded for the wrongful death.

C. **ASSAULT**

An assault is the plaintiff's reasonable apprehension of an imminent harmful or offensive bodily contact caused by the defendant's action or threat with the intent to cause either the apprehension of such contact or the contact itself.

1. **Bodily Contact**

   Bodily contact is not required for assault.

   The prototypical assault occurs when the plaintiff sees the defendant throw a punch at him. Regardless of whether the punch connects (and therefore causes a battery), the apprehension of the contact is sufficient for assault.

2. Reasonable Apprehension

A plaintiff's apprehension must be reasonable. Unlike battery, the plaintiff must be aware of or have knowledge of the defendant's act.

The defendant's apparent ability to cause harm (e.g., a "real-looking" toy gun) can be sufficient to place the plaintiff in apprehension of harm.

Even if the victim is confident that he can prevent the threatened harm, there may still be an assault.

3. Imminence

The threatened bodily harm or offensive contact must be **imminent,** i.e., without significant delay. Threats of future harm are insufficient, as are threats made by a defendant too far away to inflict any harm.

Example: If the defendant calls and threatens the plaintiff from across the city, then the threat is not imminent and therefore there is no assault.

4. Mere Words

It is sometimes said that "**mere words alone do not constitute an assault.**" However, words coupled with conduct or other circumstances may be sufficient. If the defendant is able to carry out the threat imminently and takes action designed to put the victim in a state of apprehension, there may be an assault.

Example: If the defendant sneaks up from behind the plaintiff in a dark alley and utters in a menacing voice, "Your money or your life," an assault may be complete.

5. Intent

The defendant must intend to cause the plaintiff's apprehension of an imminent harmful or offensive contact or intend to cause harmful or offensive bodily contact with the victim.

The defendant's own words, however, can negate the intent.

Example: If the defendant says, "If you were not such a good friend, I would punch you," then there is no assault.

The doctrine of transferred intent applies to assault.

6. Damages

No proof of actual damages is required. The victim can recover **nominal damages** and, in appropriate cases, **punitive damages**. If the plaintiff sustains **damages from physical harm**, such as a heart attack resulting from the assault, he may recover these as well.

D. INTENTIONAL INFLICTION OF EMOTIONAL DISTRESS

A defendant is liable for intentionally or recklessly acting with **extreme** or **outrageous conduct** that causes the plaintiff severe emotional distress.

1. **Intent**

   The defendant must intend to cause severe emotional distress or must act with recklessness as to the risk of causing such distress. Transferred intent ***does not*** apply to intentional infliction of emotional distress.

2. **Extreme or Outrageous Conduct**

   Conduct is extreme or outrageous if it **exceeds the possible limits of human decency**, so as to be entirely intolerable in a civilized society. Liability does not extend to mere insults, threats, or indignities. A defendant's conduct must be such that ordinary people would conclude that it is **"outrageous."**

   Example: As a practical joke, the defendant tells the plaintiff that his wife was killed in an accident.

   Courts are more likely to find a defendant's abusive language and conduct to be extreme and outrageous if either:

   i) The defendant is in a position of **authority or influence** over the plaintiff, such as a police officer, employer, or school official, or traditionally an innkeeper or an employee of a common carrier; or

   ii) The plaintiff is a member of a group with a **known heightened sensitivity** (e.g., young children, pregnant women, or elderly persons).

3. **Acts Directed Toward Third Parties**

   When the defendant's conduct is directed at a third-party victim, that defendant is liable if he intentionally or recklessly causes severe emotional distress to:

   i) A member of the victim's **immediate family** who is present at the time of the defendant's conduct (and the defendant is aware of such presence), whether or not such distress results in bodily injury; or

   ii) Any other bystander who is present at the time of the conduct (and the defendant is aware of such presence), if the distress **results in bodily injury**.

   Restatement (Second) of Torts § 46 (1965). (Hereinafter, "Rest. 2d § xx.")

   Example: If the defendant draws a pistol and threatens to shoot a woman in her husband's presence, and the husband suffers severe emotional distress, he may recover.

4. **Causation**

   The plaintiff may establish causation by a showing that the defendant's actions were a **substantial factor** in creating the plaintiff's distress.

   Special rules of causation apply in cases in which a bystander makes a claim of severe emotional distress. When the defendant has caused severe **physical** harm to a third party and the plaintiff suffers severe emotional distress as a result, the plaintiff can recover if:

   i) The plaintiff was **present** when the defendant inflicted the harm;

   ii) The plaintiff was a **close relative** of the injured person; and

   iii) The defendant **had knowledge** of both of the above facts.

The plaintiff does not need to prove the above if the defendant's **design or purpose** was to cause severe distress to the plaintiff.

5. Damages

The plaintiff must prove severe emotional distress beyond what a reasonable person could endure.

In many cases, the very extreme and outrageous character of the defendant's conduct itself provides evidence that the plaintiff experienced severe mental distress. In other words, the more extreme the defendant's conduct, the less evidence is required of the severity of the plaintiff's emotional distress.

If the plaintiff is **hypersensitive,** however, and experiences severe emotional distress unreasonably, there is no liability **unless the defendant knew** of the plaintiff's heightened sensitivity.

Most courts do not require the plaintiff to prove physical injury except in the case of bystander recovery when the plaintiff is not a member of the immediate family of the person to whom the defendant's extreme and outrageous conduct is personally directed (*see* § 3, *above*).

> **EXAM NOTE:** The distinction between intentional and negligent infliction of emotional distress (*see* § IV.G.1., *infra*) is often tested on the MBE.

E. FALSE IMPRISONMENT

False imprisonment results when a person acts:

i) Intending to **confine or restrain** another within boundaries fixed by the actor;

ii) Those actions directly or indirectly **result in such confinement;** and

iii) The other is **conscious of the confinement** or is **harmed by it**.

1. Confined Within Boundaries

The plaintiff must be confined within a bounded area in which the plaintiff's freedom of movement in all directions is limited. The bounded area may be large and need not be stationary. An area is not bounded if there is a **reasonable** means of safe escape.

2. Methods of Confinement

The defendant may confine or restrain the plaintiff by the use of physical barriers, physical force, direct or indirect threats (to the plaintiff, a third party, or the plaintiff's property), or by the invalid use of legal authority, duress, or the failure to provide a reasonable means of safe escape.

Shopkeeper's Privilege: A shopkeeper's reasonable (in both duration and manner) detention of a suspected shoplifter is **not** an invalid use of authority and hence is not a false imprisonment.

Furthermore, a court may find that the defendant has confined the plaintiff when he has refused to perform a duty to release the plaintiff from an existing confinement or provide a means of escape.

Example: If a child accidentally locks herself in a restroom in a restaurant, the restaurant may be liable if the restaurant intentionally fails to assist her in unlocking the door to obtain her release.

The defendant's use of moral pressure or future threats does not constitute confinement or restraint. The plaintiff is not imprisoned if she submitted willingly to confinement.

3. Time

The length of time of the confinement or restraint is immaterial, except as to the determination of the extent of damages.

4. Intent

The defendant must act with the purpose of confining the plaintiff or act knowing that the plaintiff's confinement is substantially certain to result.

If the confinement is due to the defendant's negligence rather than his intentional acts, the defendant may be liable under the rules governing negligence, but not under the intentional tort of false imprisonment. If the imprisonment occurs by pure accident and involves neither the defendant's intent nor his negligence, there is no recovery.

The doctrine of transferred intent applies to false imprisonment.

5. Damages

It is not necessary to prove actual damages (except when the plaintiff is unaware of the confinement). Punitive damages may be imposed in appropriate cases.

II. DEFENSES TO INTENTIONAL TORTS INVOLVING PERSONAL INJURY

A. CONSENT

1. Express Consent

The plaintiff expressly consents if she, by words or actions, manifests the willingness to submit to the defendant's conduct. The defendant's conduct may not exceed the scope of the consent.

a. Mistake

Consent by mistake is valid consent unless the defendant **caused** the mistake or **knew** of it and **took advantage** of it.

b. Fraud

Consent induced by fraud is invalid if it goes to an **essential** matter. If the fraud that induced the consent goes only to a collateral matter, then the consent is still valid.

c. Duress

Consent given while under duress (physical force or threats) is not valid. The threat, however, must be of **present action,** not of future action.

2. Implied Consent

The plaintiff's consent is implied when the plaintiff is silent (or otherwise nonresponsive) in a situation when a reasonable person would object to the defendant's actions.

a. Emergency situation

When immediate action is required to save the life or health of a patient who is incapable of consenting to treatment, such consent is ordinarily unnecessary. Courts generally say that consent is "implied in fact," but it probably is more accurate to say that the treatment is privileged.

Even in an emergency situation, however, a competent and conscious patient's right to refuse treatment cannot be overridden.

b. Injuries arising from athletic contests

Consent may also be implied by custom or usage (e.g., participation in a contact sport). The majority of jurisdictions that have considered the issue of when a participant in an athletic contest can recover have concluded that the injured player can only recover for a reckless disregard of a player's safety, such as a violation of a safety rule designed primarily to protect participants from serious injury.

c. Mutual consent to combat

In the case of boxing or prize-fighting, most courts hold that the plaintiff consents to intentional torts when he engages in the fighting, and is therefore precluded from recovering from any injuries sustained.

In the case of street-fighting and other illegal activities, the courts are divided. A majority holds that consent to such acts is not a defense because one cannot consent to a criminal act. The Second Restatement and a significant minority of courts now hold to the contrary, however. Rest. 2d § 60.

3. Capacity

Youth, intoxication, and incompetence each may undermine the validity of one's consent.

B. SELF-DEFENSE

1. Use of Reasonable Force

A person may use **reasonable force** to defend against an offensive contact or bodily harm that he **reasonably believes** is about to be intentionally inflicted upon him. The force used in self-defense must be reasonably proportionate to the anticipated harm. A person's mistaken belief that he is in danger, so long as it is a **reasonable mistake,** does not invalidate the defense.

2. Use of Deadly Force

The defendant may use deadly force only if he has a reasonable belief that force sufficient to cause serious bodily injury or death is about to be intentionally inflicted upon him.

3. Obligation to Retreat

A person is **not required to retreat** under the majority rule, but during the past generation, there was a trend toward requiring retreat before using deadly force unless the defendant was in (or within the curtilage of) her own home. Under the Second Restatement, a person has a duty to retreat before she may use deadly force in defense, if she can do so safely.

However, more recently, many states have adopted **"stand your ground"** statutes that extend the "no retreat" concept to **any place** the defendant might legally be by providing that a person has no duty to retreat and has the right to stand her ground and meet force with force, including deadly force, if she reasonably believes it is necessary to do so to prevent death or great bodily harm.

4. Initial Aggressor

The initial aggressor is not entitled to claim self-defense unless the other party has responded to non-deadly force with deadly force.

5. Third-Party Injuries

The actor is **not liable** for injuries to **bystanders** that occur while he is acting in self-defense, so long as those injuries were accidental, rather than deliberate, and the actor was not negligent with respect to the bystander.

C. DEFENSE OF OTHERS

One is justified in using **reasonable force** in defense of others upon reasonable belief that the **defended party would be entitled to use self-defense.** It is no longer required that the force be used to defend a member of the defendant's own family or someone otherwise under the defendant's legal protection. The defender may use force that is proportionate to the anticipated harm to the other party. He is not liable for acting on a mistaken belief that the third-party is in danger as long as his belief is reasonable.

D. DEFENSE OF PROPERTY

1. Reasonable Force Allowed

A person may use reasonable force to defend her property if she reasonably believes it is necessary to prevent tortious harm to her property.

2. Use of Deadly Force Not Allowed

Deadly force **may not be used** merely in defense of property. A person may never use a deadly mechanical device (e.g., a spring-loaded gun) to defend her property.

3. Reasonable Force to Prevent Intrusion Upon Real Property

A possessor of land may use reasonable force to prevent or terminate another's intrusion upon her land. However, the possessor may not use force to prevent or terminate the visitor's intrusion on her land if the visitor is acting under necessity (*see* § III.C.6., *infra*).

The land possessor is not liable for using force if she makes a reasonable mistake with respect to an intrusion occurring on her land.

4. Recapture of Chattels

A person may use reasonable force to reclaim her personal property that has been wrongfully taken by another. If the original taking was lawful (e.g., a bailment) and the current possessor of the property has merely retained possession beyond the period of time to which the owner consented, then only peaceful means may be used to reclaim the chattel.

5. Force to Regain Possession of Land

At common law, an owner or possessor of land was permitted to use reasonable force to regain possession of that land from one who had wrongfully taken possession of it. However, modern statutes provide procedures for recovery of realty; therefore, the use of force is no longer allowed.

E. PARENTAL DISCIPLINE

A parent may use reasonable force or impose reasonable confinement as is necessary to discipline a child, taking into consideration the age of the child and the gravity of the behavior. An educator has the same privilege unless the parent places restrictions on that privilege.

F. PRIVILEGE OF ARREST

1. Felony

a. Arrest by private citizen

A private citizen is privileged to use force (e.g., commit a battery or false imprisonment tort) to make an arrest in the case of a felony if the felony has in fact been committed and the arresting party has reasonable grounds to suspect that the person being arrested committed it.

It is a defense to make a reasonable mistake as to the **identity of the felon** but not as to the **commission of the felony.**

b. Arrest by police officer

A police officer must reasonably believe that a felony has been committed and that the person she arrests committed it. Unlike a private citizen, a police officer who makes a mistake as to the commission of a felony is not subject to tort liability.

2. Misdemeanor

In the case of a misdemeanor, an arrest may be made only if the misdemeanor is a breach of the peace that is being committed or reasonably appears about to be committed **in the presence** of the arresting party (regardless of whether it is an officer or private citizen).

III. **HARMS TO PERSONAL PROPERTY AND LAND**

A. **TRESPASS TO CHATTELS**

1. **Definition**

A defendant is liable for trespass to chattels (i.e., tangible personal property) if he **intentionally interferes with the plaintiff's right of possession** by either:

i) **Dispossessing** the plaintiff of the chattel; or

ii) **Using or intermeddling with** the plaintiff's chattel.

2. **Intent**

Only the intent to do the interfering act is necessary; the defendant need not have intended to interfere with another's possession of tangible property.

The doctrine of transferred intent applies to trespass to chattels.

3. **Appropriate Plaintiffs**

An action for trespass to chattels may be brought by **anyone with possession or the immediate right to possession** of the chattel.

4. **Mistake**

Mistake by the defendant about the legality of his actions is not a defense.

5. **Damages**

In a case of dispossession, a plaintiff may recover for:

i) The **actual damages caused** by the interference; and

ii) The **loss of use**.

In circumstances of use or intermeddling, the plaintiff may recover only when there are **actual damages**.

6. **Remedy**

The plaintiff may be entitled to compensation for the **diminution in value** or the **cost of repair**.

B. **CONVERSION**

1. **Definition**

A defendant is liable for conversion if he **intentionally** commits an act **depriving the plaintiff of possession** of her chattel or **interfering** with the plaintiff's chattel in a manner **so serious as to deprive the plaintiff of the use of the chattel**. The plaintiff's damages are the chattel's full value at the time of the conversion.

Only personal property and intangibles that have been reduced to physical form (e.g., a promissory note) can be converted.

2. Intent

The defendant must only intend to commit the act that interferes; intent to cause damage is not necessary. Mistake of law or fact is no defense (e.g., a purchaser of stolen goods is liable to the rightful owner).

Accidentally damaging the plaintiff's chattel is not conversion if the defendant had permission to use the property.

3. Interference

The defendant interferes with the plaintiff's chattel by exercising **dominion or control** over it. Examples of acts of conversion include wrongful acquisition, transfer, or detention; substantially changing; severely damaging or destroying; or misusing the chattel.

Note that if the original acquisition of the chattel was not wrongful, then the plaintiff must demand the return of the chattel before she sues for conversion.

4. Distinguishing Conversion From Trespass to Chattels

There is no specific rule as to what behavior constitutes conversion, as opposed to trespass to chattels; it is a matter of degree of seriousness. The following factors are considered:

i) The **duration and extent** of the interference;

ii) The defendant's **intent to assert a right inconsistent** with the rightful possessor;

iii) The defendant's **good faith**;

iv) The **expense or inconvenience** to the plaintiff; and

v) The **extent of the harm** to the chattel.

Generally, the greater the degree of these factors, the greater the likelihood that a conversion has occurred. Conversion is an exercise of dominion or control over the plaintiff's personal property such that the court is justified in requiring the defendant to pay the plaintiff the full value of the property.

Example: If an embittered defendant steals his ex-girlfriend's car and drives it into a lake, that is conversion. If he merely hits the hood of her car once with a hammer, that is trespass to chattels.

5. Damages

The plaintiff may recover **damages in the amount of the full value of the converted property** at the time of the conversion. Alternatively, the plaintiff may bring an action for replevin to recover the chattel.

C. TRESPASS TO LAND

Trespass to land occurs when the defendant's **intentional** act causes a **physical invasion** of the land of another.

1. **Intent**

   The defendant need only have the **intent to enter the land** (or to cause a physical invasion), not the intent to commit a wrongful trespass. In other words, the defendant **need not know that the land belongs to another.** Mistake of fact is not a defense.

   > **Example:** Assume an erroneous survey of the defendant's property leads her to believe that an annoying cherry tree is on her property when in fact it is on her neighbor's property. She intentionally enters the space where the tree is located and cuts it down. Even though she reasonably believed that the tree was on her property, she still will be liable for trespass.

   The doctrine of transferred intent applies to trespass to land.

2. **Physical Invasion**

   The defendant need not personally enter onto the plaintiff's land; intentionally flooding the plaintiff's land, throwing rocks onto it, or intentionally emitting particulates into the air over the land will each suffice.

   Additionally, the defendant's failure to leave the plaintiff's property after his lawful right of entry has expired constitutes a physical invasion.

   A trespass may be committed on, above, or below the surface of the plaintiff's land.

3. **Appropriate Plaintiffs**

   Because it is the right to possession that is being protected, **anyone in actual or constructive possession of land may bring an action for trespass** (e.g., owner, lessee, adverse possessor).

4. **Distinguished From Nuisance**

   Trespass always requires an invasion or intrusion of land; nuisance may or may not involve intrusion.

   Trespass protects the possessor's interests in the land; nuisance protects the use and enjoyment of land. *See also* § III.D., *infra*.

   If no physical object enters onto the plaintiff's land (e.g., the defendant's floodlights project onto the plaintiff's land or damage results from the defendant's blasting), the case is generally treated as a nuisance or strict liability action (discussed in §§ III.D. and V., *infra*).

5. **Damages**

   No proof of actual damages is required.

6. **Necessity as a Defense to Trespass**

   > **EXAM NOTE:** Private necessity, often referred to simply as "necessity," has been tested frequently on the MBE.

   The privilege of necessity is available to a person who enters onto the land of another or interferes with another's personal property in order to prevent injury that is substantially more serious than the invasion or interference itself. The privilege of necessity applies only to intentional torts to property.

a. Private necessity

A defendant who acts to prevent a threatened injury from some source of nature or other independent cause that is not connected with the plaintiff is said to be acting under necessity. Defendants acting under necessity have the right to use the property of others to save their own lives or more valuable property. Private necessity is a **qualified** privilege to protect a limited number of people.

1) Liability for damages caused while acting under private necessity

The property owner upon whose property the defendant (acting under necessity) trespasses cannot use self-help to exclude the defendant as a trespasser. The property owner cannot recover nominal or punitive damages.

However, most jurisdictions hold that necessity is an incomplete privilege. The property owner is entitled to recover **actual damages** even though the defendant is not a trespasser.

Example: Assume the defendant docks her valuable boat on the plaintiff property-owner's dock during a severe storm in order to prevent the destruction of the boat. During the storm, the winds knock the boat against the dock causing damage to the dock. The defendant will be liable to the dock owner for the actual damages.

b. Public necessity

Under the doctrine of public necessity, private property may be intruded upon or destroyed when necessary to protect a large number of people from public calamities, such as the spreading of a fire, the spreading of disease, or the advance of a hostile military force.

The privilege is **absolute**. As long as the defendant acts reasonably, he is not liable for any damage to the property. He is not liable even if the original entry was not necessary, as long as he **reasonably believed** that the necessity existed. The privilege lasts only as long as the emergency continues.

The privilege is available to private citizens or public officials, should the plaintiff seek to hold a public official personally liable.

c. Application to torts affecting damages to chattels

Necessity and public necessity also are privileges to the torts alleging damage to personal property, i.e., trespass to chattels and conversion.

D. NUISANCE

> **EXAM NOTE:** Although most Torts classes devote little time to this topic, the law of nuisance, particularly private nuisance, tends to be tested rather frequently on the MBE.

1. Private Nuisance

a. Definition

A private nuisance is a thing or activity that **substantially and unreasonably interferes** with another individual's **use or enjoyment** of his land.

b. Nature of defendant's conduct

The interference must be intentional, negligent, reckless, or the result of abnormally dangerous conduct to constitute nuisance.

c. Appropriate plaintiffs

Anyone with **possessory** rights in real property may bring a nuisance claim.

d. Substantial interference

A substantial interference is one that would be **offensive, inconvenient, or annoying to a normal, reasonable person in the community**. A person with special sensitivities can recover only if the average person would be offended, inconvenienced, or annoyed. Conversely, a "thick-skinned" plaintiff who is not offended, inconvenienced, or annoyed is nevertheless entitled to recover if an average reasonable person would be, although the amount of damages may be affected.

e. Unreasonable interference

The interference is unreasonable if the injury caused by the defendant **outweighs the usefulness** of his actions.

f. Distinguished from trespass

1) Physical invasion

Trespass requires a **physical invasion** of the plaintiff's property. Nuisance does not require physical invasion, but **physical invasion may constitute a nuisance.**

Example: If the defendant's factory emits particulates that settle on the plaintiff's property, the defendant may be liable for both trespass and private nuisance.

2) Substantial interference

Private nuisance requires **substantial interference** with the plaintiff's use and enjoyment of her property. Trespass, however, does not require a substantial intrusion.

Example: A defendant's merely walking onto the plaintiff's land, if unprivileged and not consented to, is a trespass.

3) Duration

Generally, a nuisance is continuous. A trespass may be a one-time event, episodic, or continuous.

g. Access to light

Historically, courts have refused to find the obstruction of sunlight as creating a private nuisance.

h. Defenses to private nuisance

Apart from challenging the elements of nuisance, the defenses available to a defendant turn on whether the defendant's conduct is intentional, negligent, or abnormally dangerous. For example, the plaintiff's negligence or assumption of the risk may be a defense to a nuisance (or reduce recovery in a comparative fault jurisdiction) resulting from the defendant's negligence.

1) Regulatory compliance

The fact that a defendant's behavior is in compliance with a statute, local ordinance, or administrative regulation is not a complete defense to a nuisance action. However, such statutory or regulatory compliance may be admitted as evidence as to whether the interference with the plaintiff's use and enjoyment of her land is unreasonable. For example, zoning regulations are typically regarded as admissible evidence in actions for nuisance, but are not determinative.

2) Coming to the nuisance

It is generally **not a defense** that the plaintiff "came to the nuisance" by purchasing property in the vicinity of the defendant's premises with knowledge of the nuisance operated by the defendant. However, the fact that the plaintiff moved to the nuisance is not irrelevant; it may be considered by the jury in determining whether the plaintiff can recover for the nuisance.

> In other words, the plaintiff's coming to the nuisance **does not entitle the defendant to judgment** as a matter of law, but is **evidence that the jury may consider.**

Conversely, ownership of land prior to the defendant's entry into the neighborhood will not, by itself, make the defendant's action a nuisance. The test is whether the defendant's action is unreasonable.

2. Public Nuisance

a. Definition

A public nuisance is an unreasonable interference with a right common to the general public. (Note: Public nuisance does not necessarily involve land, but is included in this part of the outline because of its common historical roots with private nuisance.) Typical examples of public nuisance include air pollution, pollution of navigable waterways, interference with the use of public highways, and interference with the public's use of parks or other public property.

A private citizen has a claim for public nuisance only if he or she suffers harm that is different in kind from that suffered by members the general public.

> **Example 1:** If the defendant pollutes a river, a plaintiff who fishes in the river cannot bring a claim for public nuisance. However, a plaintiff who operates a fishing camp on the banks of the river and suffers a substantial economic loss may do so.
>
> **Example 2:** A dynamiting operation causes rocks to block a public highway. All members of the community are harmed by the nuisance. Consequently, a driver who suffers economic harm, such as a loss of business, due to the blockage cannot recover.
>
> **Example 3:** Same facts as in Example 2, but in this case a rock strikes the driver's car, cracking the windshield. The driver has suffered harm different from the general community and may bring an action in public nuisance.

In most instances, state statutes or local ordinances specifically declare something to be a public nuisance. Things declared to be a public nuisance by state statutes are far more varied than those described above, including such things as running a house of ill repute or a disorderly tavern, gambling on Sundays, or growing certain types of thorny bushes.

Public authorities can either (i) seek injunctive relief to abate (prevent the continuation of) the public nuisance or (ii) criminally prosecute the defendant.

b. Applying principles derived from the law of private nuisance

The law of public nuisance is extremely vague and varies greatly from one jurisdiction to another. However, the modern trend is to transpose much of the law governing private nuisance onto the law of public nuisance. For example, most courts hold that a defendant's conduct must be (i) intentional and unreasonable, (ii) negligent or reckless, or (iii) actionable under the principles governing abnormally dangerous activities. Furthermore, the defenses available to defendants in private nuisance actions typically apply in public nuisance actions.

3. Remedies for Nuisances

a. Damages

The usual remedy for nuisance is damages. Damages include any depreciation in value of the property. All resulting harm is recoverable, including damages for reduction in the value of the real property, personal injury, and harm to personal property.

1) Utility of the defendant's conduct

Even if the utility of the defendant's conduct outweighs the gravity of the harm, damages (but not injunctive relief) may be available if the harm is serious and the financial burden of compensating for the harm would not make the defendant's continuing conduct unfeasible. In other words, while it may be reasonable for the defendant to engage in the conduct, it is unreasonable for the defendant to do so without paying for the harm done.

2) Continuing nuisance

If the nuisance is a continuing one and the court deems it "permanent," it will award the plaintiff all past and future damages. This prevents plaintiffs from returning to the court to collect damages in the future.

Occasionally, courts award **temporary damages** measured by the damages that have occurred prior to trial and within the statute of limitations. In these instances, plaintiffs may return to the court in the future to collect additional temporary damages if the nuisance continues.

b. Injunctive relief

If monetary damages are inadequate and the nuisance would otherwise continue, then courts may grant injunctive relief. In determining whether an injunction is appropriate, the courts will **"balance the equities,"** that is, weigh the social utility of the defendant's conduct against the harm caused to the plaintiff and others. However, the court need not consider the relative hardships if the defendant's sole purpose was to cause harm to the plaintiff or to violate the common standards of decency (sometimes called a "spite nuisance").

4. Abatement

a. Private nuisance

A person may enter another's land in order to abate a private nuisance after giving the defendant notice of the nuisance and the defendant refuses to act. The amount of force used may be only that which is reasonable to abate the nuisance; the plaintiff is liable for any additional damage.

b. Public nuisance

One who is entitled to recover for a public nuisance has the right to abate that nuisance by self-help, as one would with a private nuisance. However, in the absence of unique injury, a public nuisance may be abated only by public authority.

IV. NEGLIGENCE

EXAM NOTE: Approximately half of the torts questions on the MBE test the topic of negligence. In addition to memorizing the elements, be sure to know that the defendant must:

i) Fail to exercise the care that a reasonable person in his position would exercise; and

ii) Act in a way that breaches the duty to prevent the foreseeable risk of harm to anyone in the plaintiff's position, and the breach must be the cause of the plaintiff's injuries.

A. DEFINITION

Negligence is **conduct** (the commission of an act or failure to act), without wrongful intent, that falls below the minimum degree of ordinary care imposed by law to protect others against unreasonable risk of harm.

1. **Standard of Care**

    There are two basic—and sometimes competing—approaches for defining the basic standard of care in negligence.

    a. **Traditional approach**

        Most courts define the standard of care as what a **reasonably prudent person** under the circumstances would or would not do.

    b. **Restatement (Third) approach**

        The modern trend is to define negligence **as the failure to exercise reasonable care under all the circumstances,** and then use an economic or cost-benefit analysis to determine whether reasonable care has been exercised. For example, the Third Restatement calls for courts, when determining whether a person has acted without reasonable care, to weigh the following factors:

        i)   The **foreseeable likelihood** that the person's conduct will result in **harm**,

        ii) The **foreseeable severity of** any **harm** that may result, and

        iii) The **burden of precautions to eliminate or reduce the risk of harm**.

        Rest. 3d: Liability for Physical and Emotional Harm § 3.

2. **Elements of Negligence**

    A prima facie case for negligence consists of four elements:

    i)   **Duty**, the obligation to protect another against unreasonable risk of injury;

    ii) **Breach**, the failure to meet that obligation;

    iii) **Causation**, a close causal connection between the action and the injury; and

    iv) **Damages**, the loss suffered.

    > **EXAM NOTE:** When analyzing answer choices to negligence questions, look for the threshold elements. For instance, if there is no duty, then you can dismiss answer choices involving breach, causation, or damages.

B. **DUTY**

    In general, a duty of care is owed to all foreseeable persons who may be injured by the defendant's failure to follow a reasonable standard of care. An actor has a duty to exercise reasonable care when the actor's conduct creates a risk of physical harm. Rest. 3d: Liability for Physical or Emotional Harm § 7.

1. **Failure to Act**

    Generally, there is no duty to act affirmatively, even if the failure to act appears to be unreasonable. For more on this principle, and the exceptions to it, *see* § 5, *below*.

2. **Foreseeability of Harm**

Most courts today hold that if the defendant is acting affirmatively, **the foreseeability of harm to another resulting from the defendant's failure to use reasonable care is sufficient to create a general duty to act with reasonable care.** This is a change from nineteenth-century negligence law where the plaintiff was required to show an independent or autonomous source of duty, such as a contract, a statute, or a regulation.

3. **Foreseeability of Harm to the Plaintiff**

a. **Cardozo (majority) view**

The majority rule is that a duty of care is owed to the plaintiff only if she is a member of the class of persons who might be foreseeably harmed (sometimes called "foreseeable plaintiffs") as a result of the defendant's negligent conduct. According to Judge Cardozo's majority opinion in *Palsgraf v. Long Island R. R. Co.*, 162 N.E. 99 (N.Y. 1928), the defendant is liable only to plaintiffs who are **within the zone of foreseeable harm.**

b. **Andrews (minority) view**

The minority view, articulated in Judge Andrews's minority opinion in *Palsgraf*, states that if the defendant can foresee harm to **anyone** as a result of his negligence, a duty is owed to **everyone (foreseeable or not) harmed** as a result of his breach. However, the plaintiff still may not be able to recover, because a particular plaintiff's injury may not be closely enough connected to the defendant's negligence for the court to conclude that it was proximately caused by the defendant's negligence. In other words, the issue is one of duty for Judge Cardozo, but one of proximate cause for Judge Andrews. *See* § IV.E.3., *infra*. Rest. 3d: Liability for Physical and Emotional Harm § 29 cmt. n.

4. **Specific Classes of Foreseeable Plaintiffs**

a. **Rescuers**

A person who comes to the aid of another is a foreseeable plaintiff. If the defendant negligently puts either the rescued party or the rescuer in danger, he is liable for the rescuer's injuries. To the extent a rescuer's efforts are unreasonable, comparative responsibility should be available to reduce, rather than to bar, recovery by a rescuer. Rest. 3d: Liability for Physical and Emotional Harm § 32.

An emergency professional, such as a police officer or firefighter, is barred from recovering damages from the party whose negligence caused the professional's injury if the injury results from a risk inherent in the job ("firefighter's rule").

b. **Intended beneficiaries**

A defendant is liable to a third-party beneficiary if the legal or business transaction that the beneficiary is a part of is prepared negligently, and the defendant could foresee the harm of completing the transaction.

c. Fetuses

Fetuses are owed a duty of care if they are viable at the time that the injury occurred. *See* § IV.G.4., *infra*, for a discussion of "wrongful life" and "wrongful birth" claims.

5. Affirmative Duty to Act

In general, there is no affirmative duty to act. However, there are some notable exceptions to that rule:

a. Assumption of duty

A person who voluntarily aids or rescues another is liable for injury caused by a failure to act with reasonable ordinary care in the performance of that aid or rescue.

Note that some states have enacted "Good Samaritan" statutes to protect doctors and other medical personnel when they voluntarily render emergency care. These statutes exempt medical professionals from liability for ordinary negligence; however, they do not exempt them from liability for gross negligence.

b. Placing another in peril

A person who places another in peril is under a duty to exercise reasonable care to prevent further harm by rendering care or aid.

c. By contract

There is a duty to perform contractual obligations with due care.

d. By authority

One with actual ability and authority to control another, such as parent over child and employer over employee, has an affirmative duty to exercise reasonable control. Generally, this duty is imposed upon the defendant when the defendant knows or should know that the third person is apt to commit the injuring act.

Example: A parent may be liable for failing to control the conduct of a child who uses a dangerous instrumentality to injure a plaintiff.

e. By relationship

Defendants with a unique relationship to plaintiffs, such as business proprietor-patron, common carrier-passenger, employer-employee, or parent-child, may have a duty to aid or assist the plaintiffs and to prevent reasonably foreseeable injury to them from third parties.

C. THE STANDARD OF CARE

1. Reasonably Prudent Person

In most cases, the standard of care imposed is that of a **reasonably prudent person under the circumstances**. This standard is an **objective** one, measured by what a reasonably prudent person would do, rather than whether a particular defendant is acting in good faith or using her best efforts. A defendant is required to exercise the care that a reasonable person under the same circumstances (i.e., in her position, with her information and competence) would recognize as necessary to avoid or prevent an unreasonable risk of harm to another person. In determining whether particular precautions were warranted, a jury should weigh the probability and gravity of the injury against the burden of taking such precautions.

a. Mental and emotional characteristics

Under this standard, the defendant is presumed to have average mental abilities and the same knowledge as an average member of the community. The defendant's own mental or emotional disability is not considered in determining whether his conduct is negligent, unless the defendant is a child. In other words, **a mentally disabled person is held to the standard of someone of ordinary intelligence and knowledge**.

Most courts hold that if a defendant possesses special skills or knowledge, she is held to a higher standard, i.e., she must exercise her superior competence with reasonable attention and care.

b. Physical characteristics

The defendant's particular physical characteristics (e.g., blindness) are taken into account in determining the reasonableness of the defendant's behavior. The reasonableness of the conduct of a defendant with a physical disability will be determined based upon a reasonably careful person with the same disability. Rest. 3d: Liability for Physical and Emotional Harm § 11. For example, a blind pedestrian must act as any other reasonable blind person would act under the circumstances.

c. Intoxication

Intoxicated individuals are held to the same standards as sober individuals unless their intoxication was involuntary.

d. Children

The standard of care imposed upon a child is that of a **reasonable child of similar age, intelligence, and experience.** Unlike the objective standard applied to adult defendants in negligence actions, the standard applicable to minors is more subjective in nature because children are unable to appreciate the same risks as an adult.

However, a child engaged in an adult activity, such as driving a car, is held to the same standard as an adult. Courts regard children of a particularly young age as incapable of negligent conduct. Under the Third Restatement, children under the age of five are generally incapable of negligent conduct. Rest. 3d: Liability for Physical and Emotional Harm § 10.

2. Cost-Benefit Analysis

In many cases, courts describe the primary factors to consider in determining whether the defendant has acted negligently to be:

i) The foreseeable likelihood that the defendant's conduct would cause harm;

ii) The foreseeable severity of any resulting harm; and

iii) The defendant's burdens (costs or other disadvantages) in avoiding the harm.

In fact, the Third Restatement defines negligence using these terms rather than the reasonable person standard.

3. Custom

a. Within community or industry

Evidence of custom in a community or industry is admissible as evidence to establish the proper standard of care, but such evidence is not conclusive. The entire community or industry may be negligent.

b. Safety codes

Safety codes promulgated by industries, associations, and governmental bodies for the guidance of operations within their respective fields of interest are admissible to prove custom.

c. Professionals

A professional person (e.g., doctor, lawyer, or electrician) is expected to exhibit the **same skill, knowledge, and care as another practitioner in the same community.** A specialist may be held to a higher standard than a general practitioner because of his superior knowledge. In other words, for these defendants, being consistent with custom precludes liability as a matter of law.

d. Physicians

1) Local vs. national standard

Traditionally, physicians were held to the "same or similar" locale rule of custom: did the physician's actions comport with those customarily employed by doctors in the same locale or in similar localities?

During the past forty years, however, many jurisdictions have changed to a national standard: did the physician conform her conduct to the customary practice of the average qualified practitioner?

Some jurisdictions now require **medical specialists** to comply with the national standard while holding general practitioners to the same or similar locale standard.

2) Informed consent

Physicians are under a specific obligation to explain the risks of a medical procedure to a patient in advance of a patient's decision to consent to treatment. Failure to comply with this "informed consent" doctrine constitutes a breach of the physician's duty owed to the patient and is actionable as medical malpractice (medical negligence). Doctors are **not** under an obligation to disclose when the:

i) Risk is a **commonly known** risk;

ii) Patient is **unconscious**;

iii) Patient **waives or refuses** the information;

iv) Patient is **incompetent** (although the physician must make a reasonable attempt to secure informed consent from a guardian); or

v) Disclosure would be **too harmful** to the patient (e.g., would upset the patient enough to cause extreme illness, such as a heart attack).

A **majority** of jurisdictions hold that the required level of disclosure of risks is governed by custom among medical practitioners. However, a significant **minority** holds that the physician must disclose any "material risk," that is, any risk that might make a difference to a reasonable person in deciding whether to proceed with the surgery or other medical treatment.

4. Negligence *Per Se*

> **EXAM NOTE:** Negligence per se has been heavily tested on the MBE.

a. Basic rule

i) When a criminal or regulatory statute (or an administrative regulation or municipal ordinance) imposes upon any person a specific duty for the protection or benefit of others;

ii) If the defendant neglects to perform that duty;

iii) He is liable in negligence **to anyone in the class of people intended to be protected by the statute**;

iv) **For any accidents or harms of the type the statute was intended to protect against**, and

v) That were proximately caused by the defendant's violation of the statute.

In most jurisdictions, the violation of the statute establishes either negligence as a matter of law or a rebuttable presumption of negligence.

A majority of courts hold that a violation of a state or federal regulation or a municipal ordinance may also result in negligence *per se*. A minority of jurisdictions hold that violation of a regulation or an ordinance is merely evidence of negligence.

b. Proof of defendant's compliance not dispositive

Generally speaking, compliance with a statute, regulation, or ordinance does not prove the absence of negligence. However, sometimes, if the defendant's conduct complies with certain types of federal regulatory statutes, such as those establishing comprehensive regulatory schemes, compliance with the federal requirements may pre-empt common law tort actions.

c. Defenses

1) Compliance impossible

Even in those jurisdictions where negligence *per se* results in negligence as a matter of law, the defendant can avoid liability by proving that compliance was either **impossible** under the circumstances or that an **emergency** justified violation of the statute.

2) Violation was reasonable under the circumstances

The defendant's violation of a statute is excused and is not negligence if the violation is reasonable in light of the defendant's **physical disability** or incapacitation, if the defendant is a **child**, or if the defendant exercises **reasonable care** in attempting to comply with the statute. Rest. 3d: Liability for Physical and Emotional Harm § 15.

In addition, if the statute imposes an obligation only under certain factual circumstances that are not usually present, and the defendant is **not aware** that these circumstances are present and further proves that his ignorance was reasonable, then the defendant's violation of the statute is excused for purposes of negligence *per se*.

Finally, if the requirements of the statute at issue were presented to the public in a **confusing** manner (e.g., extremely vague or ambiguous), then the defendant's violation is excused. Rest. 3d: Liability for Physical and Emotional Harm § 15.

d. Violation by plaintiff

The violation of a statute, regulation, or ordinance by a plaintiff may constitute contributory negligence per se. The same requirements apply.

5. Standards of Care for Specific Classes of Defendants

a. Common carriers and innkeepers

Under the common law, a majority of jurisdictions held common carriers (e.g., planes, trains, buses) and innkeepers to the highest duty of care consistent with the practical operation of the business. Under this approach, common carriers and innkeepers could be held liable for "slight negligence."

A majority of courts continue to hold **common carriers** to this higher standard. However, most courts today hold that an **innkeeper** (hotel operator) is liable only for **ordinary negligence**.

Note, however, that the Third Restatement approach is slightly different: common carriers and innkeepers must exercise reasonable care toward their passengers and guests. While generally there is no affirmative duty to act, common carriers and innkeepers have a duty to act based on a special relationship. They must use reasonable care under the circumstances with regard to risks that arise out of the relationship with their passengers and guests. Rest. 3d: Liability for Physical and Emotional Harm § 40.

> **EXAM NOTE:** Be certain to apply the carriers and innkeepers standards only to customers or guests.

b. Automobile drivers

In most jurisdictions, automobile drivers owe ordinary care to their guests as well as their passengers (those who confer an economic benefit for the ride). However, a minority of jurisdictions distinguish between the two with "guest statutes," which impose only a duty to refrain from gross or wanton and willful misconduct with a guest in the car. Proof of simple negligence by the driver will not result in recovery by the plaintiff-guest.

c. Bailors and bailees

A bailment occurs when a person (the bailee) temporarily takes possession of another's (the bailor's) personal property, such as when a driver leaves his car with a valet. The duty of care that must be exercised by a bailor or bailee varies depending on the type of bailment.

1) Bailor's duty

The bailor has a duty to inform the gratuitous bailee only of **known** dangerous defects in personal property but must inform a bailee for hire of defects that are known or **should have been known** by the bailor had he used reasonable diligence.

2) Bailee's duty

When a bailor receives the sole benefit from the bailment, the bailee has a lesser duty to care for the property and is liable only if he has been grossly negligent. In contrast, when a bailee receives the sole benefit from the bailment, he must exercise extraordinary care for the bailor's property. Slight negligence on the bailee's part will result in liability for any injuries to the property from failure to properly care for or use it. In a bailment for mutual benefit, the bailee must take reasonable care of the bailed property.

d. Modern trend

The modern trend has been to get away from distinctions in the level of care and to regard the relationship between the parties as simply one of the circumstances in the light of which conduct is to be measured by the standard of reasonable care.

e. Emergency situations

The applicable standard of care in an emergency is that of a reasonable person in the same situation. In other words, less may be expected of the reasonably prudent person who is forced to act in an emergency, but only if the defendant's conduct did not cause the emergency.

6. Possessors of Land

The term "possessors of land" as used here includes owners, tenants, those in adverse possession, and others in possession of land. The fact that a plaintiff is injured while on someone else's land does not affect the liability of a defendant other than the land possessor. Only land possessors are protected by the rules limiting liability to trespassers or licensees. Everyone else—for example, easement holders (e.g., a utility company with power lines on the land) or those licensed to use the land (e.g., hunters)—must exercise reasonable care to protect the trespasser or the licensee.

In general, possessors of land owe a duty only to those within the boundaries of their land. The duty to entrants on the land includes:

i) **Conduct** by the land possessor that creates risks;

ii) **Artificial conditions** on the land;

iii) **Natural conditions** on the land; and

iv) Risks created when any of the **affirmative duties** discussed in § IV.B.5., *supra*, are applicable.

a. Two approaches

Approximately one-half of all jurisdictions continue to follow traditional rules that provide that the standard of care owed to land entrants depend upon whether the land entrant is an invitee, a licensee, or a trespasser.

Courts in the other half of jurisdictions now hold that a reasonable standard of care is owed to all invitees and licensees (abolishing the distinction between how these two groups are treated). The Third Restatement also follows this approach. However, a majority of jurisdictions adopting this "reasonable-care-for-all" approach continue to provide separate rules for trespassers.

b. Trespassers

A trespasser is one who enters or remains upon the land of another **without consent or privilege** to do so.

1) Traditional approach

A landowner is obligated **to refrain from willful, wanton, reckless, or intentional misconduct** toward trespassers.

a) Spring-guns and other traps

The use of a "spring-gun" or other trap set to expose a trespasser to a force likely to inflict death or grievous bodily injury will lead to liability for the land possessor. The land possessor cannot do indirectly what he would be forbidden to do directly, e.g., shoot the trespasser.

b) Discovered trespassers

Land possessors owe a duty toward **discovered or anticipated trespassers** to warn or protect them from **concealed, dangerous, artificial conditions.** There is no duty to warn of natural conditions or artificial conditions that do not involve risk of death or serious bodily harm. Land possessors also have a duty to use reasonable care while conducting activities on their land, as well as to control the activities of third parties on their property.

c) Undiscovered trespassers

Land possessors generally owe no duty to undiscovered trespassers, nor do they have a duty to inspect their property for evidence of trespassers.

Note that, in a majority of jurisdictions, when a landowner **should reasonably know** that trespassers are consistently entering his land (e.g., frequent trespassers using a footpath to cut across the corner of the property), the landowner owes a duty to the trespasser, regardless of the landowner's actual knowledge, as if the trespasser were a licensee.

d) Attractive nuisance

> **EXAM NOTE:** Attractive nuisance has been heavily tested on the MBE.

Under the "attractive nuisance" doctrine, a land possessor may be liable for **injuries to children** trespassing on the land if:

i)   An artificial condition exists in a place where the owner knows or has reason to know that **children are likely to trespass**;

ii) The land possessor knows or has reason to know that the condition poses an **unreasonable risk** of death or serious bodily injury to children;

iii) The children, because of their youth, do not discover or **cannot appreciate the danger** presented by the condition;

iv) The utility to the land possessor of maintaining the condition and the burden of eliminating the danger are **slight compared to the risk of harm** presented to children; and

v)   The land possessor fails to exercise **reasonable care** to protect children from the harm.

2)   Modern and Third Restatement approach

A few states now take the approach that land possessors owe trespassers, like all other land entrants, a reasonable standard of care under all the circumstances. Of course, the fact that the land entrant is trespassing, particularly if he is undiscovered, is one fact that the jury may consider in deciding whether the land possessor has exercised reasonable care.

The Third Restatement § 52 provides that although a duty of reasonable care is owed to trespassers, only the duty not to act in an intentional, willful, or wanton manner to cause physical harm is owed to **flagrant trespassers** who are not imperiled and unable to protect themselves. A burglar in a home would be a flagrant trespasser but someone injured while walking in a public park at midnight, despite the presence of a posted notice that the park was closed after dusk, would not be. This distinction has not been widely adopted by the courts.

c.   Invitees: traditional approach

An invitee is either:

i)   A **public invitee**—Someone invited to enter or remain on the land for the purposes for which the land is held open to the public; or

ii) A **business visitor**—Someone invited to enter or remain on land for a purpose connected to business dealings with the land possessor.

A land possessor owes an invitee the duty of reasonable care, including the duty to use reasonable care to **inspect** the property, **discover** unreasonably dangerous conditions, and to **protect** the invitee from them.

However, the duty of reasonable care owed to an invitee does not extend beyond the scope of the invitation, and the invitee is **treated as a trespasser** in areas beyond that scope.

1) Non-delegable duty

The land possessor's duty to invitees is a non-delegable duty. For example, even if a store owner hires an independent contractor to maintain the escalator in her store, she will remain liable if the contractor negligently fails to properly maintain the escalator. This same principle of non-delegable duty applies under the modern approach (discussed below) where the land possessor owes most land visitors a duty of reasonable care.

2) Recreational land use

In some jurisdictions, a land possessor who opens his land to the public for recreational purposes is not liable for injuries sustained by recreational land users so long as he does not charge a fee for the use of his land, unless the landowner acts willfully and maliciously or, in some jurisdictions, with gross negligence.

d. Licensees: traditional approach

A licensee is someone who enters the land of another with the express or implied permission of the land possessor or with a privilege. Examples of licensees include:

    i) **Social guests**—Note, they may be "invited," but they are still licensees, not invitees;

    ii) Those whose presence is **tolerated** by the land possessor such as children that routinely cut across the land on their way home from school; and

    iii) **Emergency personnel** such as police, firefighters, and emergency medical technicians.

The land possessor has a duty to either **correct or warn** a licensee of **concealed dangers** that are either **known** to the land possessor or which **should be obvious** to her. The land possessor **does not have a duty to inspect** for dangers. In addition, the land possessor must exercise **reasonable care** in conducting activities on the land.

e. Invitees and licensees: modern and Restatement approach

Approximately one-half of all jurisdictions and the Third Restatement now require the land possessor to exercise **reasonable care under all circumstances to all land entrants except trespassers** (or in the case of the Third Restatement, all land entrants except for "flagrant trespassers." *See* § 6.b., *above*). The land possessor must use **reasonable care to prevent harm posed by artificial conditions** or conduct on the land.

If the land possessor is commercial, he also must use reasonable care to prevent harm to the visitor posed by natural conditions. A non-commercial land possessor must use reasonable care to prevent harm posed by natural conditions only if the possessor is aware of the risk or the risk is obvious.

f. Liability of landlords and tenants

Because the obligations associated with property are owed by the possessor of the land, a lessee assumes any duty owed by the lessor once the lessee takes possession.

1) Landlord's liability

The landlord remains liable for injuries to the tenant and others occurring:

    i) In **common areas** such as parking lots, stairwells, lobbies, and hallways;

    ii) As a result of **hidden dangers** about which the landlord **fails to warn** the tenant;

    iii) On premises **leased for public use**;

    iv) As a result of a hazard caused by the landlord's **negligent repair**; or

    v) Involving a hazard the landlord has **agreed to repair**.

2) Tenant's liability

As an occupier of land, the tenant continues to be liable for injuries to third parties arising from dangerous conditions within the tenant's control, regardless of whether the land possessor has liability.

g. Off-premises victims

A landowner generally does not owe a duty to a person not on the premises (e.g., passerby, owner of adjacent land) who is harmed by a **natural condition** on the landowner's premises. An exception exists, however, with respect to trees in urban areas.

With respect to an **artificial condition,** the landowner generally owes a duty to prevent an unreasonable risk of harm to persons who are not on the premises. Similarly, with respect to an activity conducted on the premises by the owner or by someone subject to the owner's control, the landowner generally owes a duty of reasonable care to persons who are not on the premises.

h. Sellers of real property

Sellers of real property owe a duty to disclose to buyers those concealed and unreasonably dangerous conditions known to the seller. These are conditions that the buyer is unlikely to discover upon reasonable inspection. The seller's liability to third parties continues until the buyer has a reasonable opportunity, through maintenance and inspection, to discover and remedy the defect.

D. BREACH OR VIOLATION OF DUTY OF CARE

1. Burden of Proof

The plaintiff must establish all four elements of negligence (duty, breach, causation, damage) by a **preponderance of the evidence**. A breach of duty occurs when the defendant departs from the conduct expected of a reasonably prudent person acting under similar circumstances. The evidence must show a greater probability than not that (i) the defendant failed to meet the required standard of care, (ii) the failure was the proximate cause of the injury, and (iii) the plaintiff suffered damages. The plaintiff can demonstrate such failure by introducing evidence of the required standard of care through custom and usage, violation of a statute, or *res ipsa loquitur*.

2. *Res Ipsa Loquitur*

Under the doctrine of *res ipsa loquitur*, the trier of fact may infer the existence of the defendant's negligent conduct in the absence of direct evidence of such negligence. *Res ipsa* is **circumstantial evidence** of negligence that does not change the standard of care.

> **EXAM NOTE:** *Res ipsa loquitur* does not apply if there is direct evidence of the cause of the injury.

a. Traditional requirements

Under the traditional standard for *res ipsa loquitur*, still used in many jurisdictions, the plaintiff must prove that:

   i)   The accident was of a kind that **ordinarily does not occur** in the absence of negligence;

   ii) It was caused by an agent or instrumentality within the **exclusive control** of the defendant; and

   iii) It was not due to any action **on the part of the plaintiff**.

b. Modern trends

Even under the traditional requirements, courts often generously interpret the "exclusive control" requirement.

> **Example:** The defendant hires an independent contractor to clean and maintain his store premises. The plaintiff is injured when she slips on a floor negligently left wet by an independent contractor. Courts will find that the duty to maintain the premises open to the public is a non-delegable duty, such that the defendant continued to be in "exclusive control." Therefore, *res ipsa loquitur* can be used to find that the defendant breached a duty of reasonable care.

1) Medical malpractice

In medical malpractice cases where several physicians, nurses, and other medical personnel have access to the plaintiff during surgery, a small number of jurisdictions apply *res ipsa loquitur*, finding that each defendant has breached a duty of care unless he can exonerate himself. In the absence of such exonerating evidence, the courts hold all defendants jointly and severally liable. *See, e.g., Ybarra v. Spangard*, 25 Cal. 2d 486 (1944).

2) Product liability

In negligent cases involving products, even if the product passes through many hands—those of the manufacturer, the distributor, the retail store, and the consumer/user—if the manufacturer wrapped the package or it is clear that any negligence took place during the production process, **many courts ignore the exclusivity requirement**.

3) Comparative fault jurisdictions

Courts in the vast majority of jurisdictions that have adopted comparative fault also are inclined to loosely apply the third requirement—that the harm must not be due to any action on the part of the plaintiff (whether such action constitutes contributory negligence or not)—because such a requirement would otherwise be in tension with the law holding that the plaintiff's contributory negligence is no longer a total bar to recovery.

c. Third Restatement

In light of the fact that the majority of jurisdictions generously apply the traditional requirements for *res ipsa loquitur,* the *Restatement (Third) of Torts* has re-articulated the requirements of the doctrine in the following manner:

The fact finder may infer that the defendant has been negligent when:

i) The accident that caused the plaintiff's harm is a type of accident that ordinarily happens as a result of negligence of a class of actors; and

ii) The defendant is a relevant member of that class of actors.

Rest. 3d: Liability for Physical and Emotional Harm § 17.

However, because the Third Restatement was only recently adopted, few courts have adopted this precise articulation of the doctrine.

d. Procedural effect of *res ipsa loquitur*

If the plaintiff establishes a prima facie case of *res ipsa*, then the trial court should deny the defendant's motion for a directed verdict and the issue of negligence must be decided by the trier of fact. In most jurisdictions, *res ipsa* does not require that the trier of fact find negligence on the defendant's part. It simply establishes an inference of negligence sufficient to avoid dismissal of the plaintiff's action.

E. CAUSATION

The plaintiff must prove that the defendant's actions were both the actual cause (also known as the factual cause or "cause-in-fact") and the proximate cause (i.e., within the scope of liability) of the plaintiff's injury.

1. Cause In Fact

a. "But-for" test

If the plaintiff's injury would not have occurred **but for** the defendant's tortious act or omission, then the defendant's conduct is a factual cause of the harm. If the injury would have occurred despite the defendant's conduct, then there is no factual cause.

b. Multiple and/or indeterminate tortfeasors

The "but-for" test of causation often will not work if:

i)   There are multiple tortfeasors and it cannot be said that the defendant's tortious conduct necessarily was required to produce the harm;

ii) There are multiple possible causes of the plaintiff's harm but the plaintiff cannot prove which defendant caused the harm; or

iii) The defendant's negligent medical misdiagnosis increased the probability of the plaintiff's death, but the plaintiff probably would have died even with a proper diagnosis.

1) Substantial factor

Where "but-for" causation does not work in either the multiple tortfeasor or the medical misdiagnosis situation, many courts substitute a "substantial-factor" test, i.e., "Was the defendant's tortious conduct a substantial factor in causing the plaintiff's harm?"

The *Restatement (Second) of Torts* promoted the substantial-factor test, but the Third Restatement is highly critical of it and drops it. Under the Third Restatement, in cases in which several causes or acts may have contributed to the plaintiff's injury, each of which alone would have been a factual cause of the plaintiff's injury, each cause or act is regarded as a factual cause of the harm. Rest. 3d: Liability for Physical and Emotional Harm § 27.

Note: The substantial-factor test is still used in most jurisdictions, at least in some context.

2) Concurrent tortfeasors contributing to an individual injury

Where the tortious acts of two or more defendants are each a factual cause of an indivisible injury to the plaintiff, the defendants are jointly and severally liable.

3) Alternative causation

If the plaintiff's harm was caused by (i) one of a small number of defendants—usually two and almost never more than four or five, (ii) each of whose conduct was tortious, and (iii) all of whom are present before the court, then the court may shift the burden of proof to each individual defendant to prove that his conduct was not the cause-in-fact of the plaintiff's harm.

4) Concert of action

If two or more tortfeasors were **acting pursuant to a common plan or design** and the acts of one or more of them tortiously caused the plaintiff's harm, then all defendants will be held jointly and severally liable.

Example: Two defendants agree to a drag race and one of them injures another driver or a passenger during the race. Both will be held jointly and severally liable to the plaintiff.

c. Loss of chance of recovery

When a physician negligently misdiagnoses a potentially fatal disease and thereby reduces the patient's chance of survival, but the patient's chance of recovery was less than 50% even prior to the negligent misdiagnosis, the plaintiff ordinarily cannot prove that but for the physician's negligence the plaintiff's death would not have occurred. A majority or substantial minority of courts now hold that the plaintiff can recover reduced damages on the basis of "loss of chance of recovery."

Under this theory, the plaintiff can recover an amount equal to the total damages recoverable as a result of the decedent's death multiplied by the difference in the percentage chance of recovery before the negligent misdiagnosis and after the misdiagnosis.

Example: If the plaintiff's total damages are $1,000,000, his chances of survival were 40 percent without the negligent misdiagnosis, and his chances of survival after the misdiagnosis were 25 percent, then the plaintiff will recover $150,000 ($1 million x (40%-25%)).

2. Causal Linkage

Most often, when the plaintiff proves that the defendant's tortious conduct was a **but-for cause** of his injury, he also implicitly proves that the defendant's conduct increased the probability that plaintiff would be harmed.

However, in a few cases (including some included in past MBE questions), it is purely coincidental that the defendant's tortious conduct was the but-for cause of the plaintiff's injury.

Example: If a passenger in a car is injured because the wind happens to blow down a tree and the car is positioned under the tree at the moment it falls only because the driver has been traveling at an unreasonably unsafe speed, it can technically be stated that the passenger would not have been injured but for the driver's negligent speeding. However, most courts would find that the driver should not be found to be a cause of the accident under the doctrine of causal linkage, i.e., the driver's conduct did not increase the probability that the plaintiff would be harmed.

3. Proximate Cause (Scope of Liability)

In addition to proving actual causation, the plaintiff must prove that the defendant's tortious conduct was a proximate cause of her harm. Some courts and the Third Restatement replace the proximate causation terminology with the issue of whether the plaintiff's harm was within the "scope of liability" of the defendant's conduct. A defendant's liability is limited to those harms that result from the risks that made the defendant's conduct tortious. Rest. 3d: Liability for Physical and Emotional Harm § 29.

> **EXAM NOTE:** Remember that there must be factual cause for proximate cause to exist, and if factual cause exists, then proximate cause exists unless there are intervening acts.

a. Limitation on liability

The basic idea of proximate causation (or, scope of liability) is that there must be limits on liability for the tortious acts of the defendant. There are two sub-issues in proximate causation:

1) Which plaintiffs can recover?

a) Majority rule

Recall that a majority of jurisdictions hold that the defendant does not owe a duty of care to the plaintiff unless the plaintiff is among the class of victims who might **foreseeably be injured** as a result of the defendant's tortious conduct. *See* § IV.B.3., *supra*.

b) Minority/Restatement rule

In the minority of jurisdictions—and in the Third Restatement—which plaintiffs can recover is determined by whether harms to them were proximately caused by the defendant's tortious conduct or were within the scope of liability of the defendant's conduct.

Under the Andrews test, whether the plaintiff's harms are proximately caused by the defendant's conduct requires consideration of the following factors:

i) Is there a **natural and continuous sequence** between cause and effect?

ii) Was the one a **substantial factor** in producing the other?

iii) Was there a **direct connection** without the intervention of too many intervening causes?

iv) Was the cause **likely to produce** the effect?

v) Could the defendant have **foreseen** the harm to the plaintiff?

vi) Is the cause **too remote** in time and space from the effect?

2) Types of risks

The second proximate cause (scope of liability) issue is whether the plaintiff is able to recover for the specific type of risk that harmed the plaintiff. For example, even if the court decides that a duty of care is owed to a specific plaintiff, a ship owner, because there is a foreseeable risk that a defendant stevedore's dropping of a plank into the hold of a ship might dent the ship, is the defendant still liable when the dropped plank unforeseeably causes vapors in the hull of the ship to ignite, totally destroying the ship? Again, there are two approaches:

a) Direct cause

A majority of American courts hold that the plaintiff can recover when the defendant's tortious acts are the **direct cause** of the plaintiff's harm—a cause **without the intervention of independent contributing acts**. In deciding whether the plaintiff can recover for a particular type of harm, these courts look at many of the same factors that Judge Andrews considered in *Palsgraf*. These jurisdictions hold that the foreseeability of the type of harm does not necessarily preclude liability.

b) Unforeseeable type of risk

A strong minority of American jurisdictions hold that whether a plaintiff can recover for a particular type of risk is determined by whether or not that particular risk is **foreseeable as a result of the defendant's tortious conduct**. If it is not, then there is no proximate cause and the plaintiff cannot recover.

b. Extent of damages

Even though a strong minority of jurisdictions holds that the type of risk that produces the plaintiff's harm must be foreseeable, under the "thin skull" or "eggshell skull" rule and the "shabby millionaire" rule, the **extent of the damages need never be foreseeable**.

c. Intervening and superseding causes

Many proximate cause questions involve intervening and superseding causes.

1) Intervening cause

An intervening cause is a factual cause of the plaintiff's harm that contributes to her harm after the defendant's tortious act has been completed.

2) Superseding cause

A superseding cause is any intervening cause that **breaks the chain of proximate causation between the defendant's tortious act and the plaintiff's harm**, thereby preventing the original defendant from being liable to the plaintiff.

a) Foreseeability

Most courts hold that an **unforeseeable** intervening cause is a superseding cause that therefore breaks the chain of causation between the defendant and plaintiff. Examples of foreseeable intervening forces include subsequent medical malpractice, disease, or accident; negligence of rescuers; normal forces of nature; or efforts to protect a person or property. Examples of unforeseeable superseding causes include extraordinary acts of nature ("Act of God") and criminal acts and/or intentional torts of third parties.

b) Negligent intervening causes

As a general guideline, **negligent intervening acts are usually regarded as foreseeable** and do not prevent the original defendant from being held liable to the plaintiff.

Example: The defendant negligently injures the plaintiff in an auto accident. The plaintiff seeks treatment for the resulting broken leg and the treating physician commits malpractice that results in the amputation of the leg. Because the original driver-defendant's negligence was a but-for cause of the amputated leg and because medical malpractice is foreseeable, the driver's negligence is also a proximate cause of the amputated leg and he may be held liable for damages caused by the entire injury including the consequences of the amputation.

c) Criminal intervening causes

Criminal acts of third parties are generally regarded as **unforeseeable superseding causes,** and therefore break the chain of causation between the original defendant's negligence and the plaintiff's harm.

However, if the duty breached by the defendant is one of **failing to use reasonable care to protect the plaintiff** and the plaintiff is harmed by a **criminal act**, the original defendant remains liable.

Example: If a middle-school student is assaulted during a field trip and her parents are able to prove that her teacher failed to use reasonable care to protect her, then the fact that the intervening cause of her harm, the assault, was criminal will not preclude the student and her parents from holding the school liable.

d) Effect of non-superseding intervening causes

If the intervening negligent act is not a superseding cause, the original defendant and the actor responsible for the intervening negligent act can be held jointly and severally liable to the plaintiff.

EXAM NOTE: Remember that the original tortfeasors remain liable unless the results of an intervening negligent act are **unforeseeable**. In particular, keep in mind that medical malpractice is foreseeable, and therefore it is not a superseding cause that breaks the chain of causation and insulates the defendant from liability.

F. DAMAGES

1. Actual Damages

The plaintiff must prove actual harm, i.e., personal injury or property damages, in order to complete the requirements of liability for negligence. Unlike actions for intentional torts, nominal damages are not recoverable in negligence actions. In addition, a plaintiff who suffers only economic loss without any related personal injury or property damage cannot recover such loss through a negligence action. However, once a plaintiff has proven non-economic injury, he is entitled to recover both economic and non-economic damages. Attorney's fees and interest from the date of damage are not recoverable in a negligence action.

2. Compensatory Damages

The general measure of compensatory damages is compensation that would make the victim whole, as if he or she had never suffered the injury.

3. Mitigation of Damages, Avoidable Consequences

The plaintiff must take reasonable steps to mitigate damages. Although sometimes phrased as a "duty to mitigate," this "duty" is not an obligation that the plaintiff owes to the defendant but instead is a limitation on the plaintiff's recovery due to the failure to avoid harm that could have been avoided by the use of reasonable effort after the tort was committed. For example, if the victim fails to use reasonable care to treat a wound, resulting in infection and the loss of a limb, she ordinarily will not be able to recover for the infection or lost limb. In a contributory-negligence jurisdiction, the failure to mitigate precludes the plaintiff from recovering for any additional harm caused by aggravation of the injury. In a comparative-negligence jurisdiction, the failure to mitigate is taken into account, but it does not categorically prevent recovery.

4. Personal Injury: Categories of Damages

The typical categories of damages recoverable in a personal injury action include:

i) Medical and rehabilitative expensive, both past and future;

ii) Past and future pain and suffering (e.g., emotional distress); and

iii) Lost income and any reduction in future earnings capacity.

Under the **"eggshell-skull rule,"** the defendant is liable for the full extent of the plaintiff's injuries that may be increased because of the plaintiff's preexisting medical condition or vulnerability, even if the extent is unusual or unforeseeable.

5. Property Damage

a. General rule

When the plaintiff's real or personal property is injured or destroyed by the defendant's tortious conduct, the general rule is that the plaintiff may recover the difference between the fair market value of the property immediately before the injury and immediately after the injury.

b. Cost of repairs

In the case of tortious harm to personal property, most courts also allow the cost of repairs as an alternative measure of damages, provided that the cost of repairs does not exceed the value of the property.

c. Household items

In the case of household items, such as clothing and appliances, courts often hold that replacement value is the measure of damages.

6. Collateral-Source Rule

a. Traditional rule

Under the traditional rule, benefits or payments provided to the plaintiff from outside sources (such as medical insurance) are not credited against the liability of any tortfeasor, nor is evidence of such payments admissible at trial.

b. Modern trend

Since the 1980's, a majority of states have passed statutes that either eliminate the collateral source rule entirely or modify it substantially. Payments made to the plaintiff by the defendant's insurer are not considered payments from a collateral source and such payments are credited against the defendant's liability.

7. Punitive Damages

The plaintiff may be entitled to punitive damages if he can establish by clear and convincing evidence that the defendant acted willfully and wantonly, recklessly, or with malice. Punitive damages are also available for inherently malicious torts (such as intentional infliction of emotional distress, which requires outrageous conduct).

G. SPECIAL RULES OF LIABILITY

1. Negligent Infliction of Emotional Distress

A plaintiff can recover for negligent infliction of emotional distress from a defendant whose negligence creates a foreseeable risk of physical injury to the plaintiff if the defendant's action causes a **threat of physical impact** that in turn causes emotional distress. The emotional distress generally must result in some form of bodily harm (e.g., a heart attack).

Note that it is also possible for a defendant to inflict severe emotional distress that results in physical symptoms without the threat of physical impact, such as when a physician negligently misdiagnoses a patient with a terminal illness that the patient does not have, and the patient goes into shock as a result.

a. Threat of impact

The threat of physical impact that causes distress must be directed at the plaintiff or someone in his immediate presence.

b. Zone of danger

Generally, a plaintiff must show that he was within the **"zone of danger" of the threatened physical impact**—that he feared for his own safety because of the defendant's negligence. A plaintiff who was a bystander also generally cannot recover for emotional distress caused by witnessing the serious injury to (or death of) another person, unless the bystander is within the zone of danger.

c. Witnessing harm to close relative

There is a trend toward allowing recovery for a bystander plaintiff outside the zone of danger if the plaintiff:

i) Is closely related to the person injured by the defendant;

ii) Was present at the scene of the injury; and

iii) Personally observed (or otherwise perceived) the injury.

A majority of jurisdictions would be unlikely to expand liability to an unmarried cohabitant. However, some jurisdictions do allow engaged cohabitants to recover.

d. Physical symptoms required

The majority rule is that damages for negligent infliction of emotional distress without accompanying **physical symptoms** (e.g., nightmares, shock, ulcers, etc.) are not recoverable.

e. Exceptions to physical-injury requirement

There are exceptions to the physical-injury requirement in cases of misinforming someone that a family member has died and the negligent mishandling of a corpse.

f. "Parasitic" damages

A plaintiff who is the victim of a tort that causes physical injury may also add emotional distress as an element of damages (sometimes known as "parasitic" damages).

> Compare to intentional infliction of emotional distress, when the plaintiff must prove more than negligence (intentional or reckless extreme or outrageous conduct) but need not prove any physical injury.

2. Wrongful Death and Survival Actions

a. Wrongful death actions

A decedent's spouse, next of kin, or personal representative may bring suit to recover **losses suffered as a result of a decedent's death** under wrongful death actions created by state statutes. Under typical statutes, the recoverable damages include the **loss of support** (income) as a result of the decedent's death, as well as the **loss of companionship, society, and affection** experienced by the surviving family members, **but not pain and suffering**. Recovery, however, is limited to what the deceased would have recovered had he lived. Additionally, the decedent's creditors have no right to institute a claim against the amount awarded.

b. Survival actions

Survival statutes typically enable the personal representative of a decedent's estate to pursue **any claims the decedent herself would have had at the time of her death**, including claims for damages resulting from both personal injury and property damage. Such claims often involve damages resulting from the tort that injured the decedent and later resulted in her death.

> **Example:** If the decedent was negligently injured by the driver of another automobile and lingered—out of work, in the hospital, and in extreme pain—for a year before passing away, his estate would be able to recover for his **medical expenses** from the time he was injured until his death, his **loss of income** during this time, and for the **pain and suffering** he experienced.

Most states do not allow survival of tort actions involving intangible personal interests (such as defamation, malicious prosecution, or invasion of privacy) because they are considered too personal to survive the decedent's death.

> If a jurisdiction recognizes both wrongful death and survival actions, there is no double recovery.

3. Recovery for Loss Arising From Injury to Family Members

a. Spouses

One spouse may recover for loss of consortium and services as a result of injuries to the other spouse resulting from the defendant's tortious conduct.

b. Parent-child

A parent may recover damages for loss of services if a child is injured due to the defendant's tortious conduct. A number of jurisdictions allow a parent to recover for loss of the child's companionship in a wrongful death action if the child is killed, but only a few jurisdictions allow a parent to recover for such damages if the child is injured but lives.

Similarly, many jurisdictions allow a child to recover for loss of the parent's companionship in a wrongful death action but most do not allow the child to recover such damages if the parent is injured but lives. In a wrongful death action, the child's claim for loss of support resulting from the decedent's death will be brought by the statutorily-designated adult family member as part of the wrongful death action.

c. Limitations

The amount of damages recoverable in a derivative action (an action arising solely because of tortious harm to another) for interference with family relationships is reduced in a comparative-fault jurisdiction (and eliminated in a contributory-negligence jurisdiction) by the injured family member's contributory negligence. Thus, if the damages recovered in the injured family member's own action are reduced by the plaintiff's comparative fault, the damages recoverable by his family members in their derivative action will also be reduced.

4. "Wrongful Life" and "Wrongful Birth" Claims

a. Wrongful life

Most states do not permit actions by a child for "wrongful life" based on the failure to properly perform a contraceptive procedure or failure to diagnose a congenital defect, even if the child is born with a disability.

b. Wrongful birth

Conversely, many states do permit parents to recover for "wrongful birth" (failure to diagnose a defect) or "wrongful pregnancy" (failure to perform a contraceptive procedure). Generally, the mother can recover damages for the medical expenses of labor as well as for pain and suffering. In the case of a disabled child, the parents may be able to recover damages for the additional medical expenses of caring for that child, and, in some states, may recover for emotional distress as well.

H. VICARIOUS LIABILITY

Vicarious liability is a form of strict liability in which one person is liable for the tortious actions of another. It arises when one person has the right, ability, or duty to control the activities of another, even though the first person was not directly responsible for the injury.

1. **Liability of Employer for Employee's Torts**

   a. **Employer's right of control**

   As a general rule, the employer is vicariously liable for the employee's torts if the employer has the right to control the activities of the employee.

   b. **Scope of employment**

   An employer is liable for the tortious conduct of an employee that is within the **scope of employment**. Conduct within the scope of employment includes acts that the employee is employed to perform or which are intended to profit or benefit the employer.

   > Careful instructions directed to the employee do not insulate the employer from liability—even when the employee acts counter to the instructions—if the employee is acting within the scope of employment.

   1) **Intentional torts**

   An employer may be liable for the intentional tort of an employee. For example, when **force is inherent** in the employee's work (e.g., a bouncer at a bar), the employer may be responsible for injuries the employee inflicts in the course of his work. However, if an employee, acting on a longstanding personal grudge, punches a customer of the employer's store, the employer probably will not be held liable. In addition, if the **employer authorizes the employee** to act on his behalf, and the employee's position provides the opportunity to commit an intentional tort, the employer may be liable (e.g., when an employee with the power to sign contracts enters into a fraudulent contract with a third party, the employer may be liable). As with negligence, the test is whether the employee was acting within the scope of employment. Restatement (Third) of Agency § 7.07.

   2) **Detour and frolic**

   An employer may be liable for a tort committed by the employee during an employee's detour (a minor and permissible deviation from the scope of employment) but not for an employee's frolic (an unauthorized and substantial deviation).

   > **EXAM NOTE:** The employer and employee will be jointly and severally liable (*see* § IV.J.1., *infra*) for torts committed by the employee within the scope of employment.

   c. **Negligent hiring**

   An employer may be liable for the negligent hiring, supervision, entrustment, or retention of an employee. This is primary negligence; it is not vicarious liability.

   > **EXAM NOTE:** If you conclude that an employer is not liable under a vicarious-liability theory, be certain to consider whether the employer is liable in her own right for negligence.

2. Torts Committed By Independent Contractors

a. Generally no vicarious liability

Those who hire independent contractors are generally not vicariously liable for the torts of the independent contractors.

b. Distinguished from employee

An independent contractor is one hired to accomplish a task or result, but who is not subject to a right of control by the employer.

i) Independent contractors tend to have specialized skills or knowledge, e.g., physicians and plumbers; and

ii) Independent contractors tend to work for many employers, while employees more often work for a single employer.

c. Non-delegable duties

The person who hires an independent contractor remains vicariously liable for certain conduct, including:

i) Inherently dangerous activities;

ii) Non-delegable duties arising out of a relationship with a specific plaintiff or the public (i.e., activities that are inherently risky or that affect the public at large, such as construction work adjacent to a public highway);

iii) The duty of a storekeeper or other operator of premises open to the public to keep such premises in a reasonably safe condition; and

iv) In a minority of jurisdictions, the duty to comply with state safety statutes.

d. Negligence in hiring

In addition, the party hiring the independent contractor may be liable for his own negligence in selecting the independent contractor.

3. Business Partners

Partners in a joint enterprise, when two or more parties have a common purpose and mutual right of control, may be liable for the tortious acts of each other that are committed within the scope of the business purposes.

4. Automobile Owners

a. Negligent entrustment

The owner of a vehicle (or any other object that carries the potential for harm, such as a gun or lawn mower) may be liable for the negligent acts of a driver or user to whom the car or other property was entrusted if the owner knew or should have known of the user's negligent propensities.

b. Family purpose doctrine

Many jurisdictions, through either legislative enactments or judicial decisions, have adopted the family purpose doctrine, providing that the owner of an automobile may be liable for the tortious acts of **any family member** driving the car with permission.

c. Owner liability statutes

Many jurisdictions have enacted statutes that provide that the owner of an automobile may be liable for the tortious acts of **anyone** driving the car with permission.

5. Parents and Their Children

a. No vicarious liability

The general rule is that parents are not vicariously liable for their minor child's torts. **Exceptions** to this general rule include situations in which:

i) The child commits a tort while acting as **the parent's agent**;

ii) State statutes provide for the liability of parents where children commit specified acts such as **vandalism or school violence**; or

iii) State statutes require that a parent, when he signs for the child's driver license application, to assume liability for any damages caused by the child's negligent acts the child commits while driving a car.

b. Negligence of parents

Parents, however, are liable for their own negligence with respect to their minor child's conduct. A parent is under a duty to exercise reasonable care to prevent a minor child from intentionally or negligently harming a third party, provided the parent:

i) Has the ability to control the child; and

ii) Knows or should know of the necessity and opportunity for exercising such control.

In such circumstances, a parent who fails to exercise control may be liable for harm caused by the child, even though the child, because of his age, is not liable. Rest. 2d § 316.

Example: A father gives a gun to his six-year-old son. Although the son lacks the necessary maturity and judgment to operate the gun independently in a safe manner, the father allows the son to use the gun when the father is not present. The son, while aiming the gun at a toy in his yard, misses and accidentally shoots a neighbor. The father, because of his failure to properly supervise his son, can be liable for the injury suffered by the neighbor that is directly attributable to the son's conduct, even though the son himself will not be liable because of his age.

6. "Dram Shop" Liability

Many states recognize, either by statute (a "dram shop act") or by judicial decision, a cause of action against the seller of intoxicating beverages when a third party is subsequently injured due to the buyer's intoxication. Most states limit liability to situations in which the buyer was a minor or was intoxicated at the time of the sale. Some states extend liability to a social host who serves intoxicating beverages to a minor. The states are divided as to whether the cause of action is grounded in negligence or strict liability.

7. Bailment Liability

A bailor may be liable for his own negligent actions but generally is not vicariously liable for the tortious acts of his bailee, except for those limited situations described above, such as bailments involving automobiles or parents and children.

I. LIMITATION OF LIABILITY RESULTING FROM DEFENDANT'S IDENTITY OR RELATIONSHIPS ("IMMUNITIES")

Traditionally, governmental entities, charities, and family members were immune from liability. Today, these immunities have been largely eliminated, but the rules governing the liability of these defendants continue to differ from those governing other tortfeasors.

1. Liability of the Government and Its Officers

a. Federal government

Under the Federal Tort Claims Act, the U.S. government waives immunity in tort actions, with the following exceptions:

i) Certain enumerated torts (assault, battery, false imprisonment, false arrest, malicious prosecution, abuse of process, libel and slander, misrepresentation and deceit, and interference with contract rights);

ii) Discretionary functions (i.e., planning or decision making, as opposed to operational acts);

iii) Assertion of the government's immunity by a government contractor in a products liability case if the contractor conformed to government specifications and warned the government of any known dangers in the product; and

iv) Certain traditional governmental activities (i.e., postal, tax collection or property seizure, admiralty, quarantine, money supply, and military activity).

When the U.S. government waives its sovereign immunity under the FTCA, it is liable in the same manner and to the same extent that a private person under the same circumstances would be liable, but it is not liable for punitive damages.

b. State governments

Most states have waived sovereign immunity, at least partially, through legislation. Simultaneously, however, they have imposed limits on the amount of recovery and the circumstances under which the state can be held liable. They also have created procedural barriers to recover that do not exist in claims against private defendants. **State tort claims acts vary greatly** and therefore each act must be read carefully.

Unless otherwise provided in the legislation, the same terms and conditions apply to the liability of state agencies—including prisons, hospitals, and educational institutions—as to the state itself.

c. Municipalities

1) Usually governed by state tort claims act

Today, the liability of municipalities, other local governments, and their agencies usually are governed by the provisions of state tort claims acts.

2) Governmental vs. proprietary functions

Traditionally, immunity attached to the performance of traditional government functions (such as police and court systems), but did not attach when a municipality was performing a "proprietary" function that often is performed by a private company (such as utilities and parking lots).

3) Public duty rule

The public duty rule provides that there is no liability to any one citizen for the municipality's failure to fulfill a duty that is owed to the public at large, unless that citizen has a special relationship with the municipality that creates a special duty. A special relationship can be shown by:

i) Promises or actions on the part of the municipality demonstrating an affirmative duty to act on behalf of the injured party;

ii) Knowledge by the municipality's agents that failure to act could lead to harm;

iii) Direct contact between the municipality's agents and the injured party; and

iv) The injured party's justifiable reliance on the municipality's affirmative duty.

d. Government officials

1) Discretionary functions

When a government official is personally sued, immunity applies if she is performing **discretionary functions** entrusted to her by law so long as the acts are done without malice or improper purpose.

2) Ministerial functions

There is no tort immunity for carrying out ministerial acts, such as driving while on government business.

3) Highly-ranked officials

Many highly-ranked government officials, such as legislators performing their legislative functions, judges performing their judicial functions, prosecutors, and some upper-echelon officials of the executive branches, usually are absolutely immune from personal liability.

4) Federal immunity

Under the so-called "Westfall Act," 28 U.S.C. § 2679(b)(1), the remedy against the United States under the Federal Tort Claims Act for torts committed by federal employees precludes any personal liability on the part of a federal employee under state tort law.

2. Intra-Family Immunity

Intra-family immunity applies only to personal injuries, not to property damage.

a. Interspousal immunity

Traditionally, interspousal immunity prevented one spouse from suing the other in a personal-injury action. In most jurisdictions today, however, interspousal immunity has been extinguished, and either spouse can now institute a cause of action for personal injury against the other spouse.

b. Parent-child immunity

Traditionally, parents were immune from tort claims brought by their children. In recent decades, however, there has been a clear trend toward abolishing or greatly restricting parental immunity, but abrogation has proceeded more slowly than in the case of interspousal immunity.

Courts generally allow parents to be held liable in areas other than **core parenting activities**. For example, most states allow children to sue parents:

    i) For injuries arising from **automobile accidents**;

    ii) In extreme cases, such as those involving **sexual abuse and intentional tortious conduct**; and

    iii) When the parent is acting in a **"dual capacity,"** such as when the parent is a physician treating the child for an injury (medical malpractice claim allowed).

3. Charitable Immunity

Most states have either totally or partially eliminated the common-law rule of charitable immunity. Some states cap the amount of damages recoverable from a charitable institution.

J. SHARING LIABILITY AMONG MULTIPLE DEFENDANTS

1. Joint and Several Liability

a. Definition

Under the doctrine of joint and several liability, each of two or more defendants who is found liable for a single and indivisible harm to the plaintiff is subject to liability to the plaintiff **for the entire harm**. The plaintiff has the choice of collecting the entire judgment from one defendant, the entire judgment from another defendant, or recovering portions of the judgment from various defendants, as long as the plaintiff's entire recovery does not exceed the amount of the judgment.

b. Application

Examples of when joint and several liability applies include, among other instances, when:

i)   The tortious acts of two or more tortfeasors combine to produce an indivisible harm (*see* § IV.E.1.b.2., *supra*);

ii) The harm results from the acts of one or more tortfeasors acting in concert (*see* § IV.E.1.b.4., *supra*);

iii) Alternative liability applies (*see* § IV.E.1.b.3., *supra*);

iv) *Res ipsa loquitur* is used against multiple defendants (such as in a surgical setting) and the defendants are unable to identify the tortfeasor whose acts were negligent (*see* § IV.D.2, *supra*); and

v)   The employer and the employee are both held liable (*see* § IV.H.1., *supra*).

2. Contribution

If two or more tortfeasors are subject to liability to the same plaintiff, and one of the tortfeasors has paid the plaintiff more than his fair share of the common liability, he may sue any of the other joint tortfeasors for contribution, and recover anything paid in excess of his fair share.

a. Determining "fair shares"

In most jurisdictions, each party's fair share is determined by comparing how far each tortfeasor departed from the standard of reasonable care.

b. Intentional tortfeasor

Generally, a party who has committed an intentional tort may not seek contribution from another tortfeasor.

3. Several (Proportionate) Liability

A significant number of states now reject joint and several liability and instead recognize **pure several liability**, under which **each tortfeasor is liable only for his proportionate share** of the plaintiff's damages. In most jurisdictions, each defendant's share of liability is determined in accordance with how far each deviated from the standard of reasonable care. In other words, the more culpable defendant pays the higher proportion of the damages.

4. Satisfaction and Release

Once a plaintiff has recovered fully from one or a combination of defendants, she is barred from pursuing further action against other tortfeasors. The plaintiff generally may not receive double recovery.

If the plaintiff has not been wholly compensated, it is now the usual rule that a release of one tortfeasor does not release the others, but instead diminishes the claim against the others, ordinarily by the amount of compensation received from the released tortfeasor. However, a release may bar claims against other tortfeasors if either (i) the release agreement so provides or (ii) the plaintiff has been entirely compensated for his losses.

5. **Indemnification**

Indemnification is the shifting of the entire loss from one joint tortfeasor to another party.

a. **Vicarious liability**

Indemnification generally applies when one tortfeasor is vicariously liable for the other's wrongdoing. The tortfeasor who has discharged the liability is entitled to indemnity from the actual wrongdoer who was primarily responsible for the harm (e.g., an employer who pays a judgment for the tort of an employee due to the employer's vicarious liability).

b. **Complete reimbursement**

The employer can then seek complete reimbursement (indemnity) from the employee when:

i) There is a **prior indemnification agreement** between the parties (e.g., in the construction industry, a contractor may agree to indemnify a subcontractor for the latter's negligence that may occur in the future);

ii) There is a significant difference between the blameworthiness of two defendants such that **equity requires a shifting of the loss** to the more blameworthy defendant;

iii) Significant **additional harm is subsequently caused by another tortfeasor** (i.e., one defendant pays the full judgment, including for additional harm caused by the malpractice of the treating physician); or

iv) Under **strict products liability**, each supplier has a right of indemnification against all previous suppliers in a distribution chain.

Note: Indemnity in degree of blameworthiness is rejected in jurisdictions with comparative negligence systems. These states apportion damages based on relative fault, although indemnification is allowed in other instances when it is not based on degree of fault.

K. **DEFENSES TO NEGLIGENCE**

1. **Contributory Negligence**

Contributory negligence occurs when a plaintiff **fails to exercise reasonable care** for her own safety and thereby **contributes to her own injury**. Note that when a plaintiff is suing a defendant for the negligent rendering of services, such as medical services, the plaintiff's negligent conduct in creating the condition that the defendant has been employed to remedy is not taken into account.

a. **Contributory negligence: traditional rule**

At common law, and in a handful of states, the plaintiff's contributory negligence (i.e., failure to exercise reasonable care for her own safety) is a **complete bar to recovery**, regardless of the percentage that the plaintiff's own negligence contributed to the harm.

Examples of contributory negligence include:

i) A plaintiff's violation of a statute that is designed to protect against the type of injury suffered by the plaintiff. The plaintiff's violation of a statute cannot be used as a defense, however, when a safety statute is interpreted to place the entire responsibility for the harm suffered by the plaintiff on the defendant (e.g., workplace safety statutes when an injury occurs to someone not covered by workers' compensation);

ii) A plaintiff-pedestrian's crossing the street against the light; and

iii) A plaintiff driving at an unreasonable speed that deprived him of the opportunity to avoid a traffic accident.

A rescuer who takes significant risks when attempting a rescue may also be permitted to recover despite the rescuer's negligence.

Contributory negligence is not a defense to an intentional tort, gross negligence, or recklessness.

b. Last clear chance

In contributory-negligence jurisdictions, the plaintiff may mitigate the legal consequences of her own contributory negligence if she proves that the defendant had the last clear chance to avoid injuring the plaintiff but failed to do so. This doctrine has been abolished in most comparative-fault jurisdictions.

1) Helpless plaintiff

A plaintiff who, due to his own contributory negligence, is in peril from which he cannot escape is in helpless peril. In such cases, the defendant is liable if she **knew or should have known** of the plaintiff's perilous situation and could have avoided harming the plaintiff but for her (the defendant's) own negligence.

2) Inattentive plaintiff

A plaintiff who, due to his own contributory negligence, is in peril from which he could escape if he were paying attention is an inattentive or oblivious plaintiff. The defendant is liable only if she has **actual knowledge** of the plaintiff's inattention.

c. Comparative fault

Almost all jurisdictions have adopted some form of comparative fault (comparative negligence). There are two basic forms of comparative fault:

1) Pure comparative negligence

In jurisdictions that have adopted the doctrine of pure comparative negligence, a plaintiff's contributory negligence is not a complete bar to recovery. Instead, the plaintiff's full damages are calculated by the trier of fact and then reduced by the proportion that the plaintiff's fault bears to the total harm (e.g., if the plaintiff's full damages are $100,000, the plaintiff is 80% at fault, and the defendant is 20% at fault, then the plaintiff will recover $20,000).

2) Modified or partial comparative fault

A majority of comparative fault jurisdictions apply modified comparative fault. In these jurisdictions:

   i) If the plaintiff is **less at fault than the defendant**, the plaintiff's recovery is **reduced by his percentage of fault**, just as in a pure comparative fault jurisdiction.

   ii) If the plaintiff is **more at fault than the defendant**, the plaintiff's **recovery is barred**, just as in a contributory negligence jurisdiction.

   iii) In the vast majority of modified comparative fault jurisdictions, if the plaintiff and the defendant are found to **be equally at fault**, the **plaintiff recovers 50% of his total damages**. In a few modified comparative fault jurisdictions, the plaintiff recovers nothing when the jury finds the plaintiff and the defendant are equally at fault.

3) Multiple defendants

In either a pure comparative fault of a modified comparative fault jurisdiction, the plaintiff's degree of negligence is compared to the total negligence of all defendants combined.

4) Relationships to other defenses

   i) Last clear chance no longer applies as a separate doctrine in comparative fault jurisdictions.

   ii) Comparative fault will reduce the plaintiff's recovery even if the defendant's conduct is willful, wanton, or reckless, but will not reduce the plaintiff's recovery for intentional torts.

   iii) The impact of comparative fault on assumption of risk is considered in § K.2.c., *below*.

5) Illustrations

   i) Single defendant, pure comparative—Defendant is 55% negligent and Plaintiff is 45% negligent in causing the accident. They each have $100,000 in damages. Plaintiff will recover $55,000 from Defendant ($100,000 minus $45,000, which represents Plaintiff's proportionate fault of 45%), and Defendant will recover $45,000 from Plaintiff. Plaintiff will have a net recovery of $10,000 because Defendant's damages will be offset against Plaintiff's damages.

ii) Single defendant, modified or partial comparative—Same facts as above, except that Defendant will not recover anything because he was more than 50% at fault.

iii) Multiple defendants, modified or partial comparative—Two defendants are negligent: Defendant 1 is 20% negligent; Defendant 2 is 45% negligent. Combined, their negligence is 65%. Plaintiff is 35% negligent. Plaintiff can recover $65,000 from either Defendant 1 or Defendant 2 under the theory of joint and several liability. The paying defendant can then seek contribution from the nonpaying defendant. If either defendant suffered damages, he also has a right of recovery against either of the other two negligent parties because each one's negligence is less than the total negligence of the other two.

> When comparative negligence exists (either pure or modified), it supersedes all other affirmative defenses except assumption of the risk.

d. Imputed contributory negligence

Imputed contributory negligence occurs when another person's fault is "imputed" to the plaintiff to prevent or limit his recovery due to the other person's fault. For example, an employee's negligent driving may prevent or reduce an employer's recovery from a third party if the employer's car is damaged by the third party's negligence. The fault of one business partner can be imputed to another business partner as contributory negligence when the second party is suing a third party.

Imputed contributory negligence is disfavored. Imputed contributory negligence does not apply to:

i) A married plaintiff whose spouse was contributorily negligent in causing the harm, in a suit against a third party;

ii) A child plaintiff whose parent's negligence was a contributing cause of her harm, in a suit against a third party;

iii) An automobile passenger suing a third-party driver if the negligence of the driver of the car in which the passenger was riding also contributed to the accident; or

iv) An automobile owner in an action against a defendant driver for negligence when the driver of the owner's car also was negligent.

e. Distinguishing comparative fault, contribution, and several liability

Comparative fault, contribution, and several liability all involve comparing the level of egregiousness of fault of parties in tort litigation. However, each of these concepts operates in a different context.

i) Comparative fault always involves comparing the fault of a plaintiff with the fault of one or more defendants.

ii) Contribution involves comparing the degrees of fault of co-defendants in an action or as the result of a motion by one co-defendant against another co-defendant. It does not affect the liability of any of the defendants to the plaintiff.

iii) Several liability, in the minority of jurisdictions where it operates, involves comparing the levels of fault of the co-defendants. However, unlike contribution, the issue is how much the plaintiff will receive from each defendant.

> **EXAM NOTE:** The MBE frequently asks students to perform simple numerical calculations involving joint and several liability or several liability, contribution, and pure or modified (partial) comparative fault. *See* § IV.K.1.c., *infra*.

2. Assumption of the Risk

a. Exculpatory clauses in contracts

In general, parties can contract to disclaim liability for negligence. But, courts **will not** enforce exculpatory provisions:

i) Disclaiming liability for reckless or wanton misconduct or gross negligence;

ii) Where there is a gross disparity of bargaining power between the parties;

iii) Where the party seeking to apply the exculpatory provision offers services of great importance to the public which are a practical necessity for some members of the public such as medical services; or

iv) If the exculpatory clause is subject to typical contractual defenses such as fraud or duress.

Some jurisdictions require that the contract explicitly state that claims "based on negligence" are disclaimed.

Generally, **common carrier, innkeepers, and employers cannot disclaim liability for negligence**. State statutes often provide that certain additional businesses cannot disclaim liability for negligence.

Many courts now hold that **disclaimer of liability by contract negates** the fact that the defendant owes a **duty of care** to the plaintiff in the first place. This causes the plaintiff's prima facie case for negligence to fail, rather than acting as an affirmative defense of assumption of risk.

b. Participants and spectators in athletic events

In a negligence claim brought by a spectator or a participant of an athletic event or similar activity, the spectator or participant necessarily subjects himself to certain risks that are usually incident to and inherent in the game or activity. Some courts hold that the other players or facility owners therefore do not owe the spectators a duty of care; others allow the defendant to defend against the claim using the affirmative defense of assumption of the risk.

c. Unreasonably proceeding in face of known, specific risk

Traditionally, and in many jurisdictions today, a plaintiff's **voluntarily encountering a known, specific risk** is an affirmative defense to negligence that bars recovery. Most courts hold that the voluntary encountering must also be **unreasonable**.

In **contributory negligence** jurisdictions and in a minority of comparative fault jurisdictions, this form of assumption of the risk remains a **total bar** to recovery.

In most **comparative fault** jurisdictions, this form of assumption of the risk has been merged into the comparative fault analysis and merely **reduces recovery**. The plaintiff's awareness of the risk is taken into account in determining the degree to which the plaintiff is at fault, but it also can be considered in determining the reasonableness of the plaintiff's or the defendant's actions.

Consent distinguished: Consent is a defense to intentional torts, whereas assumption of the risk applies to negligence actions and actions alleging strict liability.

V. STRICT LIABILITY

A prima facie case for strict liability requires (i) an absolute duty to make the plaintiff's person or property safe, (ii) breach, (iii) actual and proximate causation, and (iv) damages.

The three general situations in which strict liability is imposed are:

i) **D**angerous activities;

ii) **A**nimals; and

iii) **D**efective or dangerous products.

MNEMONIC: **DAD**

EXAM NOTE: The "DAD" situations are the only situations in which a defendant can be liable without fault. Otherwise, strict liability is generally the wrong answer choice.

A. ABNORMALLY DANGEROUS ACTIVITIES

1. Basic Rule

A defendant engaged in an abnormally dangerous activity will be held strictly liable—without any proof of negligence—for personal injuries and property damage caused by the activity, regardless of precautions taken to prevent the harm. Rest. 3d: Liability for Physical and Emotional Harm § 20.

2. Definition of "Abnormally Dangerous"

Abnormally dangerous means that an activity:

i) Creates a **foreseeable and highly significant risk** of physical harm even when reasonable care is exercised; and

ii) The activity is **not commonly engaged in**.

In addition to these requirements, in evaluating whether an activity is abnormally dangerous, courts often consider the **gravity of the harm** resulting from the activity, the **inappropriateness of the place** where the activity is being conducted, and the **limited value** of the activity to the community.

EXAM NOTE: The focus is on the inherent nature of the activity, not how careful the defendant may or may not be in conducting the activity.

Common abnormally dangerous activities include mining, blasting, using explosives, fumigation, excavating, hazardous waste disposal, gasoline storage in residential areas, toxic chemicals and gases, and the storage of large quantities of water and other liquids.

3. Scope of Risk

Strict liability for an abnormally dangerous activity exists **only if harm that actually occurs results from the risk that made the activity abnormally dangerous in the first place**.

> **Example:** If the defendant's employee drops a heavy package of explosives, hitting the plaintiff's head, and causing a concussion, the plaintiff's claim is for negligence, not strict liability. The concussion is not the type of harm (i.e., an explosion) that makes the use of explosives an abnormally dangerous activity.

As in the case with superseding causes in negligence (*see* § V.E.3.c., *supra*), the defendant's liability can be cut off by unforeseeable intervening causes.

4. Airplanes

In the early stages of commercial aviation, the owner or operator of an aircraft was strictly liable to persons and objects on the ground that were injured by objects that fell or were dropped from the aircraft, or from the aircraft itself falling and crashing. Strict liability applied to any physical damage to the land under such circumstances.

The modern trend is to apply negligence law, not strict liability, to such accidents.

Strict liability does not apply to harm suffered by passengers or chattel within an aircraft due to a crash.

Crop dusting is also subject to strict liability.

B. THE RULE OF *RYLANDS V. FLETCHER*

A defendant is strictly liable for the consequences which occur when he "...for his own purposes brings on his lands and collects and keeps there anything likely to do mischief if it escapes, must keep it at his peril, and, if he does not do so, is prima facie answerable for all the damage which is the natural consequence of its escape." *Rylands v. Fletcher*, LR 3 HL 330 (1868) (involving the release of water from the defendant's reservoir onto the plaintiff's property). The narrow holding of *Rylands*—that an owner of property with a dam on it is strictly liable for the harm caused by the release of water due to the bursting of the dam—is still followed. However, the broader principle of strict liability for harm caused by any dangerous object brought onto property by the landowner is no longer always followed. Instead, courts usually hold that only abnormally dangerous activities are subject to strict liability.

C. ANIMALS

1. Wild Animals

A wild animal is an animal that, **as a species or a class**, is not by custom devoted to the service of humankind in the place where it is being kept. For example, a wild elephant that has been tamed and exhibited as part of a circus remains categorized as a wild animal.

a. Dangerous propensity

The possessor of a wild animal is strictly liable for harm done by that animal, in spite of any precautions the possessor has taken to confine the animal or prevent the harm, if the harm arises from a **dangerous propensity** that is **characteristic of such wild animals** or of which the owner **has reason to know**.

The plaintiff must not knowingly do anything to bring about his own injury.

b. Plaintiff's fearful reaction

Strict liability applies to an injury caused by a **plaintiff's fearful reaction to the sight of an unrestrained wild animal**, in addition to injuries caused directly by the wild animal.

c. Liability to trespassers

Licensees or invitees injured by a wild animal may recover in strict liability. A landowner is **not** strictly liable for injuries inflicted by his animals against an **undiscovered trespasser**, except for injuries inflicted by a **vicious watchdog**. Remember, however, that a landowner may be liable on a negligence theory.

2. Domestic Animals

a. Known to be dangerous

A domestic animal's owner is strictly liable for injuries caused by that animal if he **knows** or has reason to know of the animal's **dangerous propensities** and the harm results from those dangerous propensities. Otherwise, at common law, a domestic animal owner is only liable for negligence.

b. "Dog-bite" statutes

Many states have enacted "dog-bite" statutes that hold owners of dogs or other domestic animals designated in the statute strictly liable for damages resulting from personal injuries.

3. Owner's Animals on Another's Land

The owner of any animal, wild or domestic (other than household pets), is strictly liable for any reasonably foreseeable damage caused by his animal while trespassing on the land of another. The exception for household pets (the Third Restatement specifically mentions dogs and cats) does not apply if the owner knows or has reason to know that the dog or cat is intruding on another's property in a way that has a tendency to cause substantial harm. Rest. 3d: Liability for Physical and Emotional Harm § 21.

4. Plaintiff's Conduct

In a case alleging strict liability against an animal owner, the plaintiff's contributory negligence may reduce recovery in some comparative fault states, but will not eliminate recovery in a contributory negligence jurisdiction. (*See* § V.D., *infra*.)

However, if the plaintiff is aware of the dangerous propensity of an animal and taunts the animal, he may be prohibited from recovering under the doctrine of assumption of the risk.

5. Landlord's Liability

In most jurisdictions, the landlord is not liable for harms caused by animals owned by his tenants. The landlord lacks the required element of control over the animal. Some jurisdictions impose liability on the landlord based on negligence if the landlord is aware of the dangerous propensities of the dog or other animal.

D. DEFENSES TO STRICT LIABILITY

1. Contributory Negligence

In contributory negligence jurisdictions, the plaintiff's contributory negligence is not a defense to strict liability, i.e., it does not bar recovery.

2. Comparative Fault

The Third Restatement provides that the defendant's liability based on strict liability for either abnormally dangerous activities or animals should be reduced by the comparative fault of the plaintiff. However, only a minority of jurisdictions have taken this position. In the majority of comparative-fault jurisdictions, the plaintiff's contributory negligence does not reduce the plaintiff's recovery under a strict liability claim.

3. Assumption of the Risk

The plaintiff's assumption of the risk bars his recovery in a strict-liability action. This defense is also referred to as "knowing contributory negligence."

4. Statutory Privilege

Performance of an essential public service (e.g., construction of utility or sewer lines) exempts one from strict liability; however, liability may still exist under a negligence theory.

VI. PRODUCTS LIABILITY

A product may be defective because of a defect in its **design** or **manufacture** or because of a **failure to adequately warn** the consumer of a hazard related to the foreseeable use of the product.

When a plaintiff files a products liability case, he generally has at least three possible claims on which to base an action: **negligence, strict products liability**, and **breach of warranty**. Each type of claim requires different elements. (The Third Restatement provides for only a single cause of action in the absence of additional facts, and some courts have begun to adopt this approach.)

If, however, the defendant intended or knew with substantial certainty the consequences of the defect, then the cause of action could be based on an intentional tort. As with any intentional tort claim, punitive as well as compensatory damages are recoverable. The same defenses germane to each type of tort are applicable.

A. NEGLIGENCE

As with any negligence action, the plaintiff must prove duty, breach, causation, and damages to prevail.

1. Duty

The commercial manufacturer, distributor, retailer, or seller of a product owes a duty of reasonable care to **any foreseeable plaintiff** (i.e., a purchaser, user, or bystander).

2. Breach

Failure to exercise **reasonable care** in the inspection or sale of a product constitutes breach of that duty. The plaintiff must establish not only that the defect exists, but that the defendant's negligent conduct (lack of reasonable care) led to the plaintiff's harm. In other words, had the defendant exercised reasonable care in the inspection or sale of the product, the defect **would have been discovered,** and the plaintiff would not have been harmed. The plaintiff also has the option of invoking *res ipsa loquitur* if the defect could not have occurred without the manufacturer's negligence.

> The individual defendant must have breached his duty to reasonably inspect or sell. Unlike in strict products liability, the negligence of others in the supply chain cannot be imputed. Rather, the plaintiff has the burden of proving fault on the part of any particular defendant.

3. Causation

The plaintiff must prove factual and proximate causation.

> When a seller sells a product with a known defect and without giving adequate warnings about the defect, the failure to warn may be a superseding cause, breaking the chain of causation between the manufacturer and the injury.

4. Damages

The plaintiff is entitled to recover damages resulting from any personal injury or property damage. Claims for purely economic loss are generally not allowed under either a negligence theory or a strict liability theory, but must be brought as a breach-of-warranty action.

5. Defenses

The standard negligence defenses of contributory/comparative negligence and assumption of the risk apply.

B. STRICT PRODUCTS LIABILITY

Under strict liability, the manufacturer, retailer, or other distributor of a defective product may be liable for any harm to persons or property caused by such product.

> **EXAM NOTE:** Strict products liability is only one way that a manufacturer or supplier of a product can be held liable for a plaintiff's injuries. Remember also to consider breach of warranty and negligence.

1. **Elements of Claim**

    In order to recover, the plaintiff must plead and prove that:

    i)   The product was **defective** (in manufacture, design, or failure to warn);

    ii) The defect existed at the time the product left the defendant's control; and

    iii) The defect **caused the plaintiff's injuries** when used in an **intended or reasonably foreseeable way**.

2. **Defective Product**

    A product is defective when, at the time of the sale or distribution, it contains a manufacturing defect, a design defect, or inadequate instructions or warnings (i.e., failure to warn).

    a. **Manufacturing defect**

        A manufacturing defect is a **deviation from what the manufacturer intended** the product to be that causes harm to the plaintiff. The test for the existence of such a defect is whether the product **conforms to the defendant's own specifications**.

    b. **Design defect**

        Depending on the jurisdiction, courts apply either the **consumer-expectation test** or the **risk-utility test** to determine whether a design defect exists. Many jurisdictions use various hybrids of the two tests, and some states allow the plaintiff to prove a design defect under either test.

        i)   *Consumer expectation test:* Does the product include a condition not contemplated by the ordinary consumer that is **unreasonably dangerous** to him?

        ii) *Risk-utility test:* Do the risks posed by the product **outweigh its benefits**?

        Under the risk-utility test, in a majority of jurisdictions and under the Third Restatement, the plaintiff must prove that a **reasonable alternative design** was available to the defendant and the failure to use that design has rendered the product not reasonably safe. The alternative design must be economically feasible.

        Merely providing a warning does not necessarily prevent a product from being unreasonably dangerous.

    c. **Failure to warn**

        An action brought under a failure to warn theory is essentially the same as a design defect claim, but the defect in question is the manufacturer's failure to provide an adequate warning related to the risks of using the product. A failure to warn defect exists if there were **foreseeable risks of harm, not obvious to an ordinary user** of the product, which risks could have been reduced or avoided by providing reasonable instructions or warnings. The failure to include the instructions or warnings renders the product not reasonably safe.

1) Prescription drugs

Under the "learned intermediary" rule, the manufacturer of a prescription drug typically satisfies its duty to warn the consumer by informing the prescribing physician of problems with the drug rather than informing the patient taking the drug. Rest. 3d: Products Liability § 6. There are several exceptions, including, most importantly:

i) If the manufacturer is aware that the drug will be dispensed or administered without the personal intervention or evaluation of a healthcare provider, such as when a vaccine is administered through a mass inoculation; and

ii) As a result of a federal statute, in the case of birth control pills.

d. Inference of defect

A plaintiff is entitled to a *res ipsa loquitor*-like inference that a product defect existed if the harm suffered by the plaintiff:

i) Was of a kind that ordinarily occurs as a result of a product defect; and

ii) Was not solely the result of causes other than a product defect existing at the time of sale or distribution.

Rest. 3d: Products Liability § 3.

This inference is frequently applied in cases involving a manufacturing defect when the product is lost or destroyed as a consequence of the incident that caused the plaintiff's harm.

3. Plaintiffs

To bring a strict-liability action, a plaintiff is not required to be in privity of contract with the defendant. **Anyone foreseeably injured** by a defective product or whose property is harmed by the product may bring a strict-liability action. Appropriate plaintiffs include **not only purchasers**, but also **other users** of the product and even **bystanders** who suffer personal injury or property damage.

4. Defendants

> **EXAM NOTE:** MBE questions frequently involve the viability of claims against various defendants and the possibility of cross-claims among these defendants.

a. Business of seller

To be subject to strict liability for a defective product, the defendant must be in the **business of selling** or otherwise distributing products of the type that harmed the plaintiff.

b. Chain of distribution

Included as a seller are the **manufacturer** of the product, its **distributor**, and its **retail seller**.

c. Even if not responsible for the defect

As long as the seller is a commercial supplier of the product, the seller is subject to strict liability for a defective product, even if the revenue from sales of the product is not a significant portion of the seller's business. The seller is strictly liable even if the seller was responsible for the defect in any way and even when the product is not purchased directly from the seller.

d. Seller of component part

The commercial supplier of a component, such as sand used in manufacturing cement or a switch used in an electrical device, is subject to liability if the component itself is defective, but not when the component is incorporated into a product that is defective for another reason. However, the commercial supplier of a component may be liable if that supplier substantially participates in the process of integrating the component into the design of the assembled product and that product is defective due to the integration.

e. Indemnification

Ordinarily if the plaintiff recovers from the retailer solely for a product defect that existed at the time the product left the manufacturer's control, the retailer is able to recover from the manufacturer in an indemnification action.

f. Lessor

Generally, a lessor of a commercial product (e.g., car, boat, tools) is subject to strict liability for a defective product.

g. Products and services

A seller that provides both products and services generally is **liable if the defective product is consumed**, such as food at a restaurant, but not if the product is only used, such as the vendor of a balloon ride when the balloon itself is defective. Hospitals and doctors generally are treated as providing a service, rather than a product, in cases in which the defective product is used as a tool, loaned to the patient, or even implanted in the patient.

h. Exclusions

1) Casual seller

Because the seller must be in the business of selling similar products, a casual seller, such as an individual car owner who sells the car to his neighbor or an accountant who sells her office furniture to another businessperson, is **not subject to strict liability**.

2) Auctioneer

Similarly, an auctioneer of a product generally is not subject to strict liability with respect to the products auctioned.

5. Damages

As with negligence claims, the plaintiff is entitled to recover damages for any personal injury or property damage. A claim for **purely economic loss generally**

is not allowed under a strict-liability theory but must be brought as a breach-of-warranty action, as must a claim for harm to the product itself and any consequential damages arising therefrom.

6. **Defenses**

a. **Comparative fault**

In a comparative-fault jurisdiction, the plaintiff's own negligence reduces his recovery in a strict products liability action in the same manner as it is in a negligence action. For example, in a pure comparative-fault jurisdiction, the plaintiff's recovery is reduced by the percentage that the plaintiff's fault contributed to causing her injury.

b. **Contributory negligence**

In a contributory-negligence jurisdiction, the plaintiff's negligence generally is not a defense to a strict products liability action when the plaintiff negligently failed to discover the defect or misused the product in a reasonably foreseeable way, but it generally is when the plaintiff's fault consisted of unreasonably proceeding in the face of a known product defect.

Suppliers are required to anticipate reasonably foreseeable misuses of their products.

c. **Assumption of risk**

Voluntary and knowing assumption of the risk is a complete bar to recovery in contributory-negligence jurisdictions and in a small number of the comparative-fault jurisdictions. In most comparative fault jurisdictions, a plaintiff's assumption of a risk will reduce his recovery in proportion to degree of fault, but it will not be a complete bar to recovery. Assumption of the risk is a subjective standard. The plaintiff must be aware of the danger and knowingly expose himself to it.

d. **Product misuse, modification, or alteration by the user**

The misuse, alteration, or modification of a product by the user in a manner that is neither intended by nor reasonably foreseeable to the manufacturer typically negates liability. On the other hand, foreseeable misuse, alteration, or modification usually does not preclude recovery.

A majority of comparative-fault jurisdictions treat product misuse as a form of fault that reduces, but does not eliminate, the plaintiff's recovery. A significant minority of comparative-fault jurisdictions, and most contributory-negligence jurisdictions, hold that product misuse totally bars recovery.

> **EXAM NOTE:** Product misuse has been tested frequently on the MBE.

e. **Substantial change in product**

If the product substantially changes between the time it is distributed by the manufacturer and reaches the consumer (e.g., a part is reconditioned), then this change may constitute a superseding cause that cuts off the liability of the original manufacturer.

f. Compliance with governmental standards

Most often, compliance with governmental safety standards is not conclusive evidence that the product is not defective. On the other hand, the jury can consider evidence introduced by the defendant that the product complied with government standards and also evidence offered by the plaintiff on the product's failure to comply with these standards in deciding whether the product is defective.

However, if a product complies with federal safety statutes or regulations, a state tort claim act may be "pre-empted" if (i) Congress has explicitly so indicated, (ii) Congress has comprehensively regulated the field (i.e., "field preemption"), or (iii) it would be impossible for the manufacturer to comply with both the federal regulation and the requirements of state tort law.

g. "State of the art"

In failure-to-warn and design-defect cases, the manufacturer may introduce as evidence the level of relevant scientific, technological, and safety knowledge existing and reasonably feasible at the time of the product's distribution. In most jurisdictions, compliance with this "state of the art" does not bar recovery against the manufacturer as a matter of law. However, a number of states have enacted statutes providing that compliance with the state of the art is a total bar to recovery.

h. Statute of limitations issues

The statute of limitations begins to run against the plaintiff with a personal injury whenever he discovers, or in the exercise of reasonable care should discover, his injury and its connection to the product. As a result, the statute of limitations may not preclude an action against a manufacturer or other seller until many decades after the manufacture and distribution of the product. For example, asbestos-related diseases may not manifest themselves until decades after the distribution of the asbestos insulation and the plaintiff's exposure to it.

i. Contract disclaimers, limitations, and waivers

A **disclaimer** or limitation of remedies or other contractual exculpation (i.e., waiver) by a product seller or other distributor **does not generally bar** or reduce an otherwise valid products liability claim for personal injury.

> **EXAM NOTE:** The immunity created by workers' compensation statutes protects only the plaintiff's employer from most tort claims brought by the victim. It does not provide any immunity for other defendants. Frequently the plaintiff-employee is injured while working with a defective machine tool or with a toxic substance, such as asbestos insulation. Workers' compensation does not bar his claim against the manufacturer of these products.

C. WARRANTIES

Products liability actions brought under warranty theories generally may be brought not only against a retailer of a product, but also against a manufacturer or distributor of goods, at least when damages are sought for personal injury or property damage.

1. **Implied Warranties**

    a. **Two types**

        1) **Merchantability**

            The implied warranty of merchantability warrants that the product being sold is **generally acceptable and reasonably fit for the ordinary purposes for which it is being sold**. The seller must be a merchant with respect to the kind of goods at issue.

        2) **Fitness for a particular purpose**

            The implied warranty of fitness warrants that a product is fit for a particular purpose, but only if the **seller knows the particular purpose** for which the product is being purchased and the buyer **relies on the seller's skill or judgment in supplying the product**.

    b. **Claims**

        Any product that fails to live up to either of the above warranties constitutes a breach of the defendant's warranty; the **plaintiff need not prove any fault** on the defendant's part.

        The plaintiff may recover damages for personal injury and property damage, as well as for **purely economic loss**.

        Alternative versions of the Uniform Commercial Code provisions governing warranties provide differing versions of who can recover. For example, the most restrictive UCC provisions allow only the purchaser or a member of her family or household to recover, while a more inclusive variation essentially allows any foreseeable victim to recover.

2. **Express Warranties**

    An express warranty is a guarantee—an **affirmation of fact or a promise**—made by the seller regarding the product that is part of the **basis of a bargain**. A seller is liable for any breach of that warranty, regardless of fault. Damages for personal injury or property damage are recoverable.

3. **Defenses to Warranty Claims**

    a. **Disclaimers**

        Although the seller generally can disclaim warranties, in the case of **consumer goods, any limitation of consequential damages for personal injury is prima facie unconscionable**.

        In the case of express warranties, a disclaimer is valid only if it is consistent with the warranty, which it usually is not.

b. Tort defenses

1) Assumption of risk

Most jurisdictions hold that the plaintiff's unreasonable, voluntary encountering of a known product risk bars recovery.

2) Comparative fault

Most comparative-fault jurisdictions reduce recovery based on warranty claims in the same way they would strict products liability claims.

3) Contributory negligence

In contributory negligence jurisdictions, most courts hold that contributory negligence does not bar a plaintiff's warranty claim, except when the contributory negligence consists of the unreasonable encountering of a known risk (i.e., the overlap between contributory negligence and assumption of risk).

4) Product misuse in implied warranty claims

With or without using the language of "product misuse," most courts find that product misuse prevents recovery under the implied warranty of merchantability where the product is warranted to be fit for "ordinary purposes."

5) Failure to provide notice of breach

A warranty claim generally fails if the plaintiff fails to provide the seller with notice of the breach of warranty within the statutorily required time period (where applicable) or a reasonable period of time.

VII. DEFAMATION, INVASION OF PRIVACY, AND BUSINESS TORTS

A. DEFAMATION

A plaintiff may bring an action for defamation:

i) If the defendant's **defamatory language**;

ii) Is **of or concerning** the plaintiff;

iii) Is **published** to a third party who **understands** its defamatory nature; and

iv) **Damages** the plaintiff's reputation.

For **matters of public concern**, the plaintiff is constitutionally required to prove fault on the part of the defendant. If the plaintiff is either **a public official or a public figure,** the plaintiff must prove actual malice.

1. Defamatory Language

Language that diminishes respect, esteem, or goodwill toward the plaintiff, or that deters others from associating with the plaintiff, is defamatory. The plaintiff may introduce extrinsic facts to establish defamation by innuendo.

An opinion is actionable if the defendant implies that there is a factual basis for that opinion. *See Milkovich v. Lorian Journal Co.*, 497 U.S. 1 (1990); *Gertz v. Welch, Inc.*, 418 U.S. 323 (1974).

2. "Of or Concerning" the Plaintiff

A reasonable person must believe that the defamatory communication refers to this particular plaintiff and holds him up to scorn or ridicule in the eyes of a substantial number of respectable members of the community.

If the defamatory language applies to a group, then a member of the group can maintain a defamation action only if the group is so small that the matter can reasonably be understood to refer to that member, unless there is other evidence that the language refers to that particular member.

A deceased individual cannot be defamed. A corporation, partnership, or unincorporated association may be defamed if the language prejudices it in conducting its activities or deters others from dealing with it.

3. Publication

a. To a third party

Publication of defamatory matter is its intentional or negligent communication to a third party, i.e., to someone other than the person being defamed.

Example: If an employer confronts her employee in a face-to-face conversation where no one else is present or can overhear the conversation and tells him that he is being fired because he embezzled company funds, there is no publication and no defamation.

EXAM NOTE: MBE questions on defamation often center on the publication requirement. Remember that the statement must be **intentionally or negligently made to a third party**. Beware of fact patterns in which the publication requirement is not met, such as those involving a third party learning about the statement through no fault of the defendant's, or when no third party hears the statement at all.

b. Republication

A person who **repeats** a defamatory statement may be liable for defamation even though that person identifies the originator of the statement and expresses a lack of knowledge as to the truthfulness of the statement.

c. Internet service providers

A federal statute provides that internet service providers are not publishers for purpose of defamation law.

4. Constitutional Requirements

Since the Supreme Court's opinion in *New York Times v. Sullivan,* 376 U.S. 254 (1964), which held that the First Amendment affects the plaintiff's right to recover under the common-law tort of defamation, constitutional requirements now underlie many aspects of defamation law. These constitutional requirements affect fundamental aspects of defamation law in various ways depending on (i) the category into which the plaintiff fits and (ii) the nature of the defamatory communication.

a. Public official

A public official is someone in the hierarchy of government employees who has, or appears to have, **substantial responsibility for or control over the conduct of government affairs**. **Candidates for public office** are also treated as public officials.

b. Public figure

The constitutional requirements are the same when the plaintiff is a public figure as when she is a public official. There are two ways in which a plaintiff may be categorized as a public figure:

i) *General purpose public figures*—Plaintiffs who occupy positions of such **persuasive power and influence in society** that they are deemed public figures for all purposes; and

ii) *Limited purpose or special purpose public figures*—Plaintiffs **who thrust themselves to the forefront of particular public controversies** in order to influence the resolution of the issues involved. These plaintiffs are treated as public figures **if the defamatory statement relates to their participation in the controversy**, but they are treated as private figures if the defamation relates to any other matter.

c. Private individual

1) Matter of public concern

If the plaintiff is a **private individual** (neither a public figure nor a public official) and the statement involves a matter of **public concern**, the defendant is entitled to **limited constitutional protections**, though not as significant as those available when the person being defamed is either a public official or a public figure.

2) Not a matter of public concern

If the plaintiff is a **private individual** and the statement is a **not a matter of public concern**, then there are **no constitutional restrictions** on the law of defamation. However, many states now apply the same principles of defamation law to all cases involving private individuals as plaintiffs.

5. Falsity

a. Matters of public concern

If either (i) the defamatory statement relates to a matter of public concern or (ii) the plaintiff is a public official or a public figure, the plaintiff must prove that the **defamatory statement is false** as part of her prima facie case.

b. Private individual plaintiff/not a matter of public concern

At common law and in some states today, a private individual plaintiff suing for defamation regarding a statement that does not involve a matter of public concern is **not required to prove falsity** as part of her prima facie case. However, the defendant may prove the truth of the statement as an affirmative defense.

c. Opinion

A defamatory opinion cannot be the basis for a defamation action unless the opinion **implies knowledge of facts**.

> **Example:** If the defendant said, "In my opinion, John Jones is a thief," the statement would be regarded as defamatory because it implies the fact that John Jones stole something. On the other hand, the statement, "In my opinion, John Jones is a lousy artist," cannot be the basis for a defamation action because people can disagree regarding the quality of an artist's paintings.

6. Fault

a. Public official or public figure

If the plaintiff in a defamation action is either a public official or a public figure, the plaintiff is required to prove that the defendant acted with **actual malice**, that is, he either had **knowledge that the statement was false or acted with reckless disregard as to the truth or falsity of the statement**. To establish a reckless disregard for the truthfulness of a statement, the plaintiff must prove that the defendant entertained **serious doubts** about its truthfulness; mere failure to check facts is not sufficient. *New York Times Co. v. Sullivan*, 376 U.S. 254 (1964); *St. Amant v. Thompson*, 390 U.S. 727 (1968).

b. Private individual/matter of public concern

If the plaintiff in a defamation action is a private individual and the defendant's statement involves a matter of public concern, the plaintiff is constitutionally required to prove that the **defendant acted with fault—either negligence or actual malice**. *Gertz v. Robert Welch, Inc.*, 418 U.S. 323 (1974).

c. Private individual/not a matter of public concern

If the plaintiff in a defamation action is a private individual and the defendant's statement does not involve a matter of public concern, the constitutional requirements do not apply. At common law, the defendant was strictly liable. Most states today require **at least negligence** by the defendant for all defamation actions, and some now require actual malice in all defamation actions.

7. Libel and Slander Distinguished

a. Libel

Defamation by words **written, printed, or otherwise recorded** in permanent form is libel.

1) Television and radio

Today it is generally—though not universally—accepted that defamatory **radio and television broadcasts are libel,** regardless of whether they are spoken from a script.

2) Email and other electronic communication

Most courts addressing the issue have held that email messages can be categorized as **libel**. It is not yet clear whether courts will hold that tweets and text messages are libel or slander.

3) General and presumed damages

Subject to the constitutionally imposed limits on damages recoverable in a defamation action, the libel plaintiff need only prove **general damages** in order to complete the prima facie tort of libel. General damages are any damages that **compensate the plaintiff for harm to her reputation**. Under the common law, the plaintiff was entitled to recover "presumed damages" as part of general damages. The plaintiff did not need to prove that any damages actually were incurred; her lawyer only needed to invite the jury to award the damages that they believed flowed from the defendant's defamatory communication.

4) Libel *per quod*

In some jurisdictions, under the doctrine of libel *per quod*, if the nature of the defamatory statement requires proof of extrinsic facts in order to show that the statement is defamatory, the plaintiff must prove either special damages or that the statement fits into one of the four categories of statements that satisfy the requirements of slander per se.

b. Slander

Defamation by **spoken word, gesture, or any form other than libel** is slander. In order to recover for slander, the plaintiff must plead and prove either:

1) Special damages

Special damages require the plaintiff to prove that a third party **heard** the defendant's defamatory comments and **acted adversely** to her. Most often, special damages involve an economic loss to the plaintiff, e.g., loss of employment or loss of business, but they also would include such things as the plaintiff's fiancé breaking off the engagement or a friend refusing to host the plaintiff in her home after hearing the defamatory comments.

2) Slander per se

Under the doctrine of slander per se, a plaintiff alleging slander need not plead and prove special damages if the statement defaming her fits into one of four categories.

To qualify as slander per se, the defamatory statement must accuse the plaintiff of:

i) *Committing a crime.* In many jurisdictions, the crime must be one involving moral turpitude or one that subjects the criminal to imprisonment.

ii) *Conduct reflecting poorly on the plaintiff's trade or profession.* Traditionally, accusing a navigator, teacher, or holy person of being a drunk satisfied this requirement, but the same accusation against a sales person did not.

iii) *Having a loathsome disease.* Traditionally, loathsome diseases included illnesses such as leprosy or a sexually transmitted disease.

iv) *Sexual misconduct.* In modern times, examples of cases falling within this sub-category, as well as the previous one, are very rare. A few courts have held that trading sex for drugs constitutes sexual misconduct.

3) Parasitic damages

Once the plaintiff satisfies the requirements of the slander per se prima facie tort by proving either special damages or slander per se, at common law she was able to recover general damages as parasitic damages.

4) Constitutional constraints

Damages recoverable in a slander action, as well as damages recoverable in a libel action are subject to the constitutional limitations discussed below.

8. Constitutional Limitations on Damages

a. Public-official or public-figure plaintiffs

If the plaintiff is either a public official or a public figure, the plaintiff can only recover **actual damages**. Actual damages must be proved; they do not include presumed damages. However, actual damages are a broader category than special damages. Actual damages are not limited to out-of-pocket expenses, but include **compensation for impairment of the plaintiff's reputation and standing in the community, personal humiliation, and mental anguish and suffering**.

b. Private individual/matter of public concern

If the plaintiff is a private individual and the defamatory statement relates to a matter of public concern, the plaintiff is only entitled to recover **actual damages**. However, if the plaintiff proves **actual malice**, instead of mere fault, there is no constitutional limitation on her recovery of either punitive or presumed damages.

c. Private individual/not a matter of public concern

If the plaintiff is a private individual and the defamatory statement does not involve a matter of public concern, the plaintiff may recover **general, including presumed, damages without proving actual malice**. *Dun & Bradstreet, Inc. v. Greenmoss Builders, Inc.*, 472 U.S. 749 (1985).

9. **Defenses**

   a. **Truth**

   Truth is an absolute defense to a claim of defamation.

   > **Falsity as an element of a cause of action:** For a defamation action brought by a public official or figure, by a limited public figure, or by a private figure regarding a statement about a matter of public concern, the falsity of the statement is an element that the plaintiff must prove.
   >
   > **Common-law distinction:** The plaintiff need not prove fault or falsity for common-law defamation. Defamatory statements are presumed to be false, and the defendant must assert truth as a defense.

   A truthful statement is not defamatory. A statement that contains slight inaccuracies may nevertheless be considered to be true and therefore not defamatory. A statement that a person has engaged in conduct that is substantially different from the conduct in which the person did in fact engage is not considered to be true, even if the person's actual conduct was equally or more morally reprehensible.

   > **EXAM NOTE:** If a statement is true but seems like defamation, consider whether it constitutes intentional infliction of emotional distress or invasion of privacy.

   b. **Consent**

   Consent by the plaintiff is a defense, but as with other torts, a defendant cannot exceed the scope of the plaintiff's consent.

   c. **Absolute privileges**

   Statements made under the following circumstances are shielded by absolute privilege:

   i) In the course of **judicial proceedings**;

   ii) In the course of **legislative proceedings**;

   iii) Between **husband and wife**; and

   iv) **Required publications** by radio, television, or newspaper (e.g., statements by a political candidate that a station must carry and may not censor).

   > Statements made in the course of judicial proceedings must be related to the proceedings in order to be privileged; however, no such requirement exists for legislative proceedings.

   d. **Qualified (conditional) privilege**

   Statements made under the following circumstances are subject to a conditional privilege:

   i) In the **interest of the publisher** (defendant), such as defending his reputation;

   ii) In the **interest of the recipient of the statement** or a third party; or

iii) Affecting an important **public interest**.

Qualified privileges most often occur in the contexts of employment references, credit reports, and charges and accusations within professional societies and among members of religious and charitable organizations.

1) Abuse of privilege

A qualified privilege may be lost if it is abused. Generally, a privilege is abused by making statements outside the scope of the privilege or by acting **with malice**. Traditionally, the malice required was **express** malice—hatred, ill will, or spite. Today, most jurisdictions hold that **actual malice**, i.e., knowledge that a statement is false or acting with a reckless disregard as to the truth or falsity of the statement, will defeat a qualified privilege.

2) Burden of proof

The burden is on the defendant to prove that the privilege exists. It is, therefore, an **affirmative defense**. The burden is then on the plaintiff to prove that the privilege has been abused and therefore lost.

B. INVASION OF PRIVACY

The right of privacy **does not extend to corporations**, only to individuals. Additionally, because the right of privacy is a personal right, in most instances, this right terminates upon the death of the plaintiff and does not extend to family members.

Invasion of privacy is not a single tort but includes four separate causes of action.

MNEMONIC: **I FLAP (I**ntrusion, **F**alse **L**ight, **A**ppropriation, **P**rivate facts)

1. Misappropriation of the Right to Publicity

A majority of states recognize an action for the misappropriation of the right to publicity, which is based on the right of an individual to control the commercial use of his identity. The plaintiff must prove:

i) *Defendant's unauthorized appropriation of the plaintiff's name, likeness, or identity*—Most often commercial appropriation cases involve the use or the plaintiff's name or picture, but this is not required. A television or radio production might mimic the plaintiff's distinctive vocal patterns. Also, an action may be maintained when the defendant uses other items closely associated with the plaintiff, such as a specially designed car with unique markings associated with a racecar driver.

ii) For the **defendant's advantage**, commercial or otherwise;

iii) **Lack of consent**; and

iv) Resulting **injury**.

The states are split as to whether this right survives the death of the individual, with some states treating it as a property right that can be devised and inherited.

2. Unreasonable Intrusion Upon the Plaintiff's Private Affairs

The defendant's act of **intruding,** physically or otherwise, into the plaintiff's private affairs, solitude, or seclusion in a manner or to a degree **objectionable to a**

reasonable person establishes liability. Eavesdropping on private conversations by electronic devices is considered an unreasonable intrusion. Photographing a person in a public place generally is not, unless the photograph is taken in a manner that reveals information about the person that the person expects to keep private even in a public place.

Unlike the other forms of invasion of privacy, no publication is required to establish liability.

3. **Placing the Plaintiff in a False Light**

A minority of jurisdictions recognize a separate tort of false light. The plaintiff must prove that the defendant (i) **made public** facts about the plaintiff that (ii) placed the plaintiff in a **false light,** (iii) which false light would be **highly offensive to a reasonable person**.

Attributing to the plaintiff **views** that he does not hold or **actions** that he did not take may constitute placing him in a false light. Similarly, falsely asserting that the plaintiff was a victim of a crime or once lived in poverty may be sufficient for the false light tort.

Most jurisdictions require that the plaintiff prove **actual malice** by the defendant. As considered in the discussion of defamation, this may be constitutionally required in many instances.

4. **Public Disclosure of Private Facts About a Plaintiff**

a. **Elements**

In order to recover, the plaintiff must show that:

i) The defendant **gave publicity to a matter concerning the private life** of another; and

ii) The matter publicized is of a kind that:

a) Would be **highly offensive** to a reasonable person; and

b) Is not of **legitimate concern** to the public.

b. **Publicity**

The requirement of publicity in the public disclosure tort requires far broader dissemination of the information than is required under the "publication" requirement of defamation. The information must be communicated at large or to so many people that it is substantially certain to become one of public knowledge.

c. **Disfavored tort**

Because the public disclosure tort involves the dissemination of true facts, it clearly is in tension with the First Amendment's freedoms of speech and press. Accordingly, the tort is disfavored in the modern era.

d. Disclosure of dated material

Today, most courts hold that the public disclosure of even dated material—for example, a criminal conviction from decades ago—is a matter of public interest and therefore does not create liability.

5. Damages

The plaintiff need not prove special damages for any of the invasion of privacy torts. Emotional distress and mental distress are sufficient.

6. Defenses

a. Defamation defenses

The defenses of absolute and qualified privileges applicable in defamation actions also apply to privacy actions brought on "false light" or "public disclosure of private facts" grounds.

b. Consent

Consent is a defense to invasion of privacy actions. Mistake as to consent negates this defense, no matter how reasonable the mistake.

> **EXAM NOTE:** Remember that truth is not a defense to invasion of privacy, whereas it is a complete defense to defamation.

C. INTENTIONAL MISREPRESENTATION

A prima facie case of intentional misrepresentation is established by proof of the following six elements.

1. Defendant's False Representation

The misrepresentation must be of **a material fact**. Usually the defendant actively misrepresents the facts, such as through deceptive or misleading statements or pictures. Sometimes the misrepresentation occurs through the active concealment of a material fact, such as when the seller of a house places paneling over the basement walls in order to conceal that the foundation is in a terrible condition.

There generally is no duty to disclose a material fact or opinion to the other party. However, there may be an affirmative duty to disclose a fact when the other party is:

i) In a fiduciary relationship with the defendant;

ii) Likely to be misled by statements previously made by the defendant ("partial disclosure"); or

iii) (In a minority of jurisdictions) About to enter into a transaction under a mistake as to what the basic facts of the transaction are, the defendant is aware of this, and the customs of the trade or other objective circumstances suggest that the other party would expect the defendant to disclose these facts.

2. Scienter

The defendant must have known the representation to be false or must have acted with reckless disregard as to its truthfulness.

3. Intent

The defendant must have intended to induce the plaintiff to act (or refrain from acting) in reliance on the misrepresentation.

4. Causation

The misrepresentation must have caused the plaintiff to act or to refrain from acting. That is, the plaintiff must have actually relied on the misrepresentation.

5. Justifiable Reliance

The **plaintiff's reliance must have been justifiable**. Reliance is not justifiable if the facts are obviously false or if the defendant is stating a lay opinion. However, the plaintiff is under no duty to investigate the truth or falsity of the statement.

6. Damages

The plaintiff **must prove actual economic (i.e., pecuniary) loss** in order to recover; nominal damages are not awarded.

In a majority of jurisdictions, the measure of recovery in misrepresentation cases is the "benefit of the bargain" rule (the typical contract law measure of damages): how much did the plaintiff lose because the defendant's representation of facts was false?

A minority of states limit the plaintiff's recovery to his out-of-pocket losses (similar to the typical tort law measure of recovery).

The Second Restatement and a handful of states allow the plaintiff to choose between the benefit of the bargain and the out-of-pocket losses measure of damages.

Consequential damages, if proven with sufficient certainty, can be recovered.

D. NEGLIGENT MISREPRESENTATION

1. Elements and Scope

Under the law of a majority of jurisdictions, as well as that outlined in the Second Restatement:

i) The defendant, usually an accounting firm or another supplier of commercial information, who

ii) Provides false information (the "misrepresentation") to the plaintiff as a result of the defendant's negligence in preparation of the information,

iii) Is liable to the plaintiff for pecuniary damages caused by the plaintiff's justifiable reliance on the information, provided that

iv) The plaintiff is either in a contractual relationship with the defendant or is a third party known by the defendant to be a member of the limited group for whose benefit the information is supplied, and

v) The information must be relied upon in a transaction that the supplier of the information intends to influence or knows that the recipient of the information intends to influence.

Under this rule, the accountant who regularly conducts audits and furnishes financial statements and opinions routinely required by lenders, investors, purchasers or others, is not liable unless she is informed that an identified third party or third parties will be using the statement for a particular purpose.

2. Defenses

Unlike in intentional misrepresentation, in negligent misrepresentation, negligence defenses can be raised.

3. Damages

The plaintiff can recover reliance (out-of-pocket) damages, as well as consequential damages, if negligent misrepresentation is proven with sufficient certainty.

4. Distinguished From Ordinary Negligence

The ordinary rules of negligence apply when physical harm is a foreseeable result of a "negligent misrepresentation."

Example: A defendant air traffic controller is liable for ordinary negligence when he negligently gives the pilot of an airplane incorrect information about the plane's location and speed and, as a result, the passenger-parachutist jumps to his death in Lake Erie instead of at the target airfield.

E. INTENTIONAL INTERFERENCE WITH BUSINESS RELATIONS

1. Intentional Interference With Contract

a. Elements

To establish a prima facie case for intentional interference with a contract, the plaintiff must prove that the defendant:

i) **Knew** of a **contractual relationship** between the plaintiff and a third party;

ii) **Intentionally interfered** with the contract, **resulting in a breach**; and

iii) The breach caused **damages** to the plaintiff.

b. Nature of contractual relationship

The contract in question **must be valid and not terminable at will**. A contract that is voidable by one of the parties to the contract, such as due to a violation of the Statute of Frauds, may be the subject of tortious interference unless the party elects to void the contract.

c. Interference with performance other than inducing breach

The defendant may be liable whenever he prevents a party from fulfilling its contractual obligations or adds to the burden of a party's performance, even if the defendant does not induce the party to breach its contractual obligation. To be considered tortious, a defendant's actions must **substantially exceed** fair competition and free expression, such as persuading a bank not to lend money to a competitor.

d. Justification

A defendant's attempt to cause a third party to breach her contract with the plaintiff usually will be found to be justified if it is motivated by considerations of health, safety, morals, or ending poor labor conditions. For example, a defendant who tries to convince an American clothing store to stop buying fabrics from a foreign textile manufacturer known for its inhumane labor conditions will not be liable for interference with contract.

If the contract is terminable at will, the defendant's attempt to induce a third party to breach its contract with the plaintiff can be justified if the defendant is a business competitor of the third party who is in an existing contractual relationship with the plaintiff.

Some jurisdictions, rather than considering such policies as a "justification," require that the defendant's motives or means be "improper."

2. Interference With Prospective Economic Advantage

A defendant may be liable for interfering with a plaintiff's expectation of economic benefit from third parties even in the absence of an existing contract.

When there is no valid contract in place between the plaintiff and the third party, courts require more egregious conduct on the part of the defendant in order to hold him liable. A defendant who is the business competitor of the plaintiff will not be held liable for encouraging the third party to switch his business to the defendant.

Some jurisdictions require that the defendant's conduct, in order to be actionable, must be either "independently tortious" (e.g., consist of fraud or assault) or violate provisions of federal or state law. Other jurisdictions and the Second Restatement engage in a more open-ended balancing process to decide whether the defendant's conduct is improper.

3. Theft of Trade Secrets

The plaintiff must own a valid trade secret (i.e., information that provides a business advantage) that is not generally known. The owner of the secret must take reasonable precautions to protect the secret, and the defendant must have taken the secret by improper means.

F. INJURIOUS FALSEHOODS

1. Trade Libel

Trade libel imposes tort liability for **statements injurious to a plaintiff's business or products**. Unlike defamation, it is not intended to compensate for harm to the personal reputation of the owner/manager of the business. Proof of special damages is required. Damages for mental suffering are not available. The plaintiff must prove:

i) Publication;

ii) Of a derogatory statement;

iii) Relating to the plaintiff's title to his business property, the quality of his business, or the quality of its products; and

iv) Interference or damage to business relationships.

2. Slander of Title

Similar to trade libel, slander of title protects against false statements that harm or call into question the plaintiff's ownership of real property. The plaintiff must prove:

i) Publication;

ii) Of a false statement;

iii) Derogatory to the plaintiff's title;

iv) With malice;

v) Causing special damages;

vi) As a result of diminished value in the eyes of third parties.

G. WRONGFUL USE OF THE LEGAL SYSTEM

1. Malicious Prosecution

A person is liable for malicious prosecution when:

i) He **intentionally and maliciously** institutes or pursues, or causes to be instituted or pursued;

ii) For an **improper purpose**;

iii) A legal action that is brought **without probable cause**; and

iv) That **action is dismissed** in favor of the person against whom it was brought.

Most jurisdictions have extended malicious prosecution to include civil cases as well as criminal actions. The civil action is sometimes known as wrongful institution of civil proceedings.

The plaintiff may recover for any damage proximately caused by the malicious prosecution, including legal expenses, lost work time, loss of reputation, and emotional distress.

Note that judges and prosecutors enjoy absolute immunity from liability for malicious prosecution.

2. Abuse of Process

Abuse of process is the misuse of the power of the court. To recover for abuse of process, the plaintiff must prove:

i) A legal procedure set in motion in proper form;

ii) That is "perverted" to accomplish an ulterior motive;

iii) A willful act perpetrated in the use of process which is not proper in the regular conduct of the proceeding;

iv) Causing the plaintiff to sustain damages.

For abuse of process, unlike malicious prosecution, the existence of probable cause—and even whether the defendant ultimately prevails on the merits—is not determinative in precluding liability. Rather, **the essence of the tort is using the legal process for an ulterior motive, such as extorting payment or recovering property**.

Example: A local school board of education sued a teacher's union and subpoenaed 87 teachers for a hearing in order to prevent the teachers from walking a picket line during a labor dispute between the union and the board of education.

Note that abuse of process, like malicious prosecution, does not require ill will or spite, but it does require proof of damages.